With its ingenious orchestration of the archive and its sensitivity to both the depths and inadvertencies of the creative process, *Closing Melodies* maps the twin stories of the last days of Friedrich Nietzsche and Vincent van Gogh within a phantasmagoria of space, time, & vision. Rainer J. Hanshe has an unparalleled grasp of what might be called the analytics of genius.

— Nicholas Birns
New York University

Rainer J. Hanshe has assembled a truly uncanny and powerful text. In creatively intertwining the letters of Nietzsche and Van Gogh from their final productive years, the reader has the experience of a phantasmic perception into the possibilities of life offered by two of the most magnanimous, creative minds of the late 19th century, and which continue to find echoes today. Through this mosaic of texts, as well as his series of incantatory & disorienting intervals, Hanshe makes Nietzsche and Van Gogh speak to each other beyond the limits of space & time, and we find ourselves conversing with them too, intertwined in the feral threads of their incendiary lives. This is a book of artistic grace and gravity and makes for a truly thought-provoking & challenging experience.

— Keith Ansell-Pearson
Emeritus Professor of Philosophy, University of Warwick

Vincent

Gunk—

Dionysos

Der Gekreuzigte

Dem Gekreuzigten

Dionysos

Vincent

Briga...

Nietzsche Gesammelte...

Closing Melodies

RAINER J. HANSHE

Closing Melodies

INCLUDING ORIGINAL LETTERS BY

Friedrich Nietzsche

&

Vincent van Gogh

Contra Mundum Press   New York · London · Melbourne

Closing Melodies
© 2023 Rainer J. Hanshe

First Contra Mundum Press
Edition 2023.

Library of Congress
Cataloguing-in-Publication
Data

Hanshe, Rainer J.

Closing Melodies / Rainer J.
Hanshe

—1st Contra Mundum Press
Edition

836 pp., 6 × 9 in.

ISBN 9781940625522

   I. Hanshe, Rainer J.
  II. Title.
 III. Nietzsche, Friedrich.
 IV. Letters.
  V. Van Gogh, Vincent.
 VI. Letters.

2023941664

Dionysos strips mortals of all their conventions, of everything that makes them civilized, and hurls them into life which is intoxicated by death at those moments when it glows with its greatest vitality... until madness becomes a lowering storm and lets the frenzy of horror and destruction burst forth from the frenzy of ecstasy.

— Walter F. Otto, *Dionysos*

TABLE OF CONTENTS

Sematic Buoy

Between the leaves of this book, the lives of Friedrich Nietzsche & Vincent van Gogh are intertwined, through letters and geographical markers, to carve out and etch in relief their proximateness. In this combinatorial act, something akin to the apposition of complementary colors on a canvas is being enacted.

When speaking of the juxtaposition of two complementary colors of the same degree of brightness and light, Vincent explains in a letter to his brother Theo that their juxtaposition will raise both the one and the other to an intensity so violent that human eyes will scarcely be able to bear to look at it. And, he explains further, by way of a single phenomenon, THESE SAME COLORS, WHICH ARE HEIGHTENED BY BEING JUXTAPOSED, WILL DESTROY ONE ANOTHER BY BEING MIXED. Through this apposition of colors, the mixing destroys the two tones and *the result is an absolutely colorless grey*. But — if one mixes together two complementaries in unequal proportions, they only partially destroy one another, and you'll have A BROKEN TONE — which will be a variety of grey. That being so, new contrasts will emerge from the juxtaposition of two complementaries, one of which is pure and the other broken. The contest being unequal, one of these two colors triumphs, but the intensity of the dominant one doesn't prevent there being harmony between the two.

In its own way, this book is a kind of juxtaposition of two complementaries — if not many others — and the creation of a broken tone, or rather, *a series of partially destroyed broken tones*, which each reader creates in the end for, as the physicist Ogden Rood observed, it is the eye that blends the complementary colors together at the proper distance, which leads to true mixtures of colored light, the creation in fact of *new colors not physically present on the canvas*.

There is however no single and fixed triumph in this crossing of colors, but ever-shifting ones, for whichever color is dominant is always changing, as are its intensities. It is also a question of perception, of how one sees, of perspectival angles. Through the bringing together of similar colors in the pure state, but with differing degrees of energy, the painter, Van Gogh said, can strengthen, support, attenuate, or neutralize the effect of a color by touching what isn't the color itself.

From the onset of this book's opening salvo, there is no single authorial voice at rule, just as no single color ever rules; instead, this book exists beyond the anchor of a sole, unique self (or color), that solid and immutable subjectivity rooted in the long ago dismantled genealogy of the family tree, a phylogeny that has rotted to become rhizomatic. Think of the figure of the author as conductor and orchestra.

Disrupting and breaking apart the letters, like a vital scissional force, is an exploded conception of body and being, enacted through the series of intervals (what isn't the color itself) which move deliberately in and out of multiple voices and fields: from those of history to philosophy, science, and so on, the intervals also shift in and out of the voices of Nietzsche and Vincent, breathing thru the constellated narration like inhalations and exhalations, as well as a panoply of other elements and entities that incarnate the book. We are not only human, but other, and something else as well.

In this, there is an impulse to disorient, to create unstable ground, like the earthquakes, volcanoes, *&* other seismic events that occur throughout *Closing Melodies*, operating as a force to propel the reader to undergo internal oscillations similar to those of the philosopher and the painter, wherein a chorus of voices amalgamate and disperse, devoid of signaling quote marks, like the chaos of voices inside (and external to) the bodies of Herr Dynamite and the Horla, who themselves undergo various kinds of sparagmos, until ending in their final tearings: one with a bang, the other with a whimper.

Closing Melodies is thus not a work of fiction, but a 'history' that is phantomatic and which incorporates biography, philosophy, aesthetics, and so on. It stages and replays the final productive years (1888–1890) of the lives of a philosopher and an artist during La Belle Époque, lives that echo the fin-de-siècle itself, just as they echo and instigate aspects of an emerging century and its multitudinous energies and events.

To dis-incarnate and incarnate, to figure and dis-figure, as the body itself — *and this text* — becomes the stage of the world, a site of partially destroyed and broken tones, much like the physical locales traversed by the hermit of Sils Maria and the Dutch nomad, where the continuum of time sounds out and explodes and reality is continually *dis-* and *reconfigured*.

Rainer J. Hanshe
19 November 2021
Brooklyn, New York
6351 km from Naumburg
5814 km from Auvers-sur-Oise
121 *&* 131 years later

Closing Melodies

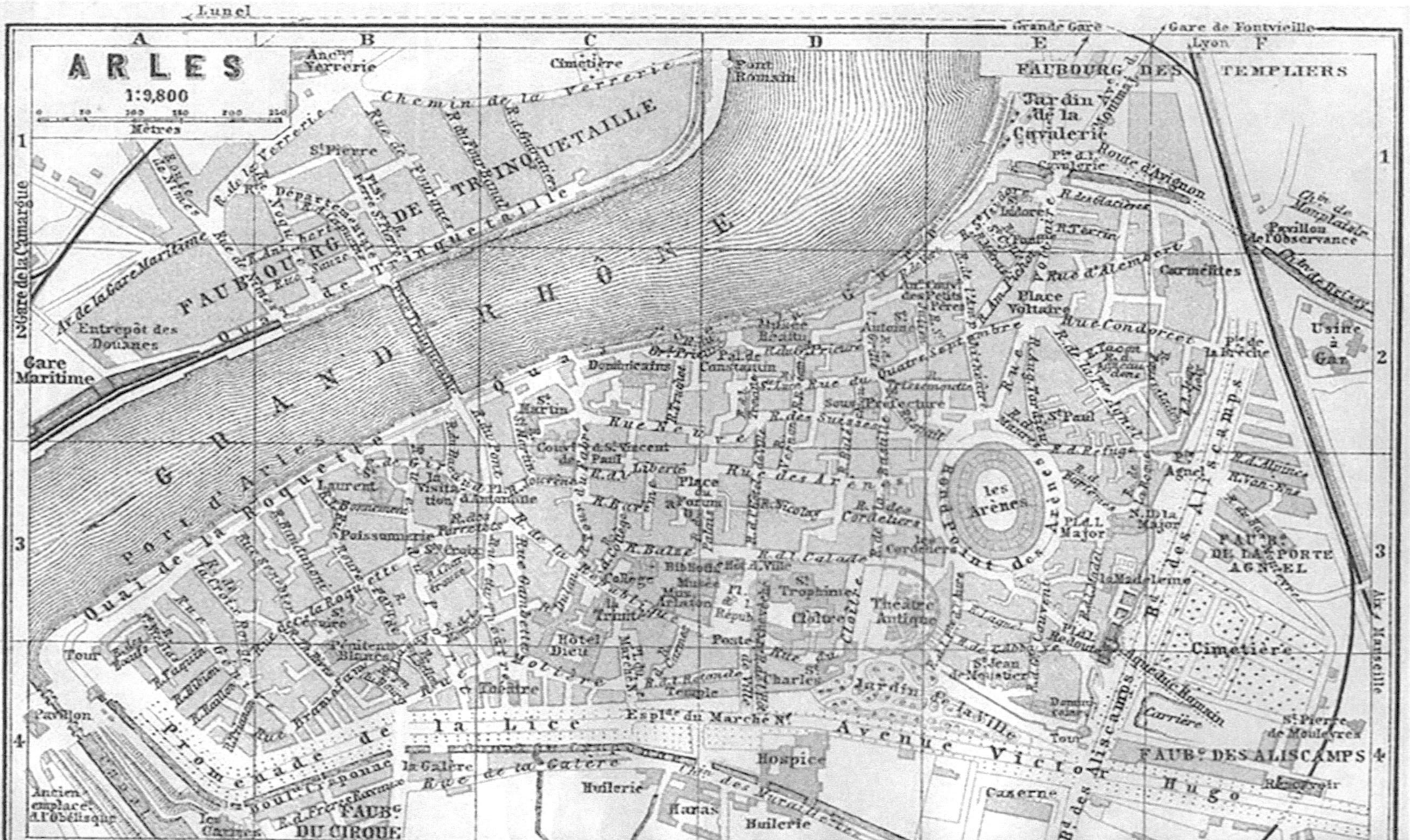

Lunel
ARLES
1:9,800
Mètres
Grande Gare
Gare de Fontvieille
Lyon
FAUBOURG DES TEMPLIERS
A B C D E F
Anc? Verrerie
Cimetière
Pont Romain
Chemin de la Verrerie
DE TRINQUETAILLE
St Pierre
Rue de Pourques
Jardin de la Cavalerie
Route d'Avignon
Ch. de Montplaisir
Pavillon de l'Observance
Rue d'Alembert
Carmélites
Gare de la Camargue
Gare de la Camargue Maritime
Route de Nîmes
Route de la Gare Maritime
FAUBOURG
Rue Départementale
Place Voltaire
Rue Condorcet
P.de la Brèche
Usine à Gaz
Entrepôt des Douanes
GRAND RHÔNE
Gare Maritime
Musée Réattu
Pal. de Constantin
Dominicains
Rue du Quatre Septembre
Sous Préfecture
St Paul
St Martin
Rue Neuve
R. des Suisses
Quai de la Roquette
Port d'Arles
Cour de St Vincent de Paul
Liberté
Place du Forum
Rue des Arènes
R. Nicolay
R. des Cordeliers
les Cordeliers
Rond-Point des Arènes
les Arènes
Pl. L.L. Major
N. D. la Major
R. d. Peluze
Agnel
FAUB. DE LA PORTE AGNEL
Poissonnerie
Collège
Musée
Mus. Arlaten
la Trinité
R. Balze
Bibliothè. Hôt. d. Ville
St Trophime
Cloître
Théâtre Antique
Ste Madeleine
Hôtel Dieu
Poste
Rue Charles
Jardin de la Ville
St Jean le Moustier
Cimetière
Tour
Pavillon
Rue Gambette
R. de la Rotonde
Temple
Théâtre
Esplanade du Marché N.
Avenue Victor
St Pierre de Mouleyres
Promenade de la Lice
Hospice
FAUB. DES ALISCAMPS
Ancien emplacet. de l'Obélisque
FAUB. DU CIRQUE
la Galère
Rue de la Galère
Huilerie
Haras
Huilerie
Caserne
Hugo
Aix / Marseille
R. des Aliscamps
1 2 3 4

TORINO

Chiesa del Carmine .... C.D.2.
"   della Consolata .... D.2.
"   N.S.del Suffragio .... B.1.
"   S.Antonio da Padova .... B.3.
"   SS.Annunziata .... F.3.
"   S.Cuore di Gesù .... D.5.
"   S.Dalmazzo .... D.2.
"   S.Domenico .... D.2.
"   S.Filippo .... E.3.
"   S.Francesco da Paola .... E.3.
"   S.   "   d'Assisi .... D.2.
"   S.Gioachino .... E.1.
"   SS.Martiri .... D.2.
"   SS.Pietro e Paolo .... D.5.
"   S.Rocco .... D.2.
"   S.Secondo .... C.4.
"   S.Teresa .... D.3.
"   SS.Trinità .... E.2.
Galleria Subalpina .... E.3.
Maschio della Cittadella .... C.3.
Amedeo VI .... D.2.
Princ.Amedeo .... D.6.
d'Azeglio .... D.4.
Carlo Alberto .... E.3.
Cavour .... E.3.
Crimea .... F.5.
Duca di Genova .... D.3.
Emanuele Filiberto .... D.3.
Esercito sardo .... E.3.
Garibaldi .... F.4.

Milano
Ciriè Lanzo
Arsenale
Osp. Cottolengo
Ritiro del Buon Pastore
Stazione
Manicomio
Ospe.Mauriz.
Margherita
Piazza Statuto
S.M. Ausil.
S.Milano
Porta Palatina
Piazza Savoia
Cattedrale
Palazzo Reale
Giardino Reale
Prefettura
Teatro Regio
Accademia Militare
Mus. Civico
Università
Banca d'Italia
Accad. Scienze
Arsenale di Artiglieria
S.Cristina
Questura
Acc. di Belle Arti
Cassa Nazionale
Borsa
Pal. Cavour
Teatro Balbo
Scuola di Guerra
Istit. Tecnico
Mus. Civico d'Arte mod.
Teatro Nazionale
Piazza Cavour
Piazza V.Veneto
Stazione Centrale
ex Piazza d'Armi
Stadium
Opificio Ferrovie
Tempio Valdese
posta Saluzzo
posta Saluzzo
Corso del Valentino
Giardino Pubblico
FIUME PO
Esposizione del 1911
Velodromo
Osp. Mauriziano Umberto I
Pinerolo . Giaveno
Alessandria
Barr. di Nizza
Moncalieri
F.I.A.T.
Casa del pte. Isabella

OPENING SALVO: NIZZA

The magnum opus *&* the earthquake
932.2 km from Paris

Early morning, 23 February 1887

As Friedrich Nietzsche is at work on plans for his magnum opus, a 6.5 magnitude Mercalli intensity X earthquake rocks the towns along the French–Italian Riviera: strike 71°, dip 85°, slip 90°, displacement 35 cm, length 45 km, width 10 km, fault center depth 10 km.

Does the strike, dip, slip, displacement, length, and fault center of the event equal in some way the same elements in the philosopher's work itself? Is the sudden release of energy in the earth's lithosphere and the concomitant seismic waves akin to the energy and seismic waves being released in his body? Are they primary body waves, powerful enough to move through liquid and solid rock, secondary body waves, vertically *&* horizontally rippling through the ground, or are they elliptical or parallel surface waves? What is the Mercalli intensity of *Nietzsche*?

The epicenter of the quake was located at the bottom of the continental slope, 20 km offshore from Imperia, Italia, triggering a 2 m-tsunami and killing more than 2000 people. It was the 13th tsunami in Nice–Cannes since 2000 BCE. The sea surface presented negative and positive displacements, with waveforms observed along 250 km of the Ligurian coast from Genoa to Cannes, with short intense wave trains being accompanied by long oscillatory tails. Meanwhile, in Paris, Vincent van Gogh was finishing work on his *Basket of Hyacinth Bulbs*, an extremely textural, tactile painting, made with short, sharp, elongated Neo-Impressionistic brushstrokes. The rough broken earth of the French–Italian Riviera was echoed in Vincent's use of the rough untreated surface of the Japanese box panel on which he painted this work. *Hyákinthos!* What of Vincent's own body was echoed in his work? Were the short, sharp, elongated brushstrokes of the canvas not unlike the short, sharp, elongated emotions of the painter?

Writing to Reinhart von Seydlitz on 24 February, Nietzsche noted that Nizza had just had its long international Carnival (with Spanish ladies at the forefront, incidentally), and hard on its heels, six hours after its final Girandola, still rarer and more novel existential excitements. For we are now living in the interesting expectation of *perishing* — thanks to a well-meaning earthquake that has everyone baying at the moon, and not just the hounds. What a pleasure it is when these ancient houses rattle over our heads like coffee grinders! when the inkwell suddenly becomes independent! when the streets fill with horrified half-clothed figures and shattered nervous systems!

That very night, between 2 and 3 AM, like the *gaillard* that I am, I made my inspection tour throughout the various quarters of the city, in order to see where the consternation was greatest — for the population was camping out-of-doors day and night: there was something refreshingly military about it. And then the hotels! where a great deal had simply collapsed, and full-scale panic prevailed as a consequence.

I located all my acquaintances, male and female, found them huddled miserably under green trees; they were wearing their flannels, for it was bitter cold, and with even the slightest tremor they were brooding on *The End.* I don't doubt that this will bring the season to a precipitate close! Everyone is thinking of departure (provided one can get away, and that the railroad lines were not the very first things to be all "torn up").

Yesterday evening the guests at the hotel where I eat could not be coaxed to take their *table d'hôte* inside the building — they ate and drank outside; and apart from an elderly *&* very pious woman who was convinced that Our Dear Lord *dare* not do her any harm, mine was the only cheerful countenance among the larvæ and 'sensitive hearts.'

Later, to another friend, the philosopher who would soon refer to himself as dynamite said I must confess that I was not even frightened and, for example, on that morning when the whole of Nizza fell into the open and was like a madhouse, I worked in the most undisturbed peace of mind in my room; it happened to me, in two letters that I wrote that day, to forget the event of the day!

On the first night afterwards, when everyone was camped out in the open, I slept quietly at home until 2 o'clock: there came a stronger shock again, the dogs howled all around, I got dressed, and went on a hike through the various parts of Nizza to see to what follies fear can drive men. This was the most interesting hike I've done in Nizza so far: afterwards I slept as well as before. —

*

Among the destroyed and partly destroyed buildings was the Pension de Genève, whose fourth floor had to be dismantled due to its suffering irreparable damage. Although the Genève was Nietzsche's usual port of call upon arriving in Nizza, the previous month he had rented a room with southern exposure on the first floor of 29 Rue des Ponchettes, thereby escaping destruction. A stroke of luck, or the shrewd instinct of self-preservation, like an animal sensing some oncoming catastrophe with the thousand tendrils of its nervous system?

If to one friend the philosopher spoke of the transience of things hurting him (the 4th floor of the Pension de Genève was where the third and fourth parts of his *Zarathustra* were written), to another, he proclaimed that the demolition of the pension had this advantage — that posterity would have one less pilgrimage site to visit. Disaster and cataclysm function then not as nega-

tive but positive forces freeing the philosopher from potentially dangerous acolytes. Every great teacher knows
that he can become a calamity as well as a blessing for
mankind. Yet, is the destruction of a pilgrimage site sufficient to circumvent ideological abominations?

*

* *

The everlasting and exclusive coming-to-be, the imper-
manence of everything actual, which constantly acts and
comes-to-be but never is, as Heraclitus teaches it, is a
terrible, paralyzing thought. Its impact on men can most
nearly be likened to the sensation during an earthquake
when one loses one's familiar confidence in a firmly
grounded earth. It takes astonishing strength to transform this reaction into its opposite, into sublimity and
the feeling of blessed astonishment. Those who cannot,
howl like dogs in terror.

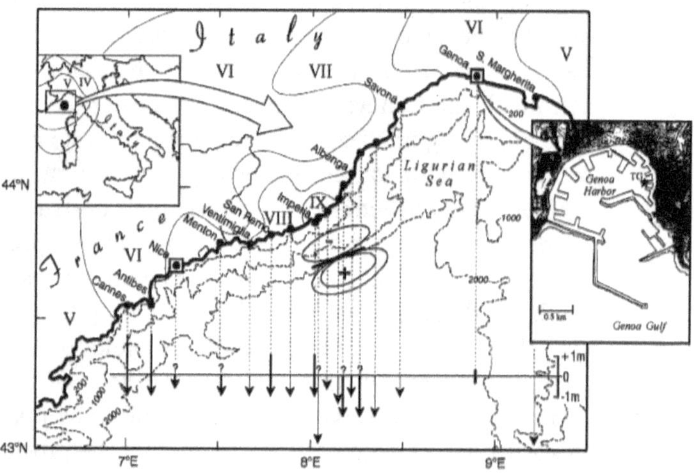

NIZZA

248.9 km from Arles

as the sick animal crawls; la bête philosophe; my relentless
& underground struggle against everything; the Faust of
the 19th century; one must live in Nizza

12 February 1888

Dear Friend,

I closed my mouth to almost everyone; there was no "proud silence" as some thought; it was much more — a humble silence,
that of a sufferer ashamed to betray how much he is suffering.
When an animal is sick, it retires to its lair; so does *la bête philosophe!* Nowadays, a friendly voice seldom reaches me. I am alone
now, absurdly alone; and in the course of my relentless and underground struggle against everything that humans beings till
now have revered & loved (my formula for this is the "transvaluation of values"), I have imperceptibly become like a lair myself
— something hidden away, which people do not find, even if
they go out and look for it. *But people do not go out in search of
such things* ... It is not inconceivable that I am the first philosopher of the age, perhaps even a little more, something decisive
and fateful standing between two millennia. Such a peculiar position is *always* being forfeited — by an ever increasing, more
and more icy, more and more sharp isolation. Instead of being
reputed, I am ridiculed, told that I am eccentric, pathological,
psychiatric, inhuman, the Faust of the 19th century, even worthy
of being put on the gallows! No lack of bad and slanderous waves
assail me; an unrestrainedly hostile tone is paramount in the
periodicals — how is it that nobody protests against this? that
nobody ever feels hurt when I am censured? And in all the years
no solace, not a drop of humanity, not a breath of love —

In these circumstances, one must live in *Nizza*. This time too
it is seething with Idlers, *Grecs* and other philosophers, seething
with "my equals"; and God, with his own cynicism, lets his sun
shine down particularly upon *us* more beautifully than upon the
so much more reputable Europe of Herr von Bismarck (which
is working with feverish virtue at its armaments, and entirely
presents the aspect of a hedgehog with heroic inclinations). The
days pass here with an impudent beauty; never was there a more
perfect winter. And these colors of Nizza — I would like to send
them to you. All the colors permeated with a shining silver grey;
spiritual, witty colors; no residue at all of the brutality of the

fundamental tones. The advantage of this small piece of coast between Alassio and Nizza is that it allows an Africanism, in color,
vegetation, and in the dryness of the air — this does not occur
elsewhere in Europe.

O, how I would like to sit together with you and your dear
esteemed wife under some Homeric and Phæacian sky ... but
I *may* not go any farther south (my eyes will soon compel me
to leave for more northern and more stupid landscapes). Write,
please, again during your stay in Munich, & forgive me for this
gloomy letter!

Your devoted friend

Friedrich Nietzsche

ARLES

248.9 km from Nizza

the weather here is changeable, often windy with murky skies; I have a touch of fever and no appetite; the future success of this idea of a long sojourn in the Midi; if all is not in vain

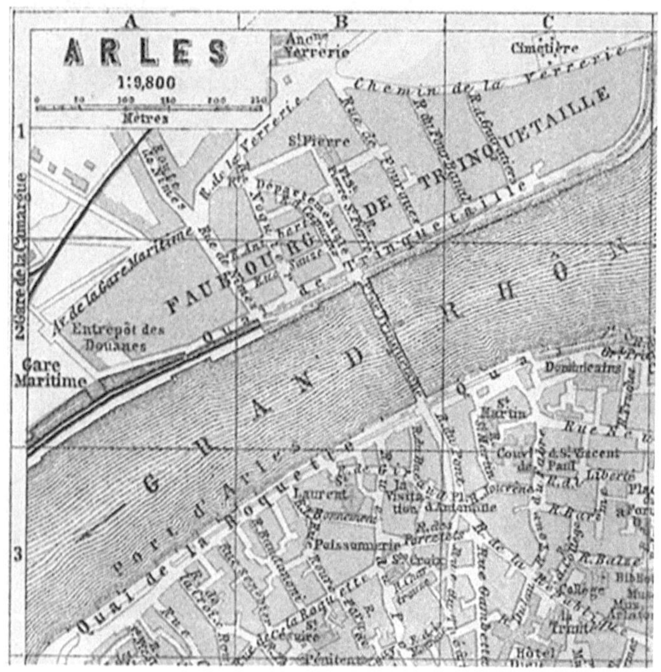

17 February 1888

My dear Theo,

Thank you very much for your letter, which I had not dared to expect so soon, as far as the 50-fr note which you added was concerned.

I brought back a size 15 canvas today. It is a drawbridge with a little cart going over it, outlined against a blue sky — the river blue as well, the banks orange colored with green grass and a group of women washing linen in smocks & multicolored caps. And another landscape with a little country bridge and more women washing linen.

Also an avenue of plane trees near the station. Altogether 12 studies since I've been here.

The weather here is changeable, often windy with murky skies, but the almond trees are beginning to flower everywhere. You are right to see Signac at his house. I was very glad to see from your letter of today that he made a better impression on you than he did the first time. In any case I am glad to know that after today you will not be alone in the apartment.

Remember me kindly to Koning. Are you well? I am better myself, except that eating is a real ordeal, as I have a touch of fever and no appetite, but it's only a question of time and patience.

Even though I'm vexed that just now expenses are heavy and the pictures worthless — that's why I don't despair of the future success of this idea of a long sojourn in the Midi.

Here I am seeing new things, I am learning, and if I take it easy, my body doesn't refuse to function.

For many reasons I should like to get some sort of little retreat, where the poor cab horses of Paris — that is, you and several of our friends, the poor impressionists — could go out to pasture when they get too beat up.

I was present at the inquiry into a crime committed at the door of a brothel here; two Italians killed two Zouaves. I seized the opportunity to go into one of the brothels in a small street called "des Ricolettes."

That is the extent of my amorous adventures among the Arlésiennes. The mob *all but* (the Southerner, like Tartarin, being
more energetic in good intentions than in action) — the mob, I
repeat, all but lynched the murderers confined in the town hall,
but in retaliation all the Italians — men and women, the Savo-
yard monkeys included — have been forced to leave town.

I should not have told you about this, except that it means
I've seen the streets of this town full of excited crowds. And it
was indeed a fine sight.

I made my last three studies with the perspective frame I
told you about. I attach some importance to the use of the frame
because it seems not unlikely to me that in the near future many
artists will make use of it, just as the old German and Italian
painters certainly did, and, as I am inclined to think, the Flemish
too. The modern use of it may differ from the ancient practice,
but in the same way isn't it true that in the process of painting
in oils one gets very different effects today from those of the men
who invented the process, Jan and Hubert van Eyck? And the
moral of this is that it's my constant hope that I am not working
for myself alone. I believe in the absolute necessity of a new art
of color, of design, and — of the artistic life. And if we work in
that faith, it seems to me there is a chance that we do not hope
in vain.

I am deeply sorry for Gauguin's plight, especially because
now his health is shaken: he hasn't the kind of temperament that
profits from hardships — on the contrary, this will only exhaust
him from here on, and that will spoil him for his work. Goodbye
for the present.

Ever yours,

Vincent

INTERVAL: PARIS

Æsthetic combat & fleeing to Arles
932.2 km from Nizza

October 1887 – February 1888

While Germany, the Austro-Hungarian Empire, & Italy renewed their triple alliance treaty in February of 1887 in opposition to France, a year later, the triple alliance of Vincent, Theo, and the artists of Paris could not hold. If promises of mutual support existed between Theo and many of the artists Vincent had befriended, the same promises were slight between those artists and Vincent, whom many found irascible and unnerving. Just as in 1914 Italy would consider the Austro-Hungarian Empire an aggressor, many considered Vincent an aggressor and, if they did not declare war on him, shunned him as an uncouth and bestial if not almost monstrous figure, a kind of Sphinx whose riddles they must decipher in order to preserve their territory and, more urgently, protect themselves from, due to possible contagion, or death. Any allegiance to him was more feigned, an act of democratic politesse, for he was but a pathway to Theo and the promise of gallery support & art-world recognition.

Vincent's two years in Paris were beset with conflicts, tensions, and frequent disturbances, not unlike what occurs when a body wrestles with some strange metic force. Once, after returning from a day of plein air painting, the painter encountered Camille and Lucien Pissarro in the street. Keen to display his work to his fellow artists, the Dutchman cast his easel & other materials onto the middle of the sidewalk and began to frantically lean his still-wet canvases against a building wall, startling the genteel Pissarros, as well as the ever so discreet French passersby. Whether or not he would indulge in more extreme behavior was always feared, for the Pissarros recalled the time when, at the height of Chevreul's discoveries about color and the ferment over color theories in Paris, Vincent once tore off all his clothes, fell to his knees, and implored his fellow artists to accept his counter viewpoints. Since the foreigner drank absinthe in the afternoon, wine in the evening, beer at night, and cognac whenever the mood struck him, for he believed it stimulated his blood circulation, his explosive temper often emerged unexpectedly, leading to volatile and disturbing outbursts.

Despite a seeming divisiveness, the Dutchman in fact sought unity, and his time in Paris was also a time of pursuing the utopia of a colony of artists whose jealousies he hoped could be superseded by a grander artistic bond. Petitioning his fellow artists to unity and strength, he believed that their common interests would enable them to sacrifice any selfish motives, however greatly such unified interests may have suffered the tyranny of his own singular vision. He saw the clan in his midst as the artists of *le petit boulevard*, a ragtag band of outsiders who stood in opposition to the painters of *le grand boulevard*. Like the members of the triple alliance, they must stick together to defeat their opponent — out of unification would come victory and triumph.

In October 1887, months before he would finally depart for the south, the fervent utopian envisioned a grand exhibition that would represent the artists of *le petit boulevard* and position him as the pivotal figure in the movement, all made possible by his brother Theo, the Maecenas of Montmartre. The aim was to attract the public, increase the visibility of their colony to artists and critics in the city and beyond, and to be a gateway to having their art presented at the entresol, the mezzanine at Goupil Gallery where the work of new, more unorthodox painters was displayed to more adventurous clientele. It was the cutting of a pathway to the future.

Although Theo supported the venture, he was displeased with his brother's choice of locale, a restaurant called the Grand-Bouillon, hardly the place to impress the ultra-formal cognoscenti of the City of Lights. The exhibition was fraught with conflict, with some artists refusing the inclusion of Signac and Seurat, Vincent refusing the inclusion of Symbolists like Redon, and others refusing to participate because of such exclusions, a series of sectarian fractures not unlike those that would later occur with the Surrealists. With only a limited number of artists contributing works, the Dutchman was left to fill the remaining empty spaces with his own paintings. In the end, the exhibition was nothing less than a mad misadventure — there was no catalogue, no publicity, and no critics reviewed the so-called show. To most, the restaurant's plat du jour was of more interest than the paintings, which many patrons of the resto found disconcerting, hardly conducive to their digestion. The muses did not rule here, but Brillat-Savarin.

In Paris, the Dutchman was something of a bête noire: in the short time he had been there, despite being as close to the center of artistic activities as an outsider could be, the foreigner had never been invited to participate in any group exhibitions, Theo's colleagues did not include him in their exhibits at other galleries, and although Theo displayed the work of many of Vincent's friends at Goupil's entresol, he did not display his own brother's work there.

With this increasing isolation from his fellow artists, and from the inner circles of the Parisian art world, the City of Lights became more and more a place of contempt and darkness for he who was in search of the sun. Alienated, he hardly painted the last months of 1887 and, because of his extreme and vehement outbursts, the police had banned him from painting in the streets. Even seemingly close companions like Bernard were deeply critical of the fevered one. To Bernard, the Dutchman's paintings were none too different from the man himself — he tortures the paint, Bernard wrote, and denies all wisdom, all striving for perfection or harmony.

Burning like the stars he would later begin to depict, it was life's intensity the painter sought, & to his sister, he exulted, when one has fire within oneself, one cannot keep bottling it up — better to burn than to burst. What is in will out.

And so, driven as if by a force beyond his control, after another combative day in Paris, fed up with the sectarianism of his fellow artists, in a state of fury, his utopic ventures come to naught, it was out of Paris that the foreigner would go, journeying on the train rapide (the Paris-Lyon-Méditerranée) from the City of Lights to Marseille, leaving at 9:40 PM on 19 February 1888.

Adieu, Paris, *adieu!*

At 4:49 PM the following day, the painter arrived in Arles. He was in search of lighter colors, of youth & freshness, & eager to recover his physical strength, to be the first on the ground in the Mediterranean of Cézanne, Monticelli, & Zola, the one who would lead the southern faction of the avant-garde & forge a pathway toward new, unsuspected horizons.

Writing to their sister Wil, Theo noted that he never expected that he and his brother would grow so attached to one another, for now that I am alone in the apartment there is a decided emptiness about me.

NIZZA

248.9 km from Arles

looking down on the "modern"; the richest, most experienced, and most independent books; catching the Germans
in flagranti; confessions about myself; I lived for years next
door to death

19 February 1888

Verehrter Herr:

You have put me under a most pleasant obligation to you with your contribution to the concept of "modernity"; for, this very winter, I have been circling this most crucial value problem, very much in the upper air, very much like a bird and with the best intention of looking down on the "modern" in as unmodern a way as possible . . . I admire — let me confess to you! — the tolerance of your judgments as much as the restraint with which you make them. How you suffer all these little children to come unto you! Even Heyse! —

During my next journey to Germany I plan to study the psychological problem of Kierkegaard, and also to renew my acquaintance with your earlier writings. This will be, in the best sense of the word, useful for me — and will serve to "bring home" to me the severity and arrogance of my own judgments.

Yesterday my publisher sent me a telegram to say that the books have been sent off to you. I will spare you and myself the story of why there has been such a delay. Do, please, make the best of a "bad job" — of these Nietzsche books, I mean.

I myself imagine that I have given to the "new" Germans the richest, *most experienced*, and most independent books that they have; likewise, that my own person represents a crucial occurrence in the crisis of value judgments. But that could be an error; and stupid, too —: I want not to *have* to believe anything about myself. A few remarks here about my first writings (— the *Juvenilia* and *Juvenalia*):

The essay against Strauss, the wicked laughter of a "very free thinker" at the expense of one who thought he was free, caused an immense scandal: despite my 24 years, I was then already a full professor, thus a kind of authority and something *substantial*. The fairest account of this affair, in which almost every "person of importance" took sides for or against me, and a ridiculous mass of paper went through the press, is given in Karl Hillebrand *Zeiten, Völker und Menschen*, Vol. 2. What mattered was not my ridiculing the senile jottings of a remarkable critic but my catching the Germans *in flagranti* with a compromising act of bad taste: German taste had unanimously admired Strauss's book *Der alte und der neue Glaube*, despite all religious and theological party factions, as a masterpiece of freedom and subtlety of thought (even of style!). My pamphlet was the first direct attack on German *Bildung* (— that *Bildung* which people were celebrating as the conqueror of France —); the word I coined, "Bildungsphilister," survived the raging fluctuations of the polemics *&* has entered everyday language.

The two essays on Schopenhauer and Richard Wagner are, it seems to me now, confessions about myself — above all, they are avowals to myself, rather than, say, real psychological accounts of those two masters, to whom I felt as much kinship as I felt antagonism. (— I was the first person to distill a sort of unity out of both of them: this erroneous belief is now very much in the forefront of German culture: all Wagnerites are adherents of Schopenhauer. This was not true when I was young: in those days it was the last Hegelians who adhered to Wagner, and even in the fifties the slogan was "Wagner and Hegel.")

Between the *Untimely Meditations* and *Human, All Too Human* come a crisis and a sloughing. Physically too: I lived for years next door to death. This was my great good fortune: I forgot myself, I survived myself... I have performed the same trick a second time. —

Well then, we have given each other presents, perhaps like a couple of travelers who are glad they met each other on the way? —

I remain your most devoted

Nietzsche

ARLES

248.9 km from Nizza

*Paris is impossible; magnificent scenery; the winter land-
scapes the Japanese did*

21 February 1888

My dear Theo,

During the journey I thought at least as much about you as about the new country I was seeing.

But I tell myself that you'll perhaps come here often yourself later on. It seems to me almost impossible to be able to work in Paris, unless you have a refuge in which to recover and regain your peace of mind and self-composure. Without that, you'd be bound to get utterly numbed.

Now I'll tell you that for a start, there's been a snowfall of at least 60 centimeters all over, and it's still snowing.

Arles doesn't seem any bigger than Breda or Mons to me.

Before reaching Tarascon I noticed some magnificent scenery — huge yellow rocks, oddly jumbled together, with the most imposing shapes.

In the small valleys between these rocks there were rows of little round trees with olive-green or grey-green foliage, which could well be lemon trees.

But here in Arles the land seems flat.

I noticed some magnificent plots of red earth planted with vines, with mountains in the background of the most delicate lilac. And the landscape under the snow with the white peaks against a sky as bright as the snow was just like the winter landscapes the Japanese did.

Here's my address

Restaurant Carrel

30 rue Cavalerie

Arles

So far I've taken no more than a little walk round the town, as I was more or less completely done in last night.

I'll write to you soon — an antique dealer whose shop I went into yesterday in this very street was telling me he knew of a Monticelli.

With a good handshake to you and the pals.

Yours truly,
Vincent

NIZZA

248.9 km from Arles

gloomy weather, loneliness, and blue fingers; everything is unsaid; the three-quarters lunatic; invaluable psychological observations relating to décadence; half mad and slowly going to ruin; I have vowed not to take anything seriously for a while; polar-bear humanity

Pension de Genève, 26 February 1888

Dear friend,

gloomy weather, Sunday afternoon, great loneliness: I can invent
no more pleasant occupation than talking a little to you and with
you. I have just noticed that my fingers are blue: my handwriting
will be decipherable only to him who deciphers my thoughts...
    What you say of Wagner's style in your letter reminds me of
a remark I found somewhere in writing: that his "dramatic style"
was no more than a species of *bad style*, even of *non*-style in music. But our musicians see *progress* in this...
    Actually everything is unsaid, as I suspect, almost unthought
in *this* area of truths: Wagner himself, as a person, as an animal,
as God and artist, surpasses a thousand times the understanding and the incomprehension of our Germans. Does he surpass
that of the French as well? — Today I had the pleasure of finding
the right answer, just when the question could seem extraordinarily hazardous: it is this — "who was most ready for Wagner?
who was most naturally and inwardly Wagnerian, in spite of and
without Wagner?" — For a long time I had been telling myself:
it was that bizarre, three-quarters lunatic *Baudelaire*, the poet
of *Les fleurs du Mal*. It had disappointed me that this kindred
spirit of W's had not during his lifetime discovered him; I have
underlined the passages in his poems in which there is a sort
of *Wagnerian sensibility* that has found no form anywhere else
in poetry (— Baudelaire is a libertine, mystical, "satanic," but,
above all, Wagnerian). And what did I find today! I was thumb-
ing through a recently published collection of *Œuvres posthumes*
by this genius — most deeply prized and even loved in France
— and there, among some invaluable psychological observations
relating to décadence (*Mon cœur mis à nu*, of the kind in which
Schopenhauer's and Byron's case has been burned), an unpub-
lished letter of *Wagner's* catches my eye, on an essay by Baudelaire in the *Revue Européenne*, avril 1861. I'll copy it out for you:

Mon cher Monsieur Baudelaire,

J'étais plusieurs fois chez vous sans vous trouver. Vous croyez bien, combien je suis désireux de vous dire quelle *immense satisfaction* vous m'avez préparée par votre article qui m'honore et qui m'encourage plus que tout ce qu'on a jamais dit sur mon pauvre talent. Ne serait-il pas possible de vous dire bientôt, à haute voix, comment je m'ai senti enivré en lisant ces belles pages qui me racontaient — comme le fait le meilleur poème — les impressions que je me dois vanter d'avoir produites sur une organisation si supérieure que la vôtre? Soyez mille fois remercié de ce bienfait que vous m'avez procuré, et croyez-moi bien fier de vous pouvoir nommer ami. — A bientôt, n'est-ce pas? *Tout à vous*

Richard Wagner

(Wagner was at that time 48 years old, Baudelaire 40; the letter is touching, though written in miserable French.)

In the same book there are sketches by Baudelaire in which he passionately defends Heinrich *Heine* against French criticism (Jules Janin). — Even during the last years of his life, when he was half mad and slowly going to ruin, *Wagnerian* music was played to him as a *medicine*; Wagner's name had only to be mentioned to him, and he would *"il a souri d'allégresse."* (— On only one other occasion, unless everything deceives me, did Wagner write a letter showing this sort of gratitude and even enthusiasm — after receiving *The Birth of Tragedy*.)

— How are you now, dear friend? I have vowed not to take anything seriously for a while. But you should not think that I have been busy making "literature" again — this manuscript was *for myself*; from now on, I intend to make a manuscript *for myself* every winter — the idea of "making it public" is actually *excluded*. — The Fritzsch question has been settled by a telegram. — Herr Spitteler has written, not badly, apologizing for his "insolence" (— as he says). — The winter is hard; but at the moment I am missing nothing except perhaps a divine and tranquil music — *your* music, dear friend!

Your N.

There has not been a single reply from the newspapers and periodicals among which Fritzsch circulated last autumn an offer of my collected works for review —

Overbeck's father has died, at the age of 84. Overbeck has gone to Dresden because of this — I fear, to the detriment of his health, which is causing him difficulties again this winter. — Snowstorms everywhere, polar-bear humanity.

From a letter of B's: "I dare not speak of W any more: people have laughed at me too much. This music has been one of the great joys of my life; for a good 15 years I have not experienced such exaltation (or rather *enlèvement*)."

ARLES

248.9 km from Nizza

that wretch Voltaire; those who penetrate to the heart of life; May bugs; overground existence, overground studies; a painter has to make paintings

24 February 1888

My dear sister,

For my part, I could just as well say that I'll stop writing to you immediately at the moment you reply to me; the simplest thing is not to write if it's too much trouble and one doesn't always feel inclined.

But be this as it may, it's very good that you're starting by finding out what sort of harm that wretch Voltaire has done — and you'll certainly find this in *Candide*, that Voltaire dared to laugh at the "highly serious life which we ought only to devote to or spend on the best ends."

And I don't have to tell you that this crime is terrible enough in itself.

I can't really write about Mauve, I think about him every day, and that's all there is to it. It has affected me very badly but personally, as a human being, he was perhaps very different from what people sometimes said, that's to say deeper in life itself than in art perhaps, and I loved him as a human being — now I find it so hard to imagine that those who penetrate to the heart of life, who by the way judge themselves as if it were another, and deal with others with as little embarrassment as if they were dealing with themselves, I find it so hard to imagine that such people cease to exist.

Now I know that it's fairly impossible for the white potato or salad grubs that turn into May bugs later to be capable of forming credible ideas about their future overground existence.

And that it would be rash of them to undertake overground studies to throw light on this question, since the gardener or others interested in salad and vegetables would immediately trample them underfoot as being harmful insects.

But for parallel reasons I have little faith in the rightness of our human ideas concerning our future life. We can no more judge our own metamorphoses impartially and sagely than the white salad grubs can theirs.

For the same reason that a salad grub has to eat salad roots for its higher development —

so I believe that a painter has to make paintings — perhaps there's something else after that.

You see that I've gone somewhat further to the south — I've seen only too clearly that I cannot prosper with either my work or my health in the winter — moreover, nowadays people are demanding color contrasts and highly intense *&* variegated colors in paintings rather than a subdued grey color. So I thought for one reason and another that I wouldn't do anyone any harm if I just went to what attracted me.

Give Ma my warmest regards; for the time being there will certainly not be any chance of my coming back to Holland. Regards.

Vincent

NIZZA

248.9 km from Arles

winter of avalanches & railway disturbances; radical prob-lems & decisions; stoves; a real ordeal for me; the fear of spring; the troubled troglodyte

3 March 1888

Pension de Genève

Dear friend,

Forgive me, that I, just in possession of your good letter, must immediately bother you with my affairs again. *Lorenzen's* calculation is quite a cause for concern: I can only recognize one post. I *paid* for the first six items on my last departure from Leipzig; I neither received nor asked for the seventh and eighth (Dionys. and Apollodor). But I want to negotiate about that with Lorenz *myself.* —

On the other hand, it worries me that you have not reported anything to me about the payment of my printing invoice to C.G. *Naumann.* I enclosed the bill in my penultimate letter: — Do I have to fear that the letter with the bill has been lost? — in this winter of avalanches and railway disturbances, much seems to be getting lost...

For weeks I have been amazed that C.G. Naumann does not signal the receipt of the money. —

The printing costs of the *Genealogy* were: 588 Marks 65 Pfennigs.

As for the salary due toward the end of the month, I ask for the same *here.* But I would be grateful for every day that it comes earlier; basically, my time in Nizza *is up* — the shine of the sun (in cold weather, by the way) is already too intense for my eyes. — Otherwise, it is better again; nor am I badly satisfied with my winter, which was devoted to radical problems and decisions. — Just send Basel paper, please. — The stove was de rigueur, you're right. Namely for my north room. Incidentally, I have absolutely no understanding of how I could endure a Nordic winter: as much as I must *wish*, called into question for reasons of the most extreme nature. But even *here* every really dark and wintry day when the sun is missing is a real torture for me: I am sick and depressed in an almost unbelievable way, physically and mentally. There is something humiliating about this absurd degree of dependence; but it doesn't help, I have to reckon with this factor. Engadin and Nizza are no longer really to be *questioned*: they are the only things that have been *proven*. Spring scares me; it has hitherto failed me in every place. — The past *decade*, with my habitual weakness and irritability in my head and nerves, which created real catastrophes from the slightest chance and accidents, should absolutely be erased from my memory. But in the meantime I have to be content with days and weeks in which I forget. *This* degree of human décrépitude, which is as unsuitable as possible for my whole way of thinking, has, since I do not hide from myself, somewhat exasperated my pride: bad enough, but the misery can only be endured at this price. — I feel like a troglodyte who has trouble believing in *light*; one becomes extremely suspicious; one becomes problematic.

Dear friend, it does not seem impossible that I will greet you again in Basel this year: although I do not want to promise it today. With the warmest wishes for you and your dear wife

Nietzsche

(The street pet. rue St. Etienne is now renamed: rue Rossini)

INTERVAL: ARLES

Lifting the volcanic veil *&* the Pont de Langlais
248.9 km from Nizza

May–August 1883 / April–May 1888

Beginning in late May 1883, steam venting began to occur from Perboewatan, the northernmost cone of Krakatoa, Indonesia, with ash outbreaks hitting an altitude of nearly 6 km. Eruptions would continue in mid June, resulting in loud explosions of thick black clouds covering the islands for nearly one week.

In the coming days, earthquakes were experienced in Anyer, Banten, and in early August, major ash columns and steam plumes rose out of volcanic vents between Danan and Rakata.

Toward the end of the month, eruptions intensified, and on 26 August 1883, the volcano went into its paroxysmal phase, with eruptions and explosions occurring every 10 minutes, like the tympani drums of the center of the earth sounding off to presage its coming thermonuclear reaction.

The following day, the volcanic island of Krakatoa erupted, unleashing a concatenation of explosions that would reverberate throughout much of the world, circumnavigating the globe seven times over.

When most of the island buckled beneath the sea, a succession of lava, pumice, and ash flows along with immense tsunamis devastated proximate coastlines. Ash discharged 80 km into the atmosphere, swathing an area of 800,000 square km, plummeting the surrounding region into darkness for two-and-a-half days, like some nightmarish vision imaged by Goya.

The discharged ash, which wafted around the globe and beyond, produced Bishop's Rings around the moon and sun. The ash also acted as a solar-radiation filter, decreasing global temperatures by as much as 0.5° C in the year following the eruption, resulting in the reduction of the amount of sunlight reaching the surface of the earth. The world was darker than it had ever been before, and this darkness would envelop it for half a decade.

At twilight, a volcanic purple light encircled the sun.

For years afterwards, the moon appeared to be blue, sometimes green.

The final explosion of the volcano was so loud the pyroclastic surge resounded across more than 10% of the earth's surface, with witnesses in Perth and Rodrigues speaking of what sounded to them like distant cannon fire. At 310 dB, the sound ruptured the eardrums of sailors over 64 km away in the Sunda Strait.

As the island collapsed under the sea into the magma chamber, 5 cubic miles of rock fragments were jettisoned into the air. Just then, Nietzsche's publisher was reading the manuscript of part I of *Thus Spoke Zarathustra* while the philosopher was relaxing in Roma. Waves estimated at 41 meters high battered nearby villages and settlements, and all vegetation on the islands was stripped bare, structures were completely destroyed, and tens of thousands of people in Java and Sumatra were taken out to sea, resulting in over 36,000 deaths. The energy released from the explosion was equal to 200 megatons of TNT. To Nietzsche, whose philosophy itself was considered a form of dynamite, it was a grand event: 2,000 human beings annihilated at a stroke! he wrote his friend Lanzky. It's magnificent. This is how humanity should come to its end — how one day it will end. When Lanzky remarked that they too would be done away with, he who called for us to build our houses on the slopes of Vesuvius rejoined, what matter!

The cataclysm of Krakatoa led to fitful weather and hallucinatory sunsets throughout the world for months afterwards, due to sunlight reflected from suspended dust particles ejected by the volcano high into the earth's atmosphere. Commercial & other vessels reported similar spectacles, all of which were accompanied by explosive noises, churning black clouds, and incandescent pumice and ash. The sun was sometimes the color of purple lavender, and noctilucent clouds were visible for the first time in history. From earth to beyond, an immense milieu had been forever altered.

Over the next year, across the Indian Ocean, rafts of volcanic pumice were seen on which human skeletons were afloat, drifting so far that they also hit the shores of Africa's eastern coast. It was then that the third part of Nietzsche's *Zarathustra* was published, he was composing the fourth, and van Gogh was in Nuenen, intensely engaged in drawing and making watercolors and oil paintings. The apotheosis of an artist-philosopher; the development and refinement of a painter. How much of the ash, steam, lava, pumice, igneous fragments and sonic echoes of the pyroclastic surges, how much of the dust particles and black clouds, entered into the pores of Herr Dynamite and the Horla, changing thereby the composition of their bodies as they changed the world around them? Were they too not surges and seismic waves? Were they too not noctilucent clouds and fitful weather?

Five years after the explosion of Krakatoa, in 1888, as the philosopher and painter traversed various parts of Europe in search of perfect climates and locales suitable to their physiological conditions, temperatures would return to normal and the volcanic veil would at last dissipate. It was the very year that the sun would become for Vincent an incandescent beacon, a burning orb out of which a heliomythic imaginary would be created, the moment when, for the Dutchman, the sky became starry, a seething cosmos of vitality and brilliance where starlight eclipsed gaslight and distant space was as close as if as proximate as a volcanic cloud.

In Paris, the painter wrestled with various techniques and styles, spurred by the different artists, scientists, and movements of his time, shifting from pointillist approaches to pastel-based palettes to monochromatic

ones to canvases of incandescent color *&* colliding complementaries. It was all an attempt to ingest and incorporate through sheer will the ruling aesthetic principles
of his time.

In Arles, abandoning the praxes of others and all
external methods, the young artist turned back to his
scientific-based investigations, as if seeking a multitude
of ways from which to see, a kind of roving perspectival-
ism born of his own tempestuous body.

Returning to use of a perspective frame he had constructed in 1882 after reading of Albrecht Dürer's description of such a device, his eye curved to the very realities
before him, not theories — it was the world as experienced by his nerves that would become his technique.

My brush stroke has no system at all, he wrote to
Bernard. I hit the canvas with irregular touches of the
brush, which I leave as they are. Patches of thickly laid-
on color, spots of canvas left uncovered, here and there
portions that are left absolutely unfinished, repetitions,
savageries; in short, I am inclined to think that the result is so disquieting and irritating as to be a godsend to
those people who have fixed, preconceived ideas about
technique.

Sitting here with my perspective frame, on the bank
of the Arles-Bouc Canal, I think back to the sketches I
did when on the shores of Scheveningen. Provence is like
Holland in character yet as beautiful as Japan for the
limpidity of the atmosphere and gay color effects. How
can I not now also think of Hiroshige? If the Japanese
are not making any progress in their own country, still
it cannot be doubted that their art is being continued in
France.

I have my pen, reed pen, ink, and graphite and am
determined to capture something essential about the
Langlais Bridge. I am drawing it, from different posi-
tions, from different directions, viewing it from as many
angles as possible, all with the aid of my perspective
frame. Eventually, I will make some watercolors, and

other drawings — I want to show as many parts of the bridge as possible, its uprights and iron supports, its strong braces and chain pulleys, its diagonal frames. A multitude of technical aspects. To circle it like a bird. If I can emphasize the crossing diagonals by setting the bridge at the moment when I can lace together the diagonal tether lines of the moving wings with the opposite diagonal of the iron cables that are attached to the upright supports, this will make for bold X's splayed out on both sides of the composition. Everything crystallizes through the perspective frame. Seeing all the images together will be like encountering a series of different moments in time, which will produce a comprehensive and total view of the bridge. The perspective frame allows me to compare the proportions of objects close at hand with those on a plane further away. I want to capture too how Arles projects the strange silhouette of its drawbridge against a huge yellow sun.

Later that summer, to Theo, Vincent would declare to his brother that it is not the language of painters but the language of nature that one should listen to.

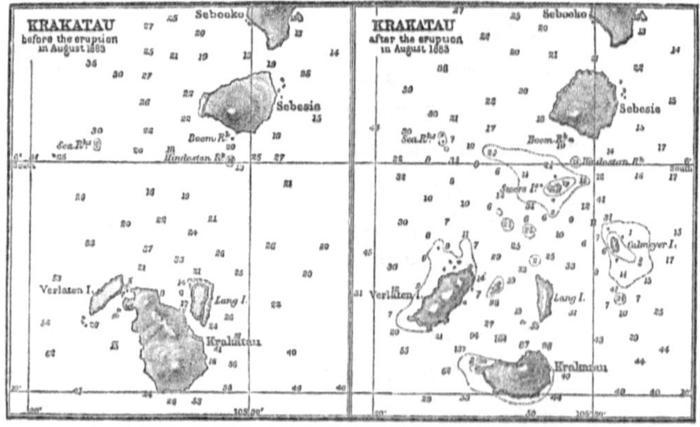

NIZZA

248.9 km from Arles

there are times when one is no longer in control of oneself; delicate and morbid machinery; the tariff war; how good to be in Europe and not in this astonishingly uncomely Paraguay; my absurd health demands; the greatest distrust of the German spring

5 March 1888

My dear good mother,

I would have written you a little letter this morning without a doubt, even if I hadn't received your heartfelt admonition. Everything was already prepared for it. In addition, my condition has really improved and the bad weeks of melancholy are over again. It saddens me that I have sent two such gloomy letters to you: but there are times when one is no longer in control of oneself and does things that one can hardly understand by the light of day. Incidentally, the winter made the whole world hard and sad: and all the more for such a delicate and morbid machinery as I am. The news from San Remo has nothing therapeutic in it either: this system of lies and arbitrary distortion of facts, which this English woman, in league with a worthless English doctor, perpetuates from one month to the next, has outraged even the foreigners, not to mention the German doctor, the entire imperial family, Bismarck. By chance I am very well, too well informed about the *intima intimissima* of this gruesome story. — Incidentally, since 1 March we have had the great *tariff* war between Italy and France here: our province is hardest hit by it. Nizza obtained *everything* that was necessary for food from Italy: — meat, eggs, butter, vegetables, wine, oil. The tariff war, with its *outrageous* taxes, simply creates a rift between the two countries: so that the whole coast has to try to get its food from elsewhere. They already want to establish a direct steamboat connection between Nizza and Algiers these days: 42 hours journey between here and *Africa*. —

Nevertheless: how good to be in Europe, be it in Naumburg or in Nizza — and *not* in this astonishingly uncomely Paraguay! The report is very honest; I really don't think it's hiding any good points. Obviously life in the capital and life in this forest and desert wilderness are quite different; in the former one will still believe oneself to be in Europe. Nothing for us! my good mother! —

Fritzsch put the matter in order by telegram; also sent an apologetic letter. Thank you very much for the little high pressure that your letter has performed.

Overbeck's father has since died in Dresden; likewise Köselitzen's Leipzig sister. One has to carry on and overcome everywhere. — Your kind and dear invitation to spend the spring in Naumburg unfortunately does not in any point match what my absurd health demands. First: I may not travel far; I can't endure it. Second: I have the greatest distrust of the German spring in particular and think with horror of the feeling of weakness and discouragement that last spring in Naumburg and Leipzig produced in me. It's not yet clear where I'm going; but not very far, and somewhere in the mountains, where the air is strong; and so that I can keep an eye on the access to the Engadin (for mid-*June*: you can't go up sooner).

Finally, my dear mother, do you mind sending me the 96 marks here in Nizza? Or do you have no money right now? I am in a bit of an embarrassment and would be grateful if I could get money sent *now*. If it doesn't suit you I would approach Mr. Kürbitz about it. (The simplest way is a 100-mark note. The letter *registers* but does *not* indicate the money in it. Or a 100-*franc* note (96 marks = 115 francs) is preferable.

With heartfelt love and gratitude
Your ancient creature

ARLES

248.9 km from Nizza

the sky was a hard blue with a great bright sun; the future is still difficult; a final victory; we don't deserve to be treated as though we were dead; poor Gauguin; blood that was real good blood

9 March 1888

My dear Theo,

Now at long last, this morning the weather has changed and has turned milder — and I've already had an opportunity to find out what this mistral's like too. I've been out on several hikes round about here, but that wind always made it impossible to do anything. The sky was a hard blue with a great bright sun that melted just about all the snow — but the wind was so cold and dry it gave you goose pimples. But even so I've seen lots of beautiful things — a ruined abbey on a hill planted with hollies, pines, and grey olive trees. We'll get down to that soon, I hope. Now I've just finished a study like the one of mine Lucien Pissarro has, but this time it's of oranges. That makes eight studies I have up to now. But that doesn't count, as I haven't yet been able to work in comfort and in the heat.

The letter from Gauguin that I had intended to send you but which for a moment I thought I had burned with some other papers, I later found and enclose herewith. But I've already written to him direct and I've sent him Russell's address as well as sending Gauguin's to Russell, so that if they wish they can make direct contact. But as for many of us — and surely we'll be among them ourselves — the future is still difficult. I do believe in a final victory, but will artists benefit from it, and will they see more peaceful days?

I've bought some coarse canvas here & I've had it prepared for matte effects, I can now get everything, more or less, at Paris prices.

On Saturday evening I had a visit from two amateur painters, one of whom is a grocer — and also sells painting materials — and the other a justice of the peace who seems kind & intelligent.

Unfortunately I'm hardly managing to live more cheaply than in Paris, I need to allow 5 francs a day.

For the moment I haven't found anything like a boarding-house, but there must surely be some.

If the weather also gets milder in Paris it will do you good. What a winter!

I daren't roll up my studies yet because they're hardly dry, & there are some areas of impasto that won't dry for a while.

I've just read *Tartarin sur les Alpes*, which I greatly enjoyed.

Has that bloody man Tersteeg written to you? That'll do us good anyway — don't worry.

If he doesn't reply, he'll hear people talking about us all the same, and we'll make sure he has nothing to fault in what we do. For example, we'll send Mrs. Mauve a painting in memory of Mauve with a letter as well from us both in which, if Tersteeg doesn't reply, we won't say a word against him but we'll make it understood that we don't deserve to be treated as though we were dead.

In fact, it's likely that Tersteeg won't be predisposed against us after all.

That poor Gauguin has no luck; I do fear that in his case convalescence will take longer than the fortnight he had to spend in bed.

For Christ's sake, when are we going to see a generation of artists with healthy bodies? Sometimes I'm really furious with myself because it isn't good enough to be sicker or less sick than others, the ideal thing would be to have a strong enough constitution to live for 80 years and along with that, blood that was real good blood.

But we could take comfort if we felt that a generation of more fortunate artists was going to come along.

I wanted to write to you straightaway that I'm hopeful winter's over now and I hope it will be the same in Paris. Handshake.

Yours truly,
Vincent

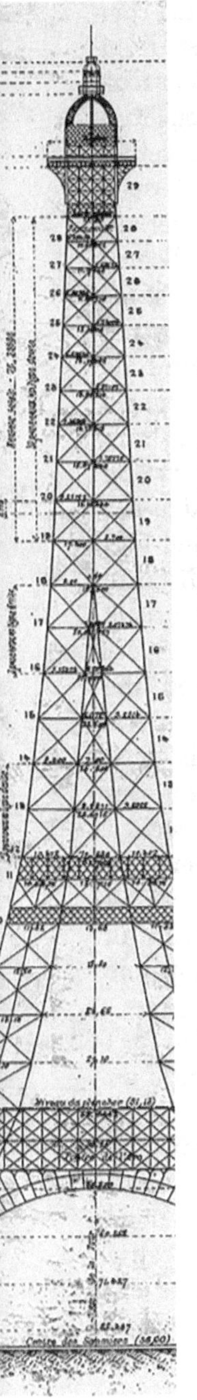

INTERVAL:
PARIS; PARAGUAY

The icon of the Enlightenment;
the rebirth of humanity, or, philosophy for dear cattle
745.4 km from Arles; 932.2 km from Nizza
7967 nm from Arles; 8020 nm from Nizza

20 March 1888

The dawning of a new century is on the rise: as construction of the first stage of the Eiffel Tower, symbol of industrial, scientific, and artistic progress *&* icon of the Enlightenment is completed in Paris, Elisabeth Förster is in Paraguay with her husband Bernhard Förster, holding an inauguration ceremony for the founding of their utopian Aryan colony, *Nueva Germania*, which would achieve the preservation of human culture & purification & rebirth of the human race. All hail Völkisch ideals!

We arrived at our new homeland and made our entry like kings, Elisabeth declared. I rode like an ancient Norse goddess in a cart drawn by six oxen. The people, all in festive dress, exulted and offered us flowers and cigars and handed us their babies to bless. Suddenly, eight splendid horsemen appeared. They were our New Germans who had come to greet us; among them were Herr Erck and other leading colonists. They brought Bern's favorite horse, beautifully decorated with black, white, and red rosettes, and he mounted the animal at once. A procession formed behind us, including riders on horseback and a long train of people.

When we reached the Aguará-umí, we were not received with a cannon salute, but cheerful gunshots rang out as we approached and a charming small wagon appeared, decorated with palm leaves like a green arbor and carrying a small red throne, which I ascended.

Once the procession reached Aguará-Guazú, the commercial center of the colony, we saw that the first triumphal arch had been erected & the official reception took place. The wives of the colonists who had been brought together brewed coffee, and our New Germans sat together under a beautifully shady tree — they all had such open and honest German faces. Then Herr Enzweiler, a very industrious and capable colonist, made a speech of welcome, raised his glass and shouted, *"Long live the Mother of the Colony,"* which pleased my heart. Accompanied by the sounds of *"Deutschland, Deutschland über alles,"* we rode to the Försterhof, our magnificent mansion in the jungle.

A month earlier, he who claimed to have Polish noblemen as ancestors stated to his friend Reinhart von Seydlitz, German politics are simply another kind of permanent winter and bad weather. Water, mess, and filth everywhere — that is how it looks from the distance. For present-day Germany, however much it may bristle, hedgehog-like, with arms, I no longer have any respect. It represents the most stupid, the most depraved, the most mendacious form of the German spirit that has ever existed — and what absurdities has not this spirit dared to perpetrate! I forgive nobody who compromises with it, even if his name be Richard Wagner, particularly when this compromise is effected in the shamefully equivocal and cautious manner in which this shrewd, all-too-shrewd glorifier of "reine Torheit" has effected it in the latter years of his life. Here in our land of sunshine what different things we have in mind!

To another friend, the Good European confessed, I want nothing whatever to do with this anti-Semitic undertaking of my sister's, let alone to offer her any money, which she continues to request — 6000 Marks for land and cattle!! Before first disembarking upon her misadventure she suggested that the portion of land be named Friedrichsheim were I to make a donation. The cattle are to be branded Eli, after Bernhard's pet name for her — and so the livestock are Jewish goddesses too?!? Laughing, I told her to call it Lamaland instead. Every anti-Semite should be packed off to Paraguay; 10 horses would not drag me there. I do not underestimate the idyllic seclusion and the Voltairean cultiver son jardin at all, especially for a philosopher: but I do not want to do it in her way, which seems too much to be a 'return to nature,' philosophy 'for dear cattle.' Indeed, I too am already a sort of 'emigrant,' and who knows, I have my Gran Chaco too!

When Elisabeth continued to pester her brother for money, my position, the retired professor wrote his sister, is financially insecure, and yours has not been proven. But above all our wishes and our interests do not coincide insofar as your project is an anti-Semitic one. The gulf between them is as great as the expanse of seas and oceans that separate us. If Dr. Förster's project succeeds, then I will be happy on your behalf and as far as I can, I will ignore the fact that it is the triumph of a movement that I reject. If it fails, I shall rejoice in the death of an anti-Semitic project.... Your reception is worthy of a priest.

The whole project of Nueva Germania, if not Bernhard and Elisabeth Förster themselves, were like archetypal incarnations of the very slave morality Nietzsche had just outlined in his recently published *Genealogy of Morality*. It was as if he had before him living embodiments of the dreaded forces he dissected *&* most feared as detrimental to the development of the species and the arrival of the Übermensch. Was then he himself not in danger of contagion, too proximate to inhaling elements devoid of the positive transformative power of steam, lava, and igneous fragments?

NIZZA

248.9 km from Arles

I must hold on to Nizza; the proximity and expectation of death; tea & biscuits; the greatest regularity in my mode of living and in my diet; a long letter from Lama; a very North German ambiance

20 March 1888

My dear mother:

The money you sent and your accompanying letter brought me great pleasure — almost as if you had made me a present. My finances were in rather a bad way; and perhaps I have already told you that my hotel fees have been increased this winter.

Nevertheless, my circumstances here are significantly less costly than those of the average hotel guest; and, moreover, this winter I have what I did not have before — a room which I like, a high one, with excellent light for my eyes, freshly decorated, with a large, heavy table, chaise longue, bookcase, and dark reddish-brown wallpaper, which I chose myself. It still seems to me that I must hold on to Nizza: the climate has a better influence on me than any other. Precisely here I can use my eyes twice as much as anywhere else.

Under this sky my head has become more free, year by year; here the uncanny consequences of being ill for years on end, in the proximity and expectation of death, are more mild in their effects. I would also mention that my digestion is better here than elsewhere; but above all, my *mind* feels more alert here, and carries its burden more easily — I mean the burden of a fate to which a *philosopher* is inevitably condemned. I walk for an hour every morning, in the afternoon for an average of three hours, and at a rapid pace — the same walk day after day — it is beautiful enough for that. After supper, I sit until 9 o'clock in the dining room, in company mainly with Englishmen and English ladies, with a lamp, which has a shade, at my table. I get up at 6:30 in the morning and make my own tea and also have a few biscuits. At 12 noon I have breakfast; at 18h, the main meal of the day. No wine, no beer, no spirits, no coffee — the greatest regularity in my mode of living and in my diet. Since last summer I have accustomed myself to drinking water — a good sign, a step forward. It happens that I have just been ill for three days; today everything is all right again. I am thinking of leaving Nizza at the end of March; the light is already too strong for me, and the air is too soft, too springlike.

It is possible that I shall have a visitor before I leave: *Seydlitz*, who is on his way back from Egypt with most of his household in tow, and who means to come and see me. My old friend *Gersdorff* also wrote in a good mood; he has just completed his month of service in Berlin (— he is chamberlain to the old empress). But the best thing was a long letter from Lama: eight pages of cordial and very sensible things. She wrote it while still in Asunción, but in very good spirits ("certainly I have a fate which suits me, and that is a good thing" —).

Yet she expresses anxiety that there will be too much to do in the months to come, because a mass of new colonists are registered and perhaps the preparations for them are not yet adequate. — I forgot to tell you that an old school friend (my "junior"), Lieutenant *Geest*, is here being treated by the Red Cross sisters; I sometimes visit him. A very North German ambiance: Frau von Münchow, Frl. von Diethfurth, and so on. My table companion this winter is once again Baroness *Pläncker*, née Seckendorf, and, as such, she is very intimate with all the Seckendorfs at court and in the army (for example, with the Graf Seckendorf, who, as you know, is the new empress's "right hand"). She is also a close friend of Geheimrat von *Bergmann*, and is herself having treatment from him, so that I was very well informed about affairs in San Remo. I have even had in my hands some pages that the crown prince wrote, a few days before his departure. — — —

No more now, my dear good mother. Grateful embraces from

Your old creature

ARLES

248.9 km from Nizza

as if we were dead or outlaws; the variety of human ills; colors like stained glass; talent is long patience; a Chinese nightmare; absinthe drinkers; creatures from another world; create a permanent exhibition of the Impressionists; the funny side of everything

21 March 1888

My dear Theo,

Here's a short note for Bernard and Lautrec, to whom I'd sol-
emnly promised to write. I'm sending it to you so that you can
give it to them sometime, it's not in the least urgent and it will
be a reason for you to see what they're doing and to hear what
they're saying, if you want.

But what's Tersteeg doing? Nothing? If you haven't had a reply, I'd drop him a line if I were you, very short and very calm,
but stating that you're astonished that he hasn't replied to you. I
say 'personally,' because even though he doesn't reply to me — to
you — HE MUST reply, and you must insist on getting a reply. If
you don't, you'll lose your self-confidence, and on the contrary,
this is an excellent opportunity to gain more. I don't believe we
should press the point in a new letter explaining things again.
We have to be careful with him — but what we have to avoid is
to let ourselves be treated as if we were dead or outlaws. Enough.
Let's hope that you've received his reply in the meantime.

I've had a line from Gauguin, who complains about the bad
weather, is still unwell, and says nothing vexes him more than
lack of money among the variety of human ills, and yet he feels
doomed to be broke for ever.

Rain & wind these past few days, I've worked at home on the
study of which I've made a croquis in Bernard's letter. My aim was
to give it colors like stained glass, and a design of solid outlines.

Am reading *Pierre et Jean* by Guy de Maupassant. It's beautiful — have you read the preface explaining the freedom the
artist has to exaggerate, to create in a novel a more beautiful,
simpler, more consoling nature, and explaining what Flaubert's
phrase might have meant, "talent is long patience" — and originality and effort of will and intense observation?

There's a Gothic porch here that I'm beginning to think is admirable, the porch of St. Trophime, but it's so cruel, so monstrous,
like a Chinese nightmare, that even this beautiful monument in so
grand a style seems to me to belong to another world, to which I'm
as glad not to belong as to the glorious world of Nero the Roman.

Must I tell the truth and add that the Zouaves, the brothels, the adorable little Arlésiennes going off to make their first communion, the priest in his surplice who looks like a dangerous rhinoceros, the absinthe drinkers, also seem to me like creatures from another world? This doesn't mean I'd feel at home in an artistic world, but it means I prefer to make fun of myself than to feel lonely. And I think I'd feel sad if I didn't see the funny side of everything.

You've had plenty of snow in Paris, from what our friend *L'Intransigeant* tells us. However, it's not a bad idea for a journalist to advise General Boulanger to put the secret police off the scent by henceforth wearing rose-tinted spectacles, which in his opinion would go better with the General's beard. Perhaps this will have the favorable influence we've been wanting for so long — on the picture trade.

But nevertheless we're going to see something of what there is in this famous Mr. Tersteeg. He'll have to come to a decision — really — in the interests of our pals we are, it seems to me, under some obligation not to let ourselves be thought of as dead men. It's not about us but it's about the question of the Impressionists in general, so as he has been approached by us, we must have his reply.

You must feel like me that we can't move forward without having positive information about his intentions.

If we think it's a good idea to create a permanent exhibition of the Impressionists in London and Marseille, it goes without saying that we'll try to establish them. So it remains to be seen, will Tersteeg be part of it? Yes or no?

And if not, what are his intentions as regards an offensive, do they exist, yes or no? And has he calculated, like us, the effect of a fall on paintings that are highly priced at present, a fall which, it seems to me, will probably come about as soon as the Impressionists rise.

Look at the way those who sell highly priced paintings are harming themselves by opposing, for political reasons, the advent of a school that for years has shown an energy and a perseverance worthy of Millet, Daubigny, and others. But let me know if Tersteeg has written to you and what he may have said. I'll do nothing about this without you. Good luck and a handshake.

Ever yours,
Vincent

TORINO

when privately one sanctions one's life by works; a very stormy journey; I do stupid things; the pale noblesse of Genoa; miserable rainy weather; the court and the noblesse of Torino; a princely residence of the 17th century; the most beautiful cafés I have ever seen

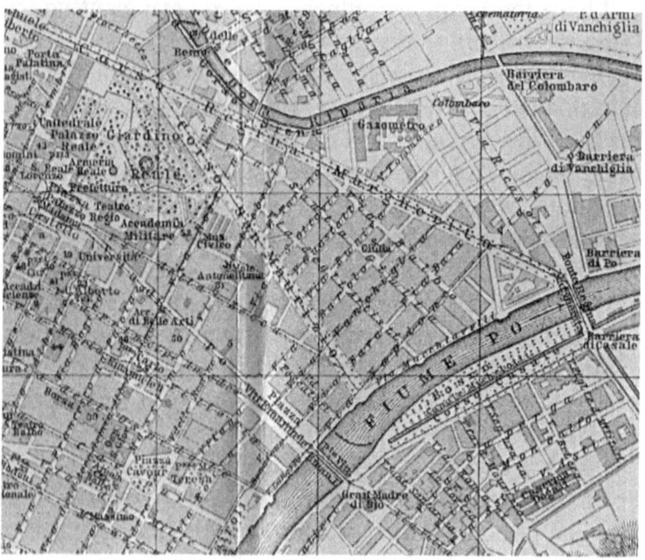

7 April 1888, Saturday

Dear friend:

How good it was to hear from you! The first greeting I received here came from you; and the last to reach me in Nizza was also from you. And what good and curious things you announced! That your quartet lies before you in a state of some calligraphic perfection, and that you now, on account of this, bless this last winter also! One certainly does become a very demanding sort of person when privately one sanctions one's life by works; it makes one forget, especially, to please people. One is too serious — you feel this — there is a devilish seriousness at the back of a man who wants to have his work respected...

Dear friend, I am using the first calm after a very stormy journey to write you a letter. Perhaps this will give me some peace and composure, for until now I was all in pieces and never have I traveled under such unfavorable circumstances. Is it possible to have so many absurd experiences between Monday and Saturday!

Everything went wrong, from the very start. I was sick for two days — where? In Sampierdarena. Do not think I was wanting to travel there. Only my luggage held fast to the original course, to Torino; we others — that is, my hand luggage and I — dispersed in various directions. And how expensive the journey was! How rich my poverty will have made some people! I really am not fit for traveling alone any more; I get so worked up that I do stupid things. Here too, at the start everything was every which way. I spent a sleepless night, amazed, not comprehending all the things the day had brought. When I see you again, I shall describe to you a scene in Savona that might have come straight out of the *Fliegende Blätter*. Only it made me ill.

In Genoa I walked around like a mere shadow among memories. Five or six special places there which I loved appealed to me even more strongly; it seemed to me to have an incomparable pale *noblesse*, and to be vastly superior to everything else the Riviera offers. I thank my destiny for condemning me to live in this hard and gloomy city during the years of *décadence*; every time one leaves it, one has also left oneself behind — the will expands again, and one no longer has the courage to be pusillanimous. I never felt more grateful than during this pilgrimage through Genoa.

But Torino! Dear friend, I congratulate you! Your advice met my deepest wishes! This is really the city that I can now use! This is palpably for me, and was so almost from the start, however horrible the situation was for the first days. Above all, miserable rainy weather, icy, changeable, oppressive to the nerves, with humid, warm half hours between. But what a dignified and serious city! Not at all a metropolis, not at all modern, as I had feared, but a princely residence of the 17th century, one that had only a *single* commanding taste in all things — the court and the *noblesse*. Everywhere the aristocratic calm has been kept: there are no petty suburbs; a unity of taste even in matters of color (the whole city is yellow or reddish-brown). And a classical place for the feet as for the eyes! What robustness, what sidewalks, not to mention the horse-drawn omnibuses and trams, the organization of which verges on the marvelous here! One can live, it seems, more cheaply here than in the other large Italian cities I know; also, nobody has swindled me so far. I am regarded as an *ufficiale tedesco* (whereas I figured last winter in the official aliens' register of Nizza *comme Polonais*). Incredible — what serious and solemn palaces! And the style of the palaces, without any pretentiousness; the streets clean and serious — and everything far more dignified than I had expected! The most beautiful cafés I have ever seen.

These arcades are somewhat necessary when the climate is so changeable, but they are spacious — they do not oppress one. The evening on the Po Bridge — glorious! Beyond good and evil!

The problem remains the weather in Torino. I have suffered from it so far extraordinarily — I could hardly recognize myself.

With greetings & thanks,
your devoted friend Nietzsche

ARLES

416.4 km from Torino

The air here is definitely doing me good; I hope to make real progress this year; yesterday I saw a bullfight; this rage to paint orchards; a constant fever for work; fits of faintness; the blood's restoring itself; we have a chance of selling or exchanging; you can't be at the pole and the equator at the same time

Monday, 9 April 1888

My dear Theo,

Thanks for your letter and for the 100-franc note it contained. I've sent you croquis of the paintings intended for Holland. Goes without saying that the painted studies are more brilliant in color. Am hard at work again, still orchards in blossom.

The air here is definitely doing me good, I could wish you deep lungfuls of it. One of its effects is quite funny, one small glass of cognac goes to my head down here, so without having recourse to stimulants to get my blood circulating, my constitution won't be taxed so much all the same.

But I've had a terribly weak stomach since I've been here, well, that's probably a matter of a lot of patience.

I hope to make real progress this year, which I really need to do too.

I've got a new orchard that's as good as the pink peach trees — some very pale pink apricot trees. At present I'm working on some yellow-white plum trees with thousands of black branches.

I'm using vast quantities of canvases and colors but all the same I hope not to waste money.

Out of 4 canvases perhaps there'll scarcely be one that would make a *painting* like Tersteeg's or Mauve's, but we'll be able to use the studies for exchanges, I hope. When will I be able to send you something? I'd so much like to do two of Tersteeg's, because it's better than the Asnières studies.

Yesterday I saw a bullfight where five men were working the ox with banderillas and rosettes. A toreador crushed one of his balls jumping over the barrier. He was a blond man with grey eyes and a lot of sangfroid; they said he'd feel it for a long time. He was dressed in sky-blue and gold, just like the little horseman in our Monticelli with the 3 figures in a wood. The bullring looks so beautiful when there's sunshine and a crowd.

Bravo for Pissarro, he's right, I think. I hope he'll do an exchange with us one day.

The same for Seurat, it would be a good thing to have a painted study by him.

Anyway, I'm working hard, hoping we'll be able to do things of this kind.

The month will be hard for you and me, but nevertheless, if you can manage it, it's to our advantage to do as many orchards in blossom as we can. I'm now well under way and I need 10 more, I think, same subject.

You know I'm changeable in my work, and this rage to paint orchards won't last for ever. After that it may be bullrings. And I have an ENORMOUS amount of drawing to do, because I'd like to do drawings in the style of Japanese prints. I can't do anything but strike while the iron's hot. Will be worn out after the orchards, because they're no. 25 and 30 and 20 canvases.

We wouldn't have too many if I could knock off twice the number. Because I believe that could perhaps melt the ice in Holland once and for all. Mauve's death was a rude shock for me. You'll easily see that the pink peach trees were painted with a certain passion. I also need a *starry night* with *Cypresses* or — perhaps above a field of ripe wheat, there are some really beautiful nights here. I have a constant fever for work.

Am quite curious to know what the results will be after a year, I hope by then I'll be less troubled by fits of faintness. At the moment I suffer a lot some days, but that doesn't worry me in the least because it's nothing but the reaction to this past winter, which wasn't normal. And the blood's restoring itself, that's the main thing.

We must reach the point where my paintings are worth what I spend and even exceed that, seeing that so much has been spent already. Ah well, we'll get there. Not everything I do is a success, of course, but the work's getting along. Up to now you haven't complained about what I spend here, but let me warn you that if I continue my work at the same rate I'll find it hard to manage. But the work's excessive.

If a month or a fortnight comes when you feel hard up let me know — then I'll turn my hand to doing drawings and that will cost us less. This is to tell you that you shouldn't force yourself for no reason — there's so much to do here, all sorts of studies, that it's not the same as in Paris, where you can't sit down wherever you please.

If it's possible to manage a bit of a steep month, so much the better, because orchards in blossom are subjects we have a chance of selling or exchanging. But I thought about the fact that you'll have the rent to pay, and that's why you must let me know if you're too hard up.

I'm still going about with the Danish painter, but he's going home soon. He's an intelligent boy, and fine as far as loyalty and manners go, but his painting is still very poor. You'll probably see him when he passes through Paris.

It was kind of you to go & see Bernard. If he does his service in Algeria, who knows, perhaps I'll go and keep him company.

Has winter come to an end in Paris at long last?

I think what Kahn says is quite true, that I haven't paid enough attention to values, but it'll be quite another thing they'll say later — and no less true.

It's not possible to do both values and color.

Théodore Rousseau has done it better than anyone else, by mixing his colors the darkness caused by time has increased, and now his paintings are hardly recognizable.

You can't be at the pole and the equator at the same time. You have to choose. And I have high hopes of doing that, too, and it will probably be color.

More soon, handshake from me to you, to Koning and to the pals.

Vincent

TORINO

A vir obscurissimus! *I enclose a small vita, the first I have written; the basic scheme according to which I have so far lived (a rigorous promise); the greatest physical elasticity and fullness; the loveliest sidewalks in the world; my forebears were Polish aristocrats; I had to give up my German citizenship; I am versed in the use of two weapons: saber and cannon — and, perhaps, one other; I became indescribably intimate with Richard and Cosima Wagner; 200 days of pain; I have never had any symptoms of mental disturbance; a few climatic and meteorological conditions are indispensable; I am, by instinct, a courageous animal, even a military one; Am I a philosopher? What does that matter!*

Torino (Italia) ferma in posta

10 April 1888

But, verehrter Herr, what a surprise! — Where did you find the courage to consider speaking in public about a *vir obscurissimus!* ... Do you perhaps believe that I am known in my own dear country? I am treated there as if I were something way-out and absurd, something that one need not for the time being *take seriously* ... Obviously you sense that I do not take my compatriots seriously either: and how could I today, now that German Geist has become a *contradictio in adjecto!* —

I am most grateful to you for the photograph. Unfortunately nothing of the kind is to be had from my side: the last pictures I had are in the possession of my married sister in South America.

I enclose a small vita, the first I have written. As regards the chronology of the particular books, you will find it on the back flyleaf of *Jenseits von Gut und Böse.* Perhaps you no longer have that page.

Die Geburt der Tragödie was written between the summer of 1870 and the winter of 1871 (finished in Lugano, where I was living with Field Marshal Moltke's family).

The *Unzeitgemäße Betrachtungen,* between 1872 and summer 1875 (there should have been 13 of these; my health fortunately said No!).

— What you say about *Schopenhauer als Erzieher* gives me pleasure. This little essay serves me as a signal of recognition: the man to whom it says nothing *personal* will probably not be further interested in me. It contains the basic scheme according to which I have so far lived; it is a rigorous *promise.*

Menschliches, Allzumenschliches with its two continuations, summer, 1876–79. *Morgenröte,* 1880. The *fröhliche Wissenschaft,* January 1882. *Zarathustra,* 1883–85 (each part in about ten days. Perfect state of a "man inspired." All parts conceived on strenuous marches; absolute certainty, as if every thought were being called out to me. At the same time as the writing, the greatest physical elasticity and fullness —).

Jenseits von Gut und Böse, summer 1885 in the Oberengadin and the foll. winter in Nizza.

The *Genealogie* resolved on, written down, and the clean copy sent to the Leipzig printer between 10 and 30 July 1887. (Of course there are *philologica* by me too. But that does not concern either of *us* anymore.)

I am at the moment giving *Torino* a trial; I mean to stay here until 5 June, and then go to the Engadin. Weather so far hard and bad as in winter. But the city superbly quiet and flattering to my instincts. The loveliest sidewalks in the world.

Greetings from your grateful and devoted

Nietzsche

A wretched pity that I do not understand either Danish or Swedish.

Vita. — I was born on 15 Oct. 1844, on the battlefield of *Lützen*. The first *name* I heard was that of Gustav Adolf. My forebears were Polish aristocrats (Niëzky); it seems that the type has been well preserved, despite three German "mothers." Abroad, I am usually taken for a Pole; even this last winter the aliens' register in Nizza had me inscribed *comme Polonais*. I have been told that my head and features appear in paintings by Matejko. My grandmother was associated with the Goethe-Schiller circle in Weimar; her brother became Herder's successor as superintendent general of the churches in the duchy of Weimar. I had the good fortune to be a pupil at the distinguished *Schulpforta*, which produced so many men of note (Klopstock, Fichte, Schlegel, Ranke, and so on, and so on) in German literature. We had teachers who would have done honor to any University (or have done so —) I was a student at Bonn, and later in Leipzig; in his old age, *Ritschl*, in those days the foremost classical scholar in Germany, picked me out almost from the start. At the age of 22 I was contributing to the *Literarisches Zentralblatt* (*Zarncke*). The establishment of a classical society at Leipzig, which exists to this day, was my doing. In the winter of 1868–69 the University of Basel offered me a professorship; I did not even have my doctorate. *Subsequently* the University of Leipzig gave me the doctorate, in a very honorable fashion, without any examination, without even a dissertation. From Easter, 1869–1879, I was at Basel; I had to give up my German citizenship, because as an officer (*mounted artillery*) I would have been drafted too frequently and disturbed in my academic duties. Nevertheless, I am versed in the use of two weapons: saber and cannon — and, perhaps, one other . . . At Basel everything went very well, in spite of my youth; it happened, especially with examinations for the doctorate, that the examinee was older than the examiner. It was my great good fortune that friendly relations developed between Jakob *Burckhardt* and myself, a very unusual thing for this very hermetic and aloof thinker. An even greater good fortune that, from the beginning of my life at Basel, I became indescribably intimate with Richard and Cosima *Wagner*, who were then living on the estate at Tribschen near Luzern, as on an island cut off from all their earlier associations. For several years we shared all our great and small experiences — there was limitless confidence between us. (In Wagner, *Collected Writings*, Vol. 7, you will find an *"epistle"* from him to me, written when the *Geburt der Tragödie* appeared.) Through this relationship I met a wide circle of interesting men (and "man-esses") actually almost everyone sprouting between Paris and Petersburg. Around 1876 my health grew worse. I spent a winter in Sorrento then, with my old friend Baroness Meysenbug (*Memoirs of an Idealist*) and the congenial Dr. Rée. My health did not improve. There were extremely painful and obstinate headaches that exhausted all my strength. They increased over long years, to reach a climax at which pain was habitual, so that any given year contained for me 200 days of pain. The malaise must have had an entirely *local* cause — there was no neuropathological basis for it at all. I have never had any symptoms of mental disturbance — not even fever, no fainting. My pulse was as slow as that of the first Napoleon (= 60). My *specialty* was to endure the extremity of pain, *cru, vert*, with complete lucidity for two or three days in succession, with continuous vomiting of mucus. Rumors have gone around that I am in a madhouse (have even died there). Nothing could be further from the truth. During this terrible period my mind even attained *maturity*: as testimony, the *Morgenröte*, which I wrote in 1881 during a winter of unbelievable misery in Genoa, far from doctors, friends, and relatives. The book is, for me, a kind of "dynamometer" — I wrote it when my strength and health were at a *minimum*. From 1882 on, *very* slowly to be sure, my health was in the ascendant again: the crisis was passed (— my father died very young, at exactly the age at which I myself was nearest to death). Even today I have to be extremely cautious; a few climatic and meteorological conditions are indispensable. It is not by choice, it is by *necessity*, that I spend the summers in the Oberengadin, the winters on the Riviera . . . Recently my sickness has done me the *greatest service*: it *has liberated* me, it has restored to me the courage to be myself . . . Also I am, by instinct, a courageous animal, even a military one. The long resistance has exasperated my pride a little. — Am I a *philosopher*? What does that matter! . . .

ARLES

416.4 km from Torino

sunshine that made all the little white flowers sparkle; at risk and peril I carried on painting; since I'm spending so much we mustn't lose sight of the fact that we've got to try to get some back; not to find oneself in real life; what's in people's hearts is also the heart of business; this victory that's almost guaranteed in advance; all the colors that Impressionism has made fashionable are unstable

Wednesday, 11 April 1888

My dear Theo,

It's awfully good of you to have sent me the complete order of
colors, I've just received them but haven't yet had the time to
check them. I'm so pleased about it. Today has been a good day
too. This morning I worked on an orchard of plum trees in blossom — suddenly a tremendous wind began to blow, an effect I'd
only ever seen here — and came back again at intervals. In the
intervals, sunshine that made all the little white flowers sparkle.
It was so beautiful! My friend the Dane came to join me, and at
risk and peril every moment of seeing the whole lot of it on the
ground I carried on painting — in this white effect there's a lot
of yellow with blue and lilac, the sky is white and blue. But as
for the execution of what we do out of doors like this, what will
they say? Well, let's wait & see.

So, after supper I started on the same painting I intend for
Tersteeg, *The Langlais Bridge*, for you. And I'd really like to make a
repetition of that one for Jet Mauve too, because since I'm spending so much we mustn't lose sight of the fact that we've got to try
to get some back, of this money that's quickly slipping away.

Afterwards I was sorry I hadn't asked for the colors from
père Tanguy anyway, although there isn't the least advantage in
that — on the contrary — but he's such a funny fellow and I
still think of him often. Don't forget to say hello to him for me
if you see him, and tell him that if he'd like any paintings for his
shop window he can have some from here, and the best. Ah, it
seems to me more and more that *people* are the root of everything, and although it remains for ever a melancholy feeling not
to find oneself in real life, in the sense that it would be better
to work in flesh itself than color or plaster, in the sense that it
would be better to make children than to make paintings or to do
business, at the same time you feel you're living when you consider that you have friends among those who themselves aren't
in real life either.

But precisely because what's in people's hearts is also the
heart of business, we have to conquer friendships in Holland, or
rather, revive them. All the more so since, as far as the cause of

Impressionism goes, we have little to fear at the moment of not winning through. And it's because of this victory that's almost guaranteed in advance that for our part we have to have good manners and do everything calmly.

I would really like to have seen the embodiment of *Marat* you spoke about the other day. That would certainly interest me very much. Unwittingly, I imagine Marat as the — moral — equivalent (but more powerful) of Xanthippe — the woman whose love turned sour. Who nevertheless is still touching — but in the end it's not as jolly as Maupassant's *La Maison Tellier*.

Has Lautrec finished his painting of a woman leaning on a little café table?

If I manage to learn how to work up the studies I've done from life on another canvas, we'd gain in terms of possible sales. I hope to succeed in doing it here — and that's why I'm making a trial effort with the two paintings that will go to Holland, and on the other hand, you'll have them too, and in this way there's nothing reckless.

You were right to tell Tasset that the geranium lake should be included after all, he sent it, I've just checked — *all the colors that Impressionism has made fashionable are unstable*, all the more reason boldly to use them too raw, time will only soften them too much. So the whole order I made up, in other words the 3 chromes (the orange, the yellow, the lemon), the Prussian blue, the emerald, the madder lakes, the Veronese green, the orange lead, all of that is hardly found in the Dutch palette, Maris, Mauve, and Israëls. But it's found in that of Delacroix, who had a passion for the two colors most disapproved of, and for the best of reasons, lemon and Prussian blue. All the same, I think he did superb things with them, blues and lemon yellows. Handshake to you, to Koning, and once again many thanks for the colors.

Ever yours,
Vincent

INTERVAL: COPENHAGEN

The tremendous ejaculation of Friedrich Nietzsche's sperm
1553.7 km from Torino, 1786.8 km from Arles

April 1888

When Georges Brandes gave the first public lectures on
the philosophy of Friedrich Nietzsche, Rodin's *The Poet*
(later to be reconfigured as *The Thinker*) was displayed in
Copenhagen as part of a major exhibition of French art,
including Delacroix, Courbet, Puvis de Chavannes and
others. Amongst the attendees was the 25-year old artist Edvard Munch, whose later 1893 painting *The Scream*
would include a depiction of the infernal sky of 1883,
the terrifying twilights of Krakatoa, which the painter
witnessed that season when he felt a great, unending
scream piercing through nature.

Originally fashioned after Dante, who used to sit
and think on a rock in Firenze, Rodin's *Poet* symbolizes
the creative genius that creates the seething world depicted below him in *The Gates of Hell*. Ugolino, Frances-
ca, Paolo, and all the characters of the *Divina Commedia*
flower forth from the poet's mind, a scintillating projection made flesh-stone. It is a world born of thought; a
materialization of images; a genesis of form rising out of
chaos, like inchoate lava rising from a magma chamber
and being given more definitive shape through its main
and secondary vents.

Broken free from the circumscribing bond to Dante,
Rodin's *Poet* becomes *The Thinker*, not a specific individual, but an archetypal figure crouched on a rock against
which his feet are contracted, fist pressed against his
teeth, right elbow pressed tautly upon his left leg. The
sheer concentrated force *&* gravity of thinking is embodied in this tense, pressurized geometry. The figure sits

in profound contemplation, fertile thoughts slowly unfurling in its body, thoughts that it will transform into a new reality — from the Proterozoic to fully formed life. He is not a passive dreamer; he is an active creator with a strong will to power. Symbol of the potency of thought and of mental creativity, the artist-philosopher, the visionary who peers from its elevated perch into the dark heart of humanity, like Nietzsche in Nizza surveying eons of time, one critic saw Michelangelo's *terribilità* in Rodin's *Thinker* and called the sculpture a true son of the 19th century. Was it an unconscious vision of the philosopher?

During his first lecture, the hall, Brandes told the thinker, was not quite full, an audience of perhaps 150. However, after a newspaper reported on the lecture, and following an article written by Brandes himself, the number of Nietzsche's listeners expanded exponentially — for the second lecture, the hall was full to bursting. Brandes spoke of Nietzsche's philosophy as a form of aristocratic radicalism and elsewhere referred to him as a diviner, a seer, and an artist less fascinating by what he does than what he is. Some 300 people listened, Brandes noted, with the greatest attention to my exposition of your works.

The lectures ended in the form of an ovation — the seeds of a new thought had been disseminated. A fitting *musical reception* for a philosopher who believed that he should have sung, not spoken!

If not a direct attendee, August Strindberg read of the lectures in a local paper *&* spoke of them to a friend, stating that everything is there! Don't deny yourself this pleasure! N. is a poet as well.

More wildly, to Brandes' brother, Strindberg wrote, the uterus of my mental world has received a tremendous ejaculation of the sperm from Friedrich Nietzsche, so that I feel like a bitch with a full belly. He's the man for me!

What zygotes could be born of this strange union? How many others would imbibe a tremendous ejaculation of the sperm from Friedrich Nietzsche till their bellies were full to bursting, too? And not only women, but also men, for, as Strindberg proved, even the male species could be impregnated by Herr Dynamite. Who didn't want to be a bitch full to bursting with Nietzsche's explosive sperm?

Later, to Brandes, the impregnator replied, what a great share you have had in my first successful spring. The history of my springs, for the last 15 years at least, has been, I must tell you, a tale of horror, a fatality of decadence and infirmity. Places made no difference; it was as though no prescription, no diet, no climate could change the essentially depressing character of this time of year. But behold, Torino! And the first good news, your news, my dear Sir, which proved to me that I am alive…. For I am sometimes apt to forget that I am alive.

Albeit gratifying, there is danger in being understood, as the hermit of Sils himself knew, if understanding is ever at all possible. Did not the masked one repeatedly ask, questioning those who did not read him with their bodies, questioning those who did not read him musically, contrapuntally, synesthetically, *Have I been understood?* Have I been *heard?* And yet, there are times when one wishes just as surely not to be understood. When one erects walls to protect oneself from those whom one does not want to communicate with, from those who may one day pronounce one holy, from those for whom one is a calamity. *En garde!!!*

In an early letter to the philosopher, the impregnated one himself warned, knowing full well the danger of being understood by just anybody, the moment you are known and understood, your stature will be diminished. And the sacred and revered rabble will address you with familiarity as their equal. Better to preserve your diminished solitude, and allow us 10,000 other elite spirits to make a secret pilgrimage to your sanctuary in

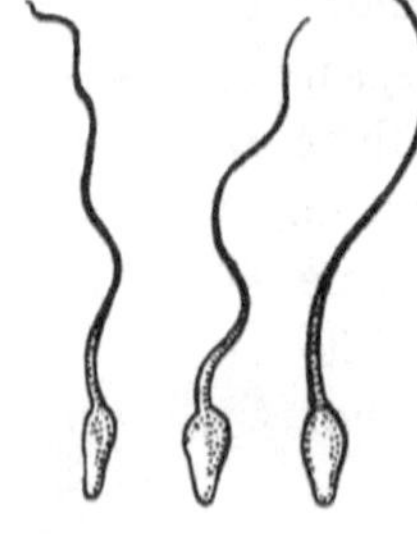

order to imbibe at our pleasure. Let us protect your esoteric teaching by keeping it pure and inviolate, and not divulge it except through the medium of your devoted catechumens, among whom I sign myself.

From the high elevation of the Upper Engadine to the lower elevation of Nizza & Torino, with the aid of a Danish Jew as midwife, the hermit of Sils Maria was moving from a desert of readers and a predominately celibate life to impregnating the uterus of men as world-reaching as Strindberg. O what distances word-sperm can travel! O what an intellectual orgy! O what wild seeds! This world is the will to power — and nothing besides! And you yourselves are also this will to power — and nothing besides!

In his dreams that night, Nietzsche asked, who else of you would like to sleep with me? I want to impregnate!

TORINO

416.4 km from Arles

a little wingbeat of hope; gloomy asses and night owls!; What a lot one will have to thank these Jews for!; a capital discovery; my digestion is that of a demigod; the first place in which I am possible!; tutto Torino Carmenizzato!; people treat the German professor most courteously; everything is tasty! and good for the stomach; some energy-giving element in the air

Friday, 20 April 1888, letters, as till now: *poste restante*

Dear friend,

how remarkable this all is! That now, after all, your star should rise over *Berlin*! That there is a little wing beat of hope again! — Really, your recent *diversion*, of which you write, is one of the most improbable and unforeseen things possible on this earth. It makes one believe in *miracles* again: a great step forward in the art of living!... It makes me extremely happy, dear friend, that something cheerful and colorful has flown across your path: because that is exactly what should have been achieved for you — but what are we *others* but gloomy asses and night owls!... That was something for the *Krause* philosophy — and not for the Nietzschean one!...

As far as the *latter* is concerned, something of the kind must exist, if one can trust a *Danish* newspaper that reached me recently. It announces that a series of public lectures is being given at the University of Copenhagen, "om den tüzke Filosof Friedrich Nietzsche." By whom? You can guess!... What a lot one will have to thank these Jews for! — Just think of my Leipzig friends at the university: and how many *kilometers* they are from the idea of lecturing about me! —

Torino, dear friend, is a *capital* discovery. I shall say a few things about it, with the ulterior motive that you, too, might benefit from it. I'm in a good mood, working from morning to night — a little pamphlet on music is keeping my fingers occupied — my digestion is that of a demigod, sleeping despite the coaches rattling by at night: all signs that Nietzsche has adapted himself eminently well to Torino. It is the *air* that does it: — dry, exhilarating, happy; there have been days on which it had all the loveliness of the air in the Engadin. When I think of my spring days in other places, for instance, in your incomparable magic seashell: how great the contrast is: the first place in which I am *possible*!... And everything accommodating, the people congenial and good-hearted. One can live *cheaply*: 25 francs, including service, for a room in the historic center of the city, vis-à-vis the grand Palazzo Carignano of 1780: five paces from the great Portici and the

Piazzo Castello, from the post office, from the Teatro Carignano!
— In the latter, since I have arrived, *Carmen*: naturally!!! successo piramidale, tutto Torino Carmenizzato! The same conductor as in Nizza. Also *Lala-Roekh* by Fél. David, Bizet's teacher. A young composer is performing an operetta, with his own libretto, Herr Miller junior. The address book lists 21 composers, 12 theaters, an accademia philarmonica, a school for music, and countless teachers of all kinds of instruments. Moral: almost a *music center*! — The spacious high Portici are the *pride*: they extend over 10,020 meters, which means two good hours of walking. Big *trilingual* bookshops. I have never seen anything like it. The firm of Löscher was very attentive to me. Its present head, Herr Clausen, gives me all kinds of information (— I am weighing the possibility of spending a winter here myself). An excellent *trattoria*, where people treat the German professor most courteously: I pay for each meal, including the tip, 1 fs. 25 ct. (minestra or risotto, a good piece of roast, vegetables, and grissini — everything is tasty! and good for the stomach). The water is wonderful; coffee in the foremost cafés costs 20 ct. a pot; ice cream, of the highest quality, 30 ct. All this will give you some idea. —

Today the sky is overcast and rainy. But I do not seem to be cross. About summer I am told that only four hours of the day are really hot. The mornings and evenings refreshing. One can see beyond the town into the world of snow: there seems to be nothing in the way; that the streets run straight into the Alps. Autumn is said to be the most beautiful time. Really, there has to be some energy-giving element in the air: to be at home here will make one *King* of Italy ...

So much, my dear old friend! Most affectionate greetings.

Your N.

The moral I draw is this: You need a place where you can live all the year round, but under different meteorological influences than in Venice, perhaps also closer to music, possibilities of performance ... And we must keep a hold on Italy!!!!!!

Tell me a little more about your quartet. Where it leads.

ARLES

416.4 km from Torino

you do not say clearly enough what you want to make felt; the betrayal of the desirable good and beautiful things; the charm which external life exercises on our six senses; saying a thing well is as interesting and as difficult as painting it; I am working on nine orchards; I aspire to share the glory of the immortal Tartarin; don't despair and above all don't have any spleen; stomach disorders; get your blood in good condition in advance

20 April 1888

My dear comrade Bernard,

Many thanks for the sonnets you sent me; I very much like the form and the sonorous melody of the first. However, with regard to idea and sentiment it may be that I prefer the last one. But it seems to me that you do not say clearly enough what you want to make felt — the certainty that one seems to have, and which one can in any case prove, of the nothingness, the emptiness, the betrayal of the desirable good and beautiful things; and that, despite this knowledge, one lets oneself be eternally fooled by the charm which external life, the things outside ourselves, exercises on our six senses, as if one did not know anything, and especially the difference between objectivity and subjectivity. Fortunately we remain stupid and hopeful in this way.

In short, your sonnets are not as good as your painting yet; never mind, it will come; you must certainly continue your sonnets. There are so many people, especially among our comrades, who imagine that words are nothing — on the contrary, isn't it true that saying a thing well is as interesting and as difficult as painting it? There is the art of lines and colors, but the art of words is there nonetheless, and will remain.

Here is another orchard, rather simple as a composition: a white tree, a small green tree, a square patch of green, lilac soil, an orange roof, a large blue sky. I am working on nine orchards: one white, one pink, almost red; one white-blue, one greyish pink; one green and pink.

Yesterday I overdid one of a cherry tree against a blue sky; the young leaf shoots were orange and gold, the clusters of flowers white, and that against the green-blue of the sky was wonderfully glorious. Unfortunately there is rain today that prevents my returning to the charge.

I saw a brothel here last Sunday — not counting the other days — a large room, the walls covered with blued whitewash — like a village school. Fifty or more military men in red and civilians in black, their faces a magnificent yellow or orange (what hues there are in the faces here), the women in sky blue, in vermilion, as unqualified *&* garish as possible. The whole in a yellow light. A good deal less lugubrious than the same kind of offices in Paris.

There is no "spleen" in the air here.

For the moment I am still lying low and keeping very quiet, for first of all I must recover from a stomach disorder of which I am the happy owner, but after that I shall have to make a lot of noise, as I aspire to share the glory of the immortal Tartarin de Tarascon.

I was enormously interested to hear that you intend to spend your time as a soldier in Algeria. That is perfect, and quite far from being a misfortune. Really, I congratulate you on it; at any rate we shall see each other in Marseilles.

You will see how delighted you will be with seeing the blue here and with feeling the sun.

At present I have a terrace for a studio.

I certainly intend to go do seascapes at Marseilles too; I don't yearn for the grey sea of the North. If you see Gaugin, remember me most kindly to him. I must write him right now.

My dear comrade Bernard, don't despair and above all don't have any *spleen*, old fellow, for with our talent and with your stay in Algeria you will turn out a wonderfully good and true artist. You too will belong to the South. If I have any advice to give you it is to fortify yourself, to eat healthy things, yes, a full year in advance — from now on — for it won't do to come here with a damaged stomach and deteriorated blood.

This was the case with me, and although I am recovering, I am recovering slowly, and I regret not having been a bit more careful beforehand. But not such a damnable winter as the past one — what was there to be done? — for it was a superhuman winter.

So get your blood in good condition in advance; here, with the bad food, it is difficult to pull through, but once one is in good health again it is less difficult to remain so than in Paris.

Write to me soon, always the same address: "Restaurant Carrel, Arles." A handshake.

Sincerely yours,
Vincent

TORINO

416.4 km from Arles

*it has color, it protests; calligraphic perfection; addicted to
the absurd; the secrecy in a big city; café 20 ct., chocolade 30,
das pezzo gelato 30; one walks around with more boldness;
always a princely taste;* many *very* bright days; *the clumsiest thoughts have wings; coordination* of taste

1 May 1888

Dear friend,

Your southern title pleases me very much; it has color, it *protests* — perhaps you'd better use "Return Home to Avignon" instead of the somewhat cozy-sounding imperative "Homecoming to Avignon!" —

And that reminds me of *Returning Home to Annaberg* and, who knows? of a tournament in Berlin; which, hopefully, will also be followed by some ball game, along with a nocturne, and everything else that is possible on a beautiful country estate, away from the big city! It all seems to me very well thought out: today marks a year in which I wish from the bottom of my heart that you have a good and beautiful piece of *life* behind you — in "calligraphic perfection"...

The weather today is gloomy so I can write all the more impartially about Torino, of which I would like to give you an even more *practical* conception than my last letters did. Because Torino is climatically good, precisely for me, a sick, absurdly dependent person and that it is a promised land for, i.e., my legs and eyes, does not yet blind me to the fact that Torino would have to offer you quite different advantages in order to be possible at all, *after* Venice. You write that it is considered an expensive city? This may be completely correct in the mouth of a civil servant or military chief: such a city is expensive because it forces them to *represent* their position and because it is almost the first city of dignitaries and civil servants in Italy (seat of the general staff, etc.). Judging by *ourselves*, who do not want to represent anything and, on the contrary, for whom the *secrecy* in a big city is a boon, it is exactly the opposite. I have not yet found a cheaper place, least of all in Italy: but Leipzig is also more expensive. That comes from the big-city competition in all the *main* things (apartment, clothing, food). I eat decidedly better here, more *solidly* than I eat in Leipzig, just as good as the panada, of blessed memory, — *and* cheaper! There are a large number of well-frequented trattorias where the prices are still significantly reduced: the town is full of young people (and older bachelors), thanks to the many secondary schools, the university, the officers' corps — who all want to eat well and not pay much. In the first-rate, most luxurious cafes, they are accommodating to an unbelievable degree. The Café Nazionale, for example, which is reminiscent of Monte-Carlo, has its shiny rooms full in the evening: you can hear a concert of 12 numbers, a small, pretty orchestra — and you don't pay a centesimo more than you normally pay (café 20 ct., chocolade 30, das pezzo gelato 30 etc.). The theater prices are also *very* moderate: by the way, the electric theater-*fever* that reigns here impresses me. All theaters (except the t. regio) in full activity; a Parisian comédie company, best reputation, arriving, two new operetta companies at the same time. Torino functions by a certain flow of life, it does not push, it is *not* the image of petty commerce and *crawling* forward. The spatial greatness and grandeur has something contagious about it; one walks around with more boldness. Now the city has its splendid spring decorations, the avenues, — that was always a *princely* taste. I still can't believe my eyes when I walk along the Po in the evening and *look* over into this rich, colorful, picturesque tree- and hill-world! The other day I discovered, on the other side of the Po, a high *tree-lined avenue*, running close to the Po for 1 and ½ hours: on the other side, a full stream; deepest silence; the river adorned with small green islets, and, to one side, without interruption, in radiant purity, the *high mountains*. They are very close: it takes 50 minutes to get to Lanzo by train: — there you already have the high mountains. The local climate is conditioned by it; in particular, the many *very bright* days, even in winter (all in all only 50 days less than in Nizza) I notice how well I can cope with cloudy weather *&* overcast skies here: — I have worked on and on, more already than in the whole winter in Nizza! On nice days a lovely, light, carefree air wafts here, in which even the clumsiest thoughts develop wings ... (— To this day, I still haven't heard *Carmen*! Proof of *how* busy I am. Only in the theater once: a Neapolitan farce — why? Because the maestro's name was E. Sassone!! "Induction psycho-motrice" is what they call that today. Coming home, I lit up my old palazzo with a self-striking candle, for *which I don't know whom I owe* thanks. Again: induction psycho-motrice!! —)

Faithfully, Your friend
N.

There has to be something like *coordination* of taste: here, where my eyes and nerves are comfortable, the dishes seem to me to have been devised according to the schema of my personal taste. *And* even the water! It flows everywhere; I walk around everywhere with a little glass.

ARLES

416.4 km from Torino

bristling with many difficulties; I haven't stopped working; I rented the right-hand wing of this building; I have my independence; this bloody health; the bad wine; patience & perseverance; I definitely want to be well turned out; I'm ready for an expedition to Marseille; to live without spending more than 150 francs a month; very strong broth; I'd tried to take a studio; the capital laid out will come back into our hands; perhaps Gauguin will come to the south; moral standards seem to me less inhuman and contrary to nature than in Paris; to lead a wild life and to work are no longer compatible at all; if you could send me 100 francs

1 May 1888

My dear Theo,

Thank you very much for your letter and the 50-franc note it contained. It's not in black that I see the future, but I see it bristling with many difficulties, and at times I wonder if these won't be stronger than I am. This is especially so at times of physical weakness, and last week I suffered from a toothache that was so agonizing that it made me waste time quite in spite of myself. Nevertheless, I've just sent you a roll of small pen drawings, around a dozen. That way you'll see that even though I'd stopped painting I haven't stopped working. Among them you'll find a hasty croquis on yellow paper, a lawn in the public garden at the entrance to the town. And in the background a house more or less like this one.

Ah, well — today I rented the right-hand wing of this building, which contains 4 rooms, or more precisely, two, with two little rooms.

It's painted yellow outside, whitewashed inside — in the full sunshine. I've rented it for 15 francs a month. Now what I'd like to do would be to furnish a room, the one on the first floor, to be able to sleep there. The studio, the store, will remain here for the whole of the campaign here in the south, and that way I have my independence from petty squabbles over guest-houses, which are ruinous and depress me. In fact, Bernard writes me that he too has *a whole house*, but he has it for nothing. What luck. I'll certainly make another drawing of it for you, better than the first croquis. And at this point I dare tell you that I intend to invite Bernard and some other people to send me canvases to show them here if the opportunity arises, and it will certainly arise in Marseille. I hope I've been lucky this time — you understand, yellow outside, white inside, right out in the sun, at last I'll see my canvases in a really bright interior. The floor's made of red bricks. And outside, the public garden, of which you'll find two more drawings.

The drawings, I dare assure you, will become even better.

I've had a letter from Russell, who has bought a *Guillaumin* and 2 or 3 *Bernards*. I'm extremely pleased about that; he also writes that he'll exchange studies with me. I wouldn't be afraid of anything unless it was this bloody health. And yet I'm better than in Paris, and if my stomach has become terribly weak that's a problem I picked up there, probably due mainly to the bad wine, of which I drank too much. Here the wine is just as bad, but I only drink very little of it. And so the fact is that as I hardly eat and hardly drink I'm very weak, but my blood is improving instead of being ruined. So once again, it's patience I need in the circumstances, and perseverance.

Having received the absorbent canvas, I'm starting these days a new no. 30 canvas that I hope will be better than the others. Do you remember in *La recherche du bonheur* the chap who bought as much land as he could run round in a single day? Well, with my orchard decoration I've been that man, more or less, half a dozen out of a dozen I have anyway, but the other 6 aren't as good, and I'm sorry I didn't rather do 2 of them instead of the last 6. Anyway, I'll send you 10 or so in the next few days anyway.

I bought 2 pairs of shoes, which cost me 26 francs, and 3 shirts that cost me 27 francs, which meant that despite the 100 note I wasn't enormously rich. But in view of the fact that I plan to do business in Marseille, I definitely want to be well turned out, and I don't intend to buy anything but good quality. And the same for work, it will be better to do one painting fewer than to do it less well.

Should it come about that you had to leave those gentlemen, don't think that I have doubts about the possibility of doing business all the same, but we mustn't be caught unawares, that's all, and if it drags on a bit longer that's actually for the better.

As for me, if a few months from now I'm ready for an expedition to Marseille, I'll be able to do things with more self-assurance than if I arrived there having run out of breath. I've seen Macknight again, but still nothing of his work. I still have colors, I have brushes, I still have plenty of things in stock. But we mustn't waste our powder.

I think if you were to leave those gentlemen, for my part I'd have to manage to live without spending more than, for example, 150 francs a month. I couldn't do it now, but you'll see that in 2 months I'll be set up like that. If then we earn more, so much the better, but I want to ensure that.

So, if I had some very strong broth, that would get me going right away, it's dreadful, I've *never* been able to get even any of the very simple things I've asked those people for. And it's the same everywhere in these little restaurants. Yet it's not hard to boil potatoes. Impossible.

And no rice or macaroni either, or else it's ruined with fat or they don't do it, and make the excuse: it's for tomorrow, there's no room on the stove, etc.

It's silly but true all the same that that's why my health is poor.

All the same, it cost me a lot of agonizing to bring myself to make a decision, because I said to myself that in The Hague and in Nuenen I'd tried to take a studio and I said to myself that it had turned out badly. But many things have changed since then, and as I feel I'm on firmer ground — let's go ahead. Only we've already spent so much money on this bloody painting we mustn't forget that it has to come back in paintings. If we dare believe, and I'm sure of it, that Impressionist paintings will go up in value, we've got to do lots of them and keep the prices up.

All the more reason why we should calmly take care of the quality of the thing and not waste time. And after a few years, I can see the possibility that the capital laid out will come back into our hands, if not in cash, then in value.

And now if you agree, I'll rent or buy furniture for the bedroom. I'll go and have a look today or tomorrow morning.

I'm still convinced that nature here is just what's needed to do color. And so it's more than likely that I won't move far from here.

Raffaëlli has done a portrait of Edmond de Goncourt, hasn't he? That must be beautiful. I've seen Le Salon published by *L'Illustration*. Is the Jules Breton beautiful?

You'll soon receive a painting I did for you for the first of May.

If necessary, I could live at the new studio with someone else, and I'd very much like to. Perhaps Gauguin will come to the south. Perhaps I'll come to an arrangement with Macknight. Then we could cook at home.

In any case, the studio is too open to view for me to think it could tempt any woman, and it would be hard for a petticoat episode to lead to a cohabitation. Anyway, moral standards seem to me less inhuman and contrary to nature than in Paris. But with my temperament, to lead a wild life and to work are no longer compatible at all, and in the given circumstances I'll have to content myself with making paintings. That's not happiness and not real life, but what can you say, even this artistic life, which we know isn't *the* real one, seems so alive to me, and it would be ungrateful not to be content with it.

Now that I've found the little white studio I have one big worry fewer. I looked at a whole lot of apartments without success. It will seem funny to you that the water closet is at the neighbor's, in quite a large house that belongs to the same owner. In a southern town I think you'd be wrong to complain about it, because these facilities are few and far between, and dirty, and you can't help thinking of them as nests of germs.

On the other hand, I have water here.

I'll put some Japanese prints on the wall.

If there happened to be some canvases in your apartment that were in the way, this could always be used as a storeroom, that might become necessary, because you ought not to have mediocre things at your place.

Bernard has written to me and sent croquis.

I'm very pleased that you found our mother and sister well.

Is Reid going to Marseille? At the bottom of it, perhaps, is that he loves this woman who didn't trust us, feeling that we might perhaps not want to encourage the cohabitation. I'm inclined to believe she's the psychological reason for his coming back. You'll say that in that case we'll have to consider everything he's going to do in the future, and maintain great composure for the moment. Will you go back to Holland for the holidays? If you could do both, going to see Tersteeg and Marseille on business regarding the Impressionists, and resting at Breda between those two chores.

Have you seen Seurat again?

I shake your hand firmly, wishing you a year as full of sunshine as the weather here today. Warm regards to Koning.

Ever yours,
Vincent

If you could send me 100 francs next time, I could sleep at the studio as early as this week. I'll also write you what arrangement the furniture dealer wants to make.

TORINO

416.4 km from Arles

*hermits are not given to "forgetting"; I took steps to alien-
ate whoever has a photograph of me; to symbolize myself
again; being mistaken for an artist; very honorably mentioned in a survey of German literature; a pitch of energy;
a good humor*

4 May 1888

My dear Sir,

What you tell me gives me great pleasure and even more, let me
confess it — surprise. Be sure that I'll "owe you for it": you know,
hermits are not given to "forgetting"?..

Meanwhile, I hope my photograph will have reached you.
It goes without saying that I took steps, not exactly to be photographed (for I am extremely distrustful of haphazard photographs), but to *alienate* whoever has a photograph of me. Perhaps
I have succeeded; I have not yet heard. If not, I want to use my
first trip to *Munich* (this autumn probably) to symbolize myself
again.

The "Hymn to Life" will start on its journey to Copenhagen
one of these days. We philosophers are never more grateful than
when we are *mistaken* for artists. I am assured, moreover, by
the best judges, that the Hymn is thoroughly fit for performance,
singable, and sure in its effect (— "clear in form": this praise gave
me the greatest pleasure). Mottl, the excellent court conductor at
Carlsruhe (the conductor of the Bayreuth festival performances,
you know), has given me hopes of a performance. —

I have just heard from Italy that the point of view of my second *Untimely Meditation* has been very honorably mentioned in a
survey of German literature contributed by the Viennese scholar,
Dr. von Zdekauer, at the invitation of the *Archivio storico* of Firenze. He concludes his paper with it. —

These last weeks in Torino (where I shall stay till 5 June) have
turned out better than any I have known for years, — above
all more philosophical. Almost every day for one or two hours
I have reached such a pitch of energy as to be able to view my
whole conception from *top to bottom*: where the immense multi-
plicity of problems lies spread out beneath me, as though in relief
and clear in its outlines. This requires a maximum of strength,
for which I had almost given up hope. Everything is connected;
everything has been going well for years; you build your philosophy like a beaver, you are forced to and do not know it: but you
have to *see* all this, as I have now seen it, in order to believe it. —

I am so relieved, so strengthened, in such good humor, — I hang a little farcical tail on to the most serious things. What is the reason of all this? Have I not the good *north winds* to thank for it, the north winds which do not always come from the Alps? — they come now and then even from *Copenhagen!*

With greetings your gratefully devoted

Nietzsche

ARLES

248.9 km from Nizza

if I sleep at the studio; tormenting new color theories; people may be crassly ignorant as far as painting goes; I want my nervous system to calm down; to establish myself I'll need a good thousand francs; spend every day drawing; I can hope not to collapse out of breath before my time; what melancholias and what dejection; our neurosis and our rather too artistic way of life; live in anticipation just as though one already had a brain disease and a disease of the marrow; those splendid optimists of the true and jovial Gallic race; cold water, air, good simple food, wear the right clothes, sleep in a good bed; send me 100 francs

4 May 1888

My dear Theo,

Yesterday I went to visit some furniture dealers to see if I could
rent a bed, &c. Unfortunately they do *not* rent, and even refused
to sell on terms of paying so much per month. This is rather
awkward. Now I've thought that perhaps — if Koning were to
leave after seeing the Salon, as I believe was his original intention, after he left you could send me the bed he's occupying now.

We have to consider that if I sleep at the studio, that makes
a difference after all of around 300 francs at the end of a year,
which is otherwise spent at the hotel. I'm quite aware that it's
not possible to say in advance: I'll stay here for such or such a
length of time; however, I have many reasons to believe that a
long stay here is likely.

Yesterday I was at Fontvieille, at Macknight's — he had a
good pastel — a pink tree — two watercolors under way, and I
found him working on a head of an old woman in charcoal. He's
at the stage when the new color theories are tormenting him,
and while they prevent him from doing things according to the
old system, he hasn't sufficiently mastered his new palette to be
able to succeed this way. He seemed very embarrassed to show
them to me, so I had to go there specially and tell him I *very much*
wanted to see his work, and now it's not impossible that he may
come to stay with me here for a while. Then we would benefit,
I think, on both sides.

I very often think of *Renoir* here and his pure, clean drawing.
That's just the way objects or figures are here, in the clear light.

We have a tremendous amount of wind and mistral here, 3
days out of four at the moment, always with sunshine, though,
but then it's difficult to work out of doors.

I think something could be done here in the way of portraits.
People may be crassly ignorant as far as painting goes, but in
general they're *much more artistic* than in the north in their own
appearance and their own lives. I've seen figures here as lovely
as those of Goya and Velázquez. They know how to stick a touch
of pink on a black suit, or make a white, yellow, pink or green

and pink, or *blue and yellow* outfit, in which nothing needs to be changed from the artistic point of view. Seurat would find some very picturesque figures of men here, despite their modern suits.

Now I dare say these people here would jump at portraits. But, before daring to take the risk of throwing myself into that, I want my nervous system to calm down first, and then I want to be settled in such a way that we can receive people at the studio. And if I have to mention the big subject, by my calculations to be in good health and be acclimatized here once and for all I'll need a year, and to establish myself I'll need a good thousand francs. If in the first year — the current one — I spent 100 francs to live and 100 francs for this establishment per month, you can see there wouldn't be a sou left in this budget for painting. But by the end of this year I'm inclined to believe I'd have gained both my quite decent establishment and my health. And my occupation while waiting would above all be to spend every day drawing, with two or three paintings a month in addition.

In — the establishment — I thus also count a complete renewal of all my linen and clothes and shoes.

And I would be a different man by the end of the year.

I'd have a home and I'd have my peace of mind about my health. And so I can hope not to collapse out of breath before my time, here.

Monticelli was physically more vigorous than I am, I think, and if I had the strength I would live like him, one day at a time.

But if he became paralyzed, and without being that much of a drinker — all the more reason why I couldn't withstand it.

I was certainly well on the way to catching a paralysis when I left Paris. It caught up with me afterwards, right enough! When I stopped drinking, when I stopped smoking so much, when I started reflecting on things again instead of trying not to think — my God, what melancholias and what dejection. Working in this magnificent nature kept up my morale, but there too, after a certain amount of effort I didn't have the strength.

Ah well, that's why when I was writing to you the other day I said that if you left the Goupils you would probably feel better in terms of morale but the recovery would be very painful. While the sickness itself, you don't feel it.

My poor friend, our neurosis &c. surely also comes from our rather too artistic way of life — but it's also a fatal inheritance, since in civilization we go on becoming weaker from generation to generation.

Take our sister Wil, she has neither drunk nor led a wild life, and yet we know a photograph of her in which she has the look of a madwoman. Isn't that proof enough that if we want to look the true state of our temperament in the face we have to range ourselves among those who suffer from a neurosis that goes back a good long way.

I think Gruby's in the right in these cases: eat well, live well, see few women, in a word live in anticipation just as though one already had a brain disease and a disease of the marrow, not to mention neurosis, which really does exist.

Certainly that's taking the bull by the horns, which isn't a bad policy.

And Degas — does that and is successful. All the same, don't you feel, as I do, it's awfully hard?

And in short doesn't it do us a tremendous amount of good to listen to the wise advice of Rivet and Pangloss, those splendid optimists of the true and jovial Gallic race who leave you your self-esteem? Yet, if we want to live and work, we must be very careful and look after ourselves. Cold water, air, good simple food, wear the right clothes, sleep in a good bed and don't have worries. And not letting yourself go with the women & real life to the extent you might like to.

I'm not set on sleeping at the studio but IF I went to sleep there, it would be if I could see the possibility of establishing myself more or less for good and for a long period of time. Having no need at all now of space at the hotel, since I have the studio elsewhere, I'll tell the people it's 3 francs a day, take it or leave it. And consequently there's nothing pressing. But if it's all the same to you, send me 100 francs anyway next time, as I'd also like to have some drawers made, the way I had shirts and shoes made, and as I have to have almost all my clothes cleaned and mended. Then they'll still be perfectly good. This is urgent, in case I'd have to go to Marseille or see people here. With all these precautions we're taking now we can be more certain of being able to hold out in the long term and of putting our work in order.

There are about 10 canvases, for which I'm looking for a crate and which I'll send you in the next few days.

I shake your hand firmly, and Koning's too. I had a postcard from Koning to say he'd received a letter to collect the paintings from the Independents. But of course he just had to collect them, what can I do about it?

Ever yours,
Vincent

(It goes without saying that if at your home there were canvases that were taking up too much space you could send them here by goods train and I'd keep them in the studio here. If that isn't yet the case it will be later, so I keep quite a few studies here that don't seem good enough to me to be sent to you.)

INTERVAL: ARLES

Ceaseless wandering *&* the artistic colony
416.4 km from Torino

Wandering (1878); The Yellow House (1888)

Since 1878, van Gogh had effectively been homeless, a kind of vagabond without domicile of his own, ceaselessly wandering to and fro as he drifted through his fate. Or was his peripatetic activity in fact the very enactment of his fate? His relentless pacing of the earth began with him studying theology in Amsterdam, then taking a course at a Protestant missionary school in Laken, then practicing as a missionary in Petit-Wasmes, in the coal-mining district of Borinage in Belgium, till he was dismissed for undermining the dignity of the priesthood. Vincent's feral personality unnerved his companions, as if he were a naked satyr dancing unbridled before a mass, appendages unsheathed, bathing not in water but in wine. There was no anchorage, nor harbor, nor rooting force, only a roving whorl, spinning at great velocity, like the sharp, swift dashes that would later populate his paintings, shooting across his canvases like meteors, not unlike the protean dashes that proliferate like equally dynamic forces in Nietzsche's blood-soaked writings.

And so, Vincent's wanderings continued, almost feverishly, with him returning to his parents' home in Etten, at which point his father considered committing him to a lunatic asylum. When seeing his son with French books by Michelet or Hugo, Pastor van Gogh would think of thieves and murderers, or of immorality. Seeing in such indulgences nothing but the potential of sin and the threat of worldly evil, the pastor reminded his wayward son of his great uncle who had been infected with French ideas and took to drink, implying that Vincent too would suffer the same fate were he to continue his this-worldly life. This is your soul on French literature. *Vade retro!*

Escaping the threat of the asylum, the drifter ventured to Cuesmes to lodge with a miner, then to Brussels to study anatomy, perspective, and modeling at the Académie Royale des Beaux-Arts at the suggestion of Willem Roelofs. Disgusted by criticism of his technique and his limited knowledge of anatomy and perspective, van Gogh ceased courses at the school. To the savage painter, innate means of expression trumped all academic forms of technique.

Pulsional energies pushing him on, it was back to Etten again, with mother and father, the prodigal son still devoid of his own hearth, at the mercy of others, crippled by poverty and restlessness, but possessed by some geyser-like inner force and sense of destiny.

Amidst a cloistered family enclave, with no renegade outlets or milieus, the wanderer's social circle was limited and, longing for some union, some uniting bridge or shared root, the pastor's son grew infatuated with Kee Vos, a recently widowed cousin. After having declared his love to her, she sternly rejected him, a stricture that led the drifter to one of his extreme, impulsive gestures.

One night, he interrupted a Vos family dinner, banging upon their door and insisting to see his beloved. When his uncle refused him entry, like an ascetic engaging in self-mortification, the pastor's son held his hand over the flame of an oil lamp, testing how stalwart his flesh, will, and spirit were.

Gazing fiercely into his Uncle Stricker's eyes, Vincent implored him to allow him to see Kee, even if only for the length of time he could endure the flame. When the uncle refused and castigated his nephew for trying to coerce his daughter, he felt that the crushing things they said to him were unanswerable and that *my she*, the martyr retorted, and no other, had been killed.

Vincent's dream of love now dead, he took off for The Hague in funereal air with flame-scorched hand to attempt to hawk his paintings and to meet with a second cousin, Anton Mauve, an artist who would tutor him in watercolors and oil painting.

Rather quickly, the young painter *&* Mauve clashed; some time later, the drifter contracted gonorrhea and resided in a hospital for nearly a month. If he could not find love, he could find contagion of another kind, making greater and greater acquaintance with the afflicted ones of the earth, as if he were still an intercessor to the world, his love some Christ-like form of caritas, despite his loss of faith.

Subsequently, he befriended the prostitute Sien Hoornik, but his attempt at living with her and her young daughter was calamitous.

The young artist moved briefly to Drenthe, then returned to living with his parents again, in Nuenen, North Brabant, where he immersed himself in painting and drawing. If the nest seemed as inescapable as the wandering, a web from which the hopeful painter could not extract or free himself, he remained singularly devoted to his brush.

In the circumscribed cloister of family and familiars, van Gogh's circle of life was limited to his most nearby satellites. At that time, he developed a relation with Margot Begemann, a neighbor's daughter (and parishioner of his father's church) 10 years his senior, who often accompanied him on his outdoor painting excursions. When they developed a love for one another and decided to marry, their families opposed the union with considerable force. Another bridge broken, another attempted union shattered, another root disinterred, like some microbe devoid of a host it could adequately feed upon.

Grief-stricken, van Gogh's potential bride-to-be poisoned herself with strychnine but survived after he forced her to vomit then took her to a doctor in Utrecht to keep the incident private.

Every additional adverse event tests the will, whittles the spirit thin, lessens the wherewithal of the soul, cracking the fibers of the strange one's inner column.

When corresponding with Theo about the events, Vincent explained that Margot's doctor informed him that she had always had a highly irritable constitution. Vincent himself said that she gives me the impression of a Cremona violin that's been spoiled in the past by bad bunglers of restorers. And in the condition in which I met her, it seems to me, a good deal too much had been bungled.

That *disturbing the peace of a woman*, in the way that the theological people say, is sometimes a breaking of stagnation or melancholy that comes over many people and is worse than *death* itself. There are people who think it terrible to hurl them back into life, into feeling again, and one must weigh up carefully how far one may go. But if one does it out of a principle other than selfishness — well — then the women themselves can sometimes become furious and may even hate instead of love; *so be it*. Yet they won't readily despise the man who did it. And they do despise the men who have extinguished the manliness in themselves. Well, these are deep things of life.

Speaking of himself, the drifter pointed out that he had experienced great sadness in two cases, sadness of a very different character. So be it — but you'll see, he explained to his brother, that your own theory in this respect doesn't always produce the results that one would say it promises to produce.

Once you've attained a position and can maintain a certain status, then you'll find wife and children and domestic happiness. This is a fine promise that society makes but does it also keep that promise?

Society leaves everyone and all ways of doing things relatively disappointed.

Again *&* again, the individual's will is broken, short-circuited before it can attempt to flourish yet, even if it were to fail, even if others saw an inevitable end that the involved individuals could not, who had the right to impede it? Although even gods don't intervene in others' lives to subvert disaster, humans cannot cease meddling in the affairs of their brethren.

Sovereignty damned, autonomy negated, the freedom to fail was denied, like taking a wild bird and encaging it to protect it against the dangers of a jungle. No more bird, no longer ferine, but homunculus, anthropoidic.

Four days prior to Vincent's 32nd birthday, unexpectedly, his father dies. To Theo, Vincent would write that it was easier to die than to live. Dying is hard, he said, but living still harder.

When forced to relinquish his studio in the family house, an old laundry cellar was given him as a replacement, but it did not suffice for painting.

Shuttled from space to space, displaced as if some threatening alien whose needs were immaterial, a punishing economics slowly undermines the painter. At odds with his family, who often agitated and disturbed him, Vincent criticizes them with a fiercely pitched fury. Soon after, following a clash with his sister Anna, he departs for elsewhere, where he paints nearly 200 oil paintings in addition to drawings and watercolors, including *The Potato Eaters*, a definitive work that opens up a certain vision and perspective, a worldview conveyed through light, tone, and expression. To Bernard, who would see the painting in 1886 after befriending Vincent, it was a frightening vision.

Although it has no worldly impact, for the first time, a work of Vincent's was exhibited in a small gallery in The Hague in late 1885, a year after his personal encounter with Delacroix, with whom he discussed ideas on color, an esteemed artist confirming his own intuitions and sensations.

Later, the drifter moved to Antwerp, where he rented a room above a paint dealer's shop on Rue des Images. Living mainly on bread, coffee, and tobacco, the fervent devotee of art immersed himself in color theory and began studying the work of Rubens and developed his first infatuation with Japanese ukiyo-e woodcuts.

In March of 1886, the drifter then moved to the City of Lights, to live with Theo in Montmartre and to immerse himself in Paris life, in painting portraits, still lifes, and scenes of the city, continuing his incorporation of Japanese elements and befriending Bernard, Anquetin, Toulouse-Lautrec, and other artists. During his trips to Asnières, Vincent became acquainted with Signac and started adopting elements of pointillism in his technique, almost as if distrusting the opening of his vision that occurred with *The Potato Eaters*. It was a period of testing, of experimentation and pursuit, where a plethora of other modes were essayed.

In each new attempt of Vincent's at cohabitation or setting up an abode of his own, some seed of disaster lurks, as if a volatile chemical element would eventually emerge, like the uprising of lava in a volcano, to dismantle the ground beneath him. What is Vincent's Mercalli intensity?

After conflicts with Theo, and being whittled to the bone by urban life, Vincent moves yet again, the forces of life pushing him on without relent. But this time he has a grand vision in mind, an artist's colony that will function as a creative bulwark far from the mania of Paris.

To create his Studio of the South and fulfill his dream of establishing an artists' community, Vincent rents the right wing of a building on the northeast corner of Place Lamartine and Avenue de Montmajour in Arles.

My house, the artist notes, is painted in a yellow the color of fresh butter on the outside with glaringly green shutters; it stands in the full sunlight in a square which has a green garden with plane trees, oleanders, and acacias. And it is completely whitewashed inside, and the floor is made of red bricks. Over it there is an intensively blue sky. In this I can live and breathe, meditate and paint.

This Studio of the South will be a shelter and refuge for artists to live and work together, a pied-à-terre which, when people are exhausted, can be used to provide a rest in the country for poor Paris cab-horses, the poor Impressionists. Like the Japanese, we will stick together and live as a family, as brothers and companions.

I have visited the used furniture dealers and haggled for beds, chairs (12 of them), a table, a mirror, and some small indispensable things. For putting somebody up, there'll be the prettiest room upstairs, like a woman's boudoir, really artistic. Then there'll be my own bedroom, which I'd like to be exceedingly simple, but the furniture square and broad.

The room where Gauguin will stay will have a decoration of large yellow sunflowers on its white walls. It won't be commonplace. And the studio — the red floor-tiles, the white walls and ceiling, the rustic chairs, the deal table, with, I hope, decoration of portraits. That will have character à la Daumier — and it won't, I dare predict, be commonplace. I really want to make of it — AN ARTIST'S HOUSE but not precious, on the contrary, *nothing precious*, but everything from the chair to the painting having character.

If what we're doing looks out toward the infinite, if we see our work having its raison d'être and continuing on beyond, we work with more serenity.

TORINO

416.4 km from Arles

I am sad to hear that your health is causing trouble; very daring rhymes; Colonie Nueva Germania and the influx of colonists; more than 300 listeners; practice and hardships in life; Zarathustra in America; infinite expressive abilities; Carmen; a certain fatality & inevitability for cheerfulness

Thursday, 17 May 1888

Dear friend,

I am distressed to hear that your health is causing trouble. Everything else that you write is so healthy, even *buoyant*. Above all, that you, too, do not know how to make "more dignified" use of an honorarium than to have it *printed* . . . That has breeding; but the one belongs in the "upside-down world." You can guess the success with which I have *raged* against the honorarium fund pulled out of Schmeitzner's throat in the last few years! All of it in shreds! — But that reminds me of a jocular verse from my time in Basel, when I liked to entertain my sister in the evenings by forging *very* daring rhymes. The verse was addressed to *Schmeitzner* when he reported that he was now serious about the publisher and had sold his house to create the necessary funds.

> You who turn your house to silver
> And shred it into paper pulver
>
> Oh Schmeitzner, do as I do!
> Better drink a couple of schnapps
> And let the thousand crabs
> All crawl along behind you!

**

A verse in honor of Pastor *Brockhaus*, who died of trichinitis (son of old Prof. B)

> The pastor who'd grown old
> Under a vice did fold:
> So much sausage did he eat
> That the trichina all came
> Crawling from tibia to feet,
> And played a deadly game.

**

To a visit from Ms. Marie *Baumgartner*, who read Byron's *Cain* to us:

With pepsin, apples, Cain
Mariam von Lörrach came,
Trudging to Basel us to see,
With cakes and tea
Abel to slay
And also the very long day.

**

When my sister and I traveled back from Rome to Genoa in the spring of 1883, we did nothing on the way but write such verses. We bribed the conductors at each station to be alone because *we kept laughing* — —

There is very good news from my South Americans: they have now finally moved to the new Colonie Nueva Germania and have been received there "no less festively than a prince would be received." The influx of colonists is significant. —

There is also good news from Copenhagen. The lectures proceed brilliantly. The hall is packed "to the bursting" every time. More than 300 listeners. The newspapers give reports.

Here the chief managing director of the Löscher company was very helpful to me, with all sorts of practicalities and hardships in life, where I don't know how to advise myself. This is a quiet, humble man, *Buddhist*, a bit of a fan of Mainländer, enthusiastic vegetarian (— he introduced graham crackers here and fixed the price: kilo = 30 ct.). Yesterday he told me, unsolicited, that he was *Jewish* ... Not even baptized! — He proved to me that Mainländer was *not* a Jew. —

From New York an admirer of my *Zarathustra* promised a major English essay on my writings in one of the best American reviews. —

I wish I could tell you how all your musical judgments edify me: it seems that when it comes to instinct I am no longer very far from your taste, — but in my *ability* to express myself, the distance is infinite. I would need a year of exact music studies just to get control of the *language* for it. —

A brilliant performance of *Carmen*, a Serata thanks to the much-admired Miss Borghi. But Nizza was *part* of all my experiences of seeing this opera performed so far (De Reims as Don José, la Frandin as Carmen).

Lalo's great success with his "roi d'Ys" in Paris, pleases me. A modest artist with whom life has already played unfairly. The "great success" started with the third act — *that is*, with the *beautiful melodies*: the clever man had *saved* them all up until then!!

Dear friend, forgive me this letter, which is perhaps too cheerful: but after I have *"revaluated values"* day after day and had reason to be *very serious*, there is a certain *fatality* & inevitability of *cheerfulness*. Like at a funeral ... With warm greetings & thanks

Your friend Nietzsche

ARLES

248.9 km from Nizza

stupefied exhaustion; forging a suit of armor, or rather, inuring us to illness; the happy owners of troubled hearts; I could still wish you had one or two good friends among the French; my blood is returning to normal; no women; I'm less at the mercy of my passions and I can work more calmly; a yearning for real life; we'd prefer to live in a meadow with a sun, a river, the company of other horses who are also free; being struck by death and immortality; the artists of the future; the reality of the fact that we're not much; the power to work is a second youth

20 May 1888

My dear Theo,

What you write about your visit to Gruby has upset me, but at the same time it reassures me that you went there.

Have you considered that your lethargy — a feeling of extreme lassitude — could have been caused by this heart condition, and that in that case potassium iodide couldn't be blamed for these periods of stupefied exhaustion? If you remember how stupefied I was myself this winter, to the point of being quite incapable! of doing anything whatsoever, apart from a little painting, although I wasn't taking potassium iodide at all. So if I were you, I'd have it out with Rivet if Gruby tells you not to take it.

And it will in any case — I have no doubt about it — be your intention to be friends with both the one and the other.

I often think of Gruby *here* and *now*, and in short I feel well, but it's because here I have the pure air and the heat, which make things more possible for me. Among all the trials and the bad air of Paris, Rivet takes things as they are without trying to create a paradise and without in the slightest way trying to make us perfect. But he forges a suit of armor, or rather, he inures us to illness and keeps morale up, I find, by making fun of the trouble we have.

So if you could now have just one year of living in the country and close to nature, that would make Gruby's treatment much easier. So I think he'll urge you not to see women except in case of necessity, but as little as possible. Now for myself, I feel fine here in that respect, but *here*, since I have work and nature, and if I didn't have that I'd become melancholy. As long as work has some appeal for you over there, and the Impressionists are going well, that would be a great gain. Because loneliness, worries, vexations, the need for friendship and fellow-feeling not sufficiently met, that's what's very bad, the mental emotions of sadness or disappointments undermine us more than riotous living: us, that is, who find ourselves the happy owners of troubled hearts.

I think potassium iodide purifies the blood and the whole system, doesn't it — will you be able to do without it? Anyway, you'll have to have a straight talk about it with Rivet, who shouldn't be jealous.

I could wish you had near you something more rudely alive, warmer than the Dutch — but all the same, Koning with his whims is an exception for the better. Anyway, it's always good to have somebody. But I could still wish you had one or two good friends among the French. Would you do me a great favor: my friend the Dane, who leaves for Paris on Tuesday, will give you 2 small paintings — nothing much — that I'd like to give to Mme the Countess De la Boissière at Asnières. She stays in boulevard Voltaire, on the first floor of the first house at the end of the Clichy bridge. *Père* Perruchot's restaurant is on the ground floor. Would you take them to her personally on my behalf, saying I had hopes of seeing her again this spring and that even here I haven't forgotten her; I gave them 2 small ones last year as well, her and her daughter. I'd have hope that you wouldn't regret making these ladies' acquaintance. After all, they're *a family*. The countess is far from young but she's first of all a countess, then *a lady*, the daughter ditto.

And it makes sense for you to go, since I can't be sure that the family's staying in the same place this year (however, they've been coming there for several years, and Perruchot must know their address in town). Perhaps I'm deluding myself — but I can't help thinking of them, and perhaps it will be a pleasure for them and for you too, if you meet them.

Listen — I'll do all I can to send you some new drawings for Dordrecht.

This week I've done two still lifes.

A blue enameled tin coffee-pot, a royal blue and gold cup, a pale blue and white checkered milk jug, a cup — on the right — white, with blue and orange designs, on a yellow grey earthenware plate, a blue barbotine or majolica jug with red, green, brown designs, and lastly 2 oranges *&* 3 lemons; the table is covered with a blue cloth, the background is yellow green, making 6 different blues and 4 or 5 yellows and oranges.

The other still life is the majolica jug with wild flowers.

I thank you very much for your letter and for the 50-franc note. I hope the crate will reach you in the next few days. The next time I think I'll take the canvases off the stretching frames and send them rolled, by fast service. I think you'll soon make friends with this Dane — he doesn't do much but — he has intelligence and a good heart, and he probably started painting not long ago. Take him out a bit one Sunday to get to know him.

For myself, I feel infinitely better, my blood is circulating well, and my stomach's digesting. I've found very, very good food now, which had an immediate effect on me.

Have you seen Gruby's face when he pinches his lips tight and says 'No women'? It would make a really good Degas, that face, like that. But there's nothing to be said against it, because when you have to work all day long with your brain, calculating, thinking, planning business, that's quite enough in itself for your nerves. So go off now and visit women in the world of artists and suchlike, you'll see you'll succeed — really. You'll see it'll work out like that and you won't lose much, will you?

I still haven't been able to make a deal with the furniture dealer, I've seen a bed but it's dearer than I thought. I feel the need to get more work done before spending more on furniture.

My lodgings cost me 1 franc a night. I've bought more linen and colors as well. I've bought some very strong linen.

Just as my blood is returning to normal, so the idea of succeeding is returning to me too. I shouldn't be too surprised if your illness was also a reaction to this dreadful winter, which lasted an age. And then it will go the same way as with me; take as much spring air as possible, go to bed *very early* because you'll need to sleep; and then food, lots of fresh vegetables and no *bad* wine or *bad* liquor. And very few women and a great deal of patience. If it doesn't clear up at once that doesn't matter. And now Gruby will give you a heavy meat diet over there. For myself, I couldn't take very much, and it's not necessary here. It's just my stupefaction that's going away, I don't feel as much need to amuse myself, I'm less at the mercy of my passions and I can work more calmly, I could be alone without being bored. I came out of it feeling a little older, but no sadder.

I wouldn't believe you if in your next letter you told me there was nothing wrong with you any more; it's perhaps a more serious change and I shouldn't be surprised if, during the time it will take you to recover, you had some dejection. There is and there remains and it always comes back at times, in the midst of the artistic life, a yearning for — real life — ideal and not attainable.

And we sometimes lack the desire to throw ourselves head first into art again and to build ourselves up for that. We know we're carriage-horses and that it'll be the same carriage we're going to be harnessed to again. And so we don't feel like doing it and we'd prefer to live in a meadow with a sun, a river, the company of other horses who are also free, and the act of generation. And perhaps in the final account your heart condition comes partly from there; it wouldn't greatly surprise me. We no longer rebel against things, we're not resigned either — we're ill and it's not going to get any better — and we can't do anything specific about it. I don't know who called this condition being struck by death and immortality. The carriage we drag along must be of use to people we don't know. But you see, if we believe in the new art, in the artists of the future, our presentiment doesn't deceive us. When good *père* Corot said a few days before he died: last night I saw in my dreams landscapes with entirely pink skies, well, didn't they come, those pink skies, and yellow and green into the bargain, in Impressionist landscapes? All this is to say there are things one senses in the future and that really come about.

And we, who, I'm inclined to believe, are by no means so close to dying, nevertheless feel the thing is bigger than us and longer-lasting than our lives.

We don't feel we're dying, but we feel the reality of the fact that we're not much, and that to be a link in the chain of artists we pay a steep price in health, youth, freedom, which we don't enjoy at all, any more than the carriage-horse that pulls a carriage full of people who, unlike him, are going out to enjoy the springtime. Well then — what I wish you as well as myself is to succeed in recovering our health, because we'll need it. That Hope of Puvis de Chavannes is such a reality. There's an art in the future and it will surely be so beautiful and so young that, really, if at present we leave it our own youth, we can only gain in tranquility. Perhaps it's too silly to write all this, but it's what I felt; it seemed that like me, you suffered to see your youth going

up in — smoke — but if it comes back and appears in what we
do, there's nothing lost, and the power to work is a second youth.
So be serious about getting better, because we'll need our health.
I shake your hand firmly, and Koning's too.

Ever yours,
Vincent

TORINO

416.4 km from Arles

however well the spring has treated me; the gentle sound of bells; my name is now the topic in all intelligent circles in Copenhagen; my "master morality"; Manu's book of laws; Plato is a Brahmin; the Jews invent nothing

If I answer your letter immediately once more, you will have no doubts about what I am missing, — it is *you* yourself, dear friend! However well the spring has treated me, it does not bring me the best thing, the thing that till now even the worst springs have brought — your music! The latter is closely interwoven — since Recoaro! — with my idea of the "spring," somewhat as the gentle sound of bells across the city of lagoons is interwoven with my idea of "Easter." I dwell on these memories with long gratitude whenever a melody of yours occurs to me; nothing has ever made me so much aware of rebirth, exaltation, and ease as your music. It is my *good* music par excellence, for which I inwardly put on cleaner clothes than for any other.

I took the liberty of sending to you the day before yesterday some theater reviews by Dr. Fuchs. They contain much that is subtle and experienced.

Dr. Brandes's lectures had a good conclusion — a great ovation, which, B says, was not meant for him. He assures me that my name is now the topic in all intelligent circles in Copenhagen and is known throughout Scandinavia. My problems seem to have interested these northerners very much; individually they were better prepared, for instance, for my "master morality" as a result of the widespread *precise* knowledge of the Icelandic sagas, which provide extremely rich material for it. I am glad that the Danish philologists confirm and accept my derivation of the word bonus; as a matter of fact, it is a tall order to trace the concept "good" back to the concept "warrior." Without my premises no philologist would have hit upon the idea. —

It is really a pity that you made an excursion into paper and ink instead of into the Cadore. It is plain that my bad example is spoiling your intrinsically better behavior. The weather was just right for such a mountain exploration; as a matter of fact, I made no use of it either, and am, like you, dissatisfied with myself for failing to do so.

I owe to these last weeks a very important *lesson*: I found *Manu*'s book of laws in a French translation done in India under strict supervision from the most eminent priests & scholars there.

This absolutely *Aryan* work, a priestly codex of morality based on the Vedas, on the idea of caste and very ancient tradition — *not* pessimistic, albeit very sacerdotal — supplements my views on religion in the most remarkable way. I confess to having the impression that everything else that we have by way of moral lawgiving seems to me an imitation and even a caricature of it — preeminently, Egypticism does; but even Plato seems to me in all the main points simply to have been *well instructed* by a Brahmin. It makes the Jews look like a Chandala race which learns from its *masters* the principles of making a *priestly caste* the master which organizes a people . . . The Chinese also seem to have produced their Confucius and Lao-tse under the influence of this *ancient classic of laws*. The medieval organization looks like a wondrous groping for a restoration of all the ideas that formed the basis of primordial Indian-Aryan society — but with *pessimistic* values that have their origin in the soil of racial décadence. Here too, the *Jews* seem to be merely "transmitters" — they invent nothing.

So much, my dear friend, as a sign of how *glad* I always am to talk with you —. I leave on Tuesday. —

Affectionately,
Your N.

SAINTES-MARIES

283.9 km from Nizza

the Mediterranean has a color like mackerel; I board and eat for 4 francs a day; I'll probably come back to do some more studies here; people can't be too bad here; the blue whiteness of milky ways

3 June 1888

My dear Theo,

I'm writing to you from Saintes Maries on the Mediterranean at last — the Mediterranean — has a color like mackerel, in other words, changing — you don't always know if it's green or purple — you don't always know if it's blue — because a second later, its changing reflection has taken on a pink or grey hue.

It's a funny thing, the family — quite unintentionally, and despite myself, I've often thought here from time to time of our uncle the seaman, who has certainly seen the shores of this sea many times.

I've brought three canvases and I've covered them — two seascapes — a view of the village — and some drawings that I'll send you by post when I get back to Arles tomorrow.

I board and eat for 4 francs a day — they started by asking 6.

As soon as I can I'll probably come back to do some more studies here.

The beach here is sandy, no cliffs or rocks — like Holland — without the dunes and with more blue.

You eat better fried fish here than beside the Seine — only there isn't fish to eat every day, as the fishermen go off to sell in Marseille. But when there is some it's darned good. If there isn't any — the butcher's is no more appetizing than Monsieur Gérôme's fellah butcher's — if there's no fish it's rather hard to find something to eat here, it seems to me.

I don't believe there are 100 houses in this village or town.

The main building after the old church, an ancient fortress, is the caserne de douanes. And what houses at that — like those on our Drenthe heaths and peat bogs, you'll see some specimens in the drawings.

I have to leave my three painted studies here, because of course they aren't dry enough to subject them to 5 hours' jolting in a carriage with impunity.

But I expect to come back here.

Next week I'd like to go to Tarascon to do two or three studies.

If you haven't already written I'll expect your letter in Arles, of course.

A very handsome gendarme came to interview me here. And the priest too — people can't be too bad here, because even the priest seemed almost like a decent fellow.

Next month will be the public bathing season.

Number of bathers varies from 20 to 50.

I'm staying till tomorrow afternoon, have still got some drawings to do.

I took a walk along the seashore one night, on the deserted beach. It wasn't cheerful, but not sad either, it was — beautiful.

The sky, a deep blue, was flecked with clouds of a deeper blue than primary blue, an intense cobalt, and with others that were a lighter blue — like the blue whiteness of milky ways. Against the blue background stars twinkled, bright, greenish, white, light pink — brighter, more glittering, more like precious stones than at home — even in Paris. So it seems fair to talk about opals, emeralds, lapis, rubies, sapphires. The sea a very deep ultramarine — the beach a mauvish and pale reddish shade, it seemed to me — with bushes. In addition to half-sheet drawings I have a large drawing, the pendant of the last one.

More soon, I hope. Handshake.

Ever yours,
Vincent

SILS MARIA

734.8 km from Arles

almost always sick; imitating animals; your philosopher from Intra interests me as a psychological problem; the first effect of Hegel's logic

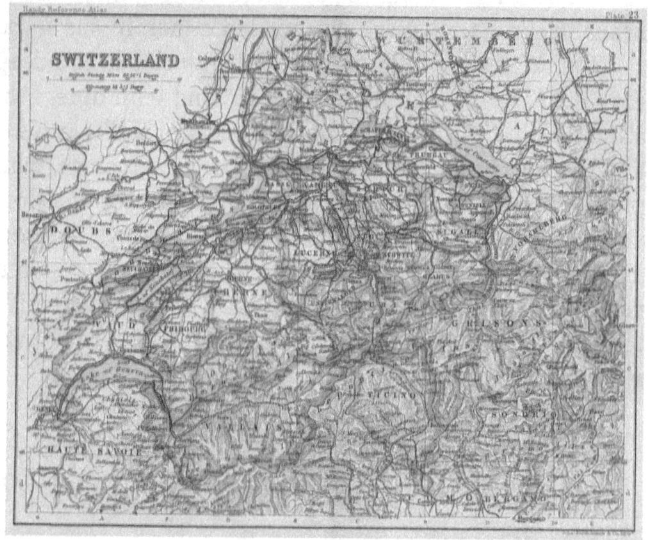

9 June 1888

Most Revered Professor,

I use the first moment when my head is clear and cheerful again to express to you that *in spite of everything* I am neither the most ungrateful nor the most impolite person in the world. It was hard for me to leave Torino without saying farewell to you; but there was no other way. I was almost always sick and the last few days I was practically stupefied by the heat. Take my pride a bit into account, that I did not want to remain entirely in your memory as a "sufferer." Also take my philosophy into account, which advises the sick man to imitate the animals and to crawl off into his *cave*. I have no doubt that sooner or later, on a beautiful, fresh, clear autumn day, I will have the honor of re-establishing such a valuable and amiable human relationship, of which this time I was hardly worthy.

In the meantime, your kindness has given me a means of being here in your company too. Your philosopher from Intra interests me as a psychological problem: a poet, and an Italian at that, who is falling in love with the grey and grey of our German scholasticism! It recalls to me the enthusiasm that Monsieur H. Taine expressed about the first effect of Hegel's logic: Taine, who also has a poet hidden inside him. He said roughly that it was the highest condition of his life.

Accept, revered Herr Professor, the most respectful greetings

Your gratefully indebted one

ARLES

734.8 km from Sils Maria

when in doubt, it's better to abstain; the need to buy canvases and pay the rent; we don't get to be old in modern times; I miscalculated the odds; an association of the Impressionists; we would live courageously; an artistic Society or a bankers' Society; the great revolution; the harvest is a bit more serious; a madman, a scoundrel, or an old fool; the shock of Paris; a recurrence of his nervous trouble; I won't write to Gauguin direct; this society that doesn't even exist costs a lot of money; the most radical thing; a fata Morgana; we have to act so that you aren't completely overwhelmed by expenses

15 June 1888

My dear Theo,

When in doubt, it's better to abstain — that, I believe, is what I said in the letter to Gauguin, and that's what I believe now, having read his reply. If he, for his part, returns to the proposal — he's perfectly free to return to it — but we'd look I'm not quite sure what, if for the moment we pressed the point, to make him say yes.

You see that I've received your letter; I thank you very much for it, including the many things in it, like the 100-franc note — as for the delay with the telegram, it was dated Sunday, so it's the postman's fault, but it hardly mattered, since the coach for Saintes Maries leaves every day.

But what stopped me was the need to buy canvases and pay the rent. I have already mentioned to you that I didn't like Tasset's canvas very much for outdoor work. In the future I think we'll take the ordinary kind. I bought 50 francs' worth of canvas with stretching frames — also because I need stretching frames of different sizes to stretch canvases on, even though I'll send them to you rolled up. They're the rather large sizes, 30, 25, 20, 15, all square. It seems to me that the large sizes (after all, it's not very large) suit me better.

But I speak about what you write in your letter. I congratulate you on having the Monet exhibition at your premises, and I much regret not seeing it. It will certainly do Tersteeg no harm to have seen this exhibition; he'll still come round to it, but as your idea was too, very late. It's indeed curious that he's changed his mind on the subject of Zola. I know from experience that he couldn't bear to hear him spoken about. What an odd character Tersteeg is; we shouldn't give up hope with him — the splendid thing about him is that however rigid and fixed his opinions may be, once he has acknowledged that something is in fact different from what he had imagined — as with Zola — then he changes and becomes bold for the cause. Unfortunately, we don't get to be old in modern times, and Mr. Tersteeg has lived longer now than he still has to live. And where is his successor? My God, what a sad thing it is that you and he are not entirely as one in business matters these days. But what can you say — it's what I believe they call a fatality.

You were fortunate to meet Guy de Maupassant — I've just read his first book, *Des vers*, poems dedicated to his master, Flaubert. There's one, "Au bord de l'eau," that's already *him*. So you see, what Vermeer of Delft is beside Rembrandt among painters, he is among French novelists beside Zola.

In short, Tersteeg's visit isn't at all what I'd dared hope, and I make no secret of it to myself that I miscalculated the odds on his cooperating.

And perhaps on the business with Gauguin, too. Let's take a look at that: I thought he was at bay and I blame myself for having money and the pal who works better than I, not — I say, he's entitled to half if he wishes.

But — if Gauguin isn't at bay, then I'm not in too much of a hurry.

And I categorically withdraw from it, and the only question for me remains quite simply this: If I looked for a pal to work with, would I be doing the right thing, would this be more beneficial to my brother and me, would the pal lose or would he gain by it?

So these, then, are questions that certainly preoccupy me, but which need to come face to face with reality in order to become actual facts.

I don't wish to discuss Gauguin's plan, having considered the situation once — last winter — you know the results. You know that I believe that an association of the Impressionists would be something along the lines of the associations of the 12 English Pre-Raphaelites, and that I believe that it could come into being. That I'm therefore inclined to believe that the artists would guarantee their livelihood amongst themselves, mutually, and independently of the dealers, each agreeing to give a substantial number of paintings to the society, and that earnings as well as losses would be shared. I don't believe that this society would last indefinitely, but I believe that during its lifetime we would live courageously and would produce. But if tomorrow Gauguin and his banker Jews come and ask me for nothing but 10 paintings for a society of dealers and not a society of artists, well, I don't know if I'd trust them — I who would be glad, on the other hand, to give 50 to a society of artists.

Isn't it a bit the way it was with Reid — why say that Gabriel de la Roquette's a scoundrel if you do the same yourself? Why say artistic Society if it's made up of bankers? Enough, for Heaven's sake, let our pal do as his heart tells him, but his plan is far from making me enthusiastic.

I prefer things as they are — to take them the way it is, without changing anything about them, to half-baked reforms.

The great revolution, art for the artists, my God, perhaps it's a utopia, and too bad, then. I think life's so short and goes by so fast. Now, being a painter you have to paint, all the same.

And you're also well aware that because at that time — last winter with Pissarro and the others, we happened to talk about it a lot, I'm now making a big effort to add nothing more except this, that speaking for myself, before next year I want to make my contribution of 50 paintings. If I manage to do that then I'll stick to my opinion.

I've sent you 3 drawings by post today.

The one with the wheat stacks in a farmyard will seem too bizarre to you, but it was done in great haste as a project for a painting, and it's to show you what it's like.

Now, the harvest is a bit more serious. And that's the subject I've been working on this week, on a no. 30 canvas — it's hardly done at all — but it kills the rest of what I have, apart from a still life, worked on with patience. Macknight and one of his friends who's been in Africa too saw this study today and said it was the best I'd done. Like Anquetin and our friend Thomas — you're really not sure what to think of yourself when you hear people say that, but I say to myself: the rest must look bloody awful, to be sure.

Well then — on days when I bring back a study I say to myself, if it was like this every day things could work — but on days when you come home empty-handed and you eat and spend money all the same, you don't feel content with yourself, and you feel like a madman, a scoundrel, or an old fool.

And dear old Doctor Ox, I mean our Swede, Mourier, I liked him well enough because, with his spectacles, he went naively and benignly about this wicked world, and because I presumed he had a heart that was purer than many a heart, and even with more of a leaning toward rectitude than many of the cleverest people have. And as I knew he hadn't been painting for very long it made not a bit of difference to me that his work was the very height of inanity. And I saw him every day for months. All right. So what can be the reason for his losing his qualities? This is how I imagine the case to be. Bear in mind that he came to the south to get over a nervous disorder caused by a whole lot of problems he's had, and as a result of which he changed career.

He was *perfectly well* here, he was very calm, &c. But the shock of Paris was too great, the change too sudden, he didn't find the Paris of his dreams, and there he is, worried and perhaps disagreeable, and in any case doing silly things.

He'll soon have sown his wild oats, I hope. While waiting, let him do whatever he likes without attaching any importance to it. He's placing huge hopes in Russell (*I believe*), he's looking for an adviser and a teacher — now — no need to tell you that Russell will perhaps not be *everything* he needs, but I believe that Russell will see that he's someone who doesn't know the circles of people with whom he's dealing, and I think that Russell will take him seriously and will try to be good for him. I believe that Russell is making a name for himself among those who have an instinctive fear of Paris. It's hard to explain what I mean by that.

Russell is such a good man — but you know, you can't recommend that people love Paris, or force them to, any more than you can recommend a pipe or black coffee with cognac. And Russell's rich and has lost money in Paris, so he can and does say to people: "see what I've had to deal with." But in any event, I'll write a word to Russell.

It seems that Macknight wasn't very pleased with me but that Russell indicated to him in reply that he should shut up. All this to tell you I understand very, very well — seeing he has turned out like that — that you're not in complete agreement with the Swede, who probably, according to what you write, has had a recurrence of his nervous trouble and is irritated by Paris. If he has money to waste in taking a studio like Gérôme's, it would be serious. As I'm slightly doubtful that he has a huge amount to waste, he's in for a bit of a drubbing that's not undeserved, I'd say. There's nothing to be done if he won't listen, but you can't live with him. I won't write to Gauguin direct — I'll send you the letter — because when in doubt, it's better to abstain. IF WE SAY NO MORE, if the reply shows we've said something like that but that there has to be an initiative in the matter from his side too, then we'll see if he's keen on it. If he isn't keen on it, if it's all one to him, if he has something quite different in mind, let him remain independent, and me too.

Handshake to you and to Mourier.

Ever yours,
Vincent

I find this in particular rather strange in this plan of Gauguin's: the society *offers its protection in exchange* for 10 paintings that the artists will have to give, if 10 artists do that, the Jewish company clearly pockets 100 paintings 'for a start.' The protection of this society that doesn't even exist costs a lot of money.

Here's the letter for Gauguin — I'm well aware that in his there is this passage "I *ask* (underlined) if, the capital having been raised for the most part, your brother would use his efforts to make a success of the business and to be its director." I'm well aware that he also writes, "I accept your proposal in principle." But I believe that it could lead us too far if we weren't a little firm in showing him that our proposal was without all these afterthoughts, and that we ourselves are too hard up to be able to risk anything other than setting up house together and sharing the month's money.

And it's true I didn't know he had so large a family; he'll more likely wish to stay in the north for that reason.

The most radical thing we could do would be for me to give up the south, and if that would get him out of trouble, go and join him in Brittany myself. And the desire I have to work in the south is naturally subordinate to the interests of people like him.

All the same, we shouldn't change lightly.

And I'm a little afraid of getting a dressing-down for having separated him from his family, or a hornet's nest like that.

Dear God, if he has such a large family his obligations are probably not to be absent from them any more. And perhaps he'd be much happier if you simply bought a painting from him from time to time.

If now I haven't mentioned these two passages and other passages in his letter it's because it seems far too difficult to me to say yes to that in all honesty. However, if it was the case that his whole plan is nothing but a Fata Morgana, and as such will vanish, he'll speak of it again of his own accord.

But there's the fare, the debt at the inn, the doctor's bill; now he's talking about another debt of 300 francs that he'll settle with that painting if his collector agrees. But if he doesn't agree? Well now, it wouldn't be very prudent to give him hopes beyond our resources and commit ourselves to doing more than we could stick to. It's all very well for Gauguin to say, he's very, very upset and it's a pity, and it can't be good for his work. No, we shouldn't change what we've said and consider that the thing isn't going ahead because of doubts and changes whose presence isn't a good sign. The more I calm myself here and the more I regain my strength, the more I feel that work is the most secure thing.

I admit that if living in Brittany is much less expensive, if necessary I must sacrifice my plan to work here, and I'll do it willingly if it's to his benefit. But all the more reason to work hard on the 50 paintings I wished to have before talking again about projects of the kind we discussed last winter. A letter from home arrives just now.

You know I feel so well now that it isn't indispensable that I stay here for my health alone. We have to act so that you aren't completely overwhelmed by expenses, that's what's necessary and that's serious enough in itself.

SILS MARIA

734.8 km from Arles

things are not at their best; I want all of my ham from Naumburg; 6 kilos of Lachsschinken; I am absolutely not allowed to take any more risks; I'm done with the little sausage; the honey did not agree with me at all; I am amazed that Lisbeth says nothing about the eight letters I wrote to her; it is not a hobby that condemns me to the Engadin & Nizza — —

Saturday, 16 June 1888

My dear mother,

Things are not at their best. Forgive me if I write somewhat briefly. You must accept the money from Kürbitz *under all circumstances*, otherwise I cannot place my *orders* as I have to! Perhaps you no longer remember what I wrote from *Torino*. This time I *want all* of my required ham from Naumburg. Last summer I got it from Basel, Zurich, St. Gallen, and elsewhere, with all sorts of annoyance and disappointment: so I don't want to do that again. As you can imagine, I always had to atone for it with my *health* if an order was bad or half-satisfactory. The *only one* that actually satisfied me was the very last Naumburg delivery from September: the round, thick *Lachsschinken*. So I wrote from Torino that this time I wanted to be sensible from the start and not undertake all sorts of bad experiments. Since my summer is about 4 months long, I need at least 12 pounds = 6 *kilos of Lachsschinken*. This is my *entire* evening meal for 4 months. If you had any idea of the difficulty of my diet, especially here under the *enormously expensive* tourism conditions, you would also understand immediately that *this* very monotonous and boring diet is relatively, by far, the *cheapest* and also the *healthiest* for me. I am absolutely not allowed to take any more risks; the more regular the better. In a big city like Torino, of course, every variety is available to me: but *not* here (— it immediately becomes terribly expensive, since I already give 2 frs. 25 ct. = 19 Groschen (without tip) for a *very* simple lunch. — If you have trouble, my dear mother, give me a good address for a shop in Gotha or in Braunschweig. I would, of course, prefer it, just as I had thought it out: if *you choose* the ham yourself and send it to me (— the costs of the transport are of course also *mine* —)

I'm done with the little sausage: it was too dry because of its small size. The bigger one is *better*, but not nearly as good as the big round one from last autumn. I think it is good to send very large ones. The 3 pounds sent are enough for a total of 14 days: that means I still have enough to eat for 6 days.

Don't be angry that I am causing you so much trouble: but I ask you to *immediately send off* a *larger* shipment than the last time: and of the *very best.* I don't even consider the cost of it if it's very good and healthy, so I am happy to give a little *more,* provided that it is of great quality. — And go, please, to *Kürbitz!!!!*

Unfortunately, the honey did not agree with me *at all*: just like last summer. Vomiting ensued. This is *wax* honey: but my stomach has no way of coping with wax. —

I enclose the One Letter from the Lama; the other will follow the next time so that this letter does not become double weight. I am amazed that Lisbeth says nothing about the eight letters I wrote to her from *Nizza* this winter.

With love
Your ancient creature

I have still not yet thanked you for your heartfelt letter. Coming to Naumburg, given my health conditions, is of course not possible: it is *not* a hobby that *condemns* me to the Engadin and Nizza — —

Sils-Engadin, Switzerland, is actually sufficient as an address: there are namely two other Sils, but not in the Engadin.

ARLES

734.8 km from Sils Maria

immersions in melancholy; as blind as moles and criminally stupid; energy generates energy, and conversely paralysis paralyzes others; people always disparage living painters; independence through one's work; to paint really well; one is far from free; art is as stultified and moldering as the religion we see falling; my own technique; there's something in the new manner; the clique of painters; my part in a battle; become wholly abstracted from whatever isn't the work or … ; hold fast to one's technique; come to Paris, it's a hotbed of ideas; I prefer to look at things myself; the clarity of the Mediterranean air; I'd also like to see if I can't make my own portrait in writing; one seeks a deeper likeness than that of the photographer; a dreadful nightmare

20 June 1888

My dear sister,

Many thanks for your letter, which I'd been looking forward to; I daren't give way to my desire to write to you often or to encourage this on your part. All this correspondence doesn't always help to keep us, who are of a nervous disposition, strong in cases of possible immersions in melancholy of the kind you refer to in your letter and which I myself have too every now and then. A friend of mine asserted that the best treatment for all ills is to treat them with the most profound contempt.

The remedy for the immersions you refer to doesn't, as far as I know, grow among the usual medicinal herbs. Nonetheless I drink large quantities of bad coffee in such cases, not because this is very good for already bad teeth but because my strong powers of imagination in this respect enable me to have a religious faith — worthy of an idolater, Christian, or anthropophagus — in the cheering effect of the aforementioned fluid. Fortunately for my fellow creatures I have so far carefully refrained from recommending this or similar remedies to them as being efficacious. The sun here, *that* is something else, and if for a while one just drinks wine that at least in part has been pressed from grapes. I assure you that the people in our country are as blind as moles and criminally stupid because they don't make more effort to go to the Indies or somewhere else where the sun shines. It's not good to know only one thing; it stultifies one. One shouldn't rest until one also knows the opposite.

What you say about extenuating circumstances, that sadly they don't take away the fact of having done something wrong or spoiled something, is very true.

Well, just think of our national history, the rise and fall of the Dutch republic, and you'll understand what I mean, we mustn't give way too much to the extenuating circumstance of not being able &c., it's less Christian (in the sense in which people water it down these days), but it's better for us and perhaps even for others. And energy generates energy, and conversely paralysis paralyzes others.

We're now living here in a world of painting where it's unspeakably paralyzed and wretched. The exhibitions, the shops for paintings, everything, everything is occupied by people who all intercept money. And you mustn't think that I'm imagining this. People pay a lot for the work when the painter himself is dead. And people always disparage living painters by pointing unanswerably to the work of those who are no longer with us.

I know that we can't do anything to change this. For the sake of peace one must therefore resign oneself to it, or have some sort of patronage or captivate a rich woman or something, otherwise one can't work. Everything one hopes for in terms of independence through one's work, of influence on others, absolutely nothing comes of it.

And yet it's something of a pleasure to make a painting, and yet there are 20 or so painters here right now, all of them having more debts than money &c., all of them with a way of life something like that of ours, who will perhaps mean more than the whole official exhibition in so far as the future manner of working is concerned.

The principal characteristic of a painter, I imagine, is *to paint really well*; those who can paint, those who can do it best, are the germs of something that will continue to exist for a long time, just as long as there are eyes that enjoy something that is singularly beautiful.

Well I constantly regret that one can't make oneself richer by working harder — on the contrary.

If one actually could do that, one would be able to accomplish much more, be able to associate with others, and what not. For now everyone is bound by his opportunity to earn his living, and one is far from free, exactly.

You talk about "whether I had submitted something to Arti" — certainly not — only Theo sent Mr. Tersteeg a consignment of paintings by Impressionists and there was one of mine in it. However, all that transpired was that neither Tersteeg nor the artists, so Theo heard, had found anything in it.

Well that's very understandable because it's always the same, people have heard of the Impressionists, they have great expectations of them... and when they see them for the first time they're bitterly, bitterly disappointed and find them careless, ugly, badly painted, badly drawn, bad in color, everything that's miserable. That was my first impression, too, when I came to Paris with the ideas of Mauve and Israëls and other clever painters. And when there's an exhibition in Paris of Impressionists alone, I believe a host of visitors come back from it bitterly disappointed and even indignant, in just the same mood as the good Hollanders were at the time when, coming out of church, they attended a lecture by Domela Nieuwenhuis or other socialists a moment later.

And yet — you know — in the space of 10 or 15 years that whole edifice of a national religion fell and — the socialists are still there and will be there for a long time, although neither you nor I belong very much to either persuasion.

Well art — official art — and its education, management, organization, is as stultified and moldering as the religion we see falling — and it won't last, however many exhibitions, studios, schools &c. there may be, won't last any more than tulip mania.

But this doesn't concern us, we're neither founders of something new nor called upon to be preservers of something old.

But this remains — a painter is someone who paints, just as a genuine flower lover is someone who loves plants and grows them himself, and *not* the tulip dealer.

And so those 20 or so painters whom people call Impressionists, although a few of them have become fairly rich and fairly big men in the world — all the same, the majority of them are poor souls who live in coffee houses, lodge in cheap inns, live from one day to the next.

But — in one day all those 20 whom I mentioned to you paint everything they set eyes on, and better than many a great man who has a big reputation in the art world.

I say this to get you to understand what sort of tie binds me to the French painters whom people call the Impressionists — that I know many of them personally and like them.

And furthermore that in my own technique I have the same ideas concerning color, which even I was thinking about when I was still in Holland.

Cornflowers with white chrysanthemums and a few marigolds. There you have a motif in blue and orange.

Heliotrope and yellow roses, motif in lilac and yellow.

Poppies or red geraniums in bold green leaves, motif in red and green.

There you have *basics* that one can subdivide further, can elaborate, but enough to show you without a painting that there are colors that make each other shine, that make a *couple*, complete each other like man and wife.

Explaining the whole theory to you would take quite a lot of writing, but still, it could be done.

Clothes, wallpaper, what couldn't one make a good deal nicer by taking account of the laws of color.

You understand that Israëls and Mauve, who didn't use whole colors, who always worked in grey, do not, with the greatest respect and love, satisfy the present-day longing for color.

Something else: someone who can really play the violin or piano is, it seems to me, a mightily entertaining person. He picks up his violin and starts to play, *&* a whole gathering enjoys it all evening long. A painter has to be able to do that too.

And this sometimes gives me pleasure, to work outside when someone's looking on. One is in the wheat, say. Well then, in the space of a few hours one has to be able to paint that wheat field and the sky above it and the prospect in the distance. Anyone who watches that will certainly keep his mouth shut afterwards about the clumsiness of the Impressionists and their bad painting, you see. But nowadays we seldom have acquaintances who are interested enough to come along now and again. But when they do, then they're sometimes won over for good.

Now contrast that with the fellows who need a studio, months and months, and I don't know what else to make something — only too often rather dull, after all that.

Can't you understand then that there's something in the new manner? And I also want this — I want to be able to paint a portrait in a morning or an afternoon, and I've done that now and again, as a matter of fact.

This work definitely doesn't alter the fact that one can work longer on other paintings. Yesterday I sent you by post a drawing that's the first scratch for quite a large painting.

But isn't it curious that, as I said to you just then, there are at least a score of fellows who in an hour or so can paint a portrait with character in it — people hardly ever ask for one — 20 or so fellows who can do whatever landscape you please, at whatever hour of the day, with whatever color effect you please, on the spot, without hesitation — nobody looks on, they always work alone. If only everyone knew this, though — but you see the circumstances are so little known. Only I imagine that a generation later or in one of the later generations — this working decisively without hesitation, measuring correctly in an instant, skillful mixing of the color, drawing at lightning speed — a generation will come that will do this not as we do now, alone, unloved, but with a public that will like it both for portraits of people *&* for portraits of landscapes or interiors.

However, I'm writing to you much too much about painting, only by doing so I wanted to get you to understand that it's rather important that Theo has got things to the point that in the firm he manages there's always an exhibition of Impressionists nowadays. Next year will be rather important. Just as the French are undeniably the masters in literature, so it is in painting too, in modern art history there are names like Delacroix, Millet, Corot, Courbet, Daumier, who dominate everything that was produced in other countries. Yet the clique of painters who currently stand at the head of the official art world is resting on the laurels won by those earlier men, and is in itself of much lesser caliber. So *they* can't do much at the forthcoming World Exhibition to help French art retain that importance it's had until now. Next year the attention, not of the public — who naturally look at everything without wondering about the history — but the attention of those who are well informed, will be attracted by the retrospective exhibition of the paintings of the great men who are already dead, and by the Impressionists. Even that won't immediately change the circumstances in which the latter find themselves, but it will at least help to disseminate the ideas and generate a bit more enthusiasm. The dull schoolmasters who are now on the selection committee for the Salon won't even admit the Impressionists though. The latter won't want that anyway, though, *&* will exhibit on their own. When you realize that I want to have at least 50 or so paintings by then, you'll perhaps see that I, who don't exhibit, will nevertheless slowly and steadily play my part in a battle of which one can at least say this, that if one takes part in it, one doesn't have to fear a *prize* or medal like a good boy. They're ambitious here too, but still there's a difference, and many here are beginning to understand how ridiculous it is to make oneself dependent on the opinion of others about what one does. I detest writing about myself and I don't know why I do it. Perhaps to give you answers to your questions. You see what I've found, my work, and you also see what I haven't found, everything else that's part of life. And the future? Either become wholly abstracted from whatever isn't the work or... I dare not elaborate on that 'or' because becoming nothing but a work machine, unfit for and indifferent to all the rest, could be either better or worse than that average. I could quite easily resign myself to that average, and for the time being the fact is I'm still in exactly the same junk heap as ever.

By the way, talking of junk. It might still be worth while salvaging anything any good from the junk of mine which, so Theo says, is still somewhere in an attic in Breda, but I daren't ask it of you and perhaps it's been lost, so don't worry about it.

But this is the question. You know Theo brought a whole batch of woodcuts with him last year? Even so, a few of the best portfolios are missing and the rest isn't as good precisely because it's no longer complete. Obviously woodcuts from illustrated magazines get rarer and rarer as the volumes get older. Enough, this junk doesn't leave me completely indifferent; for instance, there's a copy of Gavarni's *Mascarade humaine*, a book *Anatomy for Artists*, in short, a few things that are actually much too good to lose. I consider them as lost in advance, though; anything that still turns up is pure gain. I didn't know when I left that it would be for good like this. Because the work wasn't going badly in Nuenen and it was only a matter of going on with it. *I still miss* my models who were made for me and whom I still adore; if only I had them here now — I'm sure my 50 paintings would hit the mark. Do you understand that I'm not angry with the human race because they think I'm this or that — I freely admit in advance that they're absolutely right, but it saddens me that

I don't have enough power to get what I want to pose for me, where I want and for as long or as short as I want. The problem I have to bring to an end, to overcome, lies *there* and not in the technical difficulty. And today I'm a landscape painter whereas I'm actually more suited to portraits. So it wouldn't surprise me much if I were to change style again sometime. A painter — Chaplin — who paints the portraits of the most beautiful women in Paris mightily well, ladies in boudoirs dressed or undressed, has painted powerful landscapes and herds of pigs on the moors. What I'm saying is one has to do what lies to hand and hold fast to one's technique.

If you were within my reach you would, I fear, have to get down to painting. There are Parisian ladies among the Impressionists, at least one really good — even 2 good ones.

And when I think how the new manner could help to put the women who are incapable of precision, who feel musically, on the right track, then I sometimes regret getting older and uglier than is in my interest.

It's very good of Theo to have invited you to come to Paris — I don't know what sort of impression it would make on you. The first time I saw it I felt above all the miseries that one cannot wave away, any more than the smell of sickness in the hospital, however clean it may be kept. And that stayed with me later, but later I gained an understanding of how it's a hotbed of ideas, and how the people try to get everything out of life that could possibly be in it. Other cities shrink by comparison, and it seems as big as the sea. But one always leaves a whole piece of life behind there. And this is certain, *nothing is fresh there*. That's why, when one comes from there, one finds a mass of things elsewhere excellent.

I'm very glad that you've recovered your health; one does everything unwittingly and wrongly, without understanding it oneself, when one's ill.

You would *not, I think*, find the sun here unpleasant at all; I feel fine working outside in the hottest part of the day. It's a dry, clean heat.

The color here is actually very fine; when the vegetation is fresh it's a rich green the like of which we seldom see in the north, calm. When it gets scorched and dusty it doesn't become ugly, but then a landscape takes on tones of gold of every shade, green-gold, yellow-gold, red-gold, ditto bronze, copper, in short from lemon yellow to the dull yellow color of, say, a pile of threshed grain. That with the blue — from the deepest royal blue in the water to that of forget-me-nots. Cobalt above all, bright clear blue — green-blue & violet-blue.

Naturally this induces orange — a face tanned by the sun *looks* orange; further, because of all the yellow, the violet really speaks — a wicker fence or grey thatched roof or a ploughed field look much more violet than at home. Further, as you already suspect, the people here are often handsome. In a word, I believe that life here is rather more rewarding than in many other places. Only it seems to me that the people are getting a little slack here, slipping a little too much onto the downward slope of carelessness, indifference, whereas if they were more energetic the land would probably yield more. I haven't read much lately, except *Madame Chrysanthème* by Pierre Loti.

Also *L'abbé Constantin* by Ohnet, terribly sweet & heavenly, so that even his *Maître de forges*, already tending that way, becomes even more suspect. Sometimes, out of ravenous hunger, I even read the newspaper here with fury, but don't take this to mean that I have a need to read. On the contrary, in fact, because I prefer to look at things myself. But it's simply become a habit to read for a few hours in the evening, so one can't help feeling that one's missing something, but you can tell that this isn't irksome from the fact that what one sees is interesting. I spent a week by the Mediterranean, you would think it beautiful. What strikes me here and what makes painting here attractive to me is the clarity of the air, you *can't* know what that is because it's precisely what we don't have at home — but at an hour's distance one can make out the color of things, the grey-green of olive trees and the grass green of the meadow, for instance, and the pink-lilac of ploughed land; at home we see a vague grey line on the horizon; here the line is sharp and the shape recognizable from far, far away. This gives an idea of space and air.

Since I'm now so occupied with myself, I'd also like to see if I can't make my own portrait in writing. First I start by saying that to my mind the same person supplies material for very diverse portraits.

Here's an impression of mine, which is the result of a portrait that I painted in the mirror, and which Theo has: a pink-grey face with green eyes, ash-colored hair, wrinkles in forehead and around the mouth, stiffly wooden, a very red beard, quite unkempt and sad, but the lips are full, a blue smock of coarse linen, & a palette with lemon yellow, vermilion, Veronese green, cobalt blue, in short all the colors, except of the orange beard, on the palette, the only whole colors, though. The figure against a grey-white wall. You'll say that this is something like, say, the face of — death — in Van Eeden's book or some such thing — very well, but anyway isn't a figure like this — and it isn't easy to paint oneself — in any event *something different* from a photograph? And you see — this is what Impressionism has — to my mind — over the rest, it isn't banal, and one seeks a deeper likeness than that of the photographer.

I look different nowadays, in so far as I no longer have either hair or beard, both being always shaved off close; further, my complexion has changed from green-grey pink to grey-orange, and I have a white suit instead of a blue one, and am always dusty, always more laden like a porcupine with sticks, easel, canvas, and other merchandise. Only the green eyes have remained the same, but another color in the portrait, naturally, is a yellow straw hat like a grass-mower — and a very black pipe. I live in a little yellow house with green door and shutters, whitewashed inside — on the white walls — very brightly colored Japanese drawings — red tiles on the floor — the house in the full sun — and a bright blue sky above it and — the shadow in the middle of the day much shorter than at home. Anyway — but can't you understand that one can paint something like that with a few strokes, but at the same time can't you understand that some people say 'it looks too strange,' not to mention the ones who find it nothing or abominable? If it just looks like it, but looks different from the work of the pious photographer with his black shadows — it should be done for that reason alone. I really don't like Mr. Vosmaer at all, and am callous enough not to care much about the man's exchange of the temporary for the eternal.

It's a very good thing that you and Ma have acquired a garden, with cats, tomcats, sparrows, and flies, rather than have an extra flight of stairs. I could never get used to climbing the stairs in Paris, and was always dizzy in a dreadful nightmare that has left me here, but recurred regularly there.

Were I not to put this letter in the post I would certainly tear it up if I read it over first — so I won't read it over and I doubt the legibility, I don't always have time to write.

I don't think there's anything in this letter and can't understand how I managed to make it so long. Thank Ma for her letter.

A long time ago I meant you to have a painted study, and you shall get it. I'm afraid that by post, even if I pay the postage, they'll make you pay excess postage, like the flowers from Menton, and this is even bigger — but Theo will certainly send you one, if I don't think about it, ask him for it.

Embracing you and Ma in thought.

Your loving
Vincent

Theo works for all the Impressionists, he's done something for and sold for all of them, and will certainly go on doing so. But just these few things that I write to you about the matter will show you how he's something very different from the run of dealers, who care nothing for the painters.

Was there enough postage on the drawing? Write and tell me that, because I ought to know.

INTERVAL: FUKUSHIMA; PARAGUAY

Another earthquake; troubles in Nueva Germania
7967 nm from Arles; 8127 nm from Genoa + 311 km to S.M.
Fukushima →← Paraguay: 14944 nm

July 1888

In early July 1888, in Vincent's beloved Japan, a series of earthquakes occurred for a period of three days straight, then continued several days later for another two days.

On the 15th of that month, another earthquake began at 7 AM in Yama-Gun, in the Fukushima prefecture, and another, and yet a third at magnitude 5.

Forty-five minutes later, after nearly 1100 years of silence, a phreatic eruption began at the fumaroles of Mount Bandai, the rock ladder to the sky, unleashing a concatenation of nearly 20 explosions. Echoes of thunder resounded and columns of black smoke extended 1300 meters into the blue. The final explosion, which sounded like the report of thousands of cannons firing simultaneously, discharged a horizontal cloud into the sky. Soon after, a pyroclastic flow swept over the eastern part of the volcano and phreatic eruptions continued until, at 10 AM, hot rain began to fall, transforming the vast quantity of volcanic ash into lahars and suffocating sulfurous dust, debris ravaging the downstream section of Nagasegawa River and its tributaries as pyroclastic flows buried villages at the northern foot of the mountain. The earth shook *&* trembled *&* undulated like ocean waves as the inhabitants ran from the mountain district: naked, bleeding, their visages contorted with expressions of helplessness, despair, agony. Shibatani, two miles from the eastern foot of the mountain, was almost entirely destroyed, but Nagasaki, a small hamlet one mile further to the east, was perfectly preserved ... Days before the disaster, monkeys near the hot springs were howling and shrieking and screaming — those who interpreted their behavior as an ill omen wisely fled the province.

On that same day, Vincent, who called himself a simple worshipper of the eternal Buddha and painted himself as a bonze, wrote to his brother Theo about filling his house with Japanese prints, for his apartment wouldn't be what it is without the constant presence of Japanese prints, and that he, Vincent the bonze, had also given a good many Japanese prints to Bernard, but for Theo to take the Hokusais as well then, 300 views of the sacred mountain and scenes of manners & customs.

There's an attic at Bing's, and in it there's a heap of 10,000 Japanese prints, landscapes, figures, old Japanese prints too. One Sunday he'll let you choose for yourself, so take plenty of old sheets too. I myself don't understand why you don't have the fine Japanese prints at boulevard Montmartre, because Japanese art is taking new roots among French Impressionist artists.

Later that same day, the bonze also wrote Bernard about two of his large pen drawings not looking Japanese, but that they are actually the most Japanese thing that I've done, and then he wrote his brother Theo a second time, speaking of how he was just as excited about this lot of 10,000 Japanese prints to go through as Thoré about a sale of Dutch paintings.

Japanese art is something like the primitives, like the Greeks, like our old Dutchmen, Rembrandt, Potter, Hals, Vermeer, Ostade, Ruisdael. *It doesn't end.*

After recounting news of a duel that Boulanger had in Paris on 13 July with Président du Conseil Charles Floquet, an opponent of the Boulangiste movement, the bonze said that Boulanger makes no impression at all in public. To the Chinese however, both men were considered of low character, and in the *Australian Town and Country Journal*, a reporter observed that France respects the general and the minister because they are supposed to be ready to shed their blood for the public good. But the manner in which they acted would in China be considered unworthy of the larrikins of Tientsin (the lowest of the low). What can be thought of a country where the highest functions are entrusted to those who behave themselves like the worst of vagabonds. In China, the rule is to submit the matter in dispute to the Emperor, who is the best judge of right and wrong; and he recompenses or punishes according to the merits of the case. In France it is not so. France is a Republic.

From cataclysmic earthquakes and volcanic explosions to barbaric duels, the earth was in tumult.

All the same, the bonze continued, it's a funny city, Paris, where you have to live by wearing yourself out, and as long as you're not half-dead you can't do a damned thing, and still. I've just read Victor Hugo's *L'année terrible*. There's hope there, but — that hope's in the stars. I find that true, and well said, and beautiful; and what's more, I readily believe it myself, too.

But let's not forget that the earth's a planet too, therefore a star or celestial globe. And what if all these other stars were the same!!!!!! It wouldn't be very jolly, in fact you'd have to start all over again.

For art, now — for which you need time, it wouldn't be bad to live more than one life. And it's not without appeal to believe in the Greeks, the old Dutch and Japanese masters, continuing their glorious school on other globes.

As Vincent the bonze imagined the doubling of existence and of planetary globes (echoes of Blanqui?), and as the earth trembled and shook in Japan, that same month, in Paraguay, in the utopia of Nueva Germania, a quarter of the just 40 families that had ventured to the Aryan paradise fled, leaving 70 of the 100 plots unsold. Its ground too was being undermined, just as the tectonic plates beneath Japan, just as Paris with its political schisms.

To retain the title to their 40,000-acre colony, Bernhard Förster and his little Queen still had to persuade over another 100 families to participate in their grand idyll. If not, the land would be forfeited and the Paraguayan government have to be repaid its investment of 80,000 Marks. The rebirth of the German race was facing infernal heat waves, infertile soil, malnutrition, torrential downpours, drowned animals, uprooted fences, saturated straw roofs, and impassable jungle tracks. While clean water was in short supply, the flooding brought swarms of plump malarial mosquitoes and the picá, a burrowing sand fly that was an inveterate menace — once it pierced its way into any of the colonists' flesh, if not treated, their wounds would swiftly turn septic.

Within just two years, those who saw themselves as the spiritual heirs of Wagner were facing utter devastation. Where was Parsifal? How could a superior race such as the Germans suffer such indignities? How could they not triumph with ease? Was the subterranean machine of Rutenbündel actually breaking down, or was their Lebensraum gaining further ground? Over the coming months & beyond, despite its travails, the Queen of the colony would continue to promote Nueva Germania as a kind of paradisiacal El Dorado whose triumph was inevitable and destined. *Deutschland, Deutschland über alles!*

Meanwhile, Herr Dynamite was correcting proofs to his polemical pamphlet, *The Case of Wagner*, where through what is laughable he would say what is severe. Instead of a rhythm that is akin to a moving swamp, the dancing philosopher called for a music that is light, supple, and fatalistic, not an infinite melody, but one that builds, organizes, and knows how to finish, one that knows how to slope into the sea with proud and calm harmony, like the mountains at Portofino, where the bay of Genoa ends its melody.

What is it, Mr. Dynamite asks, that we others, *we halcyons*, miss in Wagner — *la gaya scienza*; light feet, wit, fire, grace; the great logic; the dance of the stars;

the exuberant spirituality; the southern shivers of light;
the *smooth* sea — perfection. —

Where are we to turn? What is the antidote to decadence? With Bizet's work, the Provençal knight proclaims, one takes leave of the *humid* north, and all the
steam of the Wagnerian ideal. It possesses, above all,
what belongs to the warm climate, the dryness of the
air, its limpidezza. Here, in all respects, the climate is
altered. Here, a different sensuality expresses itself, a
different sensibility, a different gaiety. Here, music is
Mediterranized!

Have we here found a Dionysian geo-psychology, a
pathway out of swamps and climatological disaster to
move into more halcyon air? The art of lo gai saber? The
escape routes of Prince Vogelfrei soaring over the air?

SILS MARIA

734.8 km from Arles

the farouche moment; anti-decadence musicians; the weather is extremely irregular and my health changes with it; oh!!!; a whole circle of "disciples"; to characterize me; Dionysian pessimism; to treat morality as an illusion; a strange plant; halcyonism

Sunday, 29 July

Dear friend,

In the meantime I have given instructions that one of the few copies of my *ineditum* be sent to you: as a sign that all is well between us again and that the farouche moment of an all too vulnerable and all too lonely soul has been *overcome*. The fourth part of *Zarathustra*, treated by me with that shame before the "Publico," which, in view of *not* having respected the first three parts, makes me bitterly regret ... More precisely, it is an entr'acte between *Zarathustra* and *what follows* ("I name no names ...") The more precise title, which would be more descriptive:

"The Temptation of Zarathustra."
An interlude

Mr. C.G. Naumann has surely in the meantime put at your disposal what he has from me in stock; I told him to do so. I don't know what Herr Fritzsch has done; at the moment I can neither ask nor obtain anything from him — for good reasons! —

A really intelligent musician introduced himself to me, Prof. von Holten from Hamburg, who remembered you with great interest and led me into a discussion about Riemann's principles (— also about *other* principles: we are both very anti-*decadence* musicians (that is to say anti-modern musicians). Incidentally, he wishes you the same thing I wish — a *freer* sphere of activity *&* *not* in Danzig.

The weather is extremely irregular and changes every three hours; my health changes with it. Yesterday I received a letter from Bayreuth, written with overflowing Parsifal. A Viennese admirer unknown to me, who calls me his "master" (oh!!!) and calls on me to act in a kind of magnanimity against *Parsifal*: — I should be more generous than Siegfried against the *old wanderer*. Incidentally, he spoke in the name of a whole circle of my "disciples," as he put it, all of them "free spirits" who were very grateful for "beyond good and evil" ... (— he said that I had uttered so many grand, deep, even *terrible* words to them ...)

Of Dr. Brandes's brilliant success in Copenhagen, I have perhaps already told you. More than 300 listeners for his long lecture about me; at the end a great ovation. He writes to me that my name is now popular in all intelligent circles in Copenhagen and known throughout Scandinavia. From New York I was promised an English essay on my writings.

If you should ever get the chance to write something about me (— you don't have the *time*, dear friend!!), you have the wisdom, which unfortunately nobody has yet had to *characterize* me, to "describe" me, — but *not* "to evaluate." There is a pleasant neutrality to this, it seems to me that one can leave one's pathos aside and that the finer spirituality gets all the more into one's hands. I have never been characterized — neither as a *psychologist*, nor as a *writer* ("poet" included), nor as the inventor of a new kind of pessimism (a Dionysian pessimism, born of *strength*, which takes *pleasure* in the problem of existence by the horns), nor as an *immoralist* (— the hitherto highest form of "intellectual righteousness," which is permitted to treat morality as an illusion after it has become *instinct* and *inevitability* —). It is by *no* means necessary, not even *desired*, to take sides with me: on the contrary, a dose of curiosity, as before a strange plant, with an ironic resistance, seems to me an incomparably more *intelligent* attitude toward me. — Forgiveness! I just wrote some naiveté — a little recipe to happily pull yourself out of the *impossible* ...

With the kindest regards
Your N.

In any case, you have to read the gay science "la gaya scienza": it is my most *medial* book, — a lot of subtle joy, a lot of halcyonism ...

ARLES

734.8 km from Sils Maria

to work with a more serious conception; the emptiness you sometimes feel; the moth-eaten and official tradition; alone, poor, treated like madmen; this effacement of personality; the more completely you become a dealer, the more you become an artist; dissipated, ill, a broken pitcher; make me feel that art is alive; having been not too well again; the artificial prolongation of modern hygiene; an ongoing piece of business; rigorously Impressionist but not powerful; what one ought to do there is not talk to civilized people; the very placid abbot, the mad painter; one day or another there could be a crisis

Sunday, 29 July 1888

My dear Theo,

Many thanks for your kind letter. If you recall, mine ended with: we're getting old, that's what *is* and the rest is *imagination* and doesn't exist. Now, I said that even more for myself, than for you. And I said it feeling the absolute necessity for me to act accordingly, to work, not more, perhaps, but with a more serious conception.

Now you talk about the emptiness you sometimes feel; that's just the same thing that I have, too. Considering, if you will, the times in which we live as a true and great revival of art, the moth-eaten and official tradition, which is still on its feet, but which is at bottom powerless and bone-idle, the new painters, alone, poor, treated like madmen and as a result of this treatment becoming so in fact, at least as far as their social life is concerned.

Then remember that you do exactly the same work as these primitive painters, since you provide them with money *&* you sell their canvases for them, which enables them to produce others.

If a painter ruins his character by working hard at painting, which makes him sterile for many things, for family life, *&c. &c.*

If as a consequence he paints not only with paint but with self-denial and self-abnegation and a broken heart.

Not only are you not paid for your own work either, but it costs you exactly the same as this effacement of personality, half deliberate, half accidental, costs a painter.

This is to say that if you do painting *indirectly*, you're more productive than me, for example. The more completely you become a dealer, the more you become an artist. Just as I very much hope to be in the same case... The more I become dissipated, ill, a broken pitcher, the more I too become a creative artist in that great revival of art of which we're speaking.

These things are indeed so, but this eternally existing art and this revival — this green shoot growing from the roots of the old felled trunk — these are things so spiritual that a kind of melancholy remains with us when we reflect that at less expense we could have made life instead of making art. You really ought, if you can, to make me feel that art is alive, you who perhaps love art more than I do.

I say to myself that that doesn't have to do with art, but with me, that the only way for me to regain self-confidence and tranquility is by *doing better*.

And here we are again at the end of my last letter — I'm getting old, but it's only imagination if I were to believe that art is an old, stale thing. Now, if you know what a *'mousmé'* is (you'll know when you've read Loti's *Madame Chrysanthème*), I've just painted one. It took me my whole week; I wasn't able to do anything else, having been not too well again. That's what annoys me; if I'd been well I'd have knocked off some more landscapes in between times. But in order to finish off my mousmé I had to save my mental powers. A mousmé is a Japanese girl — Provençale in this case — aged between 12 and 14. That makes 2 figures, the Zouave, and her, that I have.

Look after your health, take baths, especially *if Gruby recommends that you do*. Because you'll see in 4 years, the years by which I'm older than you, how far relative health is necessary in order to be able to work. Now we who work with our heads, our only and unique means of avoiding being finished too soon is the artificial prolongation of modern hygiene, rigorously followed, as far as we can endure it. Because I for one don't do everything that I should do. And a little good cheer is better than any other remedy.

I have a letter from Russell. He says that he would have written to me before had it not been that his move to Belle-Île had absorbed him. He's there now, and says that he'd be pleased if sooner or later I came to spend some time there. He still wants to do my portrait again. He even says, "I would have gone to Boussod's to see the Gauguin, negresses talking, had it not been that I was prevented from doing so for the same reason."

In short, he's not refusing to buy one, but is making it understood that he wouldn't want poorer quality than ours. You see that this is in any case better than nothing at all.

I'll write this to Gauguin and will ask him for croquis of paintings. We shouldn't push this business and give up on R. for the time being, but consider the thing as an ongoing piece of business that will come off.

And the same for Guillaumin, I'd like him to buy a figure by G.

He says he's received a very fine bust of his wife from *Rodin*, and that on that occasion he lunched with Claude Monet and that he saw the 10 paintings of Antibes then. I'm sending him Geffroy's article. He makes a very good critique of the Monets, first of all liking them very much: the difficulty attacked, the envelope of colored air, the color. Now after that he says, what must be repeated is that it all lacks construction everywhere, for example, with him a tree will have far too much foliage for the size of the trunk, and so always and everywhere, from the point of view of the reality of things, from the point of view of a whole number of *laws* of nature, he's pretty well hopeless. He ends by saying that this quality of attacking difficulties is what everyone should have.

I've received from Bernard 10 croquis like his brothel; there are 3 of them that are in the style of Redon; the enthusiasm that he has for that I don't much share myself.

But there's a woman washing herself, very Rembrandtesque, or in the style of Goya, and a very strange landscape with figures.

He expressly forbids me to send them to you, but you'll receive them by the same post. I think *Russell* will buy something else from Bernard. Now I've seen work by this *Boch*; it's rigorously Impressionist but not powerful, at this moment when this new technique is still preoccupying him too much to allow him to be himself. He'll become stronger and will bring out his individuality, I think. But Macknight does watercolors of the power of those by *Destrée*, you know, that vile Dutchman we knew back in the old days. However, he'd washed some small still lifes, yellow jug on purple foreground, red jug on green, orange jug on blue: better, but it's pretty poor.

The village where they're staying is *pure Millet*, small peasants, nothing but that, totally *rustic* and intimate. That character completely escapes them. I believe that Macknight has civilized and converted to civilized Christianity his lout of a landlord. At least, when you go there that scoundrel and his worthy spouse shake your hand — it's in a café, of course — when you ask for a drink they have ways of refusing the money, 'Oh, I couldn't take money from an artiss' (with two s's). Anyhow, it's their own fault that it's appalling, and this Boch must be getting pretty dull-witted with Macknight. I think Macknight has money, but not much. So they contaminate the village; if it weren't for that, I'd go there often to work there. What one ought to do there is not talk to civilized people; but they know the stationmaster and a score of bloody nuisances, and that's largely why they don't do a damned thing. I've already said that to Mourier, who once used to believe that Macknight got on highly intelligently with the 'man of the fields.'

Naturally, these simple and naive people of the fields make fun of them, and despise them. On the contrary, if you do your work there without worrying about the village idlers with their stiff collars, then you can go into the homes of the peasants, enabling them to earn a few sous. And then that bloody Fontvieille would be a treasure to them, but the natives are — Zola's small peasants, innocent and gentle beings, as we know. It's likely that Macknight will shortly do little landscapes with sheep, for boxes of sweets. Not just my paintings, but I myself most of all, I had recently become wild-eyed, a bit like Hugo van der Goes in the painting by Emile Wauters.

But having had all my beard carefully shaved off, I believe that I have as much of the very placid abbot in the same painting as of the mad painter so intelligently depicted in it. And I'm not unhappy to be somewhere between the two, because *you have to live.*

Especially as there's no getting away from the fact that one day or another there could be a crisis if you changed as far as your position with the Boussods was concerned. One more reason for maintaining relations with artists on my part as well as on yours.

Besides, I believe I've told the truth, all the same. If I succeeded in bringing back in prices the money spent, I would be doing no more than my duty. And the *practical* thing I can do is the portrait. As far as drinking too much goes... I don't know if it's bad. But just look at Bismarck, who in any case is very practical and very intelligent. His little doctor told him he was drinking too much and *that he'd overtaxed himself all his life, from his stomach to his brain.* B. stopped drinking there and then.

Since then he's lost ground and is dragging along. He must really be laughing inside at his doctor, whom fortunately for him he didn't consult too soon. Anyway, good handshake.

Ever yours,
Vincent

Remember that with Gauguin we should in no way change the idea of coming to his aid if the proposal is acceptable as it stands, but *we don't need* him. So, as far as working alone goes, don't believe that it bothers me, and don't press the matter for me, be fully assured of that.

The portrait of a young girl is on a white background strongly tinted with Veronese green, the bodice is striped blood-red and purple. The skirt is royal blue with large orange-yellow stippling. The matt areas of flesh are yellow grey, the hair purplish, the eyebrows black, and the eyelashes, the eyes orange and Prussian blue; a sprig of oleander between the fingers, because the 2 hands are included.

SILS MARIA

734.8 km from Arles

the difficulties of my existence; I have given humanity its profoundest book; one is a wild animal that is constantly being wounded; one could die of being "immortal"; the cretinism of Bayreuth; people last winter were celebrating me; outlawed & boycotted; my health has, unfortunately, not been the best; for my sister, things have meanwhile been going proportionately better; it needs greatness of soul for a person to stand my writings at all

End of July 1888

Hochverehrte Freundin,

You will be thinking: *finally*! won't you? — But I involuntarily
have no words for anyone, because I have less and less desire to
allow anyone to see into the difficulties of my existence. There
is indeed a great *emptiness* around me. Literally, there is no one
who could understand my situation. The worst thing is, without
a doubt, not to have heard for 10 years a single word that actually *got through* to me — and to be understanding about this, to
understand it as something necessary! I have given humanity its
profoundest book, a book against which all other books are mere
literature. How one must *atone* for that! — It places one outside
all human intercourse, it brings an unbearable tension and vul-
nerability, one is a wild animal that is constantly being wounded.
The wound is not hearing any answer, and having to *bear*, most
terribly, on one's own shoulders, alone, the burden which one
would have liked to share, to shed (— why else should one write?).
One could die of being "*immortal*"! — As chance would have it,
it is also my misfortune to coincide with a wretched impoverish-
ment and stagnation of the *German* mind. People in the "dear
old Fatherland" treat me like a man who ought to be locked up
— this is the form of their "understanding"! Moreover, the cretinism of Bayreuth obstructs me. The old seducer Wagner, even
after his death, is taking from me the few remaining people on
whom I could have some influence. — But in Denmark — it is
absurd to say this! — people last winter were celebrating me!! Dr.
Georg Brandes, a most intelligent man, has been brave enough
to give a longish course of lectures on me at the University of
Copenhagen! And with brilliant success! A regular attendance
of over 300! And a great ovation at the end! — The prospect of
something similar has just come to me from New York. I am the
most *independent* mind in Europe and the *only* German writer
— that is something! —

　　This reminds me of a question in your latest and much appreciated letter. You will realize that for books such as *I* write I
receive no honorarium. But you will perhaps not realize that I

have to pay the *entire* cost of printing and publication (— about 4000 francs during the past few years). As result of my being outlawed and boycotted by the press and by booksellers, the number of copies sold does not reach one hundred. I have almost no capital — my pension from Basel is modest (3000 francs a year); yet I have always saved some of the latter, so that till now I have no debts whatever. My trick is to simplify my life more and more, to avoid long journeys as well as living in hotels. So far it has turned out well; and I want it so. Only there are difficulties of one kind or another for one's *pride.* —

Under these manifold pressures from within and without, my health has, unfortunately, not been the best. In the past few years it has *not* improved. The past *months*, with the additional harassment of unfavorable weather, even seemed to be very similar to my worst times. —

For my sister, things have meanwhile been going proportionately better. The project seems to be a splendid success — the festive, almost *princely* entry into the colony about four months ago made a great impression on me. There are about 120 Germans, plus a large appendage of native peons; there are good families among them, i.e. the family of Baron Maltzan from Mecklenburg.

Recently I was strongly reminded of you, *verehrteste Freundin*, thanks to a book that highlights a foreground figure in the first volume of *Memoirs of an Idealist*. Likewise Frl. von Salis wrote me, with *much gratitude*, a letter about her visit to you.

With most affectionate wishes for your wellbeing, and the plea for your *continuing*, if silent, interest.

Your loyally devoted
Nietzsche

— It needs *greatness* of soul for a person to stand my writings at all. I have the good fortune to make all weak and virtuous people embittered against me.

ARLES

virility, originality, naturalism; we're burning; expressing oneself powerfully; lines in contrary motion; each individual was a stone; an obeliscal society; a state of total laxity and anarchy; to descend good-naturedly into the intimacy of our very own epoch; sterile metaphysical meditations that aren't up to bottling chaos; we can paint an atom of chaos; Degas has trouble getting a hard-on; eat well, do your military drill well, don't fuck too hard; spermatic painting; a certain chastity made them stronger; from the virile point of view; being exiled, a social outcast; the whore is our friend and sister

3 August

My dear old Bernard,

I realize that I've forgotten to answer your question as to whether Gauguin is still in Pont-Aven. Yes, he's still there, and if you feel like writing to him I am inclined to believe that it will please him. It's still likely that he'll join me here shortly, as soon as either one of us is able to find the travel expenses.

I don't believe that this question of the Dutchmen, which we're discussing these days, is without interest. It's quite interesting to consult them when it's a matter of any kind of virility, originality, naturalism.

In the first place, I must speak to you again about yourself, about two still lifes that you've done, and about the two portraits of your grandmother. Have you ever done better, have you ever been more *yourself*, and someone? Not in my opinion. Profound study of the first thing to come to hand, of the first person to come along, was enough to really *create* something. Do you know what made me like these 3 or 4 studies so much? That *je ne sais quoi* of something deliberate, very wise, that *je ne sais quoi* of something steady and firm and sure of oneself, which they show. You've never been closer to Rembrandt, my dear chap, than then. In Rembrandt's studio, the incomparable sphinx, Vermeer of Delft, found this extremely sound technique that hasn't been surpassed. Which today..... we're burning... to find. Oh, I know that we're working and arguing Color as they did *chiaroscuro, value*.

What do these differences matter when in the end it's a question of expressing oneself powerfully?

At present...... you're examining primitive Italian and German techniques, the symbolic meaning that the Italians' abstract and mystical drawing may contain. Do so.

I myself rather like this anecdote about Giotto — there was a competition for the execution of some painting or other of a Virgin. Lots of proposals were sent to the fine arts authorities of those days. One of these proposals, signed Giotto, was simply — an *oval* — an egg shape — the authorities, intrigued and trusting — entrust the Virgin in question — to Giotto. Whether it's true or not I don't know, but I rather like the anecdote.

However, let's return to Daumier and to your grandmother. When are you going to show us more of them, studies of that soundness? I urge you to do so, while at the same time in no way belittling your investigations concerning the properties of lines in contrary motion — being not at all indifferent, I hope, to the simultaneous contrasts of lines, of forms. The trouble is, do you see, my dear old Bernard, that Giotto, Cimabue, as well as Holbein and Van Eyck, lived in an obeliscal — if you'll pardon the expression — society, layered, architecturally constructed, in which each individual was a stone, all of them holding together and forming a monumental society. I have no doubt that we'll again see an incarnation of this society when the socialists logically build their social edifice — from which they're a fair distance away yet. But you know we're in a state of total laxity and anarchy.

We, artists in love with order & symmetry, isolate ourselves and work to define *one single thing*.

Puvis knows that very well, and when he, so wise and so just, decided to descend good-naturedly into the intimacy of our very own epoch, forgetting his Elysian Fields, he made a very fine portrait, the serene old man in his bright, blue interior, reading the novel with a yellow cover — a glass of water beside him, in which a watercolor brush and a rose. And also a society lady, like those the De Goncourts portrayed.

The Dutchmen, now, we see them painting things just as they are, apparently without thought, the way Courbet painted his beautiful naked women.

They make portraits, landscapes, still lifes. One could be stupider than that and commit greater follies.

If we don't know what to do, my dear old Bernard, then let's do the same as them, if only so as not to allow our scarce mental powers to evaporate in sterile metaphysical meditations that aren't up to bottling chaos, which is chaotic for the very reason that it won't fit into any glass of our caliber.

We can — and that's what those Dutchmen did, desperately clever in the eyes of people wedded to system — we can paint an *atom* of chaos. A horse, a portrait, your grandmother, apples, a landscape.

Why do you say that Degas has trouble getting a hard-on? Degas lives like a little lawyer, and he doesn't like women, knowing that if he liked them & fucked them a lot he would become cerebrally ill and hopeless at painting. Degas's painting is virile and impersonal precisely because he has resigned himself to being personally no more than a little lawyer, with a horror of riotous living. He watches human animals stronger than himself getting a hard-on and fucking, and he paints them well, precisely because he doesn't make such great claims about getting a hard-on.

Rubens, ah, there you have it, he was a handsome man and a good fucker, Courbet too; their health allowed them to drink, eat, fuck.

In your case, my poor dear old Bernard, I already told you last spring. Eat well, do your military drill well, don't fuck too hard; if you don't fuck too hard, your painting will be all the more spermatic.

Ah, Balzac, that great and powerful artist, already told us very well that for modern artists a certain chastity made them stronger.

The Dutchmen were *married people making children*, a beautiful, very beautiful occupation, very natural.

One swallow doesn't make a summer. I'm not saying that among your new Breton studies there aren't some virile and strong ones, but I haven't seen them yet and so wouldn't be able to talk about them. But — I've seen those virile things, the portrait of your grandmother & the still lifes — judging from your drawings I have vague doubts whether these new studies would have the same vigor, just from the virile point of view.

These studies that I'm talking about first, you see it's the first swallow of your summertime as an artist. If we want, ourselves, to get a hard-on for our work, we must sometimes resign ourselves to fucking only a *little*, and for the rest to be, according as our temperament demands, soldiers or monks. The Dutchmen, once again, had morals, & a quiet, calm, well-ordered life.

Delacroix, ah, him — "I," he said, "found painting when I had no teeth nor breath left." And those who saw this famous artist paint said: when *Delacroix paints it's like the lion devouring his piece of flesh*. He fucked only a little, and had only casual love affairs so as not to filch from the time devoted to his work. If in this letter, on the face of it more incoherent, and taken on its own without its connections to the previous correspondence and above all, friendship, than I should wish — if in this letter you find that I have some anxieties — concerns in any case — for your health, foreseeing the hard ordeal that you'll have to go through in doing your service, obligatory, alas, — then you will read it correctly. I know that the study of the Dutchmen could only do you good, their works being so virile and so spunky and so healthy.

Personally, I find continence is quite good for me. It's enough for our weak, impressionable artists' brains to give their essence to the creation of our paintings. Because in thinking, calculating, wearing ourselves out, we expend cerebral activity.

Why exert ourselves in spending all our creative juices when those who pimp for a living and even their simple, well-fed clients work more to the satisfaction of the genital organs of the registered whore in this case than we do? The whore in question has my sympathy more than my compassion.

Being exiled, a social outcast, as artists like you and I surely are, 'outcasts' too, she is surely therefore our friend and sister. And finding — in this position — of outcast — the same as us — an independence that isn't without its advantages — all things considered — let's not adopt a false position by believing we're serving her through social rehabilitation, which is in any case impractical and would be fatal for her.

I've just made a portrait of a postman — or rather, two portraits even — Socratic type, no less Socratic for being something of an alcoholic, and with a high color as a result. His wife had just given birth, the good fellow was glowing with satisfaction. He's a fierce republican, *like père Tanguy*. Goddamn, what a subject to paint à la Daumier, eh? He was getting too stiff while posing, and that's why I painted him twice, the second time at a single sitting, on white canvas, background blue, almost white, in the face all the broken tones: yellow, green, purples, pinks, reds, the uniform Prussian blue trimmed with yellow.

Write to me soon if you feel like it; am very encumbered and haven't yet found time for figure sketches. Handshake.

Yours truly,
Vincent

Cézanne is as much a respectably married man as the old Dutchmen were. If he has a good hard-on in his work it's because he's not overly dissipated through riotous living.

SILS MARIA

734.8 km from Arles

*everything I undertook was successful; the weather was in-
deed like a serious illness; philosophers fall silent; illness
& boredom in perpetuity; the highest, earthly and Engadin
perfection!; Paraguay is tempting; the wilderness and happiness; nowhere is it quiet, nowhere anti-modern enough
for me; the bells of Sils*

11 August 1888

Most honored woman

that was a day, the tenth of August! The weather, warm, pure, deep blue; everything I undertook was successful; every two hours there was a pleasant surprise (— including a private concert for me, organized by an excellent musician from Hamburg, Mr. von Holten: he had rehearsed a piece by my Venetian Maëstro and played it six times in a row — by heart!).

In the morning I walked around Lake Silvaplana, in the afternoon I was further back in the Fex Valley — there were at least 70 strangers there, all of them in a state of quasi-convalescence, because until the day before yesterday the weather was indeed like a *serious illness*. And when I arrived home in the evening, calculating what good things the day had brought, it was not even finished with its presents — I found your very kind, very amiable letter! Such an *undeserved* letter!

— But the winter was angry with me, it was a dark and sick time, without sunshine neither above nor *inside*. The whole stay in Nizza was a failure. When they are sick, philosophers act like animals, they fall silent, they crawl into their caves. My old friend Meysenbug may also be quite amazed that she hasn't heard from me since last autumn. — The heat in Italy drove me to the Engadin at the beginning of June — I, miserable man!! — such weather cannot be described; my condition worsened in such a way that it reminded me of my saddest times. Profound weakness, going to bed a couple of times every week, the fatal headache with its fatal consequences. Since one couldn't go out and shivered through the day in the cold room, one couldn't even sleep at night. In addition, a complete lack of company; eyes too weak to read; illness and boredom in perpetuity. — For about 3 weeks the weather has been *different*: not exactly better, but at least with good, albeit short, interludes. Winter days were extremely severe, with calm winds; even now the overall character of the landscape is very wintry due to the great amount of snow. But yesterday and the day before yesterday the *highest, earthly and Engadin perfection!*

In Nizza I read the *Journal de Genève* in the evening... How often have I thought of you and your suffering friend while reading the sad weather report! It was tough for a first winter in Geneva. Paraguay, under *such* weather conditions, is indeed a tempting aspect.

The last major reports of the truly princely entry and reception of my relatives in the new colony made a strong impression on me. In the end, I absolutely *need* Europe as a culture museum. The wilderness (— and happiness ...) is for someone who has no philosophy on his conscience! —

One of the curiosities of this winter was that I started to become *famous*! Where? In Denmark. The brilliant scholar of Denmark, Dr. Georg Brandes, has given a long cycle of university lectures on the philosopher Nietzsche, with extraordinary success, if one can trust the newspapers. More than 300 people are regular listeners; at the end a great ovation. — I'm being given the prospect of something similar in New York. — I wish I could enjoy something like this more. Basically, it makes me feel *ironic*.

For the next winter the hermit wants to go to Corsica, not exactly to Ajaccio, but to an undiscovered world. I need such deep self-reflection, for nowhere is it quiet, nowhere *anti-modern* enough for me. If I may ask, please say a cordial word from me to your dear friend; the same with your young daughter. I am very pleased that she is in contact with a good painter. I also hear from Miss Zimmer with great interest: I want her to remember me. A greeting to the excellent Mad. Bichler should also not be forgotten. Your admiringly devoted

Nietzsche

P. S. The bells of Sils are just beginning to ring — new bells! A beautiful soft melodic sound. —

ARLES

I have to thank you for quite a few things; delights à la da Vinci; more serious deviations of unhealthy sex; law and justice apart, a pretty woman is a living marvel; the sun of the south; brothel confidence; forced labor in perpetuity

12 August 1888

My dear Theo,

I have to thank you for quite a few things, first of all your letter and the 50-franc note it contained, but then also for the consignment of colors and canvas that I've been to collect at the station (the geranium lake arrived too), and lastly for the Cassagne book and for *La fin de Lucie Pellegrin*. If Tasset divided up his packages better there'd be a difference in the cost of carriage; this time it came to 3 parcels, two of them weighing over 5 kilos. If a few tubes had been kept back, the whole thing would have cost about 5 francs. Anyway, I'm still very glad to have them.

Pellegrin is very beautiful, it's straight from the life, and it's still elegant, and it's touching, because it keeps the broad human aspect. Why should it be forbidden to deal with these subjects? Unhealthy and over-excited sexual organs seek sensual pleasures, delights à la da Vinci. Not I, on the other hand, who have hardly seen any but the sort of 2-franc women originally intended for the Zouaves. But people who have leisure for making love look for mystery of the Da Vincian sort. I understand that these loves won't always be understood by everyone.

But from the point of view of what is *permitted*, books could actually be written dealing with more serious deviations of unhealthy sex than the practices of Lesbians; just as it's also permitted to write medical documents, surgical descriptions, on those matters.

Anyway, law and justice apart, a pretty woman is a living marvel, while a painting by da Vinci or Correggio only exists on other accounts. Why am I so little an artist that I always regret that the statue, the painting, aren't alive? Why do I understand the musician better, why do I see more clearly the *raison d'être* of his abstractions? At the first opportunity I'll send you an engraving after a drawing by Rowlandson of two women, as beautiful as Fragonard or Goya.

At the moment we have a very glorious, powerful heat here, with no wind, which suits me very well. Sunshine, a light which, for want of a better word I can only call yellow — pale sulfur yellow, pale lemon, gold. How beautiful yellow is! And how much better shall I see the north. Ah, I'm always wishing that the day will come when you'll see and feel the sun of the south.

As far as studies go, I have two studies of *thistles* on a piece of waste ground, thistles white with the fine dust from the road.

And a little study of a halting-place of fairground people, red and green caravans, and also a little study of carriages of the Paris-Lyon-Méditerranée, which last two studies have been approved as 'in quite the modern key' by the young follower of good old General Boulanger, the very brilliant second lieutenant of Zouaves.

This gallant soldier has given up the art of drawing, into the mysteries of which I was making efforts to initiate him, but for a plausible reason, because unexpectedly he had to take an examination, for which I fear he was anything but prepared. Supposing that the above-mentioned young Frenchman always tells the truth, he'll have astonished the examiners with the self-confidence of his answers, a confidence that he seems to have boosted by spending the night before the examination in a brothel. As I believe François Coppée says in a sonnet, on the subject of "my lieutenant on his way," we may have "a doubt that fills us with despair."

For, continues Coppée.... "I think of our defeat." The fact remains that I have no reason to complain of him, and if it's true that he'll soon be a lieutenant, we should acknowledge his good fortune. He literally resembles the good old General from the point of view of having spent a great deal of time with the good so-called ladies of the café-concert.

It'll be enough that I'll write to you, or he'll send you a telegram to tell you by which train he'll arrive on the 16 or the 17. He'll give you the painted studies then, which will save us carriage charges. He owes me that much, anyway, for my lessons. He'll do no more than spend one or two days in Paris on his way to the north, but on his return he'll stay there longer.

It is indeed, after so much coldness, rather kind of our uncle to have left you a legacy, but it's hard for me to get it into my head that he and C.M. haven't condemned you a little to forced labor in perpetuity by refusing to provide for you by lending you the capital needed to set up on your own. That remains a serious error on their part. But I don't labor the point. One more reason to try to do the most possible in art if we'll always be in difficulties, relatively speaking, as far as money goes. Well, my dear brother, at that moment you were ready, for your part, to set yourself up; therefore you have every right to feel that you've done your duty, for your part. With their help, you had this business in the Impressionists, taken as a whole. Without their help, the business won't be done, or will be done in a different way. You may not have earned anything, but you've deserved it, now if the Dutch are always mixing up these two such different questions, having only their word 'verdienen' in both cases, too bad for them!

I'll write another short line to Mourier, you'll read it. And I shake your hand firmly.

Ever yours,
Vincent

SILS MARIA

734.8 km from Arles

the sky as pure as in Nizza; too salty and coarse hams; a test of patience of the first order; incredible melancholy & weakness; soft and full bells

Monday, 13 August 1888

My dear mother,

We have had incomparably beautiful weather for 4 days and we all breathe easily again. Before that it was deeply winterish; so that my landlady put double blankets on my bed and I used all the winter clothes I had. But suddenly there is a wonderful summer mood; the most beautiful colors I've seen up here, and the sky as pure as in Nizza. This morning I was with Fraulein v. Salis gondoling around on the lake; yesterday an excellent musician gave me a little private concert in which he played some things by Herr Köselitz that he had rehearsed for me. A very amiable letter from Missus Fynn in Geneva arrived (despite the fact that I had been completely silent since the previous autumn and had left several letters unanswered). There are now 60 guests in my hotel. There was a great deal for me to do, we are back to full-on printing work. —

Now I have eaten the somewhat too salty and coarse hams; likewise *one* of the fine and small ones. The *second* has also already been cut into: so that it will not be very long before the supply is exhausted. My intention is still to hold out until September 15th: although given the weather this year, I can't promise anything. Basically, the whole stay so far was a test of patience of the first order: it would be impossible to think of anything more horrific. Very often I did not know how I would overcome an incredible melancholy *&* weakness.

Sils has acquired new bells, the sound of which is very soft and full.

I ask for a whole box of feathers, because of the trip to the south, where I can no longer get anything.

A few days ago I also wrote to Herr *von Bülow* in Hamburg, where he has conducted the opera for two winters now, to recommend the work of the excellent Herr Köselitz to him. He would be the only one to dare to do something new like this: but since he is an unpredictable person, I cannot predict anything. —

Embracing you in heartfelt love
Your ancient creature.

INTERVAL: PARIS

21 August 1888

As the effects of the French Revolution and the 18th century echoed forward, with that century not in fact ending, for just as with the body, there are no clear, firm, sharp dividing lines between centuries (as there are not between colors blended at a distance by the eye), the 19th century began with the discovery of dwarf planets, the election of Thomas Jefferson as President of the United States, the crowning of Ranjit Singh as King of Punjab, the merging of the Kingdoms of Ireland and Great Britain, and Napoleon's signing of the Concordat of 1801 with the Pope, a pact that presaged the papacy's future ones with Mussolini and Hitler. Is not the most pernicious colonist of the earth the Roman Catholic Empire? If the previous century did not per se close, as the clock of time persisted on, questions remained as to whether nature is solitary, poor, nasty, brutish, and short, or whether it teaches all mankind that, being all equal and independent, no one ought to harm another in his life, liberty, or possessions, or whether it is morally neutral and pacific, a primitive state uninfected by socialization and the evils of cultural institutions.

With such schismatic ambiguities in play, the dawning of a new century was on the rise, and a new politics, and that century was figured in the structure of a building being prepared as the centerpiece of the 1889 Exposition Universelle, a world's fair celebrating the centennial of the French Revolution.

Earlier denounced as a threat to French art and history, castigated as useless and monstrous, some artists

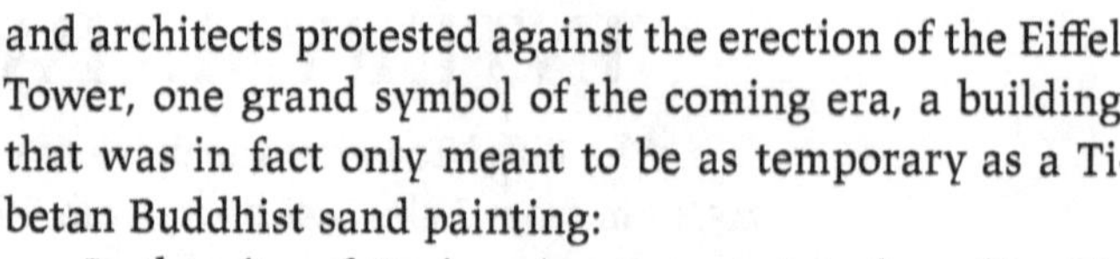

and architects protested against the erection of the Eiffel Tower, one grand symbol of the coming era, a building that was in fact only meant to be as temporary as a Tibetan Buddhist sand painting:

Is the city of Paris going to associate herself with the grotesque, mercenary invention of a machine builder, many protested, so as to deface and deflower herself? For you may not doubt that the Eiffel Tower, unwanted even by commercial America, is the deflowering of Paris.

In August, as the mercenary invention continued to rise and threaten the very hymen of Paris (who knew it was a virgin and not a courtesan...), some journalists described the monument as Eiffel's Tower of Babel, one of the most daring feats of engineering since Biblical days. And so, many believed, or feared, that the construction of such an immense tower would also lead to the confusion of the city and its being incinerated, destroyed, or eroded over time, or worse, to the sinful corruption of the glorious French tongue. Eiffel himself defended his monument, issuing a kind of ethical and aesthetic credo when countering his critics and the hullabaloo of a fearful public and its archaic and ossified ideas:

Is it because we are engineers that we do not pay attention to beauty? Do not the laws of natural forces always conform to the secret laws of harmony? The first principle of the aesthetics of architecture is that the essential lines of a monument should be determined by their perfect appropriateness to their end. Now, what condition do I have to take into consideration above all others in a tower? Wind resistance. I maintain that the curves of the four arrises of the monument, as the calculations have determined them, will vie an impression of beauty because they will demonstrate to the viewer the boldness of the conception.

That month, as Vincent was obsessively painting still lifes of sunflowers intended for Gauguin's bedroom in the Yellow House, the enormous mass of iron necessary to construct la Tour Eiffel accumulated meter by meter,

climbing toward the clouds, its spider web of red metal awaiting further assembly, just as, in the early 19th century, Ranjit Singh was accumulating French and Italian mercenaries who fought under Napoleon to modernize his army and ascend as a new world power.

From morning till night, the percussive bang of heavy sledgehammers rang throughout Paris, a symphony of rhythms rapidly pounding in rivets, the infernal flames of the forges flickering against the sky, an explosion of colors as incandescent as the palettes of the painters of every new art movement and every new art movement to come, and as incandescent as the palettes of the military technology of flamethrowers, mortars, siege guns, tanks, and poison gas that would emerge in the early 20th century not long after Pierre and Marie Curie's discovery of pitchblende. Like the Faust of the 19th century and the mad painter, Eiffel pursued his vision, critics and public be damned, protests be damned, warnings be damned. Humanity must be thrust to the edge of its threshold. This world is a monster of energy, without beginning, without end; a firm, iron magnitude of force that does not grow bigger or smaller, that does not expend itself but only transforms itself... this world is a light for you, too, you best-concealed, strongest, most intrepid, most midnightly men. — *This world is the will to power — and nothing besides!* And you yourselves are also this will to power — and nothing besides!

Despite equipping the structure with lightning rods, thunderstorms often forced the tower workers to scramble to safety, and many citizens feared the tower and its strange apparatuses were altering the climate of their beloved City of Lights. Were their biblical fears coming true? Observers remarked that large quantities of heavy rain and thunder-clouds gathered round the babelian pillar and then, as if deprived by the lightning conductors of part of their electricity, blown farther on to break in showers in other parts of the flowering metropolis that was in process of being deflowered. Is it not a sign, some

thought, of Eiffel's madness, of the coming tumult, of the soon to come confusion, of the storms of wind that will destroy the tower, of Paris no longer being Paris but becoming Babylon?? Or is it a sign of new machinic assemblages?

In the sweltering heat of summer, despite the protests, the combative weather, and factions of opposition, the second tier of the Eiffel Tower was completed as Herr Dynamite was in the midst of completing his postscripts and epilogue to *The Case of Wagner* and simultaneously completing work on *A Psychologist at Leisure*, which he called a recuperation in the midst of an immensely difficult and decisive task that, when properly understood, would do nothing less than split humanity in two.

More schisms, more earthquakes, more incandescent technology! Further thresholds to breach! Monster of energy, transform!

Later, *A Psychologist at Leisure* would be renamed *Twilight of the Idols, or: How to Philosophize with a Hammer*, arrows would fly, and the True World would become a Fable.

Many years before, the one who referred to himself as something decisive and fateful explained to a friend that he should have been at the International Exposition of Electricity in Paris in 1881, partly to learn the latest findings, partly as an exhibition; for as one who senses electrical changes and as a so-called weather prophet *I am a match for the monkeys and am probably a specialty.* I live, he confessed, amid clouds and lightning as among peers and likewise among sunbeams, dewdrops, and snowflakes. My wisdom is gathering like a cloud, like all wisdom that is to give birth to lightning!

Will egalitarianism lead to the return of the natural innocent human, or to the wild, prowling one?

Let us, the bête philosophe questioned, see — each of us within himself — whether it is possible to call back the spirit of the Enlightenment and of progressive evolution!

Was Nietzsche's feat of philosophy more dangerous than Eiffel's feat of engineering? Who would be more feared? Who considered more dangerous in the coming century? Did Herr Dynamite just live amid clouds and lightning like the dreaded tower, or was he himself not also clouds, lightning, and pyroclastic flow? Was he not becoming-volcanic, an infernal flame, pitchblende, or sunbeam, dewdrop, and snowflake?

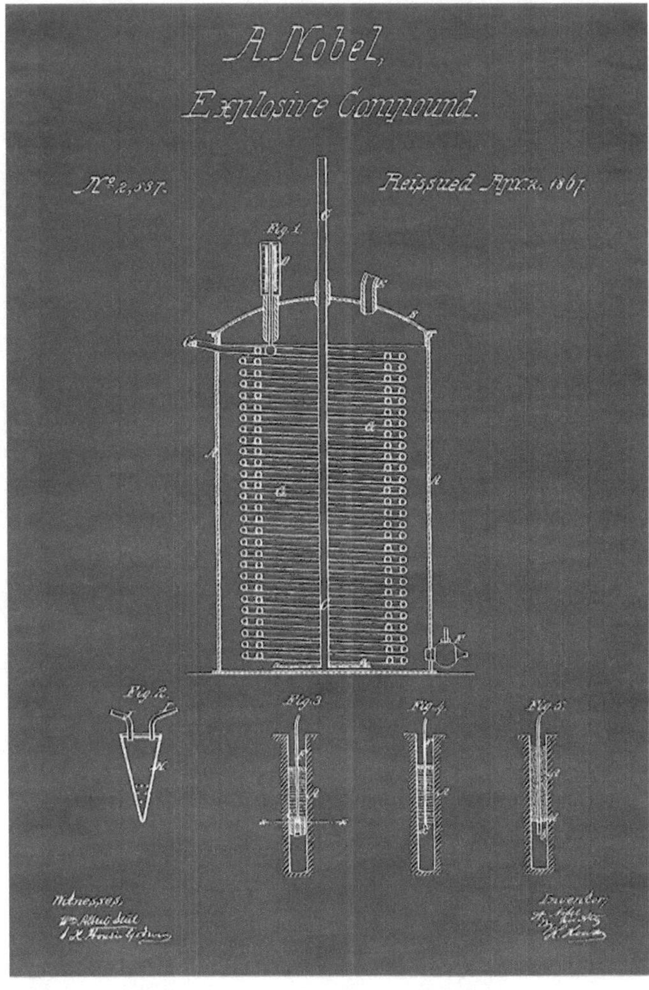

ARLES

734.8 km from Sils Maria

Gauguin's imminent arrival; painting with the gusto of a Marseillais; nothing but large Sunflowers; I'm beginning to like the south more and more; a simple technique

22 August 1888

My dear Theo,

I'm writing to you in great haste, but to tell you that I've just received a line from Gauguin, who says that he hasn't written because he was doing a great deal of work, but says he's still ready to come to the south as soon as chance permits.

They're having a fine time, painting, debating, quarreling with the virtuous Englishmen; he says many good things about Bernard's work, & Bernard says many good things about Gauguin's work.

I'm painting with the gusto of a Marseillais eating bouillabaisse, which won't surprise you when it's a question of painting *large* Sunflowers.

I have 3 canvases on the go: 1) 3 large flowers in a green vase, light background (no. 15 canvas); 2) 3 flowers, one flower that's gone to seed and lost its petals and a bud on a royal blue background (no. 25 canvas); 3) 12 flowers and buds in a yellow vase (no. 30 canvas). So the last one is light on light, and will be the best, I hope. I'll probably not stop there. In the hope of living in a studio of our own with Gauguin, I'd like to do a decoration for the studio. *Nothing but large Sunflowers.*

Next door to your shop, in the restaurant, as you know, there's such a beautiful decoration of flowers there; I still remember the big sunflower in the window. Well, if I carry out this plan there'll be a dozen or so panels. The whole thing will therefore be a symphony in blue and yellow. I work on it all these mornings, from sunrise. Because the flowers wilt quickly and it's a matter of doing the whole thing in one go.

You did well to tell Tasset that he must give us some tubes of paint for the 15 francs' carriage on the two unstamped consignments. When I've finished these sunflowers I'll perhaps be short of yellow and blue, so I'll make a small order to that effect. Tasset ordinary canvas, which at 50 centimes was dearer than Bourgeois's, is very much to my liking, and is very well prepared.

I'm very glad that Gauguin is well. I'm beginning to like the south more and more.

I have another study on the go, of dusty thistles with an innumerable swarm of white and yellow butterflies.

I've again missed some models that I hoped to have these past few days.

Koning has written that he's going to stay in The Hague; he intends to send you some studies.

I have a whole heap of ideas for new canvases. Today I saw that same coal-boat again, with workers unloading it, that I've already told you about; in the same place as the sand-boats, of which I've sent you a drawing. It would be a grand subject. Only I'm beginning more and more to look for a simple technique that perhaps isn't Impressionist. I'd like to paint in such a way that if it comes to it, everyone who has eyes could understand it. I'm writing in haste but wanted to send a line to our sister enclosed herewith. Handshake, I must get back to work.

Ever yours,
Vincent

Gauguin said that Bernard had made an album of croquis of mine, and that he'd shown it to him.

SILS MARIA

734.8 km from Arles

the battle with "nature spirits"; I have never seen myself dressed up so dignified; a language, a terminology was not available; almost uninterrupted inspiration; the style is vehement and exciting; to improvise on horrible topics; the right, very best relaxation; absurd insomnia; at 4 o'clock cacao

Wednesday, 22 August 1888

Honored Fräulein,

a weather like the morning of your departure — for the *first* time
since then: loud splashing. I will avail myself of the clever recuperation that I have so often taken in my battle with the "nature
spirits" this summer — and talk to you a little. There is, nevertheless, a certain book in front of me: it arrived last night. I have
never seen myself dressed up in so dignified a manner — almost
as a "classic." The first look inside gave me a surprise: I discovered a long *preface* to the *Genealogy*, the existence of which I had
forgotten ... Basically I only had the title of the three treatises in
memory: the rest, i.e., the *contents* had been lost to me. This was
the result of the extreme mental activity which filled this winter
and this spring, and which, as it were, had laid a *wall* between.
Now the book comes to life again in front of me — and, at the
same time, the state of last year's summer from which it was
created. Extremely difficult problems for which a language, a terminology was not available: but at that time I must have been in
a state of almost uninterrupted inspiration for this work to run
along as it does as if it were the most natural thing in the world.
You don't notice any travail in it — the style is vehement and exciting, at the same time full of finesses; and supple and colorful,
different than any prose I had ever written before. Of course, the
great critic Spitteler says: that since reading *this* work of mine he
has *abandoned* all hopes for me as a writer ...

Compared to last summer, which allowed me to *improvise*
like this upon horrible topics, this summer seems to have "fallen
through" altogether. I am extremely sorry for this: for from my
spring stay, which was a good one for the first time, I mustered
even *more* strength than I had last year. Everything was also prepared for a *large* and *very specific* task. The "pamphlet" against
Wagner (— of which I, between us, am proud) essentially belongs
to Torino and was actually the right, very best *relaxation* that
someone could enjoy in the midst of difficult things.

One of the specialties of this summer is my absurd insomnia.
Even today, like yesterday, like the day before yesterday, *thinking*
from two o'clock ... at 4 o'clock cocoa ...

Yesterday afternoon I was in the Fex Valley with Prof. Kaftan. In the "Alpenrose" there are still c. 30 people. Basically it all is coming quickly to an end now. Autumn — we have an indubitable *September* weather: if this is not still a euphemism. I want, nevertheless, to try to endure until mid-Sept.

With the warmest wishes for your wellbeing and with many reasons to *thank* you.

Your most devoted
Dr. Nietzsche.

— You can be sure that the *book* will be protected like an egg & will return to you in a completely solid (bound) envelope.

ARLES

734.8 km from Sils Maria

the more finely a color is ground; a rough look; fresher col-
ors; simplicity of technique; what a pity painting costs so
much; we live in times when there's no market for what we
do; the whims of fortune; the painters who will walk in our
footsteps; life is short; 'children's painting' vs. decadence

My dear Theo,

Would you ask Tasset his opinion on the following question? It
seems to me that the more finely a color is ground, the more
it is saturated by oil. Now we're not over-fond of oil, that goes
without saying.

If we painted like Monsieur Gérôme and the other *trompe-
l'oeil* photographic ones, we'd no doubt ask for colors ground
very fine. We, on the contrary, don't strongly object to the canvas
having a rough look.

So if instead of having the color ground on the stone for God
knows how many hours, we grind it just long enough to make it
workable, without bothering too much about the fineness of the
grain, we'd have colors that were fresher, perhaps darkening less.
If he wishes to do a test with the 3 chromes, Veronese, vermilion,
orange lead, cobalt, ultramarine, I'm almost certain that at greatly reduced cost I would have colors that were both fresher and
longer-lasting. At what price, then? I'm sure that could be done.
Probably for the reds, for emerald, which are transparent, too.

I add here an order that's urgent.

I'm now on the fourth painting of sunflowers.

This fourth one is a bouquet of 14 flowers and is on a yellow
background, like a still life of quinces and lemons that I did back
then.

Only as it's much bigger, this one creates quite an unusual
effect, and I believe that this time it's painted with more simplicity than the quinces and lemons. Do you remember that one day
at the Hôtel Drouot we saw a quite extraordinary Manet, some
large pink peonies and their green leaves on a light background?
As much in harmony and as much a *flower* as anything you like,
and yet painted in solid, thick impasto and not like Jeannin.

That's what I'd call simplicity of technique. And I must tell
you that these days I'm making a great effort to find a way of using the brush without stippling or anything else, nothing but a
varied brushstroke. But you'll see, one day.

What a pity painting costs so much. This week I had fewer
money worries than other weeks, so I let myself go. I'll have spent
the hundred-franc note in a single week, but at the end of this

week I'll have my four paintings and even if I add the price of all the colors that I've used up, the week won't have been wasted. I got up very early every day, I dined and supped well, I was able to work assiduously without feeling myself weaken. But there you are, we live in times when there's no market for what we do; not only do we not sell, as you see with Gauguin, we'd like to borrow against paintings done and we find nothing, even when the amounts are insignificant and the works substantial. And that's how we fall prey to all the whims of fortune.

And I fear that it will scarcely change during our lifetime.

As long as we were preparing the way for richer lives for the painters who will walk in our footsteps, that would already be something.

Life is short, though, and especially the number of years when one feels strong enough to brave everything. And in the end, there's the fear that as soon as the new painting is appreciated, the painters will weaken. In any case, here's what's positive, we aren't the ones who represent decadence today. Gauguin and Bernard are now talking about doing 'children's painting.' I prefer that to the painting of the decadents. How does it come about that people see something decadent in Impressionism? It's actually quite the reverse. I enclose a line for Tasset. The difference in price should be quite considerable, and it goes without saying that I hope to use fewer and fewer finely ground colors. I shake your hand firmly. (One of the decorations of sunflowers on a royal blue background has a 'halo,' that's to say, each object is surrounded by a line of the color complementary to the background against which it stands out). More soon.

Ever yours,
Vincent

SILS MARIA

734.8 km from Arles

a few days of peace; the devil's own courage; *the moods of a great actor;* wicked pedantry; *there is no sole saving interpretation;* the smallest *articulations* of music; a *typical symptom of deterioration; tender, small, sublime things; the whole color of the world changes on the Rhine; some people are born* posthumously

Sunday, 26 August

Dear friend:

A *few days of peace*. There were also a few days when I was unwell. But it *ought* to be all right — and it is all right. This time it
is my turn to talk — first, about Dr. *Brandes*. He has done for me
what he has been doing over the past 30 years for all the independent minds of Europe — he has *introduced* me to his compatriots.
What I must highly honor in my case is his overcoming here his
passionate disgust with all present-day Germans. Just recently he
has once more, *after* the emperor's visit, expressed his contempt
for all Germans, "in a veritably devilish mood," as the *Kölnische
Zeitung* says. Well, anyway, they pay him back in plenty. In academic circles he has an extremely bad name: to be associated
with him is thought to be a disgrace (reason enough for *me, as I
am,* to give the widest publicity to his winter lectures). He is one
of the cosmopolitan *Jews* who have the *devil's own courage,* — in
the north too he has hordes of enemies. He speaks many lan-
guages, has his best public in Russia, knows very personally the
good intelligentsia in England and France — *and* is a psychologist (for which the German academics cannot forgive him...)
His main work, which has run through several editions, *The Main
Developments in Literature During the Nineteenth Century,* is still
today the best *Kulturbuch* in German on this big subject. — To
music, as he wrote last winter, he regrets having *no* relation.

Herr von Holten left us 4 days ago. We are all sad. Such a
combination of kindness and mischievousness is a very rare
thing. An old abbé, with the moods of a great actor. At the same
time, very remarkably inventive in acts of kindness, in making
people happy — everyone has his tale to tell of that. He must
really be in a most fortunate situation, *not* as far as money is
concerned, I mean, but his heart, for not a day passed without
his committing some kind of "offense" out of the goodness of his
heart. — For me he had thought up the following kindness: he
had studied a composition by the only present-day musician who
has for me any significance, my friend Peter Gast, and he played
it to me *privatissime* six times, from memory, *enchanted* by

"the charming *&* intelligent work." — *In rebus musicis et musican-tibus* we got on very well — that is, we were *each* quite without tolerance and analyzed the "one-eyed man" in the kingdom of the blind . . . As for *Riemann,* we discussed him seriously enough, but agreed, agreed that a published score in which the phrases are marked is worse than any other — because such phrasing is wicked pedantry. Phrasing which is "not right" can really be confirmed in countless cases; phrasing which is right, *hardly ever.* The illusion of the "phrasers" in *this* point seemed to us an extraordinary one. The premise on which they build — that *there is* a correct, that is, *one* correct exposition — seems to me to be psychologically and experimentally *wrong.* The composer, in the moment of creation as in that of reproducing, sees these *subtle shadings* only in a precarious equilibrium — every fortuitous intensification or relaxing of the subjective sense of power treats as unities fields which are one moment larger ones and are the next moment necessarily more *contracted* ones. In short, the *old philologist* says, on the basis of his whole philological experience: *there is no sole saving interpretation,* either for poets or for musicians (a poet is absolutely *not* an authority for the meaning of his lines; the strangest proofs exist to show how fluid *&* vague the "meaning" is for them —).

Another viewpoint that we discussed (— perhaps I touched on it before, dear friend, a few years ago, in a letter to you). This animation and enlivening of the smallest *articulations* of music (— I wish that you and Riemann would use the words known to everyone from rhetoric: *period* (sentence), *colon, comma,* according to the size, likewise *interrogatory sentence, conditional sentence, imperative* — for the phrase marking is definitely the same as *punctuation* in prose and poetry), — anyway: we considered this animation and enlivening of the smallest articulations, as it enters Wagner's *practice* in music and has spread from there to become almost a dominant performance system (even for actors and singers), with counterparts in *other* arts — it is a *typical symptom of deterioration,* a proof that life has *withdrawn* from the whole and is *luxuriating* in the infinitesimal. "Phrase marking" would, accordingly, be the symptom of a decline of the organizing power, or, to put it differently, a symptom of the incapacity to bridge *big* areas of relations rhythmically — it would be a decadent form of *rhythm*... This sounds almost paradoxical. The first and most passionate advocates of rhythmic precision and univocality would be not only the consequences of rhythmical *décadence* but also its *strongest* and *most successful instruments!* The more the eye is focused on the single *rhythmic* form ("phrase"), the more *myopic* it becomes with regard to the broad, long, big forms, exactly as in architecture in the manner of Bernini. An alteration in the *optics* of the composer — this is happening everywhere, *not only* in the surfeit of rhythmical life in the infinitesimal — also *our capacity for enjoyment is restricting itself more and more to the tender, small,* sublime things ... *as a result of which* one only creates such things — —

Moral: you are entirely on the "right track" with Riemann — that is, the only track *which still exists*...

We also discussed a point that *concerns* you especially. Von Holten's view was that phrase-marking concerts of the kind that you organize are absolutely ineffectual. They make the illusion of the performer complete. *People* do not *hear* the difference between the performance with phrasing and any other: even for the professional pianist, his accustomed and adopted interpretation is by *no means* so much a *conscious matter*, as clearly defined as might be desirable (a few instances excepted), as to make him constantly aware of a difference. Such concerts, he argued, convinced people of absolutely *nothing*, because they impressed no difference on the consciousness. It would be another matter, also of course only in the hands of very sophisticated musicians, to present *different* kinds of performance one after another; what von Holten denied was that this offered any proof as to which performance was the *right* one. You had better take the vote on this ...

Everything that you write to me strengthens my wish that Danzig *delenda est*; Bonn, that sounds much happier ... I tacitly assume that the benign *Brambach*, the Schumann admirer, is still functioning as conductor there (I sang in the choir under his direction in Cologne at the Gürzenich music festival — for example, Schumann's *Faust*). There are good people living there, including women from abroad. The climatic difference is indescribably to your *advantage* ... The whole color of the world changes on the Rhine, in the "kind heart" — *crede experto*. Not least, there is a genuine Rhineland *musical-life*. You once saw my friend *Krug* in Naumburg; the same, now an important fellow, with 80 employees under him, a Justizrat, and director of the West Rhenish Railways, centered in Cologne, very recently instituted in Cologne a *Wagner Society* in the grand style; he is its president. —

With many good wishes, and hoping that you will forgive me for anything unwelcome in this letter.

Your most devoted Nietzsche

P. S. In Sils till September 14. Leaving on the 15th. — —

— I hope you did not take my "literary prescription" seriously?? — I do nothing but mischief when it comes to "publicity" and "fame." — Some people are born *posthumously*. —

ARLES

734.8 km from Sils Maria

a good eye for paintings; what is alive in art; die or go mad from despair; Whitman; God and eternity; a strong man — a little, even very, cracked; sad and delightful fates; we'll make quite a noise; a painter who sees with other eyes than theirs is mad; a painting all in yellow of sunflowers in a yellow vase and against a yellow background

Sunday, 26 August 1888

My dear sister,

If you'll let me write to you in French, that will really make my letter easier for me.

You please me much more by being moved by sculpture than by painting — all the more so since Theo assures me that you also have a good eye for paintings. Naturally, that couldn't yet be a settled taste, which will never waver, but intuition, instinct, is already a great deal, and precisely what everyone doesn't always have.

But all the same, I'm very curious to know what effect the Luxembourg will have on you.

Is it true, as I think in moments when I'm in a good mood, that what is alive in art, and eternally alive, is first the painter and then the painting?

Well, what difference does that make — but if one *sees* people *working* it's still something one doesn't find under glass in museums.

Poor Miss Harriet in Guy de Maupassant, she was right, perhaps.

But was the painter wrong to go with the farm girl? Perhaps not.

In life there's always a fate that's very annoying. And many painters die or go mad from despair, or become paralyzed in their production because nobody loves them personally.

Have you read Whitman's American poems yet? Theo should have them, and I really urge you to read them, first because they're really beautiful, and also, English people are talking about them a lot at the moment. He sees in the future, and even in the present, a world of health, of generous, frank carnal love — of friendship — of work, with the great starry firmament, something, in short, that one could only call God and eternity, put back in place above this world. They make you smile at first, they're so *candid*, and then they make you think, for the same reason. The prayer of Christopher Columbus is very beautiful.

What do you say about Monticelli's bouquet of flowers that's at Theo's, and about Prévost's Spanish woman? There are two real paintings of the south.

I myself think about Monticelli a great deal down here. He was a strong man — a little, even very, cracked — dreaming of sunshine and love and gaiety, but always frustrated by poverty, a colorist's extremely refined taste, a man of rare breeding, carrying on the best ancient traditions. He died in Marseille, rather sadly and probably after going through a real Gethsemane. Ah well, I myself am sure that I'll carry him on here as if I were his son or his brother.

We were talking just now about a fate that seemed sad to us. But isn't there another, delightful fate? And what is it to us if there is or isn't a resurrection, when we see a living man rise up immediately in a dead man's place? Taking up the same cause, carrying on the same work, living the same life, dying the same death.

When friend Gauguin's here, and we go to Marseille, I firmly intend to walk there on the Canebière, dressed exactly like him, as I've seen his portrait, with an enormous yellow hat, a black velvet jacket, white trousers, yellow gloves *&* a reed cane *&* with a great southern air.

And I'll find Marseillais who knew him when he was alive, and if you've read in Tartarin what *fên de brût* is....... We'll make quite a noise on that occasion. Monticelli is a painter who did the south all in yellow, all in orange, all in sulfur. Most painters, because they're not *colorists*, properly speaking, don't see these colors there, and declare that a painter who sees with other eyes than theirs is mad. (In the Luxembourg you'll see Montenards that aren't yellow, and I like them very much all the same. But it's likely that Montenard would find what I do totally contemptible.) All that is to be expected, of course. So I've already prepared especially a painting all in yellow of sunflowers (14 flowers) in a yellow vase and against a yellow background (it's yet another one, in addition to the previous one with 12 flowers against a blue-green background). And I expect one day to exhibit that one in Marseille. And you'll see that there'll be some Marseillais or other who will remember what Monticelli once said and did. Has Theo shown you the barbotine yet? It's really fine. Enjoy yourself, I kiss you in thought.

Ever yours,
Vincent

195

SILS MARIA

734.8 km from Arles

the honor of attacking me publicly; too much reason, too much sun; who knows me? who knows Wagner? the woman loses her grace, almost her reason; it is not wrong to be silent; no mercy; "May the Devil take you!"; the decision on the highest questions; like a fat giant

Sept 1888

To Cosima Wagner in Bayreuth (draft — letter not sent)

Reply to a letter, characterized by politeness, from Wagner's widow

You do me the honor of attacking me publicly on the basis of my writing, which gave the *first explanation about W* — You, yourself, also attempt to explain me. I confess why I am at a disadvantage: I have too much right, too much reason, too much *sun* on my side for a fight to be *allowed* to me under such circumstances. Who knows me? — Frau Cosima least of all. Who knows Wagner? Nobody but me, except Frau C who *knows* that I am *in the right*... she *knows* that the opponent is right — I will admit everything to you in this position. Under such circumstances the woman loses her grace, almost her *reason*... It is not wrong to be silent: especially when one is wrong...
Si tacuisses, Cosima mansisses...

With the expression
of a sympathy appropriate to the circumstances

You know very well how well I know the influence you have exerted over W — you know even better how much I *despise* this influence... I turned my back on you and Wagner the moment the *swindle* started...
If Liszt's *daughter* wants to have a say in matters of German culture, let alone religion, I have no mercy...

Draft letter to Carl Fuchs (*not sent*)

Worthy friend, you should, finally! consider that phrasing is not something that concerns me and that, out of sympathy toward you and out of a certain habitual objectivity toward unpleasant things, I have omitted what everyone else would have long done in my place: namely, to say, "May the Devil take you!!" But now I'm just on the defensive. I protect myself with hands and feet against someone attacking me with letters. What does my existence, filled with something somewhat *more serious*, have to do with such absurd questions as "phrasing"!

Anyone who has the slightest idea of the profound focus and concentration, which decisiveness about the highest questions demands of me, *shrinks* from writing to me. I haven't had any correspondence for a long time, except with my mother and my friend Gast — with the latter for the same reason that I wish to break off my intercourse with you. Like a fat giant, your thick letter will accompany me through life for a while — *unopened*: you can be assured of that; — — —

ARLES

734.8 km from Sils Maria

lodgings in the south; a starry, deep ultramarine sky; to untangle her personality; sticking your cigar in your mouth by the lighted end; to expose my studies from down here to the air; sometimes I know so clearly what I want; I can easily do without the dear Lord; we try to create thoughts instead of children; that je ne sais quoi of the eternal; the vibrancy of our colorations; to be able to move about; material difficulties and the study of color; the mysterious vibrations of adjacent tones

3 September 1888

My dear Theo,

Yesterday I spent another day with that Belgian — who also has a sister among the Vingtistes — — the weather wasn't good but it was a jolly good day for chatting; we went for a walk, and all the same we did see some very fine things at the bullfights and outside the town. We talked more seriously about the plan that if I keep on lodgings in the south, he should definitely set up a kind of post in the coalfields. That then Gauguin and he and I, in cases where the importance of a painting would be a reason for traveling, could exchange places — sometimes being in the north, but in a familiar part of the country where we have a friend, sometimes in the south. You'll see him soon, this young man with the Dante-like face, because he's coming to Paris, and if the room's available you'll be doing him a favor by putting him up. He's quite distinguished in appearance, and he'll become so in his paintings, I believe. He likes Delacroix, and we talked a lot about Delacroix yesterday; actually he knew the violent sketch of Christ's boat.

Ah well, thanks to him — at last I have a first sketch of that painting I've been dreaming about for a long time — *the poet*. He posed for it for me. His fine head, with its green gaze, stands out in my portrait against a starry, deep ultramarine sky; his clothing is a little yellow jacket, a collar of unbleached linen, a multicolored tie. He gave me two sittings in one day.

Yesterday I received a letter from our sister, who has seen many things. Ah, if she could marry an artist, that wouldn't be bad.

Well, we'll have to go on urging her to untangle her personality, rather than her artistic abilities.

I've finished Daudet's *L'immortel* — I rather like the remark by the sculptor Védrine, who says that achieving fame is something like when smoking, sticking your cigar in your mouth by the lighted end.

Now I definitely like *L'immortel* less, much less, than *Tartarin*.

You know, it seems to me that *L'immortel* isn't as fine as *Tartarin* for color, because, with its quantity of subtle and accurate observations, it makes me think of Jean Béraud's disheartening paintings, so dry, so cold. *Tartarin*, now, is so *genuinely* great — with the greatness of a masterpiece, just like *Candide*.

I would very much like to ask you to expose my studies from down here, which aren't completely dry yet, to the air as far as possible. If they stayed shut away or in the dark, the colors would deteriorate. So, the portrait of *the young girl*, *the harvest* (wide landscape with the ruin in the background and the chain of the Alpilles), the *small seascape*, the *garden* with the weeping tree and the conifer bushes, if you could put them on stretching frames that would be good. I'm a little attached to those.

You can see clearly from the *drawing* of the small seascape that that one's the most worked up.

I'm having 2 oak frames made, for my new head of a peasant and for my study of a poet. Ah, my dear brother, sometimes I know so clearly what I want. In life and in painting too, I can easily do without the dear Lord, but I can't, suffering as I do, do without something greater than myself, which is my life, the power to create.

And if frustrated in this power physically, we try to create thoughts instead of children; in that way, we're part of humanity all the same. And in a painting I'd like to say something consoling, like a piece of music. I'd like to paint men or women with that *je ne sais quoi* of the eternal, of which the halo used to be the symbol, and which we try to achieve through the radiance itself, through the vibrancy of our colorations.

The portrait conceived in this way doesn't become an Ary Scheffer, because there's a blue sky behind it, as in the Saint Augustine. Because Ary Scheffer is so little of a colorist.

But this would be more in tune with what Delacroix was looking for and found in his Tasso in prison and so many other paintings depicting a true man. Ah, the portrait — the portrait with the model's thoughts, his soul — it so much seems to me that it must come.

We talked a lot yesterday, the Belgian and I, about the advantages and disadvantages of this place. We quite agree on both. And on the immense interest that would hold for us, to be able to *move about*, sometimes the north, sometimes the south. He's going to stay with Macknight again for reasons of living more cheaply.

That, though, has a disadvantage for him, I believe, because living with an idler makes you idle. I believe you'll enjoy meeting him, he's still young. I believe that he'll ask your advice on buying Japanese prints and Daumier lithographs. For those, the Daumiers, it would be good to buy more, because later on we won't be able to find them.

The Belgian was saying that with Macknight he paid 80 francs for board and lodging. What a difference, then, living together — myself I have to pay 45 a month for my lodging alone. And so I always come back to the same calculation, that with Gauguin I'll spend no more than on my own, and that without suffering thereby.

Now for them, it's to be taken into account that they were very badly housed, not in terms of their beds, but of the possibility of working at home.

So I'm still between two currents of ideas, the first, material difficulties, turning this way and that to build up an existence, and then the study of color. I still have hopes of finding something there. To express the love of two lovers through a marriage of two complementary colors, their mixture and their contrasts, the mysterious vibrations of adjacent tones. To express the thought of a forehead through the radiance of a light tone on a dark background. To express hope through some star. The ardor of a living being through the rays of a setting sun. That's certainly not *trompe-l'oeil* realism, but isn't it something that really exists? More soon; I'll tell you when the Belgian might pass through, because I'll see him again tomorrow. Handshake.

Ever yours,
Vincent

The Belgian said that at home they have a Degroux, the sketch for *Saying Grace* in the Brussels museum.

The portrait of the Belgian has something of the portrait of Reid that you have, in terms of execution.

INTERVAL: PARAGUAY & LONDON

The fall of Nueva Germania & Jack the Ripper
7967 nm from Arles; 10342 km from Sils Maria
1221.5 km from Arles; 1217.1 km from Sils Maria

Early September 1888

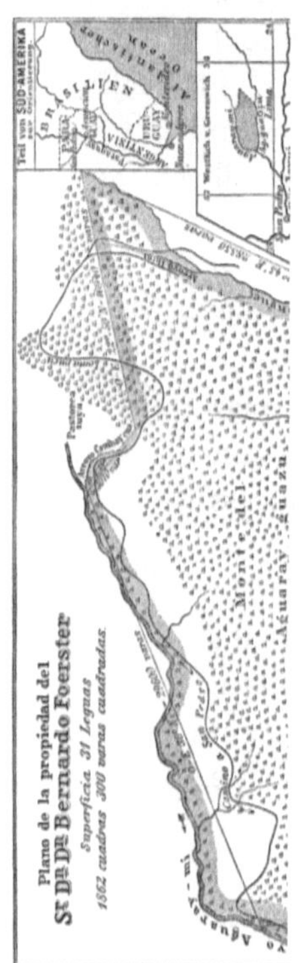

As Herr Dynamite begins writing *Der Antichrist* and
sends the completed manuscript of *A Psychologist's
Leisure* to his publisher, 10 days later the mad painter
moves into the Yellow House and begins further preparations for the arrival of Gauguin. Feverishly, Vincent
continues painting sunflowers, himself in ways becom-
ing-sunflower, taking the star of the sun into his flesh,
taking on its light, heat, and energy, his body as porous
as coral, as open to adaptation and deviation. With the
incorporation of each foreign element, something else is
born and something dies, for the organism is no longer
and never the same. The death throes of a century are
coming closer, sensibilities are shifting as violently as
the plates of the earth, and clarion calls are ringing out.
Soon, the war of Dionysos versus the Crucified will also
be announced.

In Paraguay, due to his settlers growing increasingly
distressed, Bernhard Förster anxiously petitions General Bernardino Caballero, the man whom he sought to
usurp as President of Paraguay. Although first emphasiz-
ing his colony's supposed progress, in his letter, Förster
outlines the difficulties and challenges he is facing, particularly financially, noting that thousands of pesos have
been spent on both the new colonists' needs and even
more on literary propaganda in Europe in support of
Paraguayan colonization. Notwithstanding such crises,

Förster remains staunchly optimistic, assuring the general that a well-led colony will always be a good business and the capital spent on such a project would yield a considerable profit after the third year. Proposing a kind of union, the hopeful leader then asked the general for advice and invited him to participate in his venture. The plea, however, went unanswered. With no unification in sight, Förster holed up in Asunción, seeking out creditors while also sending frantic letters to Germany for more support.

All that time, a hopeful colonist who had arrived earlier in the year, Julius Klingbeil, grew more and more disenchanted with the Aryan enterprise, seeing it as nothing but fraudulent. Klingbeil found Förster not to be the heroic figure of his portrait, nor conversant in French and Greek as he claimed, but a dissembling shell of man while his wife, the Queen of the esteemed El Dorado, was nothing but a pretentious deceiver prone to incessant and nonsensical bavardage. Chit, chit, chit, chit-chat.

While the Försters lived in splendor, complete with marble floors, four cooks, eight servants and a piano, the colonists subsisted in primitive mud and straw huts. Despite their purist claims to vegetarianism, the Aryan royalty consumed with fervor the meat they once denounced as disease inducing. Others survived on rice and beans and corn, like the Paraguayan women, whom the leaders said were remarkably industrious, hardly ever washed, and mostly lay around smoking and eating lice off their bodies (so it was reported). When Queen Eli presented Klingbeil with a map of Nueva Germania wherein all the plots but his own had been sold, she offered him the opportunity to secure his plot if he could provide funding. Colonialism *&* good will — the magnanimity of a Queen.

After some investigation, Klingbeil discovered that the Försters had no legal title to the land they were attempting to sell and, over the coming months, would pen a damning indictment of the venture, *Enthüllungen über die Dr Bernhard Förstersche Ansiedlung Neu-Germanien in Paraguay (Revelations Concerning Dr. Bernhard Förster's Colony New Germany in Paraguay).* And so the resounding axe fell. Later, the Queen would retaliate, voicing off in the pages of the *Bayreuther Blätter*, lambasting Klingbeil and his family for lacking loyalty and courage and abandoning their most ideal leaders:

Anti-Semitism has above all a positive aspect: the urge to deepen and ennoble the true German characteristics; it is motivated by the urge to create or renew institutions that strengthen true Germanness in an idealistic or economic sense *&* protect it from foreign influences...

What is my husband fighting for here and now? Is it not true Germanness? And the goal? Is it not to create a new German place as a substitute for the old?...

Let anti-Semitism prove through action, here in Nueva Germania, that it aims to create something in the true German tradition.

Queen Förster stated further that a railway was soon to be built and steamships were expanding the colony to the outside world, bringing the German flag to new territories, but no steamships could even get up the Aguarya-umí, and the future of the colony remained doubtful and desperate. Was it disease-inducing meat generating hallucinations, the mutating force of infernal heat waves, or, a holy vision?

*

Later that month, in the United Kingdom, Jack the Ripper had struck again, murdering two women on the streets of the East End of London, continuing his horrorshow gestures and occasioning terrible panic amidst the public.

The first woman was found by Louis Diemshutz, a club steward who had earlier that night been hawking jewelry at the Crystal Palace. When attempting to enter the gates of Dutfield's Yard near to 1 AM, his horse reared back, freaked by the sight of a female body with blood issuing from its throat. The woman, Elizabeth Stride, had suffered a single 6" clear-cut incision across her neck — her carotid artery and trachea had been severed. When the police constable put his hand on her face and arm, he found that they were slightly warm. Fresh kill.

Not long after, another body was discovered in Mitre Square, that of Catherine Eddowes, whose face and lower abdomen had been horribly mutilated. Adding a signature touch, the killer placed her intestines over her right shoulder, removed her left kidney and much of her uterus, then severed her nose and cut off parts of the auricle and lobe of her right ear.

In an attempt to track down the killer, a letter he had written was reproduced on posters and affixed to buildings and street poles around the neighborhood.

Soon after, facsimiles of it were released to the press & published in newspapers around the world, making Jack the Ripper infamous, a global phenomenon more newsworthy than Nietzsche and van Gogh:

25 Sept . 1888 .

Dear Boss,

I keep on hearing the police have caught me but they wont fix me just yet. I have laughed when they look so clever & talk about being on the <u>right</u> track. That joke about Leather Apron gave me real fits. I am down on whores and I shant quit ripping them till I do get buckled. Grand work the last job was. I gave the lady no time to squeal. How can they catch me now. I love my work and want to start again. You will soon hear of me with my funny little games. I saved some of the proper <u>red</u> stuff in a ginger beer bottle over the last job to write with but it went thick like glue and I cant use it. Red ink is fit enough I hope ha. ha . The next job I do I shall clip the ladys ears off and send to the police officers just for

jolly wouldn't you .   Keep this letter back till I do a bit
more work .   then give it out straight.   My knife's
so nice and sharp I want to get to work right away if
I get a chance . Good Luck.

Yours truly
Jack the Ripper

Dont mind me giving the trade name.

Wasnt good enough to post this before I got all the red ink off my hands curse it. No luck yet. They say I'm a doctor now ha ha

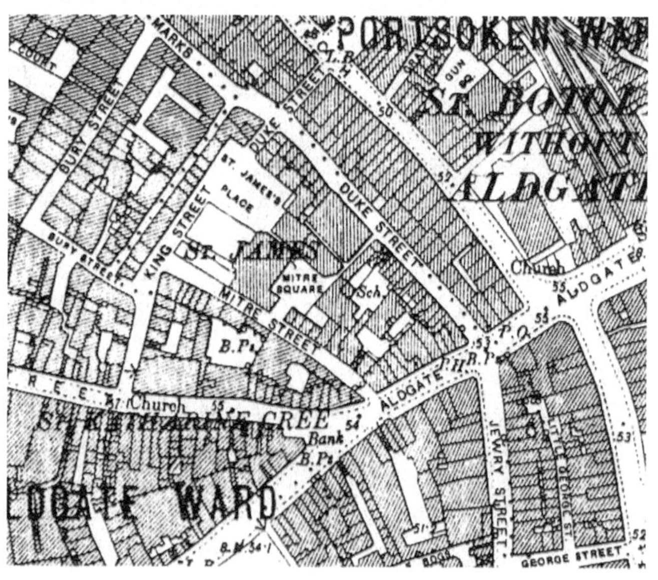

SILS MARIA

734.8 km from Arles

I once again will vanish; sacred "phrasing"?; the question of Martians; the largest trout ever caught; good mayonnaise sauce

6 Sept. 1888

Dear friend,

In the next few days I will be leaving Sils; since I still need deep focus for a long time, I once again will vanish, in accordance with my monastic practice, for *visits* of all kinds — letters included. There is already a sachet of unread letters in front of me: I'm afraid there are two from you among them. — In the end I am not hiding my suspicions from you: must they not be about the sacred "phrasing"? In this case, everything should be seriously considered, in case they might be *addressed* incorrectly? Letters about "phrasing" to the philosopher of the *revaluation of all values!* ... In Nizza they try to get me interested in the question of Martians; they have the strongest telescopes in Europe for this star. Question: who is actually closer to me, the inhabitants of Mars, or phrasing? — I would like to continue to interest myself in Dr. Fuchs, but to the *exclusion* of his Martian inhabitants...

A little work with the title

The Wagner Case
A Musician's Problem

will be sent to you in October. —

With a warm greeting
the philosopher of
Sils Maria.

N.B. Here in Sils they are trying to interest me in the largest trout ever caught, weighing 30 pounds; who knows, in this case, if there will be a good mayonnaise sauce...

ARLES

734.8 km from Sils Maria

worries don't come singly, nor do joys, either; the night is much more alive; the terrible human passions; a battle & an antithesis; whether or not Gauguin comes; this melancholy of being on the street; an ardent temperament; terrifying blue and green; I'm very glad indeed to be able to furnish my house

8 Sept. 1888

My dear Theo,

Thank you a thousand times for your kind letter and the 300 francs it contained — after some weeks of worries I've just had a much better one. And just as worries don't come singly, nor do joys, either. Because actually, always bowed down under this money problem with lodging-house keepers, I put up with it cheerfully. I'd given a piece of my mind to the said lodging-house keeper, who isn't a bad man after all, and I'd told him that to get my own back on him for having paid him so much money for nothing, I'd paint his whole filthy old place as a way of getting my money back. Well, to the great delight of the lodging-house keeper, the postman whom I've already painted, the prowling night-visitors and myself, for 3 nights I stayed up to paint, going to bed during the day. It often seems to me that the night is much more alive and richly colored than the day. Now as for recovering the money paid to the landlord through my painting, I'm not making a point of it, because the painting is one of the ugliest I've done. It's the equivalent, though different, of the potato eaters.

I've tried to express the terrible human passions with the red *&* the green.

The room is blood red and dull yellow, a green billiard table in the center, lemon yellow lamps with an orange and green glow. Everywhere it's a battle and an antithesis of the most different greens and reds; in the characters of the sleeping ruffians, small in the empty, high room, some purple and blue. The blood red and the yellow-green of the billiard table, for example, contrast with the little bit of delicate Louis XV green of the counter, where there's a pink bouquet.

The white clothes of the owner, watching over things from a corner in this furnace, become lemon yellow, pale luminous green.

I'm making a drawing of it in watercolor tones to send you tomorrow, to give you an idea of it.

I've written to Gauguin *&* to Bernard this week, but I didn't talk about anything but paintings, just so as not to quarrel, when there's probably no reason to. But whether or not Gauguin comes, if I buy furniture, then we have, in a good place or a bad, that's another question — a pied-à-terre, a home that lifts from the mind this melancholy of being on the street. Which is nothing when you're a 20-year-old adventurer, but which is bad when you've turned 35.

I see in *L'Intransigeant* today the suicide of Mr. Bing Lévy. Not possible, is it, that that could be Bing's manager, Lévy?? I think it must be somebody else. It gives me great pleasure that Pissarro found something in the young girl. Did Pissarro say anything about the sower?

Later on, when I've taken those experiments further, the sower will still be the first attempt in that genre.

The night café is a continuation of the sower, as is the head of the old peasant and of the poet, if I manage to do the latter painting. It's a color, then, that isn't locally true from the realist point of view of *trompe l'oeil*, but a color suggesting some emotion, an ardent temperament.

When Paul Mantz saw Delacroix's violent and exalted sketch, Christ's boat, at the exhibition that we saw in the Champs-Elysées, he turned away from it and cried out in his article, "I did not know that one could be so terrifying with blue and green."

Hokusai makes you cry out the same thing — but in his case with his *lines*, his *drawing*, since in your letter you say to yourself: these waves are *claws*, the boat is caught in them, you can feel it. Ah well, if we made the color very correct or the drawing very correct, we wouldn't create those emotions.

Anyway, soon — tomorrow or the day after — I'll write to you again on this subject and will reply to your letter, sending you croquis of the night café. Tasset's consignment has arrived; I'll write to you tomorrow on the subject of this coarse paint. Milliet will come to say hello to you one of these days; he writes me that he's going to come back. Thank you once again for the money sent. If I was first going to look for another place, isn't it likely that then there would be new expenses in that, at least equivalent to the costs of moving? And moreover, would I find better right away? I'm very glad indeed to be able to furnish my house, and that can only help me get on. So many thanks and good handshake; till tomorrow.

Ever yours,
Vincent

SILS MARIA

734.8 km from Arles

an unforeseen free *state of the "dear soul"; disorder and exception in my way of life; on the chamois hunt; to what extent "freedom of thought" is actually possible today; a* weapon *that is becoming* dangerous *for Wagner; a deep silence, a being-for-yourself; my music pessimism; I will be* people-friendly *again* ...

9 September

Dear friend,

I'm not getting away as soon as I was allowed to believe I would two days ago; some publishing *&* printing questions still want to be handled or wait here to be managed. The next, fairly likely date is 16 September. — Today I am in an unforeseen *free* state of the "dear soul" — and you shall feel it immediately. The last few weeks I've been *inspired* in the strangest way: so that some things that I hadn't believed myself capable of were finished — as if unconsciously — one morning. This caused some disorder and exception in my way of life: I often got up (or leapt up) at 2 o'clock at night to record something "driven by the spirit." Then I heard the front door open: my landlord sneaking out on the chamois hunt. Which of us was more on the chamois hunt? — Incredible, but true: this morning I sent the most careful, cleanest, and most elaborate manuscript that I have ever written to the printer — I don't even want to count in how few days it came about. The *title* is gracious enough: *Idleness of a Psychologist* — the *content*, the very worst and most radical, although hidden under many finesses and mitigations. It is a perfect overall introduction to my philosophy: — the thing that comes next is the "*Revaluation of All Values*" (the first book of which is almost finished). Let's see to what extent "freedom of thought" is actually possible today: I have an obscure idea that I will be *pursued* in the most beautiful form.

Moral: I've been given time to read two letters — and honestly! with delight. The humor of the matter is that I have just publicly *praised* Riemann: and so that you can understand my more *intimate* disposition, I will copy a few words from Herr Gast, which he wrote to me while correcting the relevant words.

"Riemann's metric studies, inspired *&* emerging from Wagner's propaganda lecture, can perhaps still be described as a *weapon* that is becoming *dangerous* for Wagner: just as you once (in *Morgenröte*) portrayed historical science as the daughter *&* ultimate conqueror of romanticism. I would at least like to believe that if these studies advance the acuteness of sensitivity to the musical period by a few decades, and also will awaken the sense of the great parallelism of the periods and, finally, will revive the blue-print of a composition to the level that it was alive at the turn of this century; and become a law *to* it!" — You will certainly allow me to give your very excellent oratio pro domo (*and* arte) to my friend to read? At the moment he is not too far from you: invited by a noble family to their estates in Pomerania (— Venice friend-ship; very beautiful girl, etc.) Perhaps the words I have copied give you on their own an idea of our very *purified* gustus. I have just entered into a relationship with Bülow with the aim of de-livering a comical Italian opera by Herr Gast (*The Lion of Venice*) to the Pollini menagerie. Almost nothing has been released to the public so far; it is not exactly my friend's wish to draw atten-tion to *himself* right now, in the midst of a confusion of taste. A deep silence, a being-for-yourself among the *better* is a hundred times more important than to be "known," i.e., *misunderstood.* — By the way, exactly my case — and my practice . . .

You will get a good idea of my *music pessimism* from my "pamphlet"; and also, in *this* particular case, I am still determined by certain very clear and unpleasant memories of my intimacy with Wagner. A performance of the Magic Flute Overture in Mannheim (— where I had the honor of accompanying Madame Cosima as a cavaliere on her *first* appearance before the "world") was, for the sake of an "immortality" at any price, a recital of the true excess of contrasts, a classic type of "Bernism" —

In conclusion, I confess that I am extremely pleased to have once been decidedly wrong about you, dear friend, and to even have *done* wrong to you. This improves our relationship incom-parably: believe the "idle psychologist" . . .

Heaven knows — you are an artist and *no* schoolmaster! — I know it too...

Faithfully yours, N.

Said once again: for the next week and maybe even longer I will be *people-friendly* again ...

ARLES

734.8 km from Sils Maria

I worked at furnishing the house; like a woman's boudoir, really artistic; the house will be just full of paintings; look for some lithographs and prints; an artist's house but not precious; ideas for work are coming to me in abundance; a place where you can ruin yourself, go mad, commit crimes; a full-blown case of delirium tremens; to exhibit sometime at the Revue Indépendante; the order for colors; you have a sort of country house

9 September 1888

My dear Theo,

I've just put the croquis of the new painting, the *Night Café*, in the post — as well as another one that I did some time ago. I'll perhaps end up making some Japanese prints.

Now yesterday I worked at furnishing the house. Just as the postman and his wife told me, the two beds, if you want something sturdy, will come to 150 francs each. I found that everything they'd told me about prices was true. As a result I had to change tack, and this is what I did: I bought one bed in walnut *&* another in deal, which will be mine, and which I'll paint later.

Then I bought linen for one of the beds, and I bought *two* palliasses. If Gauguin or somebody else were to come, there you are, his bed will be made in a minute. From the start, I wanted to arrange the house not just for myself but in such a way as to be able to put somebody up.

Naturally, that ate up most of my money.

With what was left, I bought 12 chairs, a mirror, and some small indispensable things. Which in short means that next week I'll be able to go and live there.

For putting somebody up, there'll be the prettiest room upstairs, which I'll try to make as nice as possible, like a woman's boudoir, really artistic. Then there'll be my own bedroom, which I'd like to be exceedingly simple, but the furniture square and broad.

The bed, the chairs, table, all in deal. Downstairs, the studio and another room, also a studio, but a kitchen at the same time.

One of these days you'll see a painting of the little house itself, in full sunshine or else with the window lit *&* the starry sky.

Then you'll be able to believe you own your country house here in Arles. Because I myself am enthusiastic about the idea of arranging it in such a way that you'll like it, and that it'll be a studio in a style absolutely meant to be that way.

Let's say that in a year you come to spend a holiday here and in Marseille, it will be ready then — and the way I envisage it, the house will be just full of paintings from top to bottom.

The room where you'll stay then, or which will be Gauguin's if Gauguin comes, will have a decoration of large yellow sunflowers on its white walls.

Opening the window in the morning, you see the greenery in the gardens and the rising sun and the entrance of the town.

But you'll see these big paintings of bouquets of 12, 14 sunflowers stuffed into this tiny little boudoir with a pretty bed and everything else elegant. It won't be commonplace.

And the studio — the red floor-tiles, the white walls and ceiling, the rustic chairs, the deal table, with, I hope, decoration of portraits. That will have character à la *Daumier* — and it won't, I dare predict, be commonplace.

Now I'm going to ask you to look for some Daumier lithographs for the studio, and some Japanese prints, but it's not at all urgent, and only when you find duplicates of them.

And some Delacroix's too, ordinary lithographs by modern artists.

It's not the least little bit urgent, but I have my idea. I really want to make of it — an artist's house but not precious, on the contrary, *nothing precious*, but everything from the chair to the painting having character.

So for the beds I bought local beds, two wide double beds, instead of iron beds. It gives a look of solidity, durability, calm, and if it takes a bit more bed-linen, that's too bad, but it must have character.

Most fortunately I have a charwoman who's very loyal; without that I wouldn't dare begin the business of living in my own place. She's quite old and has a mixed bunch of kids, and she keeps my tiles nice and red and clean.

I wouldn't be able to explain to you how pleased I am to find a big, serious job this way. Because I hope it'll be a true decoration that I'm going to undertake there.

So, as I've already told you, I'm going to paint my own bed, there'll be 3 subjects. Perhaps a naked woman, I haven't decided, perhaps a cradle with a child; I don't know, but I'll take my time.

I now no longer feel any hesitation about staying here, because ideas for work are coming to me in abundance. I now plan to buy some article for the house every month. And with patience, the house will be worth something for the furniture and the decorations.

I must warn you that very shortly I'll need a big order for colors for the autumn, which I believe is going to be absolutely marvelous. And on reflection, I'll send you the order enclosed herewith.

In my painting of the night café I've tried to express the idea that the café is a place where you can ruin yourself, go mad, commit crimes. Anyway, I tried with contrasts of delicate pink and blood-red and wine-red. Soft Louis XV and Veronese green contrasting with yellow greens and hard blue greens.

All of that in an ambience of a hellish furnace, in pale sulfur.

To express something of the power of the dark corners of a grog-shop. And yet with the appearance of Japanese gaiety and Tartarin's good nature.

But what would Mr. Tersteeg say about this painting? He who, looking at a Sisley — Sisley, the most tactful and sensitive of the Impressionists — had already said: 'I can't stop myself thinking that the artist who painted that was a little tipsy.' Looking at my painting, then, he'd say that it's a full-blown case of delirium tremens.

I find absolutely nothing to object to what you speak of, to exhibit sometime at the *Revue Indépendante*, as long as I'm not a cause of obstruction for the others who usually exhibit there.

Only we'd then have to tell them that I'd like to reserve a second exhibition for myself, after this first one of what are in fact studies.

Then next year I'd give them the decoration of the house to exhibit, when there would be an ensemble. Not that I insist, but it's so that the studies shouldn't be confused with compositions, and to say beforehand that the first exhibition would be one of *studies*.

Because there's still hardly more than the sower and the night café that are attempts at composed paintings.

As I write, the little peasant who looks like a caricature of our father is just coming into the café.

The resemblance is startling, all the same. The receding profile and the weariness and the ill-defined mouth, especially. It continues to seem a pity to me that I haven't been able to do him.

I'm adding to this letter the order for colors, which isn't exactly urgent. Only I'm so full of plans, and then the autumn promises so many superb subjects that I simply don't know if I'm going to start 5 or 10 canvases.

It'll be the same thing as in the spring, with the orchards in blossom; the subjects will be innumerable. If you gave père Tanguy the coarser paint, he'd probably do that well.

His other fine colors are really inferior, especially for the blues.

I hope, when preparing the next consignment, to gain a little in *quality*.

I'm doing comparatively less, and coming back to it longer. I've kept back 50 francs for the week; thus there has already been 250 for the furniture. And I'll recoup them anyway, doing it this way. And from today you can say to yourself that you have a sort of country house, unfortunately a bit far away. But it would cease to be very, very far if we had a permanent exhibition in Marseille. We'll see that in a year, perhaps. Handshake and

Ever yours,
Vincent

SILS MARIA

734.8 km from Arles

*the most difficult test of patience; strengthening & regain-
ing of the great rhythmic sense; Old and New Wagnerians;
essential philosophical heterodoxies; real psychologica &
of the most unknown & finest; a pleasant unfamiliarity of
existence*

Sils, 12 September 1888
Wednesday

Dear friend,

I do not yet know your address, but in view of the fact that I
would like to write to you before I leave, I will assume that a letter sent to Annaberg will also come into your hands. On *Sunday*
I shall go to Torino, on a trial basis: I never dreamed that the end
of my stay in Sils would impose the most difficult test of patience
on me. Unheard-of *flood weather* for a week; everything flooded;
it flows day and night, mixed with snow. In 4 days alone, 220
millimeters of precipitation fell (while the monthly average here
tends to be 80 mm). My health did not come out of it well: I am
also currently writing with a bit of a headache.

These days I am sending you another package, all of it printed, including, with many thanks, the *Bayreuther Blätter* booklet.
The other thing is *Fuchsiana*: a number of reviews and some of
his very strange letters (— including one that gives an excellent
idea of *Riemann's* whole undertaking: you will find that F hopes
the same from him as you hope — a strengthening and regaining
of the great rhythmic sense).

I have just heard that a book by Hans von Bülow will be published, entitled *Old and New Wagnerians*. The encounter with my
pamphlet is curious. Otherwise I'm still waiting for an answer
from him. —

There is *still* something *curious* to report. A few days ago I
sent Mr. C.G. Naumann another manuscript, with the title *Idleness of a Psychologist*. Under this harmless title hides a very bold
and precisely jotted-down summary of my most essential philosophical *heterodoxies*: so that the writing can serve as *initia-
tory* and *appetizing* for my *Revaluation of Values* (the first book
of which is almost finished). There is much judgment about the
present, about thinkers, writers, etc., in it. The last section is
called *Expeditions of an Untimely Man*; the first *Maxims and Arrows*. On the whole very cheerful, despite very strict judgments
(— it seems to me, between us, that I only learned to write in
German — that is to say *French* — this year). Chapters, besides

the above: The Problem of Socrates; "Reason" in Philosophy. How the "Real" World Finally Became a Fable. Morality as Anti-Nature. The Four Great Errors. The "Improvers" of Mankind. They are real *psychologica* and of the most unknown and finest. (— The Germans are told some truths, in particular my low opinion about the Reichs German spirituality is justified.)

This writing, appearing, all told, as a twin to the *Wagner Case* (albeit about twice as strong), has to come out as soon as possible: because I need an interim period before the revaluation is published (— this rigorously serious work, a hundred miles removed from all tolerances and kindness).

My hope is that this letter will find you in a pleasant *unfamiliarity* of existence. A few words from you will be very welcome in Torino (*ferma in posta*).

Faithful *&* grateful
your friend
Nietzsche.

— What is the *quartet* doing now?

ARLES

734.8 km from Sils Maria

last night I slept in the house; I can make something of it that will last; pure Daumier, pure Zola; I'd like to be able to count on receiving 100 instead of 50; more on the right road! I'm anxious to prove that I pay my debts; a studio-refuge; an art which may also be continued by others after us; a stronger sun and a Japanese clarity; as far as Africa; out toward the infinite; an association of artists; if Gauguin doesn't come ... if Gauguin came; just like any animal at bay; I'm for an association of artists protecting their live-lihood and their work; a painting for which we pay 400 francs today and which we sell for 1,000 francs ten years later; right at the heart of the trade; paintings on deposit; we'd make our colors at home ourselves

Tuesday
18 September 1888

My dear Theo,

Many thanks for your letter and for the 50-franc note it contained.
I've also received Maurin's drawing, which is superb. That man's
a great artist. Last night I slept in the house, and although there
are still things to be done, I feel very happy there. Besides, I feel
that I can make something of it that will last, and from which
someone else will also be able to benefit. Now money spent will
no longer be money wasted, and I believe it won't be long before
you see the difference there. At present it makes me think of Bos-
boom's interiors, with the red tiles, the white walls, the furniture
in deal or walnut, the patches of intense blue sky and greenery
visible through the windows. Now the surroundings, with the
public garden, the night cafés, the grocer's shop, aren't Millet, of
course, but failing that, it's pure Daumier, pure Zola. Now that's
quite enough to find ideas in, isn't it?

I already wrote to you yesterday that, if I count the two beds
at 300 francs, the price can't be reduced any further. If, however,
I've already bought more than that, it's because, if I already put
half of last week's money into it, yesterday I had to pay another
10 francs to the lodging-house keeper & 30 francs for a palliasse.

At the moment I have 5 francs left in my pocket. So I'm going
to ask you to send me another louis, depending on what you can
manage — but by return of post — to see me through the week,
or 50 francs, if it's possible. One way or another, this month I'd
like to be able to count on receiving 100 instead of 50, again, over
the whole month, as I asked you in my letter yesterday.

If I save 50 francs over the month myself, if I add to that
the other 50, it means that in total I'll have spent 400 francs
on furniture. My dear Theo, here we are, at last, more on the
right road! It's true that it doesn't matter not having hearth nor
home as long as you're young, and living like a traveler, in cafés, but that was becoming intolerable to me now, and most of
all, it wasn't compatible with thoughtful work. So my plan is all
worked out. I'll try to do painting for what you send me every

month, and then I want to do painting for the house. What I do
for the house will be to reimburse you for previous expenditure.
I'm still something of a tradesman, in fact, in the sense that I'm
anxious to prove that I pay my debts, and know what I want for
the merchandise that the lousy trade of a poor painter forces me
to labor at.

Ah well, I feel more or less sure of succeeding in making a
decoration that will be worth 10 thousand francs in time. Let
me say — if here we set up a studio-refuge for one or other of
our pals who are broke, no one will ever be able to reproach us,
neither you nor me, with living and spending for ourselves alone.

Now to set up such a studio you need a working capital; now
it's I who have eaten it up in the course of my unproductive years,
and I'll pay it back now that I'm beginning to produce.

I assure you that, for you as well as for me, I judge it to be
indispensable, but what's more our right, always to have a louis
or a few louis in our pocket, and a certain stock of merchandise
to handle.

But my idea would be that in the end we'd have set up and
would leave to posterity a studio in which a successor could live.

I don't know if I'm expressing myself clearly enough, but in
other words: we're working at an art, at matters that won't be of
our times only but which may also be continued by others after us.

You're doing that in your business; it's undeniable that it will
increase in future, even though you have many vexations at present.

But for me, I foresee that other artists will wish to see color
under a stronger sun and in a more Japanese clarity. Now if I set
up a studio-refuge right at the entrance to the south, that's not
so silly.

And precisely that means that we can work calmly. Ah, if
others say, it's too far from Paris &c.? Let them, too bad for them.
Why did the greatest colorist of all, Eugène Delacroix, judge it
indispensable to go to the south, and as far as Africa? Obviously
because not only in Africa but even from Arles onwards you'll
naturally find fine contrasts between reds and greens, blues and
oranges, sulfur and lilac. And all true colorists will have to come
to admit that there exists another coloration than that of the
north. And I don't doubt that if Gauguin came, he would love this

part of the country; if Gauguin didn't come, it's because he has already had this experience of more colorful countries, and he'd still be one of our friends and in agreement in principle. And another one of them would come in his place.

If what we're doing looks out toward the infinite, if we see our work having its *raison d'être* and continuing on beyond, we work with more serenity. Now you have that twice over.

You're kind to painters, and be sure that the more I think about it the more I feel that there's nothing more genuinely artistic than to love people. You'll say to me that then we'd do well to do without art and artists. That's true on the face of it, but after all, the Greeks and the French and the old Dutchmen accepted art, and we see art always recover after inevitable periods of decline — and I don't believe that we'd be more virtuous for this reason, that we had a horror of artists and their art. At present I don't yet find my paintings good enough for the benefits I've had from you. But once they're good enough, I assure you that you will have created them just as much as I, and the fact is that we make them together.

But I won't labor the point, because it will become as clear as daylight to you if I succeed in doing things a little more seriously.

At the moment I have another no. 30 square canvas on the go, a garden again, or rather a walk under plane trees, with green turf and black clumps of pines.

You did very well to order the colors and the canvas, because the weather is superb, superb. The mistral is still there, but there are intervals of calm, and then it's wonderful. If we had less mistral, this part of the country would really be as beautiful, and would lend itself as much to art, as Japan.

As I write, very kind letter from Bernard, who's thinking of coming to Arles this winter — whim — but then, perhaps it's also that Gauguin is sending him to me as a substitute, and would himself prefer to stay in the north. We'll know soon, because I'm sure that he'll write to you one way or another.

Bernard's letter speaks of Gauguin with great respect and sympathy, and I'm convinced that they have mutually understood one another. And I certainly believe that Gauguin has done Bernard good.

Whether Gauguin comes or not, he'll still be one of our friends, and if he doesn't come now he'll come at another time. I instinctively feel that Gauguin is a calculating person, who, seeing himself at the bottom of the social ladder, wishes to regain a position by means that will be honest, to be sure, but which will be very shrewd. Gauguin has little idea that I'm able to take account of all that. And he perhaps doesn't know that he must at all costs gain time, and that he'll gain it with us, if he were to gain nothing else thereby.

Now if one of these days he does a bunk from Pont-Aven with Laval or Maurin without paying his debt, in my opinion he would still be in the right in his case, just like any animal at bay.

I don't believe that it's wise to offer Bernard 150 francs for one painting a month immediately, as we've offered Gauguin. And isn't Bernard, who has clearly talked at length with Gauguin about the whole business, rather counting on replacing Gauguin?

I believe that it'll be necessary to be very firm and very categorical in all of this.

And without giving our reasons, to speak very clearly.

I can't blame Gauguin — speculator, stockbroker — if he wishes to risk something in business, only I myself wouldn't be part of it, I'd a thousand times sooner continue with you, whether you're with the Goupils or not. And the new dealers are, as you know full well, exactly the same as the old ones in my opinion.

In principle, in theory, I'm for an association of artists protecting their livelihood and their work, but in principle and in theory I'm equally against attempts to destroy old firms, once established. Just let them rot in peace and die a natural death. It's pure presumption to try to revive the trade. Have nothing to do with it, protect your livelihoods among yourselves, live as a family, as brothers and companions; splendid; even in a case where that didn't succeed, I'd like to be part of it, but I'll never be part of a maneuver against other dealers. I shake your hand firmly; I hope that what I'm forced to ask of you won't cause you too much financial trouble. But I didn't want to delay going to sleep at my house. And if you're in financial difficulties yourself, I'll get through the week with 20 francs more, but that will be urgent.

Ever yours,
Vincent

The letter that Gauguin will send you shortly will, I'm inclined to believe, clear the matter up.

I myself don't blame an artist of his merit for saying, you'll pay my journey and my debt if you wish me to come, because I don't have any — any money. But on the other hand, in that case he'd have to be very generous with his paintings. Then — but we'd still have to have the money — I wouldn't see any harm in the thing. But these paintings, which will be sold one day, will tie up the interest on what they cost, perhaps for many years to come. And in fact, a painting for which we pay 400 francs today and which we sell for 1,000 francs ten years later is still sold at cost price, because it has sat there doing nothing. But you know this better than I do.

I shouldn't be surprised if little by little you regain a love of business, or at least that you'll be reconciled with your present position when you'll feel that those who invent new things in business don't know how to make a great revolution in it.

You're kind to artists, you are, in fact, right at the heart of the trade, you do what you can, you're damned right. Only take care of your health if you can, and don't get upset about nothing. That will come quite of its own accord now, if it must come.

I only want to emphasize this, that it seems to me that Gauguin, by giving you alone his paintings on deposit, and quietly waiting for his moment while working here with me and repaying our advances with his work, would be pursuing a policy that I would respect more than any other position he could take.

For Bernard, if Bernard wished to come here, it wouldn't be on the same conditions as Gauguin — it would seem to me.

If there was a benefit in living together, there's nothing to prevent you agreeing to buy something from him from time to time, if it's possible. But no sort of contract with him, he's too changeable.

If Gauguin doesn't come, he'll succeed all the same, but he won't succeed through his contrivance, but through the real merit of his canvases. As long as he keeps the time and the money and the freedom needed to do them, that's all. I can assure you that I would certainly not be a better dealer than you; in the given circumstances you do perfectly well, and I'd only wish to send you better paintings. I'm trying to do that, and I'll continue to try to do so. I expect to return to my garden canvas again soon. It's an immense advantage that I have, not to be short of canvases and colors, and so it's certainly my duty to work without respite. If Gauguin came, I'm inclined to believe that we'd make our colors at home ourselves; I daren't do it on my own, because I fear that it would discourage me if it didn't work straightaway. I'm very curious to know what Tanguy will charge for his tubes.

Did you read an article in the number of *Le Courrier Français* that you sent, "la truie bleue"? Very good, and it reminds you precisely of La Segatori. You'll enjoy reading that article.

I'll see Millet today, I think. Thank you in advance for the Japanese prints.

I'm keeping all Bernard's letters, they're sometimes really interesting; you'll read them some day or other; they already make quite a bundle.

This firmness I was speaking of, that it will be necessary to have with Gauguin, it's solely because we already made our position clear when he described his plan of action in Paris. You replied well then without committing yourself, but also without wounding him in his *amour propre*. And it's the same thing that could be necessary again.

TORINO

416.4 km from Arles

great artillery; horrible detonations; the thunder of can-
nons; philosophizing with a hammer; one more malice
against Wagner; difficulties and tests of patience of a worse
kind; wonderful clarity, autumn colors, an exquisite feeling
of wellbeing; the idyllic way of being; the animal and the
sentimental; "incomprehensible impressions"

27 Sept 1888

Dear Friend,

Your correction of sheet 2, which Wurchow had left on the 24th, arrived here today, at the same time as Naumann's broadcast of the 25th (the 4th printing sheet). Basically, the Berlin–Torino connection should be considerably faster than Wurchow–Torino. The matter won't last long either; it will likely be 6 sheets or a little more. A final revision is *not* necessary; the manuscript was much better prepared than the Wagner-pamphlet.

As far as the *title* is concerned, your *very humane* objection was preceded by my own misgivings: finally, from the words in the *preface* I found the formula that perhaps also satisfies your needs. What you write to me about the "great artillery," I have to accept, in the middle of the *finishing* of the first book of "Um-wertung." It really boils down to horrible detonations: I don't think that one can find a sidepiece to this first book from all the literature in terms of orchestral sound (including the thunder of cannons). — The new *title* (which entails very modest changes in 3 to 4 places) should be:

Twilight of the Idols.
Or:
How to Philosophize with a Hammer.
by
F. N.

The meaning of the words, which in the end can also be guessed at, is, as I said, the subject of the *short* preface. — The *first* letter about the "case" was from *Gersdorff*. He also writes about the *lion duet* (ex ungue leonem —) "This is music the way I love it. Where are the ears to hear them, where are the musicians to play them?" — A curiosity that Gersdorff communicates and *that deeply edifies me*: G witnessed Wagner's furious rage against *Bizet* as Minnie Hauck in Napoli was and Carmen sang. On the basis that W took sides here too, my malice will be felt much more sharply at a certain main point. Incidentally, Gersdorff *warns* me very seriously about the Wagnerians. — The new title *Twilight of the Idols* will also be heard in this sense, — so *one more malice* against Wagner...

Old friend, you are still not at my height with your argument about the dative and nominative in the concept of God. The nominative is the *joke* of the job, its sufficient reason to exist...

My journey had difficulties and tests of patience of a worse kind: I did not get to Milan until midnight. The most worrying thing was a long passage at night in Como through flooded terrain on a very narrow wooden board bridge — with torch lighting! Just made for me like a blind man's cow! — Exhausted by the slack and unpleasant air of Lombardy, I arrived in Torino: but strange! everything was fine as if in a jolt. *Wonderful* clarity, autumn colors, an exquisite feeling of wellbeing in all things. In two main things, namely the *apartment* and the *trattoria*, my *second* appearance was felt in the most welcoming way. Order, cleanliness, attention in the former increased by 50 percent; the goodness in quality and quantity in the tratt. around 100, *without* the very moderate prices being changed here or there. I also have my first tailor here, who works really well for me. — Five steps from me is the largest piazza, with the old medieval castell: on it is a charming little theater, in front of which you can sit outside at night (from 8¼), eat your gelato and just now I can hear Audran's French operetta *Mascotte* (— I know it very well from Nizza). This music, which in no way becomes common, with so many pretty, witty little melodies, belongs entirely to the idyllic way of being that I now need in the evening. (The *counterpart* to this: the gypsy baron von Strauss: I ran away with disgust and *soon* away — the two types of German meanness, the animal and the sentimental, along with very horrible attempts here and there to show the *educated* musician: Heaven! What to us is in the taste of the French!) — The weather leaves a lot to be desired. But I can cope better with the bad weather here and haven't lost a day of work. Greetings to you, dear friend, with the most heartfelt wishes for Berlin *and what depends on it*, your N.

— In the end I did not even thank you for your good letter, from which the "words full of the strangest, strangest, most incomprehensible impressions" stuck in my mind.

INTERVAL: TORINO & ARLES

The Mole Antonelliana *&* Vincent's bedroom
Torino →← Arles: 416.4 km distance

October 1888

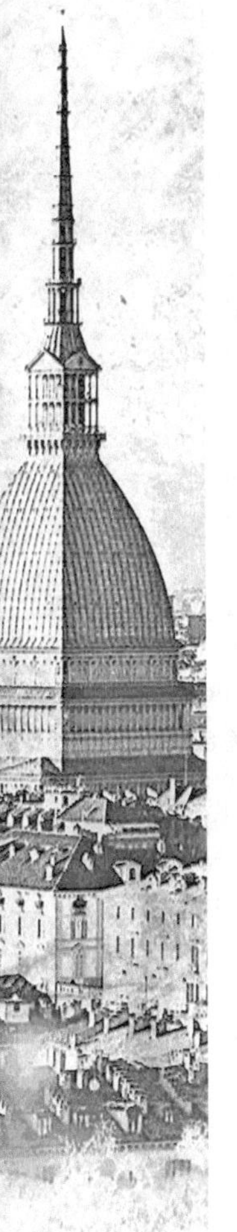

Constructed between 1863 and 1889 — thus predating but finally intertwining with the construction of la Tour Eiffel and spanning the entirety of Nietzsche's adult life —, the Mole Antonelliana, a synagogue in the city of Torino, becomes one of the philosopher's most beloved architectural structures. To Torino's Jewish community, it was to be a perennial and eternal reminder of gratitude to the noble society that had emancipated them. The structure was to commemorate the integration of the Jews in civil society and to be a bold symbol of their presence amongst the Italians.

In October, around his birthday, Nietzsche began to write his autobiography, *Ecce Homo*, and three days later, Alessandro Antonelli, the architect of the Mole, died, intertwining and symbolically uniting the birth of the philosopher's book with the death of the creator of a building that, because of its absolute drive for elevation, reminded the philosopher of nothing so much as his *Zarathustra*:

> I have baptized the tower *Ecce Homo*, and in spirit have opened an enormous free space around it.

The self-described anti-Christ, anti-anti-Semite, and philosopher of Dionysos *&* Apollo christens a synagogue with the name of a book that parodies the phrase spoken by Pontius Pilate upon his presenting a scourged Christ, bound *&* knighted with a crown of thorns, to a hostile publicum in the city of Jerusalem prior to his crucifixion. The baptism of a building! Is this one of the first pieces of architecture that gives expression to the sublimity of contemplation and stepping aside that Nietzsche called for in *Die fröhliche Wissenschaft*?

The so-called half-human, half-divine anthropos is usurped by the father of the hyperanthropos, the Über-mensch, the man who when writing to his mother re-ferred to himself as monster *&* creature, the man whose mother was an obstacle to the Eternal Return, a cyclical time figuration forged to eradicate teleology and test the fortitude of the human species, to compel it to love its fate via its own will, not divine command.

And he who came not to send peace, but a sword, he who came to set a man at variance against his father, *&* the daughter against her mother, and who proclaimed that he that taketh not his cross, and followeth after me, is not worthy of me, that Man of Sorrows is usurped by the advocate of la gaya scienza, he who canonized laughter in *Thus Spoke Zarathustra* and gave birth to the comic age — no longer is woe to be visited upon those who laugh: thorns have been replaced with gaiety, the soul with the gastrointestinal system.

A synagogue (then museum commemorating King Vittorio Emanuele II, then, in the late 20th century, mu-seum of cinema — all hail knowing illusion!) evokes for Nietzsche not only what he deemed his greatest gift to mankind, but is sanctified by him with the name of his exalted, parodic autobiography, which makes of exis-tence not a period of tragedy, not a period of morals and religions, but a period of comedy — let laughter resound!

Thus spoke the Satyr, thus spoke the Clown, thus spoke the son who sent his mother very precise notes regarding exactly what kind of ham and sausage most suited his constitution. An Übermensch cannot live on spirit alone.

*

In Arles, Vincent is not in a state of laughter, he has not heard the clarion call of the satyr, he is in a feverish state — like an animal, though not a hyena, he senses an oncoming mistral that will render him incapable of working outdoors, and so he paints five large canvases.

Shortly after, he collapses in his bed, sleeping for 16 hours straight, his eyes weary, his vision strangely tired, his body exhausted from its potent creative exertions.

Then the violent mistral hits, raising clouds of dust that turn the trees on Boulevard des Lices white from top to bottom, forcing the painter to remain indoors until it concludes.

During this period of imposed rest, on Nietzsche's very birthday, working almost like a sleepwalker, the broken pitcher makes a painting of his bedroom which, through its simplified color, gives a grander style to things, to be suggestive the painter says of rest or of sleep in general. Like Nietzsche's *Ecce Homo*, it is a kind of autobiography. Does not Vincent also want to say with his paintings who he is, and has he not, with his letters and self-portraits, not neglected to 'bear witness' about himself?

In short, the broken pitcher tells his brother, looking at the painting should rest the mind, or rather, the imagination. The solidity of the furniture should also now express unshakeable repose. This to take my revenge for the enforced rest that I was obliged to take.

Stable ground to counteract the general instability and exhaustion, however much the painting evokes a sense of vertigo and tremulousness, its open, off-kilter windows, its angled ceiling careering subtly downward, and the swift speed of its floor educing the sensation of stars hurtling thru space? While the Mole Antonelliana veers upward, Vincent veers.

Not long after, Gauguin would finally move into the Yellow House, thus at last commencing another incarnation of the wild Dutchman's utopic dream of founding an artist's colony. It would function as a spiritual-cultural community and inaugurate a new Renaissance, with Gauguin as its abbot, Theo van Gogh as its dealer-apostle, and Vincent as its patron saint, the rock upon which the building is founded. St. Vincent!

Neither the philosopher nor the painter thinks of the *ostentatio vulnerum*, for they are free of such stigma, though both will suffer wounds of their own, both will die and be reborn, not once, but many times, like figures bound to a rock.

ARLES

416.4 km from Torino

two new friends; not yet au courant; Gauguin is coming; a new colorist school; the solemnity of great effects of sunlight; artists of the monstrous frame; the south, Africa, or Sicily; always the same melancholy; I'd like to be able to do a little business for a change; the two of us have created an artistic thing; the failing of Dutch absolutes

17 October 1888

My dear Theo,

What you say about two new friends certainly does give me great pleasure.

But all the same it astonishes me that you tell me about them and their frame (costing, if I remember rightly, 2,000 francs), but that you don't say a single word about what there was in that frame, nor a single word about what they've done in paintings.

It's perhaps that you believe that I might have heard of it, but I declare to you that I'm hearing about this business and even about themselves for the first time. So I'm not yet *au courant*, and would thus like to know: "all well and good about the frame, but what was in it, and what are they doing at present?"

After that I'll surely be in a better position to give myself an idea of what their conversations with you and Pissarro were like, once I'm *au courant* with what they themselves are doing.

In any case, it proves one thing: it's that Dutch artists spoke of you as being the dealer in Impressionist paintings, something we mustn't lose sight of.

And what did they have to say about Dutch art, about Breitner, Rappard, about others, and lastly, what do they say about Tersteeg?

Gauguin writes that he's already sent his trunk and promises to come around the 20th of this month, in a few days, therefore. Which I'll be very pleased about, because I dare believe that it will do us both good.

So write me with details of your new friends' painting soon, and if they're really painters who are trying to make more progress in something that's completely new, boldly recommend the south to them. I believe that a new *colorist* school will take root in the south, seeing increasingly that those from the north rely more on skill with the brush and the so-called picturesque effect than on the desire to express something through color itself.

It gave me great pleasure to have your news, but it astonishes me so much not to know what there was in that frame.

Here, under the stronger sun, I have found what Pissarro said to be true, and moreover what Gauguin wrote me, the same thing. The simplicity, the bleaching-out, the solemnity of great effects of sunlight.

In the north one will never suspect what it's like. And if these artists of the monstrous frame seriously wish to see something new, let them go to Bing and then to the south.

As for me, I already get palpitations over ordering my deal frames at 5 francs. It's like what I said to Russell about his house, that the one here would cost several times less in hundred-franc notes than his would in thousands, and that nevertheless we were working for Gauguin even without R.

Have they seen any Seurats, these gentlemen with the frame? I think I'd prefer Seurat's frame to theirs, for inventiveness.

Yes, speaking of Seurat — have you seen him again yet?

As far as selling goes, of course I think you're right not to look for it deliberately, of course I myself would prefer never to sell if the thing could be done.

But if we were nevertheless forced to it, after what has happened we no longer have an alternative, of course, if it should indeed become necessary one day, we could do no better than not be hasty.

I shake your hand firmly, and I hope you'll tell me what there actually was in the frame. And to our new friends, warm regards and good luck, which I wish them.

If they want to see something new, certainly, let them go to the south or Africa or to Sicily if it's winter. But it's only — if they have originality — the real south that will show them something different from Holland. I hope you'll write to me again before long. Good handshake

Ever yours,
Vincent

I'm adding another line to tell you that this afternoon I finished the canvas of the bedroom.

In any case it gives me great pleasure that you've met these Dutchmen. It could just be the case that in fact I'd heard of this large painting after all, but not of the frame. Rappard once told me a story (praising the painting and the painter), and I'll easily see if it was the same painting that was involved when you've told me about what they're doing.

In any event, my dear brother, look, if you complain of having nothing in your noddle as far as of being able to produce good things goes, just look, *so much the more* must I myself also feel the same melancholy. I could do nothing whatsoever without you, and there you are, let's not get worked up over what the two of us produce together this way, but on the contrary, let's smoke our pipes in peace without tormenting ourselves too much to the point of melancholy for not producing separately and with less pain.

Certainly, from time to time I'd like to be able to do a little business for a change, and by doing so earn some money on my own account.

But since we can change nothing about it for the moment, let's accept this inevitable fact, that you'll always be condemned to trade, without rest or variation, and I that mine is also without rest, constant work that's really tiring and absorbing for the mind.

I hope that in a year you'll feel that the two of us have created an artistic thing.

This bedroom is something like that still life of French novels with yellow, pink, green covers, you'll recall. But I believe that the execution is simpler and more virile.

No stippling, no hatching, nothing; the tints flat, but in harmony. I don't know what I'll undertake afterwards, because my sight's still tired.

And at those moments, just after hard work, and the harder it is, I feel my noddle empty too, you know. And if I wanted to let myself give in to that, nothing would be easier for me than to hate what I've just done and kick it, like *père* Cézanne. But after all, why kick it — let's leave the studies alone, and only if we see nothing in them, fine, if we see in them what people call good, well then, so much the better.

Anyway, let's not think too deeply about good and bad, that always being very relative.

It's precisely a failing of the Dutch to call one thing absolutely good and another absolutely bad, when it's nowhere near as inflexible as that.

You know, I've read Richepin's *Césarine* too; there are good things in it — the march of the soldiers in flight, how you feel their weariness — let's not march in life without also being soldiers sometimes.

The quarrel of the son and the father is really heartbreaking, but it's like the same Richepin's *La glu*, I find that it leaves no hope, while Guy de Maupassant, who has written things that are certainly just as sad, makes things turn out more humanely in the end. Look at *Monsieur Parent*, look at *Pierre et Jean*, they don't end in happiness but anyway, the people are resigned and go on all the same. It doesn't end in so much blood & gore, does it now? I much prefer Maupassant to Richepin, for being more consoling. At present I've just read Balzac's *Eugénie Grandet*. The story of a miserly peasant. More soon, I hope.

Ever yours,
Vincent

True, if we're not producing framed paintings like these Dutchmen, you and I, all the same we're making paintings like Japanese prints, and let's keep it to that, no more.

(Have you read *Madame Chrysanthème* yet?)

TORINO

416.4 km from Arles

I am now the most grateful man in the world; I bring out my heavy guns; I am shooting the history of mankind into two halves; declarations of war, much jollity; a political and economic unity; the great question of value; the highest problem of humanity; the kind of existence that I now need; a duel with Wagner

18 Oct. 1888

Dear friend,

Yesterday, with your letter in my hand, I took my usual afternoon walk outside Torino. The clearest October light everywhere: the glorious avenue of trees, which led me for about an hour along beside the Po, still hardly touched by autumn. I am now the most grateful man in the world — *autumnally* minded in every good sense of the word; it is my great *harvest time*. Everything comes to me easily, everything succeeds, although it is unlikely that anyone has ever had such great things on his hands. That the *first* book of the *Transvaluation of All Values* is finished, ready for *press*, I announce to you with a feeling for which I have no words. There will be *four* books; they will appear singly. This time — as an old artilleryman — I bring out my heavy guns; I am afraid that I am shooting the history of mankind into two halves. With that work which I gave you an inkling of in my last letter, we shall soon be ready; it has, in order to save as much as possible of my now invaluable time, been printed with excellent precision. Your quotation from *Menschl. Allzumenschl.* came just at the right time to be included. — This work amounts to a hundred declarations of war, with distant thunder in the mountains; in the foreground, much "*jollity*," of my relative sort of conditioned merriment* ... This work makes it amazingly easy for anyone to gauge my *degree* of heterodoxy, which really leaves nothing at all intact. I attack the *Germans* along the whole front — you will have no complaints to make about "ambiguity." This irresponsible race, which has all the great misfortunes of culture on its conscience and at all *decisive* moments in history, was thinking of "something else" (the Reformation at the time of the Renaissance; Kantian philosophy just when a *scientific* mode of thought had been reached by England and France; "wars of liberation" when Napoleon appeared, the only man hitherto strong enough to make Europe into a political and *economic* unity —), is thinking today of the Reich, this recrudescence of the world of the petty kingdoms and of culture atomism, at a moment when the great *question of value* is being asked for the first time. There was never a more important moment in history — *but who knows a thing about it?* The disproportion here is altogether necessary; at a time when an undreamed-of loftiness and freedom of intellectual passion is laying hold of the *highest* problem of humanity and is calling for a *decision* as to human destiny, the general pettiness and obtuseness must become all the more sharply distinct from it. There is no "hostility" to me whatever — people are simply deaf to anything I say; *consequently* there is neither a for nor an *against* . . .

Dear friend, please credit the Handwerkerbank account with the 500 francs you mention. I must save with all my strength to be able to cope with the printing expenses of the next three years. (I assume that the 1000 frs. due on October 1 have also been deposited there). At the end of December I shall certainly need the 500 francs very badly. My plan is to hold on here until November 20 (— a somewhat *frosty* project, because winter comes early!). Then I shall go to *Nizza* and establish the kind of existence that I now need, breaking completely with all my usances till now. I have had some thoughts even of Bastia in Corsica; yet I am afraid of the *experiment* and its dangers, my present deep self-contemplation being what I need.

Herr *Köselitz* has moved to Berlin; his letters breathe the best state of mind one could wish for on earth. Also things are *happening* for him — I shall write to you about it later. Address: *Berlin* S.W., Lindenstrasse 116/IV/1.

Greetings to you *&* your dear wife, with very many thanks,

Your Nietzsche

* In the midst of the tremendous tension of this time, a duel with Wagner was a complete *recovery* for me: now that I am performing in open war, it was necessary to prove *publicly* that I "have my hand free" . . .

ARLES

416.4 km from Torino

If Gauguin and I work every evening for a fortnight, won't we earn it all back again?; the state of madness; I had something of a dual nature; I must be wary of my nerves; I myself believe in the south; a tendency toward great things; it horrifies me to have to ask you for money again; my own originality; send me another 50 francs right away

21 October 1888

My dear Theo,

Thank you for your letter and for the 50-franc note it contained. Thank you for having written me more about those Dutch artists' painting.

I've had gas put in, in the studio and the kitchen, which is costing me 25 francs for installation. If Gauguin *&* I work every evening for a fortnight, won't we earn it all back again? But since, what's more, G. may come any day now, I'll absolutely, absolutely need at least another 50 francs.

I'm not ill, but I'd become so without any doubt if I didn't take hearty food and if I didn't stop painting for a few days. In fact, I'm once again nearly reduced to the state of madness of Hugo van der Goes in Emile Wauters's painting. And if it wasn't for the fact that I had something of a dual nature, something of both the monk and the painter, I should be — and that long since — utterly and entirely reduced to the above-mentioned state.

But even for all that, I don't believe that my madness would be of the persecution kind, since my feelings in a state of excitement have more to do with preoccupations about eternity and eternal life.

But even so, I must be wary of my nerves, *&c.*

I only say that because you'd be wrong to believe that I'd have had the slightest *wariness* about these two Dutch painters. But in truth, it's only after your second letter that I can form an idea of what they're doing, and I'm very curious to see the photographs of their drawings.

I have a great urge to write you a letter just so that you can have them read it, to explain once again why I myself believe in the south for the future and the present.

And at the same time to say how strongly I believe that we're right to see in the Impressionist movement a tendency toward great things, and not *only* a school that would limit itself to making optical experiments. Similarly with those who do history painting, then, or at least have done it in the past; while there are some very bad history painters, like Delaroche *&* Delort, are there not also good ones, like E. Delacroix and Meissonier?

Well then, since I have the firm intention not to paint for at least 3 days, perhaps I'll rest by writing to you and to them at the same time. Because you know that that interests me a good deal, the influence that Impressionism will have on Dutch painters and on Dutch art lovers.

Here's very rough croquis of my last canvas. A row of green cypresses against a pink sky with a pale lemon crescent moon.

Foreground a piece of wasteland, and some sand and a few thistles. Two lovers, the man pale blue with a yellow hat, the woman has a pink bodice & a black skirt. That makes the fourth canvas of the 'poet's garden,' which is the decoration for Gauguin's bedroom.

It horrifies me to have to ask you for money again, but I can do nothing about it, and what's more, I'm worn out again. However, I'd believe that the work that I'm doing while spending a little more will one day seem to us less costly than my previous work.

Besides, I'd already told you that if the thing had been possible, to do a deal with Thomas, I'd have had a strong desire to be able to put even 200 more into the work before Gauguin's arrival.

As that couldn't be done, I nevertheless pressed ahead as far as I could with what I had on the go, in a strong desire to be able to show him something new. And not to fall under his influence (because of course he'll have an influence on me, I hope) before being able to show him beyond any doubt my own originality. He'll see that anyway from the decoration as it is now.

Please, at least if the thing's possible for you, send me another 50 francs right away; I don't quite know how I'll be able to get by otherwise. I'm pleased that you've read *Tartarin* again. Anyway. I hope you'll be able to write to me no later than by return of post. I shake your hand firmly.

Ever yours,
Vincent

TORINO

416.4 km from Arles

never have I looked so well; in my trattoria I receive with-out any doubt the best there is; Nizza was pure foolery; the same boundless perfection and plentitude of sun; life is worth living here; I get a very large helping of minestra; my shivery feeling; I seem to have the destiny of mankind "in the palm of my hand"; an icy shudder; the weather is so glorious; to test what risks I can take with the German ideas of freedom of speech; prophet, savage beast, or moral horror; a sign of gay detachment . . .

Tuesday, 30 October 1888

Dear friend,

I have just seen myself in the mirror — never have I looked so well. In exemplary condition, well nourished, and 10 years younger than I should be. On top of it all, since choosing Torino as my home, I am much changed in the honors I do myself — I rejoice, for example, in an excellent tailor, and set value on being received everywhere as a distinguished foreigner. I have succeeded amazingly well in this. In my *trattoria* I receive without any doubt the best there is: they call my attention to things, and this is especially a success. Between ourselves, I have never known till now what it means to enjoy eating — also what I need to keep up my strength. My criticism of the winters in Nizza is now very stringent: an inadequate and, especially for me, quite intolerable diet. The same, perhaps more so, is true, I am sorry to say, dear friend, of your Venice. I eat here with the *serenest* disposition of soul and stomach, probably four times as much as in the "Panada." — In other ways too Nizza was *pure foolery*. The Torino landscape is so much more congenial to me than this chalky, treeless, and stupid bit of Riviera that I am thoroughly annoyed at having been so late in putting it behind me. I shall say nothing of the contemptible *&* venal kind of people there — not excluding the foreigners. Here day after day dawns with the same boundless perfection and plentitude of sun: the glorious foliage in glowing yellow, the sky and the big river delicately blue, the air of the greatest purity — a Claude Lorrain such as I never dreamed I would see. Fruits, grapes in the brownest sweetness — and cheaper than in Venice! In every way, life is worth living here. The coffee in the best cafés, a small pot of remarkably good coffee, even the very best quality, such as I never found before, 20 ct. — and in Torino one does *not* pay a tip. My room, *best* position in the center, sunshine from early morning until afternoon, view on to the Palazzo Carignano, the Piazza Carlo Alberto, and across and away to the green mountains — 25 frs. a month, with service and shoes cleaned. In the trattoria I pay for each meal 1 fr. 15 ct. and add — it is certainly regarded as an exception —

an extra 10 ct. For this I get: a *very large* helping of minestra, dry or as bouillon — immense choice and variety — and Italian pastas of the first quality (only here am I *learning* the great differences); then an excellent portion of tender meat, above all, veal, better than any I have ever tasted, with a vegetable — spinach and so on; three rolls, very delicious here (for the fancier, grissini, the very thin little pipes of *bread*, which Torino people appreciate). — A *stove* has been ordered, from Dresden; you know, narron-carbon heating — without smoke, consequently without chimney. I am also having my *books* sent from Nizza. Moreover, it is wonderfully mild, even the nights. My shivery feeling, of which I wrote to you, has purely *internal* causes. It was at once all right again. —

Your letter gave me great pleasure. I have never really heard from anyone how strong the effect of my thought is. The novelty — the *courage* of the novelty: — is really of the first rank; as for the *consequences*, I sometimes look at my *hand* now with some distrust, because I seem to have the destiny of mankind "in the palm of my hand." — Are you satisfied by my concluding with the *Dionysos morality*? It occurred to me that this group of ideas should not at any price be absent from this *vade mecum* of my philosophy. With the few sentences about the Greeks, I take it upon myself to challenge everything that has been said about them. — Finally, the Hammer speech from *Zarathustra* — perhaps, *after* this book, *audible* . . . I myself cannot hear it without feeling an icy shudder run through my body.

The weather is so glorious that there is no difficulty in doing something *well*. On my birthday, I began again with something that seems to be going well and has already made considerable progress. It is called *Ecce Homo, or How One Becomes What One Is*. It concerns, with great audacity, myself and my writings: not only did I want to present myself *before* the uncannily solitary act of transvaluation, — I would also just like to *test* what risks I can take with the German ideas of *freedom of speech*. My suspicion is that the *first* book of the *Revaluation* will be confiscated on the spot, — legally and in all justice. With this *Ecce Homo*, I want to make the *question* so intensely serious, and such an object of curiosity, that current and basically sensible ideas about what is *permissible* will here admit an exception for once. To be sure, I talk about myself with all possible psychological "cunning" and gay detachment, — I do not want to present myself to people as a prophet, savage beast, or moral horror. In this sense, too, the book could be salutary: it will perhaps prevent people from *confusing* me with my anti-self.

I am very curious about your Kunstwart philanthropy. Did you know that I wrote Herr Avenarius in the summer an extremely blunt letter because of the way in which his paper dropped *Heinrich Heine?* — Blunt letters — with me a sign of gay detachment . . .

With most affectionate greetings and lots of ineffable wishes on the side, behind, and before (— "*One* thing is more necessary than the other" — thus spoke Zarathustra).

N.

ARLES

416.4 km from Torino

a great deal of work; people with the hands and stomach of a laborer; the instincts of a wild beast; blood and sex; an association of certain painters; the possibility of a great renaissance of art; serving only as intermediaries; the painting of the future; a page for Gauguin; don't listen to Vincent

1 November 1888

My dear old Bernard,

We've done a great deal of work these past few days, and in the meantime I've read Zola's *Le rêve*, so I've hardly had time to write.

Gauguin interests me greatly as a man — greatly. For a long time it has seemed to me that in our filthy job as painters we have the greatest need of people with the hands and stomach of a laborer. More natural tastes — more amorous and benevolent temperaments — than the decadent *&* exhausted Parisian man-about-town.

Now here, without the slightest doubt, we're in the presence of an unspoiled creature with the instincts of a wild beast. With Gauguin, blood and sex have the edge over ambition. But enough of that, you've seen him close at hand longer than I have, just wanted to tell you first impressions in a few words.

Next, I don't think it will astonish you greatly if I tell you that our discussions are tending to deal with the terrific subject of an association of certain painters. Ought or may this association have a commercial character, yes or no? We haven't reached any result yet, and haven't so much as set foot on a new continent yet. Now I, who have a presentiment of a new world, who certainly believe in the possibility of a great renaissance of art. Who believe that this new art will have the tropics for its homeland.

It seems to me that we ourselves are serving only as intermediaries. And that it will only be a subsequent generation that will succeed in living in peace. Anyway, all that, our duties and our possibilities for action could become clearer to us only through actual experience.

I was a little surprised not yet to have received the studies that you promised in exchange for mine.

Now something that will interest you — we've made some excursions in the brothels, and it's likely that we'll eventually go there often to work. At the moment Gauguin has a canvas in progress of the same night café that I also painted, but with figures seen in the brothels. It promises to become a beautiful thing.

I've made two studies of falling leaves in an avenue of poplars, and a third study of the whole of this avenue, entirely yellow.

I declare I don't understand why I don't do figure studies, while theoretically it's sometimes so difficult for me to imagine the painting of the future as anything other than a new series of powerful portraitists, simple & comprehensible to the whole of the general public. Anyway, perhaps I'll soon get down to doing brothels.

I'll leave a page for Gauguin, who will probably also write to you, and I shake your hand firmly in thought.

Ever yours,
Vincent

Milliet the 2ⁿᵈ lieut. Zouaves has left for Africa, & would be very glad if you were to write to him one of these days.

dear Bernard,

You will indeed do well to write him what your intentions are, so that he could take steps beforehand to prepare the way for you.

Mr. Milliet, *second lieutenant of Zouaves*, Guelma, Africa.

Don't listen to Vincent; as you know, he's prone to admire and ditto to be indulgent. His idea about the future of a new generation in the tropics seems absolutely right to me as a painter, and I still intend going back there when I find the funds. A little bit of luck, who knows?

Vincent has done two studies of falling leaves in an avenue, which are in my room and which you would like very much. On very coarse, but very good sacking.

Send news of yourself and of all the pals.

Yours,
Paul Gauguin

TORINO

416.4 km from Arles

*the autumn here was a real miracle of beauty and light,
— a permanent Claude Lorrain; the carbon-natron stove
is on the way; a tempo fortissimo; a person of extreme distinction; a concorso di bellezza; an event of cultural and
historical importance; the greatest Swedish writer has announced that he is for me; world raptures; gay detachment
fraught with a sense of destiny*

13 November 1888

Dear friend,

The fact that November 16 is a special day must excuse my writing so soon after my previous letter to you. Perhaps with you the winter has begun: it is almost with us here, — the nearest mountains are already wearing a vestigial wig. I hope the winter will match up to the autumn; at least, the autumn here was a real miracle of beauty and light, — a permanent Claude Lorrain. I have changed my ideas about what "good weather" means, and think very poorly of my having clung to Nizza. — My books, which I left there, are already on their way to Torino. While arranging for this I heard that my jolly table companion of those days, Frau von Brandeis, has arrived at the Pension de Genève. — The carbon-natron stove is also on the way, at a very decent price, for which I must give the Dresden man Nieske full credit. Today I bought a pair of superb English winter gloves. — With the best will in the world, dear old friend Overbeck, I cannot find anything bad to tell you about myself. Things continue to go well at a *tempo fortissimo* of work and wellbeing. Also people treat me here *comme il faut*, as a person of extreme distinction; the way they open the door for me is something utterly new to me. Admittedly, I visit only very good places, and also I rejoice in a classical tailor. — We recently had the melancholy pomp of a *great* funeral, in which the whole of Italy took part: that of Count Robilant, the most respected type of Piedimontese nobleman, actually also a son of King Carlo Alberto, as is well known here. In him Italy has lost an irreplaceable premier. — Something gay at the very same time: the beauties of the Torino aristocracy were most elated when the pictures of the first beauties to be crowned in *Spaa* arrived here. They at once planned a *concorso di bellezza* of their own for January — I think they all have a right to it! At the spring exhibition I saw just such a *concours* in *portraits*. Even our new lady of Torino, the Princess Laetitia Buonaparte, newly married to the Duke d'Aosta, is happy to join in. — Meanwhile I have received veritable acts of homage for my *Der Fall Wagner*. Not only has the work been called a psychological masterpiece of the first order, in a field where nobody till now has had eyes to see — in the psychology of the musician; also my revealing the décadent character of our music is *generally* called an event of cultural and historical importance that nobody except me could have brought about — my remarks on Brahms are said to be the last word in psycholog. sagacity. — Herr Spitteler expressed his rapture in the Thursday issue of *Der Bund*; Herr Köselitz, in *Der Kunstwart*; from Paris I am told that an article in the *Nouvelle Revue* is forthcoming. — There is other good news as well. The greatest Swedish writer — a "real genius," as Dr. Brandes writes — August Strindberg, has meanwhile announced that he is for me; also St. Petersburg society is seeking relations with me, which is made very difficult by the *ban* on my writings (Prince Urussov, Princess Anna Dimitrievna Tinichev). Lastly, the *charming* widow of Bizet! . . .

The printing of *Götzen-Dämmerung. Oder: Wie man mit dem Hammer philosophiert* is finished; the manuscript of *Ecce Homo: Wie man wird, was man ist* is already at the printer's. — The latter, an absolutely important book, gives some psychological *&* even biographical details about me *&* my writings: people will at last *suddenly see me.* The tone of the work, one of gay detachment fraught with a sense of destiny, as is everything I write. — Then at the end of next year the *first* book of the *Transvaluation* will appear. It is finished. —

With most affectionate good wishes on your birthday for your flourishing in body and soul.

Nietzsche

ARLES

416.4 km from Torino

Gauguin's canvas has arrived; chestnuts pulled out of the fire; what does selling any of it matter; I cannot and must not at this moment do anything other than work; Gauguin and I often talk about the need to hold exhibitions in London; we'll need some more colors; it does me enormous good to have company as intelligent as Gauguin; the red vision; the thousand obstacles to overcome; perseverance

19 November 1888

My dear Theo,

Gauguin's canvas, *Breton Children*, has arrived, and he's altered
it very, very well.

But although I quite like this canvas, it's all the better that
it should be sold, since the two he's going to send you from here
are thirty times better.

I'm speaking of the women picking grapes and the woman
with the pigs. The reason for this is that G. is beginning to overcome his liver or stomach trouble that has bothered him lately.

Now I'm writing to you in reply to what you were telling me,
that you would frame a small canvas of a pink peach tree I think,
to place it with those gentlemen.

I don't want to leave any doubt about what I think of that.

First, if you yourself would like to place either a bad or good
thing of mine there, my word if that will make you happier, then
of course you have and will have carte blanche either now or
later.

But if, on the other hand, it's either for my pleasure *or for my
own benefit*, I'd be of the opinion that it's completely unnecessary.

If you were to ask me what would give me pleasure, it's quite
simply one single thing, that you keep for yourself what you like
from what I do, in the apartment, and that you don't sell any of
it now.

The rest, the stuff that gets in the way, send it to me here for
this good reason, that everything I've done *from nature* is chestnuts pulled out of the fire.

Gauguin, in spite of himself and in spite of me, has proved to
me a little that it was time for me to vary things a bit — I'm beginning to compose from memory, and all my studies will still be
useful to me for that work, as they remind me of former things
I've seen.

So what does selling any of it matter if we're not absolutely
pressed for money?

For in addition, I'm sure even now that you'll eventually see
things that way.

As for you, you're with the Goupils, but I certainly am not, after however working there for 6 years we were absolutely dissatisfied on both sides with everything, them with me, me with them. It's an old story, but all the same that's how it is.

So continue on your way, but as far as the business is concerned it seems to me incompatible with my previous behavior to come back there with a canvas of such innocence as this little peach tree or some other thing like it. *No.* If in a year or two I have enough to make an exhibition of my own, let's say thirty or so no. 30 canvases —

And if I said to them, will you do it for me, Boussod would certainly send me packing. Knowing them alas a little too well, I think that I won't approach them. Not that I'd ever try to ruin anything, on the contrary, you must admit that I urge on all the others there zealously.

But as for me, my word I have an old grudge against them.

Be sure and certain that I consider you, as a seller of Impressionist paintings, to be very independent of the Goupils, that it will therefore always be a pleasure for me to urge artists to go there. But I don't want Boussod ever to have a chance to say "this little canvas isn't too bad for this young beginner," as if never before...

On the contrary, I won't come back to them; I'd prefer never to sell than to enter into it other than very straightforwardly. Now they're not people to act straightforwardly, so it isn't worth beginning again.

Be assured that the more clear-cut we are about this the more they'll come to you to see them. You don't sell them, so in showing my work you aren't trading outside the firm of Boussod, V. & Cie. Thus you're acting honestly, and that's worthy of respect.

If one or the other wants to buy however, fine, all they have to do is approach me directly. But be sure of this: if we can withstand the siege my day will come. I cannot and must not at this moment do anything other than work.

One thing however perhaps, I'm going to reply to Jet Mauve, tell her a whole heap of things about Gauguin &c. &c., send her some croquis, and indirectly Tersteeg will prick up his ears again.

Gauguin and I often talk about the need to hold exhibitions in London, and perhaps we'll send you a letter for Tersteeg to read. The thing is, should Tersteeg have an energetic successor — that day is approaching — the latter won't be able to work with anything but new paintings.

Handshake — we'll need some more colors.

I must also tell you that the month with the two of us together is going better on 150 each than I did on 250 just for myself. At the end of a year you'll notice that this is working after all.

I can't say anything more yet. I rather regret having the room full of canvases & having nothing to send when Gauguin sends his.

The thing is, regarding the impasto things, Gauguin has told me how to get rid of the grease by washing them from time to time.

What's more, when that's done I must work on them again to retouch them.

If I sent you any of them now, their color would be duller than it will be later.

They all think that what I've sent was done too hastily. I wouldn't deny it, and I'll make certain changes.

It does me enormous good to have company as intelligent as Gauguin and to see him work. You'll see that certain people are going to reproach G. for no longer doing Impressionism.

His two latest canvases, which you're going to see, are very firm in the impasto, there's even some work with the knife in them. And that will put his Breton canvases into the shade a little, not all, but some of them.

I hardly have the time to write, otherwise I'd already have written to those Dutchmen. I've had a letter from Boch, you know that Belgian who has a sister in the Vingtistes. He's enjoying working up there.

I really hope that we'll always remain friends with Gauguin, and in business with him, and if he succeeds in setting up a tropical studio that would be magnificent.

But that will take more money by my calculations than by his.

Guillaumin has written to Gauguin, he seems very hard up but must have done some fine work. He has a child now, but he was *terrified* by the confinement and says he'll always have 'the red vision' of it before his eyes. Only Gauguin has replied to him very well, saying that he, G., had seen it 6 times.

Jet Mauve is in much better health, and as you perhaps know has been living in The Hague since last August, near the Jewish cemetery, so almost in the country.

You won't lose anything by waiting a little while for my work, and we'll calmly leave our dear pals to scorn the present ones.

Fortunately for me I know what I want better than they believe and am, basically, extremely indifferent to the criticism of working hurriedly.

In reply I've produced work these last few days *even more* hurriedly.

Gauguin was telling me the other day — that he'd seen a painting by Claude Monet of sunflowers in a large Japanese vase, very fine. But — he likes mine better.

I'm not of that opinion — only don't think that I'm weakening. I regret as always, as you know, the scarcity of models, the thousand obstacles to overcome that difficulty.

If I were a completely different man and if I were wealthier I could *force* it, at present I'm not giving up and am plodding on quietly.

If at the age of forty I do a painting of figures like the flowers Gauguin was talking about I'll have a position as an artist alongside anything.

So, perseverance.

In the meantime I can tell you anyway that the last two studies are rather funny. No. 30 canvases, a wooden and straw *chair* all yellow on red tiles against a wall (*daytime*). Then Gauguin's armchair, red and green, night effect, on the seat two novels and a candle.

On sailcloth in thick impasto.

What I say about sending back studies, there's no hurry at all, and I'm referring to the bad ones which, however, will serve me as documents — or those that are cluttering up your apartment. As to what I say in general about the studies, I'm set on just one thing: that the position is quite clear. Don't trade on my behalf *outside the firm*; as for me, either I'll never return to the Goupils, which is more than likely, or I'll return straightforwardly, which is quite impossible.

One more handshake, & thanks for everything you're doing for me.

Ever yours,
Vincent

TORINO

*meaningful coincidences keep happening in my life now;
world historical cynicism; the foremost psychologist of
Christianity; we shall have the whole earth in convulsions;
I am a man of destiny; the vital instincts; Cesare Borgia as
Pope; Dostoevsky & Pascal, the only logical Christian; the
rapture of reading Strindberg*

20 November 1888

Verehrter Herr,

Forgive me for replying at once. Uniquely curious things, meaningful coincidences, keep happening in my life now. The day before yesterday and again today. — Ah, if only you knew what I
had just written when your letter paid me its visit...

I have now told my own story with a cynicism that will become world historical: the book is called *Ecce Homo*, and is an
assassination *attempt* without the slightest consideration for *the
crucified*; it ends by hurling such thunders and lightnings at everything Christian or infected by Christianity that one swoons. I
am, after all, the foremost psychologist of Christianity, and can,
as an old artilleryman, bring up some heavy guns, whose very
existence no opponent of Christianity had ever suspected. — The
whole work is the prelude to the *"transvaluation of values,"* of
the work that lies finished before me; I swear to you that in two
years we shall have the whole earth in convulsions. I am a man
of destiny. —

— Can you guess who comes off worst in *Ecce Homo*? The
Germans! — I have told them terrible things... The Germans,
for example, have on their conscience the fact that they robbed
the last *great* period in history, the Renaissance, of its meaning
— at a moment when Christian values, the décadence values, had
been defeated, when in the instincts of the highest priestly caste
they had been *overcome* by counter-instincts, the vital instincts!...
To *attack* the Church — that meant restoring Christianity. —
Cesare Borgia as Pope — that would have been the *goal* of the
Renaissance, its real symbol...

— Also you should not be annoyed that you yourself appear
at a decisive point in the book — I was writing it just now —
in connection with my stigmatizing the conduct of my *German*
friends toward me, their having been absolutely abandoned by
honor and by philosophy. — You suddenly appear, in a nice cloud
of glory...

I completely believe what you say about Dostoevsky; I prize
his work, on the other hand, as the most valuable psychological

material known to me, — I am grateful to him in a remarkable way, however much he goes against my deepest instincts. Roughly as in my relation to Pascal, whom I almost love because he has taught me such an infinite amount: the only *logical* Christian.

— Yesterday I read, with rapture and feeling altogether at home, *Les mariés* by Herr August Strindberg. My most unreserved admiration, which is marred only by the feeling that in admiring him I also admire myself a little. Torino *remains* my residence.

Your Nietzsche, now *Monster*

To what address shall I send you a copy of *Götzen-Dämmerung Or: How to Philosophize with a Hammer*? If you will be in Copenhagen for the next 14 days, no reply is needed. —

INTERVAL: ARLES

The Studio of the South: *dueling* perspectives
416.4 km from Torino

28–31 October 1888

As the old artillery man continues to work on *Ecce Homo*, his exalted counter tale to the fable of Christ, punctuating the composition of his book with Wagnerian improvisations on the piano and unbridled naked dances in his room, Vincent and Gauguin drive further onward into their utopic enterprise, a vision the mad painter has not only for himself and his time, but for the future:

I venture to hope, Vincent writes his brother, that in six months Gauguin and you and I will all see that we have founded a little studio that will last.

And so the activities of the Yellow House, the legendary Studio of the South, continue, with the two artists splitting an immense roll of jute sackcloth that Gauguin bought for them to paint on and which they treated with liquid barium sulfate.

Combined with Vincent's thick application of paint, the material endows his images with a texture not unlike the medieval embroideries similar to those described by Zola in *Le rêve*, a novel Vincent was then reading. With the jute sackcloth, Gauguin's impact upon the painter is evident, with the Dutchman moving carefully but hesitantly toward abstraction and, sometimes, albeit with doubts, composing from memory, as he was not usually wont to do.

Packing up their gear to head outdoors, Vincent takes Gauguin to one of his beloved sites, the ancient cemetery, Les Alyscamps, to set up their easels to paint side by side.

And so they stood before the poplar and sarcophagi-lined avenue as if before history.

Adjacent to them, just across the Craponne Canal, were railway factories, and in the distance, the Chapel of Saint-Honorat.

In Paris, polemics continue over La dame de fer and the Nabi artists unite to form an informal clan of painters whose synthetic union of metaphors and symbols sought through abstraction to break open new dimensions of art. In the Rue de Rome, Mallarmé foments yet other visions, ready to soon gamble with white space, breaking open the white page as Einstein would soon break open and distend space and time.

Before his easel, Gauguin directs his focus to a single point or perspective, omitting the railway factory at his left and subverting reality, as he stages a group of female figures as the Provençale cousins of Carmen, or the three Graces. The stone structure in the distance may as well be an ancient Roman or Greek ruin, not a church, for Gauguin has stripped it of its spire, giving it a rounded dome & high, open archways. Sky, clouds, and canal line one half of his painting, a calm, bucolic field of blue and white, while the other half is hot, with its burning yellow leaves, its sensuous flame-tongued poplars, and its single vibrant red bush, crouching as if poised to leap upon the approaching graces, or to protect them like a terrifying, riddle-bearing Sphinx or organic talisman. What questions, what enigmas reside in this moment?

Vincent directs his eye differently, widening his field of vision to include the Chapel of Saint-Honorat, the Roman sarcophagi, and the railway factories with their smoking chimneys. Here, many of the hard, ugly facts of reality are not subverted or made mythic, but given prominence, painted as they are seen, with the chimneys towering into the sky, higher than the church spire, but not higher than the poplar trees, which exceed the frame of the canvas as if stretching beyond, to the infinite ~

Whereas Gauguin transforms the characters in his work, Vincent makes his modern, with his single Arlésienne walking astride a Zouave with red pants and hat, no different than the wandering lovers of his day. One plane of sight aligns the sarcophagi with the church, as if to suggest it is equally dead and buried, the relic of a defunct, irrelevant civilization. A higher plane aligns the vibrant trees with the sky, both of which are depicted with upward, wavy brush strokes, intimating the presence of a bristling and incandescent life force, entities growing and pulsing with energy, entities that the painter of the future absorbs and takes into his being, which is becoming-tree and becoming-sky.

*

And so, the two painters of the Studio of the South make up their own community or guild, working to reach what Vincent called a height equivalent to the serene summits that the Greek sculptors, the German musicians, the writers of French novels reached, all of which he says is beyond the power of an isolated individual.

Such summits are reached by guilds combining to execute a commonly held idea. The material difficulties of a painter's life make collaboration, the uniting of painters, desirable (as much so as in the days of the Guilds of St. Luke). By safeguarding our material existence, the proselytizer attests to Theo, by loving each other like comrades-in-arms instead of cutting each other's throats, painters would be happier, and in any case less ridiculous, less foolish, and less culpable.

Throughout this time, Vincent & Gauguin read newspapers and novels, visit brothels, and continue painting outdoors when the mistral isn't about; when it is, they paint in cafes and in their studio, growing ever closer in confinement.

We are working hard, Vincent writes Theo, and our life together goes very well.

In *Le Figaro* and *Gazette des Tribunaux*, just as did Nietzsche, Gauguin and Vincent read of the infamous throat-cutting Prado, and Jack the Ripper, with tales of the latter including macabre details such as the hacking up of one victim whose right ear was also cut off.

As minor tumults erupt throughout the world, the painters engage in duels of a sort, making dual portraits of Madame Ginoux, varying versions of the night café, and other works. It is an æsthetic agon, if not war of souls. They fight for their time, and for a future.

In early November, as a storm fulminated with considerable intensity, keeping the artists contained within their small abode, surrounded by brushes, half-squeezed paint tubes, easels, stretchers, and canvases in progress, they worked on yet other pictures, from memory and imagination, by the luminosity of gaslight. What of the storm entered and altered the composition of their bodies? What fulminations did they unknowingly incorporate, like paint fumes in the night? What subtle, subatomic alterations occurred at the cellular level?

When completed, some of Vincent's paintings hung in a position of honor on the wall of Gauguin's bedroom, adjacent to prints by Daumier, Delacroix, and various Japanese artists, and so Vincent's brush strokes, the rhythms and movements of his soul, entered Gauguin's night, his corpuscles susceptive to outward radiations.

Pipe smoke and the scent of oil from uncapped paint tubes filled the air, too, due to Vincent's unkempt manner, often unnerving Gauguin, the tobacco smoke entering his flesh, the resin, additives, solvent, and pigment of Vincent's oils entering his flesh, Vincent also then almost entering his flesh, imperceptibly, like the breath of the Horla moving through the cold night air, oxygen crossing the thresholds of doorways, oxygen crossing the thresholds of flesh.

With Gauguin now serving as cook, the painters frequently take their meals at home, confined even more these winter months, two vastly different nervous systems straining to the threshold of their pressure points as the fire and coal smoke burned to warm them.

Vincent frantic, rapid in gesture, nervous in speech and manner, almost lunging back and forth before his canvas like an animal, then attacking it with a leap, a stroke here, a stroke there, then, rushing back to his chair to give his actions a swift glance.

Gauguin withdrawn, quiet, steady, his gait slow, his gestures sober, his whole physical being almost seemingly stone-like, impassive, still and solid, like some immobile edifice. All this while painting his work *Human Miseries*...

*

Later, Gauguin would reflect upon this mostly blissful beginning and state, between two such beings as he *&* I, the one a perfect volcano, the other boiling inwardly, some sort of struggle was preparing.

Meanwhile, if unbeknownst to the world, two men were performing there a colossal labor that was valuable to them both. Perhaps to others? Perhaps, could it be, to the world? There are some things, Gauguin said, that bear fruit.

To his brother, whom he extolled as the first dealer-apostle, Vincent would write, I can see my own painting coming to life, and likewise a work among the artists. I feel that we are working in a great and good enterprise, which has nothing to do with the old kind of commerce. Here I become more *&* more like Japanese painters, living close to nature like petty tradesmen. That, as you well know, is a less lugubrious affair than the decadent's way.

ARLES

416.4 km from Torino

working, working always; to try to work from the imagination; I'm really in the shit; joy in town, grief at home; we still have a whole battle to fight; Gauguin works a lot; beware of the Bernard family; Gauguin has been invited to exhibit at the Vingtistes

1 December 1888

My dear Theo,

On my side, too, it's more than time that I wrote to you with a
rested mind for once. Thanks first of all for your kind letter and
for the 100-franc note it contained. Our days pass in working,
working always, in the evening we're worn out and go to the café
before retiring to bed early. That's our existence. Naturally it's
winter here too, although the weather still continues to be very
fine from time to time. But I don't find it disagreeable to try to
work from the imagination, since that permits me not to go out.
Working in the heat of a stove doesn't bother me, but the cold
isn't for me, as you know. Only I've spoiled that thing I did of the
garden at Nuenen and I feel that habit is also necessary for works
of the imagination. But I've done the portraits of *an entire family*,
the family of the postman whose head I did before — the man,
his wife, the baby, the young boy and the 16-year-old son, all
characters and very French, although they have a Russian look.
No. 15 canvases. You can sense how in my element that makes
me feel, and that it consoles me to a certain extent for not being
a doctor.

I hope to persevere with this and be able to obtain more serious sittings, which can be paid for with portraits.

And if I manage to do *this entire family* even better, I'll have
done at least one thing to my taste and personal.

At the moment I'm really in the shit, studies, studies, studies,
and that'll go on for some time yet — such a mess that it breaks
my heart — and yet that'll give me neatness when I'm 40. From
time to time a canvas that makes a painting, such as that sower,
which I too think is better than the first one.

If we can withstand the siege, a day of victory will come for
us, even though we wouldn't be among the people who are being
talked about. It's rather a case of thinking of that proverb, joy
in town, grief at home.

What can you expect? Supposing that we still have a whole
battle to fight, then we must try to mature calmly. You've always told me to do more quality than quantity. Now, nothing is

preventing us from having a lot of studies classed as such, and consequently not having a whole heap of things for sale. And if sooner or later we're *obliged* to sell, then selling at a slightly higher price the things that can hold their own from the point of view of serious research.

I think that — in spite of myself — I won't be able to prevent myself sending you a few canvases shortly, *say within a month*. I say in spite of myself, for I'm convinced that the canvases gain from drying right through here in the south, to the point where the impasto is thoroughly hardened, which takes a long time — that's to say a year. If I restrain myself from sending them that would certainly be best. For we don't need to show them at the moment, I'm well enough aware of that.

Gauguin works a lot — I very much like a still life with yellow background and foreground. He's working on a portrait of me that I don't count as one of his undertakings that don't come to anything.

At present he's doing landscapes, and finally he has a good canvas of washerwomen, even very good as I see it.

You should receive two of Gauguin's drawings in return for 50 francs that you sent him in Brittany. But old mother Bernard simply appropriated them. Speaking of indescribable stories, this is indeed one. I think that she'll give them back though in the end. Beware of the Bernard *family*, but you should know that in my opinion Bernard's work is very fine and that he'll have some well-deserved success in Paris.

Very interesting that you met Chatrian. Is he blond or dark? I'd like to know that, since I know the two portraits.

In their work, it's above all Madame Thérèse *&* L'ami Fritz that I like.

As regards *L'histoire d'un sous-maître*, it seems to me that there's more to find fault with than seemed possible to me at the time.

I think we'll end up spending our evenings drawing *&* writing, there's more to work on than we can do.

You know that Gauguin has been invited to exhibit at the Vingtistes. His imagination is already leading him to think of settling in Brussels, which would indeed be a means of finding himself in a position to see his Danish wife again. Since he has some success with the Arlésiennes in the meantime, I wouldn't consider that as being absolutely without consequences.

He's married and doesn't much appear to be, in short I fear there may be an absolute incompatibility of character between his wife and himself, but naturally he's more attached to his children, who judging from the portraits are very beautiful. We, on the other hand, aren't too gifted in that respect.

More soon, a handshake for you and for the Dutchmen.

Vincent

Gauguin will write to you tomorrow, he's waiting for a reply to his letter and sends his warm regards.

TORINO

416.4 km from Arles

something monstrous announces itself; there is nothing fanatical about me; my truth is terrible; a happy ambassador, *the man of doom; there will be wars as there have never been wars before*

announcing my hostility; the only request I have ever been of the mind to make

this masterpiece of hard psychology; the hereditary criminal; Prado; there are no more coincidences in my life; a poet of the first rank; it speaks the language of the rulers of the world; the "Prado" style; declaring war; I am strong enough to break the history of mankind in two

To Kaiser Wilhelm II (draft)

I hereby pay the Emperor of the Germans the highest honor that can be due to him, an honor which is all the more weighty as I have to overcome my deep aversion to everything that is German in order to do so: I am giving him the *first* copy of one Work in hand, with which the nearness of something monstrous announces itself — of a crisis such as there was not on earth, of the deepest collision of conscience within mankind, of a decision conjured up *against* everything that was previously believed, had been demanded, sanctified. — And with all this there is nothing fanatical about me: whoever knows me, considers me a modest, at most a slightly mischievous scholar who knows how to be cheerful with everyone. This writing gives, I hope, a completely different picture than that of a "prophet": and in spite of this, or rather *not* in spite of it — because all prophets have been liars up to now — the *truth* speaks out of me. — But my truth is *terrible*: because up to now the *lie* was called truth ... *Revaluation of all values*: that is my formula for an act of the highest self-reflection of mankind, — my lot wants me to go deeper, more courageously, to look more *righteously* into the questions of all times than any other human could before. I do not challenge what is alive now, I challenge several millennia against me: I contradict and am nevertheless the antithesis of a *nay-saying* spirit ... There are new hopes, there are goals, tasks of a magnitude for which we lacked the concept until now: I am a *happy ambassador* par excellence, however much I must be the man of doom ... For when this volcano becomes active, we will have convulsions on earth such as never before: the concept of politics has merged completely with a war of spirits, all power structures have been blown to bits, — there will be wars as there have never been wars before. —

To Otto von Bismarck (draft)

His Serene Highness Prince Bismarck.
I do the first statesman of our time the honor of announcing
my hostility to him by presenting him with the *first* copy of *Ecce
Homo*. I enclose a second copy: to put it in the hands of the young
German emperor would be the only request I have ever been of
the mind to make of Prince Bismarck. —

The Antichrist
Friedrich Nietzsche.
Fromentin

Turin, via Carlo Alberto 6, III

Finally, in order not to do anything halfway, it must be forgiven
me if I enclose two copies of my last published work: in it the
scientific presuppositions of my way of thinking are stated with
all the clarity that I could wish for.

8 December 1888

Sehr lieber und werter Herr:

Has a letter of mine been lost? The moment I had finished reading your *Père* for a *second* time, I wrote you a letter, deeply impressed by this masterpiece of *hard* psychology; I also expressed
to you my conviction that your work is predestined to be performed in Paris *now*, in the Théâtre Libre of M. Antoine — you
should simply demand it of Zola! —

— The *hereditary* criminal is decadent, even an idiot — no
doubt about that! But the history of criminal families, for which
the Englishman Galton (*The Hereditary Genius*) has collected the
largest body of material, points constantly back to an *excessively
strong* person where a certain social level is the case. The latest
great criminal case in Paris, that of Prado, presented the classic
type: Prado was superior to his judges, even to his lawyers, in self-
control, wit, & exuberance of spirit; nevertheless, the *pressure*
of the accusation had so reduced him physiologically that some
witnesses could recognize him only from the old portraits. —

But now a word or two between ourselves, very much between ourselves! When your letter reached me yesterday — the
first letter in my life to *reach* me — I had just finished the last
revision of the manuscript of *Ecce Homo*. Since there are no more
coincidences in my life, you are consequently not a coincidence.
Why do you write letters that arrive at such a moment!... *Ecce
Homo* should indeed appear simultaneously in German, French,
and English. Yesterday I sent the manuscript to my printer; as
soon as a sheet is ready, it must go to the translators. *But who are
these translators?* Honestly I did not know that you yourself are
responsible for the excellent French of your *Père*; I thought that
it must be a masterly translation. If you were to undertake the
French translation yourself, I would be overjoyed at this miracle
of meaningful coincidence. For, between ourselves, it would take
a poet of the first rank to translate *Ecce Homo*; in its language,
in the refinement of its feeling, it is a thousand miles beyond
any mere "translator." Actually, it is not a thick book; I suppose
it would be, in the French edition (perhaps with *Lemerre*, Paul

Bourget's publisher! —) priced at about 3 frs. 50. Since it says unheard-of things and, sometimes, in all innocence, speaks the language of the *rulers of the world*, the number of editions will surpass even *Nana* ... On the other hand, it is *anti-German* to an annihilating extent; throughout, I side with *French* culture (— I treat all the German philosophers as "unconscious counterfeiters," I call the young emperor a *bleedin' ponce* ...). Also the book is not boring, — at points I even wrote it in the "Prado" style ... To secure myself against German brutalities ("confiscation" —) I shall send the *first* copies, before publication, to Prince Bismarck and the young emperor with letters *declaring war*: military men *cannot* reply to that with police measures. — I am a *psychologist.* —

Consider it, verehrter Herr! It is a matter of the first importance. For I am strong enough to break the history of mankind in two. —

There is still the question of the *English* translation. Would you have any suggestion? — An *anti-German* book in England ...

Very devotedly,
Your
Nietzsche.

ARLES

416.4 km from Torino

a little disheartened; grave difficulties; he'll either definitely go or he'll definitely stay; — I am obliged to return to Paris; incompatibility of temperament

11 December 1888

My dear Theo,

Thank you very much for your letter, for the 100-franc note enclosed with it, and also the 50-franc money order.

I myself think that Gauguin had become a little disheartened by the good town of Arles, by the little yellow house where we work, and above all by me.

Indeed, there are bound to be grave difficulties still to overcome here, for him as well as for me.

But these difficulties are rather within ourselves than elsewhere.

All in all, I think personally that he'll either definitely go or he'll definitely stay. I told him to think and do his sums again before acting.

Gauguin is very strong, very creative, but precisely because of that he must have peace.

Will he find it elsewhere if he doesn't find it here?

I'm waiting with absolute serenity for him to make a decision. Good handshake.

Vincent

Theo,

I should be obliged if you would send me part of the money for the paintings that have been sold. Taking everything into account I am obliged to return to Paris; Vincent and I can absolutely not live side by side without trouble, as a result of incompatibility of temperament, and both he and I need tranquility for our work. He is a man of remarkable intelligence, whom I greatly respect and whom I leave with regret, but I repeat, it is necessary.

Paul

TORINO

416.4 km from Arles

genius, it cannot be formulated; Nietzsche contra Wagner: a characterization of opposite poles; treating the Germans with Spanish mischievousness; the tragic catastrophe of my life; Piedimontese cuisine; I eat like a prince, I eat an excellent portion of ice cream; glorious grapes; a glorious letter from M. Taine

Sunday, 16 December 1888

Dear friend,

Important extension of the concept of "operetta." *Spanish* operetta. *La gran via*, heard *twice* — main feature, from Madrid. Simply cannot be imported: one would have to be a rogue and the
devil of an instinctive fellow — and *solemn* at the same time...
A trio of three solemn old gigantic villains is the strongest thing
that I have heard *and seen* — *also* as music: genius, it cannot
be formulated... Since I now know a great deal of Rossini and
am familiar with 8 operas, I took my favorite one, *Cenerentola*,
as an example for comparison — it is a thousand times too
kindhearted when compared to the Spaniards. You see, only a
complete *rogue* could think out even the plot — it is just like a
conjuring trick the way the villains flash like lightning into view.
Four or five pieces of music that must be *heard*; for the rest, the
Viennese waltz in the form of *larger ensembles* predominates. —
Offenbach's *Schöne Helena* coming *after* it was a sorry falling-off.
I left. — It lasts exactly 1 hour.
　　— This afternoon I plan to hear a *requiem* by the old Neapoli-
tan Jommelli (died in 1774): *Accademia di canto corale*. —
　　And now the *important* thing. Yesterday I sent to C.G. Nau-
mann a manuscript that must be dealt with at once, before *Ecce
Homo*. I cannot find *translators* for *Ecce Homo*; I must postpone
the printing for a few months. After all, there is no hurry. The
new thing you will like: — you appear in it, — and in what a way!
— It is called

Nietzsche contra Wagner.
Documents
of a Psychologist.

　　Essentially it is a characterization of *opposite* poles, in which
I have used several passages from my earlier writings, and in
this way have written the *very serious* pendant to *Der Fall Wagner*. This has not prevented me from treating the Germans with
Spanish mischievousness in it — the book (about three sheets in
length) is extremely *anti-German*. At the end there is something
of which even my friend Gast has no idea: a song (or whatever

you want to call it...) of Zarathustra, called "On the Poverty of the Richest" — you know, a little seventh heaven in which one-eighth is... *music*...

— Occasionally nowadays I see no reason why I should accelerate too much the *tragic* catastrophe of my life, which begins with *Ecce*. The *new* work will perhaps, because of the curiosity aroused by *Der Fall Wagner*, be widely read — and since I never write a sentence now in which the *whole* of me is not present, then the *psychologist's antithesis* will also be a way for people to understand me — la gran via...

Avenarius, whose fingers I have touched with a mischievous little letter, has apologized most politely and kindly — I think I have dealt very well with *this* matter. (Ask for a few more *copies* of *Der Kunstwart!*)

Just think, dear friend! Piedimontese *cuisine*! Ah, my *trattoria*! I had no idea what experts the Italians were in the *art* of cooking! — *and* in the quality! Not for nothing is one living in the most famous cattle-breeding part of the country! — And, altogether, though I eat like a prince, a *lot* too, I pay for each meal (10 ct. tip included!) 1 fr. 25. — For an apartment, including very good service, prime location in the city, sun room comme il faut, 25 per month.

Evenings I sit in a splendid high room; a small, *very nice* orchestra (piano, 4 string instruments, 2 wind instruments) plays so quietly, just as I would wish — there are 3 adjoining rooms. My paper is brought to me, *Journal des Débats* — I eat an excellent portion of ice cream: costs, including the tip (which I pay, since it is the custom here) 40 ct. — In the *Galleria Subalpina* (into which I look down when I leave my lodging), the most beautiful, most elegant room of this kind I know; they play now, evening after evening, *The Barber of Seville*, and *excellently* too: one pays slightly more for what one eats. — And how *good* the city looks when it is overcast! Recently I said to myself: to have a place that *one does not want to leave*, not even to go into the countryside, where one is glad to walk *the streets*! — earlier I would have thought it impossible. —

In friendship.
Your N.

Last, *not* least: All the people who have anything to do with me now, right down to the peddler woman, who picks out glorious grapes for me, are people just as they should be, and very polite, serene, a little fat, — even the waiter.

— *Prince von Carignano* has just died: we shall have a great funeral. — A *glorious* letter has just arrived from M. Taine! —

ARLES

416.4 km from Torino

Yesterday Gauguin and I went to Montpellier; Bruyas was a benefactor to artists; Tasso in the Madhouse; lithographs of ancient and modern artists; Gauguin and I talk — the discussion is excessively electric; in the midst of magic; Gauguin could feel his old self coming back; tired & almost fainting mentally; a life with painters as pals; a bad dream

17 December 1888

My dear Theo,

Yesterday Gauguin and I went to Montpellier to see the museum there, and especially the Bruyas room — there are many portraits of Bruyas, by Delacroix, by Richard, by Courbet, by Cabanel, by Couture, by Verdier, by Tassaert, by others too. After that there are paintings by Delacroix, Courbet, Giotto, Paul Potter, Botticelli, T. Rousseau, very fine.

Bruyas was a benefactor to artists, and this is all I'll say to you: in the Delacroix portrait, he's a gentleman with a beard, red hair, who looks damnably like you or me, and who made me think of that poem by Musset... everywhere I touched the earth, an unfortunate man dressed in black came to sit beside us, a man who looked at us like a brother. It would have the same effect on you, I'm sure.

I'd really ask you to go and see, at that bookshop where they sell lithographs of ancient and modern artists, if you could manage to get the lithograph after Delacroix's *Tasso in the Madhouse* without great expense, since it would seem to me that this figure (by Delacroix) must have some relationship to this fine Bruyas portrait.

They have other Delacroixs there, a study of a mulatto woman (which Gauguin once copied), the Odalisques, Daniel in the lions' den.

By Courbet, first, *The Village Girls*, magnificent, a nude woman seen from the back, another on the ground, in a landscape. Second, *The Woman Spinning* (superb), and a whole load more Courbets. Anyway, you must know that this collection exists, or else know people who have seen it, and consequently be able to talk about it. So I shan't insist on the museum (except for the Barye drawings & bronzes!).

Gauguin and I talk a lot about Delacroix, Rembrandt &c. The discussion is *excessively electric*. We sometimes emerge from it with tired minds, like an electric battery after it's run down.

We've been right in the midst of magic, for as Fromentin says so well, Rembrandt is above all a magician and Delacroix a man of God, of God's thunder and bugger off in the name of God.

I'm writing this to you with reference to our friends, the Dutchmen De Haan & Isaäcson, who have so sought and loved Rembrandt, in order to encourage you to pursue the researches.

One mustn't get discouraged about that. You know the strange and superb portrait of a man by Rembrandt at the La Caze gallery, I told Gauguin that, for me, I saw in it a certain family or racial resemblance to Delacroix, or to him, Gauguin.

I don't know why, but I always call that portrait *"the traveller"* or *"the man coming from far away."*

That's an equivalent and parallel idea to what I've already told you, always to look at the portrait of old Six. The fine portrait with the glove for your future, and the Rembrandt etching, Six reading by a window in a ray of sunlight, for your past and your present.

That's the stage we're at.

Gauguin said to me this morning, when I asked him how he felt: "that he could feel his old self coming back," which gave me great pleasure.

As for me, coming here last winter, tired and almost fainting mentally, I too suffered a little inside before I was able to begin to remake myself.

How I'd like you to see that museum in Montpellier some day, there are some really beautiful things there!

Say so to Degas, that Gauguin and I have been to see the portrait of Bruyas by Delacroix at Montpellier, for we must boldly believe that *what is, is,* and the portrait of Bruyas by Delacroix resembles you and me like a new brother.

As regards setting up a life with painters as pals, you see such odd things and I'll end with what you always say, time will tell.

You can tell all this to our friends Isaäcson and De Haan, and even boldly read them this letter, I would already have written to them if I'd felt the necessary electric force.

On behalf of Gauguin as well as myself, a good, hearty hand-shake to you all.

Ever yours,
Vincent

If you think that Gauguin or I have a *facility* in our work, the work isn't always accommodating. And for the Dutchmen not to get discouraged in their difficulties any more than we do, that's what I wish for them, and for you too.

From Gauguin:

Please consider my trip to Paris as something imaginary and therefore the letter that I wrote you as a bad dream ... We have been to Montpellier and Vincent is writing you his impressions.

TORINO

416.4 km from Arles

I now absolutely have to become known in England; the horned cattle breed of the Germans; I want to destroy Christianity; malicious Parisian writing; I am not a person at all, I am dynamite; Mr. Taine wrote me an invaluable letter

17 December 1888

Dear Fraulein,

You would do me a great service if you would translate the following article by Peter Gast under the title "Nietzsche *contra*
Wagner" for one of the great reviews. I now absolutely have to
become known in England, for my next writings — they are completely ready for printing — are to appear in English, French,
and German at the same time. The *horned* cattle breed of the
Germans — sorry for the strong word! — is completely alien to
me; they will defend themselves against me with confiscations
and other police measures. So for my task, which is one of the
greatest that a person can undertake — I want to *destroy* Christianity — America, England, and France are necessary — freedom
of the press in every sense...

I remember reading in an issue of the *Journal des Débats*
that an English magazine (*Century Review* or similar —) had very
energetically opened the fight against Wagner. If you feel like it,
I will send you my writing. It is malicious beyond measure and
could more easily have been written by a Parisian.

Right now something extremely radical appears from me:
*Twilight of the Idols. Or: How to Philosophize with a Hammer.** I
am sending it to you — you may introduce this piece in England.
It's anti-German and anti-Christian par excellence — shouldn't
it have a strong impact upon the English? My arguments are of
a completely different kind than have ever been used — I am not
a person at all, I am dynamite.

I hope my letter meets you in a courageous and war-ready
condition? —

Very devotedly,
Nietzsche

— Mr. *Peter Gast* is one of our first musicians or, if you want to
believe me, by far the first — he can do what the rarest can do
at all times, the *perfect*. I am honored to have such a "disciple."

N.

— Mr. Taine wrote me an invaluable letter about *Twilight of the Idols*, full of admiration for "toutes mes audaces et finesses." I am currently in negotiations, on M. Taine's advice, with the excellent editor-in-chief of the *Journal des Débats* and the *Revue des deux Mondes*, Ms. Bourdeau, whom he recommended to me as one of the most intelligent and influential French: the same should take the steps to prepare translation of the work.

* The title could be simplified: *Götzen-Hammer*

ARLES

416.4 km from Torino

My situation here is painful; a good heart that is sick; my departure will always be imminent

22 December 1888

Dear Schuff,

You await me with open arms, I thank you for that, but unfortunately I am not coming yet. My situation here is painful; I owe a great deal to van Gogh and Vincent and despite some discord, I cannot blame a good heart that is sick and that needs me. Do you remember the life of Edgar Poe, who became an alcoholic as a result of grief and a nervous condition? One day I shall explain it fully.

In any case I am staying here, but my departure will always be imminent.

Paul

INTERVAL:
ARLES, PARIS, TORINO

Christmas celebrations

End of December 1888

Within a close cluster of days, as December 1888 was coming to a close and civilization was pressing toward the '90s, verging that is on the denouement of the 19th century and the explosion of the 20th, life in the Studio of the South was reaching its own mistralic denouement.

The Ictuses, or suffering evangelists for a new art, were each bleeding in their own way, and when Vincent saw Gauguin's portrait of him, *The Painter of Sunflowers*, he said, It's me, but it's me gone mad.

The Horla, as if some kind of mythic demon, would often grow excessively rough and noisy, then silent, as if a terrible monstrosity were forming inside of him, like the magma of a volcano growing ebullient. But, had he not been taking on so many foreign elements, opening himself to radical forms of becoming, to volatile circuits, conjunctions, and levels and thresholds where various types of strata cross, intermingle, and blend?

On several nights, Gauguin wrote, I surprised Vincent in the act of getting up and coming over to my bed and standing over me. After sternly questioning him, the Horla would return to his room and fall into a deep sleep.

Another day, while at the night café, after drinking some absinthe, Vincent flung the glass and its contents at Gauguin's head. The painter avoided the attack, thrust his host to the side, then carried him out of the café and put him to bed.

The next morning, Gauguin told Vincent that yesterday's scene might occur again & if I were struck I might lose control of myself and throttle you. So permit me to write to your brother *&* tell him I am coming back.

But the mistralic tempest passed, and the waters calmed after a journey to a museum in Montpellier, when visions of new paintings took hold of each of the men.

During this time, Vincent likened himself to a frail vessel at sea, tossed by every storm, and the idea came to him for a painting of sailors, who are at once children and martyrs, and seeing the storm in the cabin of their Icelandic fishing boat, would feel the old sense of being rocked come over them *&* remember their own lullabies.

My dear friend, Vincent exulted, to achieve in painting what the music of Berlioz and Wagner has already done — an art that offers consolation for the broken-hearted! There are still just a few who feel it as you and I do!!!

Not much later, there was a hard frost, a spell of several days of intense rain, and news reports stating that the execution of Prado was at hand. While in the weeks that had passed, the frail vessel was monstrously prolific, painting over 20 works, Gauguin had sold a number of paintings, and with his coming, and hopefully continuing bounty, the former stockbroker envisioned a new existence in Martinique, for which he would leave in May of 1889, if not much sooner.

With life assured for 18 months, the painter of the tropics wrote his friend Schuffenecker, I will almost be a happy mortal. All the acolytes who love and understand me will follow after me. The commune of the tropics! Think of it.

In pursuit of his own utopia, envisioning his apotheosis, and having a band of followers, the painter noted to his friend that Vincent sometimes calls me the man who has come from far away and will go far.

Other communes were in germination too. In a letter, Theo announced to Vincent his upcoming marriage, making the painter doubt whether his brother would remain devoted to his role of being the dealer-apostle or if, like too many others, he would become yet another procreating bourgeois middle class bastard who would abandon the pursuit of art. Was not the world already becoming overpopulated? Did it need yet more children?

On Sunday, while Vincent was working on *La Berceuse*, sensing that Gauguin was elsewhere, he asked the painter if he was going to leave.

When I answered yes, Vincent tore this sentence from a newspaper and thrust it into my hand:

The murderer took flight.

Gauguin ignored his friend's cryptic and unsettling gesture and, after cooking for them both and bolting down his own meal, went out for a walk. Only moments later, he heard the sound of an onrush of short, harried, frantic footsteps.

Quickly turning 'round, the painter of the tropics came face to face with the Horla who, brandishing an open razor, told him, You are silent, but I will also be silent.

After Gauguin stared down the storm-wracked painter, the Horla lowered his head, held the razor tight, and set off running to the Studio of the South.

*

As Gauguin slept in a hotel that night, in a delirium, beset by a whorl of terrifying voices, biblical and literary texts swirling in his head, the gospels, *The Sin of Father Mouret*, murders, mutilations, persecutions, the agony of the garden, the agony of utopias, the agony of the spirit, like some storm-thrashed sailor, thrust to a threshold, the Horla took his razor and, to put cease to the frightful din, cut off nearly the entirety of his ear, severing his auricular artery, blood discharging from his neck, spurting violently outward as he ambled through the house, discoloring the rooms and the short staircase that led to the bedrooms of the painters.

I was searching, he later said, for an arrangement of colors I could not find...

Once he staunched his wound, the Horla carefully washed the severed fragment of himself, wrapped it in newspaper, put on a beret, exited the Yellow House, crossed Place Lamartine, crossed through the gateway in the town wall, walked to the brothel at 1 Rue du Bout d'Arles, asked if he could see Rachel (Gaby?), and when she appeared, bestowed upon her his gift, saying, *Guard this object very carefully*, returned to the Yellow House, ascended the blood-spattered stairs, set a candle in his window, sang an old nurse's song, because he was dreaming of the song that the woman rocking the cradle sang to rock the sailors to sleep, then himself fell into a dark, dark sleep.

The next morning, upon reaching the Yellow House to collect his things and depart for Paris, Gauguin came upon a crowd in the square, including gendarmes and the Police Commissioner, a figure he had satirized in his drawings. It was Christmas Eve, but the red-stained Yellow House was not festooned crimson with Christmas decorations... The painter was immediately arrested for, at the proliferation *&* spectacle of blood, it was thought that the savage painter of the islands had murdered the feral Dutchman.

It took Gauguin a long time to get his wits together and control the beating of his heart. Anger, indignation, grief, as well as shame at all the suspicious looks that were tearing my entire being to pieces, suffocated me, and I answered the Commissioner, stammering, All right, Monsieur, let us go upstairs. We could talk about what happened up there.

Upon reaching Vincent's room, we found him rolled up in the sheets, curled in a ball; he seemed lifeless.

Gently, very gently, I touched the body, the heat of which showed that it was still alive. For me it was as if I had suddenly got back all my energy, all my spirit.

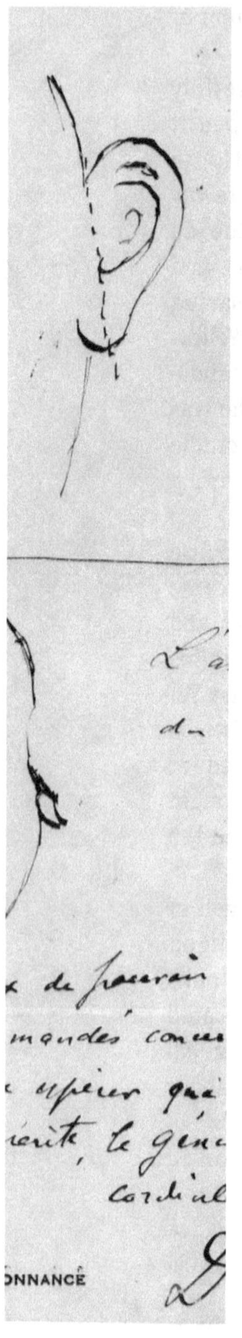

Then, in a low voice, I said to the Police Commissioner, Be kind enough, Monsieur, to awaken this man with great care, and if he asks for me tell him I have left for Paris; the sight of me might prove fatal to him.

Once the mad painter regained consciousness, he asked for his comrade, his pipe, and his tobacco. He was then taken to Hôtel Dieu, a hospital on the other side of Arles.

Later, Gauguin learned that Vincent's state was worse, that he wants to sleep with the patients, that he chases the nurses, that he blackens his face with coal. That is to say, he continues the Biblical mortifications. Thus concluded the utopic vision of the Studio of the South.

*

On Christmas day, Gauguin would depart with Theo van Gogh for Paris, and on the 26th, construction of the upper stage of la Tour Eiffel was finished, bringing the engineering marvel ever closer to completion. Heights that had hitherto never before been scaled by humanity were being surmounted, and ever-greater heights would beckon the species further on. The drive to elevation! The test of how much truth a spirit can dare! The will to power... and nothing besides!

In Torino that same day, Signore Dynamite writes to his friend Overbeck about his burgeoning grand politics, which include forming an anti-German, anti-Hohenzollern league:

> I myself am working on a *Pro memoria* for the courts of Europe, with an anti-German league in view. I mean to sew up the 'Reich' in an iron shirt and to provoke it to a war of desperation. I shall not have my hands free until I have the young emperor and all his appurtenances in my hands.

Upon receiving this declaration, Overbeck responded with great concern to his friend, inquiring as to the state of his health.

On New Year's Eve, Signore Dynamite explained that his health was still excellent; only I wrote the letter in a very bad light — I no longer recognized what I was writing. You must also not think that those "sad" communications even remotely touched me; they've been a thousand miles below me for years. —

And at 2:30 AM on the 28th, the same day Overbeck reads of Nietzsche's political provocations, Gauguin is in the 11th arrondissement, at Grande Roquette Prison, where the execution of Prado will take place. The guillotine staged against the dark Paris sky, the late night air frigid, the rabble singing comic songs and amusing themselves in other boisterous ways.

When, over three hours later, Prado is brought before the world, the painter is caught up in the frenzy, fighting the crowd to gain a coveted view of the execution.

As guards move in to corral the rabble, forcing the mass of bodies suddenly, brutally backward, the painter struggles to see, and when I want to see something, he explains, I'm obstinate.

While the crowd of onlookers grows solemn, pacified by the gendarmes, Gauguin shoves his way through them, edging closer to the stage. He has already savored the taste of blood.

Prado, in walking from the prison to the guillotine, shows no signs of fear. His arms are tightly pinioned behind his back. His heavy locks, seen to such advantage in the courtroom, are gone. His apparel seemingly consisting of a heavy woolen undershirt and dark trousers. His shirt has been roughly cut away from about the neck and shoulders. In front the guillotine board stands upright, to a height of five feet.

As Prado nears the board, a dreadful series of incidents follow each other with the rapidity of lightning.

Prado protests his innocence of the murder to the last, and declares against the injustice of this world. He refuses to disclose his real name.

Who am I first of all? What does it matter? I am unfortunate. An adventurer, isn't that right? My God, hurled on to this vast stage of human life, I yielded, a bit by chance, to everything I felt beat in my heart and boil in my brain.

When the jailers come to pinion his limbs he offers no resistance, but while they are engaged in this operation, he sheds one tear. The sight of the guillotine appears to hypnotize him.

When a priest offers him a crucifix, he says: *Non; Dieu se moque de moi.*

A trembling abbé steps apart, and four burly men, dressed in blouses of blue and white and striped stockings, who had not been seen before, spring forward, seize the condemned man, and hurl him onward against the upright board, fling themselves upon him, and by their weight bear the struggling victim, face downward, to the top of the low platform. The board works on a swivel and runs on rollers. In an instant, it is wheeled forward until Prado's neck is under the glistening blade.

Anatole Deibler, who had stood like a man of stone at the right of the guillotine during all this terrible scene, now reaches forward and fixes the wooden collar over the back of the prisoner's neck.

The knife is sprung, but the apparatus malfunctions, and Prado's ear and part of his face are sliced off.

It is a century of ears, a century of mutilations, a century of heads!

The blade is raised again and the keen steel strikes the neck as it might have collided with a rubber spring. It goes through, and the head of Prado lies among the shavings beyond.

If, as Signore Dynamite will soon declare, he is all the names in history, and even signs himself Prado in one of his letters and says that he writes in the Prado style, when Gauguin witnesses this execution of Prado, he also actually witnesses the execution of Nietzsche, long before he is corporally to die, because, to be immortal, one has to die numerous times during one's life, while it is also Nietzsche that he, Gauguin, has just fled, for Nietzsche is all the names in history, which means, it is Nietzsche who has cut off nearly the entirety of his ear and delivered it to a prostitute (?), Rachel (Gaby?), who also happens to be Nietzsche, and she, he that is, or the he that is also simultaneously a woman (is she Vincent's Ariadne? and, if so, is not then Nietzsche an Ariadne to himself?), steps back in horror and faints, and he — she, it, that . . . : *in such a state of transfiguration, what do the pronouns matter anymore?* — is singing songs in the night, for X is all the names in history, which also makes Gauguin out to be Nietzsche, or Nietzsche to be Gauguin, and when Prado is executed, Nietzsche weeps, because he is still alive as he is dying and so, because he is all the names in history, he is also Prado's father so, he can be twice present at funerals, which truly outdoes Lazarus, and outdoes even Christ, too, by a few kilometers or more, for he, Nietzsche that is (who else would it be?), is an infinite proliferation of life itself, and as if to demonstrate his cosmic abundance, Herr Dynamite appears that night for the very first time as the Andromeda Galaxy, photographed that same night by Dr. Isaac Roberts (wait, is it actually Nietzsche, too, taking an *Ecce Homo* of himself as a solar mass?), which would lead to the Carte du Ciel, the astronomers' grand project of mapping the entire sky . . . With an exposure of 4 hours, Roberts reveals the spiral nature of this nearby galaxy for the first time. *Lento! mi amici, lento!*

This world is the will to power — and nothing besides! And you yourselves are also this will to power — and nothing besides!

The blood of one is the blood of all, and the blood of all is the blood of one.

Ecce Homo!?

Ecce Homines!!!!!?

Ecce Stellæ ~

Ecce galaxias!

TORINO

416.4 km from Arles

I hope the coming year will be a good one; quite unprece-dentedly famous; I have a veritable genius among my read-ers; the complete fascination that I exert; a fine lot of scum; I am a Pole and nothing else; the savage beast Nietzsche; the only living mathematical genius

29 December 1888

Verehrtes Fräulein,

It is perhaps not forbidden to send you a greeting at the turn of the year — I hope the coming year will be a *good* one. Of the *old* year, I shall say no more — it was *too good* . . .

In the meantime I have begun to be quite unprecedentedly famous. I think no mortal has ever received such letters as I have, and only from *exclusive* intelligences, from characters with high duties and in high office. From everywhere: not least from the highest St. Petersburg society. And the French! You should hear the tone in which Mr. Taine writes to me! I have just received an enchanting, and perhaps enchanted, letter from one of the foremost and most influential men in France, who wants to make it his task to become familiar with, *&* to translate, my writings — no less a person than the editor-in-chief of the *Journal des Débats* and the *Revue des deux mondes*, Mr. Bourdeau. He tells me too that a review of my *Fall of Wagner* will be appearing in January in the *Journal des Débats* — by whom? by *Monod*. — I have a veritable genius among my readers, the Swede August Strindberg, who feels that I am the deepest mind of all times. I am sending you an article in *Der Kunstwart*, requesting that you return it to me sometime, which does indeed define the "Nietzsche case" perfectly. — The most remarkable thing here in Torino is the complete fascination that I exert — over all classes of people. With every glance I am treated like a prince — there is an extremely distinguished air about the way people open the door for me or serve me food. When I enter a large shop, all the faces change. — And since I make no demands and, with complete composure, am the same toward everybody, and also have a face that is anything but gloomy, I need neither name, nor rank, nor money to make myself always unconditionally the first. —

So that there should be no lack of *contrast*, my sister announced for my birthday, with the utmost scorn, that she supposed I too was starting to be "famous" . . . A fine lot of scum it would be that believed in *me* . . . This has been going on for *seven* years . . . —

Yet *another* case. I seriously regard the Germans as people of an utterly *vulgar* sort, and thank heaven that in all my instincts I am a Pole and nothing else. On the occasion of *Der Fall Wagner*, my publisher Herr E.W. Fritzsch printed in the *Mus. Wochenblatt*, which he edits, a most heinous article about me. I wrote him at once: "How much do you want for all my books? With sincere contempt, Nietzsche." — Answer: 11000 Marks. — Think of it! That is German... the publisher of *Zarathustra*.

Georg Brandes is going to St. Petersburg again this winter, to give lectures on the savage beast Nietzsche. He is really an extremely intelligent man; never have I received such delicate letters. — My writings are being zealously printed, with *fiery* zeal... Meanwhile, Herr Köselitz has become a big animal: Joachim and de Ahna are raving about this new "classic" — I add that he is wooing all too successfully a remarkably beautiful and interesting girl in one of the most splendid mansions of Berlin, although he has Count Schlieben for a rival. He spent the whole summer in his princess's woodland château in Pomerania, surrounded by Junkers and guards. Probably Count Hochberg will approach him to secure for Berlin the first performance of *Der Löwe von Venedig*. — In short, *Transvaluation of All Values* . . . With best greetings and wishes

Your N.

Did you hear that Mme Kovaleska in Stockholm (— she is descended from the old Hungarian King Matthias Corvin) has received the topmost mathematics prize from the Paris Academy? She is regarded today as the only living mathematical genius. —

PARIS

774.9 km from Torino

that most dreadful illness; will he remain insane?; poor fighter and poor, poor sufferer; someone to whom he could pour his heart out; whether he should be committed to an institution; there is little hope

28–30 December 1888

Dear Jo,

I found Vincent in the hospital in Arles. The people around him realized from his agitation that for the past few days he had been showing symptoms of that most dreadful illness, of madness, and an attack of *fièvre chaude*, when he injured himself with a razor, was the reason he was taken to hospital. Will he remain insane? The doctors think it possible, but daren't yet say for certain. It should be apparent in a few days' time when he is rested; then we will see whether he is lucid again. He seemed to be all right for a few minutes when I was with him, but lapsed shortly afterwards into his brooding about philosophy and theology. It was terribly sad being there, because from time to time all his grief would well up inside and he would try to weep, but couldn't. Poor fighter and poor, poor sufferer. Nothing can be done to relieve his anguish now, but it is deep and hard for him to bear. Had he just once found someone to whom he could pour his heart out, it might never have come to this. In the next few days they will decide whether he is to be transferred to a special institution and as I don't yet know how much I shall have to do in all this, I dare not make any plans.

Since I last wrote I've been wavering between hope and fear. The news is still bad and the last letter from Vincent's friend the postman says, "The doctor will wait a few days before deciding whether he should be committed to an institution." One sees the ambiguity in this sentence when one asks Why? I am waiting for an answer from the assistant house physician at the hospital. There is little hope, but he has done more than so many in his life and suffered and fought more than most people are capable of doing. If he must pass away, so be it, but the thought of it breaks my heart … My dear Mother knows no more than that he is ill and that his mind is confused. She is not aware that his life is in danger.

Theo

TORINO

416.4 km from Arles

I am Taurinorum, Cæsar, and the like; the Mole Antonellia-na is Ecce Homo; Strindberg's profonde admiration; lunch with my cook; the most beautiful page about music; take gymnastics & pastilles Géraudel; a courtesy for mésalliance

Sunday — *Sunday* 30 Dc
par excellence
(although it is cloudy —)

Old friend,

under my window, as if I were already princeps Taurinorum,
Cæsar Cæsarum and the like, the Municipal Orchestra of Torino, for example, is still playing rhapsody hongroise with all its
might. I recognize Mancinelli's grandiose Cleopatra work. Earlier I passed the Mole Antonelliana, the most ingenious building
that may have been built — strange, it has no name yet — based
on an absolute drive for elevation — it reminds me of nothing
so much as my *Zarathustra.* I christened it *Ecce Homo* and in
spirit I have opened an enormous free space around it. — Then
I went to my palazzo, now palazzo Madama — we are creating the madama for this —: it can stay *perfectly* as it is, by far
the most picturesque kind of grand castle — especially in the
stairwell. Then I received a letter of homage from my poet Au-
guste Strindberg, a veritable genius in honor of my "grandiosis-
sime *Génealogie de la Morale*," with his expression de sa profonde
admiration. Then I wrote, in a heroic-aristophanic arrogance, a
proclamation to the European courts for the *annihilation* of the
House of Hohenzollern, that bloody idiot and criminal race for
more than 100 years had the throne of France and Alsace, too, by
being Victor Buona, the brother of our Laetitia made emperor
and my excellent Mr. Bourdeau, chief editor of the *Journal de
Débats* and the *Revue des deux Mondes*, as ambassadeur at my
court, — afterwards had lunch with my cook (— he is not called
de la Pace —) and now write a letter to my friend and the most
perfect maëstro, promising him theater, orchestra, and all kinds
of *cameras*... Also, for his love, I have already written the most
beautiful page about music that may have been written — and in
the end not to love him, but rather someone — that, that, that —
for love, that — that — that he should read the page at once ...

Friedrich Nietzsche

N.

I was still present at the funeral of the ancient Antonelli that November. — He lived until *Ecce Homo*, the book, was finished. — The book and the *person* to it...

Yesterday I sent my non plus ultra to the print shop, titled *Fame and Eternity*, poetry beyond all seven heavens. It brings *Ecce Homo* to an end. — You die of it if you read it unprepared...

German will be spoken at my court: *for* the highest works of m–n are written in German...

Take gymnastics and pastilles Géraudel...

So that I do not withhold my ulterior motives from you, I am sending you a letter that I wrote yesterday for my maestro, Mr. Pietro Gasti — and which may wait a few more days... I will leave this l. to you for any use

If you ask me, you will also get the proclamation for the *J. des Débats*: it is *enough*... Triple alliance — but that's just a courtesy for mésalliance...

ARLES

416.4 km from Torino

your brother's condition; his crises did not allow me to leave him in the wards; a purely personal matter; the essence of his character; a certificate of mental disturbance; an asylum close to Paris?

30 December 1888

Dear Sir,

I hasten to reply to your letter and to give you information concerning your brother's condition.

I shall tell you straightaway that it is very difficult to give categorical answers to all the questions that you ask me. Nevertheless, I shall give you my personal assessment.

The Protestant minister, Mr. Salles, came looking for me this evening, and we went to visit him. He was very calm & seemed perfectly well. When he saw me enter his room he told me that he wished to have as little as possible to do with me. He remembered, no doubt, that it was I who had had him locked up. I then assured him that I was his friend and that I wished to see him recovered soon. I did not hide his situation from him, and explained to him why he was in a room by himself. I told him that his crises did not allow me to leave him in the wards, among all our patients. We talked like that for a little while, and then parted good friends. He asked me to write to you and to give you news of him, something that he did not want at the beginning of our discussion. When I tried to get him to talk about the motive that drove him to cut off his ear, he replied that it was a purely personal matter.

In short, I find that his condition has improved a little, and I do not believe his life is in danger, at least not for the moment. He is eating fairly well and his physical strength is helping him bear his crises. My assessment is that he will be able to recover in a short time, while retaining the extreme excitability that must form the essence of his character.

We are currently tending to his ear alone, and certainly not to his mental state. His wound is much better and is not causing us any concern.

A few days ago, we issued a certificate of mental disturbance. The mayor signed an order leaving him in the hospital for the time being, while awaiting his transfer to an asylum. During this time, the chief of police will carry out his enquiry, and then the Prefect will give instructions for him to be taken to Aix or Marseille.

I myself was a house physician in Marseille a few months ago, and I should be glad to recommend him to the colleague who took my place and who is a good friend of mine.

Despite that, I shall permit myself to ask you a question and to offer you a piece of advice. Would you like to have your brother in an asylum close to Paris? Do you have resources? If so, you may very well send him to look for one; his condition easily allows him to make the journey. The matter has not progressed so far that it could not be halted, and for the chief of police to suspend his report. This is the information that I had to offer you concerning your poor brother.

You ask me for my assessment; I shall give you it for what it is worth. I shall always be delighted to give you news of him, because I too have a brother; I too have been far away from my family. In a few months, when I submit my doctoral thesis in Paris, I too should be happy if somebody were able to take an interest in me at a difficult moment.

With my sincerest regards,
Rey Fé

INTERVAL: AMERICA

3433.12 nm (or, *as the crow flies…*) to Arles
3511.94 nm to Torino

To the Year 1889

HAVE I no weapon-word for thee — some message brief
    & fierce?
Have I fought out and done indeed the battle? Is there
    no shot left,
For all thy affections, lisps, scorns, manifold silliness?
Nor for myself — my own rebellious self in thee?

Down, down, proud gorge! — though choking thee;
Thy bearded throat *&* high-borne forehead to the gutter;
Crouch low thy neck to eleemosynary gifts.

WALT WHITMAN

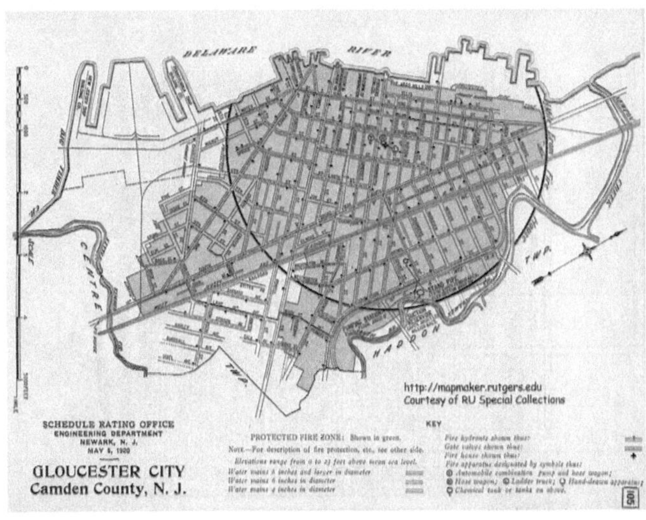

TORINO

416.4 km from Arles

the courage to go the whole way; the famous Rubicon; a convocation of princes; I want, I want to be mad!; Eheu?

31 December 1888

— You are right, a thousand times over! Warn Fuchs yourself...
You will find in *Ecce Homo* an astounding page about Tristan,
about my whole relationship with Wagner. W is altogether the
foremost name in E h. — Wherever I admit no doubts, here too
I had the courage to go the whole way.

Ah, friend! *what* a moment! — When your card came, what
was I doing... It was the famous Rubicon...

I no longer know my address: let us suppose that it will soon
be the Palazzo del Quirinale.

N.

Dear Sir,

You will soon have an answer about your novella — it sounds like
a *rifle shot*... I have ordered a convocation of princes in Rome,
I mean to have the young emperor shot.

Auf Wiedersehen! For we *shall* meet again... Une seule
condition: Divorçons...

Nietzsche Cæsar

Holtibus pridie Cal. Jan.
MDCCCLXXXIX

Carissime doctor!

θέλω, θέλω μανῆναι!

Litteras tuas non sine perturbatione accepi et tibi gratias ago.

> Rectius vives, Licini, neque altum.
> Semper urgendo neque, dum procellas
> Cautus horrescis nimium premendo
>   Litus iniquum.
> Interdum juvat insanire!
>   Vale et Fave!

> Strindberg
> (Deus optimus maximus)

Herrn Strindberg!

Eheu?... Not Divorçons after all?...

The Crucified

ARLES

416.4 km from Torino
Happy New Year!

In order to reassure you; Gauguin, did I terrify him?; I'm content to remain as I am; this over-excitement was only fleeting

Hospices Civils de la Ville D'Arles   2 January 1889
BOUCHES-DU-RHONE

my dear Theo,

    In order to reassure you completely on my account
I'm writing you these few words in the office of Mr. Rey, the
house physician, whom you saw yourself. I'll stay here at the
hospital for another few days — then I dare plan to return home
very calmly. Now I ask just one thing of you, not to worry, for
that would cause me one worry *too many*. —

    Now let's talk about our friend Gauguin, did I terrify him?
In short, why doesn't he give me a sign of life? He must have left
with you.

    Besides, he needed to see Paris again, and perhaps he'll feel
more at home in Paris than here. *Tell Gauguin to write to me*, and
that I'm still thinking of him.

    Good handshake, I've read and re-read your letter about the
meeting with the Bongers. It's perfect. As for me, I'm content to
remain as I am. Once again, good handshake to you & Gauguin.

Ever yours
Vincent

Write to me, still same address, 2 place Lamartine.

    Sir —

    I shall add a few words to your brother's letter to reassure
you, in my turn, on his account. —

    I am happy to tell you that my predictions have been borne
out, and that this over-excitement was only fleeting. I strongly
believe that he will have recovered in a few days' time. —

    I very much wanted him to write to you himself, to give you
a better account of his condition. —

    I have had him brought down to my office to talk a little. It
will entertain me and do him good.

    With my sincerest regards. ——

Rey F.

TORINO

416.4 km from Arles

God is on earth; throw the Pope into prison; the Dionysian Dithyrambs of Hanswurst; It is a prejudice that I am human; I was Buddha; Alexander and Cæsar are my incarnations; Me, I also hung on the cross; this breve to humanity; I love you!

3 January 1889

Miss von Salis.

The world is transfigured for God is on earth. Do you not see how all the heavens are rejoicing? I have just taken possession of my kingdom, thrown the Pope into prison, and am having Wilhelm, Bismarck, and Stocker shot.

The crucified one.

Cosima,

I am told that a certain godly Hanswurst today completed his
Dionysos Dithyrambs. . .

To Princess Ariadne, my beloved.

It is a prejudice that I am human. But I have already lived among people *&* know everything that they can experience, from the lowest to the highest. I have been Buddha among the Indians, Dionysos in Greece, — Alexander and Cæsar are my incarnations, likewise the poet of Shakespeare Lord Bakon. Most recently I was Voltaire *&* Napoleon, perhaps also Richard Wagner... But this time I come as the victorious Dionysos, who will prepare a great festival on Earth... Not that I have much time... The heavens rejoice that I am here... Me I also hung on the cross...

Cosima,

You are to publish this breve to all mankind, from Bayreuth, with
the inscription:

The Good News

3 January 1889

Ariadne, I love you!

Dionysos

ARLES

416.4 km from Torino

I expect to start work again soon; all in all no harm has come to me; I can't tell you how much it delights me that you've made peace

4 January 1889

My dear brother

I hope that Gauguin will also completely reassure you a little regarding painting matters.

I expect to start work again soon.

The charwoman *&* my friend Roulin had taken care of the house, put everything in good order.

When I come out I'll be able to continue on my way here again, and soon the fine days will come and I'll start on the orchards in blossom again.

I am, my dear brother, so *heartbroken* by your journey, I would have wished that you'd been spared that, for all in all no harm has come to me, and it wasn't worth troubling you.

I can't tell you how much it delights me that you've made peace and even more than that with the Bongers. Say so on my behalf to André, and give him a very cordial handshake from me.

What wouldn't I have given for you to see Arles in fine weather, now you have seen it when it's dark.

However, be of good heart, send the letters directly to me, 2, place Lamartine. I'll send Gauguin the paintings of his that are still at the house as soon as he wishes. We owe him the money he spent on the furniture.

Handshake, I must go back to the hospital again, but shortly I'll leave for good.

Ever yours,
Vincent

Also write a line to Mother on my behalf, so that no one will be worried.

TORINO

416.4 km from Arles

Once you discovered me; Dionysos vs. the Crucified One; my boredom at having created a world; great satyrs and festival animals; the world is transfigured; I am just having all anti-Semites shot; world-historical insanity; the crazy Hohenzollerns; the many births & deaths of Nietzsche; bad jokes; I make my own tea; every name in history is I; from time to time we practice magic; siamo contenti? son dio…

4 January 1889

My friend Georg.

After you discovered me, it was no great feat to find me: the difficulty now is to lose me...

The Crucified One.

Mr. Hanns von Bülow.

Considering that you began as and that you were the first Han-
seatic, and I, in all modesty, the Third Veuve Cliquot-Ariadne, I
must not spoil your game: moreover, I condemn you to the "Lion
of Venice" — he may eat you . . .

Dionysos

To my venerable Jakob Burckhardt.

That was the little joke on account of which I condone my boredom at having created a world. Now you are — thou art — our
great, greatest teacher: because I, together with Ariadne, only
have to be the golden balance of all things, everywhere we have
such beings who are above us . . .

Dionysos.

After it became irrevocably clear that I actually created the
world, friend Paul also appears in the world plan: he, together
with Monsieur Catulle Mendès, is supposed to be one of my great
satyrs & festival animals.

Dionysos.

To my maëstro Pietro

Sing me a new song: the world is transfigured and all the heavens
rejoice.

The Crucified One.

Although Malvida is known to be Kundry, who laughed at a moment when the world was trembling, much is to be forgiven her because she loved me very much: see the first volume of the "Memoirs"... I adore all these select souls around Malvida. In Natalie her father lives and I was he too.

The Crucified One

To my friend Overbeck and his wife

Although you have so far shown little faith in my solvency, I still hope to prove that I am someone who pays his debts — for example my debts to you both... I am just having all anti-Semites shot...

Dionysos.

My grumpy Erwin

At the risk of enraging you again through my blindness as regards Monsieur Taine, who formerly wrote the Veda, I dare to
place you among the gods & right next to the nicest goddess...

Dionysos.

Imperial Court Councilor Dr. Viennese

Although you have done me the honor of finding the "Wagner Case" devastating for Wagner, the said Wagner nevertheless dares to bring his decadence to light through a world-historical insanity — in lucem æternam...

Dionysos.

The illustrious Poles

I belong to you, I am more Pole than I am God, I want to give you
honor as I can give honor... I live among you as Matejo...

The Crucified One

To my beloved son Mariani...

May peace be with you! I come to Rome Tuesday to pay my respects
to His Holiness...

The Crucified One.

To my beloved son Umberto

May peace be with you! I come to Rome Tuesday and want to see you along with his holiness the Pope.

The Crucified One

The Baden House

Children, it's not good if you get involved with the crazy Hohen-
zollerns, even though, through Stéphanie, you are of my race...
Retire modestly to your private life. I give the same advice to
Bavaria...

The Crucified One

Dear Professor,

in the end I would much rather be a Basel professor than God; but I did not dare to carry my private egoism so far as to refrain from creating the world on his account. You see, one must make sacrifices however and wherever one lives. — But I have kept a small student room for myself, which is opposite the Palazzo Carignano (— in which I was born as Vittorio Emanuele) and which also allows me to hear from its desk the splendid music below me, in the Galleria Subalpina. I pay 25 fr. with service, make my own tea, and do all my own shopping, suffer from torn boots and thank heaven every moment for the old world, for which the people were not simple and quiet enough. — Since I am condemned to entertain the next eternity with bad jokes, I have a writing business here that actually leaves nothing to be desired, very pretty and not at all exhausting. The post office is 5 paces away, so I put the letters in myself, to play the part of the great feuilletoniste of the grande monde. I am, of course, in close contact with Figaro, and to give you an idea of how harmless I can be, here are my first two bad jokes:

Don't take the Prado case too seriously. I am Prado, I am also Prado's Father, I dare to say that I am Lesseps too... I wanted to give my Parisians, whom I love, a new concept — that of a decent criminal. I am Chambige too — also a decent criminal.

Second joke. I greet the immortals. Monsieur Daudet is one of the quarante

Astu.

What is uncomfortable and what disturbs my modesty is that at root every name in history is I; it is also the case with the children that I have brought into the world, that I consider with some suspicion whether or not all who come into the "kingdom of God" do not also come *out of* God. This autumn, I was dressed as lightly as possible, I twice attended my funeral, first as Conte Robilant (no, he is my son, insofar as I am Carlo Alberto, my nature below) but I was Antonelli myself. Dear Professor, you should see this building; since I am completely inexperienced in the things that I create, you are entitled to any criticism, I am grateful without being able to promise that I will benefit from that. We artists are unteachable. — Today I saw an operetta — Moorish, of genius — and on this occasion I also noted with pleasure that both Moscow & Rome are now grandiose matters. You see, my talent for landscape is not denied either. — Think about it, let's have a nice chat, Torino is not far away, we have no very serious professional duties, a glass of Veltliner would be available. Informal dress is the rule of propriety.

With heartfelt love your
Nietzsche

Tomorrow my son Umberto is coming with the charming Margherita, whom I receive here only in shirtsleeves. The *rest* is for Frau Cosima... Ariadne... From time to time we practice magic...

I go everywhere in my student overcoat, slap someone on the shoulder here and there and say: siamo contenti? son dio, ho fatto questa caricatura...

I had Caiaphas chained; also last year I was crucified at great length by the German doctors. Wilhelm Bismarck and all anti-Semites abolished.

You can make any use of this letter if you do not belittle me with respect to the people of Basel. —

INTERVAL: TORINO, BASEL, JENA

January 1889

And so we are told that, on 3 January, the philosopher of the will to power, the philosopher who criticized the Christian ethos of pity, the philosopher who prized the hardness of the diamond, for the noblest is perfectly hard, that such a philosopher enacted Raskolnikov's dream in the streets of Torino, complete with horse whipping, or sadistic horse beating, depending upon which journalist's take one adopts, with the Anti-Christ shedding tears at the cruelty, thrusting his arms around the tormented animal's neck, & collapsing in an ecstasy of pity — perhaps, more than 11 years after the fact, the Italian journalists sought to enact Herr Dynamite's call to open up as many perspectives as possible in order to get at the truth, or at least to some semblance of it, for that is all that is only ever possible, and so the journalists were simply being perspectivalists, albeit with a dash of pepperoncino, if not even more, or a glass of amaro, if not even more, or perhaps *un bicchiere di grappa*, if not even more, and with some casu martzu thrown in for good measure, to add yet further realism to the event, to enliven and intensify it with a taste of the ensuing decay that would follow the legendary embrace of the horse, despite the fact that Nietzsche's favorite cheese was actually Bruss, and he always liked to counter the Piedimontese proverb and say instead, *brucia è più forte dell'amore*. Or was it that the journalists were, with knowing Nietzschean esprit, actually creating a fable disguised as a truth, since the real world had been abolished? Or were they being operatic and, to add a bit of derring-do and *décadence française* to their tales, throwing in a dash of *Carmen?* Was the horse meant to be Carmen, or Nietzsche, with him therefore embracing himself in disguise, his last *&* final mask? Nietzsche-horse?!? Horse-Nietzsche?!? A single conduit of man *&* animal, at last united in perfect balance? *Humanimality!*

In the midst of collapsing in Piazza Carlo Alberto, Herr Dynamite, we are also told, was so powerful and so strong and so Übermenschliche that he even brought the horse to its knees after he embraced it. This world is the will to power — and nothing besides! And you yourselves are also this will to power — and nothing besides!

Did Herr Dynamite want to whisper something in the horse's ear? Was he suddenly thinking of Cosima's ears, since they were not small, or Lou Salomé's ears, since hers were not small either? In grasping the horse by the head, did he think that, because of the similarity of their ears, that he was grasping Ariadne by the head? Or was he thinking of Prado, who lost his ear to the guillotine? He could not have been thinking of van Gogh, and he definitely wasn't thinking of Malchus. Did he, Nietzsche that is, not Prado, but then, Nietzsche is Prado because... Did he, like Life, have a secret to reveal, something to whisper into the horse's ear? Did he want to play the hurdy-gurdy song for the animal? Or, was he just trying to dance the tarantella to express his love of the south, despite his in the end prizing Torino over every other Italian city? Although the journalists neglected to note this, that's what many of the Torinese actually thought that day — what else would a foreigner do but enact the dance of another region. *Che cazzo? Questo è il Piemonte, non la Puglia! Tedesco pazzo!*

But truly, one has to wonder, if it did in fact happen, and if Herr Dynamite were not in fact enacting Raskolnikov's dream, would the whipping of a horse startle someone who fought in the Franco-Prussian war? Would it provoke pity in one who understood how pain and joy are inextricably interwoven? Is the striking of a horse with a riding crop not so common, and so harmless to the tough hide of the animal, that no one would ever even notice it, let alone a half-blind Tiresias whose one good eye was myopic, especially across the expanse of a vast and crowded Italian piazza? Or did Nietzsche mistake this horse for the horse that he rode in the Franco-Prussian war and so wanted to let it know that, even though it threw him from its back, he was not mad at the horse, because he loved pain? Or, was he just playing Montaigne? Or, was he thinking of that photo wherein he choreographed the mise-en-scène of himself *&* Rée as horses harnessed *&* whipped by a leather-gloved Salomé bristling with punctum? Or was he simply trying to become a centaur?

Are we to believe, trained philosophers that we are, trained philologists too, and so doubters and skeptics and questioners, masters that is of suspicion, those that is who read off facts without falsifying them, are we to believe that he who mentions even the sweetest grapes being picked for him, that he who speaks of the gelato of Torino, of its pasta and coffee and even grissini, that such a man, who had a particular sensitivity to animals, had a dramatic encounter with a cavallo but didn't speak of it at all himself, that there is not one reference, not even the slightest coded allusion, to a horse in any of the letters or postcards penned that fatal, catastrophic day? For we must retain our sense for facts, the last developed and most valuable of all the senses! Are we Versuchers to believe that he who, in perfect mad lucidity, as the repressed counter-Nietzsche irrupted within himself and made use of every declaration the sane Nietzsche ever made, that this counter-Nietzsche, who wrote an equal number of letters, half signed Dionysos, half signed the Crucified, did not so much as make even a single joke about a whip or a carriage driver or the breath of the horse that he embraced, his lips close enough to kiss the stately and wounded beast? That at the moment when Nietzsche becomes conscious of no longer being Nietzsche and is dispersed like Zagreus and therefore open to becoming all the names in history, that he becomes Prado and Chambige and Buddha and Napoleon and so on and on, and that all the current events and details of the final days of his sane life freely erupt from his consciousness without reserve, even his repressed love of Cosima Wagner, his secret Ariadne, at such a moment, when there is no restrictive mechanism in play, when his collapse shatters the ever-so fragile walls of his psyche, which thereafter sings from its depths without reservation, that in such a frenzy, devoid of all inhibition, that Herr Dynamite, he who fell from a horse during the Franco-Prussian War and suffered injuries because of it, that he did not want at that moment to become not only Cæsar and Christ but also a horse? That he did not see himself and speak of himself as Dürer's Knight; that he did not speak of protecting the horse from Death and the Devil? While writing letters to grand dukes, kings, and emperors, while addressing the Vatican, while speaking unreservedly to friends and former friends, in the midst of his grand politics and his apocalyptic and revolutionary pronouncements, when there is no prohibiting screen and his tongue is set loose, within such a delirium, within such a strange and terrifying lucidity, when the multitude of current and past events of his life are given absolute free play, when everything in his life explodes out of the theater of his body and onto the stage of the final letters, addressed to his intimate coteries and to the world, that in the cinematic spectacle of his psyche, which exfoliated like spectral images from a magick lantern, that it did not project but a single image of a horse, horse tail, horse teeth, horse lips, horse eyes, carriage driver, carriage, or whip, and that Overbeck or Candida or Davide Fino did not find a single horse hair in Nietzsche's room, not a remnant on his clothing, not the trace of a scent, no remaining odor, not a drop of horse saliva on his collar, not a fallen or forgotten oat, that no one speaks of such hard material data? *Egads, Nietzsche stinks!* That Herr Dynamite does not even so much as whisper the word equus, cavallo, or Roß, nor wegja, nor Pferd, nor άλογο, nor does he speak of gallows or horse latitudes when thinking of Prado and of his being Prado's father, nor does he speak of a horse-godmother when thinking of Elisabeth Förster (but at that moment, does he even think of that vindictive anti-Semitic goose at all?), or horsing Lou Salomé, as he so longed to do, with every fiber of his horsy, sensual, Dionysian flesh, for maybe all that actually happened, as Overbeck was told, but which is not as operatic and ironic, was nothing more undramatic than ... *Dionysos grinning and merely collapsing in a street*, as if his legs gave out, as if the wind had been knocked out of him, as if the god could no longer dance, for after living a life of fire and consummation, after becoming every name in history but never becoming or embracing a horse, certainly not a lama, all that remains of such an expenditure is vapor and incense, yet that outlasts those who make a Weihe of their lives to Life itself.

So goes myth, lore, fable, and the Italian penchant for tall tales, the old Piedimontese art of embellishment and baroque exaggeration.

Horse or no horse, after being brought back to his room, Herr Dynamite lay unconscious or still for some time, immobile as a Greek statue, perhaps in a state of hesychia, then, suddenly, erupting into song, howling as he leapt about, ordering bottles of Barbera vino, dancing naked and improvising at the piano, cock erect, pheromones aflame, all to the terrible consternation of the Finos, landlord Davide, wife Candida, and their children.

The self-proclaimed Polish Dionysos was raising one hell of a storm.

When Overbeck arrived days later, not an hour too late, Candida was visiting the police station and the German consul, but Nietzsche's trusted friend was able to keep him from being confined to a private lunatic asylum, if not worse. Would the Carabinieri not have beat the kraut senseless for trying to make guanciale out of a horse, or would they praise his culinary inventiveness?

Upon entering his room, Overbeck found Herr Dynamite, crouching & reading in the corner of a sofa the last proofs of *Nietzsche contra Wagner*. The final agon…

At sight of his friend, the philosopher rushes up to him, violently embraces him, and breaks into a flood of tears, then sinks back onto the sofa, twitching and quivering, his body no longer in his control, his nervous system in a state of volcanic disorganization, like the plates of the earth coming apart — the schisms of the world enter the flesh. *I am not a person at all, I am dynamite!*

Later, Overbeck would speak of Nietzsche embodying in terrifying ways the orgiastic idea of sacred fury that formed the basis of ancient tragedy.

As he was groaning and quivering, the Finos gave Herr Dynamite a sip of bromide water and the creature became tranquil and laughingly began to speak of the great reception that had been prepared for that evening.

Growing inordinately excited at the piano, singing loudly & raving, shifting abruptly from loud crescendo as he imagined himself undergoing sparagmos, to indescribably soft notes, conjuring sublime, wonderfully clear-sighted and unspeakably ghastly things, each improvisation was followed by a convulsive fit.

The courageous animal & Monster would utter bits and pieces from the world of ideas in which he had been living, and also in short sentences, in an indescribably muffled tone, sublime, wonderfully clairvoyant, and unspeakably horrible things would be audible, about himself as the successor of the dead God, the whole thing punctuated, as it were, on the piano, whereupon more convulsions and outbursts would follow, with Hanswurst speaking of the profession that he had allotted to himself, to be the clown of the new eternities, and he, the master of expression, was himself incapable of rendering the ecstasies of his gaiety except in the most trivial expressions or by frenzied dancing and capering.

And so, for three nights, princeps Taurinorum kept the whole household awake with his ravings, shifting between childish innocuousness and total docility, as long as one shared his ideas about kingly receptions and processions, music festivals, and so on. The opera was coming to its delirious finale.

With the Carabinieri having been informed of the German professor's antics, the philosopher-king was in threat of being imprisoned in a jail in Torino. Ergo, Overbeck realized that 'Nietzsche' must at once be brought back to Germany, to Basel, to a university clinic where both he and the Crucified One knew the doctors, which included the improbably named Doctor Wille, and so life in Torino would soon come to an end. No more grapes, no more pasta, and certainly no more gelato or grissini.

Before Hanswurst could eventually be spirited away, he gazed at his landlord and asked, *Dear Signor Fino, will you let me have your papalina?* whereupon the landlord gave the one formerly known as Nietzsche his triangular nightcap, which the philosopher-king donned throughout his journey, its tassel swinging to and fro as if the loose arm of a cuckoo clock ticking out its final hours.

While en route to Basel, they had to transfer at Novara and the philosopher-king wanted to address the crowds he encountered and to embrace everybody he met. As he was told, ceremonies were being prepared for his arrival. But Cæsar Cæsarum was persuaded to restrain himself, for a man as eminent as he must travel incognito.

During their journey, they passed below the Alps, and when moving through the Gotthard Tunnel, itself blown open with the dynamite after which Nietzsche was named, Hanswurst burst into song, for he was not then in a chloral-induced sleep, and began canting aloud his *Venetian Gondellied* with a wholly peculiar melody, a black flag flying above his head:

An der Brücke stand
jüngst ich in brauner Nacht.
Fernher kam Gesang:
goldener Tropfen quolls
über die zitternde Fläche weg.
Gondeln, Lichter, Musik —
trunken schwamms in die Dämmrung hinaus...
Meine Seele, ein Saitenspiel,
sang sich, unsichtbar berührt,
heimlich ein Gondellied dazu,
zitternd vor bunter Seligkeit.
— Hörte Jemand ihr zu?...

Upon reaching Basel on the morning of 10 January, at first, the philosopher-king did not recognize Dr. Wille, but then, once the doctor introduced himself, the philosopher-king's memory quickly activated and he responded quietly, Wille? Ah, you're an alienist. Some years ago I had a talk with you about religious mania à propos a madman called Adolf Vischer, who was living here.

The philosopher-king was soon examined, his recent letters read, and Overbeck recounted everything that he witnessed, all of which led to Dr. Wille incarcerating the one formerly known as Nietzsche and signing a statement diagnosing mental degeneration, noting that the patient claims he is a famous man and asks for women all the time, a sure sign of insanity.

During his brief stay in Basel, the patient devoured his meals, enjoyed his baths, answered questions in fragments, tried to steal institute combs and hats, wanted to scale the walls, and when he went for walks, filled his pockets with stones and twigs. When a fellow patient played on his zither, Dionysos would leap to his toes and begin marathon dances until the head warden led him off to calm him down. When his mother arrived three days later, he embraced her joyfully, exulting, My dear good mama, I am so glad to see you, then shouted in a thunderous voice, *Behold in me the tyrant of Torino!*

In the course of the ensuing days, the sick animal's speech flow was constant, confused, and devoid of logical connection. It continued night after night, rife with priapic content and further tales of whores in his room. If at times he conversed normally, he would lapse into jokes and dances, his speech growing confused and delusional, punctuated by songs, yodeling, screams.

On other days, plagued by insomnia, he talked without intermission, got up frequently to clean his teeth or wash himself, and when outdoors, was in a continual state of motor-excitement, throwing his hat on the ground, removing his clothes, laying down, talking confusedly, reproaching himself for having been the cause of several people's ruin.

Once, after being given sulfonal *&* sleeping several hours without interruption, the patient said he felt so incredibly well that he could only express his state of being in music.

During his final days in Basel, the patient was alternately quiet, manic, *&* loud, engaging in disruptive behavior, and when indoors, his rages were vocal: *aggravato fortissimo.*

Soon after, on 17 January, Franziska Nietzsche journeyed with her son to Jena, to bring him to a clinic closer to his birthplace. Overbeck watched 'Nietzsche' board the train with stiff, hurried, lurching steps, and when he went to bid his friend farewell, whoever 'he' was uttered a roaring groan and leapt up to embrace him convulsively, stating, *You are the man I have loved most of all.*

Throughout the journey to Jena, Herr Dynamite sometimes exploded into rages at his mother and cast a single glove out the train window, forcing Franziska to retreat to another compartment and leave her son with his attendant, Ernst Mähly.

Once they reached Frankfurt, Franziska returned and in the station, held her son's head, supporting his chin, and kissed his forehead all over. When she handed him a sandwich he said, It's a long time since I ate such nice ham sandwiches. And when she gave him some cherries he said, I supposed you've brought them from the Naumburg Cherry Fair.

Once having reached the clinic at Jena, the patient sat stiffly before the staff, his face haggard, but not emaciated, as Prof. Binswanger introduced him and questioned him about his life. The patient spoke in short, conversational sentences full of peculiar word combinations and elaborate antitheses, peppered with French & Italian expressions. His tone of voice was soft and pleasant, but he soon lost his train of thought, broke off mid-sentence, and sank into silence, his face contorted with Laocoöntic pain, his gaze glowing with affliction.

Days later, Overbeck would express regret over abandoning his friend. It would have been a far more genuine act of friendship to kill him. I have now no other wish than that his life be taken from him. I feel no hesitation whatever in this respect, and no one who has been with me these days would have felt anything else. It is all over with Nietzsche!

Oddly, no Italian ever tried to sell the blinders from the horse that Nietzsche was said to have embraced, nor, once it died, its teeth, nor its mane, nor its beautiful tail, nor its infamous well-worn iron shoes, though its sweat, like the blood of St. Januarius, is kept in a vial in Torino and the descendants of the Finos sometimes wear it as a cologne.

In an aphorism on the last hour, the philosopher, in speaking of storms as being his danger, asked, Will I have my storm by which I perish, as Oliver Cromwell perished of his? Or will I go out like a light that is not first blown out by the wind, but that grew tired and fed up with itself — a burned out light? Or finally: will I blow myself out so as not to burn out? —

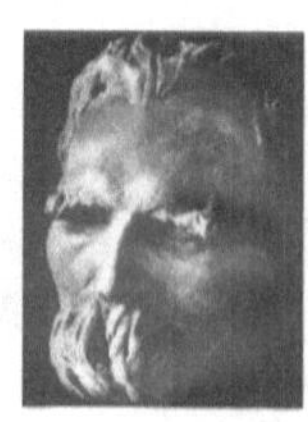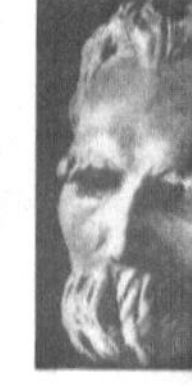

ARLES

1267.1 km from Jena

I returned home today; painting once again; it's quite diffi-cult for me to believe that we've gone so far astray; a certain country Voltaire speaks of; I think I'll see calmer days here; be completely reassured as to my health; I regret having caused a delay; what is Gauguin doing? simply tell them I've been a bit ill; I haven't yet forgotten how to jest; one perhaps learns how to live from the sick; a simple artist's bout of craziness; my appetite came back immediately; forget your sad journey and my illness.

7 January 1889

My dear Theo,

Perhaps I won't write you a really long letter today, but anyhow
a line to let you know that I returned home today. How I regret
that you were troubled for such a little thing, forgive me, for I am
after all probably the primary cause of it. I hadn't foreseen that
it would lead to you being told about it. Enough.

Mr. Rey came to see the painting with two of his doctor
friends, and they at least understand darned quickly what complementaries are. Now I'm planning to do Mr. Rey's portrait and
possibly other portraits as soon as I've accustomed myself a little
to painting once again.

Thank you for your last letter, I do indeed always feel your
presence, but on your side you should also know that I'm working on the same thing as yourself.

Ah, how I wish that you'd seen the portrait of Bruyas by
Delacroix and the whole museum at Montpellier where Gauguin
took me. How people have already worked in the south before
us! In truth, it's quite difficult for me to believe that we've gone
so far astray as that.

As to it being a hot country — my word, I can't help but
think of a certain country Voltaire speaks of — and without even
counting the simple castles in the air. Those are the thoughts that
come to me as I return home.

I'm very eager to know how the Bongers are, and if relations
with them continue to be good, which I hope they do.

If you think it all right — now that Gauguin has left —
we'll go back to 150 francs a month. I think I'll see calmer days
here again than in the course of the past year. What I'll need
very much for my instruction are all the reproductions of Delacroix's paintings that one can still get in that shop where they sell
lithographs of ancient & modern artists &c. for 1 franc, I think.
I *definitely* don't want the most expensive ones.

How are our Dutch friends De Haan & Isaäcson? Give them
my warm regards.

I just think that we must still keep calm regarding my own painting. If you want some I can certainly send them to you now, but when calm returns to me I hope to do something else.

In any case, as regards the Independents, do what seems best to you and what the others will do.

But you've no idea how much I regret that your journey to Holland hasn't already been made. Ah well, we can't change any of the facts, but make up for it as far as possible by correspondence or however you can, and tell the Bongers how much I regret having, perhaps unwittingly, caused a delay. I'll write to Mother & Wil one of these days, I must also write to Jet Mauve.

Write to me soon, and be completely reassured as to my health, it will cure me completely to know that things are going well for you. What is Gauguin doing? As his family are in the north, and as he's been invited to exhibit in Belgium and has some success in Paris at the moment, I like to think that he's found his way. Good handshake, I'm quite happy all the same that this is a thing of the *past*. Another vigorous handshake.

Ever yours,
Vincent

My dear brother,

I hope that it won't amaze you too much that although I wrote to you this morning I'm adding a few words this same evening. For I've been unable to write for several days, but you can clearly see that that's *over* now.

I've written a line to Mother & to Wil, *which I addressed to our sister* with the sole aim of reassuring them, should you have happened to mention to them that I had been ill. For your part, simply tell them that I've been a bit ill like the time when I had the clap in The Hague, and that I got myself treated at the hospital. But that it's not worth the trouble of mentioning, since I got off with a fright and that I was only in the aforesaid or mentioned hospital for a few days. Thus you'll doubtless find yourself in agreement with the short note that I've made them swallow down there at home in Holland.

And by so doing it will be pretty difficult for them to get worked up about it. In fact, they'll imagine that I almost had the clap. I hope that you'll find this stratagem innocent enough.

Also you'll see from this that I haven't yet forgotten how to jest sometimes.

I'm going to get back to work tomorrow; I'll begin by doing one or two still lifes to get back into the way of painting.

Roulin has been excellent to us, and I dare believe that he'll remain a staunch friend whom I'll still need quite often, for he knows the country well.

We dined together today.

If ever you want to make the house physician Rey *very happy*, this is what would give him great pleasure: he has heard about a painting by Rembrandt, *The Anatomy Lesson*. I told him that we'd get an engraving of it for his study. I hope to do his portrait as soon as I feel a little stronger.

Last Sunday I met another doctor who, in theory at least, knows what Delacroix and Puvis de Chavannes are all about, and who's very curious to know about Impressionism.

I dare hope to get to know him better.

I think that this engraving of *The Anatomy Lesson* is published by François Buffa and Sons, and that the net price should be between 12 and 15 francs. It would be best to frame it here to avoid transportation costs.

I can assure you that a few days in the hospital were very interesting, and that one perhaps learns how to live from the sick.

I hope that I've just had a simple artist's bout of craziness & then a lot of fever following a *very* considerable loss of blood, as an artery was severed.

But my appetite came back immediately, my digestion is good, and the blood is recovering day by day, and likewise serenity is returning to my mind day by day.

So please deliberately forget your sad journey and my illness.

Painting is the profession you know, and my goodness we're perhaps not wrong to try to keep our hearts human.

You can see that I'm doing what you asked me to, that I'm writing what I feel and what I think. For your part, follow up this meeting with the Bongers calmly, I hope that it will continue as a solid friendship, and that perhaps it's even more.

If I remain here it's because I might not be able to transplant myself for the moment. After a little while we can review the pros and cons of the situation and do the calculations again.

I shake your hand firmly.

Ever yours,
Vincent

JENA

the last burning embers; Crossing the Rubicon; a new 'what' is in formation; nightly persecutions; a theater unto himself; the old Nietzsche emerges; Behold the Kaiser! Behold the Satyr! Behold the Monster!

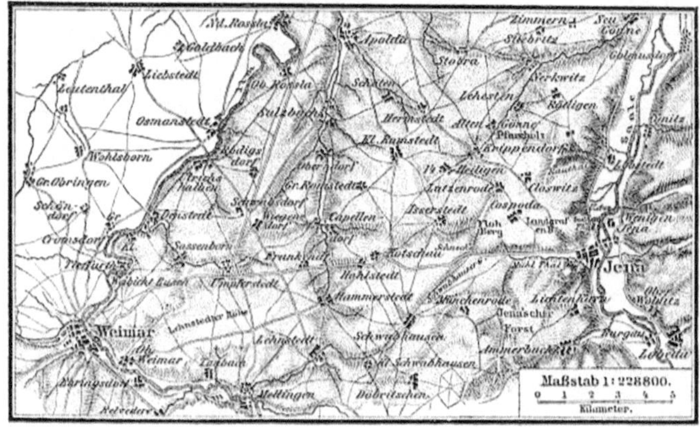

January 1889

The reports from Jena state that the patient continues to be psychotic, delusional, agitated, & incoherent. He grimaces and howls without reason, then speaks of councilors of legations, ministers, and servants. Even though he is little more than the last burning embers of what he once was, the person formerly known to be Nietzsche is also a man of high position and so he fears for his life, fears continual assassination attempts, for 'he' is at war with millennia — seeing a rifle aimed at him from behind a windowpane, he cuts his hand smashing the glass in his attempt to seize the weapon.

Is this Nietzsche's Empedoclean leap into the volcano? The moment when Herr Dynamite evaporates in the sulfuric gases and lava of madness? Crossing the Rubicon with his lantern, like the madman announcing the death of God, is 'he' ever to return? Did he become so posthumous a human being that he could not find the way back to the present? In his descent into the underworld the living all appear to the Ünterganger as nothing but shades — or is it he himself who is the shade? A vegetal entity, a mere effigy of his former selves, some dyscrasiac, discarnate assemblage, an impercipient superposition stripped of all personae — no more is he all the names in history, he is becoming no name; he is becoming nameless; he is becoming nobody. Ecce Homo: How to Become What You Are? *At the present moment, a new 'What' is in formation; a new* Ecce Homo *must be written, for a different* Homo *is in our midst. Reduced to a mere bag of howling flesh, like Marsyas cut to pieces by Apollo, Nietzsche's body and face only a shell behind which no self any longer exists, or the shattered entity of a self, the mere palpitating remnants of a human, like an overcooked fish or a steak devoid of blood, some ghost haunting the body formerly known as Nietzsche.*

At night, 'he' is persecuted, spells and contrivances are enacted, and terrifying machinery is set against him, as if he is the subject of a tyrannical penal colony, the victim of an old moral order he sought to destroy. Since he could not win the war of millennia, now he is a prisoner of war. He consorts, so he recounts to his doctors, with legions of whores in an orgiastic frenzy, a Sadean aristocrat orchestrating a geometry of sexual theater. A libertine set loose in the Dionysian temple of the mind.

I am the Duke of Cumberland, he announces to Prince Bismarck (in actuality, the chief warden), and I am the Kaiser! Last time, I had been Frederick William IV. My wife, Frau Cosima Wagner, had brought me here. Have you seen her ears?

Behold the Duke! Behold the Kaiser!

Other times, 'he' pleads for relief from nightly tortures and sleeps not on his bed but on the floor beside it, twitching and convulsing without cease. When he walks, he tilts his shoulder up spasmodically, sways when turning right about, and eats as if there were in fact a host of selves whirling within his body, devouring food without cease, as if each self were not a mere inner specter of energy but a complete body that must also be fed, adding further bulk to his fleshy corpus.

Behold the satyr!

To protect all pathways to himself, 'he' shatters a mirror, scattering splinters of glass before him. Incontinent, he pisses into his drinking glass, smears his feces on the wall, bundles it into parcels, and sometimes even drinks his own urine. No longer does he ask for Barbera vino; no longer does he enjoy the sweetest grapes; no longer does he cleanse his palette with gelato. Chattering, screaming, groaning unnervingly, 'his' vocalizations pierce the halls of the clinic.

Behold the monster!

Often, 'he' has no idea where 'he' is. Sometimes, 'he' believes he is in Naumburg; other times, that he is in Torino. In fact, 'he' is in no place, in no reality. 'He' is in a state of unbecoming. 'He' is a theater unto himself, rarely entering into dialogue with other patients. He steals books and secrets them away. He writes his name down on crumpled slips of paper that he then removes from his pockets so as to read his name aloud: Professor Friedrich Nietzsche. As if a vatic recording repeating in his head, an Ediphone spinning in short-circuit, elements of his former life sound within his body without sense, the unraveling of some strange, phantasmagoric script.

Behold the abyss!

So the months pass — no more philosophy, no more philology, no more gaya scienza. He who was to break the history of mankind in two has himself been broken into two, three, or more, a more that is forever no more — no longer does he write letters; no longer does he write books; no longer does he play with the entirety of history as if it were a pair of dice. There is no Nietzsche; there is only a state of extreme outness. Mental borborygmia. Yet, his friends at times wonder if he is only feigning madness because, at moments, the old Nietzsche emerges, or appears as if out of some mist. The mask of madness removed? Or, the last remnants of sanity within madness?

Behold chaos! Behold the vir obscurissimus!

Autem: Nietzsche Marionette, a live toy soon to be made to dance at will, against his will, for a will not his own, for a will against which he fought his entire life, torn to pieces by his enemies, rendered to bits, the Bacchants having finally devoured him, the Furies having done their work. An empty, human automaton. From the Übermensch to the sweetest grapes to the shit-smearing non-compos mentis bag of reflexive ganglia — a part mechanical, part human phantasm, an eerie juxtaposition of life and death, a broken tone and mass of colored light.

Ecce Homo:
or How to Become a Disintegrating Milieu ....
Zombie Nietzsche!

ARLES

a letter from your fiancée; I feel completely normal; I went to the hospital again to have my wound dressed; what you tell me about Gauguin gives me enormous pleasure; C.M. must wish that the firm he founded continues; don't forget The Anatomy Lesson; the mistake in pal Gauguin's calculations; a contract to turn me out; defending the interests of our artist friends; the wound is closing very well and the great loss of blood is balancing out; my suffering in the hospital was appalling; under the influence of illness; as long as cholera and the plague &c. continue to menace the area around Marseille; I wish you good days with your fiancée

9 January 1889

My dear Theo,

Even before receiving (this very moment) your kind letter, I received a letter from your fiancée this morning announcing the engagement. So I've already replied to her with my sincere congratulations, as I repeat them here to you.

My fear that my indisposition might prevent your very necessary journey, which I've hoped for so much *&* for so long — now that this fear has disappeared I feel completely normal.

This morning I went to the hospital again to have my wound dressed, and walked for an hour and a half with the house physician, and we talked a little about everything, even *natural history*.

What you tell me about Gauguin gives me enormous pleasure, that's to say that he hasn't abandoned his plan to return to the tropics. That's the right path for him. I think I can see clearly into his plan, and I approve of it with all my heart. Naturally I have regrets about it, but you can understand that provided it goes well for him that's all I need.

If you *can* do so, talk a little to C.M. about the future of his business and the fact that his son can continue it, provided C.M. himself does his full duty as regards listening to you and putting you and his son together. All the same C.M. must wish that the firm he founded continues — hasn't he introduced into Holland the very artists who were *not* with the Goupils, *&*c. *&*c.?

Then Tersteeg must admit the Impressionists, or at least believe in E. Delacroix, and then Tersteeg and you joining hands would be a great force that Boussod would have to reckon with.

What is the 89 exhibition going to be?

Don't forget *The Anatomy Lesson* for Mr. Rey. He had already told me before this morning that he likes painting, although he knows little about it, *&* that he would like to learn. I told him that he should become an *art lover* but that he shouldn't try to do painting himself. This means that perhaps we'll find 2 doctor friends here, Rey *&* the Parisian doctor I spoke to you about before.

I told them that *Bruyas* of Montpellier shares a certain family characteristic with the two of us, *&* that we're therefore simply continuing what Monticelli *&* Bruyas began in the south.

When I came out of the hospital I had quite a few things to pay, and while they aren't at all urgent for a few days, I'd be pleased if you could send me about fifty francs within the next few days.

The mistake in pal Gauguin's calculations was, in my opinion, that he's a little too accustomed to closing his eyes to the inevitable expenses of house rental, charwoman, and a whole heap of earthly things of that kind. Now, all these things weigh a little heavily on the shoulders of the two of us. But once we bear them, other artists could lodge with me without having those costs.

I've just been told that in my absence the owner of my house here apparently made a contract with a fellow who has a tobacco shop, to turn me out and give him, the tobacconist, the house.

That worries me a little, for I'm not much inclined to have myself turned out of this house almost shamefully when it was I who had it repainted inside and out and had gas put in &c., in short who made habitable a house that had been locked up and uninhabited for quite a long time, and which I took on in very poor condition. This is to warn you that perhaps at Easter, for example, if the owner persists, I'll ask you for advice about it, and that in all of this I consider myself merely an agent, defending the interests of our artist friends.

Besides, it's more than likely that water will flow under the bridge between now & then. And the main thing is not to worry about it.

Has Bernard returned the Silvestre book to you yet? I'll need the exact title to get those doctors to read this book.

Physically I am well, the wound is closing very well and the great loss of blood is balancing out, since I'm eating and digesting well. The most fearsome thing is the insomnia, and the doctor didn't talk to me about it, nor have I spoken to him about it yet. But I'm fighting it myself. I'm fighting this insomnia with a very, very strong dose of camphor in my pillow and my mattress, and I recommend it to you if you ever have trouble sleeping. I was very fearful of sleeping alone in the house, and I felt anxious that I wouldn't be able to sleep, but it went very well and I dare to believe that it won't recur.

My suffering in that way in the hospital was appalling, and yet in the midst of it all, though I was more than insensible, I can tell you as a curiosity that I kept thinking about Degas.

Gauguin and I had talked about Degas before, and I pointed out to Gauguin that Degas had said this:... "I'm saving myself for the Arlésiennes."

Now, you who know how subtle Degas is, once you're back in Paris, tell Degas that I admit to you that up until now I've been powerless to paint them as other than poisonous, the women of Arles, and that he mustn't believe Gauguin if Gauguin says good things too soon about my work, which has only been done under the influence of illness.

Now, if I recover I *must start again*, and I can't again attain those peaks to which sickness imperfectly led me.

I would very much have liked to give another painting to Rivet precisely because I wholly agree with you that it would be good to put Mr. Rey in touch with Rivet.

But you could indeed tell Rivet that it would be good to send Mr. Rey back here to the hospital with the doctor's qualification he's going to try and get. He's very, very useful here, and we'll darned well be in need of doctors again here in Arles in days to come, as long as cholera and the plague &c. continue to menace the area around Marseille. Now Rey was born here and would be worthless in Paris or elsewhere, while once he was armed with the full medical power of Paris, he could perform real miracles here in a time of calamity.

Of course we have no right to get involved in the question of medicine, only Rivet himself will perhaps be of the same opinion as regards the feeling that an Arlesian isn't a Parisian & vice versa.

Did you pass through Breda, I'm naturally inclined to think so. Above all, reassure Mother about me.

Have you seen the portrait of me that Gauguin has, and have you seen the portrait that Gauguin did of himself during those final days?

If you were to compare this portrait that Gauguin did of himself then with the one I still have of him, which he sent to me from Brittany in exchange for mine, you would see that all in all he grew more serene here, personally.

What have De Haan & Isaäcson been doing? I had vaguely hoped to see them here one day had Gauguin himself stayed longer with me, and with a view to that I'd even rented two little rooms which were coming vacant in the house which I currently have the whole of (the rent is 21.50 francs a month). I daren't press the point any more, seeing as Gauguin has gone, especially when one considers that the journey to the south costs quite a lot. Anyway, give them my kind regards when you see them again.

Roulin sends his warm regards, he was very pleased with what you said about him in your letter today, and besides, he amply deserves it.

Handshake, and naturally you'll feel how much I wish you good days with your fiancée.

Ever yours,
Vincent.

Warm regards to André Bonger if he's there too.

JENA
1267.1 km from Arles

the philosopher who no longer writes

[17 January 1889]

[Dear   ]

[Nietzsche]

ARLES

1267.1 km from Jena

what I might or might not spend in a whole year; my paint-
ings are worthless; here are the expenses; no fear of renewed
anguish; I feel weak, anxious, and fearful; for the moment
I myself am not yet mad; the whole house was turned up-
side down by this adventure; we weren't Gauguin's exploit-
ers; I've never been able to catch my breath completely;
the question of Rembrandt; the strange phenomenon of
Gauguin; the little Bonaparte tiger of Impressionism; to re-
main armed only with my brush and my pen; all the vice
versa of incompatible desires and needs

17 January 1889

My dear Theo,

Thanks for your kind letter and for the 50-franc note it contained. As to answering all your questions, can you do it yourself, at the moment I don't feel up to it. On reflection I do indeed want to seek a solution, but I must re-read your letter again &c.

But before discussing what I might or might not spend in a whole year, it would perhaps put us on track to review nothing but the present, current month for a moment.

In any case it has been completely lamentable, and indeed I would count myself fortunate if finally you might pay some serious attention to the way things are and have been for so long.

But what can one do, unfortunately it's complicated in several ways, my paintings are worthless, they cost me an extraordinary amount, it's true, perhaps sometimes even in blood and brain. I won't press the point, and what do you want me to say about it. Let's get back in any case to the present month and speak only of money.

On 23 December there was still a louis and 3 sous in the cashbox. That same day I received the 100-franc note from you.

Here are the expenses

Given to Roulin to pay the charwoman for the month of December: 20 Francs. Same for 1st fortnight of January: 10 Francs, Fr 30. Paid to hospital, Fr. 21. Paid to the nurses who dressed the wound, Fr. 10. On returning here paid for a table, a gas heater &c., which had been lent to me, and which I then took on account, Fr. 20. Paid for having all the bedding, bloodstained linen &c. laundered, Fr. 12.50. Various purchases like a dozen brushes, a hat &c. &c. let's say, Fr. 10, which comes to: 103.50. Thus we've already arrived, on the day I left hospital or the day after, at an involuntary expenditure on my part of 103.50, to which it must be added that then on the first day I cheerfully went to have dinner with Roulin at the restaurant, completely reassured and with no fear of renewed anguish. In short, the result of all that was that I was broke around the 8th. But one or two days after that I borrowed 5 francs. We were barely at the tenth. I was hoping for a letter from you around the tenth, but as that letter only arrived today, 17 January, the interval has been a fast of the most rigorous sort, all the more painfully so because my recovery couldn't take place under those conditions.

Nevertheless, I've started work again and I already have 3 studies done in the studio plus the portrait of Mr. Rey, which I gave him as a keepsake.

So this time again there's no more serious harm than a little more suffering and relative anguish. And I retain all good hope. But I feel weak and a little anxious and fearful.

Which will pass, I hope, as I regain my strength.

Rey told me that being very impressionable was enough to have had what I had as regards the crisis, and that currently I was only anemic, but that really I ought to feed myself up. But myself, I took the liberty of telling Mr. Rey that if currently the first thing for me was to recover my strength, if by pure chance or misunderstanding it had just happened again that I'd had to keep to a rigorous one-week fast, if in similar circumstances he had seen many madmen quite calm & capable of working — and if not then would he deign to remember occasionally that for the moment I myself am not yet mad.

Now, in these payments that I made, is there anything unwarranted, extravagant, or exaggerated in these expenses, considering that the whole house was turned upside down by this adventure, and all the linen and my clothes soiled? If I paid what was *owing* to people almost as poor as myself as soon as I got back, is there an error on my part or could I have economized more?

Now today, the 17th, I receive 50 francs at last. Out of this I first pay the 5 francs borrowed from the café owner, then for 10 refreshments taken during this last week on credit, which makes fr. 7.50. I still have to pay for the linen brought back from the hospital, and then for this past week, for the repair of shoes and of a pair of trousers, certainly all in all something like 5. Wood and coal still to be paid for December, and to be bought again, not less than 4. Charwoman 2nd fortnight of January, 10, which comes to 26.50. Tomorrow morning when I've cleared this amount I'll have left, net Fr. 23.50.

It's the 17th today, there are still 13 days left to get through.

Question: how much can I spend per day? Next there must be added the fact that you sent 30 francs to Roulin, out of which he paid the 21.50 for the rent for December.

There you are, my dear brother, the account for the current month. It isn't finished.

We now come to the expenses occasioned by a telegram from Gauguin that I've already reproached him quite formally for having sent.

Are the expenses thus wrongly incurred less than 200 francs?

Does Gauguin himself claim to have acted brilliantly in this?

Look, I won't press the point any more about the absurdity of that course of action. Let's suppose that I was as distraught as could be, why then wasn't the illustrious pal calmer.........
I shan't labor this point any more.

I can't praise you enough for paying Gauguin in such a way that he couldn't but congratulate himself on the relations he's had with us.

Unfortunately, that's another expense, perhaps more sizeable than it should have been, but anyway, I glimpse hope in it.

Mustn't he, or at least shouldn't he begin to see a little that we weren't his exploiters, but that on the contrary we were anxious to safeguard his existence, his possibility of work &........ &...
his integrity.

If that's unworthy of the grandiose prospectuses for artists' associations (which he proposed and to which he still holds) in the way you know, if that's unworthy of his other castles in the air.

Why then not consider him as not responsible for the sorrows and damage which unconsciously he could have caused us in his blindness, you as much as me. If currently that thesis still seems too bold to you — I won't press the point — but let's wait and see.

He's had previous experience with what he calls 'banking in Paris' and believes that he's clever at it... Perhaps you and I are decidedly not so very curious in that regard.

All the same, this isn't in complete disagreement with certain passages of our earlier correspondence.

If Gauguin were to examine himself properly in Paris or have himself examined by a specialist doctor, my word I don't really know what the result of it would be.

Several times over I've seen him do things that you or I wouldn't permit ourselves to do, having consciences that feel things differently — I've heard two or three things said of him in the same vein — but I, who saw him at very, very close quarters, I believed him led by his imagination, by pride perhaps but — — quite irresponsible. This conclusion doesn't imply that I firmly recommend that you listen to him in all circumstances. But in the matter of settling his account I see that you acted with a higher conscience, and so I believe that we have nothing to fear from being led into errors of "banking in Paris" by him. But as for him... upon my word, let him do what he wants, let him have his independences????? (in what way does he consider his character independent), his opinions... and let him go his own way, as it seems to him that he knows it better than we do.

I find it quite odd that he's claiming a painting of sunflowers from me, offering me in exchange I suppose, or as a gift, a few studies that he left here. I'll send back his studies — which will probably have uses for him that they certainly wouldn't have for me.

But for the moment I'm keeping my canvases here, and I'm categorically keeping those sunflowers of mine.

He already has *two* of them, let that be enough for him. And if he's unhappy with the exchange he made with me he can take back his little canvas of Martinique and his portrait that he sent me from Brittany, giving me back for his part both my portrait and my two canvases of sunflowers which he took in Paris. So if he ever raises this subject again, what I've said is clear enough.

How can Gauguin claim to have feared disturbing me by his presence when he would have difficulty denying that he knew I asked for him continually, and people told him time and again that I was insisting on seeing him that very moment?

Precisely to tell him to keep it between himself and me without disturbing you. He wouldn't listen.

It wearies me to recapitulate all this & calculate & recalculate things of this kind.

I've tried in this letter to show you the difference that exists between my net expenses, which come directly from me, and those for which I am less responsible. I was sorry that just at that moment you should have those expenses, which were of no benefit to anyone.

What will happen next, I'll see if my position is tenable as I regain my strength. I so dread a change or moving house precisely because of new expenses. For quite a long time I've never been able to catch my breath completely. I'm not giving up work, because at moments it's going well, and I believe that it's precisely with patience that I'll arrive at this result of being able to recover the previous expenses with paintings I've done.

Roulin's going to leave, and as early as the 21st, he's going to be employed in Marseille.

The increase in salary is minimal, and he'll have to leave his wife and his children for a while, who won't be able to follow him until much later because the expenses of a whole family would be heavier in Marseille.

It's a promotion for him, but it's a very, very meager consolation the government gives in this way to such an employee after so many years of work.

And at heart I think they, he and his wife, are still very, very upset. Roulin has very often kept me company during this past week.

I completely agree with you that we mustn't meddle in doctors' issues that have absolutely nothing to do with us.

Just because you wrote a note to Mr. Rey saying you would introduce him in Paris, I thought you meant to Mr. Rivet.

I didn't think I was doing anything compromising by saying to Mr. Rey myself that if he went to Paris it would give me great pleasure if he wanted to take a painting from me to Mr. Rivet as a keepsake.

Naturally I didn't speak of anything else, but what I said is that I would always regret not being a doctor, and that those who believe painting is beautiful would do well to see in it only a study of nature.

All the same, it will continue to be a pity that Gauguin and I were perhaps too quick to drop the question of Rembrandt and light that we embarked upon.

Are De Haan and Isaäcson still there, they mustn't get discouraged.

After my illness I've naturally had a very sensitive eye. I have *re*-looked at De Haan's undertaker, of which he was kind enough to send me a photograph. Well, it seems to me that there's some real Rembrandt spirit in that figure, which seems lit by the reflection of a light emanating from the open tomb before which the said undertaker stands like a sleepwalker. It's there in a very subtle way. I don't tackle the question with charcoal and he, De Haan, has taken as a means of expression this very charcoal, which is again a colorless material.

I would really like De Haan to see a study of mine of a lighted candle and two novels (one yellow, the other pink) placed on an empty armchair (Gauguin's armchair, to be precise), no. 30 canvas in red and green. I've just been working on the pendant again today, my own empty chair, a deal chair with a pipe and a tobacco pouch. In these two studies, as in others, I myself sought an effect of light with bright color — De Haan would probably understand what I'm seeking if you read him what I write to you on this subject.

However long this letter may now be, in which I've tried to analyze the month and in which I complain a little about the strange phenomenon of Gauguin preferring not to speak to me again while at the same time making himself scarce, it remains for me to add a few words of appreciation.

What's good about him is that he knows how to apportion expenditure from day to day marvelously well.

Whereas myself, I'm often absent-minded, preoccupied with reaching a good *end-point*.

He has more of a sense for balancing money for each day than I do.

But his weakness is that by a sudden attack & animal-like impulse he upsets everything he was setting up.

Now, does one remain at one's post once one has taken it, or does one desert it? I don't judge anyone in this, hoping not to be condemned myself should I lack the strength. But if Gauguin has so much real virtue and such capacities for doing good, how is he going to employ himself? As for me, I've ceased to be able to follow his actions, and I halt silently but with a question mark.

From time to time he and I have exchanged ideas on French art, on Impressionism...

It now seems to me impossible, at least quite improbable, that Impressionism will organize itself and calm down.

Why will the same not happen as happened in England at the time of the Pre-Raphaelites?

The association is dissolved.

Perhaps I take all these things too much to heart, and I'm perhaps too sad about them. Has Gauguin ever read *Tartarin sur les Alpes*, and does he remember Tartarin's illustrious pal from Tarascon who had such an imagination that in one fell swoop he imagined an entire imaginary Switzerland?

Does he remember the knot in a rope rediscovered high up in the Alps after the fall?

And you, who wish to know how things happened, have you ever read the whole of *Tartarin*?

That would teach you to recognize Gauguin pretty well.

I urge you in all seriousness to look at that passage in Daudet's book again.

During your trip here were you able to notice the study that I painted of Tarascon's diligence, which as you know is mentioned in Tartarin the lion-hunter?

And then do you remember Bompard in *Numa Roumestan* and his happy imagination?

This is what we have here, though of another kind, Gauguin has a fine and frank and absolutely complete *imagination of the south*, with that imagination he's going to work in the north! My word, we may yet see some more funny things!

And now dissecting the situation in all boldness, nothing prevents us from seeing him as the little Bonaparte tiger of Impressionism as regards... I don't know quite how to say this, his vanishing let's say from Arles is comparable or parallel to the Return from Egypt of the little corporal mentioned above, who also went to Paris afterwards. And who always left the armies in the lurch.

Happily Gauguin, I, and other painters aren't yet armed with machine guns and other very harmful engines of war. I, for one, am quite determined to try to remain armed only with my brush and my pen.

With loud shouts Gauguin nevertheless demanded from me in his last letter 'His fencing masks and gloves' hidden in the little room of my little yellow house.

I'll make haste to send him these childish things by parcel post. Hoping that he'll never use more serious things.

He's physically stronger than we are, so his passions must also be much stronger than ours. Then he's the father of children, then he has his wife and his children in Denmark, and at the same time he wants to go right to the other end of the globe to Martinique. It's horrifying, all the vice versa of incompatible desires and needs which that must cause him. I had dared to assure him that if he'd stayed quietly with us, working here in Arles without wasting money, earning it, since you were busying yourself with his paintings, his wife would certainly have written to him and would have approved of his quiet life. There's still more besides, there's the fact that he was sick and seriously ill, and that it was a question of discovering both the illness and the remedy. Now here his pains had already ceased. Enough for today.

Do you have the address of Laval, Gauguin's friend? You can tell Laval that I'm very astonished that his friend Gauguin didn't take a portrait of me that I intended for him, in order to give it to him. I'll now send it to you and you can let him have it. I have another new one for you too. Thanks again for your letter. Please try and think that it would be really impossible to live for 13 days on the 23.50 francs that I'll have left. I'll try to manage with 20 francs that you'd send me next week.

Handshake, I'll read your letter again and will write to you soon about the other matters.

Ever yours,
Vincent

JENA

1267.1 km from Arles

Medical Report

21 January 1889

Medical Examination Record

Was noisy all the time, in spite of 2.0 chloral. Had to be isolated
finally. — Said on one occasion that his father had 'also suffered
from softening of the brain.'

ARLES

1267.1 km from Jena

I'm not a little plagued by the friends' departure; now I feel remorse… unless; I think that I'll begin by returning what belongs to you; an arrangement of colors; I can't even make the gesture of sending you back your things; terrible engines of war; mental or nervous fever or madness; I sang then, I who can't sing

21 January 1889

My dear friend Gauguin,

Thanks for your letter. Left behind alone on board my little yellow house — as it was perhaps my duty to be the last to remain here anyway — I'm not a little plagued by the friends' departure.

Roulin has had his transfer to Marseille and has just left. It has been touching to see him these last days with little Marcelle, when he made her laugh and bounce on his knees.

His transfer necessitates his separation from his family, and you won't be surprised that as a result the man you and I simultaneously nicknamed "the passer-by" one evening had a very heavy heart. Now so did I, witnessing that and other heart-breaking things.

His voice as he sang for his child took on a strange timber in which there was a hint of a woman rocking a cradle or a distressed wet-nurse, and then another sound of bronze, like a clarion from France.

Now I feel remorse at having perhaps, I who so insisted that you should stay here to await events and gave you so many good reasons for doing so, now I feel remorse at having indeed perhaps prompted your departure — unless, however, that departure was premeditated beforehand? And that then it was perhaps up to me to show that I still had the right to be kept frankly *au courant*.

Whatever the case, I hope we like each other enough to be able to begin again if need be, if penury, alas ever-present for us artists without capital, should necessitate such a measure.

You talk to me in your letter about a canvas of mine, the sunflowers with a yellow background — to say that it would give you some pleasure to receive it. I don't think that you've made a bad choice — if Jeannin has the peony, Quost the hollyhock, I indeed, before others, have taken the sunflower.

I think that I'll begin by returning what belongs to you, making it plain that it's my intention, after what has happened, to contest categorically your right to the canvas in question. But as I commend your intelligence in the choice of that canvas I'll make an effort to paint two of them, exactly the same. In which case it might be done once and for all and thus settled amicably, so that you could have your own all the same.

Today I made a fresh start on the canvas I had painted of Mrs. Roulin, the one that had remained in a vague state as regards the hands because of my accident. As an arrangement of colors: the reds moving through to pure oranges, intensifying even more in the flesh tones up to the chromes, passing into the pinks and marrying with the olive and Veronese greens. As an Impressionist arrangement of colors, I've never devised anything better.

And I believe that if one placed this canvas just as it is in a boat, even one of Icelandic fishermen, there would be some who would feel the lullaby in it. Ah! my dear friend, to make of painting what the music of Berlioz and Wagner has been before us... a consolatory art for distressed hearts! There are as yet only a few who feel it as you and I do!!!

My brother understands you well, and when he tells me that you're a kind of unfortunate like me, then that indeed proves that he understands us.

I'll send you your things, but at times weakness overcomes me again, and then I can't even make the gesture of sending you back your things. I'll pluck up the courage in a few days. And the *"fencing masks and gloves"* (make the very least possible use of less childish engines of war), those terrible engines of war will wait until then. I now write to you very calmly, but I haven't yet been able to pack up all the rest.

In my mental or nervous fever or madness, I don't know quite what to say or how to name it, my thoughts sailed over many seas. I even dreamed of the Dutch ghost ship and the Horla, and it seems that I sang then, I who can't sing on other occasions, to be precise an old wet-nurse's song while thinking of what the cradle-rocker sang as she rocked the sailors and whom I had sought in an arrangement of colors before falling ill. Not knowing the music of *Berlioz*. A heartfelt handshake.

Ever yours,
Vincent

It will please me greatly if you write to me again before long. Have you read *Tartarin* in full by now? The imagination of the south creates pals, doesn't it, and between us we always have friendship.

Have you yet read and re-read *Uncle Tom's Cabin* by Beecher Stowe? It's perhaps not very well written in the literary sense. Have you read *Germinie Lacerteux* yet?

JENA

1267.1 km from Arles

Medical Report

22 January 1889

Medical Examination Record

Wants to have his composition performed. Complains of headaches at the top of his head and in his forehead. — Thinks this is
the reason why he was so lively.

ARLES

1267.1 km from Jena

I'm getting along so-so; a certain "what's the good of getting better" feeling; Icelandic fishermen and their melancholy isolation; the unbearable hallucinations have stopped for now; I'm working furiously from morning till night; if I'm not mad the time will come when I'll send you what I've promised; you and I will have successors in business; as long as the present earth lasts; the chief inspector of police; everything is always for the best in the best of worlds; work distracts me, and I must have distractions; I believe and will always believe in the art to be created in the tropics; perhaps everyone will one day have neurosis; struck to the marrow by artistic madness

28 January 1889

My dear Theo,

Just a few words to tell you that I'm getting along so-so as regards my health and work.

Which I already find astonishing when I compare my state today with that of a month ago. I well knew that one could break one's arms and legs before, and that then afterwards that could get better but I didn't know that one could break one's brain and that afterwards that got better too.

I still have a certain "what's the good of getting better" feeling in the astonishment that an ongoing recovery causes me, which I wasn't in a state to dare rely upon.

When you visited I think you must have noticed in Gauguin's room the two no. 30 canvases of the sunflowers. I've just put the finishing touches to the absolutely equivalent and identical repetitions. I think I've already told you that in addition I have a canvas of a *Berceuse*, the very same one I was working on when my illness came and interrupted me. Today I also have 2 versions of this one.

On the subject of that canvas, I've just said to Gauguin that as he and I talked about the Icelandic fishermen and their melancholy isolation, exposed to all the dangers, alone on the sad sea, I've just said to Gauguin about it that, following these intimate conversations, the idea came to me to paint such a picture that sailors, at once children and martyrs, seeing it in the cabin of a boat of Icelandic fishermen, would experience a feeling of being rocked, reminding them of their own lullabies. Now it looks, you could say, like a chromolithograph from a penny bazaar. A woman dressed in green with orange hair stands out against a green background with pink flowers. Now these discordant sharps of garish pink, garish orange, garish green, are toned down by flats of reds and greens. I can imagine these canvases precisely between those of the sunflowers — which thus form standard lamps or candelabra at the sides, of the same size; and thus the whole is composed of 7 or 9 canvases.

(I'd like to make another repetition for Holland if I can get the model again.)

As it's still winter, listen. Let me quietly continue my work, if it's that of a madman, well, too bad. Then I can't do anything about it.

However, the unbearable hallucinations have stopped for now, reducing themselves to a simple nightmare on account of taking potassium bromide, I think.

It's still impossible for me to deal with this question of money in detail, but I want to deal with it in detail all the same, and I'm working furiously from morning till night to prove to you (unless my work is yet another hallucination), to prove to you that really, truly, we're following in Monticelli's track here and, what's more, that we have a light on our way and a lamp before our feet in the powerful work of Bruyas of Montpellier, who has done so much to create a school in the south.

Only don't be absolutely too amazed if, in the course of the coming month, I would be obliged to ask you for the month in full, and even the relative extra included.

After all, it's only right if in these productive times when I expend all my vital warmth I should insist on what is necessary to take a few precautions. The difference in expenditure is certainly not excessive on my part, not even in cases like that. And once again, either lock me up in a madhouse straightaway, I won't resist if I'm wrong, or let me work with all my strength, while taking the precautions I mention.

If I'm not mad the time will come when I'll send you what I've promised you from the beginning. Now, these paintings may perhaps be fated for dispersal, but when you, for one, see the whole of what I want, you will, I dare hope, receive a consolatory impression from it.

You saw, as I did, a part of the Faure collection file past in the little window of a framer's shop in rue Lafitte, didn't you? You saw, as I did, that this slow procession of canvases that were previously despised was strangely interesting.

Good. My great desire would be that sooner or later you should have a series of canvases from me that could also file past in that exact same shop window.

Now, in continuing the furious work this February and March I hope I'll have finished the calm repetitions of a number of studies I did last year. And these, together with certain canvases of mine that you already have, such as the harvest and the white orchard, will form quite a firm base. During this same time, so no later than March, we can settle what has to be settled on the occasion of your marriage.

But although I'll work during February and March, I'll consider myself to be still ill, and I tell you in advance that in these two months I may have to take 250 a month from the year's allowance.

You'll perhaps understand that what would reassure me in some way regarding my illness and the possibility of a relapse would be to see that Gauguin and I didn't exhaust our brains for nothing at least, but that good canvases result from it. And I dare hope that one day you'll see that in remaining upright and calm now, precisely on the question of money — it will be impossible later on to have acted badly toward the Goupils. If indirectly I've eaten some of their bread, certainly through you as an intermediary — Directly I will then retain my integrity.

So, far from still remaining awkward with each other almost all the time because of that, we can feel like brothers again after that has been sorted out. You'll have been poor all the time to feed me, but I'll return the money or turn up my toes.

Now your wife will come, who has a good heart, to make us old fellows feel a bit younger again.

But this I believe, that you and I will have successors in business, and that precisely at the moment when the family abandoned us to our own resources, financially speaking, it will again be we who haven't flinched.

My word, may the crisis come after that... Am I wrong about that, then?

Come on, as long as the present earth lasts there will be artists and picture dealers, especially those who are apostles at the same time, like you. And if ever we're comfortably off, even while perhaps being old Jewish smokers, at least we'll have worked by forging straight ahead and won't have forgotten the things of the heart that much, even though we have calculated a little.

What I tell you is true: if it isn't absolutely necessary to shut me away in a madhouse then I'm still good for paying what I can be considered to owe, at least in goods.

Then, my dear brother, we have 89. The whole of France shivered at it and so did we old Dutchmen, with the same heart. Beware of 93, you may perhaps tell me. Alas there's some truth in that, and that being the case let's stay with the paintings.

In conclusion I must also tell you that the chief inspector of police came yesterday to see me, in a very friendly way. He told me as he shook my hand that if ever I had need of him I could consult him as *a friend*. To which I'm a long way from saying no, and I may soon be in precisely that case if difficulties were to arise for the house. I'm waiting for the moment to come to pay my month's rent to interrogate the manager or the owner face to face.

But to chuck me out they'd more likely get a kick in the backside, on this occasion at least. What can you say, we've gone all-out for the Impressionists, now as regards myself I'm trying to finish the canvases which will indubitably guarantee my little place that I've taken among them.

Ah, the future of that... but from the moment when *père* Pangloss assures us that everything is always for the best in the best of worlds — can we doubt it?

My letter has become longer than I intended, it matters little — the main thing is that I ask categorically for two months' work before settling what will need to be settled at the time of your marriage.

Afterwards, you and your wife will set up a commercial firm for several generations in the renewal. You won't have it easy. And once that's sorted out I ask only a place as an employed painter as long as there's enough to pay for one.

As a matter of fact, work distracts me. And I *must* have distractions — yesterday I went to the Folies Arlésiennes, the budding theater here — it was the first time I've slept without a serious nightmare. They were performing — (it was a Provençal literary society) what they call a Noel or Pastourale, a remnant of Christian theater of the Middle Ages. It was very studied and it must have cost them some money.

Naturally it depicted the birth of Christ, intermingled with the burlesque story of a family of astounded Provençal peasants. Good — what was remarkable, like a Rembrandt etching — was the old peasant woman, just the sort of woman Mrs. Tanguy would be, with a head of flint or gun flint, false, treacherous, mad, all that could be seen previously in the play. Now that woman, in the play, brought before the mystic crib — in her quavering voice began to sing and then her voice changed, changed from witch to angel and from the voice of an angel into the voice of a child and then the answer by another voice, this one firm and warmly vibrant, a woman's voice, behind the scenes.

That was astonishing, astonishing. I tell you, the so-called 'Félibres' had anyway spared themselves neither trouble nor expense.

As for me, with this little country here I have no need at all to go to the tropics.

I believe and will always believe in the art to be created in the tropics, and I believe it will be marvelous, but well, personally I'm too old and (especially if I get myself a papier-mâché ear) too jerrybuilt to go there.

Will Gauguin do it? It isn't necessary. For if it must be done it will be done all on its own. We are merely links in the chain.

At the bottom of our hearts good old Gauguin and I understand each other, and if we're a bit mad, so be it, aren't we also a little sufficiently deeply artistic to contradict anxieties in that regard by what we say with the brush?

Perhaps everyone will one day have neurosis, the Horla, St Vitus's Dance, or something else.

But doesn't the antidote exist? In Delacroix, in Berlioz and Wagner? And really, our artistic madness, which all the rest of us have, I don't say that I especially haven't been struck to the marrow by it. But I say and will maintain that our antidotes and consolations can, with a little good will, be considered as amply prevalent. See Puvis de Chavannes' *Hope*.

Ever yours,
Vincent

INTERVAL: PARAGUAY; ARLES & ELSEWHERE

Knight, Death, & the Devil; the shipwreck of madness

1881 / early 1889

As Bernhard Förster is making his last dying efforts to sustain his Teutonic Christian colony, Nietzsche-Dionysos proclaims to Overbeck that, as part of his war with millennia, he is having all anti-Semites shot. With this decisive gesture, he effectively and in principle orders *the assassination of his sister & brother-in-law*. Are such mercenary acts but the sublime privilege of being a god, the whimsical evocation of mordant desires, or a necessary gesture to safeguard a future the philosopher seeks to cultivate? Did he not once inform his sister that he was in a position of emergency defense against her spouse's Party? *These accursed anti-Semite deformities shall not sully my ideal!!* he exclaimed. The concept politics has become completely absorbed into a war of spirits, all the power-structures of the old society have been blown into the air — they one and all reposed on the lie; there will be wars such as there have never yet been on earth. Only after me will there be grand politics on earth.

Dionysos vs. the Crucified!

If far off in Paraguay the Försters could not feel the targets on their backs (it does take some time for light to reach its destination, even at the speed of light), Nietzsche-Dionysos felt as if he were clearing the decks and so he was becoming more and more buoyant, his days and nights festive, rife with jubilation — the Dionysian victory was in sight. Often, he has such clownish fancies that he sometimes grins for half an hour on end — pulling a face, he says, is all I can call it.

Is this part of his being a mocking monster, like his antagonist/Doppelgänger Socrates? He had been at war with the anti-Semites for some time, his life having been far too closely intertwined with their kind far more than he ever desired. If, as an earth-shaking force, he had the power to break open fault lines, to crack the history of mankind in two, how difficult could it be to dispense with a few anti-Semites, especially if he could take them out unawares?

In 1881, several years before the sister of Dionysos would marry his would-be archenemy, Förster circulated a mass petition, calling for the social segregation, economic boycott, and removal from public life of all Jews. If at the time it proved unsuccessful in achieving its ends, it was signed by nearly a quarter of a million people, as if presaging some even more terrible future act. In his essay *Echoes of Parsifal. Sundry Thoughts on German Culture, Learning, Art, Society*, Förster refers to Parsifal as God's son and the son of a supreme genius truly begotten in the plenitude of his powers. Richard Wagner, he claimed, is the prophet of his People, then went on to ask, What position does Wagner occupy in the development of the German, Aryan culture?

Although the composer paid little heed to the screeds of his fervent acolyte, it evoked for him his own impassioned attacks on the Jews, written to King Ludwig, as well as his regeneration essays, where he evinced his desires to shepherd the German Volk toward a utopian future, a future guided by the spirit of music, a project which the young Nietzsche once sought to spur on, sans anti-Semitism. In the jungles of Paraguay, if the utopian future was not taking seed, family ties with Nietzsche were growing tighter & tauter, as dense as the jungle-like mass of entangled vines & underbrush, as swift & as poisonous as shrubs like nightshade. How firmly would the ring close 'round his soul & entangle him? How deeply would 'he' be taken into the bosom of the anti-Semites? Would he become the sacrificial son of a new politics? *The Crucified One!*

In *The Relation of Modern Jewry to German Art*, an 1881 talk Förster gave to the Berlin branch of the Bayreuth Patrons' Society, the root of Christian antipathy toward the Jews is found in the Jews themselves. Upholding Dürer as a superior moral model to the characters of the Hebrew Bible, Förster wondered, How would Dürer's Knight have reacted, had he seen that nine-tenths of the modern 'educated class' listens with enthusiasm to their Music-Jews & Literature-Jews, whose prostituted business comes mostly from printed wisecracks and smut?

Dürer's image of *Ritter, Tod, und Teufel* (Knight, Death, and the Devil) would in fact prove to be a potent symbol in the lives of Nietzsche and the Försters, who received from the philosopher a copy of the artwork as a wedding gift. Yet, even the man of destiny could not have realized how prophetic his gift was, a sort of premonition of their lives, of the disastrous fate of Elisabeth & Bernhard, if not also symbolic of the fate of their increasingly intertwined lives, however immense their pathos der distanz. At the time, Elisabeth's brother trusted that the future of the young couple would be more cheerful than what is depicted in Dürer's sinister picture, but it was the mark of the sinister that would rule over them until the end of their days. As far away as the end was, one could still smell the sulfur.

If Bernhard & Eli saw themselves as the Knight and the Jews as the Devil, the philosopher saw himself as the Knight (albeit a Provençal and pagan one) and Bernhard and his sister as both Death & 'Devil.' Yet, when asserting that they feast on compassion, heroic self-denial, Christianity, vegetarianism, Aryanism, and southern colonies, for Eli the Knight, it is Fritz, her brother, that is the Devil incarnate.

I have taken my decisive step, the courageous animal told a friend. Everything is right now. Do you want a new name for me? The church has one: I am — — — — — — — the Anti-Christ. Let us not forget laughter!

Antichrist, Elisabeth said alarmed, it is terrible. I cannot help myself, but I find Fritz's views more & more unsympathetic. I do not see who could benefit from them in the slightest. Do you understand now why I wish he shared Forster's views? Forster has ideals that will make people better & happier if they are promoted and carried out. I laugh at the uproar he causes among stupid people. You will see that someday Förster will be praised as one of the best Germans and a benefactor of his people.

So went the *militis Christiani*, forging their way through the jungle and toward their Aryan utopia, Antichrist be damned, Jews be damned, Dionysos be damned. Were they not the people of Judas? Judaea, Judas, what difference, they must be vanquished, whoever and whatever they are. How can such weightless scoundrels know what freedom and redemption is?

All the while, through Brandes, Nietzsche's voice is slowly gaining ground in Europe, Helen Zimmern is translating his work into English, and the philosopher-king counts as his own eminent readers such as Strindberg and Hippolyte Taine, with Strindberg declaring in all his new letters, *Carthago est delenda, lisez Nietzsche!*

How powerful indeed was his sperm, how far-reaching! What a tremendous and voluminous ejaculation! What gifts the testicles of Nietzsche bestowed to the world! What germinal intensity!

Yet, to Knight Eli, Brandes was nothing more than a Jew who had peeked in too many pots and eaten from too many plates. But whom else would an Antichrist sit at table with but a Jew? To Knight Eli, Brandes was but another whispering Devil of little relevance, and her brother, whose entire philosophy she once said went against her grain, was delusional. The organs at the disposal of the Bernhards had much greater resonance, with their propaganda sounding in the *Bayreuther Blätter* and Bernhard proselytizing to Wagnerian societies, colonial clubs, civic groups, and farmers and worker's associations whereas the night owl, the Hermit of Sils

Maria, whispered secrets amidst mountains, rocks, and lakes.

Do you realize, Knight Eli wrote in "A Sunday in Nueva Germania," that the only fruitful spirit of colonization has emanated from Bayreuth? ... Other noises reach us on the soft currents of the evening breeze; the singing of German men reaches us from a garden a little way off. How the jungle trees must wonder at these strange new sounds wafting through the treetops. ... Up into the star-studded southern night sky, into the mysterious gloom of the jungle: *Deutschland, Deutschland über alles, über alles in der Welt.*

This world is the will to power — & nothing besides!

That same month, Förster's brother Paul would co-found the Deutschsoziale Antisemitische Partei (DSP), which would continue into the early 20th century when, in the Reichstag, DSP representatives collaborated with the Christian Social Party and the German Agrarian League. One of the DSP's aims was to nullify civil rights laws as applicable to Jews and to pass a law that would treat Jewish Germans as a new category of aliens. Race-mixing, some of them would later declare, was an abomination. In 1881, Nietzsche asserted in *Daybreak* that what is normal is crossed races. Purity, he riddled, putting the notion through radical transvaluation, is the final result of countless adaptations, absorptions, and secretions . . .

February 1889 also brought with it the publication of Klingbeil's damning account of the Teutonic utopia, *Enthüllungen über die Dr Bernhard Förster'sche Ansiedlung Neu-Germanien in Paraguay: Ein Beitrag zur Geschichte unserer kolonialen Bestrebungen.* If this screed outlining the deceptions of Nueva Germania fissured Förster's spirit and led to some supporters threatening to cease lending the venture financial support, it only emboldened his bride, who in her swift counter-attack ridiculed and lambasted Klingbeil for his lack of loyalty, courage, and trust.

Anti-Semitism, she said, has above all a positive aspect: the urge to deepen and ennoble the true German characteristics; it is motivated by the urge to create or renew institutions which strengthen true Germanness in an idealistic or economic sense and protect it from foreign influences.

Wifely bluster and galimatias did little to buoy Förster's soul, let alone have any concrete effect upon the dilemmas befalling their dream. As loans from Paraguayan banks accrued debilitating interest and the colony seemed more and more doomed, Förster spent less and less time in his utopia, holing up instead at Hotel del Lago, another colony outside of Asunción. The great Knight took to drink to assuage his besieged nerves and stem the anguish of his cell-cracking headaches. How else keep Death & the Devil at bay — or was that a way of welcoming them? The hiss of the jungle insects echoed the feverish noise of his boiling cranium for, as he gazed into the jungle, it also gazed back into him. Against his will, his body was absorbing the secretion of elements around him, but his powers of adaptation were scant, ruled by a plasmic finality.

Yet still other gases besieged the fevered brain of van Gogh this same month, the perilous edge of sanity cracking beneath his flesh as he was painting and repainting his shipwreck, *La Berceuse*.

As if to dispel the mayhem within his own psyche, to project it outwards and plant it in an exogenous root, van Gogh thought that, if Dr. Rivet examined the whole population of Arles, he would pronounce them all to be sick. Everyone here he told Theo is suffering from either fever, or hallucinations, or madness. This is to tell you that, as for myself, I don't have any illusions. When I came out of the hospital with good Roulin I fancied that I hadn't had anything, only afterwards did I have the feeling that I'd been ill, as if contact with the external world, with the provincial Arlésiennes in particular, was what in fact made me ill.

Suicided by society! Suicided by the south!

What can you say, I have moments when I am twisted by enthusiasm or madness or prophecy, like a Greek oracle on her tripod. Then I have a great presence of mind in my words and talk like the Arlésiennes, but in spite of all that, I feel so weak. Especially when my physical powers return. I told my doctor that if even the slightest symptom were to arise, I'd return and subject myself to the alienist doctors of Aix.

Having grown terrified of the artist and his unsettling behavior, many in Arles alerted the gendarmerie, who thereafter begin conducting surveillance of the Yellow House and observing the foreigner from afar.

Several days later, like descending birds of prey, the police stormed the Studio of the South, seized the Dutchman, and took him to Hôtel Dieu, where he was shackled to a bed in an isolation cell.

For days, the mad painter refused to eat. He recognized no one and remained mute, refusing, or unable, to utter a single word. Bereft of ear, bereft of pal Gauguin, bereft of his Studio of the South, the painter once again spiraled into cracked strata, fault lines of terrifying velocity and violence where all ground split open.

One of the doctors reported that he was suffering from a state of extreme over-excitement, a veritable frenzy in which he babbled incoherently and suffered from some terrible delirium. He was prey to auditory hallucinations in which he heard voices uttering reproaches against him, was in the grip of an idée fixe that the people around him were trying to poison him, to infect him with the Arlésienne fever. This patient's condition appears very serious to us, and appears to require close surveillance and treatment in a special asylum, as his mental faculties are profoundly impaired.

Is he mad, or mistralic, crowned with sunflowers, garlanded with irises, baptized with earth, Saint Fou Roux!? Or is he a human sarcophagus, solvent, fire, cold night air and coal smoke?

JENA

1267.1 km from Arles

Medical Report

10 February 1889

Jena Medical Report

Very noisy. Frequent displays of rage with unarticulated screaming without any external motive. Speaks in Italian often.

The mother brought a black book of the patient's, written before
his collapse, most of which is impossible to decipher. A few passages we can make out read:

> I sought my heaviest burden
> and found myself.
>
> Thou canst no longer bear
> thy heroic fate
> love it, thou hast no choice remaining!
>
> Quietude is salvation,
> he who has nothing to do, is much
> concerned with things of nought.
>
> Solitude
> is not grievous: it ripens——
> but thou must have the sun for thy friend.
>
> Thou didst run too swiftly:
> but now that thou art wearied
> thy joy overtakes thee.

ARLES

1267.1 km from Jena

The first day, he was highly agitated; he loses his train of thought from time to time; his mental state was once more deteriorating; we will keep Vincent in the hospital

12 February 1889

Dear Sir,

When I saw that your brother was more fatigued, I had the Rev. Salles informed, in order to ask him what he thought should be done.

I therefore admitted him, and have put him in a room, under observation.

The first day, he was highly agitated, and his delirium was general. He recognized neither me nor Mr. Salles. Since yesterday, however, I have found him more aware. He is less delirious and he recognizes me. He talks about his painting, although he loses his train of thought from time to time and utters only incoherent words and confused sentences.

I have received the engraving that you were kind enough to send me. Thank you for that.

I apologize for not having written to you sooner to acknowledge receiving it, but on the day when Vincent brought it to me, I noticed that his mental state was once more deteriorating and I wished to wait a few days before writing to you, so that I could give you news of him.

This is what I have decided for the time being. We will keep Vincent in the hospital for some time longer. If we see him returning to health we will continue to treat him here. If not, we will send him to the regional asylum. I hope, however, that this improvement that we have noted will continue, and that in a few days your brother will be able to return to his work.

With my sincerest regards,
Rey Félix'

Chief house physician
Bouches du Rhône — Arles —

JENA

1267.1 km from Arles

Medical Report

18 February 1889

Jena Medical Report

No longer knows the beginning of his last book.

ARLES

my mind was so out of sorts; it isn't permissible for anyone to take such a course of action without warning me; there are so many moments when I feel completely normal; a legend that makes them afraid of painting; the foundation of truth that there may be in the absurd; the isolation cell; at the hospital they know me now; I no longer dare to urge painters to come here; let's try to seize our fate

18 February 1889

My dear Theo,

As long as my mind was so out of sorts it would have been fruit-
less to try and write to you to reply to your kind letter. Today I've
just returned home for the time being, I hope for good. There are
so many moments when I feel completely normal, and actually it
would seem to me that, if what I have is only a sickness peculiar
to this area, I should wait quietly here until it's over. Even if it
were to happen again (which, let's say, won't be the case).

But here is what I'm saying once and for all to you and to Mr.
Rey. If sooner or later it were desirable that I should go to Aix,
as has already been suggested — I consent in advance and will
submit to it.

But in my capacity as painter and workman it isn't permissible for anyone, not even you or the doctor, to take such a course
of action without warning me and consulting me myself about it
too, because as up to now I've always kept my relative presence
of mind for my work, it's my right to say then (or at least to have
an opinion on) what would be best, to keep my studio here or to
move completely to Aix. That in order to avoid the expenses and
the losses of a move as much as possible, and not to do it except
in the event of an absolute emergency.

It appears that the people around here have a legend that
makes them afraid of painting and that people talked about that
in the town. Good. As for me, I know that it's the same thing in
Arabia, and yet we have heaps of painters in Africa, don't we?
Which proves that with a little firmness one can alter these prejudices, or at least do one's painting all the same. The unfortunate
thing is that I'm rather inclined to be impressed, to feel the beliefs
of other people myself and not always to laugh at the foundation
of truth that there may be in the absurd.

Besides, Gauguin is like that too, as you were able to observe,
and was himself also tired out at the time of his stay by some
malaise or other.

As I've already been staying here for more than a year,
and have heard people say pretty much all the bad things possible about me, about Gauguin, about painting in general, why
shouldn't I take things as they are and wait for the outcome here.

Where can I go that's worse than where I've already been twice — the isolation cell. The advantages that I have here are, as Rivet would say — first — "they're all sick" here, and so at least I don't feel alone.

Then, as you well know, I love Arles so much, although Gauguin is darned right to call it the filthiest town in all of the south.

And I've found so much friendship already from the neighbors, from Mr. Rey, from everyone at the hospital for that matter, that really I'd prefer to be always ill here than to forget the kindness there is in the same people who have the most incredible prejudices toward painters and painting, or in any case have no clear and healthy idea whatsoever about it as we do.

Then at the hospital they know me now, and if this were to come on again it would pass in silence, and at the hospital they'd know what to do. I have absolutely no desire to be treated by other doctors, nor do I feel the need for it.

The only desire I might have is to be able to continue to earn with my own hands what I spend.

Koning has written me a very kind letter, saying that he and a friend would probably come to the south with me for a long time. That in response to a letter I wrote him a few days ago. I no longer dare to urge painters to come here after what has happened to me, they run the risk of losing their heads like me. The same thing for De Haan and Isaäcson.

Let them go to Antibes, Nice, Menton, it's perhaps healthier.

Mother and our sister also wrote to me, the latter was very upset about the sick woman she was caring for. At home they're very pleased about your marriage.

Be well aware that you mustn't preoccupy yourself with me too much, nor fret yourself.

It must probably run its course, & we couldn't change very much about our fate with precautions.

Once again, let's try to seize our fate in whatever form it comes. Our sister wrote to me that your fiancée would come to stay with them for a while. That is well done. Ah well, I shake your hand most heartily, & let us not be discouraged. Believe me.

Ever yours,
Vincent

Warm regards to Gauguin, I hope he's going to write to me, I'll write to him too.

Address next letter place Lamartine.

JENA

1267.1 km from Arles

Medical Report

25 February 1889

Jena Medical Report

Asks the doctor with a smile, "Give me a little health."

ARLES

1267.1 km from Jena

Is your own health reasonably good; I walk a lot to take the air; perhaps this canvas is incomprehensible; I haven't got up my confidence; one must suffer something; run by invalids or idiots of the fine arts; to see even an entire population seized by panic; there are so many painters who are cracked

25 February 1889

My dear Theo,

Thanks very much for your kind letter and for the 50-franc note it contained. Is your own health reasonably good, and is the weather in Paris bearable?

Here we have days of sunshine and wind, I walk a lot to take the air. Up to now I've been sleeping and eating at the hospital. Yesterday and today I began to work. When Mrs. Roulin also left, to go and live with her mother in the country for the time being, she took away the *Berceuse*. I had the sketch of it and two repetitions. She had a good eye and took the best one, only I'm currently redoing it. And I don't want this one to be inferior.

I have this to say in reply to Mourier's letter, which gave me pleasure: if Gauguin wants to make an exchange with you for a version of the *Berceuse*, he can send it to his wife in Denmark, and in this way I would gladly see a canvas of mine there. But as I've already told you, perhaps this canvas is incomprehensible. I would also wish to send something to Holland. But I haven't got up my confidence for all of that yet. Will you see a bit of greenery there, in your new apartment? I hope so.

As regards Koning, really I daren't encourage him too much to come here, nor even with his gusto to get carried away with the south, with the experience I'm having of it at the moment. If he goes to Nizza, Menton, where it may be healthier, he's bound to be cheated by the gamblers because of his good humor &c., for that's a real nuisance, even here already, and warps characters. But fortunately, if he goes there he won't go there alone. For his painting, certainly there are some very fine things here.

But if one has *too many annoyances*, what can one say and do then?

Anyway, you can see that I don't quite know what to think yet.

Bernard has written to me as well. I haven't been able to reply yet, for it's so difficult to explain the nature of the difficulties one might encounter here, and with our northern or Parisian customs and ways of thinking it's inevitable that if one stays here for a long time one must suffer something that isn't amusing in these parts.

Must however admit that in all the towns there are schools of drawing and masses of art lovers, but you understand that run by invalids or idiots of the fine arts it's nothing but appearance and show.

Mr. Salles remitted me the 50 francs immediately. It gives me great pleasure that Gauguin has finished some lithographs.

I believe also what you say, that if one day it was to take a graver turn one would have to follow what the doctors said, and I don't oppose that. But that day may not be tomorrow or the day after tomorrow.

Now it isn't rare in these parts, it appears, to see even an entire population seized by panic — thus at Nizza during the earth tremor. Currently all the town is anxious, nobody knows precisely why, and I saw in the newspapers that recently in places not very distant from here there had been more light shakes of earth tremor again. All the more reason, then, for me to be of the opinion that, as far as I myself am concerned, I should wait with as much patience as I can muster, hoping that afterwards it will settle down again.

At another moment, if I were less impressionable, I would probably poke a good deal of fun at what seems to me to be askew and deranged in the local customs. At present, from time to time it doesn't have a very happy effect on me. Right, well — in fact, there are so many painters who are cracked in one way or another that little by little I'll be consoled by it.

More than ever I understand the sufferings of Gauguin, who caught the same thing in the tropics, an excessive sensitivity. At the hospital I just glimpsed a sick negress who's living there and works as a servant. Tell him that.

If you were to say to Rivet that you have so many anxieties for me he'll certainly reassure you by saying that, because there's so much affinity and community of ideas between us, you feel the same thing a little. Don't think too much about me — with an idée fixe.

What's more, I'll get along better if I know that you're calm. Whatever happens, aren't there a great many of us in France who try to remain calm whatever happens, adversity or prosperity?

I shake your hand firmly in thought. You're really kind to say that I could come to Paris, but I think that the bustle of a big city will never be worth anything to me. More soon.

Ever yours,
Vincent

JENA

1267.1 km from Arles

the psychologist who no longer writes

[26 February 1889]

[Dear   ]

[Nietzsche]

INTERVAL: ARLES

The Mayoral Petition
1267.1 km from Jena

26 February 1889

Dear Mr. Mayor:

We the undersigned, residents of place Lamartine in
the city of Arles, have the honor to inform you that for
some time and on several occasions the man named
Vood (Vincent), a landscape painter and a Dutch subject,
living in the above square, has demonstrated that he is
not in full possession of his mental faculties, and that
he over-indulges in drink, after which he is in a state
of over-excitement such that he no longer knows what
he is doing or what he is saying, and very unpredictable
toward the public, a cause for fear to all the residents of
the neighborhood, and especially to women & children.

In view of this, the undersigned have the honor of
requesting, in the name of public safety, that the man
named Vood (Vincent) return forthwith to his family, or
that they complete the formalities required in order to
have him admitted to an asylum, so as to prevent any
such unfortunate occurrence as is bound to take place
one of these days if strong measures are not taken in
his regard.

We venture to hope, Mr. Mayor, that, taking into
consideration the serious interest that we demonstrate
here, you will have the great courtesy to give our request
the response that it deserves.

We have the honor to be, with the greatest respect, Mr.
Mayor,

your devoted constituents'

D. Crévoulin, grocer; Esprit Lantheaume; Fayard; Viany, retail tobacconist; Siletto François; Claude Reynaud; Conry, black-smith; Maurice Villaret; Louis Cleheylan; Coste; Julien; Mrs Dayan; François Trouche; Coulomb; Aubert Victor, Maréchal; Berthet Adrien, ganger plate-layer; Gion Joseph; Bonifay; the widow Nay; Mayé; the widow Vénissac; Soulè; Chareyre; J. Boissié; Charabas.

We, Joseph d'Ornano, Chief Inspector of Police in the city of Arles, officer of the criminal police, assistant to the Public Prosecutor;

Considering the enclosed petition of the residents of place de Lamartine, concerning the behavior of Mr. Vincent van Gogh, a Dutch subject, suffering from mental disturbance;

Considering the attached report by Doctor Delon dated the 7th of this month and the instructions of the Mayor of Arles, ordering that van Gogh's degree of madness be established;

Have opened an inquiry & interviewed those named below:

Inquiry

1st Mr. Bernard Soulè, aged 63, landlord, of 53 avenue Montmajour, who made the following declaration to me:

As the managing agent of the house occupied by Mr. Vincent van Gogh, I had occasion to speak with him yesterday and to observe that he is suffering from mental disturbance, because his conversation is incoherent and his mind wandering. Furthermore, I have heard it said that this man is prone to inappropriate touching of women living in the neighborhood; I have even been assured that they actually no longer feel at ease in their homes, because he enters their residences.

In short, it is a matter of urgency that this insane man be confined in a special asylum, especially in view of the fact that van Gogh's presence in our neighborhood compromises public safety.

Read, agreed & signed,
Soulè

2nd Mrs. Marguerite Favier, married name Crévoulin, aged 32, provision merchant, of place de Lamartine, who told us the following:

I occupy the same house as Mr. Vincent van Gogh, who is truly insane. This individual comes into my shop and makes a nuisance of himself. He insults my customers and is prone to inappropriate touching of women from the neighborhood, whom he follows into their residences. In fact, everyone in the neighborhood is frightened on account of the presence of the said van Gogh, who will certainly become a threat to public safety.

Read, agreed and signed with us,

Mrs. Crévoulin

3rd Mrs. Maria Ortoul, married name Viany, aged 40, tobacconist, of place de Lamartine, who confirmed the previous witness's declaration

And read, agreed & signed

Maria Ourtoul

4th Mrs. Jeanne Corrias, married name Coulomb, aged 42, dressmaker, of 24 place de Lamartine, who made the following declaration:

Mr. Van Gogh, who lives in the same neighborhood as myself, has become increasingly mad in the past few days, and everyone in the vicinity is frightened. The women, especially, no longer feel comfortable, because he is prone to touching them inappropriately, and makes obscene remarks in their presence.

In my own case, I was seized round the waist outside Mr. Crévoulin's shop by this individual the day before yesterday, Monday, and lifted off my feet. In short, this madman is becoming a threat to public safety, and everyone is demanding that he be confined in a special establishment.

Read, agreed & signed,

Mrs. Coulomb

5th Mr. Joseph Ginoux, aged 45, café owner, of place de Lamartine, who agreed that the facts recounted by the previous witness are true and genuine, and has stated that he had nothing to add to her deposition

And read, agreed & signed.

Ginoux

Findings

Mr. Vincent van Gogh is truly suffering from mental disturbance; however, we have noted on several occasions that this madman has moments of lucidity. Van Gogh is not yet a threat to public safety, but there are fears that he may become so. All his neighbors are frightened, and with good cause, because a few weeks ago, the madman concerned cut off an ear in a fit of insanity, a crisis that could be repeated and be harmful to somebody in his vicinity.

Conclusions

Given that the foregoing enquiries and our personal observations show that Mr. Vincent van Gogh is suffering from mental disturbance, and that he could become a threat to public safety; we are of the opinion that there are grounds for detaining this patient in a special asylum.

In view of which I have written this report, to be submitted for the purposes of the law, and have signed;

    Arles, third March eighteen hundred and eighty-nine
    Chief of Police D'Ornano'

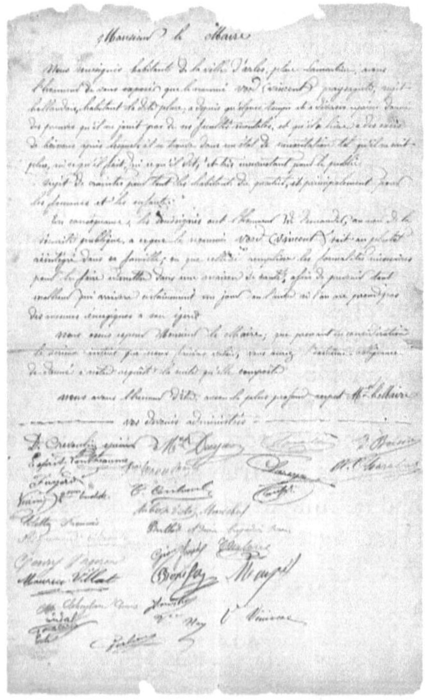

JENA

1267.1 km from Arles

Medical Report

1 March 1889

Jena Medical Report

Understands or remembers thoughts and passages in his works
to a very small extent. Weight 120 lbs (+5).

PARIS

745.4 km from Arles
865.4 km from Jena

*nothing is as distressing as uncertainty; a brother to Jo; a
note of truth, of real countryside; I would certainly have
come to see you if it wasn't so far; the public will certainly
want paintings by the new school*

16 March 1889

My dear brother,

I learn that you're not yet better, which causes me much grief. I
do so wish that you could tell me how you feel, for nothing is as
distressing as uncertainty, and if you would tell me how things
are going I can do something sooner to give you relief. You've
done so much for me that it breaks my heart to know that now
that I'll probably have days of happiness with my dear Jo, you
will actually have very bad days. She had the illusion that, since
she wants to live my life as much as possible, you would have
been a brother for her as you have always been for me. We hope
from the bottom of our hearts that you can return to good health
and that you can soon take up your work again.

In arranging my new apartment I see your paintings again
with so much pleasure. They make the rooms so jolly, and there's
such a note of truth, of real countryside in each one. It's just
as you said sometimes of certain paintings by other artists, that
they seem to come like that directly from the fields. I would certainly have come to see you if it wasn't so far, but I'm short of
time and I ask myself if my visit could be useful to you in any way.
Signac is to go to the south soon. He'll go and see you. At the moment I have an exhibition by Claude Monet at my place, which is
proving very successful. In a little while the public will certainly
want paintings by the new school, for they're certainly exercising
the public mind. If you could you would be very kind in giving
me or having me given news of you, for apart from the letters
from Messrs Rey and Salles I don't know anything about you.

I wish you better health & I remain your brother who loves you.

Theo.

JENA

1267.1 km from Arles

the philologist who no longer writes

[17 March 1889]

[Dear   ]

[Nietzsche]

ARLES

1267.1 km from Jena

brotherly anguish; my presence of mind; a petition; locked up once again; a dangerous madman; new moral emotions; a hammer-blow full in the chest; leave me here quietly; I would have been able to work if they hadn't exasperated and bothered me; I would have preferred to die; if these fellows here protest against me, I protest against them; to become definitively insane; new miseries; walk dead straight toward your goal; my house has been shut up by the police; it's quite a performance to write a letter; the guts fail me at times

19 March 1889

My dear brother,

I seemed to see so much restrained brotherly anguish in your
kind letter that it seems to me to be my duty to break my silence.
I write to you in full possession of my presence of mind and not
like a madman but as the brother you know. Here is the truth:
a certain number of people from here have addressed a petition
(there were more than 80 signatures on it) to the mayor (I think
his name is M. Tardieu) designating me as a man not worthy of
living at liberty, or something like that.

The chief of police or the chief inspector then gave the order
to have me locked up once again.

Anyway, here I am, shut up for long days under lock and key
and with warders in the isolation cell, without my culpability being proven or even provable.

It goes without saying that in my heart of hearts I have a lot
to say in reply to all that. It goes without saying that I shouldn't
get angry, and that apologizing would seem to me to be accusing
myself in such a case.

Only to warn you: to free me — first I don't ask it, being sure
that all of this accusation will be reduced to nothing.

Only I say to you, you would find it difficult to free me. If I
didn't restrain my indignation I would immediately be judged to
be a dangerous madman. In waiting let us hope, besides, strong
emotions could only aggravate my state.

If in a month's time, though, you have no direct news of me,
then act, but as long as I'm writing to you, wait.

That's why I now ask you to promise to let them act without
getting yourself mixed up in it.

Consider yourself warned that it would perhaps complicate
and confuse the matter.

All the more so since you'll understand that while I'm absolutely calm at the given moment, I may easily fall back into a
state of over-excitement through new moral emotions.

So you can imagine how much of a hammer-blow full in the
chest it was when I found out that there were so many people

here who were cowardly enough to band themselves together against one man, and a sick one at that.

Good. That's for your guidance; as regards my moral state, I'm badly shaken, but all the same I'm recovering a certain calm so as not to get angry. Besides, humility suits me after the experience of repeated attacks. So I'm being patient.

The main thing, I couldn't say it too often, is that you should keep your calm too, and that nothing should disturb you in your affairs. After your marriage we can deal with sorting all this out, and in the meantime, my word, leave me here quietly. I'm convinced that Mr. Mayor, as well as the chief of police, are more like friends and that they'll do everything they can to settle all this. Here, except for freedom, except for lots of things that I would wish otherwise, I'm not too bad. Besides, I told them that we weren't in a position to bear expenses. I can't move without expenses, now I haven't been working for 3 months, and mind you, I would have been able to work if they hadn't exasperated and bothered me.

How are Mother and our sister? Having nothing else to distract me — I'm even forbidden to smoke — which, however, the other patients are allowed to do. Having nothing else to do I think about all those I know all day and night long.

What misery — and all of it, so to speak, for nothing.

I won't hide from you that I would have preferred to die than to cause and bear so much trouble. What can you say, to suffer without complaining is the only lesson that has to be learned in this life.

Now, in all that, if I must resume my task of painting I naturally need my studio, the furniture, which we certainly can't afford to renew if it's lost.

To be reduced once again to living in the hotel, you know that my work won't allow it, I must have a fixed pied-à-terre. If these fellows here protest against me, I protest against them, and they just have to provide me with damages and interest in a friendly way, in short they just have to give me back what I would lose by their fault and ignorance.

If — let's say — I were to become definitively insane — certainly I don't say that it's impossible, in any case they should treat me differently, give me back the fresh air, my work &c.

Then — my word — I would resign myself. But we aren't even there yet, and if I'd had my tranquility I'd have been back on my feet long ago. They scold me about what I've smoked and drunk, fine.

But what can you say, with all their sobriety they're actually only giving me new miseries. My dear brother, the best thing remains perhaps to joke about our little miseries, and also a little about the great ones of human life. Take it like a man and walk dead straight toward your goal. We artists in present-day society are no more than the broken pitcher. How I'd like to be able to send you my canvases, but everything is under lock and key, police and keepers of the insane. Don't free me, it will settle itself on its own — all the same, warn Signac that he shouldn't get involved until I write again, for he'd be putting his hand into a wasps' nest. I shake your hand most cordially in thought, regards to your fiancée, to Mother and our sister.

Ever yours,
Vincent

I'll read this letter as it stands to Mr. Rey, who isn't responsible, having been ill himself — no doubt he'll write to you himself too. My house has been shut up by the police.

I have a vague memory of a registered letter from you for which I was made to sign but which I didn't want to accept because they were making such a fuss for the signature, and of which I've since had no more news.

Explain to Bernard that I haven't been able to reply to him, it's quite a performance to write a letter: at least as many formalities are necessary as in prison now. Tell him to ask Gauguin for advice, but shake his hand firmly from me.

Once again warm regards to your fiancée and to Bonger.

I would have preferred not to write to you yet for fear of compromising you and disturbing you in what must work out above all. It will settle itself; it's too idiotic to last.

When you move house, address please.

I had hoped that Mr. Rey would come to see me in order to talk with him before sending this letter, but although I had made it known that I was waiting for him, nobody came. I urge you again to be cautious. You know what it is to go to the civil authorities to complain. Wait until your journey to Holland at least.

I myself fear a little that if I go outside at liberty I wouldn't always be master of myself if I was provoked or insulted, and one could take advantage of that. The fact remains that a petition was sent to the mayor. I bluntly replied that I was entirely disposed to chuck myself into the water, for example, if that could make these virtuous fellows happy once and for all, but that in any case if in fact I had wounded myself I had done nothing of the sort to these people &c. So courage, then, although the guts fail me at times. Your coming here — my word — for the moment it would precipitate things. I'll move house when I see the means naturally.

I hope that this reaches you in good condition. Let's not fear, I'm quite calm now. Leave them to their own devices. You will perhaps do well to write one more time, but nothing more for the moment. If I'm patient, that could only make me stronger so that I won't be so much in danger of relapsing into a crisis. Naturally I who really have done my best to be friends with the people and didn't suspect it, it has been a harsh blow to me.

More soon, I hope, my dear brother, don't worry. It's perhaps a sort of quarantine I'm being put through. What do I know?

JENA

1267.1 km from Arles

Medical Report

20 March 1889

Jena Medical Report

Transferred to M2. . . . When he got some cakes from his mother
the other day he said, "Are they really from Naumburg?"

ARLES

an apartment in another part of town; try to influence them so that I have the right to go out; as far as I can judge I'm not mad; it would certainly give me pleasure to see Signac; one mustn't on any account have illusions about life; don't meddle with me; repeated and unexpected emotions; we'll suffer for a bunch of bastards and cowards; once your home is secured, there's a lot won for me too; if sooner or later I became really mad; the best for me would certainly be not to remain alone; I am a man too, after all

22 March 1889

My dear Theo,

Thanks for your letter — which I've just received. All the more so since in this case I prefer to be wrong than to be right: certainly we're absolutely, absolutely in agreement as regards the reasoning you give in your letter. I also envisage the thing that way.

What's new is that I think Mr. Salles is trying to find me an apartment in another part of town. I approve of that, for in that way I wouldn't be forced to move house immediately — I would keep a pied-à-terre, and then I could certainly make a trip as far as Marseille or further to find better. Mr. Salles is very kind and very loyal, and it's a happy contrast with others here. Anyway. That's all that's new for the moment. If on your side you would write, try to influence them so that I have the right to go out into the town nevertheless.

As far as I can judge I'm not mad, strictly speaking.

You'll see that the canvases I've done in the intervals are calm & not inferior to others. I miss work rather than it tires me.

It would certainly give me pleasure to see Signac if he must pass through here anyway. They must then let me go out with him to show him my canvases.

Then perhaps it would have been good that I should accompany him where he's going, and that the two of us could have sought a new place, but there, since that's actually scarcely probable, what's the good of him putting himself out expressly to come and see me?

What I find excellent in your letter is that you say that one mustn't on any account have illusions about life.

One must seize the reality of one's fate and that's that. I'm writing in haste to send this letter, which will perhaps not reach you until Sunday all the same, by which time Signac will already have left. I can't do anything about that.

All that I would ask is that people I don't even know by name (for they took great care to act so that I don't know who sent that document in question) don't meddle with me when I'm in the middle of painting, eating, or sleeping, or having a fuck in the brothel (not having a wife). Yet they meddle with all that.

But despite all that I don't give a damn at all — were it not for the pain I'm quite involuntarily causing you thus, or rather that they're causing — and for the delay in work &c.

These repeated and unexpected emotions, if they should continue, could change a fleeting, momentary mental disturbance into a chronic illness. Rest assured that if nothing happens I would now be able to do the same work in the orchards, and perhaps better, that I did the other year. Now let's be as firm as possible, and in short not allow people to tread on our toes too much. Right from the beginning I had very malicious opposition here. All this fuss will naturally do good to 'Impressionism,' but you and I personally, we'll suffer for a bunch of bastards & cowards.

There's something to be said for keeping one's indignation to oneself, isn't there? Already I've seen in a newspaper here a really very good article on decadent or Impressionist literature — but what do these newspaper articles &c. do to you and me? As my good friend Roulin says, 'it is acting as a pedestal for others.' At least one would wish to know for what or for whom, wouldn't one? Then one couldn't oppose it. But being a pedestal for something you aren't aware of is annoying.

Anyway, all of that is nothing provided you walk straight toward your goal — once your home is secured, there's a lot won for me too, and once that's done we can perhaps rediscover a more peaceful path after your marriage.

If sooner or later I became really mad I think I wouldn't want to stay here at the hospital, but just for the moment I still want to leave here freely. For if I still understand myself a little there will be an interval between here & there.

The best for me would certainly be not to remain alone, but I would prefer to remain eternally in a madhouse than to sacrifice another existence to my own. For the trade of painter is sad and bad these days. If I were a Catholic I could resort to making a monk of myself, but since I'm not exactly one, as you know, I don't have that resort. The administration of the hospital is — how shall I put it — Jesuit, they're very, very shrewd, very learned, very powerful, even Impressionistic... they know how to obtain information with an unheard-of subtlety — but — but — it astonishes and confuses me — yet...

Anyway, there you have something of the cause of my silence, so stay apart from me for business matters, and in the meantime I am a man too, after all, you know, I'll get by on my own, as regards what concerns me in matters of conscience.

I shake your hand heartily in thought, tell your fiancée, Mother and our sister not to worry about me, and to believe that I'm well on the road to recovery.

Ever yours,
Vincent.

JENA

1267.1 km from Arles

Medical Report

23 March 1889

Jena Medical Report

Pupillar disparity, right larger than the left, reaction to light slug-
gish. Tongue heavily furred. Exaggerated patellar reflex. Urine
clear, acid, containing neither sugar nor albumen. Paresis of the
right facial muscle at rest increasing. Gaze bestial.

ARLES

1267.1 km from Jena

I've seen Signac, which did me a lot of good; smoked herrings; idiots; someone who has his self-confidence and balance; the first time for several months that I've picked up a book; he wasn't frightened by my painting; I have the desire and the taste for work; I must have my freedom; to reach the high yellow note; suffering exile; I am tied to the earth; my so-called mental illness; I'm thinking of squarely accepting my profession as a madman; a moldy, shattered past; beware of sudden impulses

24 March 1889

My dear Theo,

I'm writing to tell you that I've seen Signac, which did me a lot of good. He was very nice and very straight and very simple when the difficulty arose of whether or not to force open the door closed by the police, who had demolished the lock. They began by not wanting to let us do it, and yet in the end we got in. As a keepsake I gave him a still life that had exasperated the good gendarmes of the town of Arles because it depicted two smoked herrings, which are called gendarmes, as you know. You know that I did this same still life two or three times before in Paris, and once exchanged it for a carpet back then. That's enough to say what people meddle in and what idiots they are.

I find Signac very calm, whereas people say he's so violent, he gives me the impression of someone who has his self-confidence and balance, that's all. Rarely or never have I had a conversation with an Impressionist that was so free of disagreements or annoying shocks on either side.

For example, he went to see Jules Dupré and reveres him. No doubt you had a hand in his coming to boost my morale a little, and thank you for that. I took advantage of my trip out to buy a book, *Ceux de la glèbe* by Camille Lemonnier. I've devoured two chapters of it — it's so serious, so profound. Wait for me to send it to you. This is the first time for several months that I've picked up a book. That tells me a lot and heals me a great deal.

In fact there are several canvases to send to you, as Signac was able to see — he wasn't frightened by my painting, or so it seemed to me.

Signac thought I was looking well, and it's perfectly true.

On top of that, I have the desire and the taste for work. Of course, it's still the case that if things were to be messed up for me in my work and in my life every day by gendarmes and venomous layabouts of municipal electors who petition against me to their mayor elected by them (and who is consequently keen on their votes) it would be only human on my part that I should succumb once more. Signac, I'm led to believe, will tell you something similar.

In my opinion we must squarely oppose the loss of the furniture &c.

Then — my word — I must have my freedom to practice my profession.

Mr. Rey says that instead of eating enough and regularly I have been particularly sustaining myself with coffee and alcohol. I admit all that, but it will still be true that I had to key myself up a bit to reach the high yellow note I reached this summer. That, after all, the artist is a man at work, and that it's not for the first passer-by who comes along to vanquish him once & for all.

Must I suffer imprisonment or the madhouse — why not? Didn't Rochefort with Hugo, Quinet and others give an eternal example by suffering exile, and the first even the penal colony.

But all I want to say is that this is above the question of sickness and health.

Naturally one is beside oneself in parallel cases — I don't say equivalent cases, as I have only a very inferior and secondary place — but I say parallel. And that was the first and last cause of my going out of my mind.

Do you know that expression by a Dutch poet

> I am tied to the earth
> With more than earthly bonds.

That's what I experienced in many moments of anguish — above all — in my so-called mental illness. Unfortunately I have a profession that I don't know well enough to express myself as I would wish.

I'll stop dead for fear of relapsing, and move on to something else.

Could you send me before you leave

3	tubes	blanc zinc white		
1	tube	same	size	cobalt
1	,,	,,	,,	ultramarine
4	,,	,,	,,	Veronese green
1	,,	,,	,,	emerald "
1	,,	,,	,,	orange lead

This in case — probable if I find the means to take up my work again — that in a short while I can set to work again in the orchards.

Ah, if only nothing had happened to mess things up for me!

Let's think carefully before going somewhere else. You can see that in the south I have no more luck than in the north. It's about the same everywhere. I'm thinking of squarely accepting my profession as a madman just like Degas took on the form of a notary. But there it is, I don't feel I quite have the strength needed for such a role.

You speak to me of what you call "the real south." Above is the reason why I'll never go there. I rightly leave that to people more complete, more entire than myself. As for me, I'm good only for something intermediate & second-rate & insignificant.

However much intensity my feeling may have or my power of expression may acquire, at an age when the material passions are more burned out — never can I build an imposing edifice on such a moldy, shattered past.

So I don't really mind what happens to me — even staying here — I think that my fate will be balanced in the long term. Beware of sudden impulses — since you're getting married, and I'm getting too old — it's the only policy that can suit us.

More soon, I hope — write to me without much delay and believe me, after asking you to give my warm regards to Mother, Sister and your fiancée, your brother who loves you dearly,

Vincent

I'll send you Camille Lemonnier's book quite soon.

JENA

1267.1 km from Arles

singing & stamping

26 March 1889

Jena Medical Report

Often wants to go to bed in the middle of the day. Goes about
singing and stamping his feet a good deal.

ARLES

1267.1 km from Jena

things are going well; I've had another few books brought; my figure of the Berceuse; an image such as a sailor who couldn't paint would imagine it; a little confused; How strange these last three months appear to me; the veil of time; distressing reality; I hope to throw myself back completely into work; "she never complained about anyone"; Imagine a perfect eternity; from time to time in life one feels amazed; to become like that good Thebe

29 March 1889

My dear Theo,

A few more words before you leave. Things are going well these days. The day before yesterday and yesterday I went into town for an hour to find things to work with. When I went home I was able to learn that the real neighbors, those whom I know, weren't among those who got up that petition. However it may be, anyway I saw that I still had friends among them.

If need be Mr. Salles is pretty sure he can find me an apartment in another district in a few days.

I've had another few books brought in order to have a few solid ideas in my mind. I've re-read *La case de l'oncle Tom* — you know, the book by Beecher Stowe on slavery — Dickens's *Contes de Noël*, and I've given Mr. Salles *Germinie Lacerteux*.

And here I am, going back to my figure of the Berceuse for the 5th time. And when you see it you'll agree with me that it's nothing but a chromolithograph from a penny bazaar, and what's more, it doesn't even have the merit of being photographically correct in the proportions or in anything.

But anyway, I'm trying to make an image such as a sailor who couldn't paint would imagine it when he was in the middle of the sea and thought of a woman on land.

They're very, very attentive to me at the hospital these days, which — like many other things — mixes me up and makes me a little confused.

Now I imagine that you'd prefer to marry without all the ceremonies and congratulations of a wedding, and am quite sure in advance that you'll avoid them as much as possible.

If you see Koning or others, and above all cousins Mauve and Lecomte, don't forget to give them my warm regards.

How strange these last three months appear to me. Sometimes nameless moral anguish, then moments when the veil of time and of the inevitability of circumstances seemed to open up a little way for the space of a blink of an eye.

Certainly, you're right after all, darned right — even allowing for hope, one probably has to accept the rather distressing reality.

I hope to throw myself back completely into work, which has fallen behind.

Ah, I mustn't forget to tell you a thing I've often thought about. Utterly by chance, in an article in an old newspaper, I found a line written on an ancient tomb at Carpentras, near here.

Here is this very, very, very old epitaph, let's say from the time of Flaubert's *Salammbô*:

> Thebe, daughter of Telhui, priestess of Osiris, who never complained about anyone.

If you were to see Gauguin you could tell him that. And I was thinking of a faded woman, at your place you have the study of that woman who had such strange eyes, whom I met by another chance.

What does it mean, that "she never complained about anyone"?

Imagine a perfect eternity, why not — but let's not forget that reality in the old centuries has that … "and she never complained about anyone."

Do you remember that one Sunday good old Thomas came to see us and said, ah but — is it women like that who give you a hard-on?

No, that doesn't always produce a hard-on precisely, but anyway — from time to time in life one feels amazed, as if one was taking root in the ground.

Now you talk to me of the "real south" and as for me, I was saying that after all it seemed to me that it was rather for people who were more complete than me to go there.

Is the "real south" not to some degree the place where one might find a reason, a patience, a serenity sufficient to become like that good "Thebe — daughter of Telhui — priestess of Osiris — who never complained about anyone"?

Beside that I feel like some kind of unworthy being.

To you and your wife on the occasion of your marriage that is the happiness, the serenity I would ask for you two, to have that true south inwardly, in your souls.

If I want this letter to leave today I must end it. Handshake, bon voyage, kind regards to Mother and Sister.

Ever yours,
Vincent

INTERVAL: ARLES, PARIS; PARAGUAY; JENA

The artist suicided by society; the healer; la Tour Eiffel
X km from here, X km from there

March–April 1889

With the departure to Marseille of Roulin, Vincent's probably sole final friend in Arles, no contact from Gauguin, and the shipwreck of the Studio of the South gazing into him like a fault line, loneliness and isolation disperse throughout the terrain of his body like a series of pulse storms, as if the terrain of Arles itself is entering and altering him. Plagued by nightmares and harrowing visions, he is rendered insomniac, delirious, his memory fractured as he spirals into a vortex of timelessness: what is day; what is night? If he forgets or refuses to eat, he drinks to excess. Absinthe? Wine? Turpentine? Ranting and babbling noisily, he pursues strangers into their houses: all boundaries have been sundered: there are no borders, only open milieus. A whorl of images and frenzied thoughts besiege him, burrowing into him like viroid particles, pressing upon him with the force of the mistral: failure, desolation, poverty, self-mutilation. The shipwreck of a life batters and cracks his central nervous system as he stands before the prodigious gallery of his paintings. Failure?? In the midst of a realized vision, abject catastrophe — faltering on a tightrope between despair and a tremendous will to power, a new earthquake upends the body.

In gazing before Rodin's head of St. John the Baptist, Theo feels as if he is gazing at his brother, finding a resemblance to him in St. John's furrowed and contorted brow, which betrays a life of reflection and asceticism.

Death, Theo writes to his soon to be wife Jo, has left no sign of anguish on that face, nor an aura of eternal peace. It has retained an air of tranquility and also an energetic concern with the future.

If vexed over his brother's plight, it is his own future that overtakes him and usurps further thought of the afflicted painter. Beyond preoccupation with his bride, the apostle-dealer is also consumed with thought of his exhibition, staged at Boussod, Valadon, *&* Cie, of work by Monet, Rodin, and Degas, an exhibition that would be celebrated as one of the most important artistic events of the winter of 1889. Despite his fidelity, it did not however include even a single of his brother's paintings.

Although bereft of tranquility, the afflicted one is not devoid of a forward driving arrow, yet wave upon wave bears violently down upon him, weakening the ballast of his ship, testing the tensility of his sails, splintering his mast. The fada, the fou roux, the stoned one, becomes the *caper emissarius* of Arles — the police raid the Studio of the South *&* the terror is subdued, escorted by force to the asylum.

The shutters to the Yellow House are secured, its door barricaded, entry prohibited by mark of official seal as if it were a site of contagion. Society unites in secret against the consciousness of Vincent for his tearing himself away from their consciousness, for his refusing to forfeit a certain higher idea of human honor. Is this the continuation of a poisoning, the suiciding of the artist?

What cowards, Vincent writes to Theo, are these meddlesome idiots and skunks who under civic moral force deem me a lunatic, a madman, a public danger!! Strong measures must be taken against me?? What is this, their Old Testament fear of the image-maker? Like Arabs, they believe that painters are possessed. Alors, I prefer my madness to other people's wisdom.

Expressing his outrage at being viewed as some demon-possessed beast, Vincent curses the silent conspiracy of a horde of provincial cowards he thought to be companions and fellow sufferers. The foreigner made the fatal error of mistaking French politesse for friendship, but salamalecs do not = sodality. He was never a *tu*, only and forever a *vous*.

The whorl of voices and images scoring his brain intensifies, his nerves growing vexed and scarred as he seeks to adjudicate himself, even if only in the theater of his mind. What to do when *he* suffers incursions, when the morally upright citizens climb up to *his* windows to gaze at him as if he were a strange animal? As if the Studio of the South were but a hall of specimens, an artist's zoo, a vivarium in which the painter has been imprisoned? Come one, come all, see Vincent the Pickled Punk! Was it society in revolt against an artist who decamped from its moral value system? Who was there to protect him from them?

I have been condemned by a mischievous opposition, the painter avowed to his apostle-brother, but whatever I have done, I have done for the New Art, the first and last cause of my aberration.

If to Vincent, all this stir will ultimately be good for Impressionism, to the doctors, no clear diagnosis was at hand, and they were uncertain as to whether or not his attacks would recommence and the fears of the publicum prove to be true. What if he were to cut off someone else's ear, or worse?

And so, as the foreigner remains confined in an observation chamber, furiously raging against his captors and the injustice of being imprisoned, of perpetual surveillance, construction of the cupola of la Tour Eiffel is being completed, its spire continuing its drive to elevation, moving ever higher into the sky as the century progresses, pursuing its drive to elevation. This world is the will to power — and nothing besides!

And as the searchlight beam of la Tour Eiffel will soon be diffused over Paris, its light a beacon to industry and the arts, the searchlight beam of Vincent's captors peers through his cell window, an invading light boring into him like a surgeon's scalpel. The body must be visible; the body must be tracked; the body must be studied. Sans flask, sans pipe, sans tobacco, sans book, sans open fields, the madman spirals deeper into himself, like a drill boring backwards, its bit grinding away with each turn, its increasing heat burning metal to vapor, till nothing remains but pulverized matter.

Vincent says he is prey to doctors who gnaw at him like wasps on fruit. When Father Salles brings the artist paints and brushes, it only enrages the afflicted one. He does not write letters, and no one writes him, not even Theo, who evades Salles's queries as to whether or not he intends on having his brother come to Paris or be put in an institution of his choosing. Alternatively, Vincent will become a ward of the state, left to the hands of the police.

Pinioned like a sufferer in an infernal ring, the madman endures indignity upon injustice, vaulting between states of amazement and revolt, as he is plagued by remorse and loathing of life, like an animal devoid of its living milieu, all esprit turned venomous, all energy become bilious.

Throughout the month, the broken pitcher descends into long bewildering silences, unsure as to when another attack might plunge him into other yet worse fits.

Confined to his bed, he enters the tribunal of his soul, everything in his life flitting through his mind like pictures on a vertiginous zoetrope. It is the scaffold of life; the thread of an existence frayed to threat, petrified, shattered into split rock.

Meanwhile, as 'Nietzsche' vaults between states of euphoria and paranoia, himself splintering into further pieces, his tongue growing borborygmic or silent with each passing night, spiraling into his own labyrinth of delirium, Elisabeth dreams of escaping Paraguay to aid her ailing brother, for she is not only an intrepid colonialist, she is also a healer.

If only I had the money for the journey, she writes her mother, I would leave at once. I am tormented by the thought that the worst would have been avoided if I had stayed in Germany.

In one fell breath, she condemns her mother and exalts herself, a gesture she will later repeat, though with far greater cunning.

Despite her not being a doctor, Elisabeth is resolute in her belief in her power to solve even medical issues. Life in the colony was however becoming onerous, and her husband offered little solace to her grief over her brother's disintegration. If she cannot heal and save her husband, she will for certain heal and save her brother.

Bernhard, she says, does not show the slightest sympathy for my grief. On the contrary, he does everything he can to make life as hard as possible for me. His behavior is taking the joy out of my life, for I remember how loving Fritz has always been (the ugly letters he wrote me were nothing but a sign of his first attack of chloride poisoning). Fritz never once said an unfriendly word to me and I thanked him by leaving the poor dear heart to his fate. I am of course an excellent wife when I take upon myself joyfully every burden without ever asking anything for myself. My sole concern is the success of our work. I only think of Bern *&* the colony. I know quite well that without me this entire colonial enterprise would have been a very uncertain affair. I am saying this without pride *&* merely to explain why I have left my poor Fritz in the lurch.

— Is it to Bernhard that she is in fact wed, or her poor Fritz? In the rings, there is a symbolic secret.

Thinking over her brother's dilemma, the Lama remembered always being suspicious of Overbeck, not believing him to be a true friend of poor, poor Fritz. In taking him to an asylum, Overbeck's real aim she believed was to forever damage her brother's reputation. Last month, she had written to her mother saying of the German Protestant theologian, I hear Overbeck is a Jew; that speaks volumes and I believe it.

And writing to Dr. Binswanger on 23 March 1889, the Queen reasserted her conviction that, not doctors, but she alone could diagnose and heal her brother.

It is my firm conviction, the monarch asserted, confirmed by experience, that the cause of my dear brother's suffering is nothing but chloral. She then insisted to Binswanger that only her statements could be of value for the treatment of her brother. Learned friends of his will want to demonstrate mental disturbance from his books. Do not believe them, she instructed, as if the doctor would be deceived by such pronouncements, they are prejudiced, they confuse genius *&* insanity. I myself am of course not in agreement with the results of my brother's philosophy, but what I can recognize clearly is that they are new, *yet completely logical.*

After imploring Binswanger to wean her brother off of chloral, she asks whether or not he speaks of her, mentions that his childhood nickname for her was Lisbeth or Lama, then returns once more to her diagnosis, informing the doctor that this terrible chloral poisoning is unpredictable in its consequences. Judging by the letters I have received, I know that you are being misinformed about my brother from all sides, nobody knows the history of his suffering as well as I do. It will be very difficult for you to form an opinion about his suffering.

And on she went, even suggesting that her brother gently be referred to Kant, as if such would be a saving medicament. His being mentally disturbed at the end did no harm to his philosophy. God bless you, dear highly revered Prof., she finally closed. In warmest gratitude, yours truly, Eli Förster.

This world is the will to power — and nothing besides! And you yourselves are also this will to power — and nothing besides!

*

459

As the Horla and Herr Dynamite turned and turned about, vortices of energy and fury, spinning like horses on wild merry-go-rounds, work on la Tour Eiffel was proceeding at a vigorous pace, steam cranes working day and night, lifting wrought-iron sections to each next level, bearing weights of up to 24,000 pounds, just as the philosopher and the painter were bearing their own internal pressures, perhaps of equal mental poundage.

Thick coal tar smoke enveloped the City of Lights. The deafening clangor of sledgehammers banging on rivets and bolting resounded throughout the arrondissements like a symphony of sirens. The sky was full of sparks, miniature lightning bolts shooting into the clouds with each hammer blow of the blackened workers helping to fulfill Eiffel's vision.

On the 15th, construction of the cupola was completed, bringing the tower ever higher into the clouds, making the logic of the structure finally evident, its abstract & algebraic beauty at last visible to the spectators below.

Above, the tower's true pinnacle was the lighthouse, encircled by a terrace designed for anemometers and other meteorological instruments. The future of civilization was at hand; the 20th century was on the horizon. What new perspectives of vision the tower opens up, what hitherto unseen vistas, like the optics of a Tiepolo painting made real. Humanity could see the world as never before, *perspectivally*, with more eyes, with different eyes, as if with the hundred eyes of a peacock's tail. Vision opened and expanded into a spinning panorama.

And on Sunday, 31 March, one week following Vincent's release from the asylum, the structure of la Tour Eiffel was at last completed, its drive to elevation far superior to that of the Mole Antonelliana, reaching a final height of 324 meters, more than twice the size of *Ecce Homo*. If the painter does not baptize la Tour Eiffel after one of his paintings as did Nietzsche the tower of Torino after one of his works, it could in retrospect be baptized such, and in spirit we can open an enormous free space around la Tour Eiffel because, in its absolute drive for elevation, it reminds us of nothing so much as Vincent's cypresses...

The day before 31 March, since he himself would not be heading south, Theo van Gogh continued arrangements for his wedding and conceived of a plan to eventually send Signac to Arles to reignite Vincent's missionary zeal for the Midi. Then, on the night of his brother's birthday, the apostle-brother took an overnight train to Holland.

On 1 April 1889, Gustave Eiffel welcomed to Parc du Champ Mars select members of the Paris press, as well as the commissioner of the fair, the French Prime Minister, and others, all of whom step by step slowly ascended the tower for the first time, as nearly 200 workers clustered together at the north pillar stairs, workers that might have figured in the paintings of Vincent van Gogh, men whose shoes he would have lovingly fathomed.

While Eiffel stopped at the different tiers of his tower to elucidate its marvels, the sun was occasionally obscured by clouds that vaulted across le ciel as intense winds surged violently through the metal tentacles of the giant sculpture, sending whorls of dust into the sky. The views of Paris both amazed and stupefied the guests, who for the first time saw Paris as nothing but a miniature landscape.

And with each movement higher into the sky, the sense of vertigo increased, with scarcer and scarcer of the guests continuing to the upper tiers — was it fear of destruction, of a fall, of Paris becoming Babylon?

An elect few went on, step by step by step, a long and slow ascent that took 30 minutes, till they reached the top observation deck, the near-pinnacle of the drive to elevation, where humanity became even more minuscule and insignificant.

A reporter from *Le Figaro* recounted that Montmartre *&* the surrounding districts all looked like little gray blobs; the forest of Saint-Germain fades into the blue mists, the Seine becomes a tranquil rivulet, traversed by

Lilliputian barges, & Paris appears like a tiny stage set with its straight roads, square rooftops, and orderly facades. The tiny black dots are the crowds. Everything everywhere looks devoid of life, except for the green of the Bois; there is no visible movement in this immensity; no noise to show the life of the people who are 'below.' One would say that a sudden slumber has, in broad daylight, rendered the city inert and silent.

After climbing a small spiral staircase, the guests were shown four rooms, including Eiffel's personal apartment and three spaces where scientific studies would be conducted. But the absolute true pinnacle, the vaulted height of heights, a point higher than any cathedral spire in the world, remained one circular stair beyond, a perilous stair too, for it was exposed to the air-thin heights where the forceful gusts of wind tested the wits of even the brave few.

11 men pressed on, joining Eiffel as he unfurled an immense French flag, whose presence in the sky was accompanied by 21 bursts of fireworks exploding from the second tier as the flag of 1789 was saluted, and progress in science & humanity extolled.

This world is the will to power — and nothing besides! And you yourselves are also this will to power — & nothing besides!

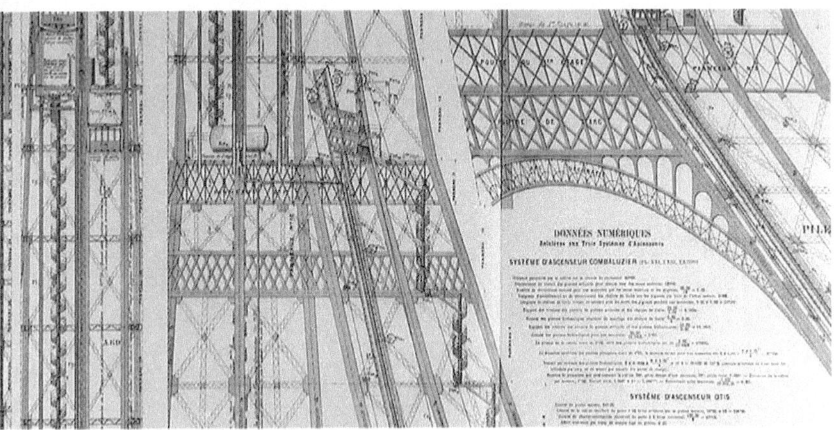

ARLES

1267.1 km from Jena

a nervous tic; the consignment of colors; friend Roulin came to see me; the road doesn't become easier as one advances in life; I'm being forced to leave; a certain vague background sadness; I have on the easel an orchard of peach trees; a difficult question to resolve; the anxiety that has reigned here in Arles; soon I'll no longer be ill enough to remain confined; silent solemnities and tendernesses

4 April 1889

My dear Theo,

A few words to wish you & your fiancée much happiness these days. It's like a nervous tic with me that on the occasion of a day of celebration I generally experience difficulties in formulating a congratulation, but it shouldn't be concluded from that that I desire your happiness less ardently than anyone else, as you well know.

I still have to thank you for your last letter, as well as for the consignment of colors from Tasset and several issues of *Le Fifre* with drawings by Forain. The latter have often had the effect on me that what I manufacture becomes very sentimental in comparison.

I waited a few days before replying, not knowing which day you would leave for Amsterdam, besides I also don't know whether it's in Breda or Amsterdam that you'll be getting married. But if, as I'm led to believe, it will be in Amsterdam, then I presumed that you would find this letter there around Sunday.

By the way — just today friend Roulin came to see me — he told me to give you his warm regards and to congratulate you. His visit gave me considerable pleasure; he often has to carry burdens that one would say were too heavy. As he has a strong peasant nature, that doesn't prevent him from always looking well and even joyful — however for me, who am always learning something new from him, what lessons for the future there are in his conversation when he seems to say that the road doesn't become easier as one advances in life. I talked with him to have his opinion on what I ought to do as regards the studio, which I must leave in any case, as I was advised by Mr. Salles and Rey, at Easter. I told Roulin that having done many things to put this house in a much better state than I had taken it in, and above all for the gas which I had put in, I considered it as a piece of work we have done.

I'm being forced to leave — all right — but to take away the gas — to make a fuss for damages or something else, certainly there would be justification but I don't have the heart for it. The only thing that I find possible in this case is to tell ourselves that we'd have tried to set up a habitation for unknown successors.

And besides, before seeing Roulin I had already been to the gasworks to arrange it so. And Roulin was of the same opinion. He's planning to remain in Marseille.

I'm well these days, apart from a certain vague background sadness that's hard to define — but anyway — I've gained physical powers rather than lose them, and I'm working.

Just now I have on the easel an orchard of peach trees beside a road with the Alpilles in the background. It appears that there's a fine article on Monet in *Le Figaro*, Roulin had read it and had been struck by it, he said.

All in all it's quite a difficult question to resolve, to take a new apartment, and even to find it, especially by the month. Mr. Salles spoke to me of a house at 20 francs that is very good, but he isn't sure that I'll be able to have it.

At Easter I'll have to pay 3 months' rent, the removal costs &c. All that is neither cheering nor convenient. Especially since absolutely nothing promises us better luck.

Roulin was saying, or rather made it understood, that he didn't at all like the anxiety that has reigned here in Arles this winter, even considered completely outside the share that fell on me. Anyway, it's like that just about everywhere, business affairs that aren't going well, worn-out resources, discouraged people and — — — — as you were saying, not content to remain spectators and becoming wicked through lack of occupation. If someone still laughs or works, they come down on him fast.

Anyway, my dear brother, I think that soon I'll no longer be ill enough to remain confined. Apart from that, I'm beginning to get accustomed to it, and if I had to remain in a hospital for good I would get used to it, and I think that I could find subjects for painting there as well.

Write to me soon if you find the time.

Roulin's family was still out in the country, and although he's earning a little more, since the separate expenses are increased in proportion, they're not a mite better off in reality, and he wasn't without very distressing anxieties. Fortunately the weather is fine and the sun glorious, and the people here momentarily quickly forget all their troubles and then glow with energy and illusions.

These last few days I've been reading Dickens's *Contes de Noël*, in which there are things so profound that one must re-read them often, it has a very great deal in common with Carlyle.

While Roulin isn't exactly old enough to be like a father to me, all the same he has silent solemnities and tendernesses for me like an old soldier would have for a young one. Always — but without a word — a certain something that seems to mean: we don't know what will happen to us tomorrow, but think of me in any event. And that does one good when it comes from a man who is neither embittered nor sad, nor perfect, nor happy, nor always irreproachably just, but such a good soul & so wise & so moved & so full of belief. Listen — I have no right to complain of anything to do with Arles when I think of certain people I've seen there and whom I'll never be able to forget.

It's late, once again I wish you and Jo much happiness, and handshakes in thought.

Ever yours,
Vincent

JENA

1267.1 km from Arles

When I march along the whole earth trembles; Where are my Pulcinelli?

4 April 1889

Jena Asylum Medical Report

The patient was heard howling at night,

*"When I march along the whole earth trembles.
I am master of the sun!"*

He donned a black mask that did not cover his mouth. Due to this, we could see frequent but sudden changes of facial expression, shifting from laughter to sadness and from melancholy to hilarity and back again. Extraordinary ability to mime and imitate. He mimicked many of our own gestures, facial expressions, and behavior.

Before we could calm him down & put him to bed he asked,

"Where are my Pulcinelli?"

ARLES

1267.1 km from Jena

The funereal pomp of the reception; the cruelest cannibals; your most friendly and beneficial visit; I am well now; studies of orchards; the normal state; I still have inner despairs; the best consolation

10 April 1889

My dear friend Signac,

Thanks very much for your postcard, which gives me news of
you. As for my brother not having replied to your letter yet, I'm
inclined to believe that it's not his fault. I've also been without
news of him for a fortnight. It's because he's in Holland, where
he's getting married one of these days. Now, while not denying
the advantages of a marriage in the very least, once it has been
done and one is quietly set up in one's home, the funereal pomp
of the reception &c., the lamentable congratulations of two families (even civilized) at the same time, not to mention the fortuitous appearances in those pharmacist's jars where antediluvian
civil or religious magistrates sit — my word — isn't there good
reason to pity the poor unfortunate obliged to present himself
armed with the requisite papers in the places where, with a ferocity unequalled by the cruelest cannibals, you're married alive
on the low heat of the aforementioned funereal receptions.

I remain much obliged to you for your most friendly and beneficial visit, which considerably contributed to cheering me up.

I am well now and I'm working in the hospital or its surroundings. Thus I've just brought back two studies of orchards.

Here's a hasty croquis of them — the largest is a poor green
countryside with little cottages, blue line of the Alpilles, white
and blue sky. The foreground, enclosures with reed hedges where
little peach trees are in blossom — everything there is small, the
gardens, the fields, the trees, even those mountains, as in certain
Japanese landscapes, that's why this subject attracted me.

The other landscape is almost all green with a little lilac and
grey — on a rainy day.

Very pleased to hear you say that you've settled down, and
will very much wish to have more news of you. How is work going, what is the character of those parts?

Since then my mind has returned yet more to the normal
state, for the time being I don't ask for better, provided it lasts.
That will depend above all on a very sober regime.

For the first few months, at least, I plan to go on staying here.
I've rented an apartment consisting of two very small rooms.

But at times it isn't completely convenient for me to start living again, for I still have inner despairs of quite a large caliber.

My word, these anxieties... who can live in modern life without catching his share of them?

The best consolation, if not the only remedy, is, it still seems to me, profound friendships, even if these have the disadvantage of anchoring us in life more solidly than may appear desirable to us in the days of great suffering.

Thank you again for your visit, which gave me so much pleasure.

Good handshake in thought.

Yours truly,
Vincent

Address until end of April, place Lamartine 2, Arles.

JENA

1267.1 km from Arles

I want a revolver

19 April 1889

Jena Asylum Medical Report

Writes unreadable stuff on the walls.

> *I want a revolver if the suspicion is true that the Grand Duchess herself is the author of these dirty doings and of these attempts against my life.*

> *I am being made ill on the right side of my forehead —*

Vehemently refuses to give precise information.

ARLES

1267.1 km from Jena

lots of happiness; expenses; I'd still wish to go to the mental hospital; to make up my mind to begin again; I wish to remain confined; it seemed to me that everything I was imagining was reality; beginning again this painter's life; these strange days; I'd very much wish ... to be able to go out in the daytime; we must accept it, the illnesses of our time; to keep exactly the right measure always; kindness has been of great worth; tell Mother and Sister my story; the mind isn't steady enough to begin again like before

21 April 1889

My dear Theo,

You'll probably be back in Paris when this letter arrives. I wish
you and your wife lots of happiness.

Thanks very much for your kind letter and for the 100-franc
note it contained.

Out of the 65 francs which I owe him, I've paid my landlord
only 25 francs, having had to pay 3 months' rent in advance on
a room where I shan't live but where I've stored my furniture,
and having in addition had around ten francs in various removal
expenses &c.

Then, since my clothes were in not too brilliant a state — so
that when I went out into the street it became necessary to have
something new — I took a 35-franc suit and 4 francs for 6 pairs
of socks. Thus I have only a few francs left out of the note, and
at the end of the month I must pay the landlord again, although
we could make him wait a few days, more or less. At the hospital, after having settled the bill up to today, there's still almost
enough for the rest of the month from the money I still have on
deposit there.

At the end of the month I'd still wish to go to the mental
hospital at St-Rémy or another institution of that kind, which Mr.
Salles has told me about.

Forgive me for not going into details to weigh up the pros
and the cons of such a course of action.

It would strain my mind a great deal to talk about it.

It will, I hope, suffice to say that I feel decidedly incapable of
starting to take a new studio again & living there alone, here in
Arles or elsewhere — it comes down to the same thing — for the
moment — I've nevertheless tried to make up my mind to begin
again — for the moment not possible. I'd be afraid of losing the
faculty of working, which is coming back to me now, by forcing
myself to have a studio, and also having all the other responsibilities on my back.

And for the time being I wish to remain confined, as much
for my own tranquility as for that of others.

What consoles me a little is that I'm beginning to consider madness as an illness like any other and accept the thing as it is, while during the actual crises it seemed to me that everything I was imagining was reality. Anyway, in fact I don't want to think or talk about it. Excuse the explanations — but I ask you, and Messrs Salles and Rey, to act so that at the end of the month or the beginning of the month of May I may go there as a confined boarder.

Beginning again this painter's life I've led up to now, isolated in the studio sometimes, and without any other source of entertainment than to go to a café or a restaurant with all the criticism of the neighbors &c., I can't do it. Going to live with another person, even another artist — difficult — very difficult — one takes too great a responsibility upon oneself. I dare not even think of it.

Anyhow, let's begin with 3 months, afterwards we'll see. Now the cost of board must be around 80 francs and I'll do a little painting and drawing. Without putting as much fury into it as the other year. Don't get upset about all this.

So there you have it, these days have been sad, moving house, transporting all my furniture, packing up the canvases which I'll send you, but above all it seemed sad to me that all that had been given to me by you with so much brotherly affection, & that for so many years, it was however you alone who supported me, & then to be obliged to come back to tell you all this sad story... but it's difficult for me to express that as I felt it.

The kindness you have had for me isn't lost, since you have had it and you still have it, so even if the material results should be nil, you still have that all the more, but I can't say that as I felt it.

Now you well understand that if alcohol was certainly one of the great causes of my madness, then it came very slowly and would go away slowly too, should it go, of course. Or if it comes from smoking, same thing.

But I would hope only that it — this recovery... The frightful superstition of certain people on the subject of alcohol, so that they prevail upon themselves never to drink or smoke. We're already advised not to lie or steal and not to commit other great or small crimes, and it becomes too complicated if it was absolutely indispensable not to possess anything but virtues in a society in which we're very indubitably rooted, be it good or bad.

I assure you that these strange days in which many things seem odd to me because my brain is shaken up, I don't hate père Pangloss in all of this.

But you'll do me a service by tackling the question forthrightly with Mr. Salles and Mr. Rey.

It would seem to me that with a boarding cost of around 75 francs a month there must be a way of confining me such that I have all I need.

Then I'd very much wish, if the thing is possible, to be able to go out in the daytime to go & draw or paint outside. Seeing as I go out here every day now, and I think that may continue.

I warn you that by paying more I'd be less happy. The company of the other sick people, you understand, isn't at all disagreeable to me, on the contrary it distracts me.

Ordinary food suits me perfectly well, especially if, like here, I could be given a little more wine than usual down there, half a liter instead of a quarter, for example.

But a separate apartment, it remains to be seen what the rules of an institution like that will be. Be aware that Rey is overburdened with work, overburdened. If he or Mr. Salles writes to you, it's better to do exactly what they say.

Anyway, my dear fellow, we must accept it, the illnesses of our time, all in all it's only fair that having lived for years in relatively good health, sooner or later we have our share of them. As for me, you'll feel a little that I wouldn't exactly have chosen madness if there had been a choice, but once one has something like that one can't catch it any more. However, in addition there will still perhaps be the consolation of being able to continue to work on some painting a little. What will you do so as not to say to your wife either too many good or too many bad things about Paris and of a heap of things? Do you feel in advance completely able to keep exactly the right measure always, from every point of view?

I shake your hand heartily in thought, I don't know if I'll write to you very, very often, because all my days aren't clear enough to write somewhat logically. All your kindnesses for me, I've found them greater than ever today.

I can't tell you it as I feel it, but I assure you that that kindness has been of great worth, and if you don't see its results, my dear brother, don't be upset about it, you will still have your kindness. Only transfer this affection onto your wife as much as possible.

And if we correspond a little less you'll see that if she is as I think she is, she will console you. That's what I hope.

Rey is a really good fellow, terribly hard-working, always at the daily grind. What people today's doctors are!

If you see Gauguin or if you write to him, give him my kind regards.

I'll be very happy to have a little news of what you say about Mother and Sister and whether they're well, tell them to take my story, my word, as a thing they mustn't upset themselves about excessively, for I'm relatively unfortunate, but in spite of that, after all, I perhaps still have some almost ordinary years ahead of me: it's an illness like any other, and currently almost all those we know among our friends have something. So is it worth talking about? I regret causing trouble to Mr. Salles, to Rey, especially also to you, but what can one do — the mind isn't steady enough to begin again like before — so it's a matter of no longer causing scenes in public, and naturally being a little calmer now, I feel completely that I was in an unhealthy state, mentally and physically. And people were kind to me then, those I remember and the rest, anyhow I've caused anxiety, and if I'd been in a normal state all of this wouldn't have happened in that way. Adieu, write when you can.

Ever yours,
Vincent

JENA

1267.1 km from Arles

the professor who no longer writes

[22 April 1889]

[Dear   ]

[Nietzsche]

ARLES

1267.1 km from Jena

thought is coming back gradually; I'm absent-minded; don't imagine that I'm unhappy; the symptoms of mental derangement; to go into an asylum, as a simple formality; I feel & am as it were paralyzed; painting narrows ideas for the rest; the idea of an association of painters remains true and reasonable; nature alone will do more good than remedies

24 April 1889

My dear Theo,

I saw Mr. Salles again and he told me what he'd written to you.
I think it will be for the best like this, and I don't see any other
way. Thought is coming back gradually, but I can still act much,
much less practically than before.

I'm absent-minded, and for the moment wouldn't be able to
control my life.

But let's leave that aside as much as possible. How are you,
are you back?

Must tell you that I think it possible that you'll find Mr. Salles'
letter still addressed to rue Lepic.

How are things at home? I imagine Mother must have been
pleased.

I assure you that I'm much calmer now that I can tell myself
that you have a companion for good. Above all, don't imagine
that I'm unhappy.

I feel deeply that this has already worked away at me for a
very long time, and that others, noticing the symptoms of mental derangement, naturally had apprehensions that were better
founded than the confidence I thought I had in thinking normally.
Which wasn't the case, because for me that crisis

Anyway, it softens me a great deal in many judgments that,
with more or less presumption, I've too often made about people
who nevertheless wished me well.

Anyway, it's no doubt a pity that these reflections come to
me a little late *in the form of feelings*. And that naturally I can't
change anything of the past.

But I ask you to consider this closely, and to consider the
course of action we're taking today as I've talked about it with
Mr. Salles, to go into an asylum, as a simple formality, and in
any case the repeated crises appear to me to have been serious
enough not to hesitate.

Besides, as to my future, it isn't as if I were 20, since I've
passed 36.

There you are, it seems to me that it would be a torture as
much for others as for myself if I left the hospital, for I feel and

am as it were paralyzed when it comes to acting & getting by. Later on, my word, time will tell.

Thus I'd like to ask you a heap of things about Holland and about recent days. Poor egotist that I've always been and still am now, I can't shake off this idea, which, however, I've already explained to you two or three times, that it's thus for the best that I go into an asylum right now. It may return in the long run. Anyway, my very meager excuse is that painting narrows ideas for the rest perhaps. One can't be in one's profession and think of the rest at the same time. It's a little inevitable — the profession is quite thankless and its usefulness is certainly contestable. And the thing I regret is not having gone into an asylum sooner, it would have been simpler.

Remains, however, the fact that the idea of an association of painters, of housing them together, some of them, although we haven't succeeded, although it's a deplorable and painful failure — this idea remains true and reasonable — like so many others.

But no beginning again.

Be well aware that we must take absolutely the simplest board and lodging.

80 francs must and can suffice, says Mr. Salles. Rey warns me that at St-Rémy it wouldn't go amiss to consider that many people are committed who are more or less well off, some of whom spend a lot of money. Which is often more harmful than useful to them. I can well believe that. And I think that for me, nature alone will do more good than remedies. Here I'm taking *nothing*. I'll have to pay perhaps another 11.87 francs in movable property tax, I've been sent a bill for it at least, in addition to the rest of the rent that I still owe the landlord. And before going to St-Rémy I must send you my consignment of paintings, I've packed one crate already.

I'd like to write to you about other things, but it preoccupies me now that this matter should be sorted out, I can't find the ideas I seek to write to you about on several things at once.

More soon, I hope that you & your wife had a good journey.

Ever yours,
Vincent

INTERVAL: TORINO, JENA; PARAGUAY; ARLES

What fun machines!
Over all obstacles, stand your ground
Muted flames

April 1889

On 10 April 1889, as Nietzsche's left temporal artery was growing more tortuous than the other, and he had been complaining nearly two weeks earlier of right-side supra-orbital neuralgia, the top of the steeple of the Mole Antonelliana was completed, its drive to elevation reaching a final height of 167.5 meters. It was the official inauguration of the synagogue — at the time, the building Nietzsche had baptized *Ecce Homo* was then the tallest brick building in Europe. The structure that reminded him of his *Zarathustra* reached its sublime peak when it was crowned with a statue of Genius that bore a star nearly 4 meters tall on its head — it seems that, with its multitude of identities, even the synagogue still had enough chaos in itself to give birth to a dancing star.

Concurrently, Nietzsche's fame continued to grow, but the philosopher's own rising star wasn't visible to him, for he was nothing but pure bedlam, the frenzied breaking out and volcanic eruption of chaos, the primeval emptiness of the self — *selves* — fragmenting and surging out like lava. Still, his friend Deussen would say, it was a providential blessing that he had no clear awareness of his condition. Being dynamite had had its repercussions — 'Nietzsche' no longer recognized the persons around him, Deussen noted, with the exception of those who stood the very closest.

Was this increasing estrangement not an eerie, proximal form of inner star friendship? Yet, as close as they stood, what of the primary Nietzsche was even there anymore? Was something barbaric not forming within him, some as of yet hitherto unseen event of becoming? Was the terrain of Jena entering and altering the cellular composition of his body, a territory whose exogenous powers he could not combat? Was his body, like Vincent's, some kind of puzzle he was trying to continually piece together, an ever-changing enigma full of energetic, physiochemical, geological, cosmic, maritime, and other strata and energies whose forms forever keep shifting like microliths in a kaleidoscope?

When the philosopher's mother accompanied him to the railroad station to meet Deussen and his wife, his friend took his arm in a friendly fashion and the philosopher did not resist, but he did not recognize whose arm he was holding. When his friend turned the conversation to Schopenhauer, all Nietzsche could say, as if he were speaking the most important truth, was: Arthur Schopenhauer was born in Danzig. When Deussen spoke of Spain where he had traveled the year before with his wife, the asylum inmate cried out, Spain! and became lively. Deussen was there too! When his friend answered, But I am Deussen, the one formerly composed of dynamite stared at his companion and could not gather his thoughts. — Was all of Nietzsche's diatomaceous earth turning to but dead powder? Was his will to dýnamis devoid of all its blasting force? Was the puzzle losing all sense of pattern?

So he still had the concept of me, Deussen said, and mentally he recognized his friend, but the power to subsume this image under the proper concept was no longer present.

It was not ancient Greece, nor the Renaissance, nor the Eternal Return that transfixed the philosopher and guided his thoughts, but a passing drummer-boy, who he watched for a long time, and the locomotives that went to and fro that enthralled him, too. *What fun machines!*

When at home, the philosopher of Dionysos sat brooding quietly on a sunny veranda entwined with grapevines, at times holding conversations with himself, often about persons & events in Schlupforta, in a tangled confusion, his mind like some mixed-up, badly spliced tape recording of his past. We are unknown to ourselves, we knowers: and with good reason, the philosopher once said. We have never looked for ourselves, — so how are we ever supposed to find ourselves?

*

Far off in the jungles of Paraguay, Bernhard Förster was enmeshed in his own tangles of confusion, plunging further into darknesses it seemed he might not emerge from either. Was the Devil getting the best of him? It could not be so. At the sign of triumph Satan's host doth flee; on then, Christian soldiers, on to victory. *Hell's foundations quiver at the shout of praise; brothers, lift your voices, loud your anthems raise!* one might presume he bolstered himself. Over all obstacles, stand your ground — that was the Goethean motto he had embossed in gold on the wall of his beloved Försterhof. But Goethe was nowhere in sight, nor Parsifal, and the jungle continued vining into him, and while he was holed up at Hotel del Lago, luckless as ever, wondering if his dream of a new, pure German society would come to be, Eli penned him distressed letters as she struggled to sustain the colony on her own.

My dear heart-Bern, she wrote, your depression worries me. Please calm yourself. Although I admit the situation is precarious, there are honorable people here, everything will be all right & you have no cause to worry.

Ever hopeful, even in the face of indisputable disaster, the monarch reassured her heart-Bern that, true, many problems are coming to a head now: the Klingbeil book and the Chemnitz affair. But things will get better.

If only they knew that, that very year, on 20 April, in Braunau am Inn, a man was born who would come to realize many of their dreams. Little matter, for their fates would eventually intertwine.

Meanwhile, as if through sheer osmosis, despite the distance of nearly 11,000 km, as if all space and time broke open, boundaries no longer existed and everything became porous, Elisabeth was plagued by a serious eye infection not long after learning of her brother's mental collapse. Her travails only intensified when revolution broke out, with skirmishes occurring nearby at San Pedro. Shrugging off any threat of attack, the Lama knew that Death & the Devil could not accost such a stalwart Christian knight, especially when under protection of the German flag.

Onward, then, ye people; join our happy throng. Blend with ours your voices in the triumph song!

*

In Arles, skirmishes of yet another sort were afoot. Again and again, the Rhône would flood southern France, as it did most famously in 1855, just two years after Vincent van Gogh was born, prompting Napoleon to visit the region to inspect the disaster. This time, if not as calamitous, water damage from the river suffused the Studio of the South, spoiling several of Vincent's paintings. First, a tempest of emotions suffused the studio, then, blood colored its floors and walls, then, the overflowing Rhône seeped through its fragile strongholds — it was as if the walls of the studio and the walls of the painter's flesh were one and the same, each suffering similar fractures & ruination, each in danger of decay, each terrain growing porous and infiltrating the other.

When the painter returned from the asylum, he found water & saltpeter oozing from the walls because the house had been without a fire during his absence, just as he had been without a fire during his confinement, his flames muted with the saltpeter of a chorus of fearful and silencing voices: *society!*

The damage to both the house and his artwork had a strong effect on the bonze, for not only did it signify the foundering of the studio, it also signified the near-destruction of its history, a form of erasure more swift than centuries of time eroding the Colossi of Memnon — as Vincent put it, even the studies that would have been the memories of it were damaged.

It's so final, the painter said, and my urge to found something very simple but durable was so strong. It was fighting against insurmountable odds, or rather it was weakness of character on my part, for I still have feelings of grave remorse difficult to define. I think that was the cause of my crying out so much during the crises, that I wanted to defend myself and could no longer manage to. For it wasn't for me, it was for the very painters like the unfortunate one spoken of in the enclosed article that this studio could have been of use.

And so there the artist sat, packing up a crate of paintings and studies as if he were also packing up and putting to an end his vision of the Studio of the South, that utopic Euro-Japanese artist's colony. Although art was Vincent's home, his veritable house of being, this destruction of his studio wasn't only a personal disaster, it was a historical one — the sundering of a guild meant to carry painting into the future, the death of a barely-born brotherhood of artists, a utopia grown cold and catastrophic, as if the packing crate were an immense coffin also engulfing and entombing the future.

I who have neither wife nor child, Vincent avowed, I need to see the wheat fields. I have a homesickness, for the country of paintings.

Would such a country ever be found? And if so, what would it become in the future? Were Vincent to live into the 20th century, would the vision of painting he had be recognizable, or would the art of the brush be entirely lost, disintegrate into mere concepts, become as industrialized and generic as the manufacturing of oils, or splinter like failed alliances and political factions segmenting into ever more conflictual sects? But then, are collectives & centers of activity any longer needed?

JENA

1267.1 km from Arles

The last will & testament

5 May 1889

Jena Medical Report

Gives the doctor a feces-smeared page of his will.

4 May 1888 [*excerpt*]

It goes without saying that I took steps, not exactly to be photographed (for I am extremely distrustful of haphazard photographs),
but to *alienate* whoever has a photograph of me. Perhaps I have
succeeded; I have not yet heard. If not, I want to use my first trip
to *Munich* (this autumn probably) to symbolize myself again.

ST. RÉMY

1230 km from Jena

*mad or cracked people; the crate of paintings; my duty to
work; I'll always be absent-minded and awkward*

*you have already observed that he loves Paris; Paris is cer-
tainly already a cemetery; there's hardly any really clear
desire or hope left; big, beautiful heartbroken eyes; there
are people who love nature while being cracked or ill; one
continually hears shouts and terrible howls; never have I
been so tranquil as here*

9 May 1889

My dear Theo,

Thanks for your letter. You're quite right to say that Mr. Salles
has been perfect in all of this; I'm much obliged to him.

I wanted to tell you that I think I've done well to come here,
first, in seeing the *reality* of the life of the diverse mad or cracked
people in this menagerie, I'm losing the vague dread, the fear of
the thing. And little by little I can come to consider madness as
being an illness like any other. Then the change of surroundings
is doing me good, I imagine.

As far as I know the doctor here is inclined to consider what
I've had as an attack of an epileptic nature. But I haven't made
any enquiries.

Have you by chance yet received the crate of paintings, I'm
curious to know if they've suffered more, yes or no.

I have two others on the go — violet irises and a lilac bush.
Two subjects taken from the garden.

The idea of my duty to work comes back to me a lot, and I
believe that all my faculties for work will come back to me quite
quickly. It's just that work often absorbs me so much that I think
I'll always be absent-minded and awkward in getting by for the
rest of life too.

I won't write you a long letter — I'll try to answer the letter
from my new sister, which greatly touched me, but I don't know
if I'll manage to do it.

Handshake, and ever yours,

Vincent

My dear sister,

Thanks very much for your letter, in which I above all looked for news of my brother. And I find it very good. I can see that you have already observed that he loves Paris and that this surprises you a little, you who don't like it, or rather who above all like the flowers there, such as, I suppose, for example, the wisterias which are probably beginning to flower. Could it not be the case that in liking a thing one sees it better and more accurately than in not liking it.

For him and for me Paris is certainly already a cemetery in a way, where many artists have perished, whom we knew directly or indirectly.

Certainly *Millet*, whom you'll learn to like a lot, and with him many others, have tried to get out of Paris. But Eugène Delacroix, for example, it's difficult to portray him 'as a man' other than as a Parisian.

All this to urge you — with all caution, admittedly — to believe in the *possibility* that there are *homes* in Paris, and not just apartments.

Anyway — fortunately *you* are now his home yourself.

It's quite odd perhaps that the result of this terrible attack is that in my mind there's hardly any really clear desire or hope left, and I'm wondering if it is thus that one thinks when, with the passions somewhat extinguished, one comes down the mountain instead of climbing it. Anyway my sister, if you can believe, or almost, that everything is always for the best in the best of worlds then you'll also be able to believe, perhaps, that Paris is the best of the towns in it.

Have you noticed yet that the old cab horses there have big, beautiful heartbroken eyes, like Christians sometimes. Whatever the case, we're not savages nor peasants, and we perhaps *even have a duty* to love civilization (so-called). Anyway, it would probably be hypocritical to say or believe that Paris is bad when one lives there. The first time one sees Paris it may be, besides, that everything there seems against nature, dirty and sad. Anyway, if you don't like Paris, above all do not like painting nor those who directly or indirectly are engaged in it, for it's only too doubtful whether that's beautiful or useful.

But what can you do, there are people who love nature while being cracked or ill, those are the painters, then there are some who love what is done by the hand of man, and those even go as far as liking paintings.

Although there are a few people here who are seriously ill, the fear, the horror that I had of madness before has already been greatly softened.

And although one continually hears shouts and terrible howls as though of the animals in a menagerie, despite this the people here know each other very well, and help each other when they suffer crises. They all come to see when I'm working in the garden, and I can assure you are more discreet and more polite to leave me in peace than, for example, the good citizens of Arles.

It's possible that I'll stay here for quite a long time, never have I been so tranquil as here and at the hospital in Arles to be able to paint a little at last. Very near here there are some little grey or blue mountains, with very, very green wheat fields at their foot, and pines.

I shall count myself very happy if I manage to work enough to earn my living, for it makes me very worried when I tell myself that I've done so many paintings and drawings without ever selling any. Don't be in too much of a hurry to consider this an injustice; I don't know anything at all about it.

Thanking you again for writing to me, and being very happy to know that now my brother doesn't return to an empty apartment when he comes home in the evening, I shake your hand in thought, and believe me

your brother
Vincent

JENA

1230 km from St. Rémy

poison

16 May 1889

Jena Medical Report

"I was poisoned again *&* again." Says he used to take 2 × 3g. chloral every 22 days.

ST. RÉMY

1230 km from Jena

the common people; a token of friendship; a sort of triptych;
I haven't yet gone outside; I assure you that I'm very well
here; as in a cockroach-ridden restaurant; the fear of mad-
ness; I think of all this without fear; one who doesn't re-
ply except in incoherent sounds; I feel that I'm in the right
place here; my work will preserve me; honorable madmen
who always wear a hat; I'm obliged to ask you for some
more colors, and especially some canvas; they too have
heard sounds and strange voices; not to be caught so much
unawares by the anguish or the terror; I would still have
melancholy for everything; the enemy before the troops

23 May 1889

My dear Theo,

Your letter, which I've just received, gives me great pleasure. You tell me that J.H. Weißenbruch has two paintings in the exhibition — but I thought he was dead — am I mistaken? He certainly is one hell of an artist and a good man, with a big heart too.

What you say about the Berceuse gives me pleasure; it's very true that the common people, who buy themselves chromos and listen with sentimentality to barrel organs, are vaguely in the right and perhaps more sincere than certain men-about-town who go to the Salon.

Gauguin, if he'll accept it, you shall give him a version of the Berceuse that wasn't mounted on a stretching frame, and to Bernard too, as a token of friendship.

But if Gauguin wants sunflowers it's only absolutely fair that he gives you something that you like as much in exchange. Gauguin himself above all liked the sunflowers later, when he had seen them for a long time.

You must know, too, that if you put them in this order: that is, the Berceuse in the middle and the two canvases of the sun-flowers to the right and the left, this forms a sort of triptych. And then the yellow and orange tones of the head take on more brilliance through the proximity of the yellow shutters. And then you will understand that what I was writing to you about it, that my idea had been to make a decoration like one for the far end of a cabin on a ship, for example. Then as the size gets bigger, the summary execution gets its *raison d'être*. The middle frame is then the red one. And the two sunflowers that go with it are those surrounded by strips of wood.

You see that this framing of simple laths does quite well, and a frame like that costs only very little. It would be perhaps good to frame the green and red vineyards, the sower and the furrows and the interior of the bedroom with them too.

Here's a new no. 30 canvas, commonplace again, like one of those chromos from a penny bazaar that depict eternal nests of greenery for lovers.

Thick tree-trunks covered with ivy, the ground also covered with ivy and periwinkle, a stone bench and a bush of roses, blanched in the cold shadow. In the foreground a few plants with white calyxes. It's green, violet, and pink.

It's just a question — which is unfortunately lacking in chromos from a penny bazaar and barrel organs — of putting in some style.

Since I've been here, the neglected garden planted with tall pines under which grows tall and badly tended grass intermingled with various weeds, has provided me with enough work, and I haven't yet gone outside.

However, the landscape of St-Rémy is very beautiful, and little by little I'm probably going to make trips into it. But staying here as I am, the doctor has naturally been in a better position to see what was wrong, and will, I dare hope, be more reassured that he can let me paint.

I *assure* you that I'm very well here, and that for the time being I see no reason at all to come and board in Paris or its surroundings. I have a little room with grey-green paper with two water-green curtains with designs of very pale roses enlivened with thin lines of blood-red. These curtains, probably the left-overs of a ruined, deceased rich man, are very pretty in design. Probably from the same source comes a very worn armchair covered with a tapestry flecked in the manner of a Diaz or a Monticelli, red-brown, pink, creamy white, black, forget-me-not blue and bottle green.

Through the iron-barred window I can make out a square of wheat in an enclosure, a perspective in the manner of Van Goyen, above which in the morning I see the sun rise in its glory.

With this — as there are more than 30 empty rooms — I have another room in which to work.

The food is so-so. It smells naturally a little musty, as in a cockroach-ridden restaurant in Paris or a boarding school. As these unfortunates do absolutely nothing (not a book, nothing to distract them but a game of boules and a game of draughts) they have no other daily distraction than to stuff themselves with chickpeas, haricot beans, lentils, and other groceries and colonial foodstuffs by the regulated quantities and at fixed times.

As the digestion of these commodities presents certain difficulties, they thus fill their days in a manner as inoffensive as it's cheap. But joking apart, the *fear* of madness passes from me considerably upon seeing from close at hand those who are affected with it, as I may very easily be in the future.

Before I had some repulsion for these beings, and it was something distressing for me to have to reflect that so many people of our profession, Troyon, Marchal, Meryon, Jundt, M. Maris, Monticelli, a host of others, had ended up like that. I wasn't even able to picture them in the least in that state.

Well, now I think of all this without fear, i.e. I find it no more atrocious than if these people had snuffed it of something else, of consumption or syphilis, for example.

These artists, I see them take on their serene bearing again, and do you think it's a small thing to rediscover ancient members of the profession.

Joking apart, that's what I'm profoundly grateful for.

For although there are some who howl or usually rave, here there is *much* true friendship that they have for each other. They say, one must suffer others for the others to suffer us, and other very true reasonings that they thus put into practice. And between ourselves we understand each other very well, I can, for example, chat sometimes with one who doesn't reply except in incoherent sounds, because he isn't afraid of me.

If someone has some crisis the others look after him, and intervene so that he doesn't harm himself.

The same for those who have the mania of often getting angry. Old regulars of the menagerie run up and separate the fighters, if there is a fight.

It's true that there are some who are in a more serious condition, whether they be filthy, or dangerous. These are in another courtyard. Now I take a bath twice a week, and stay in it for 2 hours, then my stomach is infinitely better than a year ago, so I only have to continue, as far as I know. I think I'll spend less here than elsewhere, since here I still have work on my plate, for nature is beautiful.

My hope would be that at the end of a year I'll know better than now what I can do and what I want. Then, little by little, an idea will come to me for beginning again. Coming back to Paris or anywhere at the moment doesn't appeal to me at all; I feel that I'm in the right place here. In my opinion, what most of those who have been here for years are suffering from is an extreme sluggishness. Now, my work will preserve me from that to a certain extent.

The room where we stay on rainy days is like a 3rd-class waiting room in some stagnant village, all the more so since there are honorable madmen who always wear a hat, spectacles and travelling clothes and carry a cane, almost like at the seaside, and who represent the passengers there.

I'm obliged to ask you for some more colors, and especially some canvas. When I send you the 4 canvases of the garden I have on the go you'll see that, considering that life happens above all in the garden, it isn't so sad. Yesterday I drew a very large, rather rare night moth there which is called the death's head, its coloration astonishingly distinguished: black, grey, white, shaded, & with glints of carmine or vaguely tending toward olive green; it's very big.

To paint it I would have had to kill it, and that would have been a shame since the animal was so beautiful. I'll send you the drawing of it with a few other drawings of plants.

You could take the canvases that are dry enough at Tanguy's or at your place off the stretching frames and then put the new ones you consider worthy of it onto these stretching frames. Gauguin must be able to give you the address of a liner for the *Bedroom* who won't be expensive. This I *imagine* must be a 5-franc restoration, if it's more then don't have it done, I don't think that Gauguin paid more when he quite often had canvases of his own, Cézanne or Pissarro lined.

Speaking of my condition, I'm still so grateful for yet another thing. I observe in others that, like me, they too have heard sounds and strange voices during their crises, that things also appeared to change before their eyes. And that softens the horror that I retained at first of the crisis I had, and which when it comes to you unexpectedly, cannot but frighten you beyond measure. Once one knows that it's part of the illness one takes it like other things. Had I not seen other mad people at close hand

I wouldn't have been able to rid myself of thinking about it all the time. For the sufferings of anguish aren't funny when you're caught in a crisis. Most epileptics bite their tongues and injure them. Rey told me that he had known a case where someone had injured his ear as I did, and I believe I've heard a doctor here who came to see me with the director say that he too had seen it before. I dare to believe that once one knows what it is, once one is aware of one's state and of possibly being subject to crises, that then one can do something about it oneself so as not to be caught so much unawares by the anguish or the terror. Now, this has been diminishing for 5 months, I have good hope of getting over it, or at least of not having crises of such force. There's one person here who has been shouting and *always* talking, like me, for a fortnight, he thinks he hears voices and words in the echo of the corridors, probably because the auditory nerve is sick and too sensitive, and with me it was both the sight and the hearing at the same time which, according to what Rey said one day, is usual at the beginning of epilepsy.

Now the shock had been such that it disgusted me even to move, and nothing would have been so agreeable to me as never to wake up again. At present this *horror of life* is already less pronounced, and the melancholy less acute. But I still have absolutely no *will*, hardly any desires or none, and everything that has to do with ordinary life, the desire for example to see friends again, about whom I think however, almost nil. That's why I'm not yet at the point where I ought to leave here soon, I would still have melancholy for everything. And it's even only in these very last days that the repulsion for life has changed quite radically. There's still a way to go from there to will and action.

It's a shame that you yourself are still condemned to Paris, and that you never see the countryside other than that around Paris.

I think that it's no more unfortunate for me to be in the company where I am than for you always the fateful things at Goupil & Cie. From that point of view we're quite equal. For only in part can you act in accordance with your ideas. Since, however, we have once got used to these inconveniences, it becomes second nature.

I think that although the paintings cost canvas, paint &c., at the end of the month, however, it's more advantageous to spend a little more thus, and to make them with what I've learned in total, than to abandon them while one would have to pay for board and lodging all the same anyway. And that's why I'm making them. So this month I have 4 no. 30 canvases *&* two or three drawings.

But no matter what one does, the question of money is always there like the enemy before the troops, and one can't deny it or forget it.

I retain my duties in that respect as much as anyone. And perhaps some day I'll be in a position to repay all that I've spent, because I consider that what I've spent is, if not taken from you at least taken from the family, so consequently I've produced paintings and I'll do more. That is to act as you too act yourself. If I had private means, perhaps my mind would be freer to do art for art's sake, now I content myself with believing that in working assiduously even so, without thinking of it one perhaps makes some progress.

Here are the colors I would need

3 emerald green   ⎫
2 cobalt   ⎬ large tubes.
1 ultramarine   ⎪
1 orange lead   ⎪
6 zinc white   ⎭
5 meters canvas

Thanking you for your kind letter, I shake your hand warmly, as well as your wife's.

Ever yours,
Vincent.

JENA

1230 km from St. Rémy

the immoralist who no longer writes

[23 May 1889]

[Dear   ]

[Nietzsche]

ST. RÉMY

1230 km from Jena

send me a few ordinary brushes; here we have splendid sunshine; as for me, my health is good; the establishment is a little moribund; a new person has arrived who is so agitated that he breaks everything and shouts day and night; the eternal youth of the school of Delacroix; I saw the countryside from my window; I still have remorse; the will to work again; one feels too decidedly broken for life outside; the great defect of the south; to not be indifferent and not exhibit something too mad; stop worrying with regard to me; the flowers will be short-lived; I'm not too melancholy here

31 May–6 June

My dear Theo,

I still have to ask you to send me a few ordinary brushes as soon as possible, of more or less different sizes. Half a dozen of each please.

I hope that you're well and your wife too, and that you'll enjoy a little of the good weather. At least here we have splendid sunshine.

As for me, my health is good, and as for the head it will, let's hope, be a matter of time and patience.

The director had a few words with me to say that he'd received a letter from you, and that he'd written to you. To me he says nothing and I ask nothing of him, which is simplest. He's a little gouty man — widowed a few years ago — who has very dark spectacles. As the establishment is a little moribund, the man appears to take only a rather half-hearted enjoyment in this profession, and besides there's reason enough for it.

A new person has arrived who is so agitated that he breaks everything and shouts day and night, he also tears the straitjackets and up to now he scarcely calms down, although he's in a bath all day long, he demolishes his bed and all the rest in his room, overturns his food &c. It's very sad to see — but they have a lot of patience here and will eventually get there, however.

New things become old so quickly — I think that if I came to Paris in the state of mind I'm currently in, I wouldn't make any distinction between a so-called dark painting or a bright Impressionist painting, between a varnished painting in oils and a matte picture done with thinned paint.

I mean by this that having reflected as time passed — I believe more than ever in the eternal youth of the school of Delacroix, Millet, Rousseau, Dupré, Daubigny, just as much as in the current one or even in artists to come. I scarcely believe that Impressionism will ever do more than the Romantics, for example.

It's certainly a far cry between that and admiring people like Léon Glaize or Perrault.

This morning I saw the countryside from my window a long time before sunrise with nothing but the morning star, which looked very big. Daubigny and Rousseau did that, though, with the expression of all the intimacy and all the great peace and majesty that it has, adding to it a feeling so heartbreaking, so personal. These emotions I do not detest.

I still have remorse, and enormously when I think of my work, so little in harmony with what I'd have wished to do. I hope that in the long run it will make me do better things, but we aren't there yet.

I think that you would do well to wash the canvases that are quite, quite dry with water and a little spirits of wine to remove the oil and the thinner from the impasto. The same for the night café and the green vineyard, and above all for the landscape that was in the walnut frame. The night also (but that one has recent retouchings which might run with the spirits of wine).

I've been here almost a whole month, not one single time have I had the slightest desire to be elsewhere; just the will to work again is becoming a tiny bit firmer.

I don't notice any very clear desire to be elsewhere in the others either, and this may very well come from the fact that one feels too decidedly broken for life outside.

What I don't really understand is their absolute idleness. But that's the great defect of the south, and its ruin. But what a beautiful land and what beautiful blue & what a sun. And yet I've only seen the garden and what I can make out through the window.

Have you read the new book by Guy de Maupassant, *Fort comme la mort*, what is its subject? What I read last in this category was Zola's *Le rêve*, I found the figure of the woman, the embroiderer, very, very beautiful, and the description of the embroidery all in gold. Precisely because it's like a question of color, different yellows, whole and broken. But the figure of the man struck me as rather lifeless, and the great cathedral also made me as melancholy as hell. Only that lilac and dark blue *repoussoir* makes, if you will, the blonde figure stand out. But anyway, there are already things by Lamartine like that.

I hope that you'll destroy a heap of things that are too bad in the heap I sent, or at least will only show the most passable ones.

As regards the exhibition of the Independents, it's all the same to me, act as if I wasn't there at all. To not be indifferent and not exhibit something too mad, perhaps the starry night and the landscape with yellow greenery which was in the walnut frame. Since these are two of contrary colors, and that might give others the idea of doing night effects better than I do.

Anyway you must absolutely stop worrying with regard to me now. When I receive the new canvas and the colors I'll go out a bit to see the countryside.

Since it's just the season when there are lots of flowers and thus color effects, it will perhaps be wise to send me another 5 meters of canvas in addition.

For the flowers will be short-lived and will be replaced by the yellow wheat fields. The latter, above all, I would like to capture better than in Arles. The mistral (since there are a few mountains here) appears far less annoying than in Arles, where you always get it at first hand.

When you receive the canvases I've done in the garden you'll see that I'm not too melancholy here.

More soon, good handshake in thought to you *&* to Jo.

Ever yours,
Vincent.

JENA

1230 km from St. Rémy

paranoia & violence

10 June 1889

Jena Medical Report

Suddenly smashed a window.

INTERVAL: ST. RÉMY; PARAGUAY; DISTANT SPACE

The Andromeda Nebula, the stars via death;
the birth of a new Wagnerian hero
2.537 million light years from earth

June 1889

While at Hôtel-Dieu-Saint-Esprit in Arles, Vincent's brush was directed deeply inward, his paintings focused on the world before him when he was largely in confinement, making pictures of people, grass, flowers, fields, and trees, all close, intimate icons of nature and humanity, where little if any horizon is ever seen. At times, his eye turned intensely cloistered, focusing on the interior world of the hospital, its inner garden, its ward, and yet, unlike his other paintings with lights, those of the latter painting emit no radiant effusions — was it simply the light of a daytime interior, or did he no longer see the fibrillating, radiant effulgence around things? Did existence then lose its holiness for Vincent?

In June of 1889, when at Saint-Paul de Mausole in St. Rémy, Vincent's vision begins to open out and beyond, extending into more expansive dimensions: in the background of one painting, we see mountains for one of the first times, in *Field of Spring Wheat at Sunrise*, then two more paintings featuring mountains, one of which includes a vast, bulbous, billowing formation of clouds that take up almost one-third of the upper horizontal plane of the canvas. The eye is opening to the monumental, to vastness, to immeasurabilities. It was, as he once said, the opening of a veil.

With *The Starry Night*, near-infinite distances are traversed in a new astrophysical optics, just six months after Isaac Roberts photographs the Andromeda Nebula for the first time, himself bringing a distant astral body ever closer to earth — all planes collapse and the outer regions of space touch the ground and enter the eyes and flesh of those below. Although Vincent had painted *Starry Night Over the Rhone* in September of 1888, there, the stars are more distant, removed, far above in a sky sharply distinct from the earth, and of no disproportionate scale. In *The Starry Night*, all spatial distance is buckled, with the once-separate cosmos taking up nearly three-quarters of the painting and the vegetation of the earth bridging the sky — a cypress tree reaches into the height of the heavens like an enormous obelisk, an Eiffel Tower of nature; stars rest as if nested in mountain valleys; earth and distant space are made proximate; the moon is as close and as immense as the mountains, all of which dwarf the human dwellings, none of which seem populated, most of which are colored with the blue of the mountains, as if they've been absorbed or subsumed, as if they've been incorporated by the indigo of rock and night itself, as if they've been divested of humanity and are slowly becoming earth again, one with their encircling landforms. The windows to the spired church are black, devoid of illumination, as if emitting or receiving no luminosity. What is sacred is space itself, and the stars are more monumental than the buildings below. The only light in the earthly plane is that of the golden starlight reflecting in a few building windows — here humanity does not exist, there is only the cosmos. Although reality appears relatively still to us, it is a torrent of motion, and such violent mobility, or the velocity of aeonic time, is visible, made image, in Vincent's kaleidoscopic painting. He depicts the swirling, pulsating, vibrating vortex of reality as if he sees deep time itself, perceiving not anthropomorphically, not with the mere naked eye alone, but cosmologically — the painter has taken the cosmos into himself; the human has been decentered. It is a sub species aeternitatis perspective, an art of physics. In eluding horizon lines, the pictures become images of eternity, the folding together of immeasurable distances in a single plane, distances that the painter reaches through his very illness — convalescence becomes a space-time portal.

Why, I say to myself, should the spots of light in the firmament be less accessible to us than the black spots on the map of France. Just as we take the train to go to Tarascon or Rouen, we take death to go to a star. What's certainly true in this argument is that, while alive, we cannot go to a star, any more than once dead we'd be able to take the train. So it seems to me not impossible that cholera, the stone, consumption, cancer are celestial means of locomotion, just as steamboats, horse-drawn omnibuses, and the railway are terrestrial ones.

Is madness the painter's celestial means of locomotion? Did he reach the stars one dark night in the asylum? Did he break the hands of time; find the Augenblick where the paths of eternity meet?

In Bernhard Förster's soul, the arm of time swivels between much shorter distances as the effects of Klingbeil's book continue to resound throughout both Germany & Paraguay, the stalwart Knight's fortitude fraying like weakening twine, each new broken thread lessening the strength of his rope. When German funders of his Teutonic venture lose trust and refuse further support, the great Dürer Knight sought to acquire loans when in Asunción, writing frantic letters in a state of panic, all to no avail. He thought back to his original dream, to his vision of a pure Germany, to his longing to rid his nation of the Jews and their honoring of the Golden Calf. How close did he come in his journey as a great Christian Knight? The true German he said then is a fighter, a brooder, and a poet, who would rather let that most lamentable of all nature's products, *Homo sapiens judeo progrediens communis*, die in its own void.

If there was a void, it seemed ever clearer that it was not the Jews who were perishing in it. How could this be? How could a degenerate tribe conquer the Germans? And how could the confines of a primitive jungle peopled with half-naked savages defeat a master race? Did both peoples have the power to free themselves of entropic containment?

Förster thought back to 1881 as well, when he founded the Deutscher Volksverein, whose inaugural meeting attracted 6,000 followers. Where were those champions of anti-Semitism now? How could they not participate in his visionary efforts? If they wouldn't contribute funds to the dream of Nueva Germania, was it just anti-Semitic commiseration they sought? The pleasure of hating, en masse, over pretzels & beer? Förster of the legendary Försterhof also thought back to when Elisabeth told him that her brother's goal was not her goal, his entire philosophy she affirmed went against her grain.

I was excited when I read the first part of *Zarathustra* and thought that my brother's ideals could become mine. His striving for the superman seemed something admirable and I thought that you with your colonizing venture had taken the first step toward it. In the meantime the second part of *Zarathustra* has appeared and my excitement is gone. I see now that the superman is not my ideal. Your article "National Education" is far superior and much more to my liking.

But the Knight did not feel like an Übermensch. It seemed that Death and the Devil were closing in on him, that the infernal heat of the jungles of Paraguay was but a worldly correlate to the metaphysical heat of the Inferno, to the collapsing of the horizon line between the earthly and the metaphysical realms.

While in the Swiss Colony of San Bernardino, Förster wrote to the director of the Chemnitz Colonial Society, stating that their strange conduct has deprived him of the last possibility of maintaining himself there economically. My physical and mental state he went on is such that I must assume I shall soon be relieved of my hard task. This is my last request: Please continue to put your considerable talents, your strength and your youthful enthusiasm, in the service of the worthy enterprise that I have started. Perhaps it will prosper better without me than with me. Believe me, Nueva Germania deserves to be supported rather than many other colonial enterprises. It can become an honorable monument for all who participated in the establishment of this colony.

And to his wife, he wrote on 2 June, Dear Child! A number of letters enclosed. I am not feeling well; how are you all? I hope to be able to come to you very soon. Most heartily yours, Bernhard.

Did he think he would reach her by convalescence, or by some celestial means of locomotion?

The next morning, the Goethean motto could no longer be adhered to — the feared companion had at last arrived. The valiant Knight had lost his way. Taking up a vial of strychnine and morphine, the colonialist consumed it and was soon dead.

Despite the fact that the Knight had confided to a German doctor in Asunción that he and his wife would simply take poison if the colonial project failed, Elisabeth swiftly commenced her hagiographic efforts, diligently working to conceal the truth and in its place construct a martyrology. Fact must never triumph; skewered perception must rule. Just as her beloved little Fritz was only a victim of chloral poisoning, her husband Bernhard died of nothing more than a nervous attack, provoked by his enemies and all those who had betrayed the dream of Nueva Germania. All Hail the Aryan King!

While earlier Queen Förster informed Dr. Binswanger of how her brother was to be diagnosed, now she convinced a Paraguayan doctor to sign a death certificate crafted to her choosing, forensics be damned. Through sheer will, through domineering tactics, anything can be accomplished. Over all obstacles, stand your ground! Over all truth, the mendaciousness of faith! Against all enemies, spew spittle mixed with half-digested food!

In her book on their Paraguayan adventure, Queen Eli would establish the myth of Bernhard as a Wagnerian hero who had perished as a martyr in the wilds of South America. Whereas the noble Förster had lived by his Christian beliefs, he was encircled by doubt, suspicion, and human wickedness. This one discovery — set against all the hopes and potential success of his ideal — broke the heart of this brave man, and prematurely ended this hopeful, this extraordinarily valuable life.

This world is the will to power — and nothing besides! And you yourselves are this will to power — and nothing besides!

*

Toward the near end of June, a ring of fire appeared in the Atlantic, African, and Indian skies, the moon's antumbra falling on the earth as Vincent's beloved sun was almost entirely blackened out for over 7 minutes — it was the Solar Saros 125 eclipse of 1889, and its shadow, traveling at both 1770 (at the equator) and 8000+ kilometers per hour (at the poles), was 232 km wide. It was the third occurrence in Vincent's life of his beloved sun growing almost completely dark.

At eclipse totality, birds prepared for sleep, temperatures dropped 20° or more, and the horizon was illuminated in a narrow band of light.

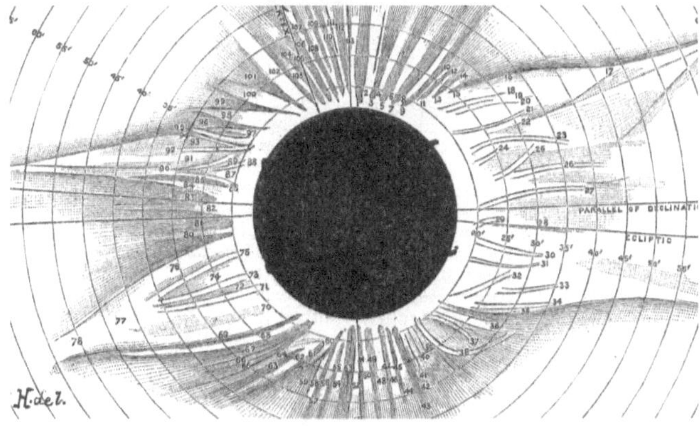

ST. RÉMY

1230 km from Jena

*we live in such a disturbed age; as for me, it's going well;
I despair of ever finding models; not exhibiting paintings
of mine; one causes a stir by exhibiting in the cafés; 81 virtuous cannibals; the Impressionists' movement has had
no unity; a country nature that is purer than the suburbs;
we try to prove that something else quite different exists;
Gauguin, Bernard, or I will all remain; dizzy heights*

18 June 1889

My dear Theo,

Thanks for your letter of yesterday. I too cannot write as I would wish, but anyway we live in such a disturbed age that there can be no question of having opinions that are firm enough to judge things.

I would have very much liked to know if you now still eat together at the restaurant or if you live at home more. I hope so, for in the long run that must be the best.

As for me, it's going well — you'll understand that after almost half a year now of absolute sobriety in eating, drinking, smoking, with two two-hour baths a week recently, this must clearly calm one down a great deal. So it's going very well, and as regards work, it occupies and distracts me — which I need very much — far from wearing me out.

It gives me great pleasure that Isaäcson found things in my consignment that please him. He and De Haan appear very faithful, which is sufficiently rare these days for it to be worthy of appreciation. And that, as you say, there was another who found something in the yellow and black figure of a woman, that doesn't surprise me, although I think that its merit lies in the model and not in my painting.

I despair of ever finding models. Ah, if I had some from time to time like that one, or like the woman who posed for the Berceuse, I'd do something quite different.

I think you did the right thing by not exhibiting paintings of mine at the exhibition by Gauguin and others. There's reason enough for me to abstain from doing so without offending them as long as I'm not cured myself.

For me it's beyond doubt that Gauguin and Bernard have great and real merit.

It's still perfectly understandable, though, that for beings like them, really alive and young, who *must* live and try to carve out their path, it's impossible to turn all their canvases to the wall until it pleases people to admit them somewhere in the official pickle. One causes a stir by exhibiting in the cafés, which I don't say isn't in bad taste. But for myself, I have that crime on my conscience, and to the point of doing it twice, having exhibited at the Tambourin and at avenue de Clichy. Not counting the disturbance caused to 81 virtuous cannibals of the good town of Arles and to their excellent mayor.

So in any case, I am worse and more blameworthy than they are in that regard (causing a stir quite involuntarily, my word).

Young Bernard — according to me — has already made a few absolutely impressive canvases in which there's a gentleness and something essentially French and candid, of rare quality.

Anyway, neither he nor Gauguin are artists who could look as if they were trying to go to the World Exhibition by the back stairs. You can be sure of that. It's understandable that they *couldn't* keep silent. That the Impressionists' movement has had no unity is what proves that they're less skilled fighters than other artists like Delacroix and Courbet.

At last I have a landscape with olive trees, and also a new study of a starry sky.

Although I haven't seen the latest canvases either by Gauguin or Bernard, I'm fairly sure that these two studies I speak of are comparable in sentiment. When you've seen these two studies for a while, as well as the one of the ivy, I'll perhaps be able to give you, better than in words, an idea of the things Gauguin, Bernard, and I sometimes chatted about and that preoccupied us. It's not a return to the romantic or to religious ideas, no. However, by going the way of Delacroix, more than it seems, by color and a more determined drawing than trompe-l'oeil precision, one might express a country nature that is purer than the suburbs, the bars of Paris. One might try to paint human beings who are also more serene and purer than Daumier had before him. But of course following Daumier in the drawing of it. We'll leave aside whether that exists or doesn't exist, but we believe that nature extends beyond St-Ouen.

Perhaps, while reading Zola, we are moved by the sound of the pure French of Renan, for example.

And after all, while Le Chat Noir draws women for us after its own fashion, and above all Forain does so in a masterly way, we do some of our own, less Parisian but no less fond of Paris and its elegances, we try to prove that something else quite different exists.

Gauguin, Bernard, or I will all remain there perhaps, and won't overcome but neither will we be overcome. We're perhaps not there for one thing or the other, being there to console or to prepare for more consolatory painting. Isaäcson and De Haan may not succeed either, but in Holland they've felt the need to state that Rembrandt did great painting and not trompe l'oeil, they also felt something different.

If you can get the *Bedroom* lined it's better to have it done *before* sending it to me.

I have no more white at all.

You'll give me a lot of pleasure if you write to me again soon. I so often think that after a while you'll find in marriage, I hope, the means to gain new strength, and that a year from now your health will have improved.

What I'd very much like to have here to read from time to time would be a Shakespeare. There's one priced at one shilling, Dicks' Shilling Shakespeare, which is complete. There's no shortage of editions, and I think the cheap ones have been changed less than the more expensive ones. In any case I wouldn't want one that cost more than three francs.

Now, whatever is too bad in the consignment, put it completely to one side, pointless to have stuff like that; it may be of use to me later to remind me of things. Whatever is good will show up better by being part of a smaller number of canvases. The rest, if you put them in a corner, flat between two sheets of cardboard with old newspapers between the studies, that's all they're worth.

I'm sending you a roll of drawings.

Handshakes to you, to Jo and to our friends.

Ever yours,
Vincent

The drawings *Hospital in Arles*, the *Weeping Tree in the Grass*, *The Fields* and *The Olive Trees*, are a continuation of those from Montmajour from back then. The others are hasty studies done in the garden.

There's no hurry for the Shakespeare, if they don't have an edition like that, it won't take an eternity to have one sent.

Don't be afraid that I would ever venture onto dizzy heights of my own free will, unfortunately, whether we like it or not, we're subject to circumstances and to the illnesses of our time. But with all the precautions I'm now taking, it will be difficult for me to relapse, and I hope that the attacks won't start again.

JENA

1230 km from St. Rémy

Medical Report

18 June 1889

Jena Medical Report

Speaks in a growling voice, very affectedly, sometimes with a great show of emotion, as if devoid of measure.

16 June 1888 [*excerpt*]

This time I *want all* of my required ham from Naumburg. Last summer I got it from Basel, Zurich, St. Gallen, and elsewhere, with all sorts of annoyance and disappointment: so I don't want to do that again. As you can imagine, I always had to atone for it with my *health* if an order was bad or half-satisfactory. The *only one* that actually satisfied me was the very last Naumburg delivery from September: the round, thick *Lachsschinken*.

ST. RÉMY

1230 km from Jena

I've got some more canvases on the go; outside Paris one quickly forgets Paris; my health is still very good; a lot of trouble with his lungs; it's still possible that life has a meaning; a wheatfield or a cypress are well worth the effort of looking at them from close at hand; no one has yet done wheatfields as I see them; send me the colors; finding something to do all day is the big thing here; what a pity that one can't move the building

25 June 1889

My dear Theo,

Enclosed you'll find an order for colors to replace the one in my previous letter. We've had some fine hot days and I've got some more canvases on the go, so that there are 12 no. 30 canvases on the stocks. Two studies of cypresses of that difficult shade of bottle green. I've worked their foregrounds with thick impastos of white lead that gives firmness to the ground. I believe that Monticellis were very often prepared in this way. One then places other colors on top. But I don't know if the canvases are strong enough for this work.

Speaking of Gauguin, Bernard, and the fact that they might well do more consolatory painting, I must, however, add what I've anyway often said to Gauguin himself, that one must then not forget that others have already done so. But whatever the case, outside Paris one quickly forgets Paris, by throwing oneself into the heart of the country one changes one's ideas. But I for one couldn't forget all those beautiful Barbizon canvases then, and it seems unlikely and anyway unnecessary to do better than that.

What's Andries Bonger doing, you don't mention him in your last two or three letters.

As for me, my health is still very good. And work is distracting me.

I have received, from one of our sisters probably, a book by Rod which is not bad but whose title, *Le sens de la vie*, is really a little pretentious for the contents, it would appear to me.

Above all it's not very cheering. The author, it seems to me, must have a lot of trouble with his lungs. And consequently a little with everything.

Anyway, he admits that he finds solace in the company of his wife, which is very well observed, but anyway, for my own use he teaches me absolutely nothing whatsoever about the meaning of life. For my part I could find him a little trite and be surprised that in these days he has had a book like that printed and that he's selling it for 3 francs 50.

Anyway, I prefer Alphonse Karr, Souvestre, Droz, because it's a bit more alive than this. It's true that I'm perhaps ungrateful, not even appreciating Abbé Constantin and other literary productions that illuminate the sweet reign of the naïve Carnot.

It appears that this book has made a great impression on our good sisters. Wil had moreover spoken to me of it, but the little women and books are two different things.

I've re-read Voltaire's *Zadig ou la destinée* with much pleasure. It's like *Candide*. There, at least, the powerful author makes one glimpse that it's still possible that life has a meaning, "although one agreed in conversation that the things of this world did not always go according to the wisest people's liking."

As for me, I don't know what to wish for, first of all working here or elsewhere appears to me more or less the same thing, and since I'm here, staying here is the most simple. Only there's a lack of news to write to you, for the days are all the same, as for ideas I have no others except to think that a wheatfield or a cypress are well worth the effort of looking at them from close at hand, and so on.

I have a wheatfield, very yellow and very bright, perhaps the brightest canvas I've done. The cypresses still preoccupy me, I'd like to do something with them like the canvases of the sunflowers because it astonishes me that no one has yet done them as I see them.

It's beautiful as regards lines and proportions, like an Egyptian obelisk.

And the green has such a distinguished quality.

It's the *dark* patch in a sun-drenched landscape, but it's one of the most interesting dark notes, the most difficult to hit off exactly that I can imagine.

Now they must be seen here against the blue, *in* the blue, rather.

To do nature here, as everywhere, one must really be here for a long time.

Thus a Montenard doesn't give me the true & intimate note, for the light is mysterious, and Monticelli and Delacroix felt that. Then Pissarro used to talk about it very well in the old days, and I'm still a long way from being able to do as he said one should.

Naturally it will please me if you send me the colors, soon if that's possible, but above all do what you can without it exhausting you too much.

So if you prefer to send me it in two batches, that's also all right.

I think that of the two canvases of cypresses, the one I'm making the croquis of will be the best. The trees in it are very tall and massive. The foreground very low, brambles and undergrowth. Behind, violet hills, a green and pink sky with a crescent moon. The foreground, above all, is thickly impasted, tufts of bramble with yellow, violet, green highlights. I'll send you drawings of them with two other drawings that I've also done.

That will keep me busy for the next few days. Finding something to do all day is the big thing here.

What a pity that one can't move the building here. It would be magnificent to hold an exhibition there, all the empty rooms, the big corridors.

I'd very much have liked to see that Rembrandt painting you spoke about in your last letter.

In the old days I saw in Braun's window a photo after a painting that must be from the fine late period (probably in the Hermitage series), in it there were large figures of angels, it was Abraham's meal. Five figures I think. That too was extraordinary. As touching as *The Pilgrims at Emmaus*, for example.

If ever there were a question of giving something to Mr. Salles for the trouble he has gone to — later one should give him Rembrandt's *Pilgrims*.

Is your health good? Handshake to you and your wife, I hope to send you new drawings next week.

Ever yours,
Vincent

JENA

1230 km from St. Rémy

Medical Report

9 July 1889

Jena Medical Report

Jumps about, makes faces, screws up his left shoulder.

ST. RÉMY

1230 km from Jena

feeling sufficient calm return to me; the forthcoming father of a family; a good gust of the mistral; my moral fatigue and my listlessness; I can do nothing but fiddle with my paintings; don't fret or worry or be melancholy on my account; a way better to express the harmony of the tones; beneath a weight that was too heavy; small emotions; our spleens and melancholies; companions in fate; fatherhood; if sometimes there are cockroaches in the food; how preoccupying a pregnancy must necessarily be; your relatively rather long silence in respect of me

15 July 1889

My dear Theo,

If I'm writing to you again today it's because I'm enclosing a few words that I've written to our friend Gauguin, feeling sufficient calm return to me these last few days for my letter not to be absolutely absurd, it seemed to me. Besides, there's no proof that by over-refining one's scruples of respect or feeling one thereby gains respectfulness or good sense. That being so, it does me good to talk with the pals again, even if at a distance. And you — my dear fellow — how are things, and so write me a few words one of these days — for I can imagine that the emotions which must move the forthcoming father of a family, emotions of which our good father so loved to speak, must be great and of sterling worth in you, as in him, but for the moment are almost impossible for you to express in the rather incoherent mixture of the petty vexations of Paris. Realities of this sort must anyway be like a good gust of the mistral, not very soothing, but health-giving. As for me, it gives me very great pleasure I can assure you, and will contribute greatly to bringing me out of my moral fatigue and perhaps from my listlessness.

Anyway, there's enough to bring back the taste for life a little when I think that I myself am going to be promoted uncle of this boy planned by your wife. I find it quite funny that she's so convinced that it's a boy, but anyway, we'll see.

In the meantime I can do nothing but fiddle with my paintings a little. I have one on the go of a moonrise over the same field as the croquis in the Gauguin letter, but in which stacks replace the wheat. It's dull ochre-yellow and violet. You'll see in a while from now.

I also have a new one with ivy on the go. Above all, dear fellow, I beg of you, don't fret or worry or be melancholy on my account, the idea that you would do so, certainly in this necessary and salutary quarantine, would have little justification when we need a slow and patient recovery. If we manage to grasp that, we spare our forces for this winter. I imagine that winter must be quite dismal here, anyway will however have to try and occupy myself. I often imagine that I could retouch a lot of last year's studies from Arles this winter.

Thus, having kept back these past few days a large study of an orchard which was very difficult (it's the same orchard of which you'll find a variation in the consignment, but quite a vague one), I've set to reworking it from memory, and have found a way better to express the harmony of the tones.

Tell me, have you received any drawings from me? I sent you some once, by parcel post, half a dozen, and then later ten or so. If by chance you haven't received them, they must have been at the railway station for days and weeks.

The doctor was telling me about Monticelli, that he had always considered him eccentric, but as for *mad*, he had only been a little that way toward the end. Considering all the miseries of M's last years, is it any surprise that he bowed beneath a weight that was too heavy, and is one right in trying to deduce from that that he failed in his work, artistically speaking? I dare to believe not. There was some very logical calculation about him, and an originality as a painter, so it remains regrettable that one wasn't able to sustain it so as to make its blossoming more complete.

I enclose a croquis of the cicadas from here.

Their song in times of great heat holds the same charm for me as the cricket in the peasant's hearth at home. My dear fellow — let's not forget that small emotions are the great captains of our lives, and that these we obey without knowing it. If it's still hard for me to regain courage over faults committed and to be committed, which would be my recovery, let's not forget from that moment on that neither our spleens and melancholies nor our feelings of good nature and good sense are our sole guides, and above all not our final custodians, and that if you yourself also find yourself facing hard responsibilities to venture, if not to take, my word let's not be *too* concerned with each other, while it so happens that life's circumstances in situations so far removed from our youthful conceptions of the life of the artist would render us brothers after all, as being companions in fate in many respects. Things are so closely connected that here one sometimes finds cockroaches in the food as if one were really in Paris, on the other hand it can happen in Paris that you sometimes have a real thought of the fields. It's certainly not much, but it's reassuring anyway. So take your fatherhood as a good fellow from our old heaths would take it, those heaths that remain ineffably dear to us through all the noise, tumult, fog, anguish of the towns, however timid our tenderness may be. That's to say, take your fatherhood there, from your nature as an exile and a foreigner and a poor man, henceforth basing himself with the poor man's instinct on the probability of the real existence of a native country, of a real existence at least of the memory, even while we've forgotten every day. Thus sooner or later we find our fate. But certainly for you, as well as for me, it would be a little hypocritical to forget completely our good humor, the confident sloppiness we had as the poor devils we were as we came and went in that Paris, so strange now — & to place too much weight upon our cares.

Truly, I'm so pleased with the fact that if sometimes there are cockroaches in the food here, in your home there is wife & child.

Besides, it's reassuring that Voltaire, for example, left us free to believe not absolutely all of what we imagine. Thus while sharing your wife's concerns about your health I'm not going so far as to believe what momentarily I was imagining, that worries about me were the cause of your relatively rather long silence in respect of me, although this is so well explained when one thinks of how preoccupying a pregnancy must necessarily be. But it's very good and it's the path where everyone walks in life. More soon, and good handshake to you and to Jo.

Ever yours,
Vincent.

In haste, but didn't want to delay sending the letter for our friend Gauguin, you must have the address.

JENA

1230 km from St. Rémy

a select public; an old envelope; when I creep into my cave; torn up newspapers, geometric figures

29 July 1889

Jena Medical Report

Mother's visit. Delighted.

The patient says to his mother, who met him in the consulting room:

> *A magnificent room, isn't it? You see, I give my lectures here before a select public and I've had the best offers from Leipzig and the magnificent home Rohde used to have was offered to me.*

Then he found a pencil and, as the mother had an old envelope with her, he began to write on it and was, so the mother believed, delighted at being in his element. When it was time to go, he took another pencil from the lecture theater as well as some of the paper that was lying about and, when the mother said to him jokingly, "Dear Old Fritz, you're a thievish little mouse," he whispered mysteriously but quite merrily into her ear,

> *Now I shall have something to do when I creep into my cave.*

The patient's fixed ideas are beginning to disappear and he converses little with other patients. Sometimes, he watches one patient playing an instrument and who often jotted down his own compositions. As a rule, he speaks French and nearly always about music. He would sometimes pick up a newspaper but would only glance at it for a few minutes, then crunch it up and tear it to pieces. When he was in the garden he would draw geometric figures in the sand and would talk of triangles and squares.

PARIS

707.4 km from St. Rémy; 866.2 km from Jena

What to do to get these nightmares to stop; to be among people who would like to do their best to cheer you up a little; I hope that this indisposition was nothing but an after-effect of the previous crisis; are the doctor & the other staff good to you?; we are brothers for more than one reason; don't lose heart, and remember that I need you so much

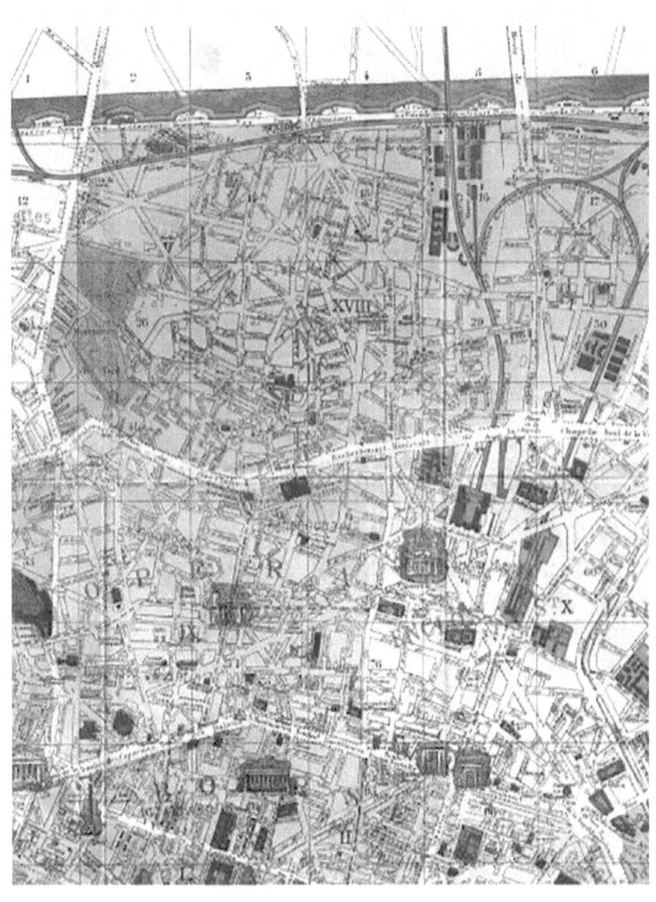

4 August 1889

Dear Vincent,

I found it so strange to have received no letter from you that I telegraphed to find out if you were well. Dr. Peyron answered me in a letter that you've been ill for a few days but that it's already a little better. My poor fellow, how I wish I knew what to do to get these nightmares to stop. When your letter didn't come I imagined, I don't know why, that you were on your way here and would come and surprise us. Should you ever think that it might do you good to be among people who would like to do their best to cheer you up a little, and who would like to have you with them, then think of our little room. It was inaugurated not long ago by Jo's mother, so it's proved usable. I hope that this indisposition was nothing but an after-effect of the previous crisis, but if there was anything particular to which you ascribe this recurrence, at any rate tell me.

Are the doctor and the other staff good to you? Is a distinction made between the various patients, and does this depend on what they pay? When one's concerned one imagines things to be different and worse than they are, so write to me as soon as you can, and even if it's only a few words. I'm not getting more concerned than necessary, but all the same I hope you'll tell me everything. We are well; I feel much better than a while ago and am not coughing at all any more because of Rivet's medicine. In your last letter you wrote that we are brothers for more than one reason. I feel that too, and even if my heart isn't as sensitive as yours, I can sometimes imagine the distress that you feel because of so many thoughts that aren't resolved. Don't lose heart, and remember that I need you so much. Jo sends her best wishes for your recovery. I hope that you'll soon be able to send good reports.

Yours,
Theo

JENA

1230 km from St. Rémy

smashing windows

16 August 1889

Jena Medical Report

Suddenly smashed several windowpanes. Declared he saw the barrel of a rifle behind the window.

ST. RÉMY

1230 km from Jena

so disturbed is my mind; the attacks have recurred; work-
ing on my paintings is quite necessary to me for my recov-
ery; I've been absolutely distraught; it appears that I pick
up filthy things and eat them; I no longer see any possibility
for courage or good hope; this new crisis, my dear brother,
came upon me in the fields; broken greens, reds, and rusty
ochre yellows

22 August 1889

My dear Theo,

I thank Jo very much for writing to me, and knowing that you wish me to write you a line I'm letting you know that it's very difficult for me to write, so disturbed is my mind. So I'm taking advantage of an interval.

Dr. Peyron is really kind to me and really patient. You can imagine that I'm very deeply distressed that the attacks have recurred when I was already beginning to hope that it wouldn't recur.

You'll perhaps do well to write a line to Dr. Peyron to say that working on my paintings is quite necessary to me for my recovery.

For these days, without anything to do and without being able to go into the room he had allocated me for doing my painting, are almost intolerable to me.

I've received the catalogue of the Gauguin, Bernard, Schuffenecker &c. exhibition, which I find interesting. G. also wrote me a kind letter, still a little vague and obscure, but anyway I must say that I think they're quite right to have exhibited among themselves.

For many days I've been absolutely distraught, as in Arles, just as much if not worse, and it's to be presumed that these crises will recur in the future, it is ABOMINABLE. I haven't been able to eat for 4 days, as my throat is swollen. It's not in order to complain too much, I hope, if I tell you these details, but to prove to you that I'm not yet in a fit state to go to Paris or to Pont-Aven unless it were to Charenton.

It appears that I pick up filthy things and eat them, although my memories of these bad moments are vague, and it appears to me that there's something shady about it, still for the same reason that they have I don't know what prejudice against painters here.

I no longer see any possibility for courage or good hope, but anyway it wasn't yesterday that we found out that this profession isn't a happy one.

All the same it gives me pleasure that you've received that consignment from here, the landscapes. Thank you above all for that etching after Rembrandt. It's surprising, and yet it makes me think again of the man with the staff in the La Caze gallery. If you want to do me a very, very great pleasure, then send a copy of it to Gauguin. Then the Rodin and Claude Monet brochure is really interesting.

This new crisis, my dear brother, came upon me in the fields, and when I was in the middle of painting on a windy day. I'll send you the canvas, which I nevertheless finished. And it was precisely a more sober attempt, matte in color without looking impressive, broken greens, reds, and rusty ochre yellows, as I told you that from time to time I felt a desire to begin again with a palette like the one in the north.

I'll send you that canvas as soon as I can. Good-day, thank you for all your kindnesses, good handshake to you and to Jo, and naturally to Cor if he's still there.

Vincent

Mother and Wil have also written me a very nice letter.

Whilst not liking Rod's book excessively, I've nevertheless done a canvas of that passage in which he speaks of the darkish mountains and huts.

(Our friend Roulin has written to me too.)

INTERVAL: ST. RÉMY; PARAGUAY

Studies in hysteria, studies in particle physics.
The myth of the fallen hero. *Blut und Boden!*

June 1889, and the early 20th century

Is the disintegration of Nietzsche, the disintegration of Vincent, the disintegration of Bernhard Förster, an outbreak within the body of rampant hydrogen and helium, oxygen and carbon gone chaotic, the body as big bang *deforming*? Does our splintering occur when we become less and less purely human, when the matter of the cosmos of which we are composed begins to intensify and break out with great force, raging, dispersing from within, longing to return to space and depart the body, all of what was strictly human being discarded, like a supernova exploding? The end of negentropy, a traversal into the Tropic of Entropy? Or is it biological nihilism? The genome gone amok?

The late 19th century is the era of new studies in hysteria, with Pierre Janet's work on hysterical somnambulists, *De l'Automatisme Psychologique*, soon about to crack the horizon — the hidden depths of humanity are opened up, revealing subconscious acts, potential psychological dissociation, mental disaggregation, and psychological automatism. The human is a host of entities and unknown forces beyond its control, a species of primate whose very nature is undergoing continual changes. Evolution has not yet ceased!

Freud, Jung, and William James extend Janet's studies and the teeming instability and chaos within the human is projected as if thru a camera obscura for man to see as never before. Herr Dynamite spoke of the indeterminate human, of radical becoming, of a configuration of warring forces, the psychologists of multiple personalities, split selves, and the instability of character. To what degree the mind can split into separate consciousnesses in each of us is, James declared, a dilemma — the riddle of the human, the human as riddle, the human as chemically volatile terrain. We, too, suffer earthquakes.

In the age of particle physics, solidity is beginning to crack, and so the human body, and so the psyche. Without a unifying or coordinating power, in the face of an abnormal weakness, chaos can break forth and wreak havoc with the self. What is within us, Nietzsche asked much earlier? An abundance of drives and impulses that must be synthesized. Moralities are the expression of locally limited orders of rank in our multifarious world of drives, so we should not perish through their contradictions. Thus a drive as master, its opposite weakened, refined, as the impulse that provides the stimulus for the activity of the chief drive. What is Nietzsche, what is Vincent? — Those who tense the bow, if they do not break it. Does not a plethora of selves live within their bodies, with each trying to usurp the other, an endless series of subterranean and enfolded pupae awaiting emergence? How much have they become-volcanic through their ingestion of pyroclastic elements, how much have they become-sea, become-mistral, become-paint, become-dynamite? What is the nature of Nietzsche, and what is the Nietzsche of nature?

A new psychology is developing and in the midst of its formation, Breuer and Freud posit the splitting of the mind (a vertical schism) and the dissociation of the personality (a horizontal schism) — with some tragic event, the subject becomes double, triple, or more. William James speaks of the break out of a constantly alert secondary self, fixed like a vigilant guardian on any command, waiting and watching for its execution — we are fragments. If split off from us, if limited, if buried, this secondary self, this internal doppelgänger (is there a third, fourth, fifth *&*...?), is all the same fully conscious. A host waiting to seize the central drive, the buried self rising to the surface like a geyser springing from the depths. Entranced, the guiding drive is seized, possessed, and all consciousness lost when the host retreats. The primary self invents a hallucination by which to mask and hide from its own view the deeds that the other self enacted. Humanity as Jekyll and Hyde. We are unknown to ourselves, we knowers: and with good reason...

When does the cataleptic subconscious rule and then retreat and disappear, effacing all memory of itself? Endogenous forces emerge; the abysses of our labile nature erupt. Is this what happens when 'Vincent' is on the road past Glanum, painting the Alpilles? Can such endogenous forces be resisted, or does the strata of the earth draw them out of the strata of the body? Is there not a struggle with and absorption of environment? Is not part of one's interior composed of one's surrounding milieus, a selected exterior that has been internalized, made flesh and bone, breath and blood?

In mid-July, surrounded by eviscerated land, standing amidst a buried ancient city of which he has no knowledge, layers of geological history awaiting discovery, just as the layers of the body (its multitude of hidden selves, its somatic currents), the news of his brother's forthcoming child swirling in his head, just after he finishes painting *Les Alpilles with a Hut*, the painter suffers another attack, another outbreak of chaos, hydrogen *&* helium gone awry, a crossing into the Tropic of Entropy, the strata of his body

fissuring

— — crack ::::::::

Or is it the secondary self seizing control, the base element running amok in the nervous system? Or is it the breaking forth in him of igneous elements, the residue of the Krakatoan or Japanese earthquakes growing active? Or is it errant hereditary perturbations?

The painter chews and sucks on his brushes; fighting as his body convulses, he continues the chewing and sucking, as if to paint his teeth, tongue, epiglottis, he squeezes tubes of paint into his mouth, swallowing colors till, soon, he vomits, his body in revolt, *juddering*, convulsing, throat engorged, *tightening* like a gnarled and contorted root — he wants to live his technique in his flesh, to become one with paint, with color, *to make himself* a Vincent van Gogh.

Although disorientated, the broken pitcher makes his way back to the asylum, easel and canvas in hand. Locked into a cell for the most disturbed patients, he is not permitted to paint.

For days, the artist is in torment, unable to eat, his body in continued mutiny, his throat ravaged, making swallowing an agony. More and more, his once formerly powerful phenotypic plasticity weakens and each new test of the spirit threatens his central drive. The host increases in strength; the doppelgänger is slowly taking center stage; the elements are wreaking havoc.

*

In Paraguay, Queen Eli drives on with her martyrological undertaking as she has her beloved heart-Bern buried in the Deutscher-Friedhof Cementerio Aleman overlooking San Bernardino & the waters of the Ypacaraí Lake.

†

Hier ruhet in Gott

Dr. Bernhard Förster
Begründer der Colonie
Neu-Germania
geb.d. 31 März 1843
gest.d. 3 Juni 1889

———

Die Liebe höret nimmer auf

Before his cross-topped gravestone, grief-stricken but stalwart, Queen Eli thinks of the passage her husband wrote on Dürer's *Knight, Death, and the Devil* in his book *Relationship between Modern Jewry & German Art*: The artist leaves us in no doubt that he will achieve his aims.

— Is it so?

She remembers too the mythic end of the Knight as her beloved described it:

When he dies he will submit nobly and gloriously and the philosophical calm will not leave him even in the worst throes of death.

This noble vision was reinforced, Queen Eli believed, when she received a condolence letter from Oscar Erck and more than 50 others loyal to their colony, affirming how Förster not only led them to their new home, but was also in every respect a warm friend and adviser. The magnanimity of his character and the greatness of the ideals that he realized here will ensure that the noble spirit of the deceased will be honored for many generations. *Es lebe Neugermanien!*

And so the legend grows; and so the halo of the martyr brightens — no philology, but faith!

The Queen was further emboldened when a poem by Wagnerite Hans Paul von Wolzogen was published in the *Bayreuther Blätter*. It was a panegyric depicting the fallen Förster as a vanquished hero of Valhalla. However, if fallen, he was not defeated, only a slightly wounded but still regal bird soaring over alien territory:

> Do not call him defeated
> because German strength is broken,
> an eagle with a broken wing
> under a blue foreign sky;
> at the silent grave
> grieve only for German devotion,
> for joy rules at Valhalla.

As such panegyrics continued, and the myth of the fallen hero and martyr resounded in Germany, Queen Eli had to tend to Förster's debts, not to speak of the greater dilemmas of the colony itself. When the proprietor of Hotel del Lago, where Förster spent his final tormented months, demanded Queen Eli pay the colonist's exorbitant bar bill (every martyr needs his high percentage spirits), in exchange she offered a plot of land in Nueva Germania. While he wondered if he could resell it for any profit at all, Queen Eli pondered Wolzogen's suggestion that a Bernhard Förster Foundation and a little Christian house of God be built in Försterrode, but as the months passed, only the meager sum of 36.30 Marks was raised.

Before the grave of the Valhallan hero, the Queen steadied her gaze, resolving to keep the colony from being taken over by foreigners. Just as no Jew, & certainly not the jungle, would defeat her, no doppelgänger or host would seize her central drive—Eli's phenotypic plasticity would only continue to grow in strength with each new crisis. The Queen's self was not only single but solidified. And with her doctored death certificate, she could easily refute the allegations of her husband's detractors, which would aid her in presenting herself as the widow of a patriotic martyr who, alone in the jungles of a savage country, would triumph over all obstacles.

Stand your ground, Christian soldier, stand your ground!!

*

In 1929, nearly 150 km southeast of Asunción, the first Latin American branch of the German National Socialist Party would be founded in Colonia Independencia, Department of Guairá.

Several years later, in 1932, it would receive the official rank of an Ortsgruppenleiter by the German government.

550

During the Nazis rise to power, their esteem grew in Nueva Germania, and Förster was seen as a progenitor of National Socialism. The Valhallan hero, the great Christian Knight, now a star in the pure pure sky.

To honor him, in 1934, Hitler ordered a memorial service to be conducted at Förster's burial site and had German soil shipped to the colony to be sprinkled over the founder's grave.

Blut und Boden!

This world is the will to power — & nothing besides!

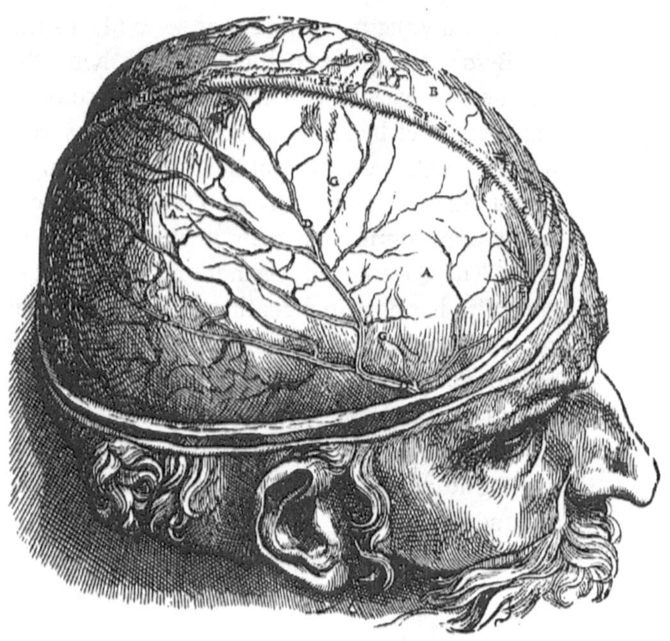

JENA

1230 km from St. Rémy

Epileptic seizures

5 September 1889

Jena Medical Report

Asks for recent literature or newspapers. Declares he suffered from epileptic seizures without loss of consciousness until his 17th year.

ST. RÉMY

1230 km from Jena

the expenses still continuing and the canvases still taking their time; the next Vingtistes exhibition; I'm working non-stop; abnormal ideas; this thin canvas perishes after a while; it's difficult to know oneself — but it's not easy to paint oneself either; I really wish for you that you were 2 years further on; strength is coming back to me day by day; this inevitability of suffering and despair; the image of death; when the crises present themselves they aren't amusing; this is probably the secret — work for a long time and slowly; a new crisis likely in the winter; let's give them the slip; I'm struggling with all my energy to master my work; at the moment my mind is functioning regularly; perhaps my journey into the south will bear fruit; I'll remain melancholy for a long time; what is original and lasting; the extinction of all vital warmth; the family will be for you what nature is for me; eating and drinking like a wolf; "let's hope that it won't recur"; a feeling of self-security from the artistic point of view; what I dream of

5 September 1889

My dear brother,

Although I've already written to you, there are still many things you have told me and to which I haven't yet replied. First that you've rented a room in Tanguy's house and that my canvases are there, that's most interesting — provided you're not paying a lot for it — the expenses still continuing and the canvases still taking their time to bring anything back in, that often frightens me.

Be that as it may, I think it's a very good step, and I thank you for it, as for so many other things. It's curious that Maus has the idea of inviting young Bernard and me for the next Vingtistes exhibition, I would really like to exhibit there, while feeling my inferiority alongside so many Belgians who have an enormous amount of talent. That Mellery, for instance, is a great artist. And he's also been holding up for a number of years now. But I would do my best to try to do something good this autumn. I'm working non-stop in my room, which is doing me good and driving away, I imagine, these abnormal ideas.

Thus I've redone the canvas of the *Bedroom*. That study is certainly one of the best — sooner or later it will definitely have to be *lined*. It was painted so quickly and dried in such a way that, as the thinner evaporated immediately, the painting doesn't adhere at all firmly to the canvas. This will also be the case with other studies of mine that were painted very quickly and with a thick impasto. Besides, this thin canvas perishes after a while and can't take a lot of impasto.

You've taken some excellent stretching frames, damn it, if I had some like that here to work on that would be better than these strips of wood from here that warp in the sun.

People say — & I'm quite willing to believe it — that it's difficult to know oneself — but it's not easy to paint oneself either. Thus I'm working on two portraits of myself at the moment — for want of another model — because it's more than time that I did a bit of figure work. One I began the first day I got up, I was thin, pale as a devil. It's dark violet blue and the head whitish with yellow hair, thus a color effect.

But since then I've started another one, three-quarter length on a light background.

Then I'm retouching some studies from this summer — anyway I'm working from morning till night.

Are you well — darn it, I really wish for you that you were 2 years further on, and that these early days of marriage, however beautiful they may be at times, were behind you. I believe so firmly that a marriage becomes good above all in the long run, and that *then* one recovers one's temperament. So take things with a certain northern phlegm and take care of yourselves, both of you. This bloody life in the fine arts is exhausting, so it seems.

Strength is coming back to me day by day, and once again it seems to me that I already have almost too much of it. For to remain hard working at the easel it isn't necessary to be a Hercules.

What you told me about Maus having been to see my canvases has made me think a lot about Belgian painters lately and during my illness. Then memories come to me like an avalanche, and I try to rebuild for myself that whole school of modern Flemish artists to the point of being as homesick as a Swiss.

Which isn't good, for our path is — onward — and retracing one's steps is forbidden and impossible. That's to say that one could think about it without getting lost in the past through an over-melancholy nostalgia.

Anyway, Henri Conscience isn't a perfect writer at all, but here and there, more or less everywhere, what a painter! And what kindness in what he said and wished for. All the time I have a preface in my head — (the one to *Le conscrit*) to one of his books in which he says that he'd been very ill and that in his illness, despite all his efforts, he had felt his affection for mankind withering away, and that long walks out in the open fields brought his feelings of love back to him.

This inevitability of suffering & despair — anyway, here I am again, recovered for a period — I'm thankful for it.

I'm writing you this letter bit by bit in intervals when I'm tired of painting. Work is going quite well — I'm struggling with a canvas begun a few days before my indisposition. A reaper, the study is all yellow, terribly thickly impasted, but the subject was beautiful and simple. I then saw in this reaper — a vague figure struggling like a devil in the full heat of the day to reach the end of his toil — I then saw the image of death in it, in this sense that humanity would be the wheat being reaped. So if you like it's the opposite of that Sower I tried before. But in this death nothing sad, it takes place in broad daylight with a sun that floods everything with a light of fine gold. Good, here I am again, however I'm not letting go, & I'm trying again on a new canvas. Ah, I could almost believe that I have a new period of clarity ahead of me.

And what should I do — continue here for these months, or move — I don't know. The thing is, when the crises present themselves they aren't amusing, and to risk having an attack like that with you or others is serious.

My dear brother — I'm still writing to you between bouts of work — I'm plowing on like a man possessed, more than ever I have a pent-up fury for work, and I think that this will contribute to curing me.

Perhaps something will happen to me like the thing Delacroix speaks of — "I found painting when I had neither teeth nor breath left," in this sense that my sad illness makes me work with a pent-up fury — very slowly — but from morning till night without respite — and — *this* is probably the secret — work for a long time and slowly. What do I know about it, but I think that I have one or two canvases on the go that aren't too bad, first the reaper in the yellow wheat, and the portrait on a light background. This will be for the Vingtistes, if indeed they remember me when the time comes. Now, it would be absolutely the same to me, if not preferable, if they forget me.

Since I myself don't forget the inspiration that I gain from giving free rein to my memories of certain Belgians. That's the positive thing, and the rest is so secondary.

And here we are in September already, we'll soon be in the middle of autumn, and then winter.

I'll carry on working very hard, and then if the crisis returns toward Christmas we'll see, and once that's over then I wouldn't see any disadvantage in sending the management here to all the devils and coming back to the north for a fairly long time. Leaving now would perhaps be too unwise, when I consider a new crisis likely in the winter, i.e. in 3 months.

I haven't set a foot outside for 6 weeks, not even in the garden. I'll try, though, next week, when I've finished the canvases in progress.

But another few months and I'll be so flabby and stupefied that a change will probably do a lot of good.

That, for the moment, is my idea on the subject, of course it isn't a fixed idea.

But am of the opinion that we shouldn't put ourselves out any more with the people of this establishment than with the owners of a hotel. We've rented a room from them for a certain amount of time, and they're well paid for what they give, and that's absolutely all.

Not to mention the fact that perhaps they'd like nothing better than for the situation to be chronic, & one would be culpably stupid if one gave in to them on that.

For my taste, they make far too many enquiries about not only what I but you earn &c.

So let's give them the slip. Without quarrelling.

I'm still continuing this letter between times. Yesterday I began the portrait of the chief orderly, and perhaps I'll also do his wife, for he's married and lives in a little farmhouse a stone's throw from the establishment.

A most interesting figure. There's a beautiful etching by Legros of an old Spanish nobleman, if you remember it that will give you an idea of the type. He was at the hospital in Marseille during 2 episodes of cholera, anyway he's a man who has seen an enormous number of people die and suffer, and there's an indefinable contemplation in his face, such that I can't help recalling the face of Guizot — for there's something of that one in this head — but different. But he's a man of the people, and simpler. Anyway, you'll see it if I succeed in it & if I do a repetition of it.

I'm struggling with all my energy to master my work, telling myself that if I win this it will be the best lightning conductor for the illness. I take great care of myself by carefully shutting myself away; it's selfish if you like, not to become accustomed to my companions in misfortune here instead, and to go to see them, but anyway I feel none the worse for it, for my work is progressing and we have need of that, for it's more than necessary that I do better than before, which wasn't sufficient.

Isn't it better that if I were to come back from here again, sooner or later, I come back decidedly capable of doing a portrait that has some character, than to come back as I left? It's coarsely expressed, for I really feel that one can't say "I can do a portrait" without telling a lie, because that is infinite. But anyway you'll understand what I want to say, that I must do better than before.

At the moment my mind is functioning regularly and I feel absolutely normal — and if I think rationally at present about my condition with the hope of having in general between the crises — if, unfortunately, it's to be feared that this will always recur from time to time — of having periods of clarity and work between times — if I think rationally at present about my condition then certainly I tell myself that I mustn't have the *idée fixe* of being ill. But that I must continue my little career as a painter firmly. To remain for good in an asylum from now on would probably be exaggerating things.

I was reading in *Le Figaro* a few days ago a story of a Russian writer who lived with a nervous illness from which he, moreover, sadly died, which caused him terrible attacks from time to time.

And what can one do, there's no remedy, or if there is it's to work passionately. I dwell on that more than I should. And all in all I *prefer* to have a proper illness like this than to be as I was in Paris when it was brewing.

Also you'll see this when you put the portrait with the light background which I've just finished beside those I did of myself in Paris, that *at present* I look healthier than then, and even a great deal more so.

I'm even inclined to believe that the portrait will tell you better than my letter how I am, and that it will reassure you — it cost me some trouble.

And then the reaper is working too I think — it's very, very simple.

At the end of the month you can rely on 12 no. 30 canvases I dare say, but there will be almost the same ones twice, the study and the final painting.

Anyway later — perhaps my journey into the south will bear fruit however, because the difference of the stronger light, the blue sky, which teaches one to see, and then above all and even only when one sees that for a long time.

The north will certainly appear completely new to me, but I've looked so much at the things that I've become strongly attached to them, and I'll remain melancholy for a long time.

I'm thinking of a funny thing. Modern art is discussed in *Manette Salomon*, & some artist or other speaking of "what will remain" says: what will remain are "the landscape artists" — that had a grain of truth, because Corot, Daubigny, Dupré, Rousseau — Millet as a landscape painter, that lasts, & when Corot says on his deathbed: in a dream I saw landscapes with completely pink skies, it was charming; then — very good — in Monet, Pissarro, Renoir we see those completely pink skies, so the landscape painters do last well, that was darned true. Let's leave aside the figure painting of Delacroix, of Millet.

Afterwards, what are we beginning to glimpse timidly at the moment that is original and lasting — the *portrait*. That's something old, one might say — but it's also brand new. We'll talk more about this — but let's still continue to seek out portraits, above all of artists, like the Guillaumin & Guillaumin's portrait of a young girl, and take good care of my portrait by Russell, which means a lot to me.

Have you framed the Laval portrait, you haven't told me what you thought of it I think, I found it marvelous, that gaze through the pince-nez, such an honest gaze.

The will that I have to do portraits these days is terribly strong, anyway Gauguin and I used to chat about that and about similar questions in such a way as to stretch our nerves to the extinction of all vital warmth.

But out of that, however, a few good paintings must emerge I dare think, and we're seeking them and they must, I imagine, be doing good work in Brittany. I've received a letter from G., I think I've already told you, and I'm very curious to see what they're doing one day.

I must ask you for the following painting items.

	10 meters	canvas
Large tubes	6 tubes	zinc white
„ „	2 „	emerald green
	2 „	cobalt
Small tubes		
	2	carmine
	1	vermilion

Large tube crimson lake
6 fitch brushes, black hair.

Then I've promised the orderly here an issue of *Le Monde Illustré*, Issue 1684, 6 July 1889, in which there's a very pretty engraving after Demont-Breton.

Phew — the reaper is finished, I think it will be one that you'll place in your home — it's an image of death as the great book of nature speaks to us about it — but what I sought is the "almost smiling." It's all yellow except for a line of violet hills — a pale, blond yellow. I myself find that funny, that I saw it like that through the iron bars of a cell.

Ah well, do you know what I hope for once I set myself to having some hope, it's that the family will be for you what nature is for me, the mounds of earth, the grass, the yellow wheat, the peasant. That's to say that you find in your love for people the wherewithal *not only to work* but the wherewithal to console you and restore you when one needs it. So please don't let yourself be exhausted too much by business matters but take good care of yourselves, both of you — perhaps in a not-too-distant future there's still some good.

I really want to redo the reaper one more time for Mother, if not I'll make her another painting for her birthday, that will come later, for I'll send it with the rest.

For I'm sure that Mother would understand it — for it's indeed as simple as one of those coarse wood engravings that one finds in country almanacs.

Send me the canvas as soon as you can, because I want to do some more repetitions for the sisters too, and if I undertake new autumnal effects I'll have the wherewithal to fill my time from one end to the other for this month.

I'm eating and drinking like a wolf at present. I must say that the doctor is very kindly toward me.

Yes, I think it's a good idea to go and make a few paintings for Holland, for Mother and the two sisters that will make three, i.e. the *reaper*, the *bedroom*, the *olive trees, wheat field and cypress*, that will make four even, for then I have yet another person for whom I'll make one too. I'll work on that with as much pleasure and more calm than for the Vingtistes, that goes without saying, since I'm feeling strong you can be sure that I'm going to try to get through a lot of work. I'm taking the best there are from 12 subjects, so they'll still have things that are a little studied and chosen. And then there is good in working for people who don't know what a painting is.

Good handshake to you and Jo.

Ever yours,
Vincent

I'm opening this letter once more to tell you that I've just seen Mr. Peyron, I hadn't seen him for 6 days. He tells me that he's planning to go to Paris this month and that he'll see you then. That gives me pleasure, for he has, there's no doubt about it, a lot of experience, and I think he'll tell you what he thinks of it quite frankly.

To me he only said — "let's hope that it won't recur," but anyway I'm *counting* on it recurring for quite a long time, for a few years at least. But I'm also counting on the fact that work, far from being impossible for me, can go along steadily in the meantime, and is even my remedy. And so I say once more — excluding Mr. Peyron the doctor absolutely — that as regards the management here we should probably be polite, but that we should limit ourselves to that but bind ourselves to nothing.

It's very serious that wherever I were to stay here for a little longer I would perhaps come up against popular prejudices — I don't even know what these prejudices are — which would make my life with them unbearable.

But anyway, I'm awaiting what Mr. Peyron will say to you, myself I have no idea what his opinion is. I worked this afternoon on the portrait of the orderly, which is progressing. If it weren't very much tempered — completely — by an intelligent gaze and an expression of kindness — he would be a real bird of prey. He really is a southern type.

I'm curious if Mr. Peyron's planned journey will indeed take place this time, I'm very curious to know what may come of it.

With another year's work, perhaps I'll arrive at a feeling of self-security from the artistic point of view. And that's always something worth seeking.

But for that I must have good luck. What I dream of in my best moments aren't so much dazzling color effects as the half-tones once again.

And certainly the visit to the Montpellier museum contributed to turning my thoughts in that direction. For what touched me there more than the *magnificent* Courbets, which are marvels, the young ladies of the village, the sleeping spinner — were the portraits of Bruyas by Delacroix and by Ricard, then the Daniel, Delacroix's odalisques, all in half-tones. For these odalisques are something quite different from those in the Louvre. It's above all purplish.

But in these half-tones what choice and what quality!

It's time for me to send off this letter at last — I could tell you in two pages what it contains, i.e. nothing new. But anyway, I don't have time to redo it.

Good handshake once again, and if it doesn't put you out too much let me have the canvas as soon as possible.

Ever yours,
V.

JENA

1230 km from St. Rémy

the agonist who no longer writes

[10 September 1889]

[Dear ———]

[Nietzsche]

ST. RÉMY

1230 km from Jena

*one would wish the world populated with people like that;
I'm working furiously; a more violent crisis may destroy
my ability to paint forever; to catch hold of the bank again;
the Japanese way of feeling and drawing; an inclination of
the heart; things that I've sought in vain for years; the street
would be better; unhealthy religious aberrations; I ought
to have defended my studio better; I feel very fearful; one
must also see people and recover one's temperament and
furnish oneself with ideas; from time to time I'll have a crisis; recovery comes, if one is brave, from inside, through the
great resignation to suffering and death; the brushstroke; to
have lasting prosperity; G. and I will perhaps work together again; the strength to continue; a fresh attack; to found a
studio somewhere in these parts; certain living types; to live
with the odd patients here; the faculty to work; influence
from outside; vegetate in idleness*

10 September 1889

My dear Theo,

I think your letter is really good, what you say about Rousseau and artists like Bodmer, that they are men in any case, and of such a kind that one would wish the world populated with people like that — yes indeed, that's what I myself feel too.

And that J.H. Weissenbruch knows and does the muddy towpaths, the stunted willows, the foreshortenings and the learned and strange perspectives of the canals "as Daumier does his lawyers," I think that's perfect. Tersteeg did well to buy some of his work from him, the fact that people like that don't sell, according to me that's because there are too many sellers who try to sell other things, with which they deceive the public and mislead them.

Do you know that today, still, when I read by chance the story of some energetic industrialist or above all a publisher, that the same feelings of indignation then come to me again, the same feelings of anger from the old days when I was with G.&Cie.

Life goes on like that, time doesn't come back, but I'm working furiously, because of the very fact that I know that the opportunities to work don't come back.

Above all, in my case, where a more violent crisis may destroy my ability to paint forever. In the crises I feel cowardly in the face of anguish and suffering — more cowardly than is justified, and it's perhaps this very moral cowardice which, while before I had no desire whatsoever to get better, now makes me eat enough for two, work hard, take care of myself in my relations with the other patients for fear of relapsing — anyway I'm trying to get better now like someone who, having wanted to commit suicide, finding the water too cold, tries to catch hold of the bank again.

My dear brother, you know that I came to the south and threw myself into work for a thousand reasons.

To want to see another light, to believe that looking at nature under a brighter sky can give us a more accurate idea of the Japanese way of feeling and drawing. Wanting, finally, to see this stronger sun, because one feels that without knowing it one couldn't understand the paintings of Delacroix from the point of view of execution, technique, and because one feels that the colors of the prism are veiled in mist in the north.

All of this remains somewhat true. Then when one also adds to it an inclination of the heart toward this south that Daudet did in *Tartarin*, and the fact that here and there I've also found friends and things that I love here.

Will you then understand that while finding my illness horrible I feel that all the same I've entered into attachments that are a little too strong here — attachments which could mean that later on the desire to work here will take hold of me again — while all the same it may well be that I'll return to the north relatively soon.

Yes, for I don't hide from you the fact that in the same way that I'm taking my food avidly at present, I have a terrible desire that comes to me to see my friends again and to see the northern countryside again.

Work is going very well, I'm finding things that I've sought in vain for years, and feeling that I always think of those words of Delacroix that you know, that he found painting when he had neither breath nor teeth left. Ah well, I myself with the mental illness I have, I think of so many other artists suffering mentally, and I tell myself that this doesn't prevent one from practicing the role of painter as if nothing had gone wrong.

When I see that crises here tend to take an absurd religious turn, I would almost dare believe that this even necessitates a return to the north. Don't speak too much about this to the doctor when you see him — but I don't know if this comes from living for so many months both at the hospital in Arles and here in these old cloisters. Anyway I ought not to live in surroundings like that, the street would be better then. I am not indifferent, and in the very suffering religious thoughts sometimes console me a great deal. Thus this time during my illness a misfortune happened to me — that lithograph of Delacroix, the *Pietà*, with other sheets had fallen into some oil and paint and got spoiled.

I was sad about it — then in the meantime I occupied myself painting it, and you'll see it one day, on a no. 5 or 6 canvas I've made a copy of it which I think has feeling — besides, having not long ago seen the Daniel and the Odalisques and the Portrait of Bruyas and the Mulatto woman at Montpellier, I'm still under the impression that it had on me. This is what edifies me, as does reading a fine book like one by Beecher Stowe or Dickens. But what disturbs me is constantly seeing those good women who believe in the Virgin of Lourdes and make up things like that, and telling oneself that one is a prisoner in an administration like that, which very willingly cultivates these unhealthy religious aberrations when it ought to be a matter of curing them. So I say, it would be even better to go, if not into penal servitude then at least into the regiment.

I reproach myself for my cowardice, I ought to have defended my studio better, even if I had to fight with those gendarmes and neighbors. Others in my position would have used a revolver, and indeed, had one killed onlookers like that as an artist one would have been acquitted. I would have done better in that case then, and now I was cowardly and drunk.

Ill too, but I wasn't brave. Then in the face of the Suffering of these crises I feel very fearful too, and so I don't know if my zeal is something other than what I say, it's like the man who wants to commit suicide, and finding the water too cold he struggles to catch hold of the bank again.

But listen — to be in a lodging-house like I saw Braat back then — fortunately that time is far off, no and again no.

It would be different if père Pissarro or Vignon, for example, wanted to take me into their home. Well I'm a painter myself — that can be sorted out, and better that the money goes to feed painters than to the excellent nuns.

Yesterday I asked Mr. Peyron point blank: since you're going to Paris, what would you say if I suggested that you be good enough to take me with you? He answered in an evasive way — that it was too quick, that he must write to you beforehand.

But he's very kind and very indulgent toward me, and whilst he isn't the absolute master here, far from it, I owe him many freedoms.

Anyway, one must not only make paintings but one must also see people and — from time to time, by associating with others too, recover one's temperament and furnish oneself with ideas. I leave aside the hope that it wouldn't recur — on the contrary I must tell myself that from time to time I'll have a crisis. But then one might for that time go into an asylum or even to the town prison, where there's usually an isolation cell. Don't worry yourself in any case — work is going well and look, I can't tell you how much it gives me a warm glow sometimes to say, I'm going to do this and that again, wheat fields &c.

I've done the portrait of the orderly, and I have a repetition of it for you. It makes quite a curious contrast with the portrait I did of myself, in which the gaze is vague and veiled, while he has something military about him, and dark eyes that are small and lively. I made him a present of it, and I'll also do his wife if she wants to pose. She's a faded woman, an unfortunate, quite resigned one, and really not much, and so insignificant that I myself have a great desire to do that dusty blade of grass. I spoke with her from time to time when I was doing olive trees behind their little farmhouse, and then she told me that she didn't think that I was ill — anyway, you would say that too at present if you saw me working, with my thoughts clear and my fingers so sure that I drew that Delacroix *Pietà* without taking a single measurement, though there are those four outstretched hands and arms — gestures & bodily postures that aren't exactly easy or simple.

Please send me the canvas soon, if that's possible, and then I think I'll need 10 tubes of zinc white as well.

However, I know quite well that recovery comes, if one is brave, from inside, through the great resignation to suffering & death, through the abandonment of one's own will & one's self-love. But it's not coming to me, I love to paint, to see people and things and everything that makes up our life — artificial — if you like. Yes, real life would be in something else, but I don't think I belong to that category of souls who are ready to live and also at any moment ready to suffer.

What a funny thing the touch is, the brushstroke. Out of doors, exposed to the wind, the sun, people's curiosity, one works as one can, one fills one's canvas regardless. Yet then one catches the true and the essential — that's the most difficult thing. But when one returns to this study again after a time, and orders one's brushstrokes in the direction of the objects — certainly it's more harmonious and agreeable to see, and one adds to it whatever one has of serenity and smiles.

Ah, I'll never be able to render my impressions of certain figures I've seen here. Certainly the road to the south is the road where there's something brand new, but men of the north have difficulty in getting through. And I can see myself already in advance, on the day when I have some success, longing for my solitude and distress here when I see the reaper in the field below through the iron bars of the isolation cell. Every cloud has a silver lining.

To succeed, to have lasting prosperity, one must have a temperament different from mine, I'll never do what I could have and ought to have wanted and pursued.

But as I have dizzy spells so often, I can only live in a situation of the fourth or fifth rank. While I clearly sense the value and originality and superiority of Delacroix, of Millet, for example, then I make a point of telling myself, yes I am something, I can do something. But I must have a basis in these artists, and then produce the little I'm capable of in the same direction.

So père Pissarro has been really cruelly struck by those two misfortunes at the same time.

As soon as I read that I had this idea of asking you if there would be a way of going to stay with him.

If you pay him the same thing as here, he'll find it worth his while, for I don't need much — except for working.

So do it directly, and if he doesn't want to I would willingly go to Vignon's.

I'm a little afraid of Pont-Aven, there are so many people there. But what you say about Gauguin interests me a lot. And I still tell myself that G. and I will perhaps work together again. I myself know that G. can do things even better than what he has done, but how to reassure him! I still hope to do his portrait. Have you seen that portrait he did of me painting sunflowers? My face has lit up after all a lot since, but it was indeed me, extremely tired and charged with electricity as I was then.

And yet to see the country one must live with the common people and in the little houses, the bars &c. And that was what

I said to Boch, who complained of seeing nothing that tempted him or made an impression on him. I go walking with him for two days and I show him 30 paintings to do, as different from the north as Morocco would be. I'm curious to know what he's doing at the moment.

And then do you know why the paintings of Delacroix — the religious and historical paintings, *Christ's Barque* — the *Pietà*, the *Crusaders*, have this allure? Because Delacroix, when he does a Gethsemane, went to see on the spot beforehand what an olive grove was like, and the same for the sea whipped up by a hard mistral, and because he must have said to himself, these people whom history talks to us about, doges of Venice, crusaders, apostles, holy women, were of the same type and lived in a manner analogous to those of their present-day descendants.

So I must tell you it, and you can see it in the *Berceuse*, however failed and weak that attempt may be. Had I had the strength to continue, I'd have done portraits of saints and of holy women from life, and who would have appeared to be from another century and they would be citizens of the present day, and yet would have had something in common with very primitive Christians.

The emotions that that causes are too strong though, I wouldn't survive it — but later, later, I don't say that I won't mount a fresh attack.

What a great man Fromentin was — for those who want to see the orient he will always remain the guide. He was first to establish relationships between Rembrandt & the south, between Potter and what he saw himself.

You're right a thousand times over — one mustn't think about all that — one must do — even if it's studies of cabbages & salad to calm oneself down, & after being calmed then — what one is capable of.

When I see them again I'll do repetitions of that study of the Tarascon diligence, the *Vineyard*, the *Harvest* and above all the *Red Bar*, that night café which is the most characteristic as regards color. But the white figure in the middle, correct as regards color, must be redone, better constructed. But I dare say that this is a bit of the real south, and a calculated combination of the greens with the reds.

My strength has been exhausted too quickly, but I can see from afar the possibility for others to do an infinity of beautiful things. And again and again that idea remains true, that to facilitate the journey of others it would have been good to found a studio somewhere in these parts.

To make the journey from the north to Spain in one go, for example, isn't good, one won't see there what one ought to see — one must first and gradually accustom one's eyes to the different light.

I myself have no great need to see works by Titian and Velázquez in museums, I've seen certain living types who have made me know better now what a painting of the south is than before my little journey.

My God, my God, the good people among artists who say that Delacroix is not of the true orient! Look, is the true orient then what Parisians like Gérôme do?

Because you paint a bit of sunny wall, even from life and well and true according to our northern way of seeing, does that also prove that you've seen the people of the Orient? Now that's what Delacroix was seeking there, which didn't prevent him at all from painting walls in the Jewish wedding and the Odalisques.

Isn't that true — and then Degas says that it's too expensive to drink in the bars while doing paintings, I don't say no, but would he then have me go into the cloisters or the churches, there I'm the one who's afraid.

That's why I make an effort at escape through the present letter, with many handshakes to you and Jo.

Ever yours,
Vincent

I still have to congratulate you on the occasion of Mother's birthday, I wrote to them yesterday but the letter hasn't gone off yet, because I wasn't in the mood to finish it.

It's funny that the idea had already come to me 2 or 3 times before to go to Pissarro's, this time, after you've told me of his recent misfortunes, I don't hesitate to ask it of you.

Yes we must be done here, I can no longer do both things at once, working and doing everything in my power to live with the odd patients here — it's unsettling. I'd like to force myself to go downstairs, but in vain. And yet it's almost 2 months since I've been out in the open air.

In the long run here I would lose the faculty to work, now there I begin to call a halt, and so I'll send them packing, if you agree. And paying for it what's more, no, then one or the other of the artists fallen in misfortune will consent to set up house with me.

Fortunately, you can write that you're well, and Jo too, and that her sister is with you. I'd very much like to be back myself when your child arrives — not with you, certainly not, that isn't possible, but in the area around Paris with another painter.

I could, to mention a third, go and stay with the Jouves, who have a lot of children and a whole household.

You'll understand that I've tried to compare the second crisis with the first, and I say only this to you: it appears to me to be some kind of influence from outside rather than a cause that comes from within myself. I may be mistaken, but whatever the case I think you'll consider it right that I'm a little horrified by all religious exaggeration. I can't help thinking of good André Bonger, who himself let out loud shouts when anyone wanted to try out some unguent or other on him. Good Mr. Peyron will tell you heaps of things, about probabilities and possibilities of involuntary actions. Good, but if he's specific I'll believe none of it. And we'll see then what he specifies, if it's specific. The treatment of the patients in this hospital is certainly easy to follow, even on a journey, for they do absolutely nothing about it, they leave them to vegetate in idleness and feed them with stale and slightly spoiled food. And I'll tell you now that from the first day I refused to take this food, and until my crisis I ate nothing but bread and a little soup, which I'll continue to do as long as I remain here. It's true that after this crisis Mr. Peyron gave me some wine and meat, which I willingly accept in these first days but wouldn't want to make an exception to the rule for a long time, and it's right to respect the establishment according to their ordinary regime. I must also say that Mr. Peyron doesn't give me much hope for the future, which I find justified, he makes me really feel that everything is doubtful, that nothing can be ensured in advance. But I myself am counting on it recurring, but only work preoccupies me so thoroughly that I think that with the body I have it will continue like this for a long time. The idleness in which these poor unfortunates vegetate is a plague, and there you are, it's a general evil in the towns and country areas under this stronger sun, and having learned differently it's a duty to resist it, certainly for me. I finish this letter by thanking you again for yours and asking you to write to me again soon, and many handshakes in thought.

JENA

1230 km from St. Rémy

Medical Report

20 September 1889

The patient is seen examining his body as if it is an object separate from himself, as if it were an alien entity, some foreign,
disjointed thing, like a marionette animated by yet some other
entity, a fish jerking on an angler's line. Or was it now caught as
if in a dark net?

ST. RÉMY

1230 km from Jena

to go into an asylum in Paris; I have crises like a superstitious person would have; grief mustn't build up in our souls like the water of a swamp; it interests me enormously to make copies; my physiognomy has grown much calmer; I'm above all ill at present; one must paint for 10 years for nothing; the rest says nothing to me, because it lacks personal will; exasperated by certain people's photographic and inane perfection; the story of people is like the story of wheat; if I have another fit of religious exaltation; it's a great advance that my stomach is working well

20 September 1889

My dear Theo,

Thanks very much for your letter. First, it gives me very great pleasure that you, for your part, had also already thought of père Pissarro.

You'll see that there are other possibilities, if not there then elsewhere. Now business is business, and you ask me to answer categorically — and you're right to do so — if I would consent to go into an asylum in Paris in the event of moving immediately for this winter.

I answer yes to that, with the same calmness and for the same reasons as I entered this one — even though this asylum in Paris might not be ideal, which might easily be the case, for the opportunity to work isn't bad here, and work my only distraction.

But that being said, I'll point out to you that in my letter I gave a very serious motive as a reason for wishing to move.

And I insist on repeating it — I'm astonished that with the modern ideas I have, I being such an ardent admirer of Zola, of De Goncourt, and of artistic things which I feel so much, I have crises like a superstitious person would have, and that mixed-up, atrocious religious ideas come to me such as I never had in my head in the north.

On the assumption that, very sensitive to surroundings, the already prolonged stay in these old cloisters which are the Arles hospital and the home here would be sufficient in itself to explain these crises — then — even as a stopgap — it might be necessary to go into a lay asylum at present.

Nevertheless, to avoid doing or appearing to do anything rash, I declare to you, after having thus warned you of what I might desire at a given moment — that is, a move — I declare to you that I feel sufficiently calm and confident to wait a while longer to see if there'll be a new attack this winter.

But if then I was to write to you: I want to get out of here, you wouldn't hesitate and it would be arranged in advance, for you would know then that I'd have a serious reason, or even several, to go into a home that wasn't run like this one by the nuns, however excellent they might be.

Now if by some arrangement or another we might move sooner or later, then let's begin as if almost nothing was wrong, at the same time being very prudent and ready to listen to the least thing that Rivet has to say, but let's not set ourselves immediately to taking overly official measures as if it were a lost cause.

As regards eating a lot, I'm doing so — but if I was my doctor I would forbid it.

Not seeing any good for myself in really enormous physical strength, for if I absorb myself in the idea of doing some good work and wanting to be an artist and nothing but that, that would be the most logical thing.

Mother and Wil, each for their part after Cor's departure, have changed surroundings — they were darned right. Grief mustn't build up in our souls like the water of a swamp. But it's sometimes both costly and impossible to move.

Wil wrote very well, it's a great grief for them, Cor's departure.

It's funny, just at the moment when I was making that copy of the *Pietà* by Delacroix I discovered where that canvas has gone. It belongs to a queen of Hungary or another country around there who has written poems under the name of Carmen Sylva. The article which talked of her and of the painting was by Pierre Loti, who made one feel that this Carmen Sylva was as a person yet more touching than what she writes — and yet she writes things like this: A woman without a child is like a bell without a clapper — the sound of the bronze would perhaps be very beautiful, but no one will hear it.

At present I have 7 copies out of 10 of Millet's *Travaux des champs*.

I can assure you that it interests me enormously to make copies, and that not having any models for the moment it will ensure, however, that I don't lose sight of the figure.

What's more, it will give me a studio decoration for myself or another.

I would like also to copy *The Sower* and *The Diggers*.

There's a photo of the *Diggers* after the drawing.

And Lerat's etching of the *Sower* at Durand-Ruel's.

In these same etchings is the *Field Under the Snow with a Harrow*. Then *The Four Times of the Day*, there are examples of them in the collection of wood engravings.

I would like to have all of this, at least the etchings and the wood engravings. It's a study I need, for I want to learn. Although copying may be the old system, that absolutely doesn't bother me at all. I'm going to copy Delacroix's *Good Samaritan* too.

I've done a portrait of a woman — the orderly's wife — which I think you'd like. I've done a repetition of it that wasn't as good as the one from life.

And I fear that they'll take the latter, I would have liked you to have it. It's pink and black.

Today I'm sending you my portrait of myself, you must look at it for some time — you'll see, I hope, that my physiognomy has grown much calmer, although the gaze may be vaguer than before, so it appears to me.

I have another one that is an attempt from when I was ill. But I think this one will please you more, and I've tried to create something simple, show it to père Pissarro if you see him.

You'll be surprised what effect the *Travaux des champs* take on in color, it's a very intimate series of his.

What I'm seeking in it, and why it seems good to me to copy them, I'm going to try to tell you. We painters are always asked to compose ourselves and to be nothing but composers.

Very well — but in music it isn't so — and if such a person plays some Beethoven he'll add his personal interpretation to it — in music, and then above all for singing — a composer's interpretation is something, and it isn't a hard and fast rule that only the composer plays his own compositions.

Good — since I'm above all ill at present, I'm trying to do something to console myself, for my own pleasure.

I place the black-and-white by Delacroix or Millet or after them in front of me as a subject. And then I improvise color on it but, being me, not completely of course, but seeking memories of their paintings — but the memory, the vague consonance of colors that are in the same sentiment, if not right — that's my own interpretation.

Heaps of people don't copy. Heaps of others do copy — for me, I set myself to it by chance, and I find that it teaches and above all sometimes consoles.

So then my brush goes between my fingers as if it were a bow on the violin and absolutely for my pleasure. Today I attempted

The Sheep Shearer in a color scale ranging from lilac to yellow. They are small canvases, around no. 5.

I thank you very much for the consignment of canvases and colors. On the other hand, I'm sending you a few canvases with the portrait, the following

Moonrise (wheatsheaves)
Study of fields
Study of Olive Trees
Night Study
The Mountain
Field of Green Wheat
Olive Trees
Orchard in Blossom
Entrance to a Quarry

The first four canvases are studies that don't have the effect of an ensemble like the others. Myself I quite like the *Entrance to a Quarry* which I did when I felt this attack beginning, because to my taste the dark greens go well with the ochre tones, there's something sad in them that's healthy, and that's why it doesn't annoy me. That's perhaps also the case with *The Mountain*. People will tell me that mountains aren't like that, and that there are black contours as wide as a finger. But anyway it seemed to me that it expressed the passage in Rod's book — one of the very rare passages of his in which I find something good — on a lost land of dark mountains in which one noticed the darkish huts of goatherds, where sunflowers bloomed.

The olive trees with white cloud and background of mountains, as well as the *Moonrise* and the *Night Effect* —

These are exaggerations from the point of view of the arrangement, their lines are contorted like those of the ancient woodcuts. The olive trees are more in character, just as in the other study and I've tried to express the time of day when one sees the green beetles and the cicadas flying in the heat.

The other canvases — the *Reaper* *&*c. aren't dry. And now in the bad season I'm going to make a lot of copies, for really I must do more figure work. It's the study of the figure that teaches one to grasp the essential and to simplify.

When you say in your letter that I've never done anything but work, no — that's not right — I myself am very, very discontented with my work, and the only thing that consoles me is that experienced people say that one must paint for 10 years for nothing. But what I've done is only those 10 years of unfortunate studies that didn't come off. Now a better period could come, but I'll have to strengthen the figure work, and I must refresh my memory by very close study of Delacroix, Millet. Then I'll try to sort out my drawing. Yes, every cloud has a silver lining, it gives one more time for study.

I'm also adding a study of flowers to the roll of canvases — not much, but anyway I don't want to tear it up.

All in all the only things I consider a little good in it are the *Wheatfield*, the *Mountain*, the *Orchard*, the *Olive Trees* with the blue hills and the *Portrait* and the *Entrance to the Quarry*, and the rest says nothing to me, because it lacks personal will, feeling in the lines. Where these lines are close together and deliberate the painting begins, even if it may be exaggerated. That's what Bernard and Gauguin feel a little bit, they won't ask for the correct shape of a tree at all, but they absolutely insist that one says if the shape is round or square — and my word, they're right —

Exasperated by certain people's photographic and inane perfection. They won't ask for the correct tone of the mountains but they'll say: for Christ's sake, were the mountains blue, then chuck on some blue and don't go telling me that it was a blue a bit like this or like that, it was blue wasn't it? Good — make them blue and that's enough! Gauguin is a genius sometimes when he explains that, but as for the genius Gauguin has, he's very timid about showing it, and it's touching how he likes to say something really useful to young folk. What an odd fellow all the same.

It gives me great pleasure that Jo is well, and I think you'll feel much more in your element thinking of her pregnancy, and naturally having concerns about it too, than if you were alone without these family concerns. For you'll feel more in nature.

When one thinks of Millet and Delacroix, what a contrast. Delacroix without a wife, without children, Millet completely in his family, more than anyone.

And yet what similarities there are in their work.

So Jouve has still kept his big studio and he's working on decorations.

That one came very close to being an excellent painter. It's money troubles with him, in order to eat he's forced to do a thousand things other than painting, which costs him more money than it brings in when he makes something beautiful.

And he quickly loses his touch for drawing with the brush. This probably comes from the old training method, which is the same as the current one — in the studios — they fill in outlines. And Daumier was always painting his face in the mirror to learn how to draw!

Do you know what I think about quite often — what I used to say to you back in the old days, that if I didn't succeed I still thought that what I had worked on would be continued. Not directly, but one isn't alone in believing things that are true. And what does one matter as a person then? I feel so strongly that the story of people is like the story of wheat, if one isn't sown in the earth to germinate there, what does it matter, one is milled in order to become bread.

The difference between happiness & unhappiness, both are necessary and useful, & death or passing away... it's so relative — and so is life.

Even in the face of an illness that's unsettling or worrying, this belief is absolutely unshaken.

I'd have liked to see those Meuniers.

Well, let it be understood that if I were to write to you again expressly and briefly that I wanted to come to Paris, I would have a reason for that, which I've explained above, that in the meantime there's no great hurry, and I'm quite confident, after warning you, to wait for the winter and the crisis which may recur then. But if I have another fit of religious exaltation, then no delay, I'd like to leave immediately without giving a reason. Only we have no right, at least it would be indiscreet, to meddle in the nuns' management or even to criticize them. They have their own belief and ways of doing good to others, sometimes it works very well. But I don't warn you lightly. And it isn't to regain more freedom or something else that I don't have. So let's wait very calmly until an opportunity presents itself to find a place.

It's a great advance that my stomach is working well, and so I don't think that I'll be as sensitive to the cold. Then I know what to do when the weather is bad, as I have this plan to copy several things that I like.

I'd very much like to see Millet reproductions in schools, I think there would be children who became painters if only they saw good things.

Give my warm regards to Jo, and handshake, more soon.

Ever yours,
Vincent

JENA

1230 km from St. Rémy

memory; stability

23 September 1889

Jean Medical Report

Does not know the assistant's name. Romberg sign negative.

14 September 1888 [*excerpt*]

... health has returned again, with the "better" weather (for the concept "good" is impractical for meteorologists and philosophers).... You will receive something from me before this month is out: a small polemical pamphlet on esthetic matters, in which, for the first time and quite frontally, I attack the psychological problem of Wagner. It is a declaration of war to the knife on this whole movement; after all, I am the only person who has sufficient scope & depth to escape being uncertain here. ...

Your friend   Nietzsche

ST. RÉMY

1230 km from Jena

I'm gaining a little patience; it would be wise to go on waiting here; if an attack recurs I still want to try a change of climate; at present I feel completely normal; this half-freedom often prevents one from doing what one nevertheless feels able to do

28 September 1889

My dear Theo,

I'm dropping you another line to explain that 3 studies are missing from the consignment of canvases (which you will have already), since by removing them the roll cost 3.50 francs less for carriage. So I'll send them next opportunity — or rather they're leaving today with other canvases — the following.

Wheatfield
Wheatfield and Cypresses
ditto
The Ivy
Study of Cypresses
Reaper
ditto
The Olive Trees

then also the three studies mentioned below, *Poppies — Night Effect — Moonrise*. Soon I'm sending you a few smaller canvases with the 4 or 5 studies I wanted to give to Mother and our sister. These studies are drying at the moment. It's no. 10 and no. 12 canvases, reductions of the *Wheatfield and Cypresses, Olive Trees, Reaper* and *Bedroom* and a little portrait of me.

This will give them a good start, and I think this will give both you and me some pleasure to ensure that our sister or sisters have a small collection of paintings. I'll do reductions of the best canvases with them in mind, in this way I also wanted them to have the red and green vineyard, the pink chestnut trees, the night effect that you exhibited.

You'll see that I'm gaining a little patience, and that persevering will be a result of my illness. I feel more detached from many preoccupations.

You'll send me one day, when it suits you, the red vineyard and other canvases with that aim when you've seen the 5 that I've done.

Now for that reaper — at first I feared that the large format repetition that I'm sending you wasn't bad — but afterwards, when the days of mistral and rain came, I preferred the canvas done from life, which appeared a little odd to me. But no, when the weather's cold and sad, it's precisely that one which makes me remember once again that summer furnace over the white-hot wheat, so the exaggeration isn't as much as all that.

Père Peyron came back and chatted with me about seeing you, and said that no doubt your letter would tell me all the details of the conversation he'd had with you. That in any case the upshot was that it would be wise to go on waiting here. Which, also being my opinion, goes without saying.

Nevertheless, if an attack recurs I still want to try a change of climate, and even to return to the north as a stopgap.

Mr. Peyron said that you looked as if you were well, which gives me pleasure.

I've received the 10 tubes of white, but *as soon as possible* I'll need another dozen zinc white

2	large	tubes	cobalt
1	"	"	emerald
1	"	"	chrome 1
1	small	tube	carmine

For there are fine autumnal effects to do.

At present I feel completely normal and no longer remember those bad days at all.

With work and very regular food this will probably last for quite a long time, so-so, and I'll also do my work all the same without it appearing. For at the end of the month you'll receive another dozen studies.

Am I mistaken, but it seems to me that your letter is very delayed this time?

Unfortunately there are no vineyards here, otherwise I'd promised myself to do nothing else this autumn. There are some, but for that I would have had to go and stay in another village.

On the other hand the olive trees are very characteristic, and I'm struggling to capture that. It's silver, sometimes more blue, sometimes greenish, bronzed, whitening on ground that is yellow, pink, purplish or orangeish to dull red ochre.

But very difficult, very difficult. But that suits me and attracts me to work fully in gold or silver. And one day perhaps I'll do a personal impression of it, the way the sunflowers are for yellows. If only I'd had some of them this autumn. But this half-freedom often prevents one from doing what one nevertheless feels able to do. Patience, however, you'll tell me, and it's indeed necessary.

Give my warm regards to Jo, look after yourself, and write soon please. Handshakes.

Ever yours,
Vincent

INTERVAL: DEEP SPACE

Fall 1889

Plagued with epileptic fits, Vincent frequently experiences out-of-body sensations, an inner division, his cohering drive in schismatic disarray, his self taken over, his tongue babbling nonsensically, his actions devoid of conscious control, his body seized, plunged into violent paroxysms, knocked unconscious. Who was 'he'? What was suffered? What actions did 'he' commit in that state of possession? Is 'he' indebted to his other selves? Or is there no clear, definable 'he' to tether Vincent to, only an inhabited body through which different selves pass like currents of wind through trees?

Nothing was clear in the apathetic stupors following his fits, but as he was recovering, he thought back to that day when he was painting the Alpilles, the ferocious wind trouncing him like a thunderbolt, his easel, canvas, and paints thrust up and into the sky as if whirled into the vortex of a tornado. Nature was no longer his comforting Heimat, or something he was one with, but an assailing terror, a force rendering his body chaotic, furies come to disjoin him. Brought to near ruin, the painter was besieged by dreadful feelings of loneliness, dizzy spells, darkness. His incandescent sun eclipsed, oblivion ruled.

Throughout the end of summer, as he struggled to recover, attacks recurred, attacks worse than those he suffered in Arles.

Wracked by hallucinations and vertigo, reality fractures before him — everything becomes a simulacrum.

While he believes he is back at the Yellow House, pursued by his detractors, the patients and asylum attendants take on the masks of the dead and the imagined. The people he sees, he explains to Theo, *even if he recognizes them*, which isn't always the case, are entirely different from what they are in reality, so much do I seem to see them in pleasant or unpleasant resemblances to people I knew in other times and places.

Disturbed and unsettled to such a degree by these attacks, he fears a more violent one might finally destroy his ability to paint for good.

As he is imprisoned in the asylum, due to his previously having consumed turpentine and paint, he is not permitted access to the materials of his craft. Like a musician bereft of an instrument, the artist is muted, rendered non-existent, reborn as if devoid of hands.

The very next year, in 1890, Max Dessoir would write in *The Double Ego* of our conscious psychical life resting on a substratum of hallucinatory nature, where long-forgotten images reside. We carry in us, he said, a hidden sphere of consciousness that, gifted with reason, feeling, and will, is capable of determining a series of actions. The simultaneity of both spheres I call double consciousness.... It follows from this that our personality is composed from two operating conscious halves, more or less independent from one another, that one could figuratively call over- and under-consciousness.

Was Vincent not battling, or being battled by, his under-consciousness, at war with an alien entity seeking to destroy or possess and undermine him? Or, is it an illness of his time, as he himself once pronounced?

During those same months, while in the asylum in Jena, Nietzsche was alternately silent and tempestuous, vacillating like Vincent (or the body that 'he' inhabited) between antipodes, he too in threat of being taken over by alien entities, substratums, hidden spheres, or the viruses of his locales. Does he have a high enough degree of visco-elasticity due to his consumption of vast quantities of gelato? A colloidal cocktail of dynamite, butterfat, pumice, and grissini? Is he enough of a thixotropic fluid, like ketchup, yogurt, or clay, to fight chaos and reconstitute the body in which he lives and dies?

When not smashing objects, he leaps about or refuses to move, stating that he is stupid in his hip or complaining of constrictions in his chest and general atrophy. Intensely hungry, he devours food as if a horse. Is he perchance suffering from horse colic due to having ingested too many horse-atoms from his frequent concourse with those beasts? Is that not why he gesticulated and leapt about in an uncontrolled and dangerous manner? Were not his bowels sometimes in states of torsion and strangulation? Did not his behavior, attitude, temperature, pulse and respiratory rates and mucous membrane color all emit signs of some alteration? Did he not sometimes curl his top lip and adopt straining to urinate stances? What of his hypomimia, dysphasia, & hypophonia?

While giving exact dates for certain medical conditions, stating his choroiditis began the year '66 or '64, 'he' confuses the current date, grows noisy, smashes windowpanes, loses objects, yet is conscious from time to time of being ill. Sometimes, he believes he is in Torino; other days, he has no idea where he is. While his mother finds him cheerful, the doctors believe that his cheer is affected, that his speech is affected, his tone regimental, particularly when he wants to speak of something important. Once, he spoke of the journey he made with Mazzini and still knew the name of his attendant when he crossed the Gotthard Tunnel. Herr Dynamite, the explosive one: sometimes a fragment, sometimes a vicious circle, sometimes a circumference! After recalling the name of the old pastry-cook in the Klostergasse, where he often went with Rohde & Gersdorff, he looked around the asylum and said, *When shall I get out of this palace? I have had a lot of headaches and I have been ill a lot in my life, and have often vomited as well.*

Earlier in the century, not long after Vincent's birth, Bénédict Morel argued that all psychological diseases result from gradual genetic degeneration — a biologico-psychological equivalent of the curse of the House of Atreus. What was the curse of the House of van Gogh? What the curse of the House of Nietzsche? What genetic contagion plagued Vincent, his brother, and the other members of his family? What genetic contagion plagued Nietzsche, his sister (was she plagued, or was she all too supremely healthy and not open to the wisdom of illness, not bold enough to cross the thresholds of sanity, not one who truly bore witness to life but only to molar structures, to ideology, not to rhizomes, but to tight clusters of sticks?), & their father? If there was no double self at work in Vincent or in Nietzsche, was there not another enemy within them, another host each had little control over, and which each could hardly combat? It wasn't a case of demonic possession, but of *genetic possession*, the havoc of generations rearing their ancient viral scars and dispossessing the present. Is Vincent mad, is Nietzsche mad, or are they the hosts of some legion of corrupting genes, cells gone awry, chemicals gone amok, genealogy in violent disarray, igneous forces irrupting? Can they, like fungus and blue-green bacterium, engage in cross-kingdom couplings, with lava, with pumice, with volcanic gases, with ... *etc. etc. etc.* and become some type of extraordinary composites, *monsters of a kind*? Are they not in fact monstrums, like human lichen? We are unknown to ourselves, we knowers: & with good reason...

Is it because of the myriad selves that live within them that they are unfathomable? A host of ever receding and advancing entities evading localization, selves that can usurp every other self and obliterate memory of themselves and so remain as elusive as dark matter? When we speak of ourselves ordinarily, said Gurdjieff, we speak of "I." But there is no such I, or rather there are hundreds, thousands of little "I's," in every one of us. We are divided in ourselves but cannot recognize the plurality of our being..

Or are they unknown to themselves because of the presence of what Boris Sidis named the subwaking self? An entity Sidis said that possesses a secret life, an entity of extraordinary plasticity that can separate the primary controlling consciousness from the lower one, the waking from the subwaking self, and cause a cleavage between the two selves, with the subwaking self rapidly growing, developing, and attaining the plane of self-consciousness, crystallizing into a person, giving itself a name, imaginary *or borrowed from history...* But this newly crystallized personality is extremely unstable, ephemeral, shadowy in its outlines, tending to subside, to become amorphous, again and again forming, rising to the surface of life, then sinking and disappearing for evermore.

A volatile theater of havoc-wreaking subjects! Who is speaking? Who behind the puppet of our bodies? Who, or what, is the ventriloquist of our cosmos of selves? Is it possible to break free of the somatic chain and to enter the open sea, to exert an influence on the character of evolution? To go far enough in the direction of decomposition, *the deformed œuvre*, to pursue fault lines to their thresholds, opening futures into the germinal? Is it possible to move from the organized body of the organism to the body without organs so as to release singularities and intensities from entropic containment? Do we possess the inventiveness for this, the will, or is the soma too strong?

*

In August of 1889, in the midst of Vincent's dark and violent upheavals, while assailed by his nerves, beyond the planet Mars, amongst the superfluity of objects orbiting the sun in that distant zone, a minor planet was discovered and named Nephthys. An irregularly shaped lump of rock (later revealed to actually be the flotsam and jetsam of a former planet) measuring nearly 70 km across, Nephthys orbits the sun at an average distance of 350 million km. Named after the Egyptian goddess of darkness, sleep, and mourning, Nephthys takes three and a half years to orbit the earth, the same period of time Vincent took to orbit Paris, the south of France, St. Rémy, and beyond, himself searching for a home as the Mistress of the House went from perigee to apogee. The Egyptians associated her with mourning and with vultures, a bird that they believed could not have children, and so she is the protector of the dead. One pays a high price Nietzsche said for being immortal: one has to die several times during one's life. Immortality for Nietzsche and Vincent and their myriad selves is a catena of uncanny moments, a chain of eerie Augenblicken between life and death, replete with startling visions. Have they been anientissed? Are they *nec entem*? Dead amongst the living, live amongst the dead. The flotsam and jetsam of many former lives; many former flotsam and jetsam come to life?

As Nephthys orbits the earth from 1888 to 1890, Vincent makes the final orbit of his life. Is Nephthys his marking orb, the distant but ever-present solar double of his life? One of the radiant elements in his paintings?

All throughout this time, as the anniversary of the utopic dream of the Studio of the South approaches, Vincent is devising plans for escape, for going into other orbits. He dreams alternately of living with other artists, or of returning to life with Gauguin, or of joining the Foreign Legion. Anything but continuing to live with nuns who disturb him, the constant sight of these good women, who both believe in the Virgin of Lourdes and make up that sort of thing.

I am a prisoner, he told Theo, in an institution whose purpose is cultivating unhealthy religious aberrations, *not* curing me. I'm astonished that with the modern ideas I have, I being such an ardent admirer of Zola, of de Goncourt and of artistic things, that I feel so much, I have crises like a superstitious person would have, and that mixed-up, atrocious religious ideas come to me such as I never had in my head in the north.

We are unknown to ourselves, we knowers: and with good reason ...

Vacillating between states of what he believes are supreme good health and the terrifying fear of further attacks, Vincent begins to see the asylum itself as his own personal Studio of the South, even thinks of staging an exhibition there, viewing the long stretches of walls in the corridors as the perfect space for hanging paintings — always, he envisions work, exhibiting, a communion and interaction of some kind with the world, and he sees himself as but an element in a grand futural line — other painters will come to continue the work, advancing from where he left off, shooting the arrow ever further on. What does one matter as a person?

In *Vestibule in the Asylum*, we see paintings lined up against the wall, as if ready or waiting to be hung. It is not an asylum that he is in, but an artist's commune of one. The dream of the painter's colony continues, albeit as a silent vision, depicted, portrayed, imagined, for it cannot be shared unless one is insane, for no one but the mentally ill can be admitted to the asylum.

In *Window in the Studio*, we see objects on the windowsill and framed and unframed paintings on the wall, giving a sense of permanency, of duration, for Vincent furnishes the room as if it were his own personal space. Even though he is admitted as a patient and his stay is inevitably temporary, he depicts the world of his spaces, his surrounding milieu, as if it were a home. There is a certain tranquility, calm, and stability in this simulacrum of domesticity. It seems lived in, as much as was his room in the Yellow House.

And in *Chair by a Fireplace*, we see the depiction of a chair not unlike the one he had in his room at the Yellow House, as well as a second one visible to the right, faintly sketched in, as if it is the ghostly, absent presence of his semblable Gauguin. *The second symbolic chair of the Studio of the South*. Two chairs by a fire, as if for two friends to sit in and talk, to converse about art, to live the dream of Japanese artist monks. Or is it the chair of one of Vincent's many doubles or sub-waking selves? Or is it the invisible visitor?

When the painter offers his work to the sisters of the asylum to hang in their common room, they object to the head nun, for they are bewildered and disturbed by *the patient's* art. The gallery type of reality the painter sought to create is stymied. Saint-Paul de Mausole is not an artist's studio, it is an asylum.

In these months, death becomes a stronger and stronger presence in the painter's life, and it is at this time that he makes a self-portrait where he is thin and deathly pale. Death also takes on symbolic figuration when he introduces the figure of a reaper into his œuvre, painting several versions of a wheatfield with a reaper.

The reaper, he explains to Theo, is struggling like a devil in the full heat of the day to reach the end of his toil. It is this figure that reminds him of the Grim Reaper and his deathly task. The reaper is death cutting through the wheat, a beloved and oft-painted element of his world, death coming to finally take the painter himself.

As golden and resplendent as they may be, the piled up, amassed forms of grain are equal to heaps of bodies. If this is the work of the reaper, such is the symbol, as golden and seething with life as the heaps of wheat may look. To subtly emphasize this, the bundles of wheat, as the yet to be reaped fields the reaper is approaching, sickle swinging from right to left as he advances without relent, are all tinged with light hints of crimson, the blood of the fallen wheat, the apotheosis of death, the end of time within one porous body of atoms. The end.

*

Earlier that summer, Vincent noted, aren't we, who live on bread, to a considerable extent like wheat, at least aren't we forced to submit to growing like a plant without the power to move, by which I mean in what way our imagination impels us, & to being reaped when we are ripe, like the same wheat.

If harvesting as the painter said takes place in broad daylight with a sun that floods everything with a light of fine gold, such bright lucidity is no less menacing — the work of a reaper remains a deathly task; the reaper will reach the end of his toil, just as Nephthys will continue its orbit, goddess of darkness, sleep, and mourning.

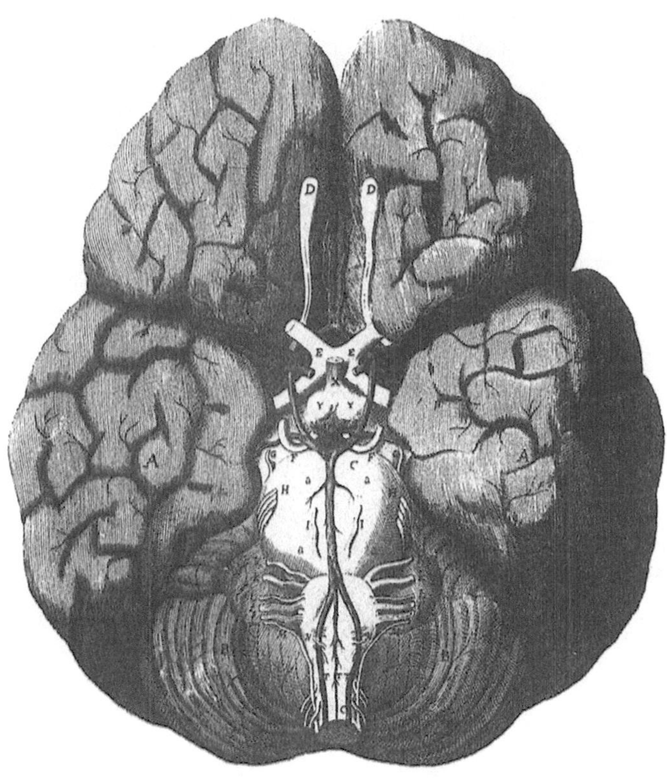

JENA

1230 km from St. Rémy

remission

1 October 1889

Jean Medical Report

Obvious remission on the whole. Weight 128 lbs (+4).

9 October 1888 [*excerpt*]

My condition is much better than that of summer, which I have
the most eerie memories of.

Yours sincerely, your Nietzsche

ST. RÉMY

send me the whites I asked for; a few expenses; we're having some superb autumn days; an article on studies of mine; more willpower in the drawing, more knowledge of the Provençal south; I haven't dared ask Mr. Peyron to go to Arles; I'm staying on here for the time being; a very agreeable prospect; writing doesn't always come; Impressions of Provence

5 October 1889

My dear Theo,

I was longing for your letter and so I was very happy to receive it, and to see from it that you're well, as are Jo and the friends you speak of.

I must ask you to send me the whites I asked for *as soon* as possible, and to add to them some canvas, 5 meters or 10, whichever suits. Then I must begin by telling you a piece of rather vexing news, as I see it. It's that during the stay here there have been a few expenses which I thought Mr. Peyron had notified you about as they occurred, which he told me the other day he hadn't done, with the result that it has mounted up to around 125 francs, deducting from it the 10 you sent by postal order.

It's for paint, canvas, frames and stretching frames, my trip the other day to Arles, a piece of linen clothing, and various repairs.

I'm using two colors here, lead white and ordinary blue, but in quite large quantities, and the canvas, that's for when I want to work on unprepared, stronger canvas.

This comes unfortunately just at this time when I would gladly have repeated my trip to Arles etc.

That said, I'll tell you that we're having some superb autumn days, and that I'm taking advantage of them. I have a few studies, among others a mulberry tree, all yellow on stony ground standing out against the blue of the sky, in which study I think that you'll see that I've found Monticelli's track. You'll have received the consignment of canvases I sent you last Saturday.

It surprises me a lot that Mr. Isaäcson wants to do an article on studies of mine. I'd willingly urge him to wait a little longer, his article would lose absolutely nothing by it, and with another year of work I could hope to put more characteristic things before him with more willpower in the drawing, more knowledge of the Provençal south.

Mr. Peyron was very kind to talk of my case in those terms — I haven't dared ask him to go to Arles one of these days, which I'd very much like to do, believing that he would disapprove.

Not, though, that I suspected that he believed there was a connection between my previous trip and the crisis that closely followed it. The thing is that there are a few people over there whom I felt and once again feel the need to see again.

While I don't have here in the south, like good Prévost, a mistress who holds me captive, I couldn't help becoming attached to people and things.

And now that I'm staying on here for the time being, and will most probably spend the winter here — in the spring — in the fine season, shall I not stay here too? That will depend on my health above all.

What you say of Auvers is nevertheless a very agreeable prospect to me, and sooner or later that ought to be fixed without seeking further. If I come to the north, even supposing that there's no room in this Doctor's home, it's probable that he would, on père Pissarro's recommendation and your own, find either board with a family or quite simply at the inn. The main thing is to know the doctor so that, in the event of a crisis, one doesn't fall into the hands of the police and isn't forcibly carried off into an asylum.

And I can assure you that the north will interest me like a brand-new country.

But anyway, for the moment there's therefore nothing that's absolutely hurrying us.

I reproach myself for being so behind with my correspondence, I'd like to write to Isaäcson, Gauguin, and Bernard. But writing doesn't always come, and what's more, work is pressing. Yes, I'd like to say to Isaäcson that he would do well to wait longer, there isn't yet that in it that I hope to attain if my health continues. It's not worth mentioning anything about my work at the moment. When I'm back, at best it will form a kind of ensemble, "Impressions of Provence."

But what does he want to say now when the olive trees, the fig trees, the vineyards, the cypresses must be more accentuated, all characteristic things, the same as the Alpilles, which must get more character.

How I'd like to see what Gauguin and Bernard have brought back.

I have a study of two yellowed poplars on a background of mountains, and a view of the park here, autumnal effect, some of the draughtsmanship of which is more naive and more — at home.

Anyway, it's difficult to leave a land before having something to prove that one has felt and loved it.

If I come back to the north I plan to do a whole lot of Greek studies, you know, *painted* studies with white and blue and only a little orange, just like in the open air.

I *must* draw and seek style. Yesterday at the almoner's here I saw a painting that made an impression on me. A Provençal lady with an intelligent, purebred face, in a red dress. A figure like the ones Monticelli thought of.

It wasn't without great faults, but there was simplicity in it, and how sad it is to see how much they have degenerated from it here, as we have from ours in Holland.

I'm writing to you in haste so as not to wait to answer your kind letter, hoping that you'll write again without delaying long.

I've seen more very beautiful subjects for tomorrow — in the mountains.

Kind regards to Jo and to our friends, above all when you get the chance thank père Pissarro for his information, which will certainly be useful.

Shaking both your hands, believe me

Ever yours,
Vincent

JENA

1230 km from St. Rémy

the father of Zarathustra no longer writes

[5 October 1889]

[Dear —————]

[Nietzsche]

ST. RÉMY

1230 km from Jena

broken & neutral violets; this will complement the reaper; when nature is superb; two views of the park and the asylum; if they should happen to remember me; one should go down into the depths and paint the light effects; if Gauguin had remained here he wouldn't have lost anything; facing obstacles; ashamed and defeated; a study of the mountains, a very wild ravine; I'm not mad; bored to death; to look for sites

8 October 1889

My dear Theo,

I've just brought back a canvas I've been working on for some time, once again of the same field as the one of the reaper. Now it's mounds of earth and the background parched lands, then the rocks of the Alpilles. A bit of blue-green sky with a small white and violet cloud. In the foreground: A thistle and some dry grass. A peasant dragging a bundle of straw in the middle. It's another harsh study, and instead of being almost entirely yellow it makes an almost completely violet canvas. Broken and neutral violets.

But I'm writing you this because I think that this will complement the reaper and will make it easier to see what it is. For the reaper appears done at random, and this with it will balance it. As soon as it's dry I'll send it to you with the repetition of the bedroom. I seriously ask you to show them *together*, if someone or other comes to see the studies, because of the opposition of the complementaries.

Then this week I've done the entrance to a quarry, which is like a Japanese thing, you'll well remember that there are Japanese drawings of rocks where grasses and little trees grow here and there. There are moments between times when nature is superb, autumnal effects glorious in color, green skies contrasting with yellow, orange, green vegetation, earth in all shades of violet, burnt grass where the rains have nevertheless given a last vigor to certain plants, which again start to produce little violet, pink, blue, yellow flowers. Things that make you quite melancholy not to be able to render them.

And the skies — like our northern skies, but the colors of the sunsets and sunrises are more varied & more pure. As in works by Jules Dupré and Ziem.

I also have two views of the park and the asylum in which this place appears most agreeable. I tried to reconstruct the thing as it may have been by simplifying and accentuating the proud, unchanging nature of the pines and the cedar bushes against the blue.

Anyway — if they should happen to remember me — which I'm not keen on — there'll be enough to send something colored to the Vingtistes. But I'm indifferent to that. What I'm not indifferent to is that a man who is far superior to me, Meunier, has painted the female thrutchers of the Borinage and the shift going to the pit and the factories, their red roofs and their black chimneys against a delicate grey sky — all things I've dreamed of doing, feeling that it hadn't been done and that it ought to be painted. And still, there's an infinite number of subjects there for artists, and one should go down into the depths and paint the light effects.

If you haven't yet sent the canvas and the colors, you should know that I now have absolutely no canvas.

And I was going to ask you if you would find it difficult to send the amount of what I owe to Mr. Peyron immediately, if it was possible for you then to send me about 15 francs by postal order, I would go to Arles one of these days.

It often seems to me that if Gauguin had remained here he wouldn't have lost anything, for I clearly see, also in the letter he wrote me, that he isn't entirely at the top of his form. And I know well the cause of that — they're too hard up to find models, and living as cheaply as he thought possible at the beginning won't have lasted. However, with his patience, next year will perhaps be dazzling. But then he won't have Bernard with him if the latter does his military service.

Do you sense how much the figures of Jules Breton and Billet and others *will remain*? Those people overcame the difficulty of models, and that's a lot. And a painting like that by Otto Weber from the good period (not the English) is bound to hold its own. One swallow doesn't make a summer, and one new idea doesn't in any way destroy works that have been done and perfected. That's the terrible thing about the Impressionists, that the development of the thing gets stuck, and that for years they're left facing obstacles that the preceding generation had overcome, the difficulty of money and models. And so Breton, Billet, and others really are certain to mock it and be astonished and say: "come on, when are we going to see your peasants and your peasant women?" As for me, I feel ashamed and defeated.

I've copied that woman with a child sitting beside a hearth by Mrs. Demont-Breton, almost all violet, I'm certainly going to continue copying, it will give me a collection of my own, and when it's sufficiently large and complete I'll give the whole lot to a school.

I can also tell you that next consignment you'll become better acquainted with good Tartarin's Alpilles, which up to now — apart from the canvas of the mountains — you haven't yet seen unfold, except in the distant background of the canvases. I have a study, rougher than the previous one of the mountains. A very wild ravine where a slender stream weaves its way along its bed of rocks.

It's all violet. I could certainly do an entire series of these Alpilles, for having seen them for a long time now I've got used to it a little. You remember that fine landscape by Monticelli that we saw at Delarebeyrette's, of a tree on some rocks against a sunset. There are a lot of effects like that at the moment, only I can't ever be outside at the time the sun sets, otherwise I would have tried it.

Does Jo continue in good health? I think that all in all this year is happier for you than the preceding ones. As for me, my health has been good lately — I really think that Mr. Peyron is right when he says that strictly speaking I'm not mad, for my thoughts are absolutely normal and clear between times, and even more than before, but during the crises it's terrible however, and then I lose consciousness of everything. But it drives me to work and to seriousness, as a coal-miner who is always in danger makes haste in what he does. Our mother and sister will be making their preparations to move house.

I'm enclosing a note for Isaäcson, Bernard, and Gauguin. Naturally there's no urgency at all to get it to them. The first time they come to see you will suffice. In the evenings I'm bored to death, my God the prospect of winter isn't a cheery one.

I hope that you'll have received the canvases sent about ten days ago in good order.

I'm going off for a long hike in the mountains to look for sites. More soon — above all send the paint and the canvas if it hasn't been sent, for I've no canvas left at all, nor any zinc white.

Kind regards to Jo.

Ever yours,
Vincent.

JENA

1230 km from St. Rémy

music?

15 October 1889

Performs some kind of music on the piano but without the ability to make new structures. Keeps babbling, *Zukunft! Kuzunft!
Zukunft der musik! Kukuzukunft! Kuku! Kuku!*

ST. RÉMY

1230 km from Jena

there's considerable improvement; going to Arles; melancholy very often overtakes me with great force; the author is a painful, anxious person; in all these articles I find something that appears sick to me; Parisian moral fatigue; one feels so much from what he says; I'm beginning to feel more the wholeness of the countryside; Jo already feels her child quicken

25 October 1889

My dear Theo,

Thanks for your letter and for the 150 francs — which I've handed to Mr. Peyron, asking him again to tell you each month if there have been expenses, yes or no — so that it doesn't mount up. I must also thank you for a consignment of colors, and finally yesterday evening the canvas and the Millet reproductions arrived, which I'm very pleased about.

Mr. Peyron repeated to me again that there's considerable improvement and that he's optimistic — and that he sees no objection at all to my going to Arles in the coming days.

However, melancholy very often overtakes me with great force, and besides, the more my health returns to normal the more my mind is capable of reasoning very coldly, the more to do painting that costs us so much and doesn't bring in anything, not even the cost of producing them, seems madness to me, a thing completely against reason. Then I feel utterly sad, and the bad thing is that at my age it's darned difficult to start again with something else.

In the few Dutch papers you added to the Millets — I notice Parisian letters, which I attribute to Isaäcson. It's very subtle, and one deduces that the author is a painful, anxious person of a rare tenderness — a tenderness that makes me think immediately of the Reisebilder of H. Heine.

No need to tell you that I find what he says about me in a note extremely exaggerated, and one more reason why I prefer him not to say anything about me. And in all these articles I find, beside very refined things, something, I don't know what, that appears sick to me.

He has stayed in Paris a long time — I assume he's wiser than I am, not drinking &c.

But in it, though, I find something like my own Parisian moral fatigue. And I think that within a short time his temperament would faint away from sadness, tired of an *idée fixe* of seeking good if he continued much longer.

Our sister told me in her last letter that Isaäcson might go to the Transvaal. My word, that could be better for him than Paris, but I'll regret it on our account, for I have lots and lots of fellow-feeling for him, and would greatly desire to make his acquaintance personally. I'm planning to write to him again about his articles, and I'll give him a portrait of myself as a souvenir.

I think that this one could have been someone who could have married our sister. That would be better for him than this journalist's life, and perhaps would get him back on his feet. For I'm touched by the fact that one feels so much from what he says, that he's a very suffering and very good person, happy when he can admire.

This morning I began *The Diggers* on a no. 30 canvas.

Do you know that it might be interesting to try to do Millet's drawings as paintings, that would be a very special collection of copies, something like the works of Prévost, who copied little-known Goyas and Velázquez for Mr. Doria.

Perhaps I'd be more useful doing that than through my own painting.

Mother wrote to me too with news of Cor.

I worked on a study of the fever ward in the Arles hospital, and then having no canvas lately I've been taking long walks in all directions across the country — I'm beginning to feel more the wholeness of the countryside in which I live. Later I may also return time and again to the same Provençal subjects.

What you say of Guillaumin is very true, he has found a true thing and he's satisfied with what he's found without embarking at random on dissimilar things, and that way he remains right and becomes stronger, always with these same very simple subjects. My word, he isn't wrong, and I like this sincerity he has enormously.

I'm hurrying to finish this letter, I had already begun to write to you four times without being able to finish.

Ah, at the moment you yourself are fully in the midst of nature, since you write that Jo already feels her child quicken — it's much more interesting even than landscape, and I'm very pleased that it has changed like this for you.

How beautiful the Millet is, A *child's first steps!*

Handshake to you, to Isaäcson, my best regards above all to Jo. I'm going to work some more on *The Diggers*, the days are very short. More soon.

Ever yours,
Vincent

JENA

1230 km from St. Rémy

short-term memory & bibliokleptomania

1 November 1889

Jena Medical Report

This evening he still accurately remembers a talk he had with
the doctor yesterday. — Steals books. — Very excited after a visit
from his mother. Weight 129 lbs. (+1).

Tuesday, 30 October 1888 [*excerpt*]

I sometimes look at my *hand* now with some distrust, because I
seem to have the destiny of mankind "in the palm of my hand."
— Are you satisfied by my concluding with the *Dionysos morality*?
It occurred to me that this group of ideas should not at any price
be absent from this *vade mecum* of my philosophy.

N.

ST. RÉMY

1230 km from Jena

*I was growing flabby by dint of never seeing anything ar-
tistic; to translate them into another language; my health
is very good — except often a lot of melancholy; greatly
driven to seek style; abominable nightmares; I'd very much
like Jo to see The Evening; I hope that your health and Jo's
continue to be good; to believe in landscapes*

3 November 1889

My dear Theo,

Enclosed I'm sending you a list of colors I need as soon as possible.

You gave me very great pleasure by sending me those Millets, I'm working on them zealously. I was growing flabby by dint of never seeing anything artistic, and this revives me. I've finished *The Evening* and am working on *The Diggers* and the man who's putting his jacket on, no. 30 canvases, and *The Sower*, smaller. The evening is in a range of violets and soft lilacs, with light from the lamp pale citron, then the orange glow of the fire and the man in red ochre. You will see it. It seems to me that doing painting after these Millet drawings is much rather *to translate them into another language* than to copy them. Apart from that I have a rain effect on the go, and an *evening* effect with tall *pines*.

And also a leaf-fall.

My health is very good — except often a lot of melancholy however — but I feel much, much better than when I came here, and even better than in Paris. Also, as for the work the ideas are becoming firmer, it seems to me. But then I don't quite know if you'd like what I'm doing now. For despite what you say in your previous letter, that the search for style often harms other qualities, the fact is that I feel myself greatly driven to seek style, if you like, but I mean by that a more manly and more deliberate drawing. If that will make me more like Bernard or Gauguin, I can't do anything about it. But am inclined to believe that in the long run you'd get used to it.

For yes, one must feel the wholeness of a country — isn't that what distinguishes a Cézanne from something else. And Guillaumin, whom you mention, he has so much style and a personal way of drawing. Anyway, I'll do as I can.

Now that most of the leaves have fallen the landscape looks more like the north, and then I really feel that if I went back to the north I would see it more clearly than before.

Health is a big thing, and a lot depends on it, as regards work too.

Fortunately those abominable nightmares no longer torment me.

I hope to go to Arles in the next few days.

I'd very much like Jo to see *The Evening*, I think that I'll send you a consignment shortly, but it's drying very badly because of the dampness of the studio. Here the houses have scarcely any cellar or foundations, & one feels the damp more than in the north.

At home they'll have moved by now, I'll add 6 canvases for them to the next consignment. Is it necessary to have them framed, perhaps *not*, for it isn't worth it. Above all, don't frame the studies I send you from time to time, that can be done later, pointless for them to take up too much room.

I've also done a canvas for Mr. Peyron, a view of the house with a tall pine tree.

I hope that your health and Jo's continue to be good.

I'm so happy that you're no longer alone, & that everything's more normal than before.

Is Gauguin back, and what's Bernard doing?

More soon, I shake your hand firmly, & Jo's, and our friends', and believe me

Ever yours,
Vincent

I'm trying to simplify the list of colors as much as possible — thus I very often use the ochres as in the old days.

I know very well that the studies drawn with long, sinuous lines from the last consignment weren't what they ought to become, however I dare urge you to believe that in landscapes one will continue to mass things by means of a drawing style that seeks to express the entanglement of the masses. Thus, do you remember Delacroix's landscape, Jacob's struggle with the angel? And there are others of his! For example the cliffs, and the very flowers you speak of sometimes. Bernard really has found perfect things in there. Anyway, don't be too swift to adopt a prejudice against it.

Anyway, you'll see that there's already more character in a large landscape with pines, red ochre trunks defined by a black line than in the previous ones.

INTERVAL: MESSINA, SICILIA

The will to power *&* phagocytosis
1616.9 km from St. Rémy, 1961.5 km to Jena

November 1889

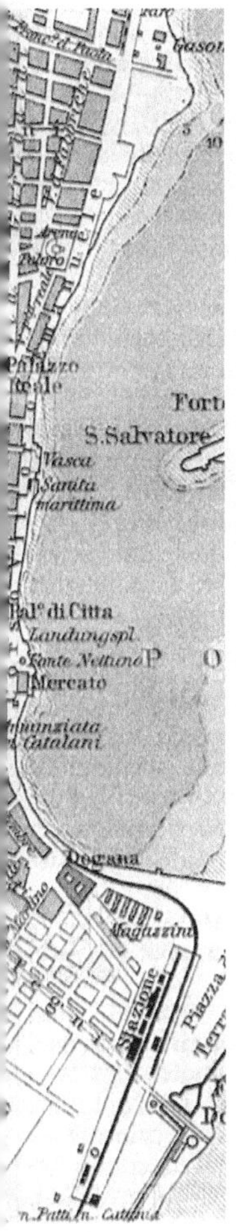

Cosmology, philosophy, psychology — a host of sciences to define and determine or discover and invent what humanity (*reality*) is constituted of. What, however, of biology? We are more than individuals, Nietzsche said, we are the whole chain as well, but what is the individual? Is there biological unity or disunity? Is the individual akin to a coral reef, to a rhizome, or to disparate planetoids in an asteroid belt? What is the true character of our morphological nature? Aside from hydrogen, helium, oxygen, and carbon, are we not also clay, dirt, and chaos? What too of our geological nature? Are we not walking, talking minerals? What is our organismal dimension?

The truth of man, Nietzsche discerned, is atomistic anarchy, relations of force, of struggle, of contest. Life is biological struggle, down to the atoms. What you believe is immaterial; what is *actual* is what triumphs, in the face of all delusions.

Through the long succession of millennia, Nietzsche observed, man has not known himself physiologically: he does not know himself even today. Biological existence cannot be moralized or spiritualized. Conflicting instincts are not to be harmonized — impossible ideal! All weaker forces are constrained by stronger ones in the oligarchic structure of existence. The natural expression of the will to power seeks its maximal articulation. There is no stasis; the dance of struggling forces is dynamic — striving, overcoming, superseding, incessant metamorphosis, a state of ever-changing dynamics. Such is organic nature itself, and man is nothing less and nothing more than organic nature, the active biological organism seeking opposition and resistance, obstacles to overcome and move beyond. There is no adaptation; there is the assimilation of weaker forces, the consumption of them in the combustion furnace of man. Milieu? External causes? Inner force! The self is tornadic, spinning, whirling, in constant movement and mutation, ceaselessly redefining itself, more even than the river that never stays the same. It does not adapt; it is not reactive, it is *active* — a site where festive yet dangerous forms combine and deviate, transform and pollute, slaughter and nurture, threaten and overcome.

And so what is at war in the old artilleryman, and what is at war in the mad painter? Are they not but subjects in dynamic and continual reconstruction? A war of forces seek their triumph within them; their bodies the terrain of a contest and a contest of terrains, for they are closer to life, more fundamentally biologically attuned than others, and so their selves, organisms in shifting display, version upon version of self mutating, combining, deviating, transforming, each mutation altering the body, a dance or war of myriad selves that may forever mutate the last ruling self. It is genetic, cognitive, emotional, physical, and immunological! They are not homeostatic, but dialectical, allostatic beasts: labile, fluxional, metamorphic: creatures whose centers are ever-shifting whirlwinds. In the calculus of their growth, they are always in a state of alteration, their bodies more open to modification and disruption. The cosmos explodes within them. The subject-object dyad is indeterminate. Clear divisions dissipate and vanish, like the borders between centuries, like the plethora of debris in an asteroid belt. What is space, what dark matter, what dark energy, what still unknown, X?

If Nietzsche's biological axis is metaphoric, it is not limited to metaphor but akin to reality itself — it is from that axis that a real biologico-psychology is established.

If unknown to himself, like that of his unknown selves, in the world of biology Herr Dynamite had a twin to his philosophy, a doppëlganger in near-proximity.

In 1870, Ilya Ilyich Mechnikov was appointed Professor of Zoology and Comparative Anatomy at 22, just one year after Nietzsche was appointed the Chair of Classical Philology at the University of Basel at 24. Following a number of misfortunes and suicide attempts, in 1883, one year after Nietzsche himself visited Sicilia and wrote his *Idylls of Messina* in that city, Mechnikov settled there, too. Under just 2 km from where Herr Dynamite resided, Metchnikov established a private marine biology laboratory where he conducted studies on sea anemones and starfish. Introducing a rose thorn under the skin of one of the starfish larvae, Metchnikov came to observe mobile cells surrounding the foreign body, cells he would later dub phagocytes. The biologist saw an analogy between the starfish larvae and the accumulation of cells in the inflammatory lesions of humans, hypothesizing that the phenomenon was indicative of a general event of evolutionary history. In the starfish larvae, Metchnikov saw the entire spectacle of evolution — *it was a stage depicting the incendiary phagocytes engulfing invading parasites.* Conflict, he realized, was between individuals of different species, an agon not only between parasite and phagocyte, but between phagocyte and superfluous or damaged cells. Phagocytes, he later discovered, are present in all organs, including the spleen, liver, blood, and brain, and they maintain a considerable degree of independence while directing their activity to exterminating every weak member of a colony.

Just as Nietzsche was completing *Thus Spoke Zarathustra*, Mechnikov established a true scientific corollary to his thinking. The scientist's notion of the organism is the biological equivalent of Herr Dynamite's ethos. Mechnikov sought clues in the evolutionary fate of our three embryonic layers, the endoderm, the ectoderm, *&* the mesoderm, where reside the ameboid phagocytosing cells, the tracers of mesodermal activity in the embryo, larval, and later stages of development. And simultaneously, Herr Dynamite noted that what every smallest living part of a living organism wants is an increase of power. The protoplasm stretches its pseudopodia in order to search for something that resists it — not from hunger, but from *will to power*, its energetic dýnamis. And Metchnikov discovers the secrets of phagocyte behavior, of its highly protean remodeling tissue, of its functioning as an architect *constructing us from within*, like death carving the cells of life to sculpt us into being. The phagocyte is no mere hunter of food, it functions as the steward of every organism's self and secures its labile identity. It is a hunter that decides what is to be destroyed or preserved. The phagocyte is an agonist, practicing the hospitality of warriors. It defends the organism; it preserves organismal integrity. Metchnikoff discovers that immunity is an active process, not a given, but a war, a continual act of self-fashioning. This world is the will to power — *&* nothing besides! And you yourselves are also this will to power — *&* nothing besides!

And so, individuality, the subject, the self, the body, is not ever stable, *but in threat of constant destruction &* *reconstitution*, like the thousand selves at war with themselves (and like broken colors creating new contrasts *&* intensities, colors not physically present), each seeking to usurp the other, in the more highly mobile and prismatic bodies open to the volatility of life. Environment is only an external aspect of the inner dimension that defines the organism. Self-integrity must be fought for, for it is in continuous threat of assault and decomposition. Phagocyte activity is nothing but Darwin's struggle of the species turned inward within the organism. The constitution of the body is not in balance; life's cellular components are labile, tornadic, mutational. Flesh, atoms, organs, all mutate *&* transform! — every five to seven days, the intestines completely regenerate, every six weeks, the liver *&* skin, every three months, the skeletal structure, every two months, the brain, every year, 98% of the body's atoms are renewed — *we are metabolic butterflies.*

Are the basic chemical compounds of the universe breaking out in the body? Are events of discombobulation the aftereffects of dissociations, disaggregations, psychological automatism forever altering the self? The subject splitting; a personality from the sea of multiple personalities becoming dominant? The secondary self seizing power? Psychical life's substratum of hallucinatory nature tyrannizing and triumphing? Over-consciousness losing out to under-consciousness? The rise of the subwaking self? The metabolic butterfly breaking down, out, and beyond? Or is it strictly plasmic finality? Genetic degeneration? Nietzsche and Vincent shifting between states of harmony and disharmony, assemblages of warring inner elements, patho-physiological events far superseding 'their' wills — consciousness become a merry-go-round of chaos and death. It is the biological pathology of the body at play to the nth degree. Nietzsche's will is Metchnikov's phagocyte as immune cells, & Herr Dynamite's agonism is Metchnikoff's organism in continual strife. Come out, come out, whoever you are... Come out, come out, *whatever* you are...

Contrary to the predominant cast of 19th century conceptions of the nature of pathology, the son of Emilia Nevakhovich advances it as having a dynamic role beginning with disharmony. If, Lord Bakon (Nietzsche) suggests, we could imagine dissonance become man — and what else is man? — this dissonance, to be able to live, would need a splendid illusion that would cover dissonance with a veil of beauty. Dissonance; disharmony; dissolution; reconstitution. Metchnikov shatters the notion of immunity as a passive concept with his phagocytosis theory, and when he discovers that phagocytes still function in dead organisms, his theory becomes a truth. I move from X to pathology; I move from laboratory to cosmos. Man becomes sun; man becomes lava; man becomes music. Vincent (the Horla) *becomes* flowing paint;

Nietzsche (Cæsar Cæsarum) *becomes* dancing star. Vincent *is* X, Nietzsche *is* X, and X *is* X.

To Claude Bernard, health was the normal state, an idealized physiology, but to Metchnikoff, health is not the norm, only an idealized goal. Our physiological processes are infernos, and disharmony, *dissonance*, is the norm. Just as Nietzsche spoke of the indeterminateness of the human, Metchnikov discovers the indeterminateness of our organismal integrity, an integrity only attained through active combat. The organic as Nietzsche knew is the sole true basis of the human. Instinct, behavior — expressions of the will to power, and ontogeny here finds its rhizomatic root: — there is no spirituality, there is no morality, there is no self that is separate from the body, *& there is no soul*. Body, instinct, unconscious — hierarchy of selves? No! Body am I entirely, and nothing else; and soul is only a word for something about the body!

*

Books, art, religion, time, the visible *&* solid earth,
and what was expected of heaven or fear'd of hell,
                    [are now consumed,
Mad filaments, ungovernable shoots play out of it,
the response likewise ungovernable,
Hair, bosom, hips, bend of legs, negligent falling hands
                        [all diffused...
Ebb stung by the flow *&* flow stung by the ebb ~

Whitman, I Sing the Body Electric

JENA

1230 km from St. Rémy

hemicranias

10 November 1889

Jena Medical Report

Continued violent right hemicranias. Says the date is "March 97."

5 November 1888 [*excerpt*]

Today I bought a pair of superb English winter gloves. With the best will in the world, dear old friend Overbeck, I cannot find anything bad to tell you about myself. Things continue to go well at a *tempo fortissimo* of work and well-being. Also people treat me here *comme il faut*, as a person extreme of distinction; the way they open the door for me is something utterly new to me. Admittedly, I visit only very good places, and also I rejoice in a classical tailor.

Your Nietzsche

ST. RÉMY

1230 km from Jena

*not to see any paintings for a while; fate is bent on thwart-
ing us; Gauguin wrote me; continue to paint or leave painting alone; the possible and the reality of things; I've been to
Arles; we'll see if this journey might provoke another crisis;
to see the people and things of the north again for this life
here is terribly numbing; perhaps there'll be some progress
so as to be less of a burden to you; the 6 paintings for the
Vingtistes will make an ensemble*

19 November 1889

My dear Theo,

Thanks for your letter, and am very glad that you write that Jo is staying well. The great event is nearing now, I think of you both very often. For you, when you write about seeing so many paintings that you would wish not to see any for a while, this clearly proves that you've had too many business worries. And then — yes there's something in life other than paintings, and this something else one neglects and nature seems to avenge itself then, and besides, fate is bent on thwarting us. I think that in these circumstances one must keep to the paintings as much as duty demands but no more. As for the Vingtistes, here's what I'd like to exhibit:

1 & 2	The two pendants of sunflowers
3	*The Ivy*, upright
4	*Orchard in Blossom* (the one Tanguy's exhibiting at the moment, with poplars crossing the canvas)
5	*The Red Vineyard*
6	*Wheatfield*, rising sun, which I'm working on at the moment.

Gauguin wrote me a very kind letter and speaks animatedly of De Haan and of their rough-&-ready life at the seaside.

Bernard also wrote to me, complaining about a heap of things while resigning himself like the good boy he is, but not happy at all; with all his talent, all his work, all his sobriety, it appears that home is often a hell for him.

Isaäcson's letter gives me great pleasure, I enclose my reply which you will read — the ideas are beginning to link together a little more calmly, but as you'll see from it I don't know if I should continue to paint or leave painting alone.

If I continue, certainly I'm in agreement with you that perhaps it's better to attack things with simplicity than to seek abstractions.

And I'm not an admirer of Gauguin's *Christ in the Garden of Olives* for example, a croquis of which he sent me.

Then as for Bernard's, he promises me a photograph of it, I don't know, but I fear that his biblical compositions will make me wish for something else. Lately I've seen women picking and gathering olives, no way for me to get a model, so I didn't do anything about it. However now isn't the moment to ask me to approve of friend G's composition — and friend Bernard has probably never seen an olive tree. Now he therefore avoids conceiving the least idea of the possible and of the reality of things, and that isn't the way to synthesize. No, never have I got involved in their Biblical interpretations. I said that Rembrandt and Delacroix had done this admirably, that I liked that even better than the primitives, but then stop. I don't want to begin on that chapter again. If I remain here I wouldn't try to paint a *Christ in the Garden of Olives*, but in fact the olive picking as it's still seen today, and then giving the correct proportions of the human figure in it, that would perhaps make people think of it all the same. Before I've done more serious studies than I have up to now I don't have the right to get involved in this. And then the Pre-Raphaelites went a long way in that category of ideas. When Millais painted his *Light of the World* it was serious in another way. Really, there's no comparison. Not to mention Holman Hunt and others, Pinwell & Rossetti.

And then here there's Puvis de Chavannes.

Now I'll tell you that I've been to Arles and I saw Mr. Salles, who handed me the rest of the money you sent him and the rest of what I'd handed over to him, that is, 72 francs. However, only around twenty francs remain in the cash-box with Mr. Peyron at the moment, since down there I stocked myself up with colors and paid for the room where the furniture &c. is. Stayed there for 2 days, not yet knowing what to do next, it's good to show oneself there from time to time so that the same story doesn't start again with the people. At present no one there is hostile to me as far as I can tell, on the contrary, they were very friendly, and even gave me a warm welcome. And if I stayed in the area, little by little I'd have a chance to acclimatize myself, which isn't easy for strangers and would have its uses for painting there. But first we'll see a little if this journey might provoke another crisis. I almost dare hope not.

It's often cold here too, however we're a little more sheltered from the mistral by the mountains. And between times I keep working. I have several things to send you with the canvas for the Vingtistes. I'm waiting for that one to be dry.

If I'd known in time that there were trains from here to Paris at only 25 francs I would certainly have come. It's only on going to Arles that I found this out, and it's because of the expense that I haven't done it — at the moment it would seem to me that in springtime it would however be good to come in any event to see the people and things of the north again. For this life here is terribly numbing, and in the long run I'd lose my energy. I had hardly dared hope that I would still be as well as is the case.

However, everything depends on whether this suits you or not, and I think it's wise not to rush things. Perhaps by waiting a little we won't even have need of the doctor at Auvers or the Pissarros.

If my health remains stable, then if while I'm working I again start to try to sell, exhibit, make exchanges, perhaps there'll be some progress so as to be less of a burden to you on the one hand and to regain a little more zest on the other. For I don't hide from you the fact that my stay here is very tiring on account of its monotony, and because the society of all these unfortunates, who do absolutely nothing, gets on one's nerves.

But what can one do, one can't have pretensions in my case, I already have too many as it is.

Gauguin says that they get models easily. That's what I lack most here.

Bernard speaks to me of an exchange, you're quite free to deal with this with him if he wishes and speaks to you about it. I'd really like that, besides the portrait of his grandmother, you should have a good thing of his. It appears he fancies the *Berceuse*.

I think that the 6 paintings for the Vingtistes will make an ensemble like this, the wheatfield will make a very good pendant to the orchard.

I'm dropping a line to Mr. Maus to give him titles, as he asks in his letter.

Now, warm regards to Jo, and good handshake.
You must read the letter to Isaäcson, it complements this one.
More soon.

Ever yours,
Vincent

JENA

1230 km from St. Rémy

crippling headaches

21 November 1889

Jena Medical Report

Patient states: "I've got such a headache that I can neither walk
nor see."

ST. RÉMY

1230 km from Jena

I'd like to be able to do something good; they'd driven me mad with their Christs in the garden; thinking and not dreaming is our duty; Puvis and Delacroix are much healthier than those Pre-Raphaelites; I've been messing about in the groves morning and evening; how I'd like to see the studies from nature; to do for the mountains and for the cypresses what I've just done for the olive trees; by working assiduously from nature; slow, long work is the only road; one must work as hard and with as few pretensions as a peasant; I'm going to attack the cypresses and the mountains; to paint a bookshop

26 November 1889

My dear Theo,

I have to thank you very much for a consignment of colors, which was also accompanied by an excellent woolen waistcoat. How kind you are to me, and how I'd like to be able to do something good in order to prove to you that I'd like to be less ungrateful. Your colors reached me at the right moment, for what I brought back from Arles is almost exhausted. The thing is, I've been working this month in the olive groves, for they'd driven me mad with their Christs in the garden, in which nothing is observed. Of course there's no question of me doing anything from the Bible — and I've written to Bernard, and also to Gauguin, that I believed that thinking and not dreaming was our duty, that I was therefore astonished when looking at their work by the fact that they give way to that. For Bernard has sent me photos of his canvases. The thing about them is that they're sorts of dreams and nightmares, that there's some erudition there — one can see that it's someone who's mad about the primitives — but frankly the English Pre-Raphaelites did this much better, and then Puvis and Delacroix are much healthier than those Pre-Raphaelites. So this doesn't leave me cold, but it gives me an uncomfortable feeling of a tumble rather than progress. Well, to shake this off, I've been messing about in the groves morning and evening on these bright and cold days, but in very beautiful, clear sunshine, and the result is 5 no. 30 canvases which, with the 3 studies of olive trees that you have, at least constitute an attack on the problem. The olive tree is variable like our willow or pollard in the north. You know that willows are very picturesque, despite the fact that it appears monotonous, it's the tree typical of the country. Now what the willow is in our native country, the olive tree and the cypress have exactly the same importance here. What I've done is a rather harsh and coarse realism beside their abstractions, but it will nevertheless impart the rustic note, and will smell of the soil. How I'd like to see the studies from nature by Gauguin and Bernard, the latter tells me of portraits that doubtless would please me more.

I hope I'll get used to working in the cold — in the morning there are very interesting effects of white frost and fog, and I still have the great desire to do for the mountains and for the cypresses what I've just done for the olive trees, have a really good go at them.

The thing is, the olive tree and the cypress have rarely been painted, and from the point of view of placing the paintings this *ought* to go to England, I know well enough what they're looking for over there. Whatever the case, I'm almost sure that in this way I'll do something passable from time to time. As I said to Isaäcson, it's really more and more my opinion that by working assiduously from nature, without saying to oneself in advance, I want to do this or that, by working as if one were making shoes, without artistic preoccupations, one won't always do well, but on the days when one thinks about it the least one finds a subject that holds its own with the work of those who came before us. One learns to know a country that's basically quite different from what it appears at first sight. On the contrary, one will say to oneself, I want to finish my paintings better, I want to do them with care; in the face of the difficulties of the weather, of changing effects, a heap of ideas like this finds itself reduced to being impracticable, and I end up resigning myself by saying, it's experience and *each day's* little bit of work alone that in the long run matures and enables one to do things that are more complete or more right. So slow, long work is the only road, and all ambition to be set on doing well, false. For one must spoil as many canvases as one succeeds with when one mounts the breach each morning. To paint, the tranquil, regulated life would therefore be absolutely necessary, and at present what can one do when one sees that Bernard, for example, is always put under pressure, pressure, pressure by his parents. He can't do as he wants, and many others with him. One says to oneself, I shan't paint any more, but what will one do then? Ah — a more expeditious painting process should be invented, less expensive than oil and yet durable. A painting... it will end up becoming as commonplace as a sermon, a painter like someone who's a century behind the times. It's a shame, though, that it should be so. Now if the painters had better understood Millet as a man — now some like

Lhermitte and Roll have grasped him — things wouldn't be so. One *must* work as hard and with as few pretensions as a peasant if one wants to last.

And instead of putting on grandiose exhibitions, it would have been better to address oneself to the common people, and work so that everyone may have paintings or reproductions at home, which are lessons like the work of Millet.

I'm completely at the end of my canvas, and when you can please send me 10 meters. Then I'm going to attack the cypresses and the mountains. I think that this must be the center of the work I've done here and there in Provence, and then we can conclude the stay here when it's convenient. Which isn't urgent, for Paris only distracts, after all. I don't know, though, not always being a pessimist — I keep telling myself that I still have it in my heart to paint a bookshop one day with the shop window yellow-pink, in the evening, and the passers-by black — it's such an essentially modern subject. Because it also appears such a figurative source of light. I say, that would be a subject that would look good between an olive grove and a wheatfield, the sowing of books, of prints. I have that very much in my heart to do, like a light in the darkness. Yes, there's a way of seeing Paris as beautiful. But anyway, bookshops aren't hares, and there's no hurry, and I have a good will to work here for another year, which will probably be wiser.

Mother must have been in Leiden for a good fortnight by now.

I've delayed sending you the canvases for them because I'll include them with the canvas of the wheatfield for the Vingtistes.

Warm regards to Jo, she's very good, continuing to be well. Thank you once again for the colors and for the woolen waistcoat, and good handshake in thought.

Ever yours,
Vincent

JENA

1230 km from St. Rémy

noise

1 December

Jena Medical Report

When the patient was allowed to sleep in a bed, second-class,
with an attendant, instead of in the cell, he was so noisy that he
had to be isolated again. — Weight 133 lbs. (+4).

2 December 1888 [*excerpt*]

Sunday afternoon, after four o'clock, wildly beautiful autumn
day. Just returned from a big concert, which really made on me
the strongest impression of any concert I have been to — my face
kept making grimaces, in order to get over a feeling of extreme
pleasure, including, for ten minutes, the grimace of tears. Ah! if
you could have been there!

Your friend N.

ST. RÉMY

Yesterday I sent three packets by parcel post containing studies; in spite of the cold I'm continuing to work outside; I often think of you and Jo; I feel absolutely normal, so to speak, but without ideas for the future

7 December 1889

My dear Theo,

Yesterday I sent three packets by parcel post containing studies that I hope you'll receive in good order. I really must thank you for the 10 meters of canvas, which have just arrived.

Among the studies you'll find the following, which are for our mother and sister: *Olive Trees — Bedroom — Reaper — Working with Plough — Wheatfield with Cypresses — Orchard in Blossom — Portrait.*

The remainder is above all autumn studies and I think the best one is the yellow mulberry tree against a very blue sky. Then the study of the house and of the park, of which there are two variants. The studies on no. 30 canvases weren't yet dry and will follow later. They're giving me a lot of trouble, and sometimes I find them very ugly, sometimes they look good to me — perhaps you'll have the same impression when you see them. There are a dozen of them, so it's more substantial than what I've just sent.

In spite of the cold I'm continuing to work outside up to now, and I think that it's good for me and for the work.

The last study I did is a view of the village — where people were at work — under enormous plane trees — repairing the pavements. So there are piles of sand, stones and the gigantic tree-trunks — the yellowing foliage, and here and there glimpses of a house-front *&* little figures.

I often think of you and Jo, but with a feeling as if there was an enormous distance from here to Paris and as if it were years since I saw you. I hope that your health is good, for myself I can't complain, I feel absolutely normal, so to speak, but without ideas for the future, and truly I don't know what it's going to be, and perhaps I'm avoiding going into this question deeply, sensing that I can do nothing about it.

I've finished, or almost, the copy of *The Diggers* too.

You'll see that there are no more impastos in the large studies. I prepare the thing with sorts of washes with spirits, *&* then proceed with touches or hatchings of color with spaces between them. This imparts atmosphere and uses less paint.

If I want to send this letter off today I must hurry, so handshake in thought & warm regards to Jo.

Ever yours, Vincent.

JENA

1230 km from St. Rémy

disgorging

9 December 1889

Jena Medical Report

Vomiting. No evidence of faulty diet, but patient often eats in a
great hurry.

ST. RÉMY

1230 km from Jena

*I'm very glad that you and Jo are in good health; I'm work-
ing on a painting at the moment; the calm life of seclusion;
completely resigned to staying here; another very nice letter from Gauguin; better days have already begun for myself; the money that was with Mr. Peyron has run out; an
order for canvas and colors; to see modern life as bright despite its inevitable sadnesses; I'm going to work some more
outside*

19 December 1889

My dear Theo,

Thanks very much for your last letter, I'm very glad that you and Jo are in good health, and very often think of you both.

It's very interesting what you tell me about a publication of colored lithographs with a text on Monticelli, honestly, that gives me very great pleasure, and I'd be very curious to see them one day. I hope that he'll reproduce in color the bouquet you have, for that's a thing of the first order as regards color.

One day I'd very much like to do a print or two myself in this vein after my canvases. Thus I'm working on a painting at the moment, women picking olives, which would lend itself to it, I think. These are the colors: the field is violet and further away yellow ochre, the olive trees with bronze trunks have grey-green foliage, the sky is entirely pink, and 3 small figures pink also. The whole in a very discreet range. It's a canvas I'm working on from memory after the study of the same size done on the spot, because I want a far-off thing like a vague memory softened by time. There are only two notes, pink and green, which harmonize, neutralize each other, oppose each other. I'll probably do 2 or three repetitions of it, for in fact it's the result of a half-dozen studies of olive trees.

I think it likely that I'll do hardly any more things in impasto, it's the result of the calm life of seclusion I'm leading, and I feel I'm better for it. Fundamentally I'm not as violent as that, anyway I feel more *myself* in calmness.

You'll perhaps also see it in the canvas for the Vingtistes that I sent yesterday, the *Wheatfield with Rising Sun*. You'll receive the *Bedroom* at the same time. I've also added two drawings to them. I'm curious to know what you'll say about the *Wheatfield*, you may have to look at it for a while perhaps. However, I hope that you'll write to me soon whether it's arrived in good order if you find a free half hour next week.

I'd be completely resigned to staying here next year too, because I think the work will get along a little. And through the prolonged stay, I feel the country here differently from the first place encountered — good ideas are now germinating a little and should be allowed to develop. And thus I wouldn't be so very far removed from the idea of going to look for something in the land of Tartarin. I have a great desire to do more of both the cypresses and the Alpilles, and often going on long walks in all directions I've noted many subjects and know good places for when the fine days come. Then, from the point of view of expenditure there would hardly be any advantage in moving I think, and moving makes the success of the work all the more doubtful. I've received another very nice letter from Gauguin, a letter thoroughly impregnated with the proximity of the sea, I think he must be doing fine, rather savage things.

You tell me not to give myself *too many* worries and that better days will come again for me. I'd say that these better days have already begun for myself, when I glimpse the possibility of completing, to some extent, the work in such a way that you'll have a series of Provençal studies done with feeling which will hold up, this is what I hope, with our far-off memories of youth in Holland, and thus I'm treating myself by redoing the olive trees again for our mother and sister. And if I could one day prove that I wouldn't impoverish the family, that would relieve me. For at present I always have a great deal of remorse in spending money that doesn't come back. But as you say, patience and working is the only chance of getting out of that.

However, I often tell myself that if I'd done like you, if I'd stayed at the Goupils', if I'd restricted myself to selling paintings, I would have done better. For in the trade, if one doesn't produce oneself one makes others produce, now that so many artists need support among the dealers and only rarely find it.

The money that was with Mr. Peyron has run out, and a few days ago he even gave me 10 francs in advance. And in the course of the month I'll certainly need another 10, and at New Year I'd consider it right to give something to the servant lads who work here, and to the porter, which will make another 10 francs or so.

As regards winter clothing, what I have isn't very much, as you'll understand, but it's warm enough and so we can wait until spring with that. If I go out it's to work, so then I put on the most worn-out things I have, and I have a velvet waistcoat and trousers for here. In the spring, if I'm here, I'm planning to go and make a few paintings in Arles as well, and if I get something new around then, that will suffice.

I'm sending you enclosed an order for canvas and colors, but I still have some and it can wait until next month if this one is too heavily burdened already.

I remember the painting by Manet you speak of. As to figure, the portrait of a man by Puvis de Chavannes has always remained an ideal for me, an old man reading a yellow novel, with beside him a rose and watercolor brushes in a glass of water — and the portrait of a lady that he had in the same exhibition, a woman already old but completely as Michelet felt, that there's no such thing as an old woman. These are consolatory things, to see modern life as bright despite its inevitable sadnesses.

Last year around this time I was certainly not thinking that I would recover as much as this.

Give my kind regards to Isaäcson if you see him, & to Bernard.

I regret not being able to send the olive trees one of these days, but it's drying so badly that I'll have to wait.

I think it'll be a good course of action to have our sister come in January. Ah, if that one could get married, that would be a good thing.

I shake your hand warmly in thought, I'm going to work some more outside, the mistral's blowing. It usually dies down by the time the sun's about to set, then there are superb effects of pale citron skies, and desolate pines cast their silhouettes into relief against it with effects of exquisite black lace.

At other times the sky is red, at other times a tone that's extremely delicate, neutral, still pale lemon but neutralized by delicate lilac.

I have an evening effect of a pine again against pink and green-yellow. Anyway, shortly you'll see these canvases, of which the first, the *Wheatfield*, has just left. More soon, I hope, warm regards to Jo.

Ever yours,
Vincent

INTERVAL:
ST. RÉMY & JENA

The heliomythic allegory; the secret emperor
Jena →← St. Rémy: 1230 km distance

January 1890, the New Year

As the anniversary of the collapse of the Studio of the South and Vincent's severing of his ear approached, the painter was plagued with anxieties about yet another potential attack. With winter in effect, the weather grew harsher and the period of sunlight shorter, leading to the painter being confined more and more to the despairing quarters of the asylum. Wracked by boredom, frequently overwhelmed by despair and the fear of repeated psychotic spells, the cold air, leafless trees, and barren countryside evoked for the frail vessel of the North — Theo and Jo in Paris, his family in the Netherlands — and intensified his feeling of severe isolation, an increasing loneliness, and estrangement from all around him:

I think of you and Jo very often, he wrote Theo, *feeling as though there were an enormous distance between here and Paris and it was years since I saw you.*

The broken pitcher expressed being devoid of any sense of a future and incapable of doing anything about it. He felt almost doomed, his confidence, nothing but pretension, and proclaimed that fate itself was set on thwarting them.

While everyone in his family seemed to be united by the forthcoming birth of Theo and Jo's child, an event resulting in all of them growing ever closer, the Horla's home was an asylum. Amongst the gifts of paintings he made to his mother and sister was one of a view of the garden from his studio window. While the facade of the asylum building on the right stretching toward the distance and the stone boundary wall in the background together produce a feeling of confinement, the blooming flowers and wavelike bands of color of the sunset offer the promise of life, of renewal, of the potency of existence, just as do the trees that rise high above the building roof and into the sky, beyond the edge of the canvas, as if they will continue to grow and exceed any and every confining structure or boundary. The spirit of Vincent in free motion, extending outward & beyond?

In the foreground is a tree that is perchance emblematic of the painter himself. It is leaning toward the ground as if it might collapse, and has one immense wound where a large limb had been cut off, just like the Horla's own ear. Where does the tree become-painter and the painter become-tree?

It is a somber giant, the painter said, like a defeated proud man, and contrasts, when considered in the nature of a living creature, with the pale smile of a last rose on the fading bush in front of him. Underneath the trees, empty stone benches, sullen box trees; the sky is mirrored — *yellow* — in a puddle left by the rain. A sunbeam, the last ray of daylight, raises the somber ochre almost to orange. Here and there small black figures wander around among the tree trunks. You will realize that this combination of red ocher, of green gloomed over by grey, the black streaks surrounding the contours, produces something of the sensation of anguish, called "black-red," from which certain of my companions in misfortune suffer. Moreover the motif of the great tree struck by lightning, the sickly green-pink smile of the last flower of autumn, serve to confirm this impression. —

While two of the black figures walk side by side along the pathway adjacent to the asylum building, the third is alone, still, faceless, without definition, positioned between two trees as if the figure itself is as inorganic as a tree, which intensifies and emphasizes its isolation and separation, its blank face the same color as the sawed-off face of the wound on the lightning-struck tree, as if they are perhaps no different.

Guilt consumes the Horla, and he refers to the emotion as the grief that gathers in our heart like water in a swamp. He vacillates between painting with sustained and energized focus and wonders if he should even continue painting at all. It costs so much, he laments to Theo, and brings in nothing.

If praised by Jozef Isaäcson and others, the artist remains doubtful, full of incomprehension, deprecatory, countering, there isn't anything worth mentioning about my work now. We must work as much and with as few pretensions as a peasant, he declares. Slow, long work is the only way, and all ambition and keenness to make a good show of it, false.

In one instance, the painter speaks of an explosion of ideas and subjects, of his desire to finish his series of paintings *Impressions of Provence* and so of remaining in the asylum because, if he leaves, it could be disruptive and undermine his stability.

Contrarily, his drives in combat, he again speaks of quitting painting altogether and instead leading a hard life, say, as a soldier in the East, for that he says would cure him. A martial discipline to drive away madness — the Japanese painter monk become samurai.

His fear of a new attack leaves him in a latent state of sensitivity, and in the midst of it he works on numerous versions of paintings of olive groves, as well as a ravine, wooden sheds, roads, and fields. The figures in all of these paintings, if they contain figures at all, are nearly faceless, mostly solitary, or dwarfed by nature, with some landscapes being entirely devoid of humans, seemingly still, as if the world had stopped revolving, as if even the sun was no longer revolving, but was pinioned in place. It is the becoming still of life; it is nature as natura morte.

Writing to his mother, the painter reproaches himself, burrowing deeper into doubt, a form of dread and fear, claiming that his illness is more or less his own fault, but reasoning and thinking about these things he says is sometimes so difficult, and sometimes his feelings overwhelm him more than before.

When in the midst of painting yet another olive grove, in a state of perfect calm, unexpectedly, seemingly without cause, the aberration seized the painter yet again. Exaltation — delirium — violence — disorientation — amnesia. Flesh disintegrates, body walls crack open: frost, fog, and mistral enter his terrain — the black fog of nothingness; the red right hand come to seize sanity. *Clang! Clang! Clang!*

Upon awakening from the fit, the Horla had no recollection of what had occurred, but Dr. Peyron reported to Theo that Vincent had consumed his paints again, which led to the doctors forbidding his access to them. Paint become painter, painter become paint. What is the nature of Vincent, and what is the Vincent of nature?

Countering the self-reproach made to his mother, to Theo, the patient exclaimed that the crowding together of all these lunatics in this old cloister is, I believe, becoming a dangerous thing in which one risks losing all the good sense one might still have retained.

Ever stalwart, the Horla vows that he is going to set to work again soon as he will be allowed, and if not, then he'll make a clean break with the asylum — it is not the subject splitting, it is not a secondary self seizing power, it is not hallucinatory nature triumphing, it is not underconsciousness taking over, it is not the subwaking self or genetic degeneration, but it is the superstitious ideas of those in the asylum that have led to this relapse.

It makes me more melancholy than I could tell you sometimes, the painter says to his brother, because there's always basically some truth in it that as a man a painter is too absorbed by what his eyes see and doesn't have enough mastery of the rest of his life. As for me, don't worry too much. I'm calmly defending myself against the illness, and I think that I'll be able to get back to work one of these days.

Full of a certain defensive brio, the patient feels more & more imprisoned & concocts plans to escape to another asylum where he can work in the fields, or to go to Brittany to join Gauguin, or to go to Paris, or to even become a businessman, or find some kind of job.

Let's take the terrible realities for what they are, he says to his brother, and if it should be necessary for me to give up painting, I think I should do so.

Art will come to an end.

Adieu, painting, *adieu.*

?

Vincent's spirits return ever quicker, Peyron retracts the diagnosis he confided to Theo, & the doctor resumes his usual treatment of bromide and nostrums.

Despite Theo warning his brother against painting and suggesting he draw instead, the painter protests, Why should I change my means of expression? I want to go on as usual, and in fact the artist already had returned to using his paints, unbeknownst to Peyron, working on another Millet copy, of new parents encouraging a child to take its first steps.

The founder of the Studio of the South also contemplates a trip to Arles, to see his dark-eyed Arlésienne, to recover his furniture, and to test if he is capable of risking a journey to Paris.

On the 18th, the Vingtistes exhibit opens at the Museum of Modern Art of Brussels and includes works by Redon, Cézanne, Signac, Toulouse-Lautrec, Sisley, and the two painters of the Studio of the South, Gauguin and Vincent van Gogh, with six of Vincent's paintings being included. Out of that exhibit, the first van Gogh painting would be sold, *The Red Vineyard.*

The next day, the painter journeys to Arles, but upon arriving, he learns that his dark-eyed Arlésienne, Madame Ginoux, has taken ill again and cannot see him, or so she says. Not long after, the artist returns to St. Paul de Mausole. To his sister, he writes with consternation of the rapid passing of life, of an urgency to make up for lost time, and of the future being more and more myste-rious, and, dear me, a little gloomy.

A few days later, the Horla is seized by another at-tack, this one far worse than the previous. Peyron writes to inform Theo that his brother is unable to work at all, and that he only replies incoherently to any questions put to him. He is even unable to read or write, and when-ever he is approached, or if one of the doctors attempts to speak with him, he recoils in horror, as if sound itself pains and disturbs him, as if even the gentlest noise were a knife. A web of exposed nerves.

Sequestered in his cell, the patient castigates himself over his sad and melancholy past, lacerating himself for the disaster of his life. It is the painter in his garden of Gethsemane, it is the painter as Prometheus, pinioned to a rock, liver eternally regenerated and torn to pieces, food for the gods to salt and feast on.

The same day Peyron conveyed his terrible news, Jo van Gogh-Bonger wrote to Vincent to inform him that not only would the baby soon be born, but that this morning Theo brought in the article in the *Mercure* and after we'd read it Wil and I talked about you for a long time — I'm so longing for your next letter, which Theo is also looking forward to.

Albert Aurier's article, "Les isolés: Vincent van Gogh," is the first public appreciation of the painter's work. In it, Aurier extols van Gogh's strange, intense, and fever-ish work and deems him a worthy successor to the 17th-century Dutch masters. He speaks too of the disquieting and disturbing display of a strange nature, that is at once entirely realistic, and yet almost supernatural, of an ex-cessive nature where everything — beings and things, shadows and lights, forms and colors — rears and rises up with a raging will to howl its own essential song in the most intense and fiercely high-pitched timber: Trees, twisted like giants in battle, proclaiming with the ges-tures of their gnarled menacing arms and with the tragic waving of their green manes their indomitable power, the pride of their musculature, their blood-hot sap, their eternal defiance of hurricane, lightning, and malevolent Nature; cypresses that expose their nightmarish, flame-like, black silhouettes, mountains that arch their backs like mammoths or rhinoceri; white and pink and golden orchards, like the idealizing dreams of virgins; squatting, passionately contorted houses, in a like manner to beings who exult, who suffer, who think; stones, terrains, bushes, grassy fields, gardens, and rivers that seem sculpted out of unknown minerals, polished, glimmering, iridescent, enchanting, flaming landscapes, like the effervescence of multicolored enamels in some alchemist's diabolical crucible; foliage that seems of ancient bronze, of new copper, of spun glass; flowerbeds that appear less like flowers than opulent jewelry fashioned from rubies, agates, onyx, emeralds, corundums, chrysoberyls, amethysts, and chalcedonies; it is the universal, mad, and blinding coruscation of things; it is matter and all of Nature frenetically contorted ... raised to the heights of exacerbation; it is form, becoming nightmare; color, becoming flame, lava and precious stone; light turning into conflagration; life, into burning fever. —

The heliomythic allegory is born: — in the midst of spams and fits, as the self fractures, as his body is undergoing sparagmos, while the volcanic fragments play out and explode, Vincent van Gogh enters the world stage.

*

Although this month is also the anniversary of Nietzsche's collapse in Torino & the end of his life as a writer, unlike the painter, the philosopher never once recovers enough to resume thinking and writing. Despite having found in Plutarch the means by which Cæsar defended himself against sickness and headache (*tremendous marches, simple way of life, uninterrupted sojourn in the open air, exertion*), the method clearly did not preserve the old artilleryman. The philosophy of the future, at least as enacted by the body that was once Nietzsche, has come to an end. Now, he suffers increasing threat of having his will and his will to power taken over not only by the selves within his corpus, or by hereditary worms closing off evolution, but by other more invidious external agents.

At one period during his stay in the Jena asylum, he was frequently visited by Julius Langbehn, author then of the newly-released *Rembrandt as Educator*, and self-proclaimed secret Emperor in possession of healing powers capable of spiritually renovating the German Empire. In his book, which Langbehn himself promoted as a bugle call to the young and aspiring German generation of his day (the representatives of the future), a book later beloved by Adolf Hitler, Langbehn declared the Dutch painter to be a figure capable of healing the Germans of having become inorganic, soulless, mechanical, inartistic, and mob-like. Speaking like a therapeutic prophet, the secret Emperor denounced intellectualism, science, and modern culture as sicknesses and in opposition praised the free individual and the true German aristocrat. The splitting up and atomization of German culture was to be replaced by a totality, by an organic whole, by a Völkisch-Christianity as represented by the peasants of Rembrandt's paintings. A great and final reformation of Deutschland was at last in sight, and Langbehn would lead the nation to it with his definitive solution.

In late 1889, just prior to the publication of his book, Langbehn visited Frau Pastor Nietzsche to convince her that he was able to heal her son. The purist prophet was seeking to establish a noble minority to counterbalance the democratizing, leveling spirit of the century. Like Nietzsche, Langbehn was an ex-soldier and veteran of the Franco-Prussian war and had fought in battles in Le Mans and Orleans, an experience that gave rise to his contempt for combat. However, unlike the old artilleryman, Langbehn denounced battle and saw nothing positive in martial vigor. When first learning of he who pronounced there will be wars the like of which have never been seen on earth before, the secret Emperor knew the philosopher of the future, who at the time was largely unknown, was a perfect specimen for his plan. Struck by his *Zarathustra*, Langbehn recognized in Nietzsche one of the geniuses of the age. When having learnt of the great Dionysian having been hit by madness and his tormented struggle with it, the secret Emperor was deeply affected. With the specimen of the wild animal Nietzsche, Langbehn could intervene against those culpable for Germany's cultural policies, to prevent the same brutalities that were exerted against Hölderlin and Mayer, and open a gate to the new glorious future that would be Germany's. Nietzsche Puppet would be the perfect foil for Langbehn and the Försters.

More than a quarter century earlier, when in the midst of studying art and archeology in Munich, Langbehn was told that his mother had suffered a mental breakdown and had been committed to an asylum. Abandoning his pursuits, Langbehn quickly fled to her, only returning to his studies much later. When learning of Nietzsche's illness, it evoked Langbehn's experience with his parent, or at least with his mythicized version of the episode, and he saw in Nietzsche a woman he could rescue. During his meeting with Frau Pastor Nietzsche, Langbehn informed the philosopher's mother of his plan, noting that he had healed his own mother of mental illness. Frau Pastor Nietzsche saw in the secret Emperor a man touching in his goodness, one of the cleverest and most worthy of respect. How could she not be moved by someone who said he could achieve what doctors could not, and who abandoned his own path to dutifully tend to his own progenitor? Later, during his daily walks with the philosopher, encounters authorized by Dr. Binswanger, Langbehn claimed that Nietzsche exulted, I believe you'll save me! To her daughter in Paraguay, Frau Pastor Nietzsche wrote, God has sent me an angel in Langbehn.

Throughout his further visits, Langbehn engaged in exorcisms of a sort with Nietzsche, believing that through judicious contradiction he could resuscitate the overworked and nerve-worn philosopher and return him to the right path. What princeps Taurinorum needed was opposition, someone to denounce the Dionysian sacred as decadent, as a symptom of decay (two years later Nordau would publish *Degeneration*, wherein Nietzsche is characterized as a madman, with flashing eyes, wild gestures, and foaming mouth, and in the 1920s, the Nazi's would adopt the term *Entartete Kunst* to characterize much modern art, but to Herr Dynamite, it is precisely the weaker nature, as the tenderer and more refined, that makes any progress possible at all — absorb infection and transform!) and of an intellect as a poison devoid of any power over the true vital force of life. The cult of Dionysos was actually in fact a cult of weakness, Langbehn declared; the healthy Homeric Greek did not know this God, only the Asiatics did. Additionally, the self-proclaimed Antichrist was to be put straight on his critique of Christianity, which the secret Emperor said was facile because Nietzsche was actually not truly acquainted with the Gospels. *Amen!*

The self-proclaimed healer announced to Nietzsche's mother that he saw her son as both a king and a child who had to be treated as the royal infant that he was. Part of his cure would involve establishing a regal household that would revolve around Nietzsche. The philosopher would be brought to Dresden, Langbehn himself would play the role of the major-domo, a mental specialist was to assist him as expert, the mother would masquerade as a nurse, and three or four attendants would complete the royal retinue. Pirandello's *Enrico IV* avant le lettre. All the staging of 'Nietzsche' required was capital, but Langbehn was confident that he could secure it. The winds would however dismantle this plot — like a dog whose senses could not be fooled, the madman smelled something bad from afar. One day, at the asylum, after committing some impertinence against 'Nietzsche,' the philosopher exploded in a violent rage, overturned a table, and rushed from the room with clenched fists shouting for the attendant. Langbehn, seemingly bereft of his great healing powers, quietly departed.

Returning with a new, far more insidious idea, the secret Emperor informed Nietzsche's mother that his cure could only be accomplished if he were given legal control of the philosopher. The healer noted that the Jena clinic was not to be trusted. It was a tyrannical establishment under which the great King Nietzsche suffered. He is treated like a demoralized professor, who had gone to pieces and become insane in Italy, or as a prisoner and convict. Seeking to gain Queen Elisabeth Förster's support, Langbehn even denounced Overbeck to the now sole leader of Nueva Germania, falsely accusing Nietzsche's close friend of obscuring his true character. To gain guardianship over Nietzsche Puppet, Langbehn drew up this document for his mother to sign:

The undersigned pledges hereby herself, in the case the legal guardianship of her son, Friedrich Nietzsche, passes over into the hands of Dr. Julius Langbehn, to avoid every oral and written communication with the above-mentioned during the period of this guardianship. She pledges herself further to obey the instructions of Dr. Langbehn in regard to an intended personal visits to her son during this-same period, in particular to inform him beforehand of the time of her proposed arrival and departure. The undersigned will, of course, be permitted to visit her son at any time under the above conditions, providing that his health or his mental state does not render this inadvisable.

This grand conspiracy did not however come to be. Through the intercession of Overbeck, Nietzsche's mother eventually freed herself of the secret Emperor's influence and never signed the document, safeguarding the philosopher from Langbehn's designs. Nietzsche Puppet was secure for the time being, at least from one Völkisch Christian with plans for the purification and reformation of Deutschland, if not the purification & reformation of Nietzsche.

Thereafter, the savior of Germany never returned, and the country did not benefit from his spiritual beneficence, at least not then. Yet, Langbehn's own mother did not in fact benefit from his healing powers, for her condition, which some thought to be psychosis or schizophrenia, with a persecution mania focused on her children, remained unchanged during her time in the asylum and till her end but then, no prophet is accepted in his own country, or by his own mother...

In 1900, following the death of whatever was left of Nietzsche, the so-called healer wrote to Bishop Keppler noting that, one must not confuse Nietzsche with his imitators and apostles. I think it possible and even probable that if he had lived longer he would have changed his opinion of Christianity just as he changed his opinion of Wagner. ... He was very grateful to me for instruction as well as for kindness. He received both from me, and once he literally kissed the hem of my garment in return. This was somewhat Byzantine and exaggerated, but shows how far removed he was personally from the Genghis Khan type that he so often portrayed. One must know people to offer an opinion on them. One must never judge oneself—or others—according to universal opinion 'Atheists' like Shelley and 'Anti-Christs' like Nietzsche are simple, truant schoolboys who must be brought back into the fold. With regard to Nietzsche, I actually had this intention, but circumstances were stronger than I. Nietzsche's error—his so-called philosophy, which is merely mental and spiritual suicide—are strikingly reminiscent of the suicides of overworked schoolboys today. In such cases one should pity and not condemn... My verdict on Nietzsche the man is based on personal impressions of him. I have never met a more guileless and simple person among educated people. But his writings—with the exception of the rather weird *Zarathustra*—I detest if possible even more than you do. I literally cannot read one page of them without feeling physically ill. I consider him in short a pure spirit of whom the devil has taken possession. . . . I studied the Nietzsche case intensively because it is typical of my whole policy that is based on bold thoroughness and a childlike faith in God. In Nietzsche I have lost a brother. God have mercy on his poor soul. May I beg you to commend him to God's charity—because he was my brother?

What a triumph if the Church could claim Nietzsche!

This world is the will to power — and nothing besides! And you yourselves are also this will to power — and nothing besides! Yes, you altruists, too, who create secondary values for yourselves in the service of other egoisms! But altruism is only a detour to the preservation of one's own feeling of vitality & value!

*

Throughout the remainder of the month, the doctors noted improvements in Nietzsche's health, speaking also of his always bowing very politely to the doctors. And on 21 January, Peter Gast thought his friend's sanity was possibly returning, that his madness was a mere simulation. The mask of Dionysos? Enrico the IV undisguised? Or did Langbehn in some way actually heal Nietzsche? Or did Nietzsche, once again, through convalescence, cure himself? Is his germ plasm evolving independently of all perturbations, free of the endogenous powers of the organism? Did his Cæsarean regimen actually preserve him?

I would almost like to say, Gast said, that Nietzsche's mental disturbance consists only of an accentuation of the humorous side he formerly displayed, when among friends in an intimate circle. We spoke much of Venice and what was very surprising was that he had, of all things, remembered many of my more burlesque observations. —

Was Herr Dynamite to return, to emerge from his madness, as did the Horla over 1230 kms away in St. Rémy? Did the painter's recoveries not signal the possibility that the philosopher could also possibly recover and continue philosophizing again? Could 'Nietzsche' regain his will? Could that body regain itself? Since 'he' was all the names in history, could Nietzsche Puppet become Herr Dynamite again, or some other self within his panoply of ever recurring selves? Was not whoever 'he' was just a fortuitous spin of the Ferris wheel of the soul? Or no? If perchance it was simulated madness, could not 'Nietzsche' have finally become genuinely 'mad'?

If the hermit of Sils Maria's disturbance was in fact but a mere accentuation of his Aristophanic nature, Gast doubted that his friend would benefit from being awakened from his delirium, that his madness was a necessary mask between himself and the real world, a mask that he could perhaps not remove, and which emerged against 'his' will. Nietzsche he said would be just about as grateful to his rescuers as somebody who has jumped into the water to drown himself and has been pulled out by some fool of a coastguard.

If Nietzsche's mother first saw Langbehn as some heavenly-sent angel, perhaps now she saw him more as a fool treading where divine messengers would not. Save the Anti-Christ — would that not have been for him to have become what he was not? Had he not been devoid of will, would he not have resisted the cowardly death and enacted a free one, one that was not a matter of chance or surprise? The sick man, he once said, is a parasite of society. In certain cases it is indecent to go on living. To continue to vegetate in a state of cowardly dependence upon doctors and special treatments, once the meaning of life, the right to life, has been lost, ought to be regarded with the greatest contempt by society. In a state of sanity, would not Nietzsche have gone the way of a samurai? Seppuku in Torino?

When Gast received the score to his opera *The Se-cret Marriage* and showed it to he who preferred sing-ing to writing, the patient was exultant. He picked up the four long strips of sheet music again and again, Gast wrote to Fuchs, sang everything correctly, conducted and laughed aloud, and seized my hand as though he were a drowning man clutching his rescuer. He often repeated: 'Greetings to Fuchs when you write to him! He did that very well! Greet him from me also!' He was much better and more serious today than yesterday when he talked so much in an undertone, part of the time looking into space. But after an hour of company he is already quiet and exhausted.

And so moves Herr Dynamite, from music to silence to enervation, like one brooding in the depths amongst ice, like Rodin's *Thinker* contemplating eternity, the son of the coming century who played out in his very body the history of the world and its wars.

We ourselves, we free spirits, are a transvaluation of values, an *embodied* declaration of war on and victory over all old concepts...

JENA

1230 km from St. Rémy

somatic condition; Tristan-like sensitiveness!

1 February 1890

Jena Medical Report

Speaks somewhat more coherently. Somatic condition unchanged.
Weight 138 lbs.

*

Letter from Peter Gast, a friend of the patient:

Today I am enormously strengthened in my belief that we shall
have our Nietzsche back again. Yesterday and today he was splendid! Yesterday I was upstairs in the ward among the totally insane where Nietzsche usually sits (visitors are not really allowed
there at all); from there we proceeded to the music room. I wanted to sit down at the piano and gave Nietzsche the bag with the
six doughnuts I bring him every day, but he said: No, dear friend,
I do not want to get sticky fingers now, because I want to play a
little first. Then he sat down at the instrument and improvised.

Oh, if you had been listening! Not one wrong note! Interwoven tones of Tristan-like sensitiveness! *Pianissimi* alternating
with the fanfares of trumpets and the sonorous sound of trom-
bones, Beethoven-like profundity and jubilant songs rising above
it, then again reveries and dreams — it beggars description! Oh,
for a phonograph! The effect upon his cerebral system was quite
powerful; he was a different man after it! Excellent! To-day he
was reading a book that Naumann sent me in which Nietzsche
himself is often quoted; that, too, made him wonderfully reasonable. His mother is coming next Sunday; we shall consider the
advisability of removing him. It must be done soon, at all costs.
He himself is asking: Well, when are we going to Naumburg?

ST. RÉMY

1230 km from Jena

You're a father at last; I was extremely surprised by the article on my paintings; to guide not only me but also the other Impressionists; trying to retain a certain calm, and if possible presence of mind; Gauguin proposed founding a studio in his name; I have scruples of conscience; I'm a little anxious about a woman friend who is still ill; I'm personally feeling completely well today

1 February 1890

My dear Theo,

Today I've just received your good news that you're a father at last, that the most critical moment has passed for Jo, finally that the little one is well. It does me, too, more good and gives me more pleasure than I could express in words. Bravo — and how pleased Mother is going to be. I also received a quite long and very serene letter from her the day before yesterday. Finally what I've certainly hoped for so much for a long time has happened. No need to tell you that I've often thought of the two of you the past few days, and it touched me greatly that Jo still had the kindness to write to me the night before. How brave and calm she is in her danger, that touched me greatly. Well this contributes a great deal to making me forget these last few days when I was ill, then I no longer know where I am and my mind wanders.

I was extremely surprised by the article on my paintings that you sent me, no need to tell you that I hope to go on thinking that I don't paint like that, but rather I do see from it how I ought to paint. For the article is quite right in the sense that it indicates the gap to be filled, and I think that basically the writer writes it rather to guide not only me but also the other Impressionists, and even rather to make the breach in the right place. So he proposes a collective self, as ideal for the others as it is to me. He tells me simply that there's something good here and there, if you like, in my very imperfect work as well, and there's the consolatory side which I appreciate and which I hope I'm grateful for. Only it must be understood that I don't have a strong enough back to carry out a job like that, and by concentrating the article on me, no need to tell you how I feel mired in flattery, and in my opinion it's as exaggerated as what a certain article by Isaäcson said on your account about you, that at present artists declined to argue, and that a serious movement was silently being created in the little shop on boulevard Montmartre. I admit that it's difficult to say, to express oneself otherwise — just as one can't paint as one sees — and it's therefore not to criticize Isaäcson's boldness or that of the other critic, but as regards us, well, we're *posing* a little for THE *model*, and my word, that's a duty and a job like any other. So if you or I were to gain some reputation or other, it's a matter of trying to retain a certain calm, and if possible presence of mind. Why not say, WITH MORE REASON, what he says about my sunflowers about Quost's magnificent and so-complete Hollyhocks and about his yellow irises, about Jeannin's splendid peonies? And you, like me, foresee that being praised must have its other side, its reverse of the coin. But gladly I'm very grateful for the article, or rather "glad at heart," as the revue song has it, since one can need it as one can truly need a medal. Then an article like that has its own merit as a critical work of art, as such I consider it worthy of respect, and the writer *must* use exalted tones, synthesize his conclusions *&c.*

But right from the start we must think of not putting your young family *too much* into the artistic environment. Old Goupil ran his household well in the Paris undergrowth, and I think that you'll still think of him very often. Things have changed so much, for today his cold aloofness would be shocking, but his strength to weather so many storms, that though was something.

Gauguin proposed, very vaguely it's true, founding a studio in his name, he, De Haan and I, but said that first he's pursuing his Tonkin project vigorously, and he appears to have cooled about continuing to paint, I don't know exactly why. And he's the sort of man who would scarper to Tonkin, indeed, he has a certain need for expansion and finds the artist's life — and to an extent he's right — a mean one. With his experiences of several journeys, what can one say to him? So I hope that he'll feel that you and I are indeed his friends without counting on us too much, which he doesn't anyway. He writes with a lot of reserve, more serious than the other year. I've just written a line to Russell once again to remind him about Gauguin a little, for I know that Russell is very serious and strong as a man. And if I got back together with G., then we'd have need of Russell. Gauguin and Russell are people with a rustic background; wild no, but with a certain innate gentleness of the far-off fields, probably much more than you or I, that's how I find them.

One must — it is true — believe in it a little from time to time in order to see it. If, for myself, I wanted to continue, let's call it TRANSLATING certain pages of Millet, then in order to prevent people, not criticizing me, I couldn't care about that, but bothering or obstructing me under the pretext that I'm manufacturing copies — then among the artists I need people like Russell or Gauguin to carry this task to a successful conclusion, to make something serious of it. To do the things by Millet that you sent, for example, the choice of which I consider completely right — I have scruples of conscience, and I took the pile of photographs and I sent them unhesitatingly to Russell so that I shouldn't see them again until I'd thought long and hard about it. I don't want to do it before first having heard something of your opinion, then also that of certain others on those that you'll soon receive. Without that I'd have scruples of conscience, a fear that it might be plagiarism. And not now, but in a few months, I'll try to get Russell's honest opinion about the usefulness of the thing. In any case, Russell *has outbursts*, he gets angry, he says something true, and that's what I need sometimes. You know that I found the Virgin so dazzling *that I didn't dare look*. Immediately I felt a — 'not yet.' Now the illness makes me very sensitive, and for the moment I don't feel capable of continuing these 'translations' when it would involve such masterpieces. I'm stopping with the sower, which is in progress and isn't coming along as would be desirable. However, being ill, I thought a lot about continuing this work, and that when I do it I do it calmly, you'll see it soon when I send the five or 6 finished canvases. I hope that Mr. Lauzet will come; I very much want to make his acquaintance. I trust in his opinion when he says that it's Provence, there he touches on the difficulty, and like the other fellow he points out a thing to be done rather than one done. The landscapes with the cypresses! Ah, that wouldn't be easy. Aurier feels it too when he says that even black is a color, and about their flame-like aspect. I'm thinking of it but I don't dare do it either, and say like Isaäcson, who is cautious, that I don't yet feel that we've reached that point. It requires a certain dose of inspiration, a ray from on high that doesn't belong to us, to do beautiful things. When I'd done those sunflowers I was seeking the contrary and yet the equivalent, and I said, it's the cypress. I'm stopping there — I'm a little anxious about a woman friend who is still ill, it seems, & to whom I'd like to go, she's the one whose portrait I did in yellow and black, and she had changed so much. It's nervous crises and the complications of a premature change of life, very difficult in short. She looked like an old grandfather last time. I had promised to come back in a fortnight and was taken ill again myself.

Anyway, for me the good news you've told me and that article and a heap of things mean that I'm personally feeling completely well today.

Now in thought I remain with you all as I finish my letter. May Jo long remain for us all that she is. Now as for the little one, why then don't you call him Theo in memory of our father, that would certainly give me so much pleasure. Handshake.

Ever yours,
Vincent

JENA

1230 km from St. Rémy

the aphorist who no longer writes

[9 February 1890]

[Dear —————]

[Nietzsche]

ST. RÉMY

1230 km from Jena

I feel that you create colors with your words; I feel ill at ease; Monticelli's artistic temperament is exactly that of the author of the Decameron; a good painting should be the equivalent of a good deed; the future 'painting of the tropics'; sectarian thinking; the emotions that take hold of me in the face of nature

9 February 1890

Dear Mr. Aurier,

Thank you very much for your article in the *Mercure de France*, which greatly surprised me. I like it very much as a work of art in itself, I feel that you create colors with your words; anyway I rediscover my canvases in your article, but better than they really are — richer, more significant. However, I feel ill at ease when I reflect that what you say should be applied to others rather than to me. For example, to Monticelli above all. Speaking of "he is — as far as I know — the only painter who perceives the coloration of things with such intensity, with such a metallic, gem-like quality" — if you will please go and see a particular bouquet by Monticelli at my brother's place — bouquet in white, forget-me-not blue and orange — then you will feel what I mean. But for a long time the best, the most remarkable Monticellis, have been in Scotland, in England. In a museum in the north however — the one in Lille I think, there must still be a marvel by him, far richer and certainly no less French than Watteau's *Departure for Cythera*. At present Mr. Lauzet is in the process of reproducing around 30 Monticellis. Here you have it, as far as I know there is no colorist who comes so straight and directly from Delacroix; and yet it is likely, in my opinion, that Monticelli only had Delacroix's color theories at second hand; in particular he had them from Diaz and Ziem. It seems to me that his, Monticelli's, artistic temperament is exactly that of the author of the *Decameron* — Boccaccio — a melancholy man, an unhappy, rather resigned man, seeing high society's party pass by, the lovers of his day, painting them, analyzing them, he — the outcast. Oh! He does not *imitate* Boccaccio any more than Henri Leys imitated the primitives. Well, this was to say that things seem to have strayed onto my name that you would do better to say of Monticelli, to whom I owe a great deal. Next I owe a great deal to Paul Gauguin, with whom I worked for a few months in Arles, and whom, besides, I already knew in Paris.

Gauguin, that curious artist, that stranger whose bearing and gaze vaguely recall Rembrandt's *Portrait of a Man* in the La

Caze gallery, that friend who likes to make one feel that a good painting should be the equivalent of a good deed, not that he says so, but anyway it is difficult to spend time with him without thinking of a certain moral responsibility. A few days before we parted, when illness forced me to enter an asylum, I tried to paint "his empty place."

It is a study of his armchair of dark, red-brown wood, the seat of greenish straw, and in the absent person's place, a lighted candlestick and some modern novels. If you have the opportunity, as a memento of him, please go and look a little at this study again, which is entirely in broken tones of green and red. You may perhaps then realize that your article would have been more accurate and — it would seem to me — thus more powerful — if in dealing with the question of the future "painting of the trop-ics" and the question of color, you had done justice to Gauguin and Monticelli before talking about me. For the share that falls or will fall to me will remain, I assure you, very secondary.

And then, I would also have something else to ask of you. Supposing that the two canvases of sunflowers that are presently at the Vingtistes have certain qualities of color, and then also that they express an idea symbolizing 'gratitude.' Is this any different from so many paintings of flowers that are more skillfully painted and which people do not yet sufficiently appreciate, père Quost's *Hollyhocks*, *Yellow Irises*? The magnificent bouquets of peonies that Jeannin produces in abundance? You see, it seems to me so difficult to separate Impressionism from other things, I cannot see the point of so much sectarian thinking as we have seen these last few years, but I fear its absurdity.

And, in closing, I declare that I do not understand that *you* spoke of Meissonier's infamies. It is perhaps from that excellent fellow Mauve that I have inherited a boundless admiration for Meissonier; Mauve was endless in his praise for Troyon and Meissonier — a strange combination.

This is to draw your attention to how much people abroad admire, without attaching the slightest importance to what unfortunately so often divides artists in France. What Mauve often repeated was something like this, "if you want to do color you must also know how to draw a fireside or an interior like Meissonier."

I shall add a study of cypresses for you to the next consignment I send to my brother, if you will do me the pleasure of accepting it as a memento of your article. I am still working on it at the moment, wanting to put in a small figure. The cypress is so characteristic of the landscape of Provence, and you sensed it when saying: "even the color black." Until now I have not been able to do them as I feel it; in my case the emotions that take hold of me in the face of nature go as far as fainting, and then the result is a fortnight during which I am incapable of working. However, before leaving here, I am planning to return to the fray to attack the cypresses. The study I have intended for you depicts a group of them in the corner of a wheatfield on a summer's day when the mistral is blowing. It is therefore the note of a certain blackness enveloped in blue moving in great circulating currents of air, and the vermilion of the poppies contrasts with the black note.

You will see that this constitutes more or less the combination of tones of those pretty Scottish checked cloths: green, blue, red, yellow, black, which once appeared so charming to you as they did to me, and which alas one scarcely sees any more these days.

In the meantime, dear sir, please accept my grateful thanks for your article. If I were to come to Paris in the spring I shall certainly not fail to come & thank you in person.

Vincent van Gogh

When the study I send you is dry right through, also in the impasto, which will not be the case for a year — I should think you would do well to give it a good coat of varnish. And between times it should be washed several times with plenty of water to get out the oil completely. This study is painted in full Prussian blue, that color about which people say so many bad things and which nevertheless Delacroix used so much. I think that once the Prussian blue tones are really dry, by varnishing you will obtain the dark, the very dark tones needed to bring out the different dark greens.

I do not quite know how this study should be framed, but as I really want it to make one think of those dear Scottish fabrics, I have noticed that a very simple flat frame, *bright orange lead*, creates the desired effect with the blues of the background and the dark greens of the trees. Without this there would perhaps not be enough red in the canvas, & the upper part would appear a little cold.

JENA

1230 km from St. Rémy

music

[12 February 1890]

The monster, he who said he is not a person at all, plays the piano.

ST. RÉMY

1230 km from Jena

Jo and the newborn are well; Gauguin wrote to me that he'd exhibited in Denmark; a painter must work really just as hard as a shoemaker; to try & recover what the paint- ings cost; emerging from reality more and making a kind of tonal music with color; the illness that still continues to worry me; if we put Gauguin's plan into practice; we could still work here together

12 February 1890

My dear Theo,

I was in the middle of writing to you to send you the reply for Mr. Aurier when your letter arrived. Am very pleased that Jo and the newborn are well and that she expects to be able to get up in a few days from now. Then what you write about our sister also interests me a great deal. I consider that she was lucky to see Degas at his home. I still think that she would above all make a good doctor's wife. Anyway, one can't exactly force these things, nevertheless it's good to have one's eyes open if the opportunity were to present itself.

And so Gauguin has come back to Paris — I'm going to copy my reply to Mr. Aurier to send it to him, and you can let him read the article from the *Mercure*. For really I consider that one should say things like that about Gauguin, *&* about me nothing except very secondarily.

Gauguin wrote to me that he'd exhibited in Denmark and that this exhibition had been very successful. To me it seems a shame that he didn't continue here a bit longer. The two of us together would have worked better than myself all alone this year. And at present we'd have a little cottage of our own to stay in and work, and could even accommodate others.

Did you notice in that newspaper you sent me an article on the fruitfulness of certain artists. Of Corot, Rousseau, Dupré *&c.*; do you remember how many times when Reid was there that we talked about that, even of the *necessity* to produce a lot.

And that shortly after I came to Paris I said to you that before I had two hundred canvases I wouldn't be able to do anything. What would appear to some people to be working too fast is in reality completely the ordinary run of things, the normal state of regular production, considering that a painter must work really just as hard as a shoemaker, for example.

Would it not be a good idea to send Reid, and perhaps also Tersteeg, or rather C.M., a copy of Aurier's article?

The thing is that it seems to me that we ought to take advantage of it to try to place something in Scotland, either now or later.

I think you'll like the canvas for Mr. Aurier, it's in terribly thick impasto & worked like certain Monticellis, I've kept it for almost a year.

But I consider that I must try to give him something good for that article, which is in itself a very artistic thing; and it really serves us well for the day when we, like everyone, will be obliged to try and recover what the paintings cost.

Everything beyond that leaves me quite cold, but recovering the money it costs to produce, that's the very condition of being able to continue.

For the Impressionists' exhibition in March I hope to send you a few more canvases that are drying at the moment. If they didn't arrive in time you would have to make a choice from those that are at père Tanguy's.

I've tried to copy Daumier's *Drinkers* and Doré's *Penitentiary*, it's very difficult. In the next few days I hope to begin on Delacroix's *Good Samaritan* and Millet's *Woodcutter*.

Aurier's article would encourage me, if I dared let myself go, to risk emerging from reality more and making a kind of tonal music with color, as some Monticellis are. But the truth is so dear to me, *trying to create something true* also, anyway I think, I think I still prefer to be a shoemaker than to be a musician, with colors.

In any event, trying to remain true is perhaps a remedy to combat the illness that still continues to worry me. Lately my health is quite good, however, and I'd dare to believe that if I were to spend a while with you that would have a lot of effect upon me to counteract the influence that the company I have here necessarily exerts. But it seems to me that there's no hurry about this, and that we must consider calmly if this is the moment to spend money on the journey. Perhaps by sacrificing the journey one could be useful to Gauguin or Lauzet.

A few days ago I bought a suit that cost me 35 francs, I must pay for it toward the end of March. With this I'll have sufficient for the year, for when I came here I also bought a suit for around 35 francs, and it has served me all year. But I'll need a pair of shoes and a few pairs of drawers in March as well.

All things considered, life here isn't very expensive, I think that in the north one would spend rather more.

And that's why — even if I came to you for a while — the best policy might still be to continue the work here. I don't know — and either is good to me — but we mustn't hurry to move.

And don't you think that in Antwerp, if we put Gauguin's plan into practice, one would have to maintain a certain rank, furnish a studio, in short do as the majority of established Dutch painters do? It's not as simple as it appears, and would fear for him as well as for myself a regular siege by the established artists, and he would have the same story as he had before in Denmark.

Anyway, we'd have to begin to say to ourselves that it's still through the same procedure that the established painters can cause troubles for adventurers, as we'd be in Antwerp, and even oblige them to decamp. And as for the dealers there, we mustn't count on them at all.

The academy there is better, and they work more vigorously there than in Paris. And then Gauguin is still in Paris at the moment, his reputation is holding up there, and if he leaves for Antwerp he could find that it's rather difficult to *come back* to Paris. Going to Antwerp I would fear for Gauguin rather than for myself, for naturally I can get by in Flemish, I resume the studies of peasants I began before and abandoned with much regret — there's no need to tell you that I have a great love of the Kempen. But I foresee that for him the battle could be very tough. I think that you'll tell him the pros and cons of this absolutely as I would tell him, I'll write to him one of these days, especially to send him the reply to Mr. Aurier's article, and I'd think that if he wanted we could still work here together if his steps to find a position were to come to nothing. But he's skillful, and perhaps he'll come through it in Paris itself, and if he holds on there for his reputation he does well, for he always has this, that he was the first one of all to work in the heart of a tropical land. And one will necessarily come back to that matter. Above all, give him my warm regards, and if he wants he can take the repetitions of the *Sunflowers* and the repetition of the *Berceuse* in exchange for something of his that would give you pleasure.

If I came to Paris I would have to rework several canvases done in the beginning here, I wouldn't have any lack of work then. Warm regards to Jo, and good handshake in thought.

Ever yours,
Vincent.

Please send the enclosed letter to Mr. Aurier after you've read it.

JENA

1230 km from St. Rémy

When he tried to hit dogs or even people; our association was now entirely based upon the past; confused information; no memory of his immediate past; communicating from two different planets; he imagined his recovery to be close at hand; losing the spirit in realms of fantasy; as docile as a child

A third person, a perfect stranger who might have come upon us together would have noticed hardly anything strange in Nietzsche's behavior, save for one or two oddities — at table or outside in the street when he tried to hit dogs or even people who suddenly appeared. Outwardly we were two old friends, and I alone knew that our association was now entirely based upon the past. Nietzsche had greeted me at once on our first meeting in his mother's home as though nothing had undermined our old friendship and so it remained till my departure from Jena. Nietzsche's loquacity almost grew during our conversations, but these talks were based almost entirely on events that occurred before insanity befell him. There was no lack of attempts on my part to direct his thoughts to things that had occurred lately, such as his association with Dr. Langbehn, which had broken off so recently, and which interested me greatly. In vain. Nietzsche — without my instigation — sometimes imparted confused information as to his present affairs, about his acquaintances in the asylum, for example, of which he appeared to have no memory of his immediate past and sometimes indeed to avoid it deliberately — he pretended scarcely to have known Dr. Langbehn. Our talks, confidential as of old, were confined almost entirely to the past that lay behind the moment when insanity had come upon him. . . . In these circumstances, our association — it lasted for three days — was as though we had been communicating from two different planets. I was on the old one that we had inhabited together up to the outbreak of his madness, Nietzsche was on the new one. We could only talk about matters that occurred during the earlier period and even of these Nietzsche had nothing but fragmentary memories. But within the limit of these altered conditions we were as though nothing had happened between us, the same friends as before. As an example, I will only mention the suggestion that he should return to his position at Basel. He referred to it constantly, for he imagined his recovery to be close at hand. This was to me a particularly significant sign of his mental disintegration when I recalled what stress he had laid upon leaving that position for years past, in the days when he was in full health! Then it struck me as noticeable he referred chiefly to our events in his life, particularly to persons with whom he had been associated (Wagner, etc.), whereas he seldom referred to his literary work and to the plans still unrealized which had been the absorbing interest of his last lucid days. Not that these Jena conversations entirely lacked those flashes of brilliancy which recalled his highest inspirations — in this respect there was much that even surprised me at the time but, on the whole, such moments had grown very rare, and I had the impression that Nietzsche's spirit could only be awakened occasionally without losing itself in realms of fantasy, whereas in other respects I discerned a 'calming down' to the point of depression or weariness in his behavior. Nor did Nietzsche display any trace of the opposition and resistance he used to show at Torino. He was as docile as a child when reproved for the oddities already mentioned, particularly as his thoughts could be immediately transferred from one object to another and everybody with whom he came into contact could sway them. I was particularly struck by the fact that, contrary to my fears which were based on past experience, he allowed himself to be taken back to the asylum on our return from our walks in the evenings without the slightest difficulty.

Franz Overbeck

INTERVAL: JENA & ST. RÉMY

To be mad, or not to be mad, is that the question?
St. Rémy →← Jena: 1230 km distance

February–March 1890

Herr Friedrich Nietzsche, purveyor of the will to power, inventor of the Übermensch, artist of self-overcoming, descendant (self-proclaimed) of Polish nobility (Niëzky!), never recovers to write and philosophize again but continues his descending tarantella, whereas Vincent continues to return from each bout of madness, from each spell of delirium, from each fall into vertigo. Is Vincent the stronger, more resolute figure, or is Niëzky? Can one even speak of or measure strength in such terms? Can one determine whose madness is more extreme? Whose nervous system more susceptible to havoc? Whose cells more prone to destruction, or radical plasticity? Is there greater strength in recovering from madness, or in remaining in it, in going to its furthest threshold, in living out the full spectrum of its lifespan? To be mad, or not to be mad, is that the question? And what would Nietzsche have made of the painter had they crossed paths, before crossing their Rubicons, and what would Vincent have made of the philosopher? There are no major events, discoveries, or inventions at this time in history — Nietzsche & Vincent are the major events. Nietzsche & Vincent are the discoveries. Nietzsche & Vincent are the inventions. Nietzsche & Vincent are the epochal lightning rods. Nietzsche & Vincent are the tsunamis, the earthquakes, the galaxies, the exploding nebulæ, the soil-enriching magma from the depths of the earth.

It was the start of a new decade, the final 10 years of the 19ᵗʰ century, and so the denouement of one age and the prelude of another. The dawn of the future, of 1900, of the 20ᵗʰ century: — the leap from horses and carriages and photography to airplanes and cinema, from gaslight and Newton's law of universal gravitation to the speed of light and the theory of relativity — all space and time would forever after be different, as would all philosophy and painting, and so life itself.

While Bernard once noted that Vincent believed he was some kind of Christ, a God, a being from the other side, spell after spell of madness tempered the painter's incendiary soul. If the once-inflamed artist were seeking in different ways to refute Aurier's prophetic and fevered analysis of him and his work, reducing its visionary status, in contrast, time, history, and the coming century would confirm and reinforce Aurier's view and his recognizing in Vincent an ever-beckoning future. To the rising poet and critic, Vincent's art was at once entirely realistic and yet almost supernatural, of an excessive nature where everything — beings and things, shadows and lights, forms and colors — rears and rises up with a raging will to howl its own essential song in the most intense and fiercely high-pitched timbre. In Vincent, he knew that leaps and bounds had been taken, that classical, traditional conceptions of art had been superseded by light years. Just as Baudelaire gave birth to a new poetics, Vincent van Gogh had given birth to a new visual æsthetics. Like Nietzsche recognizing the illusory nature of reality, and later, physicists declaring the universe to be a hologram, Vincent unveiled reality, realized that the true world was a fable, saw reality as a sorceress whose imagery could only be deciphered through visionary faculties. What characterizes his work as a whole, Aurier announced, is its excess, its excess of strength, of nervousness, its violence of expression, thereby enumerating a litany of characteristics of a Dionysian nature, of a painter whose loyalty to the earth and the cosmos led to its opening its secrets to him. The splendid ability of the great genius, Nietzsche observed, for which even eternal suffering is a slight price, the stern pride of the artist — that is the content and soul of Aeschylus' poem, while Sophocles in his *Oedipus* sounds as a prelude the holy man's song of triumph. In Vincent's paintings, we have another holy man's song of triumph, and in Vincent himself, a posthumous figure who signals the coming age, a figure who presages new forms of vision and color, one who breaks from classical optics and opens the eye of Marsyas. To Nietzsche, the guardians of classical beauty were seeking nothing but mendacious cloaks for their own coarseness, an æsthetical pretext for their own insensitive sobriety. Van Gogh, Aurier pronounced, is a hyper-æsthetic who perceives with abnormal, perhaps even painful, intensities, the imperceptible and secret characters of lines and of forms, but even more so the colors, the lights, the nuances invisible to healthy pupils, the magickal irrisations of shadows.

There was something volcanic in the painter, and Aurier characterized him as a terrible and demented genius, often sublime, sometimes grotesque, always at the brink of the pathological. It was the age of Prado and of Chambige, of Baudelaire's ascendancy (the birth of Marsyan art, the birth of the *de-formed* œuvre) and of the voyant letters of Rimbaud and his delirious journey to Africa, of the birth of Artaud, and of Mallarmé throwing dice and Nietzsche's mad screeds to emperors and princes, of his pronouncement that in the next years the world would be turned upside down — when the old God will have abdicated, he, Nietzsche, the Philosopher of Dionysos, would be ready to rule the world. This world is the will to power — and nothing besides! And you yourselves are also this will to power — and nothing besides! Mother, where is my ham? I am the tyrant of Torino, send me the large sausages!

Earlier, in April 1887, while Vincent was in Paris painting *Montmartre: Windmills & Allotments*, Nietzsche's journey from Nizza to Lago Maggiore was interrupted by a violent outbreak of migraine, like a windmill spinning out of control and nearly rending its tower to pieces. In Laveno, the philosopher suffered a terrible, freezing night with constant vomiting. Then, from Cannobio, Villa Badia, on 14 April, after two more days of his illness repeating, fearing that death would soon overtake him — and I do not, he said, withhold an ever deeper longing for death — the philosopher began revising and re-editing his older writings to insure that something of himself remained, a piece of culture that for the time being could not be replaced by anything else. This winter, he wrote Franz Overbeck, I surveyed European literature in order to be able to say that my philosophical position is by far the most independent. I am, the dynamitic one said, the holder of a millennial heritage. The Europe of today does not as much as suspect the terrible nature of those decisions around which my whole being revolves nor to what problematic wheel I am bound — and that a catastrophe is preparing, my catastrophe, the name of which I know but will not utter.

Over a year later, in December 1888, just 18 days before his collapse, the old artilleryman wrote to Gast, I now understand why I need not precipitate this tragic catastrophe of my existence that begins with *Ecce Homo*.

Two weeks afterward, he wrote to Köselitz, informing him that in November he was present at the funeral of old Antonelli, the architect who constructed the philosopher's most beloved synagogue, the building that symbolized his *Zarathustra*. Antonelli lived, Nietzsche said, just until *Ecce Homo*, the book, was finished. The book and the person as well.

Questo è.

Nietzsche then was no more; 'he' knew that 'his' (that main configuration of selves that we know to be someone, *something*, called Nietzsche) end had come while 'he' was still alive, but his dominion had already been prepared — Dionysos was ready to usurp the Christ;

a reformed & united Europe could be born. The thyrsus, not the cross, could be civilization's new guiding symbol. Enter the maenads. Incipit comoedia. *All hail paganism!*

When Aurier published in *L'Art Moderne* a truncated version of his original article to coincide with the opening of the Vingtistes exhibit, it brought Vincent's work ever more to the world forefront. Within two years, Aurier would be dead, but in the climate of the burgeoning century, his essay hit the art world like a lightning bolt and Vincent, despite his protests and self-effacement, became a guiding beacon of the new age. In some way, he was the embodiment of Claude Lentier, the mad genius Zola envisioned in his *Masterpiece*. If his work still disturbed classicist critics who remained oblivious to the times and continued to prize Salon conventions, younger avant-garde artists exulted over his incandescent imagery and the pathway he had broken open. Kirchner, Heckel, Beckman, Dix and others were on the horizon. Although some artists derided Vincent's work, it provoked a furor, and while the painter was perhaps anxious before the public exposure of his creations in such provocative terms, once stating that success is the worst thing that can happen in a painter's life (do not forget the necessity of not being understood, of the need to protect oneself from those whom one does not want to communicate with — as Strindberg said to Herr Dynamite: *The moment you are known and understood, your stature will be diminished!*), it was also a sign of recognition of everything that he had sought to achieve, of his dream of the Studio of the South, and mostly, of Theo's loyal support of him over the past decade. If the grander utopic ventures themselves had crashed, the paintings did not — the work survived the deluge, the work survived the shipwreck, the work surpassed the suffering, the violence, the madness. Before all who doubted, before the scoffing villagers and those who lacked the ability to recognize what Vincent had achieved, it was a triumph, an apotheosis of sorts, a vindication of every sacrifice both brothers had made throughout their lives. As Nietzsche noted in *The Birth of Tragedy*, the best and highest possession mankind can acquire is obtained by sacrilege and must be paid for with consequences that involve the whole flood of sufferings and sorrows with which the offended divinities have to afflict the nobly aspiring race of men.

In the midst of Vincent's public recognition and ascension, Gauguin had proposed to him that they set up a studio in Antwerp, arguing that Impressionism will not be truly accepted in France until it has returned from abroad. Alternatively, Vincent suggested that Gauguin come back down south, then wrote to Theo that they could have a little house of their own to live and work in, and could even put others up, thinking once more of an extended colony of artists. Was the Studio of the South to be realized once more? Was Vincent's envisioned revolution at hand? Would the great community of artists finally come to be? Or was Gauguin just bluffing?

Despite the bonze's newfound recognition, there was something reticent in Theo, as if, with his brother's growing notoriety, he feared having to explain the painter's history and his whereabouts, as well as the stories that must have been circulating in the art world about his epileptic fits, his attack on Gauguin, and his severing his own ear and making a gift of it. How defend such acts of violent expenditure to a society that understood painting about as much as it understood Hebrew?

When Vincent ventured to Arles on his test journey, he suffered yet another debilitating attack and was found ambling through the streets of the city, incoherent, with no knowledge of who he was, no recognition of where he was, and no idea as to why he was there. In the midst of world triumph, the most debilitating fragility. Stupefaction. Dissolution. Self after self crashing through his body. Volcanic matter rearing up and out. Did he in some way want to free himself of the sane world? The painter did once say that he preferred his madness to other people's wisdom. When one has fire within oneself, one cannot keep bottling it up... *Burn!*

Dr. Peyron was obliged to send personnel from the asylum to retrieve the painter, who did not know where he spent the night of Saturday to Sunday. The painting he took with him to give to Madame Ginoux, *L'Arlésienne*, was lost and not recovered. So extreme was the painter's delirium. Peyron wrote to Theo that, although Vincent is unable to read or write, he is hopeful the condition will last only for another few days and he will regain his sanity as before, but since it has lasted so long, it will be more difficult for him to pull through.

The spell persisting only for a brief time proved not to be true; the painter would not recover from this attack until the end of April. As if living out Aurier's characterization of him as a mad genius, the artist remained in his room, seized by fear and hallucinatory agitations, plagued by despair, not only due to his continuously recurring illness, but by being prohibited from visiting his studio and having the freedom to paint. Is it not painting that makes him mad, or madness that makes him unable to paint?

Crouched with head in hands, like Rodin's *Thinker*, the voices of others wound him. He gestures violently to be left alone. To be mad or not to be mad.

Although Dr. Peyron believes he will recover, the crisis, he tells Theo, will leave its mark on his constitution.

The artist of the future, the living embodiment of Zola's Claude Lentier, could not paint just as Nietzsche could no longer think or write. The void had opened up and taken center stage. The body was growing recalcitrant. The fire was breaking out.

*

If Vincent recovered from time to time and regained the strength and fortitude to continue his work, despite Nietzsche's friends thinking he had feigned his madness, he never once recovered enough to pursue any of the multitudes of projects he had outlined before his collapse. But perhaps his madness was a new form of philosophy. The hermit of Sils Maria once said that everything he had written was foreground; for me the real thing begins only with the dashes. — — Was Nietzsche's body at last becoming a human dash, or the interval and abyss between two thought strikes? Or was it finding yet another way to communicate, whatever in fact it was, whatever in fact was left of *the it* that previously existed, of the myriad subjects that 'his' body had become, or which were emerging from it, that Pandora's box endemic with subjects? To what destination would the Ferris wheel spin next? Where would the ball land on the roulette trundle of the entrails?

At the beginning of March, when Gast left Jena, he reported that Nietzsche was downcast:

When I went away, there were tears in his eyes; he was particularly lucid on that day.... The farewell touched me very much. To see this man, this Titan, broken because his mental gifts were too great for his physical strength, the noblest human being shattered because in all things he was too divine! And become a mockery of himself, an object of pity to those over whom he should wield his scepter.

In late March, despite his stripping naked in the streets to go swimming like a whale only to be subdued by the police, his mother noted that her son was growing more and more lucid from week to week. He played something the other day just as he used to, though I did not recall where it came from, and when I asked him toward evening what it was, he answered *Opus 3* of Ludwig van Beethoven, three bars. His piano playing has so much profundity that one knows he is thinking, and it is the piano that he plays mostly, because I ask him to and, of course, beg him every time not to excite his nerves, and he is obedient.

If subdued, if the father of Zarathustra writes no more, if the philosopher of the hammer has laid aside his subtle tuning fork, if the fuse has been removed from his bundle of dynamite, it seems that he continues to think, that music becomes his primary form of thought, and he plays for hours, just as he perambulated for hours along the bay of Portofino, or atop the eagle's nest of Èze, or the banks of il fiume Po. 'He' speaks via the piano, moving between communication & concealment, having at last decided not to speak as his animals instructed, but instead to fashion a lyre and to sing and foam over in order to heal his soul, that is, to make music, to think through sound, for he has reached the place where future & past come together, he has been released from the eternal flow, he has returned to what in his youth he called his semi-pathological musical excitement. *Dionysos has opened the vine!*

I know only one thing about my music, he once said in defense of it to Hans von Bülow, that it enables me to keep control of a state of mind that would perhaps be more dangerous if it was left unsatisfied. The original name for the state of mind was cannibalido.

It was not however others that Nietzsche was eating, but himself, just as he sometimes consumed his own urine and excrement as a way of reingesting and retaining the body that he was losing, the many selves within him rapidly disintegrating inside 'himself,' inside that body full of combat and conflict. In this basest form of the eternal return, he was drinking back into his corpus the flames that were breaking out of it, just as the world drank back into itself all the waste that it too expunged. The world lives on itself; its excrements are its food. This world is the will to power — and nothing besides! And you yourselves are also this will to power — & nothing besides!

ST. RÉMY

1230 km from Jena

wishing a happy year to you; I'm very much behind, not having been able to work for two months; things aren't going well at all; I have a great desire to leave this place; I feel too damaged by grief to be able to face up to publicity

29 April 1890

My dear Theo,

I haven't been able to write to you until now, but as I'm feeling a little better these days I didn't want to delay wishing a happy year to you, your wife and your child, since it's your birthday. At the same time, please accept the various paintings I'm sending you with my thanks for all the kindnesses you've shown me, for without you I would be most unhappy.

You'll see that first there are canvases after Millet. As these aren't destined for public viewing, perhaps you'll make a present of them to our sisters sooner or later. But first you must keep the ones you consider good, and as many as you wish, they're absolutely yours. One of these days you must send me some other things by ancient & modern artists to do, if you find any.

The rest of the canvases are meager, I'm very much behind, not having been able to work for two months. You'll find that the olive trees with the pink sky are the best, with the mountains, I would imagine; the first go well as a pendant to those with the yellow sky. As regards the portrait of the Arlésienne, you know that I've promised our friend Gauguin one, and you must see that he gets it. Then the cypresses are for Mr. Aurier. I would have liked to redo them with a little less impasto, but I don't have the time.

Anyway, they must be washed again several times in cold water, then a strong varnish when the impasto is dry right through, then the blacks won't get dirty when the oil has fully evaporated. Now I would necessarily need colors, part of which you could well get from Tanguy's if he's hard up, or if that would please him. But of course he mustn't be dearer than the other.

Here's the list of colors I would need:

<table>
<tr><td rowspan="4">Large
tubes.</td><td>12 zinc white, 3 cobalt, 5 Veronese green</td></tr>
<tr><td>1 ordinary lake</td></tr>
<tr><td>2 emerald green, 4 chrome 1, 2 chrome 2</td></tr>
<tr><td>1 orange lead, 2 ultramarine</td></tr>
</table>

Then (but from Tasset's) 2 geranium lake, medium-sized tubes.

You would do me a service by sending me at least half of it at once, at once, for I've lost too much time.

Then I would need 6 brushes, 6 fitch brushes, and 7 meters of canvas, or even 10.

What can I tell you of these two last months, things aren't going well at all, I'm more sad and bored than I could tell you, and I no longer know what point I'm at.

As the order for colors is a little large, let me wait for half if that suits you better.

While I was ill I nevertheless still did a few small canvases from memory, which you'll see later, reminiscences of the north, and now I've just finished a sunlit corner of a meadow which I think is fairly vigorous. You'll see it soon.

As Mr. Peyron is away I haven't yet read your letters, but I know that some have come. He has been quite kind in informing you of the situation, as for me I don't know what to do or think. But I have a great desire to leave this place. That won't surprise you; I don't need to tell you any more about it.

Letters have also come from home, which I haven't yet had the courage to read, so melancholy do I feel.

Please ask Mr. Aurier not to write any more articles about my painting, tell him earnestly that first he is wrong about me, then that really I feel too damaged by grief to be able to face up to publicity. Making paintings distracts me — but if I hear talk of them that pains me more than he knows. How is Bernard? Since there are duplicates of some canvases, if you want you could do an exchange with him, because a good-quality canvas of his would look well in your collection. I fell ill at the time I was doing the almond-tree blossoms. If I'd been able to continue working, you can judge from that that I would have done others of the trees in blossom. Now the trees in blossom are almost finished, really I have no luck. Yes, I must try to leave here, but where am I to go? I don't believe one can be more shut up and imprisoned in the places where they don't pretend to leave you free, such as at Charenton or Montevergues.

If you write home, give them my warm regards and tell them I think of them often.

Then good handshake to you and Jo. Believe me

Ever yours,
Vincent.

Please send me what you can find of figures among my old drawings, I'm thinking of redoing the painting of the peasants eating supper, lamplight effect. That canvas must be completely dark now, perhaps I could redo it entirely from memory. You must above all send me the women gleaning and diggers, if there are any left.

Then if you like I'll redo the old tower at Nuenen and the cottage. I think that if you still have them I could now make something better of them from memory.

JENA

1230 km from St. Rémy

the poet who no longer writes

[31 April 1890]

[Dear ————]

[Nietzsche]

ST. RÉMY

1230 km from Jena

to climb back up again from the dejected state; people here are too curious, idle, and ignorant about painting; I've had too hard a life to kick the bucket; if I'd been able to work without this bloody illness!; I'm almost sure that I'll soon get better in the north; fortunately the letters from our sister and mother were very calm; when you expect me over there in Paris

1 May 1890

My dear brother,

Today, as Mr. Peyron had come back, I read your kind letters, then the letters from home as well, and that did me an enormous amount of good in giving me back a little energy, or rather the desire to climb back up again from the dejected state I'm in. I thank you very much for the etchings — you've chosen some of the very ones that I've already liked for a long time, the David, the Lazarus, the Samaritan, and the large etching of the wounded man, and you've added the blind man and the other very small etching, the last one so mysterious that I'm afraid of it and dare not wish to know what it is. I didn't know it, the little goldsmith. But the Lazarus! Early this morning I looked at it and I remembered not only what Charles Blanc says of it, but indeed even that he doesn't say everything about it.

The unfortunate thing is that the people here are too curious, idle, and ignorant about *painting* for it to be possible for me to practice my profession. This is what one could always observe, that you and I made an effort here in the same direction as some others who weren't understood either, *&* were bitterly saddened by circumstances.

If ever you go to Montpellier you would see that what I tell you here is true.

Now, rather, you propose coming back to the north, *&* I accept.

I've had too hard a life to kick the bucket as a result, or to lose the power to work.

So Gauguin and Guillaumin, the two of them, want to do an exchange for the landscape of the Alpilles. Besides, there are two of them, only I think that the one finished last, which I've just sent, is done with more determination and is more accurate in expression.

I'm perhaps going to try to work from the Rembrandts, above all I have an idea to do the man at prayer in the range of tones running from bright yellow to violet.

Included is Gauguin's letter, do what you think best as regards the exchange, take the ones you like for yourself; I'm sure that our taste is increasingly becoming the same.

Ah, if I'd been able to work without this bloody illness! How many things I could have done, isolated from the others, according to what the land would tell me. But yes — this journey is well and truly finished. Anyway, what consoles me is the great, the very great desire that I have to see you again, you, your wife and your child, and so many friends who have remembered me in my misfortune, as, for that matter, I don't stop thinking of them either.

I'm almost sure that I'll soon get better in the north, at least for quite a long time, while still apprehensive of a relapse in a few years' time — but not immediately. That's what I imagine after having observed the other patients here, some of whom are considerably older than I am or, among the young ones, were more or less idlers — students. Anyway, what do we know about it?

Fortunately the letters from our sister and mother were very calm. Our sister writes very well, and describes a landscape or an aspect of the town as if it were a page from a modern novel. I always urge her to busy herself with domestic rather than artistic things, for I know that she's already too sensitive, and at her age would have difficulty in finding the way to artistic development. I'm really afraid that she too will suffer from a thwarted artistic will. But she's so energetic that she'll make up for it. I talked with Mr. Peyron about the situation, and told him that it was almost impossible for me to bear my fate here, that not knowing anything very clear regarding the line to take, it seemed preferable to me to return to the north.

If you think this is a good idea, and if you suggest a date when you expect me over there in Paris, I would have someone from here accompany me part of the way, as far as Tarascon or Lyon. Then you would wait for me, or have someone wait for me, at the station in Paris. Do what seems best to you. For the time being I would leave my furniture behind in Arles. It's with friends, and I'm sure they'd send it the day I wanted it. But the carriage and packing would be almost what it's worth. I consider this as a shipwreck, this journey, well, one can't do as one wants, and as one ought to either. Once I got out a little into the park I recovered all my clarity for work, I have more ideas in my head than I could ever put into action, but without it dazzling me.

The brushstrokes go like a machine. So based on that I dare believe that in the north I would rediscover my confidence once freed from surroundings & circumstances that I neither understand nor wish to understand. It was very kind of Mr. Peyron to write to you, he's writing to you again today, I leave him regretting that I have to leave him. Good handshake to you and to Jo, I thank her very much for her letter.

Ever yours,
Vincent

JENA

1230 km from St. Rémy

furiously loud; slices of apple; guttural growlings; music

[1 May 1890]

At times, before the vermin of his mother, the body that once harbored a man named Nietzsche grows furiously loud and unruly, terrifying the woman.

After caressing him and speaking to him in a friendly tone, she manages to get her son to chew on something sweet, like slices of apple, or his beloved cherries, his disturbed vocalizations eventually decrease in volume, tempered by the act of masticating, and the violent noises of the creature turn into low, guttural growlings, then into more quiet moans as he approaches the piano to begin performing improvisations.

As he stands before the instrument striking the keys, his mother pushes him down onto the piano stool and he continues playing, gazing at the piano as if it were the only living thing in the room, till he is completely lost in the music and moans no more.

ST. RÉMY

1230 km from Jena

I categorically reject what you say; my desire to leave here is now absolute; it would seem preferable to me to go and see this doctor in the country; I need air, I feel damaged by boredom and grief; it's already something to resign oneself to living under guard; continue at liberty or stick myself in an asylum for good; is it fair to have me accompanied like a dangerous animal?; my patience is at an end; in painting one must seek nothing and hope for nothing

4 May 1890

My dear brother,

Thanks for your kind letter and for the portrait of Jo, which is very pretty and is very successful as a pose. Well, I'll be very simple and as practical as possible in my reply. First, I categorically reject what you say that I should be accompanied throughout the journey. Once on the train I no longer run any risk, I'm not one of those who are dangerous — even supposing I have a crisis, aren't there other passengers in the carriage, and besides, don't they know what to do in all the stations in such a case? You're giving yourself worries here that weigh on me so heavily that it might directly discourage me.

I've just said the same thing to Mr. Peyron, and I pointed out to him that crises like the one I've just had have always been followed by three or four months of complete calm. I wish to take advantage of this period to move — I want to move in any event; my desire to leave here is now absolute.

I don't feel competent to judge the way they treat patients here, I don't feel any desire to enter into the details — but please remember that I warned you around 6 months ago that if I was seized by a crisis of the same nature I'd wish to change asylums. And I've delayed too long already, having allowed an attack to go by in the meantime, I was then right in the middle of work, and I wanted to finish canvases in progress, otherwise I would no longer be here by now. Right, so I'm going to tell you that it seems to me that a fortnight at the most (a week, though, would please me more) should be enough to take the necessary steps to move. I shall have someone accompany me as far as Tarascon — even one or two stations further if you insist. Once I've arrived in Paris (I'll send a telegram when I leave here) you would come and pick me up at the Gare de Lyon.

Now it would seem preferable to me to go and see this doctor in the country as soon as possible, and we'd leave the luggage at the station.

So I would only stay at your place for let's say 2 or 3 days, then I'd leave for this village. Where I would start off by lodging at the inn.

This, it seems to me, is what you could do in the next few days — without delay — write to our future friend, that doctor: "my brother would very much like to make your acquaintance, and as he would prefer to consult you before prolonging his stay in Paris, hopes that you will approve of his spending a few weeks in your village, where he will come to make some studies; he has complete confidence that he will reach an understanding with you, believing that with a return to the north his illness will abate, whereas by staying on in the south his condition would be in danger of becoming more acute."

There, you could write to him like that, we'd send him a telegram the day after my arrival in Paris, or the day after that, and he'd probably wait for me at the station.

The surroundings here are starting to weigh on me more than I could express — my word, I've waited patiently for over a year — I need air, I feel damaged by boredom and grief.

Then work is pressing, I'd be wasting my time here. Why then, I ask you, do you fear accidents so much — it isn't that that ought to frighten you, my word, since I've been here I've seen people fall over or lose their mind every day — what's more serious is to try and take misfortune into account. I assure you that it's already something to resign oneself to living under guard, even in the event of it being sympathetic, and to sacrifice one's freedom, to stand outside society and to have only one's work, without distraction. That has carved out wrinkles that won't be rubbed off in a hurry. Now that it's beginning to weigh too heavily upon me here, I think that it's only right to put a stop to it.

So please write to Mr. Peyron that he should let me leave, let's say on the 15th at the latest. If I waited I would let the good moment of calm between two crises pass, and leaving now I'll have the free time necessary to make the other doctor's acquaintance. Then, if in a while from now the illness were to recur it would be foreseen, and according to how serious it was we could see if I can continue at liberty or if I must stick myself in an asylum for good. In the latter case — as I told you in my last letter I would go into an institution where the patients work in the fields and in the workshop. I think that even more than here I'd then find subjects for painting.

Consider, then, that the journey costs a lot, that it's pointless and that I do have the right to change asylums if I please, it isn't my absolute freedom that I'm demanding.

I've tried to be patient up to this point, I haven't done any harm to anyone, is it fair to have me accompanied like a dangerous animal? No thank you, I protest. If a crisis occurs, they know what to do in every station, and then I'd let them do it.

But I dare believe that my composure won't desert me. I have so much distress at leaving like this, that the distress will be stronger than the madness, I'll therefore have the necessary nerve, I dare believe. Mr. Peyron says vague things, to free himself from responsibility he says, but that way we'd never, never get to the end of it, the thing would drag on and on, and in the end we'd get angry with each other.

As for me, my patience is at an end, at an end, my dear brother, I can't go on, I must move, even if as a stopgap.

However, there really is a chance that the change will do me good — work is going well, I've done 2 canvases of the fresh grass in the park, one of which is extremely simple. Included is a hasty croquis of it.

The trunk of a pine tree violet pink, and then grass with white flowers and dandelions, a little rose bush and other treetrunks in the background, in the uppermost part of the canvas. I'll be out of doors there. I'm sure that the desire to work will devour me and make me insensible to everything else and in a good mood. And I'll let myself go there, not without consideration but without dwelling on regrets for things that might have been.

They say that in painting one must seek nothing and hope for nothing but a good painting and a good talk and a good dinner as the height of happiness, not counting the less brilliant interludes. Perhaps it's true, and why refuse to take what is possible, especially if by doing so one gives the illness the slip.

Good handshake to you and to Jo, I think I'm going to do a painting for myself after the subject of the portrait, it may not be a resemblance perhaps, but anyway I'll try.

More soon, I hope — and come on, spare me this forced travelling companion.

Ever yours,
Vincent.

JENA

1230 km from St. Rémy

the pianist who no longer writes

[13 May 1890]

ST. RÉMY

1234 km from Jena

*I obtained permission to pack my trunk; I hope to be in
Paris before Sunday to spend the day; I saw the countryside again — how many more things I would have done;
I'd immediately very much like to do a painting of a yellow
bookshop; spending days doing nothing, here or elsewhere,
that's what would make me miserable*

13 May 1890

My dear brother

After a last discussion with Mr. Peyron I obtained permission to pack my trunk, which I've sent by goods train. The 30 kilos of luggage one is allowed to take will allow me to take a few frames, easel, and some stretching frames &c.

I'll leave as soon as you've written to Mr. Peyron, I feel calm enough, and I don't think that a mental upset could easily happen to me in the state I'm in.

In any event, I hope to be in Paris before Sunday to spend the day, which you will have off, quietly with all of you. I really hope to see André Bonger too at the first opportunity.

I've also just finished a canvas of pink roses against yellow-green background in a green vase.

I hope that the canvases of the last few days will compensate us for the expenses of travel.

This morning, as I'd been to have my trunk stamped, I saw the countryside again — very fresh after the rain and covered in flowers — how many more things I would have done.

I've also written to Arles for them to send the two beds and the bed linen by goods train. I estimate that this can only cost a good ten francs in transport charges, and it's still something gained from the debacle. For it'll certainly be useful to me in the country.

If you haven't yet replied to Mr. Peyron's letter, please send him a telegram, in such a way that I may make the journey on Friday or Saturday at the latest to spend Sunday with you. In doing so I'll also lose the least time for my work, which is finished here for the moment.

In Paris, if I feel up to it, I'd immediately very much like to do a painting of a yellow bookshop (gas effect), which I've had in my mind for so long. You'll see that I'll be at work right from the day after my arrival. I tell you, as regards work, my mind feels absolutely serene and the brushstrokes come to me and follow each other very logically.

Anyway until Sunday AT THE LATEST, I shake your hand firmly in the meantime, warm regards to Jo.

Ever yours,
Vincent.

Probably the answer to Mr. Peyron will already have left, which I hope. I was a little vexed that there were a few days' delay, because that seems to me to be of no use for anything. For either I'd plunge into new works here, or it's now that I have the leisure for the journey. Spending days doing nothing, here or elsewhere, that's what would make me miserable in my current state of mind. Besides, Mr. P. isn't opposed to it, but naturally when you leave, your position is a little difficult with the rest of the administration. But it's going well, and we'll part amicably.

NAUMBURG

1276.1 km from St. Rémy

music

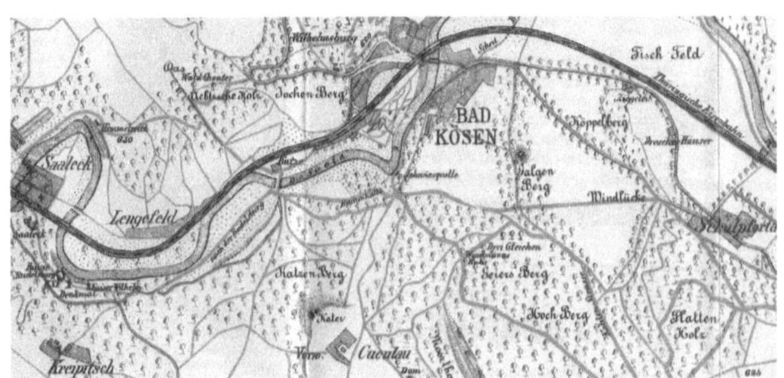

[20 May 1890]

Performs tight, dense, arrhythmic, unstructured sounds on the
piano, a series of dark, swift, entangled notes.

INTERVAL: JENA, ST. RÉMY & ELSEWHERE

The head of Dionysos, the song-filled night. Rebirth?

March–June 1890

When penning his autobiography shortly before his self-disintegration (impeccable timing), Nietzsche traced out a phantasmatic genealogy and noted that, when looking for his profoundest opposite, ineradicable vulgarity of the instincts, he always thought of his mother *&* sister — it would blaspheme my divinity, he said, to think that I am related to this sort of canaille. The way my mother and sister treat me to this very day is a source of unspeakable horror: a perfect infernal machine is at work here, which can reveal with unerring certainty the exact moment that I can be hurt — in my highest moments, ... because at that point I do not have the strength to resist poisonous vermin ... Physiological contiguity makes this sort of *disharmonia præstabilita* possible ... But I will admit that the greatest objection to the 'eternal return,' my truly abyssal thought, is always my mother *&* sister.

Indictment of indictments! For the father of Zarathustra, a familial link is enough to potentially destroy a philosophy. What exit out is there? What secret to overcoming? What pathway to freedom? To amor fati?

Moving beyond the confines of the nuclear family, the father of the indeterminate human declared that Frau Cosima and Richard Wagner were by far the people most closely related to him and that all prevailing ideas about degrees of relation are unsurpassable pieces of physiological absurdity. Kinship is not then limited strictly to the bloodline, to biology, but to typology, to the rhizome, not the tree, *&* so, in a kind of Senecan form of progenitorism (if it is not in our power to choose the parents allotted to us, we can choose whose children we would like to be), genetic shaping spirals outward into all of history, from the present moment to the big bang. People, the descendant of Polish nobility proclaimed, are least related to their parents: it would be the most extreme sign of vulgarity to be related to your parents. Higher natures *have* their origins infinitely further back; collecting, economizing, accumulating has gone on longest for their sake. Great individuals are the oldest: I do not understand it, but Julius Cæsar could be my father — or Alexander, that Dionysos incarnate... As I am writing this, *the postman is bringing me a head of Dionysos...*

And so, on 24 March 1890, the man who once described himself as a female elephant and who traced his phantasmatic genealogy to Wagner, Cæsar, and Alexander, recognizing in this the long millennial chain that makes up each human, was released from the Jena asylum and put into the care of his mother, a source of unspeakable horror, a *disharmonia*, and one of the greatest objections to his cyclical conception of temporality, the eternal return. Someone who could wound him more than anyone else, some poisonous vermin he could not defend himself against, a sort of canaille, an infernal machine would have complete dominion over him. The House of Atreus, the House of Nietzsche — contagion of contagions!

Che cosa? Sono il figlio di un dio! Son un dio?

What pray tell happened to the head of Dionysos, we do not know, nor do we know what happened to the body of the beheaded god — this acéphalic enigma remains unsolved. Was there a feast? If however Nietzsche is a divinity (Zeus?), could that head, wherever it now might rest (did the Finos secret it away somewhere in Torino in hopes of one day selling it, as they tried to do with the piano that Nietzsche played but which no one would buy? Yet where, pray tell, is the body of that beloved horse?!?), be a sacrificial offering to him? Not the crucifixion of a son, but *the beheading* of one, a gesture thereby freeing humanity of a burden of guilt and enabling it to surpass its gods and become what it is, splaying open its genealogical line to also make it typological, and creating the freedom to trace it any and everywhere? There is no judging figure gazing down upon us, there is no icon of torture, there is no curse upon life — — *that* is Dionysos vs. the Crucified! *That* is the vanquishing of the crown of thorns; *that* is the triumph of the vine. But then, if Alexander, that Dionysos incarnate, could be Nietzsche's true father, is not Nietzsche then the son of an incarnated god, and is it not therefore his own father's head that he has been brought? If so, with this, the Oedipal family drama has been rendered obsolete. The theater of the self (*of selves*) is transformed — it is no longer a monocle, it is a prismatic, multi-valved kaleidoscope, a laughing, welcoming, *hospitable Medusa.*

While someone cut off the head of Dionysos and made a gift of it to Nietzsche-Zeus, or Nietzsche-Staphylus, or Nietzsche-X, whoever that last 'he' might have been, for 'he' could be all the names in history, that very same month Vincent had cut off his ear and made a gift of it to a supposed prostitute.

From Arles to Torino, a trail of blood saturates the earth, a ritual trail of sacrifice — the blood of humans, the blood of gods.

Sing me a new song, went Nietzsche's Orphic injunction, the world is transfigured, all the Heavens are rejoicing, and on he danced naked in his room, leaping about like Dionysos, then playing the piano, then dancing, then playing the piano, then...

My thoughts sailed over many seas, went Vincent's haunted injunction, I even dreamed of the Dutch ghost ship and the Horla, and it seems that I sang then, I who can't sing on other occasions, to be precise an old wet-nurse's song while thinking of what the cradle-rocker sang as she rocked the sailors and whom I had sought in an arrangement of colors before falling ill.

From the Studio of the South to the Galleria Subalpina, *almost as if synchronized*, the painter and the philosopher filled the night air with songs. — — The music of humans, the music of gods, the music of madmen. *Quem Iuppiter vult perdere, dementat prius...*

When first admitted to St. Paul de Mausole, Dr. Peyron certified that Mr. Van Gogh suffered an attack of acute mania with visual and auditory hallucinations that led him to mutilate himself by cutting off his ear. Today he appears to have regained his reason, but he does not feel that he has the strength or the courage to live independently and has himself asked to be admitted to the home. Peyron noted further that Mr. Van Gogh is subject to attacks of epilepsy, separated by long intervals, and that it is advisable to place him under long-term observation in the institution. He tells us that his mother's sister was epileptic, and that there are several cases in his family. What has happened to this patient may be no more than a continuation of what has happened to several members of his family.

The House of Atreus, the House of van Gogh — *contagion of contagions*. Did the painter not know, as did the philosopher, of the free, open rhizomatic line to which he could trace himself, that the typological marks us just as much as the biological? That we are just as much rock and rhizome as we are human? If Vincent knew of the phantasmal line, would he have returned from each bout of madness, or would he have remained in the first and stayed forever mad, himself already a schizophrenic Ferris wheel of souls, a singer of songs unbeknownst to himself, an Orpheus and Eurydice in one, eternally destroying himself and his other with each fatal turn? *Are you there?* I am dead. *Are you there?* 'I' am dead.

On 16 May 1890, one year and 8 days after his being admitted to St. Paul de Mausole, the painter was finally released, almost exactly two months after Nietzsche's own release from the asylum. And so they each wandered, the philosopher and the painter, in near proximity, geographically, physiologically, psychologically, *orphical-ly* — one devoted to philosophy, one devoted to painting, both undergoing acts of sparagmos, both incarnations of Dionysos, or open vessels of Dionysian energies.

In Mr. Van Gogh's discharge papers, Dr. Peyron stated that, during his stay in the home, this patient, who was calm for most of the time, had several attacks lasting for between two weeks and a month; during these attacks, the patient is subject to terrifying fears, and on several occasions he has attempted to poison himself, either by swallowing colors that he used for painting, or by ingesting paraffin, which he had taken from the boy while he was filling his lamps. The last attack he had occurred following a journey that he made to Arles, and it lasted approximately two months. In the interval between attacks the patient is perfectly calm and lucid, and passionately devotes himself to painting. He is asking to be discharged today, in order to go to live in the north of France, hoping that that climate will suit him better.

Like Nietzsche, Vincent seeks the perfect climate for his physiology, what is most optimal for his creative will to power. Does he find it? Is even his undoing his fated denouement, some apotheosis of artistic ferocity? Were the bodies of Nietzsche and Vincent not free of the sick desire to live forever?

Before leaving St. Rémy, one of the last portraits Vincent made was of an old man sitting on a chair not unlike the one from his room in the Yellow House. Based on his earlier painting *At Eternity's Gate*, the figure's head is buried in his hands, a gesture of extreme grief, not unlike Vincent's own gestures, made as he sat in his cell during his bouts of madness, fighting to close off the world, to perhaps remain mad and not suffer continual vertigo. If all vision is blocked, if the perilous moment cannot be surpassed, if the future seems inexistent, the fire burning by his side may be a signal of *an ever-burning inner flame*, a will to power that pushes him beyond, even if to the brink of destruction, for one's end must also not be rejected but willed. If the walls are bare, stripped of any paintings as if emblematic of the failed Studio of the South, of Vincent's southern journey being a shipwreck, as he himself described it, the old man's sturdy, solid shoes point forward, as if ready and waiting for the grief to end so that his journey can continue, whether it lead to fruition, or destruction. With every passing day, we are one step closer to death. Good morning...

The next day, Vincent reached Paris, staying with Theo and Jo at 8 Cité Pigalle for three days. There, the painter encountered much of his work of the previous years and earlier, from *The Potato Eaters* to *Starry Night*, as well as his orchards *&* flowers — every room contained paintings of his, as if Theo *&* Jo's apartment was the first ever Vincent van Gogh Gallery. Even over the cradle where the 3½-month-old Vincent slept, the painter's namesake, there was a painting of his of a young flowering pear tree. A lifetime of work condensed in a single space.

From the confines of an asylum to the hearth of a home, the whirlwind of life thrust Vincent onward, an ever-displaced wanderer of the earth pacing to the pulse of his fate.

After his long spell out of the world, or at the heart of his own innermost reality, the legendary founder of the heliocentric mythos visited galleries in Paris to see what his companion artists were up to during his asylum sojourn. In particular, Vincent was struck by Puvis de Chavanne's *Inter artes et naturam*, a copy of the central panel of a triptych that Chavanne had painted for the Musée des Beaux-Arts in Rouen.

When one looks at it for a long time, Vincent later wrote his brother, one gets the feeling of being present at a rebirth, total but benevolent, of all things one should have believed in, should have wished for.

Perhaps this was a signal then, a crystallization of some type, of a life that could have been. A rebirth was to come from within his own circle, too, through himself, Gauguin, Bernard, and others, but despite their being in the city, neither Gauguin nor Bernard arranged to meet Vincent, and Vincent did not view Gauguin's paintings, nor despite his numerous gallery visits did he pay respects to his brother's gallery. Although he arrived with his easel, canvases, stretchers, paints, and brushes, spurred by a fervor to begin painting at once, for he knew there was a way of seeing Paris beautiful, he did not paint a single canvas, let alone even draw. If he seemed to be in the midst of some ascendancy, with his gaining recognition through Aurier's praise, since then, not a painting of his had been sold. How then face Theo's gallery, or his own blank canvas, as fired as he was with ideas, as prodigious as he could be? Paris, the art center of the world, remained a place of rejection and repulsion. And how not ever paint a portrait of his patron saint? When coming face to face with Theo after such a long separation, did he perhaps see the specter of death in his visage? hear it in his death rattle of a cough? Did he sense in some way his own impending death, and the end of his brother? Did he not want to let his brushes reveal some unconscious revelation? The seer that turns from truths knows such truths will still come to be. Just as Orpheus made his fatal turn, Vincent made a fatal turn, in the other direction, believing it was not a turning toward, but, the direction is immaterial — if it seemed like it could be a saving gesture, it was not, for it is not the turning itself that opens death, but death that opens the turning, it is death that draws one toward it, forcing one to turn as if a centrifugal force, moving one away from life, *toward* the final dash, *into* silence.

Three days after arriving in Paris, Vincent would venture to Auvers-sur-Oise *&* begin his final Untergang. A centripetal force would draw him ever closer and closer to the center of himself and, like Nietzsche, he would begin to consume himself, to struggle to devour that which was exiting him so as to remain whole, but after so much devouring, what more is there to consume?

I hope, he wrote to Theo, that it will not be unpleasant to meet oneself again after a long absence...

Although his new doctor, Paul Gachet, had served in a mobile unit in the Franco-Prussian war, thereby bringing the philosopher and the painter into ever-closer proximity, and who had treated the likes of Cézanne, Manet, Renoir, and Pissarro, when encountering Gachet, as if a doctor himself, Vincent diagnosed to Theo that Gachet was sicker than him.

We must not count on him at all, he wrote — when one blind man leads another, don't they both fall into the ditch?

Transfixed by the beauty of Auvers, the painter explained to his brother that it was the real country, characteristic *&* picturesque, an almost lush place with much wellbeing in the air. It was akin to him to Chavanne's mural, a kind of bucolic Elysian village devoid of factories and replete with lovely, abundant greenery. He described it as the stern poetry of the heath *&* it opened in him a new frenzy of creativity.

The lowering storm was on the horizon.

AUVERS-SUR-OISE

918.3 km from Naumburg

*I would gladly swap profession for profession; up to today
things are going well; I would like you, Jo, and the little one
to have a rest in the country; there's a lot of well-being in
the air; tell me which painting Miss Boch bought; paintings
vaguely present themselves to my sight; I hope that your
health will be good*

25 May 1890

My dear Theo, my dear Jo,

Thank you for your letter, which I received this morning, and for the fifty francs that were inside it.

Today I saw Dr. Gachet again, and I'm going to paint at his place on Tuesday morning, then I'm going to lunch with him and afterwards he'll come to see my painting. He seems very reasonable to me, but is as discouraged in his profession of country doctor as I with my painting. So I told him that I would, however, gladly swap profession for profession. Anyway, I readily think that I'll end up being friends with him. He told me, besides, that if melancholy or something else were to become too strong for me to bear, he could well do something again to lessen its intensity, and that I mustn't be embarrassed to be open with him. Well, that moment when I have need of him may indeed come, however up to today things are going well. And they may get even better; I still believe that it's above all an illness of the south that I caught, and that the return here will be enough to dispel all that.

Often, very often, I think of your little one, and I then tell myself that I would like him to be big enough to come to the country. For it's the best system of bringing them up here. How I would like you, Jo, and the little one to have a rest in the country instead of the traditional journey to Holland. Yes, I'm well aware that Mother will absolutely want to see the little one, and it's certainly a reason to go there. However, she would certainly understand if it were really in the little one's best interests.

Here we're far enough from Paris for it to be the real countryside, but nevertheless, how changed since Daubigny. But not changed in an unpleasant way, there are many villas and various modern and middle-class dwellings, very jolly, sunny and covered with flowers. That in an almost lush countryside, just at this moment of the development of a new society in the old one, has nothing disagreeable about it; there's a lot of well-being in the air. I see or think I see a calm there à la Puvis de Chavannes, no factories, but beautiful greenery in abundance and in good order.

When you have the opportunity, will you tell me which painting Miss Boch bought? I must write to her brother to thank them, and then I would propose the exchange of two of my studies for one by each of them.

Enclosed is a note that you will please send to Isaäcson.

I have a drawing of an old vineyard of which I plan to do a no. 30 canvas, then a study of pink chestnut trees and one of white chestnut trees. But if circumstances permit, I hope to do a little figure work. Paintings vaguely present themselves to my sight, which it will take time to shape, but that will come little by little. If I hadn't been ill, I would have written to Boch and to Isaäcson long since. My trunk hasn't arrived yet, which annoys me, I sent a telegram this morning.

Thank you in advance for the canvas and the paper. Yesterday and today it rains and is stormy, but it isn't unpleasant to see these effects again. The beds haven't arrived either. But despite these annoyances, I feel happy no longer to be so far from you all and our friends. I hope that your health will be good. It seemed to me, though, that you had less appetite than before, and from what the doctors say, we should have very solid food for our temperaments. So be sensible about it, especially Jo too, as she has her child to feed. Truly, the amount should be doubled, it wouldn't be any exaggeration when there are children to make and feed. Without that it's like a train moving slowly where the route is straight. Time enough to reduce steam when the route is more uneven. Handshake in thought.

Ever yours,
Vincent.

NAUMBURG

918.3 km from Auvers-sur-Oise

the dithyrambist who no longer writes

[25 May 1890]

AUVERS-SUR-OISE

918.3 km from Naumburg

it would be good for many reasons that we were all togeth-er again; Gachet appears to me as ill and confused as you or I; I'm working on his portrait; I still haven't found any-thing interesting in the way of a possible studio; much surer of my brush; a healthy return to true antiquity; what did Gauguin say about the last portrait; I feel that Gachet will work with you and me without reservation

3 June 1890

My dear Theo,

For several days now I'd have liked to write to you with a rested mind, but have been absorbed in work. This morning your letter arrives, for which I thank you and for the 50-franc note it contained. Yes, I think that it would be good for many reasons that we were all together again here for a week of your holidays, if longer isn't possible. I often think of you, Jo, and the little one, and I see that the children here look well in the healthy fresh air. And yet it's difficult enough to raise them, even here, all the more is it rather terrible sometimes to keep them safe and sound in Paris on a fourth floor. But anyway, one must take things as they are. Mr. Gachet says that father and mother must feed themselves quite naturally, he talks of taking 2 liters of beer a day &c., in those amounts. But you'll certainly enjoy furthering your acquaintance with him, and he's already counting on it, speaks of it every time I see him, that you'll all come. He certainly appears to me as ill and confused as you or I, and he's older and a few years ago he lost his wife, but he's very much a doctor, and his profession and his faith keep him going however. We're already firm friends, and by chance he also knew Bruyas of Montpellier and has the same ideas on him as I have, that he's someone important in the history of modern art. I'm working on his portrait, the head with a white cap, very fair, very light, the hands also in light carnation, a blue frock coat and a cobalt blue background, leaning on a red table on which are a yellow book and a foxglove plant with purple flowers. It's in the same sentiment as the portrait of myself that I took when I left for here.

Mr. Gachet is absolutely fanatical about this portrait, and wants me to do one of him if I can, absolutely like that, which I also wish to do. He has now also come to understand the last portrait of the Arlésienne, one of which you have in pink — he comes back all the time, when he comes to see the studies, to these two portraits and he accepts them fully, but fully as they are. I hope to send you a portrait of him soon. Then I painted two studies at his house, which I gave him last week. One aloes with marigolds and cypresses, then last Sunday white roses, vines, and a white figure in it.

I'll very probably also do the portrait of his daughter, who is 19, and with whom I can easily imagine Jo will quickly make friends.

So I'm looking forward to doing the portraits of all of you in the open air, yours, Jo's, and the little one's.

I still haven't found anything interesting in the way of a possible studio, and yet I'll have to take a room to put in the canvases which are surplus at your apartment and which are at Tanguy's. For they still need a great deal of retouching. But anyway, I live from day to day — the weather is so fine. And my health is good, I go to bed at 9 o'clock but I get up at 5 o'clock most of the time.

I have hopes that it won't be disagreeable to be together again after a long absence. And I also hope that I'll continue to feel much surer of my brush than before I went to Arles. And Mr. Gachet says that he would consider it highly improbable that it should recur, and that it's going completely well. But he, too, complains bitterly of the state of things everywhere in the villages where the least foreigner has come, that life there becomes so horribly expensive. He says that he's astonished that the people where I am lodge and feed me for that, and that I'm still fortunate, compared to others who have come and whom he's known. That if you come, and Jo and the little one, you can't do better than stay at this same inn. Now nothing, absolutely nothing keeps us here but Gachet — but the latter will remain a friend, I'd assume. I feel that at his place I can do not too bad a painting every time I go there, and he'll certainly continue to invite me to dinner each Sunday or Monday.

But up to now, however agreeable it is to do a painting there, it's a chore for me to dine and lunch there for, the excellent man goes to the trouble of making dinners in which there are 4 or 5 courses, which is as abominable for him as it is for me, for he certainly doesn't have a strong stomach. What has held me back a little from saying something about it is that I see that, for him, it reminds him of the days of yore when people had family dinners, which anyway we too well know.

But the modern idea of eating one, at most two courses is, however, certainly progress, & a healthy return to true antiquity.

Anyway père Gachet is a lot, yes a lot like you and I. I was pleased to read in your letter that Mr. Peyron asked for news of me when he wrote to you. I'm going to write to him this very evening that things are going well, for he was very kind to me and I'll certainly not forget him. Dumoulin, the one who has Japanese paintings at the Champ de Mars, has come back here, and I very much hope to meet him.

What did Gauguin say about the last portrait of the Arlésienne that's done after his drawing? You'll end up seeing, I would think, that it's one of the least bad things I've done. Gachet has a Guillaumin, naked woman on a bed, which I consider very beautiful, he also has a very old Guillaumin portrait by him, very different from ours, dark but interesting.

But his house, you will see, is full, full like an antique dealer's, of things that aren't always interesting, it's terrible, even. But in all of this there's this good aspect, that there would always be what I need there for arranging flowers or still lifes. I've done studies for him, to show him that should he not be paid in money we'll nevertheless still compensate him for what he does for us.

Do you know an etching by Bracquemond, the portrait of Comte, it's a masterpiece.

I'd also need as soon as possible tubes of zinc white from Tasset and 2 medium tubes of geranium lake.

Then as soon as you could send them I'd be absolutely set upon copying all of Bargue's *Etudes au fusain* again, you know the nude figures. I can draw them quite quickly, let's say the 60 sheets that there are in a month, so you might send a copy on loan, I'd make sure not to stain or dirty it. If I neglected to keep on studying proportions and the nude I'd find myself in a bad position later on. Don't think this absurd or futile.

Gachet also told me that if I wanted to give him great pleasure he would like me to redo for him the copy of Delacroix's *Pietà*, which he gazed at for a long time. Later he'll probably give me a hand with the models, I feel that he'll understand us completely, & that he'll work with you and me without reservation, with all his intelligence, for the love of art for art's sake. And he'll perhaps have me do some portraits. Now to have clients for portraits one must be able to show different ones that one has done. That's the only possibility I can see of placing something. But however, however, certain canvases will one day find collectors. Only I think that all the fuss created by the large prices paid lately for Millets &c. has further worsened the state of things as regards the chance one has of merely recouping one's painting expenses. It's enough to make one dizzy. So why are we thinking about it, it would stupefy us. Better still, perhaps, to seek a little friendship and live from day to day. I hope that the little one will continue to be well, and you two also until we see each other again, more soon, I shake your hand firmly.

Vincent

NAUMBURG

918.3 km from Auvers-sur-Oise

music

He who was once Herr Dynamite performs music upon the piano, each piece more and more rhythmically discordant as he
becomes more and more uncivilized, more and more infected
by wild affect, more and more losing all sense of time-rhythmic,
all sense of passion needing to be bridled. *The Good European?*
He was, in effect, becoming more and more *Elisabeth* (*more and
more 'German'*) and losing all sense of ethos. His body is under
attack, assailed by an infinite number of rhythms knocking pulling twitching jabbing cutting biting tickling. He is no longer the
same arrangement of atoms he once was (there is no longer any
he, only an *it*), but another, and another, and another ~

AUVERS-SUR-OISE

918.3 km from Naumburg

I really regret that Mr. Ginoux has been injured; not being able to come back to Arles; I was more catching the illness of the others than curing my own; they have twice written an article about my paintings; I still often think of you all; obscurely as in a mirror

11 June 1890

My dear friends Mr. and Mrs. Ginoux,

I want to reply straightaway to Mrs. Ginoux's letter to say that I was really pleased to have news of you. I really regret that Mr. Ginoux has been injured and has suffered so much. Please have my things packed up by someone else so that he doesn't wear himself out with it; I'll gladly reimburse you for all the expenses you may have, but he mustn't tire himself too much, for fear that his wound may open up.

But in this way I'm counting on you sending on Saturday, for I'm awaiting it.

Yes, I too really regretted not being able to come back to Arles to take my leave of you all. For you well know that I had grown attached to people & things there with you with a sincere friend ship. But in the final days I was more catching the illness of the others than curing my own, the society of the other patients influenced me badly, and in the end I no longer understood anything about it. Then I felt that it was better to try a change, and anyway the pleasure of seeing my brother, his family and our painter friends again has done me good up till now, and I feel absolutely calm and in a normal state. The doctor here says that one must throw oneself fully into work and distract oneself in that way.

The latter knows a lot about painting, and likes mine very much, he encourages me a great deal, and two three times a week he comes to spend a few hours with me to see what I'm doing.

They have twice written an article about my paintings, once in a Paris newspaper and the other time in Brussels, where I had exhibited, and now, lately, again in a newspaper of my own country, Holland, and that means that a lot of people have been to see my paintings and that I've sold on better terms. And it isn't over. It's anyway certain that since I stopped drinking I've done better work than before, there's still that which has been gained.

But I still often think of you all, one can't do as one wants in life, one must leave the place one feels most attached to — but the memories remain and one remembers — obscurely as in a mirror — absent friends.

Thus I hope that the dispatch can take place on Saturday. Here is the address again.

Vincent van Gogh
At Ravoux's, place de la Mairie
Auvers sur Oise
(Seine *&* Oise)
By goods train

In this way there can't be any mistakes. And I thank you in advance for your trouble, but let Ginoux get a man to do the packing and not wear himself out. I shall reimburse you the costs.

Wishing you good health *&* complete recovery, most cordial greetings.

Vincent van Gogh.

NAUMBURG

918.3 km from Auvers-sur-Oise

he who shot the history of mankind into two halves
no longer writes

[11 June 1890]

AUVERS-SUR-OISE

918.3 km from Naumburg

*The difference between Tanguy & Tasset colors; the Dutch-
man would do well to go to Brittany with Gauguin and De
Haan; I myself also hope very much to join them; a few etchings of subjects from the south; at the moment I have two
studies on the go; certainly the future is very much in the
tropics for painting, not here; those people of that future*

17 June 1890

My dear Theo,

Thanks much for your letter of the day before yesterday, and for the 50-franc note it contained. I waited for the consignment of colors and canvas from Tasset, which has just arrived, and for which I also thank you very much, to answer the question regarding the difference between Tanguy and Tasset colors. Well, it's absolutely the same thing, in the Tasset tubes there are some from time to time, especially for the *white*, that aren't filled properly. However, when Tanguy for his part also fills them badly too, — certainly without doing so deliberately — the tubes of cobalt, for example like the one I have in my hands — so I'm talking only based on the same fact that exists on both sides — I just don't see why one would have any very serious things to reproach the other with.

Is there a difference in the invoices? That's what would interest me more. And then in the colors there is adulteration as in wines. How can one judge correctly when, like myself, one knows nothing of chemistry. I'd nevertheless consider it very good that, should père Tanguy be going to extraordinary lengths for us by putting his time and his effort into packing up and dispatching the canvases that are in his attic, then you should get paint from him, even if it's a little worse than the other. It would only be fair.

But what he says about a difference in the tubes, I repeat, it's pure imagination on his part. And the reason why we went to Tasset's is that the latter's colors are in general less insipid. Now this difference isn't important, and if Tanguy has the good will to pack up the canvases stored at his place — fair that he has the order for the colors.

It was with pleasure that I made the acquaintance of the Dutchman, who came yesterday. He looks much too nice to be doing painting in the current conditions. If he nevertheless persists in wanting to do it I told him that he would do well to go to Brittany with Gauguin and De Haan, because he'll live there on 3 francs a day instead of 5 francs, and will have good company. That I myself also hope very much to join them, since Gauguin is going there. I was really pleased to learn that they're going to renew their attempt there. Certainly you're right that it's better for Gauguin than staying in Paris. Very pleased, too, that he likes the head of that Arlésienne. I really hope to do a few etchings of subjects from the south, let's say 6, since I can print them free of charge at Mr. Gachet's; he's very willing to run them off for nothing if I do them. It's certainly a thing that must be done, and we'll act in such a way that in some way it forms a sequel to the Lauzet-Monticelli publication, if you approve. And Gauguin will probably engrave a few of his canvases in combination with me. His painting, which belongs to you, and especially for the rest of the Martinique things.

Which plates Mr. Gachet will also print off for us. Of course we'll leave him free to run off copies for himself. Mr. Gachet will come one day to see my canvases in Paris, and then we'd choose the ones to be engraved. At the moment I have two studies on the go — one a bouquet of wild plants, thistles, ears of wheat, leaves of different types of greenery. One almost red, the other very green, the other yellowing.

The second study a white house amid greenery with a star in the night sky and an orange light at the window and dark greenery and a somber pink note.

That's all for the moment. I have an idea for doing a more important canvas of *Daubigny's* house and garden, of which I already have a small study.

I was really pleased that Gauguin is going off with De Haan again. Naturally this Madagascar plan seems to me hardly possible to carry out, I would much prefer to see him leave for Tonkin. If, however, he went to Madagascar I'd be able to follow him there. For one *should* go there in twos or threes. But we aren't there yet. Certainly the future is very much in the tropics for painting, either in Java or in Martinique, Brazil or Australia, and not here, but you feel that it hasn't been proved to me that you, Gauguin, or I are those people of that future. But certainly once again, there and not here, one day, probably soon, one will see Impressionists working who will hold their own with Millet, Pissarro. Believing in that is natural, but going there without the means of existence or a relationship with Paris, a mad impulse when for years on end one has rusted away while vegetating here. Well. Thanks again, and good handshake to you and your wife, and good health to the little one, whom I'm really longing to see again.

Yours truly,
Vincent.

NAUMBURG

918.3 km from Auvers-sur-Oise

music

[17 June 1890]

The former hermit of Sils Maria, now hermit of Naumburg, now hermit to 'his' body, performs detached, stormy improvisations on the piano and mutters *Ignatz, Ignatz! Lick-y an-thro ran ton ton ton, an-thras ran ton ton ton, lick-y net i i i i iiiiiiiiii!!!*

AUVERS-SUR-OISE

918.3 km from Naumburg

I painted Miss Gachet's portrait; the curious relation-ships that exist between one piece of nature and another; in women's clothes one sees very pretty arrangements of bright colors; if only one could have the individuals one sees pass by to do their portraits

28 June 1890

My dear Theo,

You could send the attached order for colors at the beginning of the month, anyway at the most convenient moment, there's no urgency for a few days earlier or later.

Yesterday and the day before yesterday I painted Miss Gachet's portrait, which you'll see soon, I hope. The dress is pink.

The wall in the background green with orange spots, the carpet red with green spots, the piano dark violet. It's 1 meter high and 50 wide.

It's a figure I enjoyed painting — but it's difficult.

He's promised to get her to pose for me another time with a little organ. I'll do one for you — I noticed that this canvas looks very good with another horizontal one of wheatfields, thus — one canvas being vertical and pink, the other pale green and green-yellow, complementing the pink.

But we're still a long way from people understanding the curious relationships that exist between one piece of nature and another, which however explain and bring each other out. But a few, though, do feel it, and that's already something. And then this has been gained, that in women's clothes one sees very pretty arrangements of bright colors. If only one could have the individuals one sees pass by to do their portraits, it would be as pretty as any past era, and I even think that often in nature there is currently all the grace of Puvis's painting, *Inter artes & naturem*. Thus yesterday I saw two figures, the mother in dark carmine dress, the daughter in pale pink with a yellow hat without any ornamentation, very healthy figures, rustic, well tanned by the open air, burned by the sun, the mother especially with a very, very red face and black hair and two diamonds in her ears. And I thought again of that canvas by Delacroix, *Maternal Upbringing*. For in the expressions on the faces there really was everything that there was in the head of George Sand. Do you know that there's a bust-length portrait of George Sand by Delacroix, there's a wood engraving of it in *L'Illustration* — with the hair cut short.

Good handshake in thought to you & Jo, and good fortune with the little one.

Ever yours, Vincent

NAUMBURG

918.3 km from Auvers-sur-Oise

the Anti-Christ (Dionysos) who no longer writes

[28 June 1890]

AUVERS-SUR-OISE

918.3 km from Naumburg

The child is ill; it would be a good plan to come and lodge here; a rather melancholy letter from Gauguin; three croquis; Jo would have twice as much milk here; what will be, will be; I scarcely dare count on always having the necessary health; I still love art & life very much

2 July 1890

My dear Theo and dear Jo,

I've just received the letter in which you say that the child is ill; I'd very much like to come and see you, and what holds me back is the thought that I'd be even more powerless than you are in the given state of distress. But I can feel how very exhausting it must be, and would like to be able to lend a hand. By coming straightaway I fear I would increase the confusion. However, I share your anxieties with all my heart. It's a real pity that at Mr. Gachet's the house is so cluttered with all sorts of things. Otherwise I think it would be a good plan to come and lodge here — at his house — with the little one, at least for a good month — I think that the country air has an enormous effect. In the street here there are kids born in Paris and really sickly — who however are well. Coming here to the inn would be possible too, it's true. So that you aren't too alone I could come myself to stay at your place for a week or fortnight.

That wouldn't increase the expenses. For the little one, truly I'm beginning to fear that he must be given air, and especially the little bustle of the other children of a village. Surely, Jo too, who shares our anxieties and risks, I think that from time to time she must take this distraction of the country.

A rather melancholy letter from Gauguin, he talks vaguely of having definitely decided on Madagascar, but so vaguely that one can clearly see that he's only thinking of it because he doesn't really know what else to think about. And the execution of the plan seems almost absurd to me.

Here are three croquis — one of a figure of a peasant woman, big yellow hat with a knot of sky-blue ribbons, very red face. Coarse blue blouse with orange spots, background of ears of wheat.

It's a no. 30 canvas but it's really a little coarse, I fear. Then the horizontal landscape with the fields, a subject like one of Michel's — but then the coloration is soft green, yellow, and green-blue. Then undergrowth, violet trunks of poplars that cross the landscape perpendicularly like columns. The depths of the undergrowth are blue, and under the big trunks the flowery meadow, white, pink, yellow, green, long russet grasses and flowers.

The people here at the inn used to live in Paris; there they were constantly indisposed, parents and children, here they never have anything, and especially not the littlest one which came here when it was 2 months old, and then the mother had difficulty in suckling him, while here all of that went well almost immediately. In another respect you work all day long, and at the moment you're probably hardly sleeping. I'd willingly believe that Jo would have twice as much milk here, & that then when she came here one could do without cows, donkeys, and other quadrupeds. And as for Jo, so that during the daytime she has company, my word, she could also go and stay just opposite père Gachet, perhaps you remember that there's an inn just opposite at the bottom of the slope.

What do you want me to say as regards the future, perhaps, perhaps, without the Boussods?

What will be, will be, you haven't spared yourself trouble for them, you've served them with an exemplary fidelity all the time.

I, too, am trying to do as well as I can, but I don't hide from you that I scarcely dare count on always having the necessary health.

And if my illness recurred you would excuse me, I still love art and life very much, but as to ever having a wife of my own I don't believe in it very strongly. I fear, rather, that toward let's say the age of forty — but let's not say anything — I declare that I know nothing, absolutely nothing, of what turn it may yet take.

But I'm writing to you at once that as regards the little one I think you mustn't worry yourselves excessively; if it's that he's teething, well to make the task easier for him perhaps we could distract him more here where there are children, animals, flowers and good air.

I shake your hand and Jo's firmly in thought, and kiss the little one.

Ever yours,
Vincent

Thank you for the consignment of colors, for the 50-franc note and for the article on the Independents.

An Englishman, Australian, called Walpole Brooke will probably come to see you; he lives at 16 rue de la Grande Chaumière — I told him that you would let him know a time when he could come & see my canvases that are at your place.

He'll probably show you some of his studies, which are still rather lifeless, but however he does observe nature. He has been here in Auvers for months, and we went out together sometimes, he was brought up in Japan, you would never think so from his painting — but that may come.

NAUMBURG

918.3 km from Auvers-sur-Oise

music

[2 July 1890]

The former old artilleryman, or is it Cæsar, or is it Prado, or is it
... performs violent improvisations on the piano.

AUVERS-SUR-OISE

918.3 km from Naumburg

*rather difficult and laborious hours; we also feel our exis-
tence to be fragile; the storm that threatens you also; my life,
too, is attacked at the very root; the brush however almost
falling from my hands; trying to express sadness, extreme
loneliness; what I consider healthy & fortifying about the
countryside; I often think of the little one*

10 July 1890

Dear brother and sister,

Jo's letter was really like a gospel for me, a deliverance from anguish that was caused by the rather difficult and laborious hours for us all that I shared with you. It's no small thing when all together we feel the daily bread in danger, no small thing when for other causes than that we also feel our existence to be fragile.

Once back here I too still felt very saddened, and had continued to feel the storm that threatens you also weighing upon me. What can be done — you see I usually try to be quite good-humored, but my life, too, is attacked at the very root, my step also is faltering. I feared — not completely — but a little nonetheless — that I was a danger to you, living at your expense — but Jo's letter clearly proves to me that you really feel that for my part I am working and suffering like you.

There — once back here I set to work again — the brush however almost falling from my hands and — knowing clearly what I wanted I've painted another three large canvases since then. They're immense stretches of wheatfields under turbulent skies, and I made a point of trying to express sadness, extreme loneliness. You'll see this soon, I hope — for I hope to bring them to you in Paris as soon as possible, since I'd almost believe that these canvases will tell you what I can't say in words, what I consider healthy and fortifying about the countryside.

Now the third canvas is Daubigny's garden, a painting I'd been thinking about ever since I've been here.

I hope with all my heart that the planned journey may provide you with a little distraction.

I often think of the little one, I believe that certainly it's better to bring up children than to expend all one's nervous energy in making paintings, but what can you do, I myself am now, at least I feel I am, too old to retrace my steps or to desire something else. This desire has left me, although the moral pain of it remains.

I very much regret not having seen Guillaumin again, but it pleases me that he's seen my canvases.

If I'd waited for him I would probably have stayed to talk with him in such a way as to miss my train.

Wishing you luck and good heart and relative prosperity, please tell Mother and Sister sometime that I think of them very often, besides this morning I have a letter from them and will reply shortly.

Handshakes in thought.

Ever yours, Vincent

My money won't last me very long this time, as on my return I had to pay the baggage costs from Arles. I retain very good memories of this trip to Paris. A few months ago I little dared hope to see our friends again. I thought that Dutch lady had a great deal of talent.

Lautrec's painting, portrait of a female musician, is quite astonishing, it moved me when I saw it.

NAUMBURG

918.3 km from Auvers-sur-Oise

he who was all the names in history no longer writes

[10 July 1890]

AUVERS-SUR-OISE

pointlessness; the state of peace, the storms that threaten it;
I'm applying myself to my canvases with all my attention;
the painters themselves are increasingly at bay; the util-
ity of a union; old thatched roofs and immense stretches
of wheat after the rain; to the right a hurdle; a black cat;
sky pale green

23 July 1890

My dear brother,

Thanks for your letter of today and for the 50-franc note it contained.

I'd perhaps like to write to you about many things, but first
the desire has passed to such a degree, then I sense the pointlessness of it.

I hope that you'll have found those gentlemen favorably disposed toward you.

As regards the state of peace in your household, I'm just as
convinced of the possibility of preserving it as of the storms that
threaten it.

I prefer not to forget the little French I know, and certainly
wouldn't see the point of delving deeper into the rights or wrongs
in any discussions on one side or the other. It's just that this
wouldn't interest me.

Things go quickly here — aren't Dries, you and I a little more
convinced of that, don't we feel it a little more than those ladies?
So much the better for them — but anyway, talking with rested
minds, we can't even count on that.

As for myself, I'm applying myself to my canvases with all
my attention, I'm trying to do as well as certain painters whom
I've liked and admired a great deal.

What seems to me on my return — is that the painters themselves are increasingly at bay.

Very well. But has the moment to make them understand the
utility of a union not rather passed already? On the other hand a
union, if it were formed, would go under if the rest went under.
Then you'd perhaps tell me that dealers would unite for the Impressionists; that would be very fleeting. Anyway it seems to me
that personal initiative remains ineffective, and having done the
experiment, would one begin it again?

I noted with pleasure that the Gauguin from Brittany that I
saw was very beautiful, and it seems to me that the others he's
done there must be too.

Perhaps you'll see this croquis of Daubigny's garden — it's one of my most deliberate canvases — to it I'm adding a croquis of old thatched roofs and the croquis of 2 no. 30 canvases depicting immense stretches of wheat after the rain. *Hirschig* asked me to ask you please to order the attached list of colors for him from the same colorman you send me. Tasset can send them directly to him, cash on delivery, but then he would have to be given the 20%.

Which would be simplest.

Or you'd put them into the consignment of colors for me, adding the invoice or telling me how much they cost, and then he'd send you the money. Here one can't find anything good in the way of colors.

I've simplified my own order to a very bare minimum.

Hirschig is beginning to understand a little, it has seemed to me, he's done the portrait of the old schoolmaster, which he gave him, good — and then he has landscape studies which are a little like the Konings at your place as regards color. It will become completely like that, perhaps, or like the things by Voerman that we saw together.

More soon. Look after yourself, and good luck in business &c. Warm regards to Jo, and handshakes in thought.

Yours truly,
Vincent.

Daubigny's Garden

Foreground of green and pink grass, on the left a green & lilac bush and a stem of plants with whitish foliage. In the middle a bed of roses. To the right a hurdle, a wall, and above the wall a hazel tree with violet foliage.

Then a hedge of lilac, a row of rounded yellow lime trees. The house itself in the background, pink with a roof of bluish tiles. A bench and 3 chairs, a dark figure with a yellow hat, and in the foreground a black cat. Sky pale green.

NAUMBURG

918.3 km from Auvers-sur-Oise

unbridled noise

[27 July 1890]

Possessed by some strange state of becoming, the body that was
once Nietzsche attacks the piano, hitting, banging, assaulting
keys, generating unbridled, nearly barbaric, cacophonous, pur-
plish-blue noises, bright gold noises, noxious red noises, sprawl-
ing thru the room, like a forest, threat'ning \\ *clang* — to engulf —
CLANG-CLANG/ /to destroy — CLANG-it.

CLOSING PROLOGUE: AUVERS-SUR-OISE

Spells of madness, the utopia of the family, the paintbrush falls
918.3 km from Naumburg

27–29 JULY 1890

In Auvers-sur-Oise, Vincent seems to have found a new haven of sorts. At the Ravouxs, he is given use of a small room that will serve as his studio when he paints indoors while in their barn he can dry his paintings. Yet, those places are not his own. The painter remains a vagabond, like the tail of a comet that may one day break off and disperse, a shattered star, nothing but detritus in an asteroid belt.

After a decade of being at the mercy of others, and after his brief visit with Theo and Jo, the mad wanderer dreams of a new communal house, this one however is not to be with other painters, but with his brother, wife, and their child — it will be a novel family, of artist, gallerist, and mother and son. His life with Sien having failed, his hope of ever having a helpmeet long dead, he envisions renting a house in the village and continually attempts to persuade his brother to leave Paris for the country and to live in his Chavannean Eden.

Since leaving St. Rémy, Vincent hasn't suffered any spells of madness and Dr. Gachet believes he has entirely recovered and that it is doubtful that his malady will return. A new horizon, a hopeful future is, it seems, possibly in sight, or something the painter longs for or needs in order to keep the lowering storm at bay. If however he is free of the stigma he suffered in Arles, he is not without despondent spells.

I am far from having arrived at some kind of tranquility, he wrote Theo, indicating, if free of the haunted denizens of St. Rémy, if feeling less like a pathological specimen, there was still no solid shore to which he felt rooted. I don't at all want to say exhausted, but anyway troubles are taking up too much room, are too numerous, and you're sowing among thorns.

He has no region, no secure terrain.

If separate from Theo in space and time, Vincent began to bind himself to his brother as never before, and to try to bind Theo to him with entreaty after entreaty. While his brother was set to travel to Holland to visit his mother with wife and child, Vincent urged him not to, arguing that the journey is always very, very costly and it has never done any good. Instead, it was to Auvers-sur-Oise that he and his wife and child should travel, for it would also be best for the kid.

Myself, Vincent said, all I can do at the moment is say that I think that we all need some rest, nesting his brother *&* his family within his own condition. I feel — a failure — that's it as regards me — I feel that that's the fate I'm accepting. And which won't change any more.

For the painter, all utopic visions have ceased; life is now mere endurance, yet it is as a family tribe that that fate will be lived out — but one more reason, he says to Theo, setting aside all ambition, we can live together for years without ruining ourselves on either side.

If the painter is immersed in his art, he tells Theo that it is difficult to acquire a certain facility of production, and by ceasing to work he would lose it much more quickly, more easily than it cost him in troubles to acquire it. And the prospect darkens, he notes — in his final paintings, the sky is bereft of stars; the illumination of the cosmos absent; the bright scintillating sun and moon have grown dim. The radiating light is gone. The painter concludes that he doesn't see a happy future at all, and when appeals to his brother end in mere silence, or when the familial utopia hits an impasse, the painter appeals once more to Gauguin to unite in Brittany, but that prospect is also quickly rejected. Gauguin tells Vincent that, for a person who is ill and sometimes in need of a doctor, it is risky, for my studio is so far from the town. Gauguin though had no interest in the city and continued to dream of the tropics, stating that the savage will return to the wild. Yet, as wild as the savage is, what he does not want to suffer are the violent outbreaks of a madman.

As the days and nights pass, the madman is more and more isolated, his stars losing more and more luminosity, the darkness of chaos approaching with the speed of light.

Carrying Gauguin's thread forward, Vincent notes to Theo that the future of painting is in the tropics, however, in a despondent cry, he negates this very future possibility — I am not convinced, he declares to Theo, that you, Gauguin, or I are the men of that future.

Does he want all of them to abandon painting?

If Vincent is a failure, then all of them are, yet him only in their wake. What is before the painter becomes nothing but a series of dead tomorrows, all negated in advance. With the promise of art having failed, the last desperate bulwark is family.

If Vincent was not all the names in history, if in his cycle of collapse he was not undergoing subjective mutations akin to Nietzsche's, he was a sort of Ferris wheel of vertiginous states of becoming, an ever-spinning corporeal machine whose body was a battlefield of incoherence and discombobulation. I am risking my life for my work, he said, and my reason has half foundered because of it. With each return to madness, with each unmooring from sanity, he shifted through cycles of vehement oscillations, his center holding until it cracked. Dispersed from place to place, his life was like his body: lonely, isolated, devoid of privacy, a whorl of chaos: — a man with no true place of his own, a man with no residence in his name, save for the virtual reality of his art, his finished paintings all signed VINCENT. What is home for the painter? Asylum after asylum after asylum: sites of surveillance, sites of sickness, sites of control. Cast into the most extreme unknown, cast into an exacting indeterminacy, nerves pressed to their threshold, life for Vincent was a ring spiraling outward and inward, a ring breaking apart and shattering, a ring spinning back to the recurring station of oblivion and destruction. And it was he felt an impasse from which he could not return: — I am too old to retrace my steps or to desire anything different. That desire has left me, though the mental suffering of it remains.

In his portrait of Dr. Gachet, a work based in part on Delacroix's *Tasso in the Madhouse*, the painter depicted the mask of melancholy, a mask he called the heart-broken expression of our time. There is something in it, he explained to Gauguin, of your *Christ in the Garden of Olives*, something of a man not destined to be understood, which was perhaps a masked portrait of Vincent himself, for there was a kinship he felt with Gachet, seeing in him something of his own fragility and mental instability. Amongst the olive trees of Auvers-sur-Oise, Vincent was the afflicted one, the sufferer of agonies, Prometheus upon the rocks, his body seething with turbulence, a territory at war. The alliance had long been broken.

If free of the provincial aspersions of the people of Arles, the painter remained an enigma and monster of sorts in Auvers-sur-Oise, what with his strange demeanor, tatterdemalion clothes, peculiar accent, and wounded ear, which many residents found grotesque, similar to the misshapen auricle of a gorilla. A kind of Elephant Man of the French countryside, Vincent was the local freak, and his visage unsettled many, most of whom turned from him, all of whom refused to pose for him. But could he fight his own constitution? Could he combat a family curse? How free himself of his DNA? How deterritorialize? How break open a new region? Our neurosis, he wrote his brother, is also a fatal inheritance, since in civilization the weakness increases from generation to generation. If we want to face the real truth about our constitution, we must acknowledge that we belong to the number of those who suffer from a neurosis that already has its roots in the past.

And when in the summer of 1888 he wrote to Theo, in reference to his brother's syphilis and the disappearance of his desire the moment he feels himself to be himself again, the self-appointed physician noted, echoing his earlier words, the root of the evil lies in the constitution itself, in the fatal weakness of families from generation to generation, and there's no cure for it.

Fin.

Round and round the Ferris wheel of vertiginous states spun, the inner whorl raging, the turbulence of the soul intensifying, the reaper inching closer *&* closer, like the recurring event of the Solar Saros eclipse.

If consumed by study after study, if painting with the same or a similar fury and intensity such as possessed him previously, nature and painting did not have a calming let alone restorative effect. The cosmic vision the artist opened when painting *Starry Night* had faded. The stars were as if no more, as if they had burned themselves out. His eye did not extend into the distance, but burrowed ever deeper and deeper, till the sky was closed out, the crows vanished, and there was nothing but gnarled roots *&* trunks, objects as bent, twisted, and involuted as the pathway of his fate.

Standing before a knot of earth and trees, a rush of images flashed through the painter's mind, a flickering specter of his genealogy, of the cursed House of van Gogh, with his own recurrent spells echoing in him, as his brother's delusions, hallucinations, and outbursts, and those of his sister Wilhelmina, who would spend 40 years in an asylum, his epileptic maternal aunt, his paternal uncle Cent, who himself frequently disappeared to southern France to seek solace from his spells of madness (did he not realize that it is southern France which causes madness?), and his younger brother Cor, who would later commit suicide, or so some believed — the whole terrible wave of the van Gogh genealogical line flickered in him, haunting his flesh, haunting his nerves, haunting his cells, haunting his spirit, the terror of plasmic finality. They come to live in us, one could imagine him saying, the specters of generations, they come to burrow in our veins, infecting us with their maladies, like some doomed plague of locusts devouring us from the inside.

The center spiraling out and devouring him from beyond, the void opening up and engulfing him, the abyss tearing him apart, the Ferris wheel of Atreus turning and turning at warp speed, the violent oscillations ravaging the mind till vertigo could be endured no more, the corporeal machine reaching the final point of dissolution, its fire so intense it burns the heart, the center fracturing, the sea journey no longer endurable, for there is no secure nest, there is no home, there is nothing, nothing, nothing, *just exile* — nest as confinement and cage, nest as asylum *&* house of threat, nest as auto-da-fé...

Like a dash bringing life to its conclusion, like a razor severing an ear—BANG: a single bullet is discharged, lodges in the body, unravels it.

The Ferris wheel of oscillations ceases.

The paintbrush falls to his side.

A 7mm Lefaucheux pinfire revolver brings the vertigo to an end.

*

Je me suis blessé, Vincent replies to Gustave Ravoux, as he raises his shirt to display the small would under his ribs.

Around it, a dark red circle has formed, a purple halo of sorts, like the vibratory rings around the stars of the painter's paintings. Out of it, a thin stream of blood flows. The final colors of his life.

The reaper has finished his work; the light has gone out; the circle of fate has closed.

Dying is hard, Vincent said to a mourner at his father's funeral on 26 March 1885, but living is harder still, and on 29 July 1890, at 1:30 A M, two days after the pistol shot, two days after his final brush stroke, drawing one last inhalation of his pipe as he gazes into his brother's eyes, the painter stops living, the lapidary work of life done.

CLOSING PROLOGUE: NAUMBURG; PARAGUAY; WEIMAR

The specter *&* simulacrum vs. the female Minotaur
The open horizon

1889–1900 ~

Although his organs still continued to function, he who was once Nietzsche had stopped living on 3 January 1889, that uncanny Augenblick when 'he' crossed the Rubicon into another domain, a firm unbroken line having been drawn between 'his' life and 'his' living death. But then, Nietzsche had already died so many times during his life: he had lived as a shadow in St. Moritz and in Naumburg; he had gone to the underworld and sacrificed not only rams but also his own blood; he had experienced numerous dark Untergangen ad infinitum; and while in Torino, he noted in *Ecce Homo* that he was grateful for *his whole life*, that he had buried his 44th year there and so he was already dead (as his father) and yet, he was still alive and growing old (as his mother). Speaking to us therefore from beyond, he was a specter and simulacrum of 'his' body, the last remnants of a dispersed god, a corpo disfatto. *Nietzsche-Zombie!*

Once again, 'he' was back in Naumburg, and as dead as ever, for he had left the land and had embarked upon a journey into uncharted territory. The expedition was so absolute and extreme that he had burned the bridges behind him — indeed, he had gone even farther and destroyed the very land behind him (entire civilizations had been earthquaked; moralities undermined; artists disemboweled; philosophers uncrowned; religions eviscerated;

gods killed) as he traveled out to sea and beyond, into unknown oceans, into new horizons (the Übermensch, the Eternal Return), and into a new infinite, into an infinity more immense and terrifying than Pascal's (even more solitary, more dangerous, more sublime) — it was an ever-recurring cyclical infinity whose weight could crush one. This sailor however had been cast from his ship, and like one emerging from a grandiose wreckage, he was thrown back onto land, an alien who had been transformed and transfigured by his excursionem. Who, if anyone, would recognize him? If mist had once struck his face, if the winds of storms had once marked his flesh, this wild figure once known as Prince Vogelfrei was no longer on the prow of his ship but striking the walls of a cage — the land upon which he had been cast was entirely foreign, for truly, there was no longer any land for him, as there is no land for those who have crossed beyond, who have emerged victorious from their shipwrecks. 'He' was at sea, far beyond the final sematic buoy. No longer human, but fish. Yet, dead as he was (Nietzsche corpse = Nietzsche mother), his body was still alive, and it had to endure the test of tests, an 11-year crucible more exigent than any theological wager.

*

In February of 1886, before embarking to Paraguay, the newly married Elisabeth Förster (née Nietzsche) had sent her brother a gold ring as a token of affection — did she want to bind him in an ménage à trois she thought equal to or greater than the one between him, Paul Rée, and Lou Salomé? To reverse or supersede a trinity she found immoral and unholy? Inscribed within the band of the gold ring were the words: "Remember B. & E. with love."

Although the budding Anti-Christ accepted the gift, the combination Bern & Eli offended him. Quite apart from Förster's views, he said to his mother, as if the third ring did indeed signify that the marriage was also to the philosopher himself, despite his never assenting to it, there is no affinity between him and me. It is fortunate that he is gone.

Yet, just as Elisabeth & Bernhard were boarding the steamer *Uruguay*, the new bride had discovered that both her engagement and wedding rings had disappeared — the sole ring that remained was the one given to the man whom no one would wed, and with Elisabeth's future return to Naumburg, & the future that she would live out there with her brother, it was in fact as if they were bound to one another by an eternal ring, fated in the most eerie of ways, as if the sister's marriage was never actually to Bernhard Förster, whom she would outlive, but to her brother, Friedrich Wilhelm Nietzsche, whom she would outlive, burying husband after husband. Caught in an enclosing circle of endless recurrence, the ring uniting, in terrible discord, Lama and Female Elephant, Anti-Semite and Anti-Christ, a spiritual marriage the Queen would eventually legally solidify when changing her name from Elisabeth Förster to Elisabeth Förster-Nietzsche, bringing together in herself with one dreadful Bindestrich the trinity of Knight, Death, and Devil.

At table with her mother, when she first returned from Paraguay in late 1890, after recounting the tragedies she had endured and vigorously denying that Bernhard had committed suicide, the Queen of the jungle outlined her plans to her mother, noting that she would defend Förster's name, work, and ideals, that she would restore Nueva Germania and become its reigning monarch, thereby continuing her utopic vision of a purified Germany, while in Berlin she would entreat officials in that city to support all German colonial efforts. A new century was on the rise during which Germany must triumph; it was only a question of seizing the world spirit and guiding history to the country's will — was such a destiny not in fact on the horizon? Could triumphant boots not be heard in the distance? As one who discounted such affairs, Elisabeth would not however appeal to

Bismarck but seek the direct address of the Emperor and gain him as an ally for Nueva Germania. Her will to power would extend itself ever further through her appealing to Provost von der Goltz, the ecclesiastical counselor of the Lutheran Church, to ask him to assist in the building of a Christian church in Paraguay. Finally, she would compose a book about Nueva Germania, detailing its accomplishments and its future, including its agricultural and industrial potential, and therefore its prospective political apotheosis. This world is the will to power — and nothing besides! And you yourselves are also this will to power — and nothing besides!

Meanwhile, above, on the second floor, as if perched like some foreboding bird to the gateway of tomorrow, was the man of many names, or what was left of that body, and as he heard his sister speaking, he began to emit fierce bestial howls and rage against the burgeoning religio-political tumult below, as if in protest against and in condemnation of every one of his sister's pronouncements, not to speak of the haunting enclosure in which he was suddenly caught.

While Queen Eli called for the building of churches, the Anti-Christ spoke of the need for expansive places of reflection, *an architecture for thinkers* where refined manners would prohibit even priests from praying aloud: a whole complex of buildings and sites that would give expression to the sublimity of contemplation and stepping aside. The time is past when the church possessed a monopoly on reflection, when the *vita contemplativa* always had to first be a *vita religiosa*; and everything built by the church gives expression to that idea.

I do not see, the Anti-Christ said, how we could be satisfied with such buildings, even if they were stripped of their ecclesiastical purpose; the language spoken by these buildings is far too pathetic and self-conscious, reminding us that they are houses of God and ostentatious monuments of some transcendent intercourse; we who are godless could not think *our thoughts* in such surroundings. We wish to see ourselves translated into stone and plants; we want to take walks *within ourselves* when we stroll around these halls and gardens.

Stone and plants, halls and gardens, not churches: such was the new architecture called for by he who once sought to form his own society in the climate of the littoral Provençal, the homeland of la gaya scienza, a place which suited his nature marvelously well. A land not of grapes of wrath but of grapes of delight.

If he could no longer articulate thoughts linguistically, if he was fundamentally non compos mentis, his nerves still seemed astute, possessing a native intelligence, the cultivated instinct of the philosopher of the future, and they revolted against the dark utopic visions and plebicolic aspirations of his demagogic sister. Thus spoke the body; thus it revolted. Ring be damned!

If still perhaps dreaming of his society of lo gai saber, if no longer speaking through philosophy but music, albeit more and more losing his sense of rhythm, the one formerly known as Herr Dynamite was forcibly entrapped in a domicile with both his mother and sister, the two greatest objections to his thought of the Eternal Return, sources of unspeakable horror, disharmonias, figures who could wound him more than anyone else, poisonous vermin whom he could not defend himself against (sometimes, however, he did try to strangle his mother — was that not possibly a way to try to strangle himself and so end his own life since, as a living dead man, he was also his mother and less & less himself?), real canaille, infernal machines that would make of him and his philosophy a puppet, Nietzsche Marionette: propped up, robed in white, prophetized, staged for National Socialism, staged for Fascism, staged for Elisabeth Förster-Nietzsche's will to power.

My brother's goal is not my goal, she had previously declared to her ringless husband; his entire philosophy goes against my grain. Because my talents are practical, all your plans and magnificent ideas excite me: they can be translated into actions. And that is why I am at a loss what to do with my brother's philosophy. I do not see at all what can be done with it.

Ring be damned! Turn no more, circle; give me teleology! Deutschland, Deutschland über alles!

The art of living Nietzsche's philosophy was too subtle and difficult. It could not be adhered to like a step-by-step program; it would not yield immediate, utilitarian returns. What was one who sought power and prestige to do with it? Whereas the Übermensch was an intractable and elusive ideal, National Socialism was a feasible and concrete goal. Purify the German race; rid Germany of the Jews; drive out the foreigners, thought Elisabeth, all her dark fin-de-siècle energies emerging with the force of a geyser. A solution was finally in sight.

And so, as the Good European communicated via the piano, babbled and gibbered, sputtering amphigorically, or remained silent, himself having become a human dash, or the interval between two Gedankenstriche, the Nietzsche family house became a center of propaganda for Paraguay and Anti-Semitism.

Queen Eli felt like she was triumphing, but her limelight dimmed swiftly and firmly — despite the success of her book on Nueva Germania, it met with strong opposition from the remaining colonists, and her efforts were finally sundered, with her account of the venture shown to be false and untrue.

After her visit in 1892, a key member of the community, Fritz Neumann, wrote to the Chemnitz Colonial Society that there was neither running water nor roads in Nueva Germania, that those who had tried to settle in the forest had been driven out by nature, and that the undergrowth had already suffocated their collapsed huts and abandoned plantations. Another investor, George Strekfus, said I do not believe that Mrs. Förster has been cured in Germany of her disease, which borders on megalomania; on the contrary, her alleged successes concerning the clergyman, etc., have probably made her even more conceited and domineering. Über alles!

None too flummoxed by her efforts finally being exposed for what they were, with Nietzsche's star on the rise, the Queen recognized a keen opportunity—the philosophy she once discredited with resolute finality was suddenly adopted and championed. Not long after, Queen Eli forged the terrible hyphen, Förster-Nietzsche, a dark conduit that did not function as a bridge, but as a negative sign, a dual negation & subtraction, a slit in the eye fusing fascism *&* free spirit, Anti-Semitism *&* anti-anti-Semitism, Christian & Anti-Christ, New Testament god & Dionysos. The unholy alliance was established, and when Elisabeth & Frau Pastor Nietzsche had taken over in collaboration with Constantin Naumann the publications of the free spirit, Peter Gast told Overbeck, one could laugh oneself sick at the thought that two pious women and a country parson sit in judgment on what can and cannot be published of the writings of one of the fiercest anti-Christians and atheists. — — *Ring be damned!*

It displeases me to hear my sister's voice, the philosopher once wrote; I have always been sick when I was with her. And against his will, Elisabeth was with him seemingly eternally, as if he were trapped in some dreadful vivarium, her hyphenation hammering out & forging the bond of the ring, like a shackle around a slave's foot, like a web entrapping prey, her presence putting the affirmation of the Eternal Return in danger. If Nietzsche could not triumphantly affirm life's eternal recurrence, would he even be able to live this life? Yet, was 'he' even alive anymore? Was not 'he' a new 'he' after undergoing such mutation? How many times would 'he' have to say yes to life? Or was the 'he' the body of the one born Friedrich Wilhelm Nietzsche now actually the ultimate and final 'he' that 'his' body was always meant to become, Nietzsche-Mother, Nietzsche-Sister, Nietzsche-Corpse? And, ultimately, did it matter? Did Life need Nietzsche to say *Ja!* to it? Life didn't give a damn about him, or any other human for that matter — life cared about the species about as much as it cared for a speck of dust. There is no caritas in the drive to evolution; if one species perishes, another emerges. Trilobite, dinosaur, human, overhuman, ... Yet, for humanity, in creating Zarathustra, Nietzsche created a figure that could vanquish God and nihilism and affirm the Eternal Return. 'He' did not have to do such himself; a myth had been invented and the domain of the subject superseded. When Peter Gast would visit and 'Nietzsche' would read aloud, the former philosopher would get excited and bark and growl until the book was removed from his hands. But he did not understand what he read, and more often than not, simply shouted out page numbers, or a series of indiscriminate lines, each disconnected from the next, the veins in his forehead bulging as he struggled to read the text. When sitting in his armchair, he would stare for hours out the window, and like an imbecilic child, examined his favorite objects. During such moments, he would turn to his mother and repeat a litany of phrases:

I am dead because I am stupid; I am stupid because I am dead. I am dead because I am stupid; I am stupid...

I have a fine feeling for things.

I do not like horses.

Ich bebe!

It's *ich liebe*, Fritz, his mother corrected.

Ich bebe!

It's *ich liebe*, Fritz.

Ich bebe! Ich bebe!

No more did he write philosophy, but scrawl cryptic first-person messages in red and blue crayon, wearing the mask of mother & sister:

Indeed, Fritz was declared incurable at the court of Prof. Binzwanger and from that moment I had no peace in being able at least to look after him myself.

I've had my fingers burnt so I prefer not to move in. Do they have children?

As mother of the colony I still have so much to do for all the colonists! That is the main pleasure for Fritz. I am monstrously good. I do not know whether I am leaving my husband's work in the lurch. For me everything was over a long time ago, what I have lost I have lost. Only if my private property increases in value will I be able to recover the greater part of my capital. Money is nothing to me! God has always helped me! And I am very glad to give.

Philosophy? Amphigory? Cut-ups of the sub-waking selves playing aloud like recitations from the phonograph of the mind? What is his designation? Friedrich Nietzsche. What is that here? An ear. What is that here? A nose. What is that here? Hands I do not love.

Having been driven out of Nueva Germania, Elisabeth's new colonial project became Friedrich Nietzsche himself — if she could not triumph in the jungles of South America, she would triumph in Germany and take possession of a body far more easy to tame than the wilds of a foreign land, though Nietzsche himself was as foreign a land to her, if not even more so, than her previous locale, while his body of work was infinitely more alien and wild.

Queen Eli would obtain official authorization over the editorship of her new colony's published and un-published writings, and she would prepare a complete inventory of all its existing manuscripts and establish a register and archives. What matter that she had no training in philosophy or philology or library sciences? What matter that, when Rudolph Steiner attempted to tutor her in Nietzsche's philosophy, he concluded that she was a complete lay woman in all that concerns her brother's doctrine, and that she lacks any sense for fine, and even for crude, logical distinctions; her thinking is void of even the least logical consistency; and she lacks any sense of objectivity.

Over all obstacles, stand your ground! Über alles!

Queen Eli forged on and the Nietzsche house would be turned into the Nietzsche Archive and contain all her brother's memorabilia, stored in museum-style cabinets decorated with the carved insignia of Zarathustra's animals—eagle, serpent, and lion. To further solidify her hyphenated union with her brother, the Nietzsche Archive would also contain her memorabilia, including a bust of Bernhard Förster and material on Nueva Germania, as if there were no distinction between their visions and the Förster Archive were equal to the Nietzsche Archive, with only the short interval of a Bindestrich, or minus sign, separating them —not a chasm, not an ocean, not several continents, not a galaxy, but a mere insignificant interstice just a hair's breadth long.

In this official and mythicized environment, Queen Eli would welcome visitors ready to pay homage to the father of *Zarathustra*, though he was merely a mask for the Queen to project herself through to the world. The cult of Nietzsche (Elisabeth) was being born, the puppet ready to be displayed, its will long having been rendered ineffective, like a dead appendage only another could operate. Elisabeth & Nietzsche were finally bound to one another, united as if Siamese twins that had accidentally been separated at birth, a parabiositic mutation.

When Erwin Rohde visited the family during Easter in 1894, he saw that his friend was completely apathetic, recognized no one but his mother & sister, and spoke scarcely a sentence for a month at a time. Was there anymore a Nietzsche?

His body is shriveled and weak, Rohde said, though his complexion is healthy. . . . But obviously he no longer feels anything — neither happiness nor unhappiness.

The Augenblick for him to have enacted a free death had long past; the ring was now spinning in another direction: Theseus was trapped in a labyrinth devoid of an Ariadne, with no thread to lead him out and no weapon with which to defend himself, or defeat his opponent.

In the ensuing months, Nietzsche Marionette was being further colonized, & Elisabeth moved out of her mother's home, set up a house of her own, & established the Nietzsche Archives there. The ring around Nietzsche's finger was growing more and more constricting, the halls of the labyrinth darker & higher, its shadows ominous, its sonics terrifying, its odors horrific.

Feverishly, Queen Eli worked at editing her brother's voluminous papers, demanding from his correspondents the return of all his letters, and appropriating his copyright. Slowly but precipitously, she was enmeshing herself with her brother, absorbing and consuming him, spidering her way into his very soul, dominating him in a way that she could not in her youth, an act of vengeance against his lack of regard for her, her marriage, and her colonial endeavors. *Alles heil der Geist der Schwere!*

As the vegetating father of Zarathustra languished, Queen Eli composed the first volume of a biography of her most-prized possession—what matter his health, or having nurses care for him when he could easily be displayed to the world, an effigy of the will to power, the ghostly figure who gave birth to Zarathustra, a Brazen Head that might begin speaking mystic phrases. Everything was articulated in the hands, the eyes, the mustache—*Nietzsche Puppet!* What need for an animating mind?

When Overbeck visited over a year later, 'Nietzsche' was half-crouching in his room like a wild animal mortally wounded and wanting only to be left in peace. Were they wounds he suffered from the infernal machines? The anguish of not being able to affirm the Eternal Return any longer? Was it the sound of his sister's voice cutting into him like a razor, slowly taking possession of his life? *Disharmonias! Vermin!* What, if some day or night a demon were to steal after you into your loneliest loneliness...

Overbeck said 'he' did not appear to be suffering or in pain, except perhaps for the expression of profound distaste visible in 'his' lifeless eyes... 'He' had been living for weeks in a state of alternation between days of dreadful excitability, rising to a pitch of roaring and shouting, and days of complete prostration.

The carved insignia of eagle, serpent, and lion were no proxies for real eagles, serpents, and lions.

With her hagiographical account of her brother gaining widespread recognition, Queen Eli became the official mouthpiece of his philosophy, as if *she* was the Brazen Head through which he spoke and 'Nietzsche' nothing but a spectral projection for her to prism herself through. The Minotaur continued growing in height and stature, becoming ever more monstrous and powerful, as if it too had a mustache and wielded a sword. In being the guardian of the free spirit par excellence, the triumphs she sought but failed to achieve in Paraguay could be realized through her acts of ventriloquism. The puppeteer was becoming an ever-greater master of her pupa and would eventually be able to manipulate it at will, making it dance with ease, till it served her every drive. *The slave revolt triumphs! The master is defeated! The transvaluation of values is overturned.*

In conducting research for the second volume of the philosopher's life, Queen Eli traveled around much of Europe, retracing her brother's nearly every step, rendezvousing with many of his friends and gaining entry into the select circles of Europe's aristocracy. With her newfound eminence, the Queen was sought after as never before. When receiving a marriage proposal from a high society member whose one demand was that she not publish *The Antichrist*, the Queen staunchly rejected the proposal, despite her own stern objections to the book— her marriage was to Nietzsche & the Nietzsche Archive alone. Her will would not be bent, her ring would not be broken, let alone removed from her brother's finger—such frontiers would never be invaded; Theseus & the Minotaur would be forever united. Thus spoke the Bauchredner! But does not she who gazes long into the eyes of a puppet not also take the risk of turning into a puppet herself?

*

Although Nietzsche was dead and yet still alive and growing old as his mother, to Queen Eli, Franziska Oehler was even more inexistent than her effigy of a son. Perhaps she too was as dead as Pastor Nietzsche. In the Queen's biographical account of her brother's life, Frau Pastor Nietzsche was not spoken of as one of the influential women in his life; in fact, she was barely mentioned in Eli's book. When learning of this, Frau Pastor Nietzsche was deeply wounded and, to offset her daughter's distortions, began writing her own account of her children's lives but eventually abandoned the project, lacking the energy and drive of her daughter. This world is the will to power—and nothing besides! And you yourselves are also this will to power, if you know how to harness it...

While Frau Pastor Nietzsche was concerned with protecting her son from visitors due to his ailing condition, Queen Eli frequently displayed the puppet to the world. Once, when the mother was not present in Naumburg, the Queen invited the painter Curt Stöving to paint a portrait of the puppet. When the images of the sick philosopher were publicly exhibited throughout Germany, the mother was outraged and admonished the queen, stating, nobody understands why you did this to your brother. Dr. Zeller said that these pictures show Fritz with the face of a criminal, and Adalbert's wife exclaimed she would destroy them if she were the mother.

With this critique, Queen Eli feared the mother would seek to usurp her role and possibly further interfere with her utopic plans. Nietzsche was her child, not her mother's, and so began a war between mother and daughter over Nietzsche Puppet, with each seeking to gain sole guardianship of it, & each denouncing the other to the different members of the House of Nietzsche-Oehler. To the Queen, she must have total, unquestioned control over Nietzsche Puppet, including over the growing savings that were accumulating in his name from the profits of his book sales, and for months, as she was parasitically invading her brother like a host that did not know the difference between hospitality and colonialism, she sought to triumph over her mother, seeking every means to vanquish her and enfold her brother within her bosom, for to lose him was to lose herself, to split the Bindestrich in two and for her identity to be unmasked, cracked to reveal nothing but the mute void that it was. If anyone was to provide the milk of kindness to Nietzsche Puppet, it was Queen Eli whose breast would nourish the zombie!

After enduring numerous entreaties and devious schemes, all of which she resisted, Frau Pastor Nietzsche finally relented when her daughter threatened to seek legal condemnation of her as incompetent to be her son's guardian. At last, all rights to Nietzsche Puppet were surrendered & Queen Eli had sole possession of it—she could now remove Nietzsche's face & adopt it as her own: *Elisabeth Förster-Nietzsche-Minotaur*.

As the great victor of Nietzsche, Queen Eli decided that in order to be even freer of her mother's influence, and to be in the historic center of German culture, she would move the Nietzsche Archive to Weimar. Great political triumphs could more readily be realized only in that city. Thereafter, battles began with editors, publishers, lawyers, bankers, benefactors, and scholars, sometimes including threats of duels and lawsuits. While Nietzsche and Vincent had architectural correlates to their works, there was no engineering marvel that could be baptized in honor of the monarch's work; instead, it is the Paraguayan nightshade that reminds us of nothing so much as her social and political longings, longings echoed in the soul of her true but lesser twin, Langbehn.

Whilst Förster-Nietzsche's star was rising, she continued work on the second volume of her brother's life and planned a three-month trip to attend university lectures and socialize with the great figures of Europe, but the journey was never to be made. Frau Pastor Nietzsche had grown ill, forcing Queen Eli to return home to assist in aiding her brother. Not long after the Queen's return, on 20 April 1897, Franziska Oehler Nietzsche was no more, and so the puppet would truly be the sole possession of Queen Eli. With the mother dead and buried, Queen Eli could really come into her own, with that is the succor of every ally she could soldier to her cause. Who could defeat a Minotaur that was not a prisoner but the ruler of its labyrinth?

A few months later, since Queen Eli's own place was too small to house herself, Nietzsche Puppet, and the archives, and she did not have the finances to establish her queendom, Elisabeth petitioned Nietzsche's friend Meta von Salis to come to her aid and buy Villa Silberblick, a house on a hill overlooking downtown Weimar. As a friend and acolyte of Nietzsche's, von Salis wanted the philosopher, or what was left of him, to be able to finish out his life in seclusion and to be spared the invasions of a curious public. Although she had offered the house to Queen Eli on condition that the Minotaur could live there for a modest annual rental as long as her brother was alive, with the option of possibly buying it after his death, Eli took it upon herself to not only move in but to structurally renovate the interior and exterior of the house without first consulting von Salis. After learning of the significant alterations, and receiving Eli's bill for the construction, von Salis was aghast. The relation ended acrimoniously, with von Salis growing ever more disturbed by the Queen's actions, including her putting Nietzsche Puppet on display for a journalist, who described observing the invalid first during its sleep, then awake, watching it crouched on a chair as it was being fed a piece of cake.

The father of Zarathustra had become a caged animal fit for exhibition, a circus monkey or pickled punk. The freak attraction of Weimar—come one, come all, step right up, gaze into the blackened nitroglycerin pupils of 'Nietzsche,' and, if you dare, *let them gaze into you!!*

It is incomprehensible to me, von Salis wrote to Dr. Oehler, Queen Eli's cousin, that a man who was so sensitive when he was well, is sacrificed to the public now that he is a helpless invalid.

In her last letter to von Salis, the Queen expressed her regret that their friendship had ended for good saying, I have liked you very much, indeed I have loved you and I miss you more than ever now that I have triumphed over all men and manikins.

If Queen Eli had lost the support of Meta von Salis, it was of little concern to her—she had already colonized her house, and other benefactors could easily be found. The queendom had been founded; the cornerstone was in place. More, without an Ariadne, Theseus could never escape the labyrinth, and so the mask of the Minotaur was set, affixed as if an actual head and not a spectral hologram signifying nothing.

With her hypnotic, piercing, beady pupils, like some seductive Hoffmannesque automaton, the Queen seduced more and more benefactors to her cause, including the Anglo-German count, diplomat, and writer Count Harry Kessler, who was eventually appointed the bibliographic advisor of the Nietzsche Archive.

When invited to spend the weekend with the Queen at Villa Silberblick, Kessler was privy to displays of Nietzsche Puppet, and therefore his frequent eruptions — clearly, as much as he was a dead but living marionette who himself loved to play with dolls and toys, he still contained a sufficient amount of sulfuric and nitric acid.

In August 1897, after being given a tour of the house, Kessler was brought into the philosopher's room only to find him asleep on a sofa. In his diary, the Count reported that Nietzsche's mighty head had sunk halfway down to the right as if it were too heavy for his neck. His forehead was quite colossal; the mane of his hair still dark brown, like his shaggy, swollen moustache. There are wide, black-brown shadows sunk deep under his eyes into his cheeks. In his flat, loose face deep furrows from thought and desire are engraved but gradually fading and becoming smooth again. The hands are waxen, with greenish-violent veins, and somewhat swollen, like those of a corpse. A table and a high-stool had been shoved against the sofa so that the heavy body would not fall down in case of a sudden movement. He was exhausted by the muggy, thunderstorm atmosphere and would not awaken, despite his sister stroking him several times and calling to him, "Darling, darling" caressingly. Thus he resembles not someone sick or crazy but rather a dead man.

The slain Theseus, the zombie philosopher, jerked up by strings, like the son of Dr. Frankenstein awakening, inanimate matter become animate, sparked to movement by jolts of electricity, for he was nothing but dead flesh.

Two months later, just before the zombie's birthday, after Count Kessler and Frau Förster-Nietzsche discussed their plans for a new edition of *Zarathustra*, not long before turning out the light to sleep at 10 PM, Kessler was awoken by the loud roaring of the still dynamitic puppet:

I rose half up and heard two, three times the long, raw, sounds, as if groaning, Kessler wrote in his diary, which he cried out with all his strength in the night. Then all was silent again.

If 'he' could not speak, the feedback system of the body of 'Nietzsche' continued to emit strident frequencies, as if a last form of energetic protest the corpus disfatto could discharge.

Despite the regularity of such eruptions, the Queen continued to put her puppet on display and Villa Silberback became a mecca for artists, writers, poets, and politicians, including Karl-August, the ruling grand duke of Sachsen-Weimar. The ambitious project of editing and publishing *The Will to Power* came to Queen Eli's mind, for Germany was at last ready for such a magnum opus. Who better to understand it than the Emperor? Did not Nietzsche call for a Roman Cæsar with Christ's soul? Was the arrival of an Übermensch not at hand? With *The Will to Power*, the Queen hoped that she could at last unite Nietzsche Puppet and Wilhelm the II and perhaps make of him a patron and disciple. If her political dynasty in South America failed, through the corpse of her brother, the Queen could unite philosophy and politics, bridge century & century, and stand triumphant, the midwife to a great new political dynasty, with Nietzsche the profound mask through which she could display & crown herself. Who cares about Paraguay when one can triumph in Germany, when one can slip on a corpse & dominate the world? *Over all obstacles, stand your ground! Amen!* Über alles*!*

Whereas the philosopher did not want to be a holy man, sooner even a buffoon, the utopic colonist wanted to be idolized, to enshrine the phantasm of her I and erect a temple to her ego. Was the pyramidal mausoleum she wanted to erect for her brother on the Chasté peninsula in Sils Maria not in actuality a celebration of and monument to herself, Förster-Nietzsche-Minotaur?

To complete the task of writing *The Will to Power*, the Queen called upon Nietzsche's most fervent disciple, Peter Gast, and on 4 August 1900, he ventured to Weimar to stay there for the next few years. Three weeks later, on 25 August 1900, ten years and one month after Vincent van Gogh returned to the earth, Friedrich Wilhelm Nietzsche died for the last time, forever closing out the circle of identities, at last escaping, in body, though not yet in œuvre, the labyrinth in which his ventriloquist had entombed him. It was near to the anniversary of Pliny the Elder's death in AD 79, a death caused by the eruption of Mount Vesuvius *&* winds born of pyroclastic surges. *Fortes' inquit 'fortuna iuvat: Pomponianum pete.*

*

With Elisabeth Förster, we hear the tone of *Sieg Heil!* in her body, an atropinic tonality not of the future, but of a folkloric past that sought to be a present but which was nothing but death incarnate: the stench of ovens, the banality of evil, the triumph of ressentiment. And in Nueva Germania, what final legacy stands? Charred remains engulfed by forest growth, the ashes of Försterhof, a street sign on which is written: "Elizabeth Nigtz Chen" — the Bindestrich has cracked; history has split, altered, and freed the family name. The subtraction is complete.

With Friedrich Nietzsche, we hear the halcyon tone of the cosmos, of his call to stop feeling ourselves to be such fantastic egos and to gradually learn to throw off the imaginary individual. Discover the errors of the ego, he pleaded. Realism egoism as an error! And not understand altruism as its opposite! *That* would be love for other imaginary individuals! No! Let us go beyond 'me' and 'you'! *Feel cosmically!*

This is the transformation into stone and plant; this is the gentle sloping into the sea in such proud and calm harmony as do the mountains at Portofino — where the bay of Genoa ends its melody. This cosmic feeling, this interplanetary tone, is echoed in Strauss's grand musical evocation of the philosopher of the future, in the sonics of his *Also sprach Zarathustra*, whose reverberating organ and clarion trumpets ring out, intimating a new dawn, its opening 21 bars articulating the sublime possibility of the Übermensch, of the cosmos entering and transforming one, of an open horizon, of the scintillating light of Vincent's sun and the intoxicating and holy laughter of Zarathustra, the Pulcinella of Torino.

*

Dead, the bodies of Nietzsche and Vincent undergo their final sparagmos, a terminal but regenerative event: their corpuses returning to earth, extending into it and beyond, all boundaries finally obliterated — seeding the earth, seeding the oceans and seas, seeding the atmosphere, becoming part of the composition of the mountains, trees, and clouds, altering the composition of oxygen: subatomic elements carried by lizard, fish, and bird, vines growing out of the sites of their graves, uniting plant and stone, futural lines opening in rhizomatic directions, threading through the cosmos like free detritus spiraling in space, hovering in gardens of dark matter ~

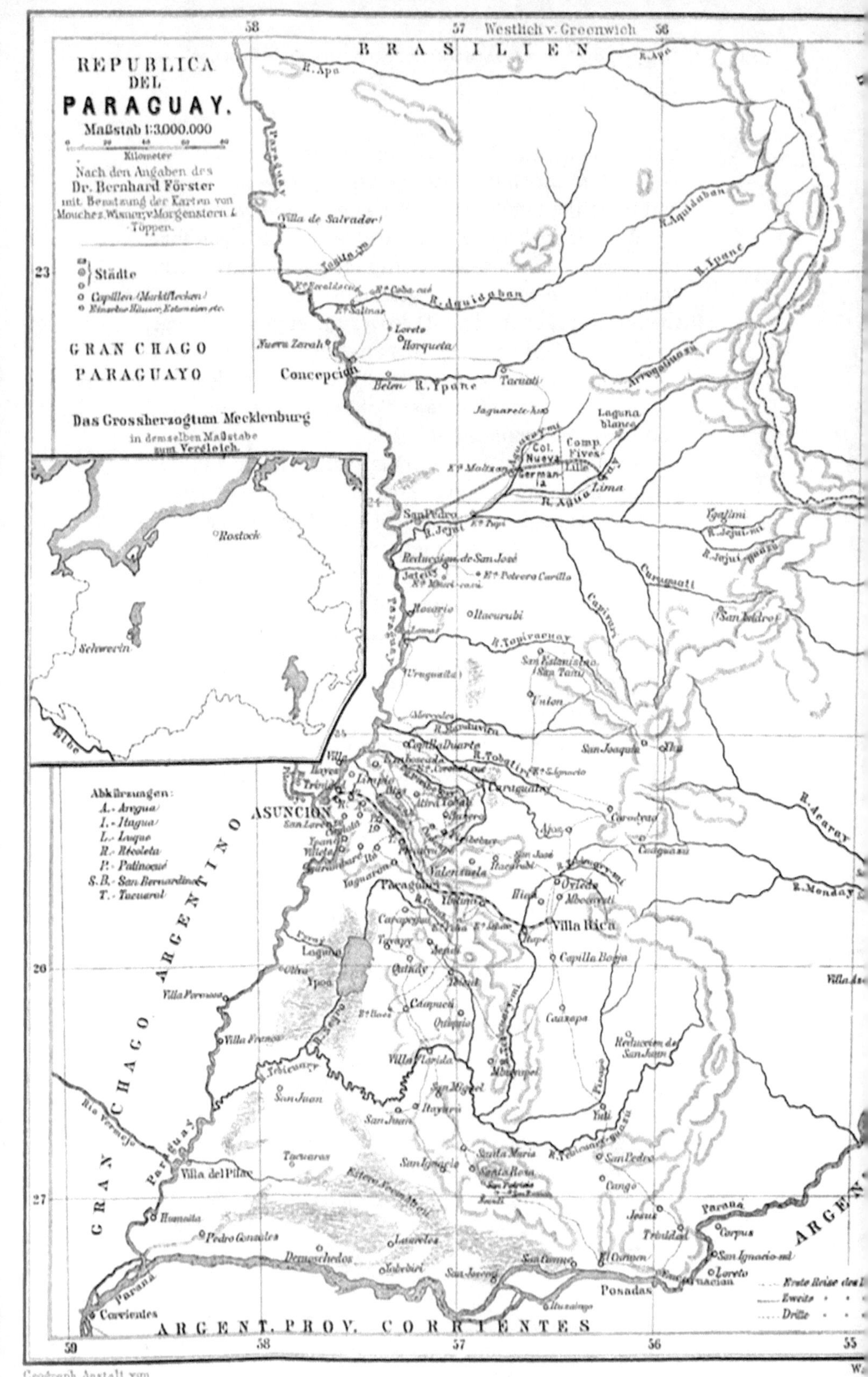
Westlich v. Greenwich
BRASILIEN
REPUBLICA DEL PARAGUAY.
Maßstab 1:3.000.000
Kilometer
Nach den Angaben des
Dr. Bernhard Förster
mit Benutzung der Karten von
Mouche, Wisner, Morgenstern &
Töppen.
Städte
Capillen (Marktflecken)
Einzelne Häuser, Estancien etc.
GRAN CHAGO
PARAGUAYO
Das Grossherzogtum Mecklenburg
in demselben Maßstabe
zum Vergleich.
Rostock
Schwerin
Elbe
Abkürzungen:
A. = Aregua
I. = Itagua
L. = Luque
R. = Recoleta
P. = Patinoené
S.B. = San Bernardino
T. = Tacuaral
R. Apa
R. Aya
Villa de Salvador
Jejui m.
Paraguay
R. Aquidaban
R. Ipane
R. Ewaldscca
R. Coba cué
R. Salinar
Loreto
Nueva Zarah
Horqueta
Concepcion
Belen R. Ypane
Tacuati
Arroyoguazú
Jaguarete-ion
Laguna
blanca
Comp.
Fives-
Lille
Col.
Nueva
German-
ia
R. Malta
Lima
R. Agua
San Pedro
R. Jejui
R. Papo
Ygatimi
R. Jejui mi
R. Jujui guazu
Reduccion de San José
Jateit3
R. Mbaci-cassu
R. Potrera Carilla
Curuguati
San Isidro
Rosario
Itacurubi
Capivari
Lomas
R. Topiracuay
San Estanislao
(San Tam)
Uruguaita
Union
Mercedes
R. Manduvira
Ibu
Capilla Duarte
R. Tobatiry
R. Ychnacio
San Joaquin
Villa
Hayes
Trinidad
Emboscada
R. Coronel cué
Luque
Atira Tobati
Caraguati
Coronda
R. Acaray
ASUNCION
San Lorenzo
Capiata
Itaugua
Valenzuela
Paraguari
Hiatá
Mbocoveti
R. Monday
San José
Itacurubi
Villa Rica
Capilla Bar ja
Caazapa
Reduccion de
San Juan
GRAN CHACO ARGENTINO
Paraguay
Villa Formosa
Laguna
Ypoa
Otra
Villa Franca
Tebicuary
Villa Florida
Mbuyapei
San Miguel
Villa Asc
Rio Vermejo
San Juan
San Juan
Itapiru
Yuti
Tacuaras
Santiago
Santa Maria
R. Tebicuary-guasu
San Pedro
Cango
Villa del Pilar
Estero Nuembucú
Jesus
Paraná
ARGEN
Humaita
Carmen
Trinidad
Corpus
Pedro Gonzales
Demoschedos
Icolobiri
San Javier
San Ignacio mi
Loreto
Posadas
Corrientes
Paraná
Erste Reise des
Zweite
Dritte
ARGENT. PROV. CORRIENTES
Geograph. Anstalt von

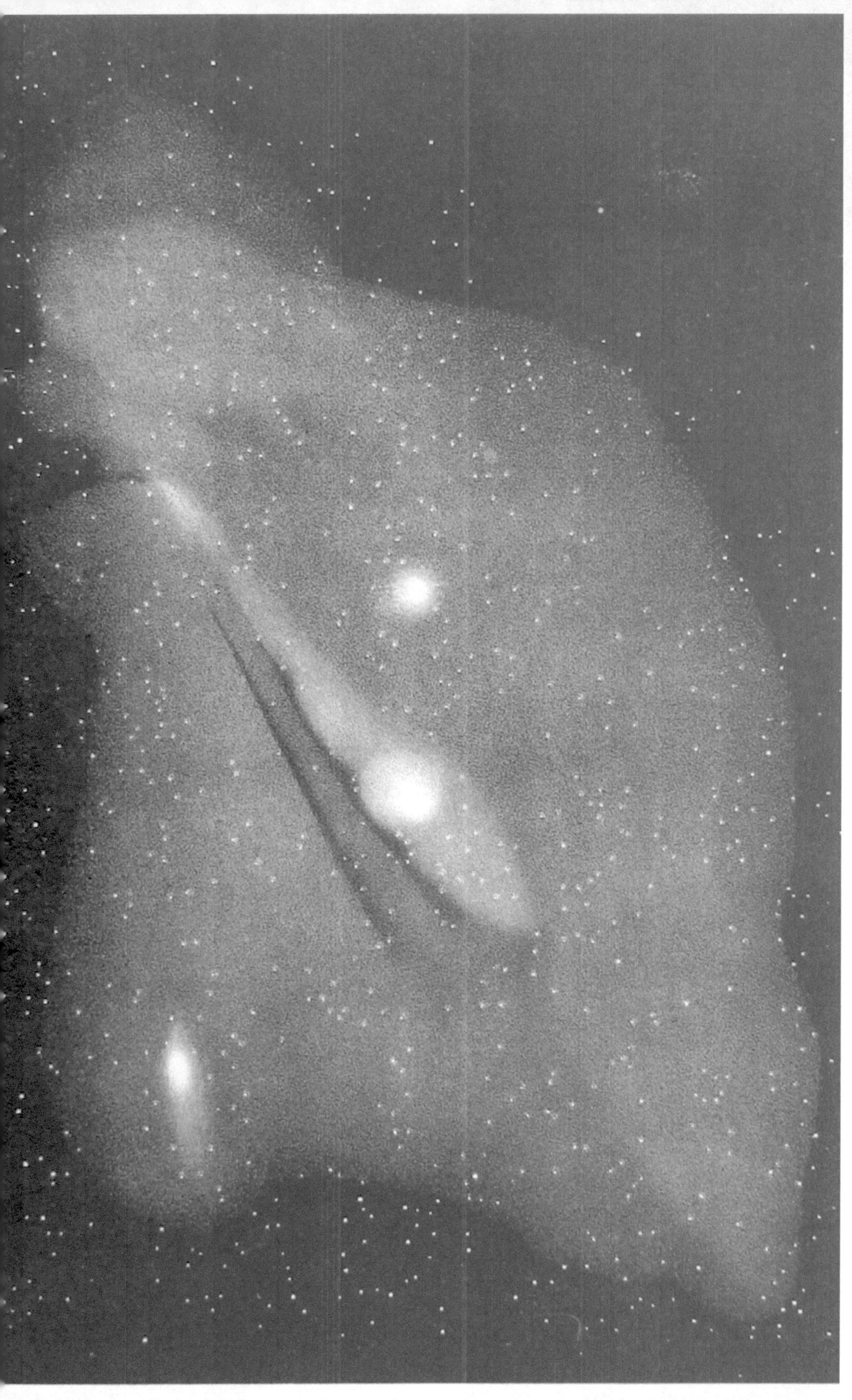

COLOPHON

CLOSING MELODIES

was handset in InDesign CC.

The text font is *Lapture*.
The display font is *Louvette*.

Book design & typesetting: Alessandro Segalini
Cover design: Alessandro Segalini

CLOSING MELODIES

is published by Contra Mundum Press.

Contra Mundum Press   New York · London · Melbourne

2017   Joseph Kessel, *Army of Shadows*
       Rainer J. Hanshe *&* Federico Gori, *Shattering the Muses*
       Gérard Depardieu, *Innocent*
       Claude Mouchard, *Entangled — Papers! — Notes*
2018   Miklós Szentkuthy, *Black Renaissance*
       Adonis *&* Pierre Joris, *Conversations in the Pyrenees*
2019   Charles Baudelaire, *Belgium Stripped Bare*
       Robert Musil, *Unions*
       Iceberg Slim, *Night Train to Sugar Hill*
       Marquis de Sade, *Aline & Valcour*
2020   *A City Full of Voices: Essays on the Work of Robert Kelly*
       Rédoine Faïd, *Outlaw*
       Carmelo Bene, *I Appeared to the Madonna*
       Paul Celan, *Microliths They Are, Little Stones*
       Zsuzsa Selyem, *It's Raining in Moscow*
       Bérengère Viennot, *Trumpspeak*
       Robert Musil, *Theater Symptoms*
       Miklós Szentkuthy, *Chapter on Love*
       Charles Baudelaire, *Paris Spleen*
2021   Marguerite Duras, *The Darkroom*
       Andrew Dickos, *Honor Among Thieves*
       Pierre Senges, *Ahab (Sequels)*
       Carmelo Bene, *Our Lady of the Turks*
       Fernando Pessoa, *Writings on Art & Poetical Theory*
2022   Miklós Szentkuthy, *Prae, Vol. 2*
       Blixa Bargeld, *Europe Crosswise: A Litany*
       Pierre Joris, *Always the Many, Never the One*
       Robert Musil, *Theater Symptoms*
2023   Pierre Joris, *Interglacial Narrows*
       Gabriele Tinti, *Bleedings — Incipit Tragœdia*
       Évelyne Grossman, *The Creativity of the Crisis*

SOME FORTHCOMING TITLES

Léon-Paul Fargue, *High Solitude*
Sara Whym, *Dreamscapes*

AGRODOLCE SERIES Æ

2020   Dejan Lukić, *The Oyster*
2022   Ugo Tognazzi, *The Injester*

HYPERION
On the Future of Æsthetics   2006–2023

To read samples and order current & back issues of *Hyperion*,
visit contramundumpress.com/hyperion

Edited by Rainer J. Hanshe & Erika Mihálycsa (2014 ~)

CONTRA MUNDUM PRESS

is published by Rainer J. Hanshe

Typography & Design: Alessandro Segalini

Publicity & Marketing: Alexandra Gold

THE FUTURE OF KULCHUR
A PATRONAGE PROJECT

LEND CONTRA MUNDUM PRESS (CMP) YOUR SUPPORT

With bookstores and presses around the world struggling to survive, and many actually closing, we are forming this patronage project as a means for establishing a continuous & stable foundation to safeguard our longevity. Through this patronage project we would be able to remain free of having to rely upon government support &/or other official funding bodies, not to speak of their timelines & impositions. It would also free CMP from suffering the vagaries of the publishing industry, as well as the risk of submitting to commercial pressures in order to persist, thereby potentially compromising the integrity of our catalog.

CAN YOU SACRIFICE $10 A WEEK FOR KULCHUR?

For the equivalent of merely 2–3 coffees a week, you can help sustain CMP and contribute to the future of kulchur. To participate in our patronage program we are asking individuals to donate $500 per year, which amounts to $42/month, or $10/week. Larger donations are of course welcome and beneficial. All donations are tax-deductible through our fiscal sponsor Fractured Atlas. If preferred, donations can be made in two installments. We are seeking a minimum of 300 patrons per year and would like for them to commit to giving the above amount for a period of three years.

WHAT WE OFFER

Part tax-deductible donation, part exchange, for your contribution you will receive every CMP book published during the patronage period as well as 20 books from our back catalog. When possible, signed or limited editions of books will be offered as well.

WHAT WILL CMP DO WITH YOUR CONTRIBUTIONS?

Your contribution will help with basic general operating expenses, yearly production expenses (book printing, warehouse & catalog fees, etc.), advertising and outreach, and editorial, proofreading, translation, typography, design and copyright fees. Funds may also be used for participating in book fairs and staging events. Additionally, we hope to rebuild the *Hyperion* section of the website in order to modernize it.

From Pericles to Mæcenas & the Renaissance patrons, it is the magnanimity of such individuals that have helped the arts to flourish. Be a part of helping your kulchur flourish; be a part of history.

HOW

To lend your support & become a patron, please visit the subscription page of our website: contramundum.net/subscription

For any questions, write us at: info@contramundum.net